A History of Indiger

A History of Indigenous Latin America is a comprehensive introduction to the people who first settled in Latin America, from before the arrival of the Europeans to the present.

Indigenous history provides a singular perspective to political, social, and economic changes that followed European settlement and the African slave trade in Latin America. Set broadly within a postcolonial theoretical framework and enhanced by anthropology, economics, sociology, and religion, this textbook includes military conflicts and nonviolent resistance, transculturation, labor, political organization, gender, and broad selective accommodation. Uniquely organized into periods of 50 years to facilitate classroom use, it allows students to ground important Indigenous historical events and cultural changes within the timeframe of a typical university semester.

Supported by images, textboxes, and linked documents in each chapter that aid learning and provide a new perspective that broadly enhances Latin American history and studies, it is the perfect introductory textbook for students.

Dr. René Harder Horst is I.G. Greer Distinguished Professor 2018 to 2021 in History at Appalachian State University in North Carolina, United States. He is author of *The Stroessner Regime and Indigenous Resistance in Paraguay*, *Military Struggle and Identity Formation in Latin America*, *El Régimen de Stroessner y la Resistencia Indígena*, and numerous articles on Indigenous history in Latin America.

'Finally, a Latin America textbook that places the lives and experiences of Indigenous peoples at its center! Horst carefully introduces theoretical and conceptual debates in accessible ways as he ably covers 500 years of history from an indigenous perspective. The book's generous sweep encompasses the diversity as well as common themes of indigenous livelihoods with close attention to native sources and voices. Centering indigenous history creates a compelling narrative thread for a coherent history that is nonetheless attentive to geographical variation and to individual experience. Unflinchingly presents indigenous peoples as both victims and protagonists. Readable, accessible, and rich in detail and analysis.'

Professor Avi Chomsky, Department of History, Salem State University, USA

'The native "voice" has long been under-emphasized in historical accounts of the New World, almost to the point of non-existence. René Harder Horst, in this fine and highly detailed work, thus offers a needed corrective. He demonstrates that the quality of the indigenous experience provides its own quite distinct legitimacy and proves, I think, that the Apristas of Peru are right in eschewing the traditional term "Latin America" in favor of the far more comprehensive "Indoamerica." We might very well learn from them as we go forward.'

Professor Emeritus Thomas L. Whigham, Department of History, University of Georgia, USA

'We have long needed an Indigenous history of Latin America. René Harder Horst is one of those rare and outstanding scholars who possesses the breadth and depth of knowledge necessary to tackle such an important but difficult subject. *A History of Indigenous Latin America* fills an important gap in the field. This engaging text will introduce students to new ways of understanding and interpreting the Americas that for far too long have been approached from a colonialist point of view. An Indigenous perspective provides a counter narrative that embraces those who are traditionally marginalized and are often left out of history. As such, this book contributes a much more complete understanding of the Americas than that to which we have previously had access.'

Professor Marc Becker, Department of History, Truman State University, USA

A History of Indigenous Latin America

Aymara to Zapatistas

René Harder Horst

NEW YORK AND LONDON

First published 2020
by Routledge
52 Vanderbilt Avenue, New York, NY 10017

and by Routledge
2 Park Square, Milton Park, Abingdon, Oxon, OX14 4RN

Routledge is an imprint of the Taylor & Francis Group, an informa business

Library of Congress Cataloging-in-Publication Data
Names: Horst, René Harder, 1967- author.
Title: A History of Indigenous Latin America : Aymara to Zapatistas /
René Harder Horst.
Description: New York : Routledge/Taylor & Francis Group, 2020. |
Includes bibliographical references and index.
Identifiers: LCCN 2019048423 (print) | LCCN 2019048424 (ebook) |
ISBN 9780415519113 (hardback) | ISBN 9780415519120 (paperback) |
ISBN 9781315228402 (ebook)
Subjects: LCSH: Latin America--History--Textbooks. |
Indians--History--Textbooks. | Indians--Latin
America--History--Textbooks.
Classification: LCC F1410 .H68 2020 (print) | LCC F1410 (ebook) |
DDC 980/.01--dc23
LC record available at https://lccn.loc.gov/2019048423
LC ebook record available at https://lccn.loc.gov/2019048424

ISBN: 978-0-415-51911-3 (hbk)
ISBN: 978-0-415-51912-0 (pbk)
ISBN: 978-1-315-22840-2 (ebk)

Typeset in Garamond
by Integra Software Services Pvt. Ltd.

Visit the eResources: www.routledge.com/9780415519120

Contents

Figures

Maps

Textboxes

Acknowledgments

I am grateful to the many Indigenous peoples throughout the Americas who shared their lives with me. Peter and Lita Naswood accompanied my year on the Navajo Reservation. Barry Dana (Penobscot and Wabanaki) and Hawk Henries (Chaubunagungamaug band of the Nipmuck people) supported my years teaching at Bates College in Maine. Francisco Cáceres, Domingo Chascozo, Feliciano García, Leonida García, Luís, Delfina, and Tino Mendoza, Miguel Mendoza, Francisco Cáceres, Alcides Pintos, and Enrique Romero are Q'om, Pilagá, and Guaraní life friends in Argentina and Paraguay. Osvaldo Pitoe and Jorge Carema (Western Guaraní), and Asque Eurides Gómez (Nivaclé), are the Indigenous artists in the Paraguayan Chaco who drew the pictures featured on the cover and in Chapter 1, and Verena Regehr kindly arranged for and sent me their work.

I am grateful to Kimberly Guinta, former senior acquisitions editor at Routledge, Taylor & Francis Group, who first believed in my dream and pedagogic need for this book. Ms. Guinta guided the initial stages, and her insights and expertise shaped the organization and content of the book in many important ways. Genevieve Aoki, Daniel Finaldi, and Rebecca Novack helped at different stages. Zöe Thompson was the editorial assistant who carefully shepherded the book through its final stages and oversaw the organization of documents and purchase of images. Alanna Donaldson was the Deputy Production Editorial Manager who oversaw the last stages. Eve Setch, publisher in Modern History, managed the final years of production. I am also indebted to the 11 anonymous scholars who made constructive and important suggestions to Routledge at different stages of the writing process. Finally, Ann King was the superb copy-editor who carefully reviewed the manuscript. While this dedicated team generously made this book come together, I am alone responsible for any errors or omissions.

Many colleagues contributed their time and knowledge to assist in compiling this textbook. At Appalachian State University I am grateful to John Craft, Professor of Graphic Arts and Imaging Technology, who designed the cover. Ed Behrend-Martínez, Michael Behrent, Rodney Duke, Jim Goff, Jari Eloranta, Scott Jessee, Lucinda McCray, Sheila Phipps, Mary Valante, and Thomas Whyte made helpful suggestions over the years. Graduate students Chris Howard and Beau Lockhard assisted with the indexes and glossary, and Gina Slagle in IT Support Services helped with technology. Donna Davis in the Department of History office kindly facilitated travel arrangements during many years of research and presentations.

Arlene Balkansky helped locate sources at the Library of Congress. Stephen Buckwalter, Louise Burkhart, Robert Carmack, Ken Coates, Jeffrey Cohen, Carlos Enrique Consalvi, Jo Crow, David Russell Edmunds, Nicola Foote, Mariana Giordano, Laura Gotkowitz, Jeffrey Gould, Greg Grandin, Peter Guardino, Jim Handy, James Howe, James LaGrand, Erick

Langer, Tito Lehaye, Erin O'Connor, Julia O'Hara, Mary Roldan, Carlos Martínez Sarasola, Sinclair Thomson, Brett Troyan, Thomas Whiggham, Yanna Yannakakis, and Alejandro Zorzin all generously shared suggestions and information. Marc Becker at Truman State University read the entire manuscript at various stages and offered valuable advice for improvements. Markus Krisetya, VP at Telegeography and a life friend, created the maps with great attention to detail. I am indebted to his expert cartography.

My late father Willis and my mother Byrdalene Horst helped me see the world from different viewpoints, offered suggestions that helped shape this textbook, and taught me to care. My wife and children endured a decade of discussions, research trips, and too many long hours in the office, yet remained extremely supportive throughout the entire process. Their insightful advice and encouragement made this textbook possible. I wish them strength in helping shape an inclusive world that is welcoming to everyone.

A Note on the Documents

Throughout the book, there are links to documents and accompanying questions for discussion. These are online resources that may be found at www.routledge.com/9780415519120.

Introduction

Indigenous People from the Southern Cone Meet an Important Person

On the evening of May 17, 1988, hundreds of Indigenous people and Bishop Luicio Alfert welcomed Pope John Paul II to the small Paraguayan town of Mariscal (Marshall) Estigarribia. Located in the dry, western Chaco, the small community was just about the most remote place that still had an airstrip to receive the papal entourage. Mariscal, as locals called the village, featured an army base and a Catholic mission to the local Indigenous people. In front of hundreds of Native people from Paraguay, Argentina, Brazil and Bolivia who had arrived to meet the Pope, the Bishop quickly took his seat and instead invited Enenlhit leader René Ramírez to the podium. Only a year before, Ramírez had led his community in their successful legal battle to recover their ancestral lands in the Chaco. Confidently delivering the most significant speech of his life, Ramírez explained to the surprised pontiff that in his country there was more land available for cows than for the Indigenous people.

> We are a living testimony to the people who have lived in these continents before they were called "Americas." We are the inheritors of their cultures and their spiritual richness. We feel strongly united together with you. We speak different languages and have different cultures and religions, yet we share the same history, the same sufferings, and the same concerns.... The Whites tell us that we must become civilized. We invite the Whites to be civilized and respect us as people, respect our communities and our leaders, respect our lands and our forests, and return to us even just a little of what they have taken away from us. We wish to be friends of all the Paraguayans. We want them to let us live in peace.[1]

John Paul II began to cry when he saw the unexpected change in the program and listened to the Indigenous testimony. The pontiff then responded to the assembly first in Guaraní: "Ymá guivéma aimese penendive; ha peina âga, aimema pendeapytepe" ("For a long time I have wanted to be with you. And now here I am, I am with you"), and then asked if they could understand him. When the assembly shouted back with a resounding "hee" ("yes" in Guaraní), John Paul II won them over by declaring that then he could also become a missionary in the Chaco. The pontiff expressed his support and called on those in power to respect Native peoples and lands.

> Your desires for general improvements are just. Most importantly, you desire respect as persons and that your human and civil rights be recognized and protected. I know the serious problems that you face, particularly in reference to your land ownership and property titles. For these I appeal to the sense of justice and humanity by those responsible so they defend the have-nots. From the beginning of evangelization in

> these lands, the Church defended the liberty and dignity of the Indigenous people, and missionaries often spoke against the abuses to which your ancestors were at times subject.... You desire to make your own choices about your people's development, and request respect for your cultures and free decisions to develop your economic and human levels by way of education that joins your traditional values with advances in today's world.[2]

The meeting with the pontiff turned into a three-day pan-Indigenous celebration. Native people discussed and compared their situations over the next three days and long into the nights as they danced, talked, and celebrated their eventful meeting with the Pope.

Embarrassed by the unexpected media victory that Indigenous people had scored, the dictator of Paraguay tried to assassinate Ramírez. The leader fled into hiding, living in the woods from food supplied by his community. Not until Stroessner's 35-year regime finally collapsed 8 months later, in January 1989, was Ramírez able to return home. My interview with the Enenlhit leader, in May 2001, was the first time in over ten years that he ventured back to Asunción. Even though by that time Paraguay boasted a democratic government, civil liberties, and a new constitution, fears of retaliation still haunted Ramírez.

René Ramírez clearly understood that his presentation to the Pope had been part of the groundswell of popular opposition to the Paraguayan regime and a milestone for Indigenous people throughout southern Latin America who desired a democratic opening.[3] Authorities at the time recognized that the encounter between the pontiff and the Indigenous people played a role in furthering the political change. Ramírez emphasized,

> My virtuous protest was that we wanted liberty in democracy and that Indigenous people be treated as humans, as people who were the original inhabitants of this country. We wanted our land, our territory, since we were no longer able to practice our culture.[4]

Scholars support this leader's declaration about growing Indigenous desires for political participation. Political scientist Donna Lee Van Cott included the Paraguayan example in her study of nations in which the militarization of relations with Native people and the resulting Indigenous responses had helped move nations away from authoritarian rule.[5] In his study of the Catholic Church and the end of the Stroessner regime, political scientist Miguel Carter noted the Indigenous meeting with Pope John Paul II as an important step in the erosion of public support for the dictator.[6] Paraguayan lawyer Esther Prieto showed that Catholic Church support for Indigenous people moved Paraguay towards a democratic future through their lobby for and inclusion in the new Constitution of 1992.[7] The Native presentation to the Pope brought together Indigenous people throughout the Southern Cone of Latin America and symbolized their growing participation in national and continental events. No longer would it be as easy for Latin American nations to marginalize Native people in their midst.

The Indigenous meeting with the Catholic pontiff featured in the introduction is an example of the awakening of Indigenous activism and protests that punctuated the last decades of the twentieth century in Latin America. From Chile to Brazil, from Paraguay to Mexico, Native people took every available opportunity to make their voices and anger heard. Only a few months later, in February 1989, an even more impressive assembly of 3,000 Kayapó people and their allies converged on the Brazilian town of Altamira to protest plans for the construction of dams along the Xingu and Iriri rivers. The project would have displaced 25,000 people in 18 Native groups from dozens of communities. Plans to develop the forest in Brazil had earlier passed unnoticed. This time though, led by Kayapó leader Raoni, with his notable lip plug and his rock star ally Sting, the massive demonstration captured widespread media attention, gained international support, and finally put the dam projects on hold. It seemed as though the world woke up and realized there were still Indigenous people in Latin America who were enduring difficult conditions. Those people were now doing something about their plight by using the media to publicize their interactions with the states within which they were enveloped. These dramatic events serve as good examples of ways in which Indigenous people in Latin America have recently captured world attention. Yet Indigenous people have been adapting to and reacting against non-Indigenous people since they first made contact with outside peoples. This book studies the histories of Latin American Indigenous people from contact up until the present, focusing on themes of resistance, adaptation, and survival.

Notes

1 "Discurso Indígena de Bienvenida Dirigida a Su Santidad," 19–21.
2 "Juán Pablo II y Los Indígenas," 26.
3 René Ramírez, Enenlhit leader, interview with author, Asunción, May 21, 2001.
4 Ibid.
5 Van Cott, *Indigenous Peoples and Democracy*, 21.
6 Carter, *El Papel de la Iglesia*, 123.
7 Prieto, "Indigenous Peoples in Paraguay," 241–242. See also Horst, "Indigenous Integration," 219.

1 Indigenous Latin America

Introductions, Methodology, and Definitions

Methodological Challenges and Historiographical Themes

The encounter between Indigenous people and John Paul II suggests that Indigenous history is fraught with controversy, much of which is reflected in the methodology and historiography of the field. This study begins with an examination of major theoretical definitions of Indigenous peoples. The most complete and yet accessible coverage is Professor Ken Coates' text *A Global History of Indigenous Peoples*, which serves as a foundation for understanding the peoples featured in this book. Additional works by historians, paleoanthropologists, sociologists, economists, anthropologists, and philosophers help frame the Indigenous histories under consideration and open up avenues for further research. When possible, the text includes Indigenous perspectives for comparison and to add analytical depth. Primary documents, such as diaries and accounts by early settlers and administrators, deepen analysis and provide options for added research throughout the study.

Another methodological challenge involved in studying Indigenous history derives from stereotypes that some people unconsciously hold about Indigenous people. In her book on pan-Maya activism in Guatemala during the last decades of the twentieth century, Kay Warren, Professor of Anthropology at Harvard University, lays out four fallacies often employed by North Americans in their formulation of Mesoamerican ethnicity. While originally presented by Warren to Mayan audiences in Guatemala, these fallacies are also helpful for a more general study of Indigenous people. The four fallacies also contrast with Warren's formulation of a more accurate approach to Native history, which she suggests as the constructionist alternative. This first chapter explores some of these erroneous yet deeply rooted stereotypes of Indigenous peoples and their histories, and suggests better alternatives for their study.

Methodological challenges also result from the fact that most of the Indigenous peoples in the Americas did not leave written records. Only the existing outside records of their actions, documented mostly by non-Indigenous people, suggest what Native goals may have been. Such accounts were usually biased and reveal even more about the writers' goals than about possible Indigenous motives and actions. For example, because Native people often struggled to resist outside control and manipulation, much of their history appears to be resistance and militancy. Furthermore, observers usually did not describe the majority of history that seemed normal; for these reasons their accounts more frequently noted these salient events of violent resistance that were traumatic and memorable. It is important to note that the majority of Indigenous people did not rebel violently and gradually joined Latin American society, so observers did not record their daily actions. Rebellions feature prominently in the book, even though most Native interactions with outsiders were peaceful: violent episodes stand out prominently because people remember the trauma and their significance.

Terminology also complicates documenting Indigenous history. The name that the original inhabitants of the Americas called themselves has changed over the years. Originally, groups called themselves by their own word for people from a certain place, as in the Aztecah, the Nahuatl word for "people from Aztlan," who organized the polity that became known as the Aztec Empire. Even the European term for the people they met in the Americas – "Indians" – is also a misnomer, since explorers thought they had arrived in India rather than having sailed into a new continent. This text therefore employs the term preferred by contemporary Native peoples, "Indigenous people," as well as "Native people" for variation. Even the designation for modern nation states is problematic, since Indigenous peoples today consider themselves to be "nations" despite not administering independent nation states.

As students engage with the history, illustrations, maps, Indigenous individuals, and artwork in this text, my hope is, first, that they will learn more about the important role Indigenous people have played in Latin America's past; second, that they will gain an awareness and a deeper understanding of these Native people; and third, that this study will awaken interest, foster new research and broaden awareness about different groups of people throughout Latin America, especially those who share Indigenous ancestry and heritage.

How to Use this Book: A Few Suggestions for Students and Instructors

This textbook is organized both chronologically and thematically to include various geographic locations and peoples over a vast amount of time. Chapters are based on roughly 50-year segments of history, from before Indigenous contacts with outsiders up until the twenty-first century, yet focus on themes within that timeframe to assist with cohesion and organization of the material. This approach emphasizes important events and periods of both Native and mainstream histories, merging them into one study focused on the role Indigenous people played in the history of the continent and how outside changes in turn affected them. It was not possible to cover everything at all times in one book. The large amount of historical material forced cuts and exclusions; the choice of what to include or leave out in such a broad history was always painful but never arbitrary. Weaving together the stories of hundreds of Native peoples whose histories changed over time as they interacted with outsiders was complicated and humbling. Choosing the events on which to focus seemed at times too dependent on the availability of sources for that period and place and not illustrative enough of the entire historical picture. I hope the book does justice to the Native experience and provides a basic framework and overview for students and teachers studying Indigenous histories in Latin America.

Each chapter outlines historical changes for Indigenous peoples during a specific time period in broader Latin American history, noting developments for Natives and outsiders and the interaction between both. In several sections, historical events and the availability of sources made it necessary to shorten or lengthen the time period under consideration by a few years; hopefully the reasons for these accommodations will be self-evident. Rather than cover everything in the chapters in class, an instructor might choose to focus on a particular subject and instead allow the text to cover the rest of the material. Specific topics, Native people or groups, as well as salient periods that hold interest particularly to a research subject, experience, or study by the instructor, could then be approached more productively as a group during class time.

Chapters present links to two Indigenous documents from or about Indigenous history during the period under consideration. These documents are located on the website accompanying the book. The documents are intended to foster discussion, deepen analysis of events, provide ideas for further research, and point to some of the available printed sources of Indigenous history. When possible, documents were dictated or written by Indigenous people themselves. During some periods, material objects serve to illustrate a people or culture when readily accessible written testimonies were absent. As you read and consider the documents, carefully analyze what the writer's goals in the excerpt may have been, to whom the writing was targeted, how it may have been received by the readers, and what historical repercussions may have resulted from the writing of the piece.

Each chapter also features two illustrations. Focused on Indigenous subjects and created by Native artists when possible, the illustrations foster discussion on a specific aspect of the period featured in the chapter. Some images are handcrafts, art, or architecture created by Indigenous people themselves. Other illustrations are pictures or art created by outsiders. In both cases, when possible, people who themselves played a role in the section's history produced the art. A few images feature places or Indigenous sites. All of them raise ideas for class discussion and illustrate aspects of themes considered in the chapters: What surprised you about the picture under consideration? What reinforced something you already knew about either Indigenous or Latin American history? What reminded you of a stereotype mentioned in this introductory chapter? How does the illustration deepen the chapter content, and what additional insights does it provide? What about or within the picture might one explore further to learn more about a related subject in either Indigenous or Latin American history?

Indigenous history provides many subjects for discussion and historical analysis. When teaching Indigenous history, I have tried to make my classes as interactive as possible and to allow plenty of space for questions, answers, commentaries, and insights. Like any history text, this book introduces many names, people, places, and subjects that will be new to students. Such is the case for any new historical field. Rather than memorizing all the new names, students could focus on the main themes that distinguish each chapter period, and employ personal research, expertise, and relations to local specialties to complement and/or illustrate chapter content. Let the book cover some details and instead classes might focus on broader themes or the intersections between Indigenous and mainstream histories. If one chooses to use films and music in class, as I often do to broaden student analysis, connect subjects with ideas in the text and again present these materials to students for discussion and analysis. In addition, if one's traditional preparation is primarily Latin American history, use one's strengths to relate to Indigenous issues and topics that arise in the text. Perhaps present mainstream events and then focus on a discussion of Indigenous actions, influence, sources, and also interpretations as they are presented in the text, or in music, art, or historical documents. Above all, enjoy both the study and teaching of this Indigenous history.

Very Different Places, Cultures, and Lives

Humans necessarily see the world from the vantage points of their own cultures and experiences. To study people who are different than ourselves requires time, energy, and a willingness to be changed, because learning why people lived or live differently than we do deepens our understanding of what it means to be human, helps us understand where we have come from, and offers new possibilities for our collective future. While few of us realize beforehand the extent that learning about other people will alter the way we view the world, in retrospect, we are never the same after we have studied other people, their ways of life, and their past. Learning Indigenous history and Indigenous perspectives on that history helps us view and understand our own history differently. In this book, we focus on the people who first populated the Americas and their descendants' experiences. This chapter explains some definitions to help frame our study of Indigenous history. Students engage some theory about our subject, explain why it is important to keep theory in mind as we study the past, explore some of our personal stereotypes about Native peoples, and establish some guidelines to help us learn the new names, geography, and events that mark Native histories in Latin America.

Framing Our Study of Indigenous History

The people who first populated the Western Hemisphere developed cultures, languages, arts, cities, governments, and explanations of their place in the world. Their cultures differed radically from the ways of life we share in the twenty-first century, yet, first and foremost, these people were also human. At the very basic level, they worried about the same practical concerns that trouble many of us today, such as: How will I earn a living and provide for my loved ones? With whom will I spend my life? How will I interact with the people around me? How much work do I actually have to do to get by? How can I enjoy my life and protect my loved ones from danger? Will I devote some of my life energies to a larger cause and purpose? Studying Indigenous history begins with the acknowledgment that our common humanity links various peoples together and makes us more similar in beliefs and goals than most of us have ever stopped to consider. Indigenous peoples have in the past lived cultures and histories quite different to those people who today share cultures descended from Europe. The variety of their histories, as well as ways in which historians have prioritized written documents to understand the past, challenges what we really know about Indigenous peoples, since most of them did not leave behind written sources about their lives. Despite our cultural differences and the historiographical challenges, though, there is much we can learn about Indigenous history as we explore their experiences in Latin America. Indigenous history is thus a different way to study Latin American history, a new way to examine the background of the entire continent.

Identity Matters

As the meeting between Native people and Pope John Paul II suggests, positions and legitimacy, as well as identity, all matter when negotiated over barriers of power and class. The Native people who met with the Pope expressed anger at continued discrimination and exclusion from political power in the countries where they lived. While they represented many different backgrounds that had traditionally divided them, Indigenous people found common experiences in the daily discrimination they faced and in their exclusion from dominant societies that governed the territories where they lived. Their group presentation to the pontiff shows also that by the late twentieth century, communications, transportation, and common languages, and especially shared experiences of

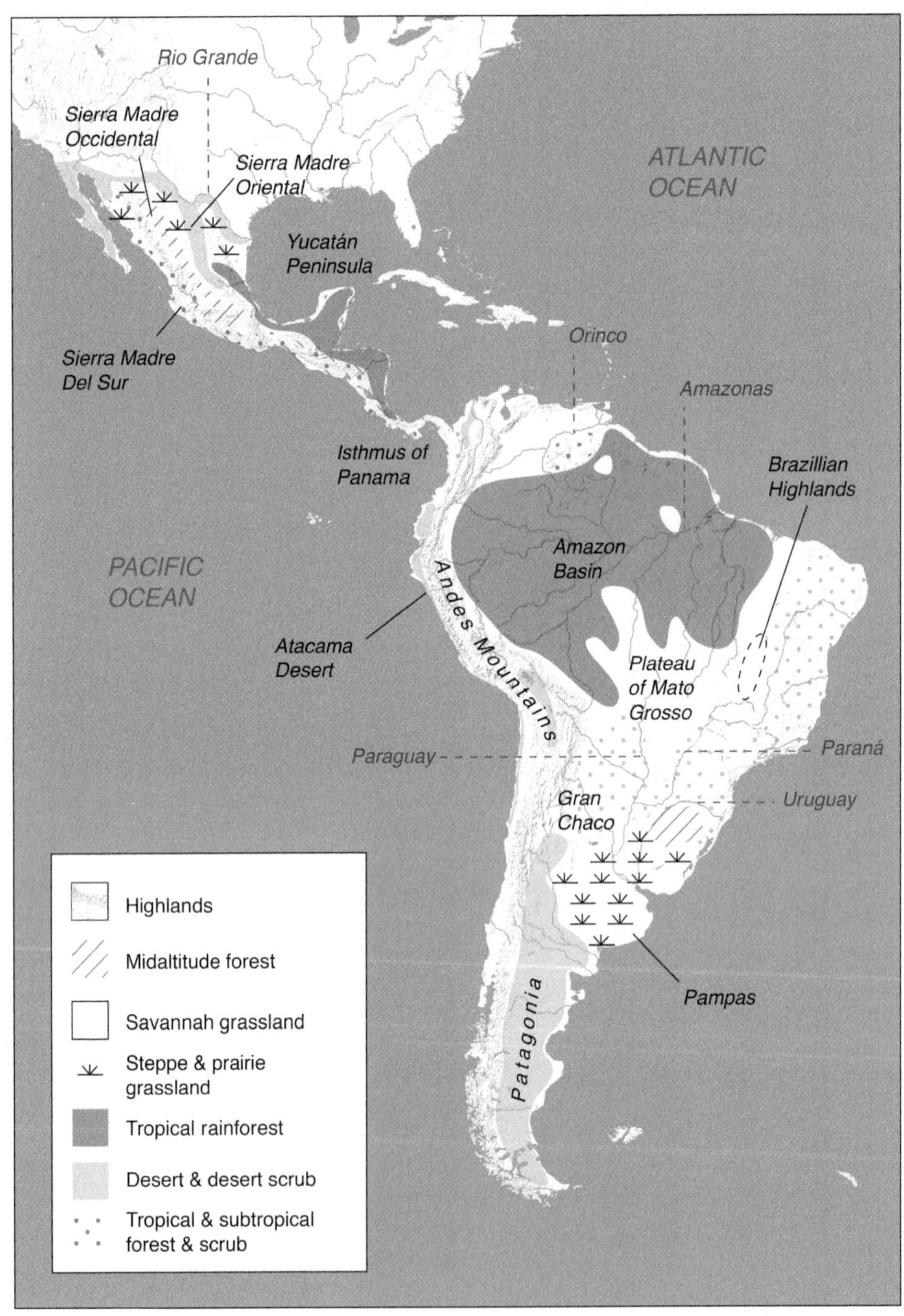

Map 1.1 Geographic Areas of Latin America

discrimination, allowed Native peoples to find common causes and to present a more united front to outsiders than ever before.

René Ramírez's meeting with me in 2001 also revealed important changes taking place within Native societies. During my initial research in 1994/1995, people had still been afraid to speak with outsiders, even though the repressive Stroessner regime had collapsed four years earlier, because of possible recrimination. Native people were especially suspicious about how outsiders would employ their testimonies. Six years later, Ramírez was clearly aware that the Indigenous meeting with the Pope had eroded regime legitimacy and had threatened the dictator, as evidenced by the seven months he spent hiding in the forest after the event because of death threats from the dictator. When I paid the leader for our interview, he demanded three times the amount that I first offered and then asked also for my little cassette recorder. Clearly, Ramírez was aware that his presentation had been important and intended me to pay him fully for his contribution to the history I was documenting. Native people were changing as they interacted more than ever with the surrounding national societies and worked to counter outside threats to their communities.

I have long been interested in Indigenous cultures and histories. While I am not Indigenous to Latin America myself, almost daily contact with them for the first third of my life helped legitimate my historical studies. My parents first taught on the Navajo reservation in Arizona, so I spent my first year of life in a hogan among the Navajo. Then my folks moved to northern Argentina to help support an Indigenous religious organization. Our family made weekly visits to Q'om, Pilaga, Mocovi, and Wichi communities, where I played with Indigenous children and learned their ways of life until I moved to the U.S. for college. During graduate work at Indiana University, I studied Indigenous Latin American and Native American histories and focused my own research on Indigenous experiences in the less-studied nation of Paraguay during the second half of the twentieth century. A Fulbright Grant funded my year of research, where I worked in archives and visited Indigenous communities throughout Paraguay to discover their experiences under authoritarian rule.

Paraguay is unique in Latin America because early colonial relations created a multicultural population that employed the Indigenous Guaraní language for intimate, daily interactions, yet used Spanish for education and formal state affairs. Guaraní served political leaders as a nationalistic tool of resistance against Paraguay's stronger neighbors Brazil and Argentina, to which Paraguay lost a devastating war in the nineteenth century, and then against Bolivia, which Paraguay defeated in a war during the Great Depression. Schools taught the Guaraní language to children as a nationalistic state-building tool.

Despite their Indigenous heritage, Paraguayans despised the people who refused to leave their Native communities and integrate into national society. Paraguayans raised lighter skinned Native children as domestic servants and troops routinely pursued Indigenous people in the forests for target practice. When international human rights agencies accused Paraguay of genocide in the 1970s, the resulting scandal brought Native conditions into the public light and forced the regime to enact pro-Indigenous legislation. Indigenous people joined forces with the Catholic Church and lower classes to overthrow the regime in 1989, and then won recognition as a minority people in the new Constitution enacted in 1992. Their pan-Indigenous mobilization, similarly visible in other nations, shows how Native people were organizing to improve their situations throughout Latin America by the end of the twentieth century. These experiences provided some of the stories that encouraged me to become an historian.

Writing Indigenous Histories: The Reasons for this Book

I have taught Latin American, Native American, and Indigenous histories for almost 20 years, trying to communicate to students what I experienced growing up in Latin America and then explored in an academic setting as a graduate student at Indiana University. In my Native American history courses, students have canoed, eaten moose from bowls they made from birch bark, and have slept in shelters under the stars at a Penobscot forest preserve in Maine to learn a bit about life outside an industrial society. We have visited museums to examine Native artifacts and practice ethnohistory, an approach that keeps in mind both past events and the cultures involved, to explore material remains left by Native peoples here in Appalachia, where I currently work. Yet the problem remains that, for my students, Latin America is very far away, and even students who had been to Cancun, Buenos Aires, or Rio had probably not visited Native communities. How then can contemporary students, who feel twice removed from the historical experiences of the Native peoples of Latin America, learn what life was and is like for these people, in both rural and urban settings, during both the colonial and the modern periods?

Many excellent general texts about Latin American history exist, which for reasons of length nevertheless only mention Native peoples in passing, or as a way to set the stage for the arrival of the Europeans at the end of the fifteenth century and to explain challenges faced by the invaders in setting up colonial society. There are also many great studies of specific groups of people, including women, peasants, African slaves, and even social outcasts, as well as excellent books on Native peoples within specific countries during defined periods of time. However, I have often wished for a general text about Indigenous history that summarizes extant information and provides a general overview of Native experiences on the continent. According to the International Work Group for Indigenous Affairs, there are 40 million Indigenous people in Latin America and the Caribbean who belong to nearly 600 Indigenous groups. Indigenous numbers were significantly larger in prehistoric times, before contact with people from other continents. Hundreds of different groups of people in the Americas enjoyed their own languages, religious beliefs, and ways of life. Some groups traded together and were allies, while others competed for resources and fought against enemies. Given the great diversity of their experiences, it is no wonder that Indigenous peoples could not join forces to counter outside threats together, as occurred during the European invasions of the sixteenth century. The circumstances of each group may have been unique, but as we will discover, Indigenous peoples also faced common challenges. This textbook links these peoples together within the broader history of Latin America to retell the continent's history from a different point of view, one where Indigenous people figure as central actors rather than passing human interest stories in an evening news brief.

Learning Indigenous Histories

Since many Indigenous groups did not leave written documents, much of what we know about their histories comes from material written by outside observers and from non-written artifacts and material culture sources that Native people left behind, such as tools, architecture, artwork, and archeological remains. This is especially the case for people living before contact with Europeans, and for people who lived in settings difficult to access or far from European and then, later, national settlements. The obvious challenge in working with these sources is that outside observers, such as explorers or priests, wrote to communicate their own perspectives. These works naturally reflect the prejudice and stereotypes of their own time period and culture. Another problem is that mostly outsiders wrote these sources, often as letters or journal entries. Because of linguistic challenges or simply a lack of interest, they rarely directly revealed what the Native people thought about the historical events in question. We can sometimes only guess at Indigenous perspectives on the events recorded by putting their known actions and responses into context. Therefore some of the history about early Indigenous experiences is at best informed guesswork or an approximation of Native intents based on recorded events, and a historian must contextualize Indigenous actions within their own observation of such actions and hope to approximate motivation, causes, and the results of occurrences long past.

An ethnohistorical approach helps clarify the past more completely because in that approach to history, scholars keep in mind the cultures and ways of life of the historical actors as they seek to explain historical events. This is the general approach taken in this text to understand Indigenous histories in Abya Yala. The name "Abya Yala" comes from the Kuna Indigenous people who today live on the Caribbean coast of Panama. The term means "land in full maturity" and "land of vital blood." Aymara leader Takir Mamani, in Bolivia, recently proposed "Abya Yala" as a name for the Americas outside European heritage; Indigenous peoples have increasingly employed the term in recent years.[1] This book uses the term to refer to Indigenous Latin America, the continent prior to European colonization.

Why Study Indigenous Peoples and their Histories?

A superficial look at Latin America suggests few reasons to study Indigenous history. After all, Europeans conquered all major Native peoples and established a new society that pushed Indigenous people to the very bottom of the new social structure. A few Europeans spoke against common abuses and noticed that Native populations were collapsing from disease, yet the importation of slaves from Africa gave the colonizers a replacement labor pool. Racism and prejudice shaped the way in which the conquerors viewed the original peoples with whom they created the Americas. During the later colonial period, Indigenous people obstructed the imposition of total European rule and did so even more as politicians shaped new countries following independence. State expansion during the twentieth century often left Natives as peasants or urban poor in the shanty towns of developing cities. Scholars have frequently relegated Indigenous people to the periphery of Latin American history, irrelevant to most important historical events that shaped the continent. So why study them?

The historical field has changed its traditional focus on European colonial and state expansion to include people who have not traditionally held political power, and the results of this shift in perspective have shaped this text. During the second half of the twentieth century, some historians studied the experiences of the common people rather than the histories of great men that dominated the field in previous centuries, providing a view of history from the bottom up. Howard Zinn's book *A People's History of the United States* is a good example of this approach. Rather than focus on the founding fathers and political leaders, the generals, and corporations that shaped U.S. history, Zinn instead looked at how Native people, the poor, women, slaves, rebels, and differing political ideologies each helped form the United States. This book

Map 1.2 Modern Political Borders in Latin America

also takes a bottom-up approach as much as possible, using an ethnohistorical perspective that employs the study of Indigenous cultures to explore how Native peoples shaped Latin America's history.

Learning Indigenous history thus shows a different side of Latin America, a new perspective of the continent's people that has all too often been ignored in traditional histories, especially after European contact. That in and of itself should be a good reason to engage the experiences of Latin American Native peoples. Yet Indigenous people have also played a central role in shaping Latin American history, and learning about their participation helps us learn about the entire continent in greater depth. From the people on the Caribbean islands who first met Columbus' expeditions, to recent Native presidents of Latin American states, Indigenous people have influenced and shaped the history of Latin America. This book outlines their influence and participation in that history. The image of X'oyep women in Chiapas, southern Mexico (see Figure 1.1) shows Native people resisting state authorities.

Figure 1.1 X'oyep Women in Chiapas, Mexico Confront Security Forces during the Zapatista Uprising in 1994. (Archivo Pedro Valtierra, Cuartoscuro Agencia de Fotografía y Editora)

Definitions: Who is Indigenous? How Can We Know?

This book begins with some definitions and theory to guide the study. Defining the term "Indigenous" helps set the framework for the scope of this work. Some people in the United States have replaced the traditional yet pejorative term "Indian" with one deemed more politically correct: "Native American." In Canada, the terms "host population" and "First Nations" for Native peoples and "settler culture" or "settler people" for European colonists are employed as a better way to explain frontier dynamics, where the settler heritage appropriated and used land that had initially belonged to the host people.

In Latin America, the term that "Europeans" used to designate the first people they met in the Caribbean was "Indians," a result of Columbus' mistaken understanding of geography: the famous explorer simply thought he had reached India in southeastern Asia. In opposition to European abuses and prejudice, as well as because they are of course simply not from India, people descended from the original Latin Americans have preferred to call themselves aboriginal, Indigenous persons, or Natives. Because in British history the term "aboriginal" often refers to the Australian colonial context, this study employs "Indigenous person" or "Native" to designate the descendants of people who lived in the Americas prior to European colonization. For simplicity's sake, I have used these designations to refer to all original peoples, despite the many differences between them. For example, the Wichi, who traditionally hunted and gathered in small groups in the western Chaco region of what is today northern Argentina, live very differently than those Native people who organized and ruled over huge political empires, such as the Aztecs, Incas, or Mayans. This book nevertheless considers them all Indigenous to the Americas because they trace their ancestry to pre-Columbian times.

Scholars argue about the exact definition of these peoples, and whether they were actually Indigenous or not according to specific theories, and the distinctions in each of their cultures are, of course, important. In *A Global History of Indigenous Peoples*, historian Ken S. Coates has summarized different definitions of Indigenous peoples and provided his own helpful summary. The link below connects to the collection of documents on Indigenous identity. This book adopts some shortcuts: if the people in question trace their ancestry to pre-Hispanic roots and consider themselves Indigenous, we honor their choice and include them as Indigenous people of Latin America.[2]

For Document 1.1: Five Documents on Indigenous Identity, visit www.routledge.com/9780415519120.

The first document for this chapter includes definitions for Indigenous peoples, beginning with some definitions used at the United Nations. The initial excerpt is by Julian Berger, who for over 20 years directed the program on Indigenous peoples and minorities at the U.N. Office of the High Commissioner for Human Rights. Berger argues that central to being Indigenous was belonging to a separate culture, including language, religion, political and moral values, art, music, and dance. What else is included in the document? What does he define as the relationship of Native peoples to colonization, conquest, and agriculture? In what ways might Indigenous political organizations differ? As you read Berger's definition, consider what "decentralized political structure" and "community level organization" would mean for Aztec or Incan rulers. Were those people not Indigenous because they ruled an empire? Almost all the definitions of "Indigenous" spell out the relationship of the minority people to the dominant society. Finally, Berger's definition allows self-identification by individuals. This point is important: to be Indigenous one must consider oneself to be a member of that group of people.

Another definition, this one from the early 1970s, comes from José Martínez Cobo, an Ecuadorian representative to the U.N. subcommittee on Indigenous peoples. How does he define the relationship between Native peoples and their traditional homelands, culture, and language? Why might Cobo have chosen this emphasis? Why might a U.N. official have emphasized individual self-identification as being so important to *indigeneity*, that is, to being Indigenous? The U.N. Commission on Human Rights, Economic and Social Council, as we read in the next document, defines "Indigenous" as being descended from people who existed before colonization and who were overrun by global capitalism. The U.N. Draft Declaration on the Rights of Indigenous Peoples did not employ this definition, because it defines Indigenous people in their relation to capitalism and to a specific territory rather than on their own terms. Another definition that frames Indigenous identity within contemporary ways of life is by the IWGIA, the International Work Group for Indigenous Affairs. This definition also frames Native peoples as disadvantaged victims of the dominant society. While their marginalization may often be the case, most Indigenous peoples have responded creatively to the challenges they face, and some have even been victors in their struggles; thus, portraying them as victims is also at times inaccurate.

Given the differences in points of views, even among experts, for our purposes this book adopts the definition of Indigenous peoples written by Ken S. Coates in *A Global History of Indigenous Peoples*, included with the documents to this chapter.[3] Coates' definition is thorough, and defines Native people in their own right and not only in opposition to outside forces. While global in design, Coates' description refers to some features that are very important to Native lives throughout Latin America: the size of group, their relation to the land and environment, mobility, sustainability, and similar historical relationships with colonial and later independent societies. Coates' definition also includes historical perspectives for Indigenous societies: both past and contemporary experiences have shaped Native people throughout Abya Yala and Latin America. History has been critically important to Indigenous people, as it is to us all. Keep Coates' definition in mind as we engage in the study of Latin American Indigenous people; let it serve as a foundation for the varieties of peoples and experiences we encounter.

Colonized and Colonizers

As several of these definitions suggest, outsiders have often defined Indigenous people based on their relationships with outside people. Sometimes stronger military or colonizing forces conquered Native people. For many of the peoples included in the U.N. definition, it would have been European colonization during the early modern times that altered the way they traditionally lived. In other cases, Native people traded products and resources with each other, and over time their use of different technologies changed their ways of life. Moves to new locations, in or near European cities, for instance, or to work in mines or on farms, gradually altered Indigenous cultures. All these life-changing events are interrelated, but necessarily influenced the way the Native people viewed themselves and, over time, their own identity. One must be careful to remember, though, that groups of humans have always interacted thus; peoples who were militarily stronger took advantage of peoples with weaker defenses to appropriate

Figure 1.2 The Conquest, Art by Eurides Gómez, Nivaclé, Paraguayan Chaco.

labor, sacrificial victims, wealth, and resources in many places in the world. Nobody invested colonization purposefully to exploit the Indigenous peoples in Latin America; it has existed since humans first organized themselves. Early groups of hominids raided each other's camps. Early biblical literature is full of examples of stronger peoples taking advantage of weaker groups. Early civilizations such as the Assyrians or Egyptians were just as used to conquest and appropriation of resources as were the later Greeks, Romans, and Europeans. Thus, accepting that similar events occurred previously and in most other contexts of human interactions helps keep the analysis of Indigenous experiences in Latin America more objective. Still, as a recent picture drawn by Nivaclé artist Eurides Gómez for this textbook suggests, visions of the Spanish conquest remain alive and present for Indigenous people in Latin America.

Cultural Complications and Stumbling Blocks

After journalist Walter Lippmann first coined the term "stereotype" in the 1920s to mean a widely held but simplified idea of particular types of people or things, society has become much more aware of how we view and think about groups of people who may differ from us. All peoples hold stereotypes of others and many of them are hurtful and harm social interaction. As people face experiences they do not understand, they create ideas and images to find meaning and impose order upon the world. Many of these thoughts are simply incorrect. Think about your personal views of Indigenous people, both in the United States and in Latin America. Indians lived in teepees and hunted buffalo and shot cowboys on the Great Plains from horseback with rifles, right? Actually, only a few peoples on the Great Plains did so, and then only for a short time, and even then only after acquiring guns and horses from the Europeans. So that image is a stereotype. Which of our ideas about Indigenous people are accurate, and which may be stereotypical or even prejudicial? What has contributed to our misunderstandings and stereotypes of Native peoples? Which stereotypes about Native peoples might you hold?

One of the first stereotypes we should disregard is the idea that Indigenous people were all the same, that they thought and acted as a single unified group, and were all products of a distant prehistoric past. We need to remember that most Indigenous peoples largely lived in small, scattered, single groups with linguistic, cultural, and religious differences from one another, rather than in a united block just because they shared the same continent. Another common stereotype is that Natives everywhere lived in small bands, were fairly ignorant, and all disappeared when hit with European "technological superiority." This image is far from reality. Just as Europeans changed as their technology developed and new understandings transformed their societies, Indigenous people did not keep on living the same as their ancestors throughout time. Another view holds that people originally in the Americas all died from diseases when they met Europeans; concurrently, that people today claiming Native heritage must be imposters out to get what money and land they can from the government. At the root of these stereotypes is a lack of historical understanding and the desire to elevate oneself above other people.

Building on the work of novelist Raymond Williams, Brazilian anthropologist Alcida Rita Ramos has identified keywords that non-Natives use to stereotype Indigenous people and their cultures. As you read through them, consider whether you have ever heard these words associated with Indigenous people and with what intent. The first of these is *child*. Explorers viewed Native people as innocent, ingenuous, good, simple, guileless, and trusting, as they would imagine a young child who showed little interest in exchange commodities like gold or silver. The epitome of this stereotype is the use of Native Americans for toys or children's movies such as *Pocahontas*. Another harmful designation is *heathen*, and it is not difficult to understand how this stereotype developed, given the missionary enterprise of European explorers. Rather than accept Indigenous beliefs and deities which they observed as legitimate, European missionary goals allowed them to cast Native people as both demonic and devoid of any beliefs. A third stereotype is *nomadic*, with all its resulting associations, such as being disordered wanderers who used land that should otherwise have been colonized for profit, or who ranged willy-nilly through the forest without a clear purpose. Moreover, what about the sedentary Indigenous peoples who lived from agriculture, even deep within the Amazon rainforest? Many Native peoples moved in order to harvest resources, but few were actually completely nomadic. Still another erroneous term is *primitive*, usually used to label Indigenous people who lived on the borders of imperial centers as crude, savage, and uncivilized. As Ramos points out, this term reflects upon the host country – Brazil in her case – in a negative way. One often also hears the stereotype *savage* applied to Indigenous people, especially in reference to their violent responses to European aggression or from various cultural practices. The reason why it is important to eliminate hurtful stereotypical terms is not only because they are incorrect but also because the people who first employed them (missionaries, journalists, anthropologists, explorers) all relegated (Indigenous) subjects to an inferior position.[4] When one reads primary sources written by these people, it is important to keep these stereotypes in mind and reflect upon the meanings and intentions behind the words.

An additional stereotype that is important to keep in mind when studying Indigenous history is self-evident but often overlooked. The many hundreds of Indigenous nations in Abya Yala when the Europeans arrived were mostly disparate and small. Each people had their own language, beliefs, customs, faith, and history of interaction with outside groups. Many groups traded with others, and imperial powers overran and conquered some peoples to exploit their resources and labor, yet most Native peoples did not interact with other groups much beyond some trading, or in war, and could not even understand or speak with other Indigenous peoples. Fragmentation because of cultural differences helps explain so much of what occurred after Indigenous people met the European explorers and colonists, and it is central to keep this diversity in mind when studying Native history.

Indigenous history and Native subjects of study are also inherently political: not as in what political party one does or does not support, but rather relating directly to state policies and their results for people within a country. As students explore how Indigenous people helped shape the Latin American countries in which they live today, or where their ancestors may have lived prior to political independence, their relationships to government leaders inevitably come under consideration. Changing political leadership, and struggles between conservatives and liberals within various state boundaries and between those countries and the United States, inevitably affected Native peoples during the nineteenth and twentieth centuries. The sale of tropical fruits and products late in the nineteenth century, opposition to populist or socialist leaders, U.S. support of military dictatorships, and the Cold War all shaped the lives of Latin Americans, including Indigenous peoples. Natives have often been people without political power; this means they did not enjoy access to a society's established structures for political representation and therefore lacked a voice or power within the country where they lived. While some Indigenous people have gained a political voice and even positions in government, the majority remain without a legitimate way to influence and shape political change. Studying their past is therefore often necessarily political.

The Indigenous population varied widely throughout Abya Yala and still does today, for both geographical and political reasons. Indigenous people today comprise 10 percent of Latin America's population. In a few countries, Natives form a political plurality and make up the relative majority, though often they have not controlled political outcomes to that extent. In Bolivia and Guatemala, Indigenous people make up over 60 percent of the population. In Peru and Ecuador, Native people comprise between 30 and 45 percent of the total population, and in Mexico 14.9 percent. Paraguay, despite widespread use of the Indigenous language Guaraní and extensive racial mixture, has a Native population of only between 2 and 3 percent. Brazil celebrates a large historical Native presence, yet Indigenous peoples today account for only 0.4 to 1 percent of the total population. More than 80 percent of Indigenous people live in five countries situated where the large Aztec, Maya, and Inca empires once flourished: Mexico, Guatemala, Ecuador, Peru, and Bolivia. Twelve Native language groups today have more than one million speakers, which together form 73 percent of the region's Indigenous population.[5] Despite demographic plurality in several countries, however, Native people have often lacked political representation and influence, with obvious results.

Constructive Ways to Approach Indigenous History and Native Responses

In her book on pan-Maya activism in Guatemala during the last decades of the twentieth century, Kay Warren, Professor of Anthropology at Harvard University, lays out four fallacies often employed by North Americans in their formulation of Mesoamerican ethnicity. While originally presented by Warren to Mayan audiences in Guatemala, these fallacies also help inform a more general study of Indigenous people. The four fallacies also contrast with Warren's formulation of a more positive approach to Native history, which she suggests as the constructionist alternative. As you read the documents in the link at the end of this paragraph, consider their implications carefully, as we will return to these ideas in different ways throughout this book.

For Document 1.2: Theory from Kay Warren, James Scott and Benedict Anderson, visit www.routledge.com/9780415519120.

The constructionist approach that Warren suggests as a positive alternative to the fallacies she lists is a more informed way to study Indigenous history. As we will see, ethnicity is indeed often the way people negotiate, represent, resist, and appropriate their identity, yet these are not all up to choice: culture, class, and politics all influence personal and group actions. This approach emphasizes keeping in mind how people exercise and challenge power: domination and subordination are central to Indigenous histories and critical to the study of "how" and not only the "why" involved in cultural change. In this approach, identifying labels are important, but obviously they change as they are "constructed, contested, negotiated, imposed, imputed, resisted, and redefined in action." This view also allows for economic and political transitions; there is no one predetermined model or pattern that applies to all peoples, but rather changing economic and political structures that affect people differently over time. Nor is ethnicity a vestige from the distant past, but is instead a product of the modern world.

Finally, ethnic identity is "continually reinvented" through the creation and changes of communities and peoples.[6] These ideas may seem like splitting hairs over theoretical concepts, yet the idea of "cultural change" rather than "cultural loss" will become more important as we explore Indigenous history. The following interview helps explain how Indigenous people can participate fully in modern society without losing their Indigenous identity. Keep these ideas in mind as we study historical change throughout Indigenous societies in Abya Yala.

Individuals: Professor Irma Velázquez Nimatuj, Ph.D.

To illustrate the idea that people can identify as Indigenous and still participate in modern society, in February 2017 I interviewed Irma Velázquez Nimatuj, a K'iche' social anthropologist from the community of Quezaltenango in Guatemala. During the time we talked in Durham, N.C., Dr. Nimatuj was teaching two courses at the Latin American Studies center at Duke University: "Indigenous Resistance & Revolution: Mexico and Central America" and a graduate course in anthropology, "Indigeneity, Ontology, Epistemology," co-taught with Diane Nelson, Professor of Cultural Anthropology. Dr. Nelson called Nimatuj "one of the most important intellectuals and activists in Guatemala."[7] Dr. Nimatuj traces her Indigenous heritage for centuries: the K'iche' nation gained influence following the demise of the Aztec Empire and her ancestors have lived in her community for at least fifteen generations. Her father traveled broadly to trade and Dr. Nimatuj thus grew up in a merchant family. Her mother did not even speak Spanish, yet nevertheless encouraged her children to attend school and to learn Spanish so they could better resist outside control. After studying to be a teacher and then attending a public university, Dr. Nimatuj worked as a reporter for a newspaper, where she had to hide her Indigenous identity to keep her job. She later attended Florida International University with a Fulbright Fellowship, the first Indigenous woman to win such academic recognition.

Continuing her studies, Dr. Nimatuj finished an MA in Anthropology at Indiana University, writing a thesis that analyzed why her K'iche' people did not hold political power. She then continued her graduate studies at the University of Texas at Austin, becoming the first K'iche' Maya woman to earn a Ph.D. in social anthropology. In her dissertation, Dr. Nimatuj analyzed how the extension of coffee onto Indigenous lands in her community had contributed to prostitution among Indigenous women. She employed Marxist theory to analyze how Latino racism contributed to the oppression of the Indigenous population. Dr. Nimatuj successfully lobbied the European Union to allow more of the proceeds from coffee harvesting to benefit the Indigenous women who did the work. In June 2002, she participated in an Indigenous march from San Marcos to the capital, Guatemala City, to lobby unsuccessfully for landownership. The following year, Dr. Nimatuj initiated a court case in the capital that made racial discrimination in Guatemala illegal. She has spoken out about human rights abuses by the military, particularly on Indigenous women, and served as a witness at a trial on behalf of 15 Maya women forced into sexual and domestic servitude by military officers during the Guatemalan Civil War (1960–1996). The recent documentary film *500 Years*, which premiered at the 2017 Sundance Film Festival, features Dr. Nimatuj in its focus on Mayan resistance and the historic genocide trial against former president Efraín Ríos Montt. Dr. Diane Nelson from Duke University explains that Nimatuj's books on Mayan struggles for land following a genocidal war are some of the best analyses of this central issue in Guatemalan history.[8]

Figure 1.3 Dr. Irma Velázquez Nimatuj. (Photo courtesy Dr. Nimatuj)

Indigenous Responses to Outside Scholars

Dr. Nimatuj's experience shows an example of ways in which Indigenous people participate actively in contemporary life without changing their Native heritage. Sometimes, however, the issue of identity is controversial, especially when heritage, political access, or even finances are involved and disputed as a result. Dr. Warren, for instance, presented her paper on the fallacies of "indianness" and constructionist alternatives in 1989 to a group of Mayan scholars in Guatemala. Her ideas provoked a heated response from leaders involved in the pan-Maya movement, who were working to reconstruct Mayan identity and influence following a devastating genocide that occurred during the 1980s. One of her most outspoken critics was the best-known Mayan intellectual of the day, Dr. Demetrio Cojtí Cuxil. By origin Kaqchikel, Dr. Cojtí has been a critic of the neocolonial nature of Guatemalan society, holds a Ph.D. from the University of Louvain in Belgium, and has worked for UNICEF. Clearly, this Mayan intellectual is influential and has been actively involved in Guatemalan society, since he served as Deputy Minister of Education between 2000 and 2004 and has taught at several universities in Guatemala, Spain, and the U.S. He is also author of numerous books on the revitalization of Mayan culture. Countering Warren, Dr. Cojtí argued that the appropriate role for foreign anthropologists was to help note continuities in Mayan culture, those essentialist features inherited from precolonial times that make Mayas Mayan, not to argue against these characteristics! This intellectual argues for the existence of a central essentialist cultural core and legacy that gives Native peoples their identity. Dr. Cojtí has also written about *ladinos*, people of mixed Indigenous and European racial heritage and another distinct ethnic group in Guatemala, presenting them as having a personality crisis resulting from the insecurity of their cultural domination.[9] Dr. Cojtí has countered attacks on Mayans as "Marxists, racists, radicals, bigots, purists," turning such criticism by instead emphasizing Mayan collective rights. Why might this Indigenous intellectual have found Warren's suggestions so offensive to his program of re-vindicating Mayan identity and furthering his people's rights? Can we employ Warren's theory, removed as we are from Guatemala, even if some Mayan intellectuals and leaders found it unhelpful for their causes? This exchange illustrates the controversial nature of Indigenous identity as Native people interact with political and economic structures.

Additional Theoretical Analysis of How People without Power Respond to Outside Control

Another scholar whose work helps us understand Indigenous history is the influential political scientist James Scott, whose work focuses on the way people without power resist those who try to control them. Scott's book *Domination and the Arts of Resistance* analyzes the strategies people employ to counter stronger authority or undesired impositions. Many of this scholar's points apply to our study, yet one important specific concept from Scott is the idea of the hidden transcript, in which people without power employ subtle ways to communicate their anger against outsiders rather than acting out directly. Indigenous peoples at times seemed to conform to expectations of the powerful in interactions, even as they employed more subtle ways to make known their disapproval or anger at the power disparities between them and the colonizers or other more powerful entities.[10] One example of this is the Napo Runa people of Tena-Archidona, in Ecuador's eastern forests, who served as colonial porters for travelers, and who also carried food supplies and products to and from the capital. Called *bestias de silla*, literally riding beasts or mules, Runa porters carried travelers on their backs as late as the nineteenth century. Sometimes, as if to show their disapproval of the job, porters dumped their traveler burdens into a swamp and made off with their goods.[11] Perhaps casting off their burdens was a not-so-hidden transcript of angry responses to unfair labor practices.

Benedict Anderson, a noted political scientist, is the author of *Imagined Communities*, a book that explores the creation of nationalism and countries in general, especially as nationalism relates to printing, languages of state, and concepts of time. Anderson's analysis helps explain the political context within which Indigenous people live. One important idea that Anderson contributes to this work are the foundational ideas for nationalism: horizontal comradeship, solidarity among whites, and a background based on a common heritage of race mixture. Who is left out of these common bonds? As students will explore in chapters 9 and 10, Anderson's analysis of young countries as they developed in Latin America helps explain how new rulers treated Native peoples. Creole functionaries who took control following independence played decisive roles in the origins of national consciousness in Latin America. Too often, their lifestyles, attitudes, and policies contrasted sharply with those they excluded from power – Indigenous people and Afro-descendants – who fought in their armies but did not receive benefits in the newly formed countries. Anderson analyzed how these new leaders artfully used the idea of their Indigenous heritage, from the Aztecs, Mayas, and Toltecs in Mexico to the Tupamaros National Liberation Movement, an urban guerrilla group active during the 1960s and 1970s. Even though these guerrillas fought in Uruguay instead of Peru, where the eighteenth-century Aymara leader Tupac Amaru had lived and fought, the Tupamaros employed Amaru's name to show resistance and forge imagined links of strength to oppose the ruling military regime.

Conclusion

The welcome that Indigenous people from Argentina, Bolivia, Brazil, and Paraguay gave to Pope John Paul II in 1988 illustrates the way in which Native peoples in Latin America were organizing themselves during the last decades of the twentieth century. Speaking to power, marching to obstruct rural development projects, demanding inclusion in the new constitutions that followed the decline of military rule across the continent, and forging broad liaisons with other Native peoples, NGOs, and politicians are all tactics that illustrate yet another awakening by Indigenous peoples that has occurred over these last several decades. Once again, Indigenous people have made their presence known and have demanded recognition by the outsiders and countries that enveloped their ancestors so long ago. For if Indigenous peoples have been profoundly changed by their relationship with the enveloping Latin American countries, by studying the history of their interaction with outsiders one also realizes the degree to which Native people have also altered the course of the entire continent. The dialectic between these peoples and outside forces changed individual lives and the experiences of entire groups of people, as well as the very courses of the empires that tried to control them and the countries that spread across the continent in place of former Indigenous lands.

Discussion Questions

1. What previous knowledge about Indigenous people do you bring to this class?
2. Which of the common stereotypes of Indigenous people have you experienced?
3. Which image of Indigenous people should be emphasized and promoted, and why?
4. What emotions and perspectives are portrayed in the depiction of the Conquest drawn by Nivaclé artist Eurides Gómez for this chapter?
5. Who holds power and influence in your community, state, and nation? What groups lack this authority and why?
6. How can Indigenous people both identify as Indigenous and still participate fully in contemporary society?
7. What insights into recent Indigenous experiences does Dr. Nimatuj provide?

Notes

1 López-Hernández, *Encuentros de los Senderos.*

2 Several theoretical texts that explain Indigenous identity in greater depth include Maybury-Lewis' *Indigenous Peoples, Ethnic Groups, and the State*, Urban and Sherzer's *Nation-States and Indians in Latin America*, and Héctor Díaz Polanco's *Indigenous Peoples in Latin America.*

3 Coates, *A Global History of Indigenous Peoples, Struggle and Survival*, 13–14.

4 Ramos, *Indigenism*, ch. 1.

5 Van Cott, *The Friendly Liquidation of the Past*, 14.

6 Warren, "Transforming Memories," 204–206.
7 "CLACS Welcomes Indigenous Rights Activist to Duke," Duke University Center for Latin America and Caribbean Studies, spring 2017. I interviewed Dr. Nimatuj on February 1, 2017 in Durham, N.C.
8 "CLACS Welcomes Indigenous Rights Activist to Duke." Available at https://latinamericancaribbean.duke.edu/clacs-welcomes-indigenous-rights-activist-duke.
9 Cojtí Cuxil, Demetrio, cited in Warren, *Indigenous Movements*, 46, 74, 230, 249.
10 Scott, *Domination and the Arts of Resistance*, 36–37.
11 Muratorio, *The Life and Times of Grandfather Alonso*, 31.

2 Indigenous Latin America

Abya Yala

Chronology

25,000 years ago to 12,000 years B.C.E.	Migration(s) over Bering Strait land bridge.

Introduction: Who is Indigenous?

Scientists largely agree that the first hominids, our distant ancestors, all came from Africa originally, so technically speaking no one is indigenous to Latin America. Paleoanthropologists (people who study early human remains) have discovered some of the earliest-known hominid bones in Ethiopia, where two huge pieces of the Earth's crust, tectonic plates named the African and Arabian plates, slowly grate against each other. Over the past 30 million years, resulting clashes gradually formed the Great Rift Valley in the Earth's crust, a deep trench that stretches from Israel south to Mozambique. Eruptions and earthquakes along this rift spewed fossils to the surface, where water and wind slowly uncover ancient hominid remains. Over the past decades, these 3-million-year-old fossils have given us a better understanding of our ancestors. It was beside a lake in Ethiopia, here, for instance, that in 1974, scientists discovered a small 3.2-million-year-old female *australopithecus afarensis* they named Lucy. This species lived alongside smaller hominids called *australopithecenes*, who eventually died out and allowed our early ancestors, the *Homo habilis*, to develop.[1] In turn, their descendants, the *Homo erectus*, lived by hunting and gathering between 1.5 million and 300,000 years ago. These forbearers of ours had much larger brains than earlier hominids, paleoanthropologists tell us, used fire and stone tools, and even ate meat. They spread from Africa up through Europe and Asia. Some of their successors were the more familiar Neanderthals, who lived in Europe between 100,000 and 40,000 years ago, and our direct ancestors, the *Homo sapiens*, eventually replaced them. Early forms of *Homo sapiens* emerged in each part of the world where there had been *Homo erectus*, and *Homo sapiens sapiens*, the most successful of these later people, eventually replaced other hominids. Does being Indigenous depend only on how long someone lives in a place? If one looks back far enough into prehistory we are all native only to Africa, so technically there are no people indigenous to the Americas.

What are the implications of such a startling conclusion? First, some might argue that people in Latin America who consider themselves Indigenous must be making up a story simply to get ahead or claim resources. One might also conclude that there would be no reason to write this book on Indigenous Latin America if we are all technically indigenous only to Africa. Third, when foreigners first arrived, land in the Americas could more easily be seen as free for their taking, since nobody could claim to be Indigenous and to have staked a prior legitimate claim to the territory. We might consider Indigenous people only as earlier migrants, despite thousands of years of occupancy between their arrival and the arrival of Europeans. If we were to adopt those points of view, it would be much easier today to dismiss Indigenous claims to better rights, given that they, like Europeans, had also arrived from elsewhere to settle a new continent. Our scientific explanations would more easily invalidate Indigenous accounts of their origins, stories of migration, descent, emergence, deluge, and creation. The discussion between Native people and scientists over Indigenous origins is thus highly charged, political, and critical to understanding people in the Americas who claim Indigenous ancestry and identity.

This chapter explores both Indigenous and scientific stories about how people first came to be in Abya Yala and explains how the story we choose to value helps shape our views about Indigenous people.

The ancestry of Indigenous peoples, and how they came to be in Abya Yala, is therefore important to both earlier and later immigrants, Natives, and others. Who is Indigenous and who is not, as well as where we all belong today, helps us understand why we live where we are, why we live like we do, how we interact with other people and our natural surroundings, and how we relate to political forces that try to control our lives. It also helps determine who is Indigenous and has the earliest claim to these continents and who should have the right to claim their lands and resources. In the following pages we engage both Indigenous and scientific stories about how people first occupied Abya Yala.

How and When did People Populate the Americas? Some Indigenous Accounts

Why does it matter when people first settled the Americas? Do people who first use the land have first claim to that territory as their property? What really determines who owns a place and its resources? Is it a piece of paper from the previous owner, a real estate agency, or the government? Or is it the person who first cleared the land or whoever officially bought the property? Is it whoever has the deadliest weapons? Did a supreme religious deity grant certain people ownership over this territory, and therefore can they claim manifest sanction for the use of force to take over the place? Before we examine the scientific account of how people first came to the Americas, this book first explores how Indigenous people explain their own origins. Their stories reveal important information about who these people are and how they see their world.

Indigenous people generally attribute their presence in the Americas to creation by a supernatural deity, to emergence out of the earth, to a deluge, or to a long migration. As historian Ken S. Coates has explained, hundreds of Native stories link a specific geographic and environmental place with a creative power and their own people and culture.[2] The following section includes explanations by several different Indigenous peoples to explain their origin.

The Maya Origin Story

The Maya people of the Yucatan Peninsula kept their religious stories in a book called the Popol Vuh, most copies of which the Spanish quickly destroyed. Later, during the eighteenth century, a priest translated a remaining copy into Spanish, including their creation stories. The Maya origin story describes three imperfect creations and a final creation that turned out so nicely that it was modified so that people would not be as perfect as God. As in the Judeo-Christian tradition, in the Maya story God also spoke the world into being through a word.

This is the account of how all was in suspense, all calm, in silence; all motionless, still, and the expanse of the sky was empty.

This is the first account, the first narrative. There was neither man, nor animal, birds, fishes, crabs, trees, stones, caves, ravines, grasses, nor forests; there was only the sky.

There was nothing brought together, nothing which could make a noise, nor anything which might move, or tremble, or could make noise in the sky.

There was nothing standing; only the calm water, the placid sea, alone and tranquil. Nothing existed.

There was only immobility and silence in the darkness, in the night. Only the Creator, the Maker, Tepeu, Gucumatz, the Forefathers, were in the water surrounded with light. They were hidden under green and blue feathers, and were therefore called Gucumatz.[3] By nature they were great sages and great thinkers. In this manner the sky existed and also the Heart of Heaven, which is the name of God and thus He is called.

Then came the word. Tepeu and Gucumatz came together in the darkness, in the night, and Tepeu and Gucumatz talked together. They talked then, discussing and deliberating; they agreed, they united their words and their thoughts.

Then while they meditated, it became clear to them that when dawn would break, man must appear. Then they planned the creation, and the growth of the trees and the thickets and the birth of life and the creation of man. Thus it was arranged in the darkness and in the night by the Heart of Heaven who is called Huracán.

The first is called Caculhá Huracán. The second is Chipi-Caculhá. The third is Raxa-Caculhá. And these three are the Heart of Heaven.

Then Tepeu and Gucumatz came together; they then conferred about life and light, what they would do so that there would be light and dawn, who it would be who would provide food and sustenance.

Thus let it be done! Let the emptiness be filled! Let the water recede and make a void, let the earth appear and become solid; let it be done. Thus they spoke. Let there be light, let there be dawn in the sky and on the earth! There shall be neither glory nor grandeur in our creation and formation until the human being is made, man is formed. So they spoke.

Then the earth was created by them. So it was, in truth, that they created the earth. Earth! they said, and instantly it was made.

Like the mist, like a cloud, and like a cloud of dust was the creation, when the mountains appeared from the water; and instantly the mountains grew.

Only by a miracle, only by magic art were the mountains and valleys formed; and instantly the groves of cypresses and pines put forth shoots together on the surface of the earth.

And thus Gucumatz was filled with joy, and exclaimed: "Your coming has been fruitful, Heart of Heaven; and you, Huracán, and you Chipi-Caculhá, Raxa-Caculhá!"

"Our work, our creation shall be finished," they answered.

First the earth was formed, the mountains and the valleys; the currents of water were divided, the rivulets were running freely between the hills, and the water was separated when the high mountains appeared.

Thus was the earth created, when it was formed by the Heart of Heaven, the Heart of Earth, as they are called who first made it fruitful, when the sky was in suspense, and the earth was submerged in the water.

So it was that they made perfect the work, when they did it after thinking and meditating upon it.[4]

How does this story differ from your own understanding of beginnings? There are interesting similarities between the Maya creation stories and the Judeo-Christian stories with which students may be more familiar: both begin with God speaking the world into existence and then creating life on Earth in an ordered sequence. God also ordered the animals to serve and be killed. The accounts soon differ, however, and Mayans believed that God tried several times before coming up with the "correctly made" humans. Both Christians and Mayans believed their ancestors gave thanks for having been created. In some ways, the Maya belief that God had to decrease human perfection resembles the Genesis story of the Tower of Babel, where God kept people in their place when they believed themselves to be too powerful. Note also the importance that women played in the Mayan story, rather than being portrayed as the cause of human evil as in the Judeo-Christian stories of origin.

The Moche Origin Story

The Moche provide another example of belief in religious sources of life. The Moche lived along the northern Pacific coast of Peru, between the Nepeña Valley north of today's Lima and the Piura Valley south of Ecuador. Their culture followed the Chavin, a pre-Inca civilization that flourished between 1500 and 200 B.C.E. Anthropologists regard the Chavin as having been the original religious culture that influenced subsequent societies in Peru. Chavin artists carved animals and gods into walls and temple rooms and hammered them onto sculptures, textiles, and ceramics. Their rulers employed images of jaguars and caimans, who lived far away in jungles on the eastern slopes of the Andes, as incarnations in human forms, showing their extensive trade networks. Chavin ways of life profoundly shaped later peoples in Peru, especially the Moche, who flourished during the first centuries of the Common Era.

Moche origin stories developed in one of the driest deserts in the world, since mountains separated them from the Amazonian breezes and the Humboldt Current kept away moist ocean winds. The centers of their life were the sea, valley vegetation, desert sands, and mountains, as well as the irrigation systems for the maize, potatoes, cotton, and rice that supplemented their diet of fish. These people did not use a written language, but painted murals on the walls of their large pyramids and buildings act as texts. They also left behind hundreds of objects of gold, silver, copper, and ceramic vessels that suggest to us ideas about their cosmology.

Figure 2.1 Coca Takers beneath Bicephalas Arc. (Christioger B. Donnan and Donna McClelland, Christopher B. Donnan and Donna McClelland Moche Archive, 1963-2011, Dumbarton Oaks, Trustees for Harvard University, Washington, D.C.)

Moche artifacts reveal another glimpse into how Native people linked their origins to the land in which they lived and to supernatural beings. The Moche followed a supreme god who wore a sunrise headdress and lived in the high mountains towering to their east. This god created the world and the Moche. He had a son, a fanged deity who represented the celestial sun star and lived on the coast. Although somewhat frightening, the son was concerned for humans and taught them how to grow maize and vegetables. Every evening, like the sun that rises over the mountains and sets in the west, the fanged god descended into the ocean to battle threatening fish, crab monsters, and demons. God the son thus protected the people from frightening threats; he fought and cut the tail off a sea monster with a lizard body and snake tail, as well as a marine bivalve monster. When the god drowned in the sea, two cormorants with human form rescued him from the ocean bottom. If god the son represented the celestial sun, the Moche perhaps believed that cormorants rescued him every night and then he reappeared in the morning in ritual sacrifice to assure the daily return of the actual sun. A lizard with a bird headdress and a human form assisted god the son in his duties, while owls and snakes helped the creator god. The Moche climbed mountains to sacrifice human victims to their creator god, but most of the images and artifacts they left are associated with the sea. Their art and stories of origin suggest that while these people raised crops and ventured into the hills, their main food came from the ocean, their source of life and daily sustenance.[5] Only their gods lived in the threatening mountains to their east, and the Pacific Ocean played a huge role in shaping their culture.

The Mixtec Origin Story

The Mixtec, who lived in what is today the western part of the Mexican state of Oaxaca where there was no commanding imperial rule, called themselves people of the rain place. They kept detailed accounts, and had an interesting story about the foundation of the Earth and the five suns, or cosmic ages. The first sun, 4-Tiger, came into existence in 955 B.C.E. and lasted for 676 years. Ocelots ate the people under this first sun, they believed, in the year 13, and all of them perished. The Mixtec sun was destroyed in the year 1-Reed. The sun that followed was 4-Wind, and after 364 years, the wind carried away trees and houses and turned all people into monkeys. Even the sun was blown away by the wind and everything perished on day 4-Wind. The third sun was 4-Rain. Fire rained on those who lived under this sun and turned them all into turkeys. All their homes burned down. Fire also consumed the sun in year 1-Flint. The next sun lasted for 676 years and the Mixtec called it 4-Water. The water lasted for 52 years and finally swallowed all the people, who became fish; the heavens collapsed on them and they all died in a single day. That devastating day was also known as 4-Water and took place in the year 1-House, a day when even the mountains were overwhelmed. The water lasted for 52 years until another sun was born. This sun is the fifth one, in which we now live; it is called 4-Movement because of the way it follows its path. Under this sun, the Mixtec predict that people will face earthquakes and hunger until their own end.[6] Note how important detailed accounting for the passing of time and changes during the different stages was for the Mixtec people, being much more precise than in any other story so far.

The Cashinawa Origin Story

The Cashinawa, a non-literate people who practiced swidden (slash-and-burn) agriculture in the Peruvian Amazon, share an interesting belief about the origin of the rainbow. "In the beginning there was neither moon, stars, nor rainbow and the nights were totally dark. This situation changed because a young girl did not want to get married. She was called Iaça." Exasperated by her obstinacy, the mother finally sent her daughter away. The young girl wandered for a long time in tears and, when she tried to return home, the old woman refused to open the door. "You can sleep outside," she yelled. "That will teach you to not want to get married!" Sobbing, the young girl ran about frantically, and beat on the door. The mother was so infuriated that she cut off her daughter's head with a bush knife, and it rolled onto the ground. She threw the body into the river. During the night, the head moaned around the hut. After wondering about its future, it decided to change into the moon. "In this way," it reflected, "I shall be seen only from afar." The head promised the mother not to bear her any ill-will, provided she gave it balls of thread; by holding one end between its teeth, it got the vulture to take it up into the sky. The eyes of the decapitated girl became the stars and her blood the rainbow. Henceforth women would bleed each month, then the blood would clot and children with black bodies would be born. But if the semen clotted, the children would be born white.[7] These people linked the rainbows they saw in the sky to the menstrual cycle. Besides a mythical origin of the rainbow, note the way the Cashinawa explained differences in skin color as the result of the clotting of "two magical essences." Stories of origins, such as the accounts of the Garden of Eden in the Jewish, Christian, and Muslim faiths, have often explained biological differences between the genders. Religious leaders in these faiths have also used such accounts to control women and their reproductive choices.

The Tukano Origin Story

In the Vaupés area of southeastern Colombia, the Tukano recount that the first humans, a man and woman, descended from the Milky Way in a large serpent canoe. Father Sun showed them how to make a magical drink to connect them with radiant powers in the heavens. The sun also gave them cassava, coca, and caapi vine to eat and drink along their journey. The golden light of the sun gave the first people the rules on how to live and how to speak. While the first men made the potion, the sun god impregnated the first woman through her eye. Her child was born in a flash of light. The woman, named Yaye, cut the umbilical cord and rubbed the baby with magical herbs to shape its body, and he became a boy who radiated golden light. The glowing infant became known as Caapi, named after the narcotic vine plant, and lived to become an old man. Each Tukano male, when becoming a man, cut a piece of his Caapi vines to release his hallucinatory powers, to join with the source of life, and thus receive his semen. In yet another version of the story, the first Tukanoan woman of creation drowned men in visions, since they viewed intercourse as a visionary experience.[8] Tukano stories of origin focus on descent from the sky and a unique connection with celestial bodies, especially the sun. They linked a celestial voyage to procreation and the reception of food from their celestial deity.

The Q'om Origin Story

The Q'om of the Gran Chaco, in what is today northern Argentina, explain the arrival of women to the world by noting that in the beginning men were still all animals. One day, Hawk led his hunting party to the forest. In the evening, they roasted their prey, storing extra meat on their thatched roofs. The following morning, after the hunters left, women came down from their home in the sky on ropes and stole all the food. When the hunters returned, they asked each other, "Who has eaten our meat?"

When the same thing happened the following day, Rabbit guarded the meat while the men hunted, but he fell asleep and never saw the women descend and steal their meat. The hunters mistreated him for not having better protected their food. The next day Parrot guarded the roasted meat after receiving instructions to watch even more carefully. From the top of a *quebracho* tree, Parrot saw the women descend as usual. "Now I see why nothing was left. There are indeed many thieves," he declared. As they stole the meat, Parrot noticed that the women had two mouths; that is, their vulvas also had teeth so they could eat both above and below. They gathered the game in a heap and sat down to enjoy it in the shade. Parrot carefully dropped a fruit on one of the women. "Look up in the tree," exclaimed the woman, "there sits my future husband, the man whom I shall marry." They all looked up at Parrot. "No," said another, "I will marry him." "No, he is going to be mine," retorted yet another. The women fought over Parrot, scratching, biting, and hitting. They even threw sticks at each other, one of which hit Parrot in the mouth, breaking the bone under his tongue and twisting his beak. Then the women returned up the ropes into the sky.

The next day, Hawk kept watch and prepared two sticks to fight the thieves. The women descended on two ropes, the young, pretty women down one and the old, ugly ones on another. They carefully examined each tree to see if they were being watched, then quickly ate the meat. Suddenly, the women saw Hawk spying and started to fight over who would marry him. "He is my husband," cried one, "I shall marry him." "He is my man, shut up," cried another. "You may marry him, but I shall kill him," shouted another woman. Soon they were all throwing sticks at Hawk, which he parried with his wings. Finally, the women grew tired and climbed the ropes to the sky. When they were high in the air, Hawk threw a stick and cut the rope, causing many women to fall back to earth. Hawk picked out two women for himself before calling the other men. The women fell with such force they were stuck under the ground. When the hunters returned, they dug out the women, each keeping the one he found. As the armadillo dug, he scratched a woman and left her blind in one eye.

The men divided the women among themselves. Hawk warned them, "take care, they have two mouths!" The men were frightened when they heard the grinding noise of the teeth in the women's vulvas. Fox declared, "I don't care, I shall do as I please." To find out what the noise was, Fox forced his wife to have sex beside a lagoon, but as they began to make love she cut off his penis and testicles with the teeth of her vulva and Fox died. A little rain fell; Fox returned to life, made himself a wooden penis, and looked for his wife. He found her at Hawk's camp, and she invited him in. But when she tried to bite his wooden penis, it was too hard and was only dented. The men made a big fire and placed the women around it with their legs spread; their teeth chattered noisily when exposed to the heat. Hawk threw rocks to break off all the woman's teeth except one (the clitoris) and declared, "Now wait, tomorrow your wives will be well again and you may safely copulate with them." The others were so afraid that their teeth withdrew and stopped making a noise. So each hunter was left with one woman and remained with the one they had found. The Q'om myths of origin help explain the importance of their practice of bilateral descent, a form of family lineage in which relatives on both the mother's and the father's sides share equal importance for emotional ties and both parents pass on family property and inheritance equally to their children.[9]

The Nahua-Speaking Peoples' Origin Stories

The Nahua-speaking peoples in Central America have some of the best-known stories of origins by migration. The Pipil and Nicarao, the first Nahuatl-descended people to reach Nicaragua, tell of a long trip out of the north to their homelands in Guatemala, El Salvador, and Nicaragua.[10] "We are not natives of this land, and it was a long time ago that our predecessors came here, and we do not remember how long ago because it was not in our time," the Nicarao in Teocatega, Nicaragua recounted to Fray Francísco de Bobadillo. In 1528 Governor Pedro Arias de Avila had sent Bobadillo to discover how the arrival of Christianity had changed Indigenous people of Nicaragua. "In that remote time there came upon them [our predecessors] a great army of people, called Olmecas," who "defeated and subjugated the natives [sic.]." The invaders imposed great tributes and demanded a large number of maidservants to take as women and to avail themselves of them. They also forced each town to give them two children daily for sacrifice, for eating, or for service, as well as 100 turkeys each day. The Olmecas used the Natives as slaves and for the "slightest discontent about their service they... shot them with arrows."[11] "Their masters kept them for these purposes and they ate them, and thus they [our predecessors] left their houses out of fear; and their masters had come from other lands, and they had subjugated them, because they were many, and for this reason they left their land." Elders counseled the people to flee and promised their gods would follow behind, guarding and defending them. When four years without rain finally made conditions intolerable, the people fled by boat along the coast of the South Sea [Pacific Ocean]. Some refugees settled in Quauhtemallan [Guatemala], while the Chorotega moved on to the Isthmus of Rivas region of Nicaragua by 800 C.E. It seems likely, scholars explain, that Nahua speakers moved into Central America in a single late prehistoric migration that lasted for seven or eight generations, and that their stories of origin reflect that prehistoric move.

The Guaraní Origin Story

Another story of origins by migration comes from the Guaraní of eastern Paraguay and southern Brazil. These people, who lived from swidden agriculture, traditionally migrated to create new fields after depleting an area of the forest. Over many centuries, Guaraní migrations in search of what they called *yvy maraneỹ*, virgin forest that had not been shaped by humans, became legendary and acquired mystical/religious dimensions.[12] Migration to find a better place shaped this people's culture.

The Andean Flood Story

The Indigenous peoples of Peru's coastal plains even share myths of a great flood that followed creation. They recount that Viracocha (God) created humans at Pachacama, a name meaning creator of the world and located close to today's Lima. Later Viracocha brought the world to an end with a great flood that covered the world's highest mountains. Even the sun hid during the flood and did not reappear until waters began to recede. All people and living things perished, except for a woman and a man who floated in a drum until finally settling at Tiahuanaco. Some versions of the flood story hold that receding waters first revealed the island in Lake Titicaca. Others relay that all humans perished in the flood and the creator then remade people out of clay, painting clothing on their bodies and giving them language, songs, seeds, and vegetables to nurture themselves. Once completed, Viracocha sent each nation underground until he summoned them forth one by one. Called by name, people emerged to populate the Earth. Later, the people viewed the places they emerged from as holy and began to worship at them, calling them a *huaca* or *guaca* (shrine), and even dressing in the colors of their painted *huaca*. Others believe that a few people escaped the flood by climbing trees and hills, or hiding in caves before emerging to repopulate the Earth.[13] It is curious to consider whether stories of origins that include parallels to Jewish and Christian stories of origins were influenced by contact with Europeans, or whether common themes emerged separately because they include ideas shared by different groups of people.

There are variations to this Andean flood story. North in Cañaribamba, the Cañares people tell that two brothers survived the flood atop mount Huacayñan, located in their land, by eating roots and herbs. After searching for food one day, the brothers returned to find their hut filled with food and *chicha* (beer). For days, provisions were replenished, until one boy finally hid and saw two *guacamayas* (parrots like macaws) enter their hut and change into two well-dressed beautiful women of royal heritage. As they began to prepare food, the boy emerged and the frightened women became birds again and flew away. The boys managed to trap the women when they next returned. Finally won over, the young women explained that Viracocha had sent them to prevent the young men from dying of hunger during the flood. The women became the youths' wives and the couples populated Cañaribamba with their offspring. The Cañares used images of the birds to remind themselves that God had rescued them from a flood.[14] How do these flood stories compare with Judeo-Christian accounts of Noah and the flood? How might flood and repopulation myths have motivated the people who shared them?

Common themes run through hundreds of similar Indigenous accounts of origins. In general, these stories link the existence of people in the world to a supernatural spirit or animal spirit that guided either human emergence from the earth, descent from the sky, survival of a great deluge, or a long migration that finally brought them to their homeland.

Indigenous peoples share many common themes of origin with peoples from major world religions. The three monotheistic faiths draw from a common tradition and believe that a spirit called God created day and night, the stars, planets, animals, and then human beings in a very short period of time. The religions share common patriarchs and matriarchs, as well as origins in the Middle East where their civilizations arose. Native stories at first glance seem different because they are new to us, but each people have their own accounts of original ancestors, early paradisiacal locations, explanations for gender differences and body functions, right and wrong, group cohesion, use of resources, relations to outsiders, and even great floods. Native people actually share many ideas from myths of origins in common with people from Europe and Asia.

How and When did People Populate the Americas? The Great Migration

Scientists have largely rejected the idea that humans first emerged at different places around the world, instead favoring the idea of a single location, likely in eastern Africa.[15] Some Indigenous peoples have reacted angrily to this thesis, arguing that it reveals prejudice against their beliefs and traditions. Scientists countered by explaining that humans reached northern Siberia 25,000 years ago, and eventually crossed into the Americas by boat or perhaps trekking across Arctic land exposed during the last ice age.[16] Animals and humans seem to have first entered the Americas about 13,000 years ago, but there are clues that they may have arrived even earlier, perhaps even 30,000 years ago, so multiple crossings at different times remain possible.[17] Resulting conflicts between Native peoples trying to protect their burial sites and the scientists, who wish to advance discoveries, have been contentious, especially as they involve governments, resources, and protected (or not) Native lands.

The Bering Strait Migration

Many scientists agree that during the last ice age the oceans shrank as water froze and left a passage between continents across the Bering Strait. People may have followed animals over the wide bridge hunting for food, and then settled in northwestern North America as early as 25,000 years ago and certainly at least by 12000 B.C.E. Humans seem to have migrated south to the continent's center between the Rocky Mountains and the glaciers over hundreds of years, but this move may have occurred even more quickly than we imagined. In southern Chile at Monte Verde, archeologists in the 1990s discovered the remains of a hide-covered wooden shelter 20 feet long, and a tool factory built beside a mastodon-butchery site, all dating to 14,800 years ago. The people who lived there transported salt and seaweed from the coast inland, and herbs for medicine from 40 miles in opposite directions, long before people were even supposed to have been in the Southern Cone.[18] As recently as March 28, 2014, *The New York Times* reported the discovery of stone tools proving that people lived at Serra da Capibara in northeastern Brazil 22,000 years ago, long before even the Monte Verde findings.[19] Further south, paleontologists reported that humans hunted giant sloths in today's Uruguay about 30,000 years ago! What scientists think they know about peopling the continent of South America is still under revision as they make further discoveries.

Indigenous People Question Science

Large anniversaries, like a twenty-fifth, fiftieth, or even a centennial draw our attention, and so it has been in the Americas. In preparation for the Columbus Quincentenary (five-hundredth) anniversary in 1992, Indigenous people started to refute the idea that Europeans had "discovered" them, and took scientists to task for their Bering Strait migration theory. One can imagine why scientific exploration angered Native peoples. Who would want their ancestor's remains disinterred for examination in a laboratory, or to be told that they had no original claim to the land where their ancestors had lived, let alone that their own accounts of their people's origins were only myths? Indigenous people throughout the continent protested scientific findings, Western history, and rediscovered the political strength of joining forces to demonstrate for a political and economic cause. In October 1991, hundreds of Indigenous leaders met in Guatemala to design a "Continental Campaign" as a collective response to the Columbus Quincentenary. Their declarations focused on their age-old presence in the Americas, their ownership of the land and rejection of Columbus having "discovered" them. "After five hundred years of oppression, exploitation, and discrimination, we Indigenous People have little to celebrate in 1992 except our resistance, and much to protest," expressed Francisco Calí, a leader from highland Guatemala. Shuar leader Rafael Pandam from Ecuador declared, "We have been struggling for five hundred years – and we are prepared to struggle for five hundred more."[20]

Many Indigenous people oppose the idea that they arrived from Asia over a land bridge thousands of years ago because it seems like an attempt to delegitimate their ownership of the land and understandings of their origins. Historian Roxanne Dunbar-Ortiz, author of *An Indigenous People's History of the United States*, has called this idea one of the myths about Native Americans, a hypothesis rather than fact: "the Bering Strait theory is an increasingly slippery slope that can at best be thought of as only one among numerous possible scenarios for the peopling of the Americas."[21] Numerous archeological and scientific findings over the past two centuries have also challenged the land bridge theory. Whether one believes the Indigenous myths of origins or gives greater

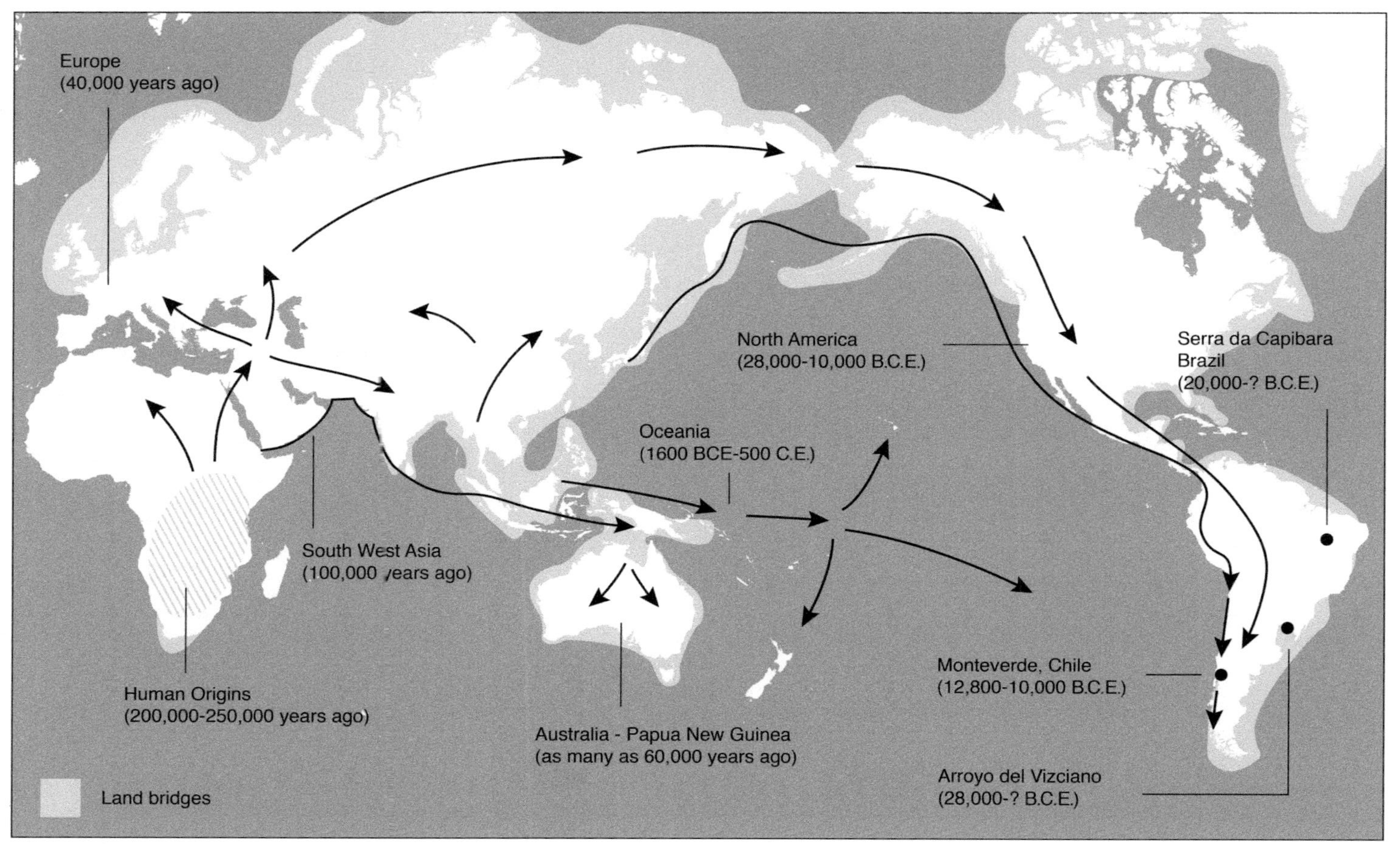

Map 2.1 Possible Migratory Routes

authority to scientific theories of origins, both suggest that Indigenous people were in the Americas thousands of years before the Europeans arrived.

Indigenous Demographics in Abya Yala

If Indigenous people spread so relatively quickly through Abya Yala and found it an abundant land teeming with life, it should not surprise us that their numbers grew rapidly. When Europeans first arrived in the Caribbean, they found the islands densely populated. On entering the Aztec capital, Spanish explorers described it as an anthill because of the many people they encountered. By the time the Europeans reached North American coasts a century later and described them as sparsely inhabited, they found land already sharply depopulated by diseases that had spread from first contacts elsewhere.[22] Clearly, these epidemics made a huge difference in the intervening century and shaped the later exploration of the Americas. Explorers' preconceptions shaped their estimations of the size of Indigenous populations, leading them to underestimate the number of Indigenous people they encountered. Even with that variable taken into account, however, the Americas seem to have been densely populated, especially where large Native empires concentrated people and resources in a relatively small space.[23]

So how many people actually lived in Latin America on the verge of European arrivals? Demographers have broadly estimated the total number of Indigenous people at European contact, and as new evidence emerges those numbers have continued to rise. What is today Mexico had the largest population, with at least 20 million people. The Andes Mountains had fewer inhabitants, yet still as many as 12 million people lived there. Semi-sedentary peoples in Central America and the Caribbean numbered as many as 5 million each. An average of scholarly estimates suggests the proximity of 54 million people in the entire Americas on the verge of contact.[24] Consider that Western Europe at the time totaled 60 to 70 million people, China alone 100 to 150 million, and all of Africa 36 to 72 million people. Demographic estimates suggest a large Indigenous population in Abya Yala prior to contact with Europeans.

The reason such demographic estimates are important is because Indigenous political issues and land claims have become controversial. A larger original population number potentially adds weight to Native claims to land, resources, and political rights. Larger numbers also make the accidental holocaust following contact that ended so many lives feel so much worse at an emotional level. With so many deaths laid at the hands of invading Europeans, one can see why demographics became politicized. The danger of employing numbers for political purposes is that ultimately, goals for such charges are politically motivated, controversial, and accomplish few results today. Perhaps it is enough to know that many millions more people lived in Abya Yala than previously imagined.

Early Indigenous Organization

A look at Abya Yala before contact reveals a multiplicity of peoples, cultures, languages, and political organizations. People lived on islands, beaches, hills, and mountains. Communities thrived along rivers and oceans, in deserts and on prairies, near glaciers, and in tropical forests. Geography played a huge role in shaping the many Indigenous cultures, languages, religions, and political organizations that varied widely throughout the continent, even as individual leaders, community decisions, and interactions among peoples also shaped their history and surroundings. This diversity of place and culture is why learning about Indigenous peoples is so interesting. What is more, archeologists are only scratching the surface of early Abya Yala.

The way in which Native people politically organized their lives in turn shaped the results of their later encounters with outsiders. The majority lived in smaller communities and hunted, gathered resources, fished, and farmed for a living. Some peoples, such as the Incas and the Mexica, had organized huge political empires by conquering or allying themselves with other peoples, yet many peoples lived independently in smaller communities. Clearly, history and geography had shaped cultures, economies, and polities everywhere in Abya Yala.

Early Indigenous Empires in Peru

What determined how far Indigenous people were able to spread their political control? As it does today, geography helped shape the size of Native political organizations. While the majority of Indigenous people lived in smaller groups, in a few places large empires extended their rule over neighboring agricultural peoples. In the Andes highlands, the bottleneck of narrow land west of the mountains, hemmed in by the high peaks and ocean, concentrated densely yet relatively isolated populations and allowed important cultures with political power in the hands of strong groups to flourish. The Chavin civilization introduced above, which seems to have focused on creating harmony with nature, spread across northern Peru after 1500 B.C.E., and its followers decorated temples to the faith as far north as Cajamarca and south to Ayacucho, leaving an extensive religious compound at Chavin de Huántar. Strong localized cultures followed the Chavin demise after 200 B.C.E., building on the Chavin cultural heritage. Important nations included the coastal Moche, who created a state in the north, and the Nazca, who lived along the southern coast. The famous Nazca lines, a series of ancient geoglyphs that outline humming-birds, spiders, monkeys, fish, sharks, and other animals, some of them several hundred meters across and visible from the air, still remain a puzzle, but the Nazca culture also included all kinds of beautiful crafts, including ceramics and textiles.

The Chavin belief system influenced the Ayacucho region, and its people invaded the valley of Cuzco between 540 and 900 C.E., leaving cultural patterns that included textiles and carvings of animals and gods that included jaguars, caimans, eagles, and snakes. The Wari Empire that followed became the largest political power in the highlands until the Incas; they adopted art motifs from the Nazca and traded their textiles as far south as Arequipa. Similarly, the Tiwanaku Empire expanded south of Cuzco into what became Upper Peru under European rule, and its capital dominated the Lake Titicaca region until 1000 C.E. Built high above the tree line, their capital city boasted platform mounds and temples. The Tiwanaku traded coca, maize, and seashells broadly with other peoples via llama trains.

Early Indigenous Empires in Mesoamerica

In the north, the mild climate and fertile terrain in today's central Mexican highlands, also called Mesoamerica, allowed the concentration of large populations and imperial structures to flourish. By 8000 B.C.E., people there had already domesticated squash, followed by chili peppers, gourds, amaranth, avocados, and maize by 3400 B.C.E. A stable food source encouraged village life and the production of ceramics. This sedentary culture allowed for larger political organization. The Ocos established some of the first villages, followed by the Olmecs on the Gulf Coast, with their political center at San Lorenzo and their

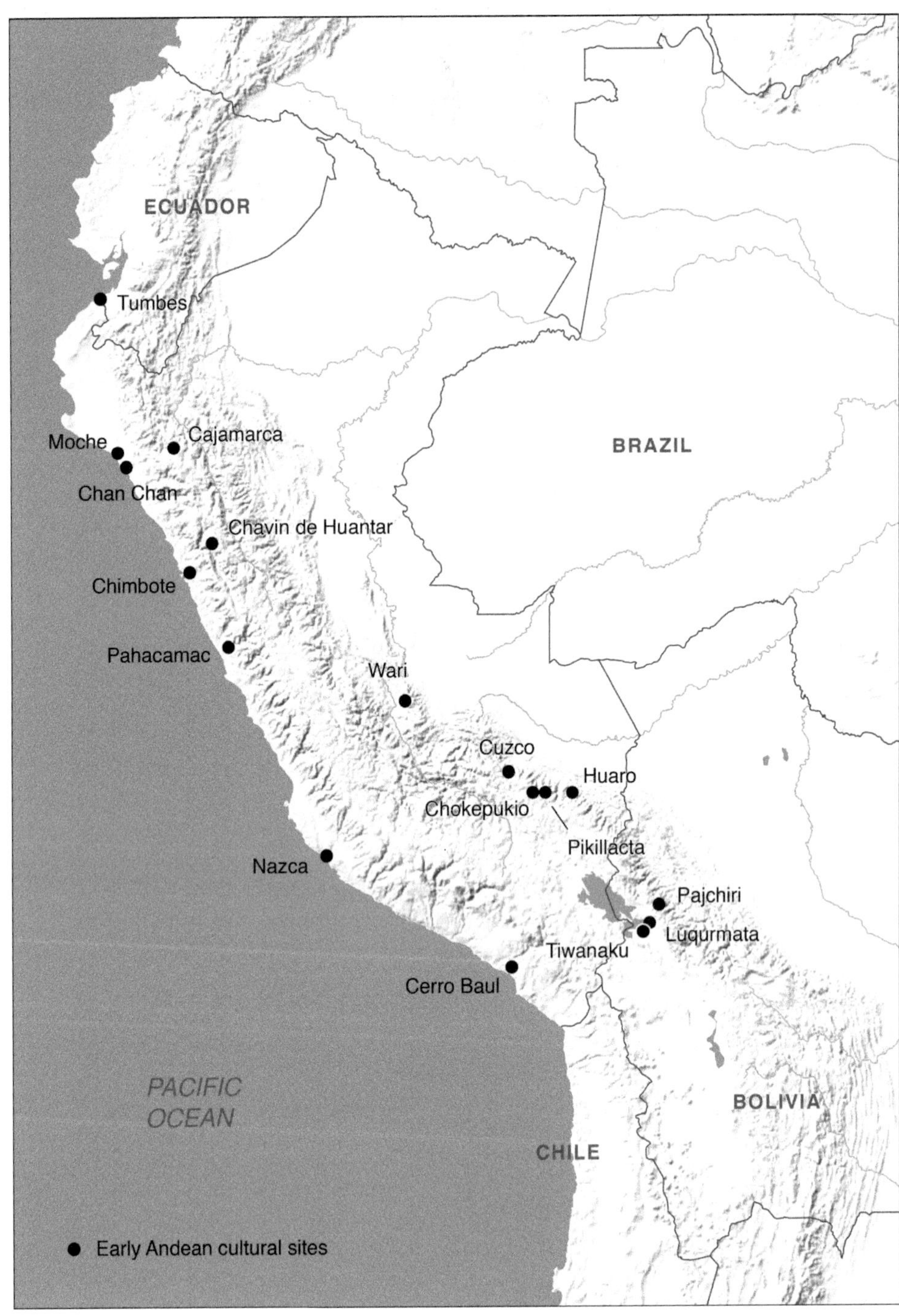

Map 2.2 Early Andean Archaeological Sites

huge carved stone heads, thought to represent Olmec leaders. Other political centers at Monte Albán, and then Teotihuacan, dominated Mesoamerica until they were eclipsed by the Maya Empire. The Maya ruled southern Mesoamerica from the Yucatan after 500 C.E. during the Classic Period. Between 800 and 900 C.E. their empire collapsed for unknown reasons, but possibly because they were too successful. Scholars have argued that increasing numbers of people overextended the ecological balance, meaning that the empire grew to include too many people for the food they could produce. Epidemics of disease may have also played a role. Maya society fragmented and their demise allowed the empire of Chichén Itzá to emerge in the south and the Toltec Empire in the north. Another strong state included Monte Albán, the Zapotec capital situated on a hill that subdued neighboring cities and even sent diplomats and ambassadors north to Teotihuacan.

These pre-Columbian peoples kept track of past events. The following document excerpt, showing the importance they gave to history, is attributed to post-conquest historian Hernando Alvarado Tezozómoc, who was descended from Aztec royalty. In the late sixteenth century he wrote about the Aztec perspective on the history of central Mexico for the Royal Court (*Real Audiencia*) of Mexico, for whom he worked as the nahuatlato (nahuatl language interpreter).

For Document 2.1: The importance of history by Tezozómoc, post-conquest historian, visit www.routledge.com/9780415519120.

Individuals: Nezahualcóyotl, Ruler of Texcoco

Born in 1402, Nezahualcóyotl grew up as part of the nobility but his life was not easy: at 16, he saw his father killed in battle by Tepanec warriors. His uncle, ruler of the Aztecs, hid the boy at Tenochtitlan during the Tepanec occupation. Captured when he tried to reclaim Texcoco, the teenager later finished his military training and education at the Aztec capital. When Tezozómoc died, Prince Nezahualcóyotl took advantage of the ensuing chaos to reclaim his inheritance. The prince allied himself with Tenochtitlan and Tacuba and they retook Texcoco. Four years later, at the age of 29, Nezahualcóyotl became king. Under his leadership Texcoco flourished and became renowned for its well-functioning government and flourishing culture. The king's new legal code comprised 80 laws divided into 4 sections, each enforced by a supreme council. The poet-king founded a university with academies in religion, astronomy, philosophy, law, history, and music. He built a new palace a half-mile square and decorated with botanical gardens on Lake Texcoco; in its 300 rooms all types of arts flourished. The king's favorite home was a villa high on a hill by the city, where gardens, canals, ponds, and swimming pools offered him a sheltered retreat. Nezahualcóyotl's rule provides a glimpse into a thriving Native kingdom and the luxurious life that only a few Indigenous nobles enjoyed before Europeans arrived.

For Document 2.2: The Flower Songs of Hungry Coyote Poet of Ancient Mexico, from the sixteenth century Codex Ixtlilxochitl, visit www.routledge.com/9780415519120.

Trends: The Aztec and Inca Empires

By the fifteenth century, two large Indigenous empires controlled the political centers of Abya Yala. The dominant people in northern Mesoamerica were the Mexica, whose capital, Tenochtitlan, on an island in Lake Texcoco, was already a century old. The dense population of the area permitted rapid growth and commerce; in 1428, the neighboring cities of Tlacopan and Texcoco allied themselves with the Mexica during the leadership of Nezahualcóyotl, poet-king of Texcoco. Over the next century, the thriving population in Tenochtitlan grew to 200,000 persons on only 13 square kilometers. Canals and dikes kept the surrounding salty water away from the fresh water that fed the *chinampas*, fields of hydroponic beds on raised artificial islands built in the lakebeds of the suburbs, where crops were grown to feed the capital's population. A complex network of canals allowed canoes to transport merchants, artisans, farmers, priests, and politicians between neighborhoods. The adjoining city of Tlatelolco boasted a thriving marketplace where over 60,000 people shopped every day. To do business, people went to the walled compound called the Sacred Precinct at the heart of the urban grid, where government officials served the needs of the teeming city. Priests staffed the Mayor Temple and hosted worshipers of an array of deities, including Tlaloc, god of rain and agriculture, and Huitzilopochtli, god of war. Merchants left the bustling capital to trade with surrounding peoples, and soldiers marched forth to bring captives and slaves back to the imperial center. Tributary communities in conquered provinces fed the capital with sacrificial victims and taxes, but shopped for their own goods in local markets. Imperial society was highly stratified; the upper classes, nobility called the *pipiltin*, lived luxuriously by heavily taxing both *macehualtin*, the commoners in the city, and the *calpulli*, rural wards. By the end of the fifteenth century, Tenochtitlan was the largest city in the world, with between 200,000 and 250,000 inhabitants, over four times the population of London, and Emperor Motecuhzoma firmly controlled millions of subjects. What an empire!

The second Indigenous empire at the time was Tawantinsuyu, the Land of the Four Quarters, controlled by the Inca high in the Andes Mountains. Composed at its core by Quechua and Aymara peoples, the empire extended in the south from Picunche territory, northernmost of the Araucanian peoples, all the way north to Omaguá territory in today's Colombia. This empire was huge, larger than any other state at the time: Ming China, Czarist Russia, Songhay in the Sahel, Great Zimbabwe in West Africa, the Ottoman Empire, and even the Mexica's Aztec Empire, were all smaller than Inca dominions.[25] The geographic sweep of the Inca was equally impressive: from Ecuador in the north to Chile in the south the Incas controlled rainforests in the upper Amazon, the deserts of coastal Peru, and some of the hemisphere's highest mountains, all the way south to Lake Titicaca. The empire was also young: rulers had built their administration on the ruins of the waning Wari and Tiwanaku states only in 1200. The Inca, as their ruler was known, personally controlled all land and property in his territory and impressed peasants into laboring for the state.

The eighth Inca, Viracocha Inca, assumed power in about 1410 C.E., extended his authority over neighboring peoples under the ruling name of Pachacuti (Earthshaker) with impressive military strength. Defeating threats by northern people, Pachacuti conquered the Vilcas and Soras to the west and quashed a revolt by the Ayaviri at Lake Titicaca and the Chumbivilca to the southwest. Giving his son Tupac Inca Yupanqui charge of the army in 1463, Pachacuti rebuilt Cuzco into a brilliant capital, codified the legal system, and institutionalized ancestor worship. His favorite son, Amaru Inca, was not an aggressive commander, so Tupac took charge instead, and in 1471 expanded the empire north to Quito. This aggressive leader sailed a navy of 20,000 soldiers on a balsa fleet into the Pacific, perhaps even reaching the Galapagos before returning to conquer the Chimu Empire, his nearest rival, as well as the peoples of highland Bolivia and northern Chile to the Maule River. With similar prowess, Tupac's son Huayna Capac succeeded his father in 1493 and took Peru's northeastern mountains, today's Ecuador, and southern Colombia. Inca roads, architecture, plazas, and accounting methods continue to amaze observers. By the time Huayna Capac died in 1527, the Spanish had reached his empire, and the European diseases were killing millions of his people, including finally himself. In only a few generations, the Inca had constructed a powerful empire renowned for its massive stone walls, paved roads, meticulous masonry, and the largest administrative system of its day, all without any wheels, gunpowder, or steel.

Mesoamerica was probably the first place in the Western Hemisphere to produce enough surplus food to support a stratified society with central political organizations, administrators, and priests, and Peru followed. Once a society can support priests and administrators who do not raise their own food, one in effect has a "civilization" and a very complex culture. As Jared Diamond has shown, abundant food production and thousands of years of change led to the invention of writing in Mexico, as it also did in China at about the same time.[26] What is more, the earliest civilizations in Abya Yala developed in very challenging environments, just as they did in the Indus Valley, Early China, Egypt, and Mesopotamia.

Indigenous Societies and Cultures Differed Broadly Throughout the Continent

The brief introduction to Abya Yala by the fifteenth century hints at hundreds of different peoples living in vastly varying ways, each one carefully adapted to their environment. From empires that skimmed wealth by force from subject peoples, to small groups of hunter-gatherers who lived in limited spaces and found their own sustenance, the social and political organization of Latin American Indigenous societies differed widely. Hundreds of languages, ways of life, religious beliefs, traditions, and customs together wove the multicultural quilt that was Abya Yala.

Consider how different Indigenous ways of life shaped their later interaction with Europeans. Hunters and gatherers had no metal or wheels, and lived in small groups where fragile environments could not support larger settlements. They had no need for large military forces. Agricultural groups could provide for larger populations. Some used metals and designed broad commercial networks to trade with distant peoples. Along oceans or

Figure 2.2 Emperor Huayna Capac, Guaman Poma de Ayala Etching, p. 112 [112]. (Royal Danish Library, GKS 2232 4 to: Guaman Poma, Nueva corónica y buen gobierno (1615))

rivers, people fished and harvested marine products, and some, as did the Incas, even explored distant shores. Where peoples had forged broad empires, they employed standing armies to subject other peoples and tax them for wealth, labor, and sacrificial victims. Some peoples in the Andes employed mammals for transportation, but llamas and alpacas were not domesticatable in the same way that horses, sheep, or cows were in Europe. In Mesoamerica, the largest mammal was the guinea pig. Imagine how many guinea pigs it would have taken to provide a standing army with sufficient protein! How would people in these different cultural circumstances have fared when confronted with an outside force, such as the Europeans, who brought steel swords, firearms, and large mammals like attack dogs and horses? As we will see, cultural arrangements and the geography that had formed them also played a huge role in shaping the way Indigenous people interacted with outsiders when they first met near the end of the fifteenth century. Contrary to intuition, as we will explore when we turn to the next chapter, the size of the Indigenous political organization or territory did not relate directly to the speed with which the Europeans conquered them when they all met.

Conclusion

Before the Europeans arrived, millions of people lived in what are today the Americas. Native people generally explain their presence in Abya Yala as the result of creation by a deity, emergence from the earth, survival of a deluge, or from a great migration. Their origin stories link people to spiritual deities, the natural environment, and to specific geographic settings. In the European tradition, scientists have explained the peopling of the American continents as the result of a great move out of Africa, across Asia, and eventually over the Bering Strait, possibly as early as 30000 B.C.E. but most likely in several migrations between 25000 and 12000 B.C.E. Spreading relatively quickly through the continents, the newcomers adapted themselves to different environmental niches where they developed unique political, cultural, and religious organizations. Geography and natural surroundings shaped the lives, languages, and cultures of these people in distinctive ways. By the time they met the Europeans, somewhere between 60 and 100 million people lived between the Rio Grande and the frozen southern tip of Abya Yala.

In two places, namely Mesoamerica and the central Andes, Indigenous people concentrated power in large states. The Olmecs, Monte Albán, and Teotihuacan formed early polities in Mesoamerica, followed by the Maya Empire between 500 and 900 C.E. and then by Chichén Itzá in the south and the Toltec Empire in the north. The Mexica, Tlacopan, and Texcoco formed the Aztec Empire in 1428, with its magnificent capital at Tenochtitlan. In the Andes, Quechua and Aymara peoples built on the ruins of earlier Chavin, Nazca, and Tiwanaku civilizations to form the powerful Inca Empire in 1438, with a standing army and the largest political organization in the world at the time.

Elsewhere in Abya Yala, Indigenous people hunted and gathered on prairies, fished the oceans, farmed along great rivers, and lived from semi-nomadic or nomadic hunting and gathering in forests and jungles where ecosystems were too fragile to support sedentary life and agriculture. The amazing variety of cultures, languages, beliefs, and political organizations kept peoples isolated and politically fragmented unless joined under the political hegemony of a conquering imperial force. These were the peoples and cultures to whom the Americas originally belonged, the people who would, toward the end of the fifteenth century, encounter very different types of people on their coasts.

Discussion Questions

1. Are scientific accounts more authoritative than Indigenous peoples' explanations for their presence in the Americas? If so, what makes them more credible?
2. What stories have people in the Judeo-Christian religious heritage told for centuries to link their people and wealth to a place and a supernatural power? How do stories of origin legitimate a people's place and power in the world?

3. How do your own relatives and ancestors explain how they have come to belong where they are? How do stories of origins empower and serve the people and the cultures who share them?
4. What does the mother's treatment of her rebellious daughter in the Cashinawa story about the origins of rainbows reveal about Cashinawa culture? How does this mythical story relate ideas about gender and respect?
5. What does the Q'om creation story tell us about gender relations in traditional Q'om society? Who enjoyed the most power? Why might people in this hunting and gathering society have originally considered men to be different types of animals, yet women to have homes in the sky?
6. Do the Guaraní accounts of a great migration to flee oppression by foreigners or to seek a better home remind you of any stories of origin in the Judeo-Christian tradition? What similarities or differences do you see?
7. Why did Indigenous people organize empires in such different places as a lake in central Mexico and a valley high in the Peruvian mountains?

Notes

1 Even older hominin remains (our direct human ancestors), dating to 3.67 million years ago, have been discovered recently in South Africa.
2 Coates, *A Global History of Indigenous Peoples*, 27.
3 Guc or q'uc, kuk in Maya, is the bird now called quetzal.
4 Goetz and Morley, *Popol Vuh*, 81–84.
5 For two good sources, see Bawden, *The Moche*, and Benson, *The Mochica, A Culture of Peru*.
6 From the *Codice Chimalpopoca, Legenda de los Soles*, fol. 76–77, 135.
7 Hoffmann, *The Seven Story Tower*, 135, 138.
8 Reichel-Dolmatoff, in *Flesh of the Gods*, 104.
9 Miller, "Toba Kin Terms."
10 Steward and Faron, *Native Peoples of South America*, 235.
11 Torquemada, 1: bk 3, 331–333; cited by Fowler, *The Cultural Evolution*, 35.
12 Melià, *El Guaraní*, 107–108.
13 Cobo, *Inca Religion and Customs*, 11–14.
14 Cobo, *Inca Religion and Customs*, 15.
15 Stringer and McKie, *African Exodus*, 24.
16 Stringer and McKie, *African Exodus*, 149; Christian, *Maps of Time*, 191; Leakey, *The Making of Mankind*, 159.
17 Christian, *Maps of Time*, 191.
18 Fernández-Armesto, *The Américas*, 26.
19 Romero, "Discoveries Challenge Beliefs," A5.
20 Winn, *Americas*, 269–270.
21 Dunbar-Ortiz and Gilio-Whitaker, "*All the Real Indians Died Off*," 21.
22 Jennings, *The Invasion of America*, 23.
23 Dobyns, "Estimating Aboriginal American Population," 395.
24 For demographic information on the Americas prior to European contact, see William Denevan, "Estimating the Aboriginal Population," 129; Denevan, *The Native Population of the Americas*, 3; Kicza, *Resilient Cultures*, 27.
25 Mann, *1491, New Revelations of the Americas*, 64.
26 Diamond, *Guns, Germs, and Steel*, 236.

3 Indigenous Encounters with Europeans

The Fifteenth Century

Chronology

201 B.C.E.	Rome defeats Carthage and takes control of Iberia for six centuries.
418 C.E.	Visigoths take over most of Iberia.
711 C.E.	The Moors from North Africa begin the conquest of Iberia.
718 C.E.	Christian forces begin the *Reconquista* against the Moors.
860 C.E.	Norse explorers reach Greenland.
1252 C.E.	Christian forces push the Moors into Granada, in southern Iberia.
1415 C.E.	Portuguese Prince Henry sails along West Africa for slaves, ivory, and gold.
1469	Princess Isabella of Castile weds second cousin Prince Ferdinand of Aragon.
1487	Portuguese explorer Bertholomeu Dias rounded Africa's southern Cape of Good Hope.
1492	Fall of Granada, expulsion begins of 500,000 Muslims and thousands of Jewish people.
October 1492	Arawak and Island Caribs meet Italian explorer Christopher Columbus.
January 1493	Chief Caonabó burns Columbus' Fort Navidad to ashes and kills his sailors.
September 1493	Columbus' second voyage to the Americas, diseases spread quickly.
1494	Spain and Portugal divide the Americas between them with the Treaty of Tordesillas.
1498	Columbus' third voyage; Arawaks distributed in *repartimientos* to pacify Spanish settlers. The Hundred Years' War between Kaal and Mutal peoples in Yucatan ends. The Mexica and their Aztec Empire become a dominant political force in central Mexico. Inca emperor Huayna Capac extends his rule north through Ecuador into southern Colombia.

Introduction

What was it like for Indigenous people on the Caribbean islands to watch Spanish explorers ride the waves in rowboats to their beaches? As a child, when my family visited Q'om, Mocobí, Pilaga, and Wichi communities in northern Argentina, elders would often tell us they had received notice of our impending visit from a bird in song, or from another animal, or, even more often, in a vivid dream. Rarely did they seem surprised when we arrived. Perhaps people have some way of sensing impending visits, or at least, they might later look back and believe they saw those signs beforehand. Still, to our Western way of thinking, these ideas seem preposterous, invented, or even deliberately deceptive. The Nahua, however, appear not to have been terribly surprised by the Spanish arrival. Instead of seeing them as supernatural, they apparently viewed them as another group of invaders with whom they would have to deal.[1] Later, after the Europeans had seized control, Native people recalled previous signs and omens that had foretold the Spaniards' arrival. During the challenging time immediately after the conquest, however, when disease was ravaging communities, death was everywhere, and the explorers were taking their wealth in what must have seemed an end-of-world cataclysm, it is not surprising to learn that in retrospect Indigenous people wanted to believe they had anticipated and expected the strange visitors.

Have We Met Before? Indigenous People Possibly Encounter Outsiders in Earlier Times

We do not really know for sure who went where and when in prehistoric times, that is to say, before we have written accounts of peoples' travels and adventures. Artifacts and even linguistic patterns, though, have allowed historians, archeologists, and anthropologists to speculate about how and when earlier peoples interacted. There is substantial evidence that people traveled around Europe and across the North Atlantic in earlier times. Norse adventurers first documented a trip around Iceland in about 860 C.E., but we know that people were sailing along Europe's coasts long before that, because already before 2500 B.C.E. people from Portugal, Spain, and France were spreading rituals and artifacts around Northwestern Europe. The Greeks reportedly reached the British Isles before 300 B.C.E. and the Romans followed. Indigenous people on Greenland first had recorded contact with Norse explorers in 860 C.E. The Vikings, after settling Greenland in the early tenth century, explored the northeastern coasts of North America. The Inuit (formerly called Eskimos) and Native peoples of Labrador and Newfoundland in Canada, whom the Vikings called Skraelings from Vinland, usually greeted Norse adventurers in the twelfth and the fourteenth centuries with what the Vikings referred to as "showers of missiles."[2] Native peoples on the northeastern coast of the Americas encountered Europeans long before the Spanish ventured across the Atlantic.

Indigenous Legends/Memories Foretell Encounters with Strangers

Following the European conquest of the late fifteenth and early sixteenth centuries, Native people throughout the Americas recollected predictions of future encounters with foreigners. The fact of the conquest, though, complicates the historical usefulness of these predictions because people did not document them in writing until long after the Europeans had arrived. An example from the United States shows how these historical forecasts worked. In North America, an Oglala Sioux holy man named Black Elk recalled one such prediction when talking to poet John Neihardt in 1930 on the Pine Ridge Reservation in South Dakota. His grandfather had once explained to his father that long before contact with whites, a Lakota holy man called Drinks

Water dreamed that the four-leggeds (buffalo) were returning into the earth and that a strange race had encircled the Lakota with a spider's web. "When this happens, you shall live in gray houses, in a barren land, and beside those square gray houses you shall starve," the holy man had predicted. The deep sorrow caused by the dream led to the healer's death. As Black Elk analyzed, "You can look about you now and see that he meant these dirt-roofed houses we are living in, and that all the rest was true. Sometimes dreams are wiser than waking."[3] This example shows how some Native Americans reconstructed past stories and events and then employed them to explain current situations.

In Latin America, numerous Native peoples recall prophecies that foretold the arrival of the Europeans. The Yekuana, who live in the headwaters of the Orinoco River and are more commonly known by their Carib-derived name Makiritare, include Europeans in their stories of origin. In fact, they credit their first grandfather Wanadi (God and culture hero, the unknowable and unseen force) with the creation of both the Fañuru (Spanish, bad white people) and the Hurunko (Dutch, good white people) right along the Upper Orinoco. Makiritare legends speak of a great flood used to punish humans for misbehaving, and of Odo'sha, the master of evil and incarnation of all negative forces in the universe, who taught people to make houses.[4] Stories relate that Odo'sha tricked and turned the Fañuru against Native peoples. At Odo'sha's urging, the Fañuru marched against the Natives, beating them with clubs and taking their villages. They stole Karakaña (Caracas) by force, claiming, "everything on Earth is ours." Then they killed Wanadi by tying him to a post. After three days, Wanadi came down from the post and went up the Orinoco to persuade more people to fight the Fañuru.[5] Note the use of New Testament symbolism within the legend, specifically the crucifixion of Jesus, to explain opposition between European conquerors and the Native people, as well as mention of Caracas, a contemporary city.

Another example of Native predictions comes from the Mayan-descended peoples in the Yucatan and their Books of Chilam Balam. These books drew from hieroglyphic Mayan texts, but like the Makiritare prophecies, authors wrote them only after the conquest in the sixteenth century. A *chilam* is a priest and prophet, and *balam* means jaguar and refers to a last name. The nine surviving books, written in Mayan with the Spanish alphabet, contain both Mayan and Christian religious texts, astrological and historical data, explanations of the Mayan calendar, ritual astronomy, and prophecies about the coming of the Europeans. Scholars believe parts of the books date to pre-conquest times. The Chilam Balam of Chumayel, for instance, describes the strangers who would come from the east, bringing Christianity and making the sky cry. As Document 3.1 shows, the book predicts that the arrival of the strangers would scatter throughout the world the women and men who sing, and all who sing, a reference to the Maya. The priests of the damned bearded strangers, the historical prophecy continues, would change the colors of one's white clothing, and their heads will be jaguars as they extend their power over all peoples. The strangers' lust and madness will mark their words and wandering, and their arrival will scatter the people of the earth, producing ruin through their greed. The sky will be toppled and the earth turned upside down, producing hunger, depopulation, and the destruction of the peoples.[6] This Mayan text, clearly written down following initial contact because of its precise descriptions of the Europeans, helped Indigenous people make sense of their changing world and empowered them throughout the conquest. These texts helped people reconcile their participation in the colonial Christian world with the preservation of knowledge of their

Indigenous traditions and past.[7] Mayan cultural heritage resistance persisted long after other peoples had fallen to Spanish control.

For Document 3.1: First Prophetic Wheel Excerpts, visit www.routledge.com/9780415519120.

The best-known Indigenous predictions about the European arrival include the Mexica forecasts about the arrival of the Spanish in Mexico. (The Tarascan people, traditional enemies of the Mexica, also believe that extraordinary events preceded the arrival of the Europeans, and also documented their stories only many years after the conquest.) The Mexica first retold these predictions to Franciscan friar Bernardino de Sahagún in the 1550s and 1560s, a long time after the actual events of the conquest. A lifetime missionary in central New Spain, Sahagún collected Native testimonies and published them in an impressive book called *General History of the Things of New Spain*. Housed in Florence after Sahagún sent it to the Pope, scholars refer to the book as the Florentine Codex. Book Twelve of this volume describes Indigenous visions, actions, speech, and emotions during the first years following the Spanish arrival. The Codex fits into this chapter, even though it dates from the early sixteenth century, because it recounts supernatural events that the Mexica recalled experiencing before meeting the Europeans.

The Mexica recounted that ten years before the Spaniards arrived, a tongue of flame appeared suspended in the sky, large and resplendent, rising in the east immediately after midnight and lasting until the morning. Narrow at the bottom and wide at the top, the flame threw off sparks that seemed to pierce the sky.[8] The second omen was that the temple of Huitzilopochtli, their god of war, caught fire and burned to ashes. Then a bolt of lightning struck the temple of Xiuteuctli, the god of fire, and it burned to the ground, though there was no thunderstorm at the time. The fourth sign was a comet that appeared during the day while the sun was shining and then divided into three shining stars. Fifth, the water of the lake of Mexico boiled up and made exploding sounds, flooding the foundations of the houses. Then, during the night, people heard the voice of a woman weeping and shouting, "O my children, where am I to take you?" The seventh omen was that hunters caught a dark bird the size of a crane, which had a round mirror in the middle of its head. The emperor gazed into the mirror and saw a multitude of people marching together, armed and prepared for war, carried on the back of deer. Then many monsters appeared as the eighth sign, with monstrous bodies, which disappeared after the emperor saw them.[9] So many frightening calamities in only a few years made a great impression on Native people in central Mexico.

These visions of omens, later interpreted to have foretold the arrival of the Europeans, clearly fit into the vein of other prophetic or apocalyptic literature, similar to the Book of Revelation, the last book of the Christian Bible. These unique types of writings frequently combine prophecies and dreams, and people write them during times of great crisis and trauma. The apparitions that Sahagún recorded were clearly extraordinary, frightening events that stood out sharply in Native memories. The passage of time may have obscured and confused the exact events as they occurred. Retold over a meal by the fire or in the marketplace over many years, one can imagine that events may even have grown magical as elders passed them on to succeeding generations. Imagine the trauma of foreign conquest, the collapse of one's empire and all its structure, and then the tragedy of the unexplainable death of millions of one's people. These accounts, retold over a long time to help explain the world in which one lived, might have taken on supernatural meanings. This is not to say, of course, that the Mexica did not experience a series of frightening events that they later associated with the arrival of the conquerors; rather, that in those seemingly calamitous years of immense collective stress, the people may have been more susceptible to ascribing the events a more magical meaning than was really there. Most important is that during the years following the Iberian conquest, as they tried to make sense of the collapse of their world, the Mexica empowered themselves by recalling the reception of mysterious omens predicting these calamitous events.

Encounters between Very Different Peoples

South and east of the Mexica, beyond the Yucatan Peninsula, the people who lived on islands in the Caribbean Sea were the first to meet the invading Europeans toward the end of the fifteenth century. The Arawak and the Island Caribs were sedentary horticulturalists who lived in small communities with their own social classes, priests, and hereditary (or sometimes elected) leaders. The Islanders cultivated corn and yams but were also fierce warriors. They descended from Amazonian people who had migrated to the northeastern coastal plain of South America, where they had lived along riverine terraces from tropical forest horticulture that included root crops, animal protein, and probably maize. These people painted their ceramics red and white. Clearly, the seas facilitated rather than hindered travel for them, since there is archeological evidence of large migrations. The Arawak first moved to the Lesser Antilles in around 3000 B.C.E. and then on to Caribbean islands in the last centuries B.C.E., where they displaced nonagricultural people from Central America who had arrived previously in around 5000 B.C.E. Throughout the first millennium C.E., the island population increased, especially after 600 C.E., when sedentary agriculturalists populated the islands.

The Arawak islanders organized themselves politically in chiefdoms that sometimes competed, yet these people had obviously developed a complex culture that offered plenty of time for sports and leisure. They built ceremonial plazas called "bayetes" or ball courts, where teams of women and men from different chiefdoms competed to prevent a ball from touching the ground by hitting it with any part of their bodies except their hands. Archeologists have found remains of at least 21 such ball courts on Hispaniola alone, the island today shared by Haiti and the Dominican Republic. Politically, Arawak villages allied themselves by the hundreds into complex chiefdoms under the leadership of leaders they called caciques; by the late fifteenth century, six such polities dominated the central areas of Hispaniola. Cacique Behecchio led western areas where Haiti's capital Port-au-Prince is located today. Caonabó ruled the territory east of Behecchio, while Higüayo dominated the island's southeast. Along the northern coast, caciques included Guacanagarí to the west, followed by Guarionex and Mayobanex in central areas.[10] These leaders shaped early relations with European explorers.

The Europeans Encountered by Indigenous People on their Coasts

Much like the Americas, by the time Iberians ventured out across the Atlantic late in the fifteenth century, their homeland was a great mixture of peoples from different traditions. The peninsula had long served as a natural bridge between continents and bodies of water; whoever controlled Iberia oversaw trade between Africa and Europe, as well as between Asia and Western Europe. The mixture of many peoples and their cultures on the peninsula over many years created the country that later interacted with the Indigenous people in the Americas. These peoples included Iberian people from Africa, Celtic people from Central Europe, Phoenician traders, Greek explorers, and Carthaginian merchants, all interested in controlling the strategic Straits of Gibraltar between the Atlantic Ocean and the Mediterranean Sea. Rome took control of the peninsula for six centuries after 201 B.C.E., during which time it imposed the Latin language and legal system upon the Iberian people. The Germanic Visigoths conquered most of Iberia in the fifth century C.E., but their weaker control allowed Moors from North Africa to conquer them in 711 C.E. The Christian crusade to retake the Iberian Peninsula by force took 700 violent years, but played a huge role in shaping the people who conquered the Americas. The reconquest of the peninsula created a crusading militaristic culture that linked Spanish Christianity with the conquest of enemies and plunder for personal enrichment. Understanding the great exchange of cultures and traditions in Iberia helps explain the way in which these Europeans later interacted with Indigenous people in the Americas.

Roman Iberia

After the Romans defeated Carthage in 201 B.C.E., they kept Iberia and forced their system of city states and Christian, Latin culture onto the Iberian peoples. Urban centers became hubs of imperial control, and artisans, merchants, the military, the clergy, and powerful families all lived in the cities. Society stratified into castes as people invested a lot of importance in owning huge amounts of land, and in differences in rank and class. Wealthy nobles and merchants in the cities lived very differently than the commoners, the vast majority of peasants and shepherds who took care of estates and sheep in the countryside. A person's occupation determined their rank and position. Below the nobles came professionals, doctors, clergy, and lawyers, who shared the noble way of life and outranked the merchants, who in turn trumped the stewards and servants, who depended on the upper ranks for sustenance. Another important Roman organizational tool was patronage, in which all families and organizations were hierarchical, top-down systems where senior male members dominated and controlled the rise of lower and younger people. Patronage and the patriarchy that sustained it allowed men with power, autocrats, to head pyramids of influence that oversaw disadvantaged people, who in turn attracted their own clients. Entire towns might benefit from one citizen who received a favor from a great man; municipalities adopted noted men as patrons to receive favors. Families divided their inheritance among legitimate children, passing on wealth to the next generation.[11] The struggles between the Visigoths and the Romans also militarized Iberian society, a trend that only grew as all the Christians fought to expel the Muslims from the peninsula.

The Moorish Influence on Iberia

When they invaded a divided Iberia in 711, the Moors brought with them a sophisticated civilization that far surpassed European achievements. They had inherited from the Islamic world many practical developments in medicine, farming, chemistry, and science. Algebra, astronomy, metalwork, paper, lacquer, cotton, silk, sugar, citrus fruits, and much of the Greek scientific advances all arrived in Western Europe with the Moors. Language and knowledge from the sciences also entered the Latin world. When Spanish speakers today say pillow (*almohada*), almond (*almendra*), neighborhood shop

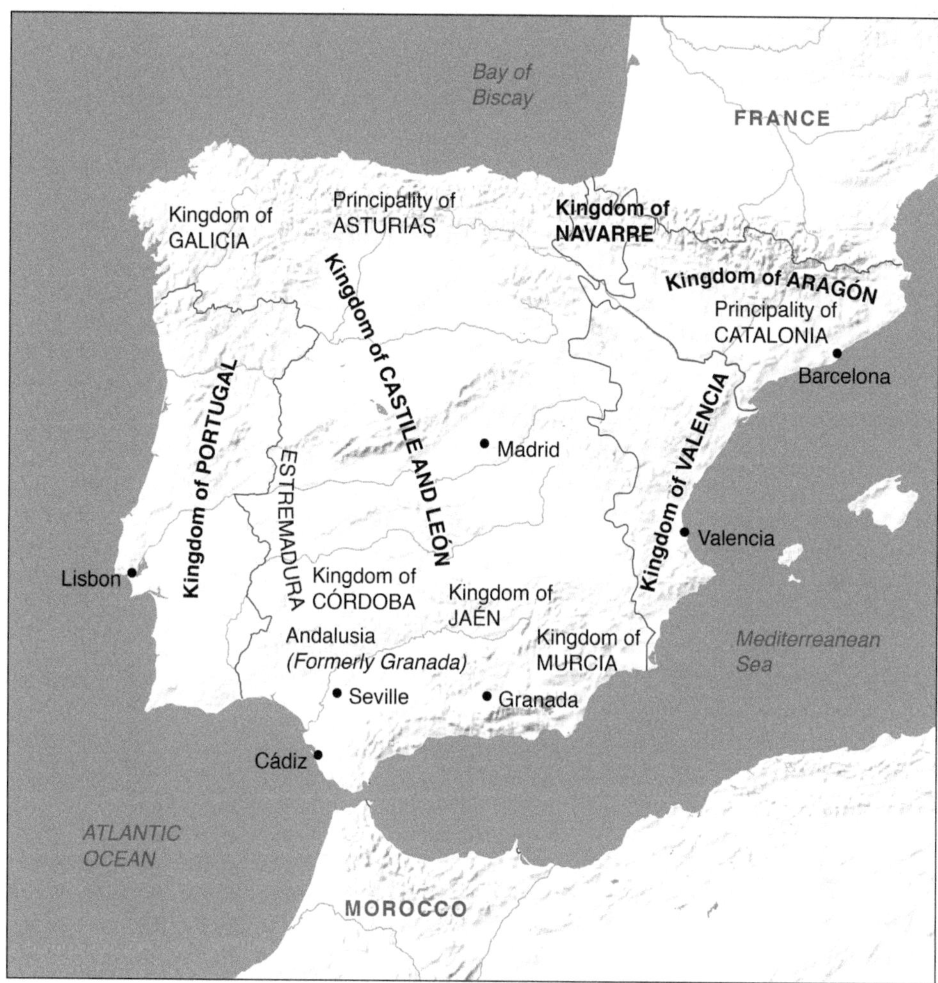

Map 3.1 Early Modern Iberia, Atlantic, and Mediterranean

(*almacén*), wire (*alambre*), and lunch (*almuerzo*), they are using words from the quarter of their language that derives from Arabic. The Moorish invaders also divided the huge Visigoth estates and distributed the land among the serfs, earning popular support. In the later years of their rule, feuding within the Moorish ruling families reversed some of their earlier advances, but their ways of life shaped the culture that Europeans carried to the Americas.

The Christian Reconquest of Iberia

Impressive scientific advances and cross-cultural interaction, though, did not overcome Christian intolerance in the end. The Iberian ways of life, grand mixtures of people, and especially the crusade mentality that Iberians developed during their long war to expel the Moors shaped the people who traveled to the Americas. The Reconquest fostered a culture of religious proselytism but especially of conquest and plunder for personal enrichment. The crusade for religious purity unleashed by the Catholics to expel the Moors and Jews from the Iberian Peninsula destroyed the advances of that progressive society. Even as Christians took advantage of Moorish women, incorporated terms from the Arabic language into their own, and benefited from the Moors' advances in science and math, the crusade mentality became the focus of their lives.

Kilometer by long kilometer, over hundreds of years, the Christian crusaders overcome Arabic territory, founded new cities, and defeated Moorish forces. The land they took was mostly too arid for farming, so the Christian nobles turned to sheep herding, using breeds from North Africa to supply Northern Europe with wool. Herders moved their huge flocks across Iberia seasonally, causing great damage to farmlands and woods. The nobles' powerful sheep organization, the Mesta, made advantageous arrangements with the Crown to protect its members' interests and over time created the emphasis on animal husbandry rather than agriculture that Iberians took to the Americas. The Crown also offered *fueros* (legal exemptions and autonomy) to the nobles as a way to encourage them to settle towns in reconquered territory. Although the struggle against the Moors was one of give and take, marked in many places by tolerance and cooperation, the military struggle gradually intensified. By 1252, the Christians had pushed the Moors into Granada, a small kingdom in the very south and center of the peninsula protected by mountains and rugged terrain. Muslim forces hung on there for another two centuries while a new power, the Spanish kingdom of Castile, took charge of the fight. Many *conquistadores* who later fought in the Americas had first fought against the Moors.

As they warred against the Moors and expanded trade, several Iberian kingdoms gained power and wealth. Portugal, along the Atlantic coast, enjoyed a long period of maritime expansion under Prince Henry, who, as a youth in 1415, was already trading with Africa for slaves, ivory, and gold. The first Portuguese trading colonies were on Madeira, west of Morocco, and then the Canary Islands, where they built sugar plantations and developed the political systems they would later use in Brazil. Portuguese exploration paid off in 1487, when Bertholomeu Dias rounded the Cape of Good Hope to reach East Africa's long-desired spices. The race to Asian wealth then began in earnest, with Portugal in the lead.

While Portuguese ships ventured south in pursuit of commerce, Castilian towns also became bustling centers of trade. To unite the collective strength of the two largest Spanish kingdoms against the enemy, in 1469 Princess Isabella of Castile wed her second cousin Ferdinand of Aragon. Joining forces, the Catholic monarchs finally defeated the Moors at Granada in 1492, expelling from Iberia Muslims and tens of thousands of people of Jewish faith. Ferdinand and Isabella and their nobles received most of the land taken from the Moors. By the end of the century, 2 to 3 percent of the people owned 95 percent of the Iberian countryside. In addition to their pursuit of land, wealth, and religious purity through crusades, the upper classes carried their traditions of patronage, patriarchy, and unequal land distribution (called *latifundia*) with them to the Americas.

Spanish History Reappraised: Why Iberian History Matters to Indigenous History

Why spend so much space on the conquerors in a book about Indigenous peoples? Iberia's history inspired the voyages of discovery and shaped their colonies in the Americas. The Reconquest exposed Europeans to people who looked and believed differently but who had a sophisticated and scientifically more advanced culture. Rather than equals, Iberians saw the Moors as just targets of conquest because of their own prejudices against darker people of other faiths. During the Reconquest they began to use thousands of African slaves, while their cities came to house the largest Jewish minority in Europe. The Iberian search for precious metals and other exportable goods from the Moors led the Europeans to exploit and treat Indigenous people in the Americas as inferior beings. In turn, these attitudes encouraged the Native people to resist the explorers as invaders. The war instilled in Iberians the mentality of taking over new lands and conquering new groups of people who were not Christians. As they occupied territory, Iberians founded new cities to secure their gains and military leaders forced their faith on the conquered Moors "in return" for their forced labor and tribute. New wealth and military prowess furthered the medieval tradition of knightly and Christian nobility. The Iberians transplanted the tradition of concentrating people in square-gridded urban areas and imposed Catholicism much as the Romans had done to Iberia. Even the Latin patriarchal system of male domination passed to Latin America, as did the militarization of society in service to imperial goals. It was this culture of conquest, plunder, religious zeal, and the destruction of pre-existing societies that Indigenous people in the Americas met near the end of the fifteenth century.

Christopher Columbus, the one explorer that children in the United States learn about from a very young age, was actually Italian rather than Spanish. He had sailed initially for Portugal, though, so his basic goal was to establish trading posts in the New World to exchange cheap trinkets with local peoples before exploring further to find better trading terms, as his nation had done along West Africa. The Catholic monarchs in Spain, though, owing to their long struggle against the Muslims, instead intended to plunder, take control, settle, and then rule any new territory they found, while converting its peoples to Christianity. The contradictions between these different goals complicated Columbus' efforts.

Indigenous Peoples of the Caribbean Discover Europeans

Rather than the "superior" Asian civilization and vast wealth fabled by European travelers like Marco Polo, the people who met Columbus' sailors in October 1492 looked very different, and the explorers were disappointed. These people were naked and seemed "poor in everything." Although some had small pieces of gold piercing their noses, nowhere did the Europeans see the vast wealth they had expected to find in Asia. Arriving first in the Bahamas, Columbus reached the coast of Cuba and then turned east and arrived at Hispaniola, but still found very little gold. From his very first meeting on October 12, the adventurer's ship's log is full of descriptions about how generous, simple, and good-natured the Arawak were, how easy it should be to make them become Christians, and what good slaves they would make.[12]

Document 3.2 is part of the journal that Columbus took to his royal patrons in January 1493 to describe his first voyage. What impressed Columbus most of all about the people he met on the islands? What exchanges did the sailors make with the Indigenous people? Analyze the language and words Columbus used to describe them. What does their interaction and journal reveal about the Indigenous people and what does the document show about the Europeans?

For Document 3.2: Excerpt from Columbus's Diary of His First Voyage, December 12, 1992, visit www.routledge.com/9780415519120.

Some of the Arawak, faced with superior firepower and perhaps with few alternatives, initially approached the Europeans compassionately. In December 1492, Guacanagarí, leader on the northern side of Hispaniola, sent Columbus a belt and mask with features of hammered gold, along with an invitation to visit his community. Then, on Christmas day, Guacanagarí received a desperate plea for help from the adventurer when his flagship *Santa María* hit a reef and sank. Guacanagarí visited Columbus aboard the *Niña* and, while his people traded gold nuggets for hawks' bells, helped the sailors to shore.[i] The chief noticed Columbus' delight at seeing the gold, and directed him toward a place in the interior of the island that he called Cibao [Cibayo], where he said even the stones were golden, and gold was so common that the people paid it little attention.[13] The Arawak leader employed a strategy often seen throughout the conquest, which was to point the Europeans elsewhere by promising them fabulous riches that lay just over the far hills or around the next river bend. Guacanagarí may also have seen the newcomers as potential allies against rival leaders in neighboring chiefdoms on the island, or as a source of trade goods to exchange with neighboring groups.

To strengthen their new alliance, Arawak from Guacanagarí's village helped the sailors build a few houses on the northwestern side of Hispaniola, close to their own town. Their assistance, though, encouraged Columbus' plan: "a Spanish empire across the sea," maintained by loyal Indigenous slaves.[14] From the new settlement, sailors continued to search for gold. Although they found very little, the Admiral nevertheless portrayed his discoveries in glowing terms. He declared the new settlement a great success, proclaiming to have "taken possession of a large town… and in it I have built a fort and defense."[15]

The Arawak people were curious about the explorers, but their attempts to interact peacefully with the Europeans failed when the explorers, finding very little gold, instead began to kidnap the Natives. In one harbor, five young Arawaks boarded Columbus' ship for a last visit, and the Admiral kept them to train as interpreters. At another stop, sailors captured seven inquisitive women and three boys on the beach. The fathers and husbands of the captives begged to come along with their loved ones, and the Admiral agreed. Two young men escaped immediately but the other captives all died later at sea.

More and more Native people became slaves as the Spanish failed to find gold. Arawak along the northern coast of Hispaniola fell captive as Columbus filled his ships with slaves for his first return to Spain. The Arawak did not go willingly. On January 11, 1493, 55 Arawak warriors refused to sell more than two of their bows when the sailors stopped along their beach to purchase weapons. In the ensuing skirmish, the Spanish sailors slashed one Native in the buttocks and shot another in the chest before the rest picked up their fallen friends and fled.[16] In all, 31 Arawak captives sailed with Columbus when he finally set off for Spain in February 1493 to show off the Natives and his small amounts of gold. Only seven Indigenous people survived the voyage, though, and the Admiral exhibited them like exotic animals in Lisbon and then in Castile. Imagine the shock the Arawak felt when they experienced a cold winter for the first time, let alone the cross-cultural and linguistic differences they experienced when Columbus displayed them to gaping audiences.

i A hawk's bell was generally 3.2 centimeters (1.3 inches) in diameter.

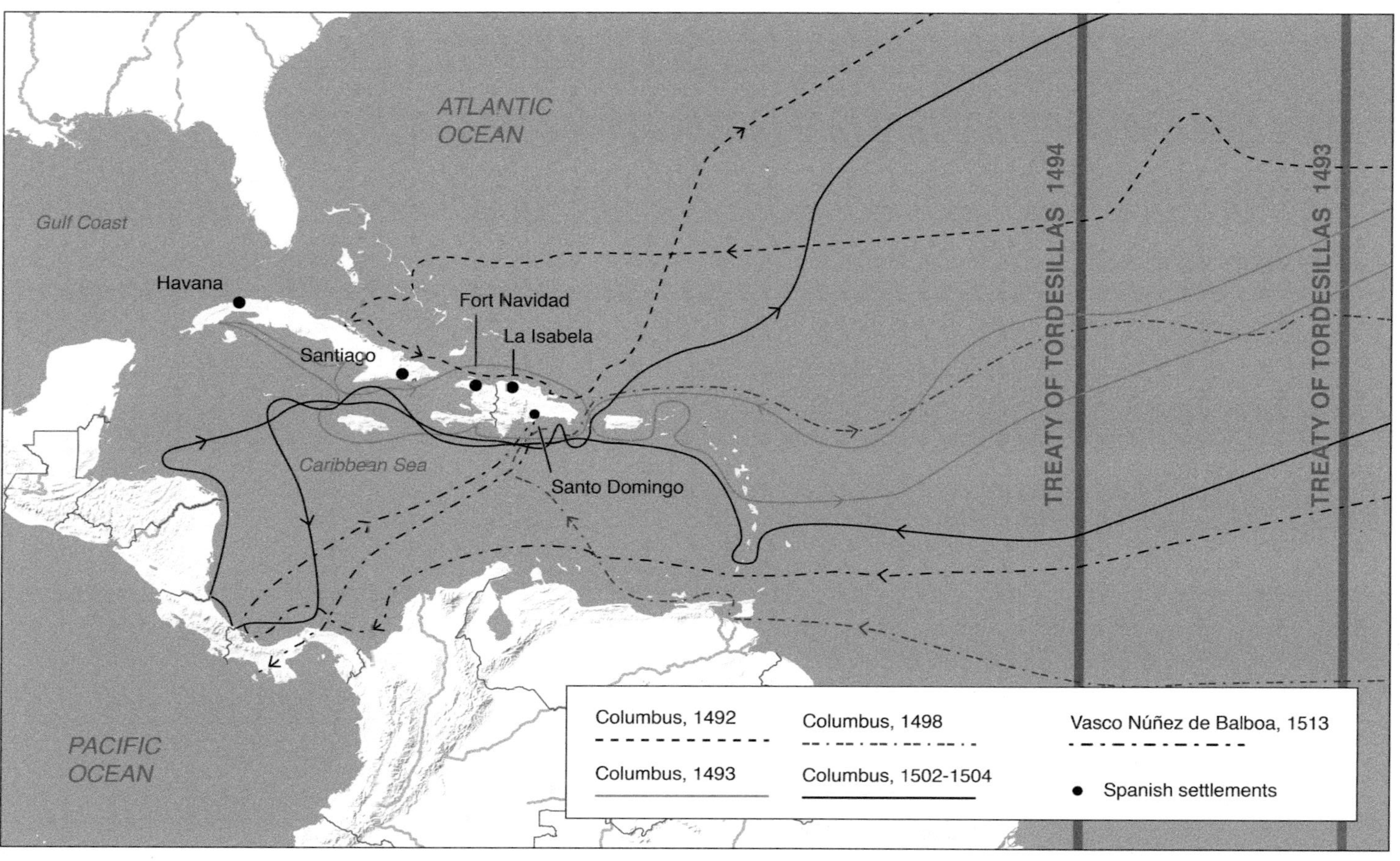

Map 3.2 Early Indigenous Interactions with Spanish Explorers in the Caribbean

Figure 3.1 Effigy Vessel, Dominican Republic, Itiba Cahubaba Blooded Aged Mother. (National Museum of the American Indian, Smithsonian Institution (12/7442). Photo by NMAI Photo Services.)

Those Arawak who lived near the new European settlement understandably grew hostile to the newcomers and responded in kind. The sailors that Columbus left behind on Hispaniola raped Native women and killed some Arawak men, but they did not survive long. In mid-January, Cacique Caonabó, whose territory lay south of Fort Navidad, burned the settlement to ashes and killed 20 of the remaining sailors. Guacanagarí, who perhaps had thrown his lot in with the explorers because they had settled near his village, defended the Spanish but received injuries in the fray. From then on, the Spanish occupation met with stiff Indigenous resistance. Cacique Guacanagarí's choices also show that the Arawak were not one united people; the different leaders looked first to the interests of their own communities and, where possible, used the Europeans to further their own geopolitical goals against rival Indigenous chiefdoms.

Individuals: Arawak Chief Caonabó

Chief Caonabó was another leader on the island, also a Western Arawak but originally from the Bahamas. Caonabó initially visited a new European settlement called La Isabela which the Spanish had founded 30 miles east of Navidad in 1493, and feigned friendship to inspect the town and prepare to destroy it. Over the next two years, the leader kept the Spaniards out of his territory, a mountainous region named Cibao, which in Arawak means "the place where rocks abound," vowing to kill all the Christians. In April 1494, the chief and four other leaders assembled over 2,000 warriors and fought an army of 400 soldiers from La Isabela, but his forces lost the battle.[17] From then on, the relationship between the Indigenous people and the newcomers only grew worse.

Caonabó finally fell prisoner to a troop of European soldiers, but only due to their deception. The following year Spain sent Alonso de Ojeda, a veteran of the conquest of Granada and a skilled swordsman, to avenge the destruction of Fort Navidad and capture Chief Caonabó. Ojeda led a troop of 400 soldiers to the interior of Hispaniola and they cunningly played their cards well. The Spanish bowed down before Caonabó and kissed his hands, praising him with loud exclamations of adulation. Under the pretext of honoring the Arawak leader, Ojeda invited Chief Caonabó to mount his warhorse, and then outfitted the leader with handcuffs of shiny metal, which Ojeda claimed were jewels that Spain's monarchs wore for special occasions. Flattered, Caonabó accepted the invitation; once handcuffed, he became Ojeda's prisoner. At one community, Ojeda arrested and sent the leader, his brother, and nephew back to Isabela in chains. He accused the chief of having asked five Native porters to carry the Spaniard's clothes across a river and then dumping them in the water before escaping. Ojeda cut the ears off his three prisoners and sent them all back to Isabela, where Columbus decapitated them in the plaza. For dumping clothes into the river! Ojeda's abuses stand as good examples of behavior outside of direct state supervision, and his colleagues helped perpetuate the abuses. The Spanish discovered gold in Caonabó's territory, built a new fort in the central highlands named St. Thomas, and began mining for precious metals. Caonabó and 600 other Arawak fell prisoner to the Spanish and traveled to Spain as slaves, but a storm sank the ships and everyone drowned, trapped by their irons in the hold.[18]

Ojeda's brutal punishment of the three Arawak illustrates what Bulgarian-French philosopher Tzvetan Todorov called the severing of the social link to government authority, in that case to royal prohibitions of abuse. Todorov's studies in history and culture theory have significantly influenced culture theory and thought history, as well as sociology, anthropology, and semiotics. The philosopher pioneered an insightful way to analyze early European treatment of Native people within his study of how the "self" discovers the "other." For Todorov, it was the vast distance from royal authority in Europe that helps explain the birth of the "modern being … restrained by no morality and inflicting death because and when he pleases."[19] Abuses by Iberian explorers in the Americas, in this view, reflected the changes sweeping through Europe. This perspective views European "barbarity" as nothing new, but rather a "quite human" heralding of the advent of modern times. Mutilation as punishment or revenge had in fact already been common in the European Middle Ages; what the Spanish initiated during the conquest,

Todorov explained, was the difference between abuses perpetuated within one's own country and in the "colony," a separation that "radically different moral laws" regulated behavior in each. These differences would only grow over the next centuries of colonization.

The Arawak Complicate Columbus' Administration and the Slave Trade

The Arawak stepped up their resistance to the Spanish after Columbus returned on his second voyage in September 1493, and their opposition complicated his trip immensely. As Europeans began to settle their island, Native people employed guerrilla warfare to stop them, but their attempts were futile because the Admiral had this time arrived with a huge entourage and orders from Ferdinand and Isabella to settle, populate, and Christianize.

Pope Alexander VI, himself Castilian and notoriously corrupt, issued the bull *Inter cetera*, granting Castile ownership of the West Indies. Another papal bull, *Piis fidelium*, charged the Castilian Crown with converting "pagans" in the overseas territories.[20] Portugal threatened war over losing any claim to the New World, so in 1494 the countries signed the Treaty of Tordesillas, an agreement that delegated all lands east of an imaginary line 370 leagues west of the Cape Verde islands to Portugal, and everything west of the line to Spain. Of course, at the time, nobody knew what they would find, but this plan supposedly offered a more even playing field on which to launch colonization. On his second trip, Columbus' 17 ships brought 1,500 colonists, five priests, soldiers, and a gaggle of adventurers. The sailors brought 20 purebred mastiffs and greyhound attack dogs to help subdue the Arawak, and the dogs roamed free on the island, devastating the smaller mammals. Horses, cattle, pigs, sheep, goats, chickens, and black rats from the ships destroyed island wildlife and plants, while spreading disease to the Native population.[21]

Columbus' second voyage of 1493 introduced the Native people to widespread disease and death. The seven Arawak who survived the first trip back to Europe and accompanied the Admiral on his travels all became ill in Spain. Three died as the ships left Cádiz to return to the Caribbean, two perished en route, and two Arawaks survived the journey, but barely escaped death. Following their arrival back in Hispaniola, both Indigenous people returned to their home communities, spreading disease to more people. The Admiral himself became sick in 1494 with "a very serious illness between pestilential and modorra [insomnia]," which almost immediately deprived him of sight, of the other senses, and consciousness, so that he was not expected to survive. It took Columbus five months to recover.[22] Over 1,000 of the 1,500 settlers who returned to Hispaniola with the Admiral on his second voyage died, and the remaining 500 faced desperate conditions; of course, the men left immediately to seek gold instead of planting crops. Influenza, typhus, smallpox, and dysentery spread so quickly through the islands that by 1496, less than one-third of the Arawak people on Hispaniola remained alive.[23] Within only two decades of initial contact, the Arawak disappeared from the Bahamas in what became the New World's first genocide caused by contact with Europe.[24] The Spanish settlers also faced death from disease, primarily dysentery. The diseases were not Columbus' fault, but his choices made the situation worse.

Faced with a massive invasion, the Arawak creatively resorted to guerrilla warfare. Even as they began to die from disease, warriors ambushed the Spanish soldiers, set fire to their supplies of food, and raided their outposts during the nights. An alliance of four Arawak groups lobbed gourds stuffed with ashes and hot peppers at the invaders to blind and choke them while warriors killed them. When attacked, Natives even destroyed their own villages and gardens to prevent the Europeans from taking their food.[25] Arawak resistance greatly complicated Spanish colonization.

Arawak resistance increased as Columbus continued to enslave them. Natives refused to cooperate when settlers tried to force them to work and search for gold. To make matters worse, the Admiral was a notoriously poor administrator; Columbus could cross an ocean, but he could not run a colony. The admiral ordered every Native person over the age of 14 to provide the equivalent of a hawk's bell filled with gold every three months, or instead to substitute spun or woven cotton. The Europeans punished failure to do so by cutting off a hand, a foot, or even by killing the Native offender.[26] To enforce their orders, the Spanish built three additional fortresses on Arawak land. Natives desperately searched through the underbrush and sand for gold, harassed Spanish settlements, or even just ran away. Finally, in desperation, Natives rose up openly against the Europeans in 1495, and their resistance doomed Columbus' administration. When he returned to Spain in February, the Admiral captured 1,500 Arawak people in a massive raid to fill his ships with slaves. The Arawak became prisoners in pens at La Isabela, guarded by dogs and soldiers. Only the healthiest people left for Spain, though, since there was room for only 500 on the ships; the healthiest remaining people became slaves for the settlers. Evicted from the pens, the Arawak nobody had chosen fled in terror. Women dropped their infants in their haste, running for miles without stopping. Only 300 of the Arawak arrived in Spain alive. Archdeacon Fonseca, the personal chaplain that the queen had charged with constructing the colonial administration, sold the slaves in Seville but most died from disease. Between 1494 and 1500, as many as 2,000 Arawak people traveled as slaves to Spain.

Native people fought openly against the Europeans between 1494 and Columbus' third voyage in 1498, as miners spread throughout the island and Spanish soldiers tried to secure their prospecting. Arawak people living under the protection of Behecchio, on the plain where today's city of Port-au-Prince, Haiti is located, faced an attack in early 1497 when Columbus' brother Bartolomé invaded their land and demanded tribute.[27] Guarionex, the leader in central Hispaniola, resented Spanish efforts to build forts south across his territory to defend the goldminers. At first, the leader negotiated to keep the peace with the Spanish, but as his people grew desperate, Guarionex fled north for protection under his ally Mayobanex. The Arawak then faced a three-month military campaign by Columbus' brother in 1498 to capture Guarionex.

The Arawak saw more and more abuses as Columbus' obsession with finding the Orient became worse as he literally lost his sanity. Turning on his own soldiers as his mental situation deteriorated, the Admiral tried to pacify rebellious settlers by giving them *repartimientos.* This arrangement, originally from the Spanish war of reconquest, granted Europeans free Native labor in return for looking after and converting them to Christianity. Later, as colonizers spread to the mainland, they began to call these grants *encomiendas*, after the Spanish term *encomendar*, to entrust. Spanish recipients became *encomenderos*, people entrusted to care for and convert the Indigenous people. The *encomienda* system was another institution repurposed from the Reconquest.

Unable to stop European enslavement, the Arawak grew desperate. Thirty people fell captive to Columbus at one point during his third trip and he confined them below deck. During the night, as the sailors prepared the ship for departure, the desperate Native people all committed suicide by hanging themselves from the low hold, bending their knees to reduce their height until they strangled. The Crown finally arrested the ailing explorer and brought him back to Spain in chains in 1499. Indigenous resistance complicated Spanish exploration and settlement, but they could not stop the onslaught of Europeans who soon occupied their territories.

Widespread Death: Early Accounts of Demographic Collapse in the Caribbean

Contact with diseases was the worst part of the European invasion of the Caribbean, because the Native peoples had no immunity and the diseases devastated their communities. Demographic historians Borah and Cook have estimated the population of Hispaniola at 8 million people prior to contact, a number that scholars have since challenged and averaged downward. Still, even the more conservative estimates suggest a large initial population on the islands.

Indigenous people also perished from cultural misunderstandings. In 1496, Jeronymite priest Ramón Pané had given six Arawak men, subjects of leader Guarionex, images of Jesus and the Virgin Mary. The priest even taught them how to pray the Hail Mary and Lord's Prayer on their knees, as well as to call on the name of Jesus when faced with tribulation and death. Mission work seemed to be progressing well. Later, though, clerics caught the same men burying the holy images in their fields. Missionaries assumed the strange practices to be purposeful desecration, so they promptly burned the Arawak men at the stake.[28] Rather than trying to defile the images, though, as the authorities believed, the men had hoped that the gods of the conquerors (symbolized to them by the crosses) would bless their corn, cassava, and bean crops.

Indigenous Peoples of Abya Yala in the Late Fifteenth Century

By the time European explorers arrived in the Caribbean, the population of the Western Hemisphere totaled around 60 million people, and a quick tour of Central and South America introduces some of the larger groups of Indigenous peoples on the eve of the European invasion. West of the Arawak homelands lies the Yucatan Peninsula, the heart of the former Mayan empire. By the fifteenth century, this civilization had long been in decline. The Hundred Years' War between the Kaal and Mutal had destroyed the center of Maya civilization, and the large Mayan cities gradually disappeared into the jungle as people abandoned them. Scholars have debated many reasons for the Mayan decline, including overpopulation, draught, and misuse of resources, all causes with some evidence in support. Perhaps Mayan leaders were unable to cope with a changing environment soon enough. Still, their cultural legacy was immensely important, and vestiges of Mayan phonetic writing, math, calendars, architecture, and art were still present throughout what became Central America.

The Mexica, to the northwest, had eclipsed the Maya by the fifteenth century and had become the dominant political force in central Mexico; Mexica territory was densely populated with up to 20 million people. Allied with other Nahuatl speakers, the Mexica's powerful Aztec Empire dominated surrounding peoples from its capital Tenochtitlan. The Mexica ruled regional ethnic states called *altepetl*, each composed of four or more *calpulli*, neighborhoods with their own gods, temples, and administrators that oversaw the collection of tribute and the distribution of land. Conquering the nearby city states of Texcoco and Tlacopan, the Mexica extended their control over the central Mexican valley and became a vast empire in 1486, when Aztec armies led by Ahuitzotl swept through Oaxaca, Guatemala, and the Gulf Coast, extending imperial control over the Triple Alliance and leaving only the Tarascans and Tlaxcalans undefeated. The Mixtecs and Zapotecs became tributaries of the Aztec rulers, by then considered deities. Moctezuma II, who became emperor in 1502, linked himself to the god of war, Huitzilopochtli, to increase his power over nobles and commoners alike. The powerful imagery centered in Tenochtitlan united his population. Over four centuries later, well-known Mexican painter Diego Rivera imagined the glories of the Aztec Empire and depicted its bustling marketplace in his famous mural *Market in Tlatelolco*, shown in Figure 3.2.

By the time the Aztecs achieved the height of their power, as many as 5 million people lived on the Central American isthmus, many of whom had displaced earlier groups. South of the Yucatan, in what became Guatemala, Natives who had been part of the Mayan Empire lived in communities with their own Mayan dialects. Larger groups included the Achi, Chorti, Ixil, Kaqchikel, K'iche', Mam, Pokoman, Q'eqchi, Tzutujil, and Xinca. The Lencas and related Care, Cerquín, and Potón peoples lived in what became Honduras. The Tawahkas, commonly known as the Sumu or Mayangna and one of the most populous Native groups in Central America, lived along the northeastern Atlantic coast. West of them along the coast lived the Tolupanes, related to the Hokan linguistic family in southwestern North America. The Chortis people lived in southwestern Honduras, and east of them in the Mosquitia region of central Honduras lived the Pech, divided into nine subgroups.[29] South, along the Pacific, in the land that became El Salvador, lived the Nahua Pipil peoples who had migrated from the north. East in what became Nicaragua, Native peoples included the Chorotega and Nicarao. Along the Pacific lived the Matagalpa and Maribio, who had displaced the earlier

Figure 3.2 *Market in Tlatelolco*, Stylized Mural of Aztec Commercial Life by Diego Rivera. (imageBROKER/Alamy Stock Photo)

Corobici.[30] The Tawahkas also lived with the Rama on the Caribbean coast. Shortly before the Europeans arrived, the Mexica established trading colonies and spread their Nahuatl language throughout the region. Many years before, around 500 C.E., the Matambú had fled to mountainous regions in what became Costa Rica to escape from the Maya. The Maleku lived in western regions surrounding the volcano Arenal, while the Bri Bri lived along the mountains of Talamanca in central Costa Rica and on the Atlantic coast near Panama.[31] Many peoples lived in the narrow isthmus that became Panama. The Talamanca, Teribe, and Ngäbe (formerly called Guaymí) – who included the Movere and Murire peoples – lived in southwestern Panama. Southeast of them lived the Embera-Wounaan. The Kuna lived in the northeast. Smaller groups of Native peoples included the Ngöbe-Buglé in the southwest, the Teribe in the northwest, and the Bokota in northeastern Panama.

South America was by this time populated by hundreds of Indigenous peoples, each also with their own way of life, beliefs, and language. Their cultures differed according to the geography where they lived. In the mountains of northwestern South America were chiefdoms or states ruled by priests and warriors, divided sharply into social classes and with large standing armies. The Chibcha controlled highland Colombia, and their capital city eventually became Bogotá. The Omagua lived from gardening and farming along 700 kilometers of Amazonian headwaters. This large group lived in hundreds of settlements, divided into two polities of thousands of people each.[32] In what became northern Venezuela and along the Caribbean coast, chiefdoms were less militaristic because geography allowed them to organize in small farming villages rather than in larger imperial structures. Their villages resembled the communities on islands throughout the Greater Antilles to which they had migrated from the Yucatan in around 2000 B.C.E.[33]

South in tropical Amazonia, Indigenous people also lived in farming villages and as small groups of hunters and gatherers. Despite the rainforest cover, the poor soil quality forced the peoples to hunt and fish to supplement their crops, so their social-political organization differed widely from the large empires to their west. It was easier to manage a small group if it remained mobile to procure food. These people farmed cassava, maize, gourds, pumpkins, beans, and cotton for hammocks or cord, and hunted sustainably, without depleting the forests, by keeping communities small. The Atlantic coast was at the time under attack by Tupi-speaking peoples, the Tupinikin and then the Tupinambá, who were migrating north from the Paraguayan basin and forcing the coastal peoples inland.[34] Tupi violence was rooted in avenging incursions onto their territory and the theft of their resources by other peoples, as well as the capture of enemy slaves. Tupian culture resembled the Europeans they would soon meet.

Tawantinsuyu, the Inca Empire, extended along the Andean mountain range. The Quechua and Aymara peoples lived at the center of the empire in today's highlands of Peru and Bolivia, ruling over many smaller groups. The eleventh emperor, Huayna Capac, extended Inca power south to central Chile and north to southern Colombia – that is further than east to west across the continental United States – and, amazingly, ruled over as many as 12 million people along 3,000 miles of some of the most challenging mountains in the world. In fact, Huayna Capac himself was leading troops against the Pasto and Popayán peoples in southern Colombia, who still refused to submit to Inca rule, when word reached him that strange people had appeared along the coasts of his empire.

South of Peru and the Atacama Desert, but still in the Andes, lived the Picunche, northernmost relatives of the Reche, who paid the Incas a rich annual tribute in gold. To thrive in the rugged terrain, they inhabited small, scattered settlements.[35] To their south, the Reche cultivated maize, used llamas as pack animals, and lived in small communities. Women oversaw agricultural production while men hunted and organized political matters. The Huilliche and Cunco were the southernmost Reche. Still to their south, on the islands at the very tip of the continent and in small family groups that harvested shellfish and marine products, lived peoples in the Yaghan linguistic family, including the Yagán, Yámana, Ona, Alakaluf, and Tequenica peoples.

North, on the prairies of the Southern Cone, lived scattered groups of guanaco hunters who, like the bison hunters of North America's Great Plains, migrated to pursue game. Because these people moved often, they did not develop farming, metallurgy, or pottery. The Patagones, Tehuelche, Querrandíes, Puelches, and even Reche ranged from south to north. The Minuane and Charruas lived in today's Uruguay. Northwest in the Gran Chaco region lived the Guaycuru peoples, including the Q'om, Mocobí, Pilagá, and the Wichi to their west. Still north of them, the Guató, Chane, Zamuco, Mbayá, Evueví, Nivaclé, Enlhit, and Enenlhit lived in the dry scrub forest called the Chaco and the Chiriguano lived to the northwest in what became Upper Peru and later Bolivia. East of the Chaco resided different Guaraní-related peoples who farmed, hunted, and gathered in the forests of what later became Paraguay and Brazil. Some of these peoples have since disappeared, yet they played a role in the historical period covered by this text.

This short introduction highlights the fact that many, many groups of Indigenous peoples lived in the Americas when the Europeans arrived. These people enjoyed their families, farmed, hunted, and fished to produce food, made alliances, struggled against opponents and invaded rival territories, chose political and religious leaders, worshiped deities, and lived in communities that differed depending on the geography. In many ways, then, Indigenous people in the Americas lived much like people indigenous to other parts of the world.

Conclusion: Memories of New Encounters

Indigenous people in the Americas resembled peoples elsewhere in the world in many ways. Still, they experienced difficulties when they met Europeans toward the end of the fifteenth century. Cultural artifacts, traveler accounts, and archeological data suggest that Native peoples interacted with people from Asia and Europe long before Columbus reached the Caribbean. Obscured in the distant past, these encounters did not enlighten the Europeans who first ventured west in the late fifteenth century. What is more, Indigenous predictions about the European arrival were apocalyptic stories created or recovered later in times of severe cultural crisis and disorder. Challenging events color the writings themselves, but the stories may have empowered the people to endure their situation.

Indigenous people met Europeans shaped by centuries of military conquest, religious crusades, and a political culture birthed by the Romans, Visigoths, and Moors. Close ties between the Vatican and the Catholic monarchs complicated early voyages of exploration, as did Portugal and Spain's differing traditions of trade and conquest. Columbus, while perhaps a brave explorer, was a notoriously poor administrator. The Admiral was ruthless with Caribbean Indigenous peoples, squeezing gold from them, enslaving and shipping them back to Iberia, and ignoring even their most basic humanity. Columbus' brothers and son followed his lead, killing to enrich themselves as they imposed Christianity upon the Natives by force. While the Spanish deceived, captured, and massacred Native Caribbeans in their search for gold, however, a vast number of the Native deaths were technically not their fault. No one at the time could have predicted or understood that contact with European diseases would produce deaths of massive proportions for Native Caribbean peoples.

By the time Indigenous people and Europeans met at the close of the fifteenth century, hundreds of Indigenous peoples lived in Abya Yala, each carefully adapted to the natural surroundings in which they lived. Like people everywhere, Natives in the Americas loved their families, and farmed, hunted, and gathered for food. Natives chose their political leaders, defended their territories and resources, worshiped their deities, fought off aggressors, and valued their cultural heritage. Some lived in small groups carefully suited to the fragile environments where they hunted and gathered. Others formed coalitions and organized vast agrarian empires that drew resources from far and wide into their political center. These peoples varied from each other even more than did European countries; different languages, arts, religions, customs, and military technology kept Native societies apart just as they did elsewhere in the world. Outsiders had ventured to the Americas before and had left traces of their voyages; this time, by the end of the fifteenth century, the invading forces seemed determined to stay.

Discussion Questions

1. Does the mixture of recent and historical traditions discredit Native prophecies of European arrivals and early interaction? If these legends were actually documented (written down) in relatively recent modern times and perhaps created after the conquest, does this invalidate the accounts as credible Native prophecies?
2. Did events in the Indigenous accounts of early encounters with Europeans really happen exactly as they were remembered and described?
3. How did the Moor invasion of Iberia shape the people who came to the Americas?
4. Analyze how Arawak and Island Carib peoples complicated early European exploration.
5. Explain why European reports differed from the reality they actually discovered.

Notes

1 Swartz, *Victors and Vanquished*, 29.
2 Skraelings, a term meaning "shriekers" or war-whoopers," was the designation that Vikings used without distinction for both Greenland Inuit and Indigenous North Americans. See e.g. Pohl, *The Viking Settlements of North America*, 51. The translation from"Eirik's Saga," in *The Vinland Sagas*, reads: "When they clashed there was a fierce battle and a hail of missiles came flying over, for the Skraelings were using catapults" (p. 99). The term "missiles" could have been anything shot through the air, including arrows, while "catapults" generally referred to stones shot from slings.
3 Nabokov, *Native American Testimony*, 17.
4 De Civrieux, *Watunna, Mitología*, 77, 173.
5 De Civrieux, *Watunna, An Orinoco Creation Cycle*, 147, 149, 150.
6 Vásquez and Rendón, *El Libro de los Libros de Chilam Balam*, 49, 52, 60–61, 62.
7 Knowlton and Aveni, *Maya Creation Myths*, 41.
8 Schwartz, *Victors and Vanquished*, 31.
9 Lockhart, *We People Here*, 51–57.
10 Wilson, *Hispaniola: Caribbean Chiefdoms*, 15.
11 De Ste. Croix, "Suffragium: From Vote to Patronage," 33–48.

12 Bergreen, *Columbus*, 14.
13 Las Casas, *Historia de las Indias*, I, 275.
14 Bergreen, *Columbus*, 84.
15 Bergreen, *Columbus*, 102.
16 Las Casas, *Historia de las Indias*, I, 304.
17 Bergreen, *Columbus*, 170.
18 Las Casas, *Historia de las Indias*, I, 406, 408.
19 Todorov, *The Conquest of America*, 145.
20 Since the fifteenth century, a papal bull has been an apostolic letter with a leaden seal issued by the Pope, signed with the title of episcopus, servus servorum Dei, meaning servant of the servants of God. Prien, *Christianity in Latin America*, 24.
21 Cunningham, "The Biological Impacts of 1492," 33–34.
22 Cook, "Sickness, Starvation, and Death in Early Hispaniola," 359.
23 Cook, "Sickness, Starvation, and Death in Early Hispaniola," 373.
24 Cunningham, "The Biological Impacts of 1492," 31.
25 Mann, *1493*, 9.
26 Las Casas, *Historia de Las Indias*, I, 417, 430.
27 Wilson, *Hispaniola: Caribbean Chiefdoms*, 16.
28 Pané, *Relación*, ch. 26.
29 *Pueblos étnicos de Honduras*, 3–20.
30 The Nahuatl-speaking peoples in Central America were known as Pipil, and by the end of the fifteenth century they lived south and east of the Bay of Fonseca. Nahuatl speakers also lived in areas that became Chinandega and between Matiare and Managua. See Newson, *Indian Survival in Colonial Nicaragua*, 30–31.
31 Conejo, *Dilema e identidad*, 5.
32 Wilson, *Indigenous South Americans*, 244.
33 Steward and Faron, *Native Peoples of South America*, 7.
34 Hemming, *Red Gold*, 24, 27, 28.
35 Faron, "Effects of Conquest on the Araucanian Picunche," 239.

4 Natives Challenge the Conquerors Yet Help Create a New World, 1500 to 1549

Chronology

1500	In August, Columbus defeats a Native rebellion at Concepción.
1500	Native people on the coast of Brazil meet Pedro Cabral.
1502	Columbus' fourth voyage to the Americas.
1508	Arawak search for gold for Ponce de León.
1510	Rebellion by peoples of Colombia and Ecuador against the Incas' forced *mit'a* labor.
1511	Settlement of Cuba, the Arawak flee to Cuba. Antonio de Montesinos denounces Spanish abuses on Hispaniola.
1512	Spanish burn Arawak Chief Hatuey to death, leading to a massive Native uprising. Laws of Burgos enacted.
1514	*Encomienda* system established.
1519	Pedro Arias Dávila executes Balboa, then searches for gold in the Gulf of Panama. Moctezuma and the Aztecs meet Hernán Cortés at Tenochtitlan.
1520	Native people in southern Abya Yala meet Magellan's fleet.
1524	Pizarro and Almagro leave to find the Inca Empire and Peru. Cortés sends 12 Franciscan friars to Nahua villages as missionaries.
1525	Cuauhtemoc, the last Aztec leader, is executed.
1527	Indigenous peoples in the Yucatan Peninsula experience Francisco de Montejo's invasion. The Inca Empire in civil war between Husacar and Atahualpa.
1530	Pizarro arrives in northern Peru.
1532	Atahualpa falls captive to Pizarro at Cajamarca.
1534–1536	Indigenous people expel all the Spanish from the Yucatan Peninsula. Pizarro grants *encomiendas* of Native people to his soldiers.
1534	In May, Inca forces lose the Battle of Teocajas in Ecuador to the Spanish.
1535	Pizarro founds Lima on the Pacific coast of Peru. New Spain becomes the first Viceroyalty. Manco Inca rebels against the Spanish in Peru.
1536	Querandí at River Plate delta meet Pedro de Mendoza.
1540	Las Casas leaves Central America for Spain to lobby for Native lives. Mixton Wars and Mixtec uprising in New Galicia, New Spain.
1541–1542	Amazonian peoples meet the Gonzalo Pizarro expedition.

1542	King Charles V enacts the New Laws to abolish the *encomienda* system.[1]
1544	Mayans in the Yucatan receive Franciscan missionaries.
1545	Discovery of Potosí silver mine in Upper Peru.
1546	The Great Mayan Revolt in Yucatan Peninsula.

Introduction: Early Indigenous Responses to the Europeans

As we have seen, the Indigenous people who met Europeans at the turn of the sixteenth century lived in many different groups throughout the Americas. Understanding Native people to have been like people in other places and times helps explain how they interacted with the Europeans. Natives loved their families, worked to feed them, decided on leaders and group actions, carefully held a balance with deities to ensure access to resources and personal well-being, defended territories and resources from aggressors, and passed on their culture and values to their children. Their sociopolitical arrangements varied from small hunting and gathering groups to large empires, and their responses to the outsiders varied as well. Some collaborated and profited. Most resisted in some way, either with outright force or through nonviolent strategies. Everywhere, Indigenous people helped shape the new world that was being born.

In much the same way, the Europeans who explored Indigenous lands were products of their environments. Seafaring, trading, exploration, and the mixture of Indigenous Iberian, Greek, Roman, Visigoth, Portuguese, Castillian, and Aragonese cultures, ways of life, and religions all shaped Iberian traditions. The *Reconquista* itself, that long crusade to slowly push Muslim and Jewish people out of the Iberian Peninsula, profoundly shaped the people who settled the Americas. Abuse, coexistence, negotiation, imposition, warring, theft, hatred, fear, and love were all part of the baggage that explorers brought with them to the Americas. Colliding forces from the two worlds were explosive and took time to stew and settle into a great social soup, that grand mixture of peoples and cultures that became colonial Latin America. By the end of the fifteenth century, Native people and Europeans had just met in a few places and were testing each other to discover how they would interact. As the new century opened, meetings became more frequent and widespread and, over the next 50 years, Indigenous people and Europeans laid the basic structure of what came to be known as colonial Latin America.

Native Peoples on Caribbean Coasts Meet the Europeans

Indigenous people in northern South America first met Europeans late in July 1498, when on his third voyage Columbus accidentally skirted the delta of the Orinoco River, in what is now Venezuela. A large canoe carrying 25 Indigenous men approached the caravel and saw the sailors dancing to a tambourine, apparently trying to lure the Natives closer. The Indigenous people were likely Guaiqueri, the dominant political force in the area. The Admiral was only 46 years old, but illness made him appear ten years older, and finding land and a large river delta was fortuitous because his sailors were exhausted. The Guaiqueri people must have felt threatened, as they fired arrows at the sailors. Later, one of their leaders visited the flagship, wearing a gold crown that he placed on Columbus' head. To the Europeans, these people looked lighter in color than people they had met in the Caribbean, and wore cotton cloths on their heads that Columbus mistook for turbans.[2] Over the next days, as the explorers met more people decorated with gold necklaces and pearl bracelets, the Admiral's spirits soared: he must have finally reached Asia. After claiming the Paria Peninsula for Spain, Columbus met "handsome," "gentle," and "tractable" people who honored him with a banquet of alcoholic beverages, bread, and fruits. Eight years after arriving in the Caribbean, however, the Admiral was still not ready to accept that he had found a new continent. Suffering from vision problems and insomnia as he explored the Gulf of Paria, Columbus concluded that the seas were lifting his ships toward the entrance to heaven. Finally, the near-loss of his ships to shallow waters and violent currents finally forced the explorer to return to Santo Domingo at the end of August. The Admiral's report that he had reached a "mighty continent that was hitherto unknown" reflected his growing self-doubt.[3]

Native Peoples in Eastern South America Encounter the Europeans

While Columbus' sanity deteriorated, more and more Indigenous people on the coasts of South America met the strange people. The Crown had commissioned Columbus' rivals to explore the Americas in peace, while treating the people with friendship. Natives on the Guajira Peninsula encountered the first of these groups in 1499, with the arrival of Alonso de Ojeda and his fleet. These people, likely the Añu, wore gold ornaments and lived in thatched houses on stilts above the water. The Spanish as a result named the area Venezuela, "Little Venice."[4] One of Ojeda's companions on that trip was Amerigo Vespucci, who even before traveling had written a fictional story claiming to have discovered the continent. His "virtual" creation of the Americas illustrates how fiction, imagination, and great distance from the authorities in an age of slow communications shaped European behavior in the lands they explored. Ojeda's infamous abuses of Indigenous people that followed became the norm; along with his colleagues' depredations, they illustrate the behavior analyzed by Todorov. Further exploration produced further abuses; one year later Vincente Pinzón, another rival of Columbus, enslaved Native people in January 1500 when he scouted the Amazon River delta.[5]

The Tupinamba, along the coasts of central Brazil, met Europeans quite accidentally in April 1500, when winds blew Portuguese Captain Pedro Cabral and his fleet off course during his voyage to trade in India.[6] By the time the sailors reached the beach in what became the State of Bahia, 20 Native men were already waiting. They imitated the sailors, who erected a cross and celebrated mass, so carefully that the traders predicted easy conversion. Pero Caminha, Cabral's scribe, predicted that "One can easily imprint on them any mark we choose, for Our Lord has given them good bodies and good faces as befit good men. If anyone is to come here, let a clergymen come along to baptize them." It was the Natives' nakedness, though, that most intrigued the traders. Caminha noted that one girl was

> all dyed [*sic.*] from head to foot in that paint; and indeed she was so well built and so well curved and her privy part (what a one she had!) was so gracious that many women of our country, on seeing such charms, would be ashamed that theirs were not like hers.[7]

Sailors tried to dress them, but the people they described as "noble savages" quickly threw off the European clothing. Along one river, sailors stumbled upon a Native dance and the Tupinamba welcomed them warmly to join in the fun. Another friendly group spent a day dancing to the sailors' tambourines. After trading feathers for paper, trinkets, and alcohol, the Tupinamba filled one of the ships with dyewood, a tree that produced a bright red dye, and Cabral sent the cargo back to Portugal when he left for India.

The Portuguese depictions of the Indigenous people as savages exemplify what Todorov has described as European concepts of the "other," as well as his analysis that discovery of the other knows several degrees. As the philosopher explained, from the "other-as-object identified with the surrounding world to the other as subject equal to the I but different from it, with an infinity of intermediary nuances." Initial Portuguese descriptions clearly portrayed Native people as "objects," the first stage in encounters with knowledge of the "other." Their celebration of mass following Cabral's landing, as well as predictions of easy conversion and attempts to clothe the Tupinamba, illustrate Todorov's conclusion that since the period of the conquest, for almost 350 years, Western Europeans have tried to assimilate the "other," to do away with an exterior alterity, and have ultimately in great part succeeded. Europeans spread their way of life and values around the world and, "as Columbus wished, the colonized peoples have adopted our customs and have put on clothes."[8] Colonial contacts, however, also changed the Europeans. As Todorov made clear, knowledge of the "other" also develops self-knowledge; gaining additional insight during the encounter facilitated European conquest and ultimately their colonization efforts.

Cabral's discovery was fortuitous for his monarch, because the territory and people he found lay clearly east of the Line of Tordesillas, within the half of the world the Pope had already designated for Portugal. For the next 30 years, the Tupinamba cut hard dyewood logs and transported them 11 to 14 miles to the coast, where they traded them with the Portuguese for axes, knives, cloth, mirrors, and tools.[9] Peoples along the Brazilian coastline also bartered with French merchants who followed the Portuguese, many of whom settled on their lands and started families of their own with Native women. The Carijó welcomed one such captain in 1503, who lived for a year with the Indigenous women as a "naked sultan" and prepared dyewood logs to ship back to Portugal.

Events: Different European Interactions with Indigenous Peoples

That French merchants in Brazil started families with Native women while trading with Europe seems surprising, given the way the Spanish had treated Indigenous people in the Caribbean. It is possible to compare how Europeans related to the people they met and then stereotype their behaviors. Because of their long history of war in the Reconquest, the Spanish generally used violence to force Native people to provide them with precious metals and then labor. The Portuguese, long engaged in Atlantic trade, at first mainly traded with Indigenous peoples. Later, they also tried to force Native people off the land or settle them into missions. As we have seen, the French likewise tended initially to approach Native peoples commercially, and even entered alliances with them when they needed allies to combat rival European nations. Yet the French also employed violence to subdue and convert Indigenous people.

The British, who arrived in North America a century later, had no interest in converting the Native people and little incentive to trade with them. In his book *The Invasion of America*, Jennings depicts British colonization as a territorial invasion fueled by greed and the desire to transplant their British culture to a more profitable location. In his words, the British "did not settle virgin land. They invaded and displaced a resident population."[10] The brutal British occupation of eastern North

America, already partially depopulated by virgin soil epidemic diseases, supports Jennings' analysis. In addition, unlike the French, the British tended not to have children and raise informal families with Native women.

While it is perhaps possible to distinguish some general differences in the ways that European peoples related with Indigenous peoples in the Americas, ultimately these approaches were all grades along the continuum of colonialism. The mercantilist parameters of the sixteenth and seventeenth centuries, created to enrich the most powerful nations, justified abuses in their interests. This does not excuse European treatment of the Native people, but an historic context helps explain how colonizers legitimated the abuses that explorations produced.

The Inca Empire Counters Internal Insurrections

West of Amazonia in the Andes Mountains, the Inca Empire was in growing disarray. Emperor Huayna Capac (Quechua for "the mighty young one") had fought since 1493 to extend his rule. Huayna Capac was unable to subdue regional rebellions and his empire began to spin out of control. Just as his armies completed the conquest of the Chachapoyas in Peru's Amazonian cloud forest region in 1510, the Huancavelicas, Quitos, Pastos, Carangues, Cayambia, and Popayán rebelled in what later became southern Colombia and northern Ecuador against the Inca labor tax called the *mit'a* or "turn." This system of rotational forced labor, distributed carefully throughout the empire, mobilized a few men each year from each unit of administration to work in the mines, build the public infrastructure, or serve in the army. The arrangement was the main source of income for the empire, but newly conquered peoples clearly resented the *mit'a* imposition.[11] Huayna Capac led his army of Qulla soldiers, conscripted from the high-altitude forests around Lake Titicaca, to repress these uprisings. Imperial forces easily defeated the elderly, women, and children left to meet them. As his troops carelessly celebrated their victory, however, Pasto warriors ambushed and killed them. In revenge, the royal forces slaughtered Pasto women and men, young and old.

Emperor Huayna Capac resettled the reconquered area with his own colonists to ensure loyalty, and then went after the remaining rebels. In one charge against a fortress, rebels dumped the emperor's litter and nearly killed him. Humiliated as he trudged back to camp on foot, Huayna Capac harangued his soldiers. Reinforced by new recruits, his army later returned in revenge and this time killed thousands of Pasto men and adolescent boys.[12]

Internal insurrections by resentful subject peoples help explain why the Incas were unprepared to throw off the Spanish invasion. Their army took years to subdue the northern rebellion with scorched-earth tactics, but veterans of the war, and especially the *kurakas* (leaders), resented their arrogant ruler and finally rebelled. At the same time, the Chiriguano in the mountains of what became Bolivia, whom the Inca had recently conquered, began to plunder imperial frontiers. The Inca's attempt to force them to supply labor and land had backfired. The Chiriguano in particular resented that their own relatives outside the imperial state boundaries were free of taxation and the *mit'a*, yet still illegally received goods distributed by the Inca state from their relatives under Inca control. The outsiders, along with the Caracaras and Candires peoples, also raided imperial

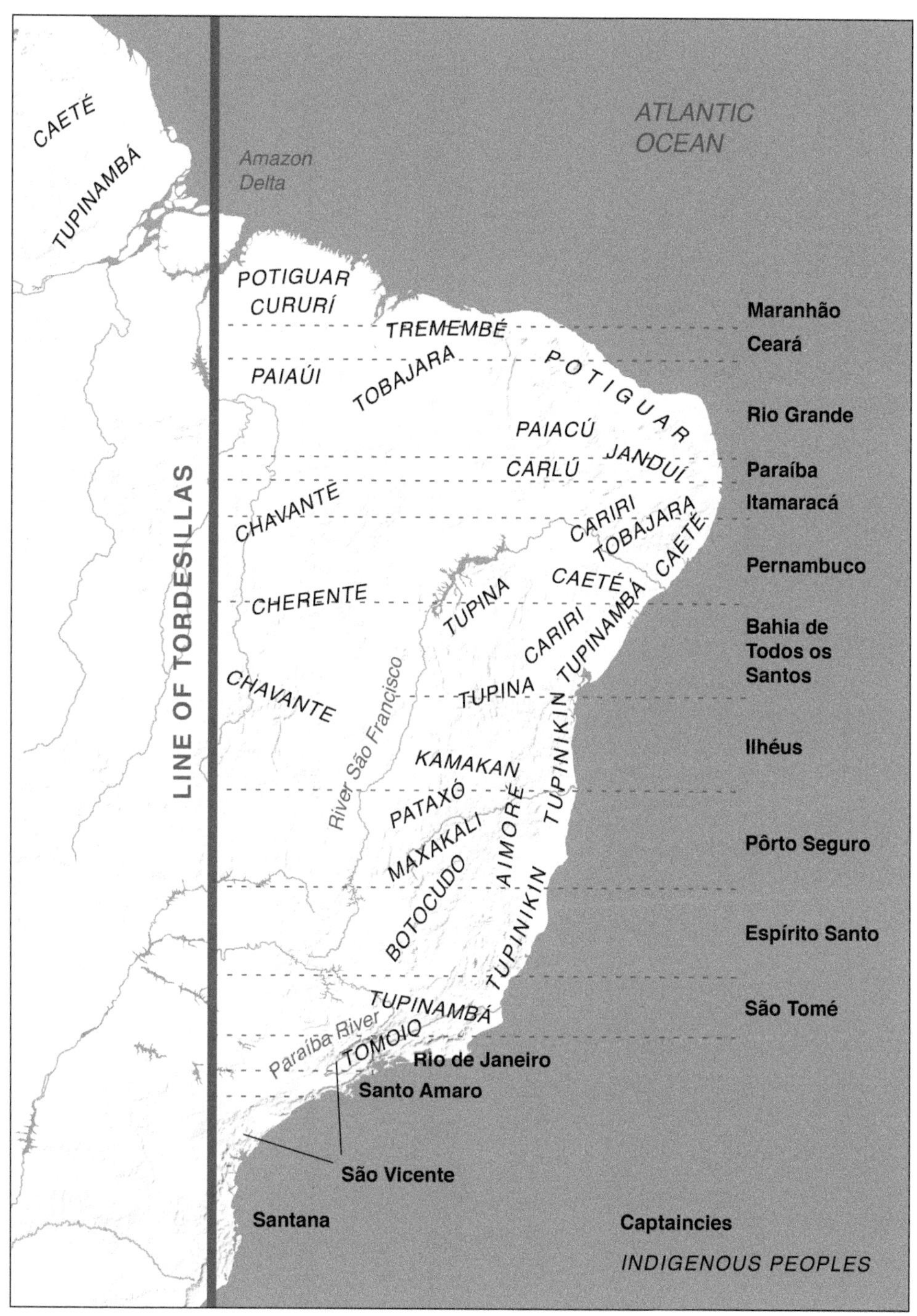

Map 4.1 Major Indigenous Populations in the Brazilian Captaincies

borders, trading their plunder with Chanes and Guaraní peoples east to the Paraguay River. The Inca used such regional divisions to control conquered peoples, yet, as subject peoples, the Chiriguano clearly tried to manipulate the Inca to their own advantage.

Indigenous Resistance Takes Off in Earnest as European Slave Raids Increase

While insurrections challenged the Inca Empire, Native people were making Spain's rule in the Caribbean increasingly difficult. More and more people fell into slavery as the new Spanish leaders increased impressment. In 1508, on Puerto Rico, Ponce de Leon forced the Arawak to mine for gold and within a year they had made him one of the wealthiest men in the colonies. To escape the forced labor and disease, the enslaved Arawak fled, but governors pursued them to the Bahamas, to Jamaica, and finally to Cuba. That same year, Pope Julius II granted Spain the right to collect tithes in return for creating a Catholic diocesan system in the West Indies, an attempt by the pontiff to solidify royal and papal authority in the Americas.

The Arawak fleeing Hispaniola joined the local Ciboney people in neighboring Cuba. Cacique Hatuey was one of the refugees. The leader gathered his people together and declared:

> You know how the Christians have stolen our lands, captured our people, taken our women and children, killed our parents, brothers, relatives, and neighbors. They killed leaders and vassals, destroying and finishing them off; and if we had not fled our lands and arrived here, we could also have been killed by them. Do you know why they do all these things?

The people all responded: "They do it because they are cruel and mean." Chief Hatuey answered, "I will tell you why: because they have a big lord who they love very much, and I will show it to you." The chief uncovered a woven palm basket full of gold and continued:

> Here you see their lord, which they serve and love; to have this lord they go to great lengths, and for him they pursue us; for him they have killed our fathers and brothers, our people and neighbors, and have taken all our goods, and for him they make us work and pursue us. For him let us party and dance, so that when they arrive this god can tell them to treat us better.

Then his people threw the basketful of gold into the river.[13] Resistance was spreading; the people of Puerto Rico, led by Cacique Agüeynaba, rose up against Ponce de Leon's rule during this time.

Cacique Hatuey fell prisoner to the Spanish in 1512, who found him by torturing his people. Then conquistadors sentenced the leader to death by incineration. The executioner asked the Arawak leader, who was tied to a post atop the firewood, to accept baptism and die as a Christian. Chief Hatuey reportedly asked why he would want to be like the Christians who were so evil. The priest promised that those who died as Christians would go to heaven to live in pleasure with God. Hatuey asked again if Christians went to this heaven, and the priest assured him that good Christians did go there. The chief refused to join Christians in heaven if indeed that is where they spent eternity.[14] Hatuey's execution led to a massive Native uprising. As many as 7,000

Indigenous warriors attacked the governor's main captain, Pánfilo de Narváez, while he was asleep, and he escaped only because the warriors looted the soldiers' clothing rather than killing them.[15] It seems unlikely that the soldiers could have so easily escaped so many angry Native people, so the Spanish account of the attack was likely exaggerated. Still, even a smaller mob moving angrily against the Spanish, after Hatuey had been on the island for such a short time, attests to his influence and following as a leader.

Colonial Impositions and Some New Advocates

As more settlers arrived in Hispaniola, which people were calling Santo Domingo after its main city, reports about the ill-treatment of the Native people reached the Spanish authorities in Seville. Dominican friars led these charges. On the Sunday immediately before Christmas 1511, in front of the leading citizens of Santo Domingo, Friar Antonio de Montesinos condemned sin among the Spanish and employed scriptures about Isaiah and John the Baptist to denounce colonists for abusing the Indigenous people. Everyone important was there: Governor Diego Columbus, royal emissaries, and the other notable people in the Church listened nervously as the priest criticized their abuses of the Indigenous people.

Preaching from John 1: 22–23, Montesinos called the settlers to repent and prepare for the arrival of the Messiah:

> There is a sterility of conscience among you on this island, and a blindness in which you live. You are in mortal danger of condemnation, not realizing the grave sins you are committing with such insensitivity. You are immersed in them and dying in them. I want you to know that I have come to this pulpit, I who am the voice of Christ on the desert of this island. And you had better pay attention, not just listen, but heed with all your hearts and all your minds. For this will be something you never heard before, the hardest, harshest, most terrifying news you ever expected to hear. This voice says you are in mortal sin for the cruelty and tyranny which you inflict on these innocent people. By what right do you hold these Indians in such cruel and horrible servitude? By whose authority have you made such detestable war on these people who lived peacefully in their lands? How can you hold them so oppressed and exhausted, without giving them food nor curing their illnesses? They die daily from the work you demand of them. Let me be perfectly clear. You are killing them to get the gold you so crave. … Are these not men? Do they not have rational souls? Are you not obliged to love them as yourselves! Don't you understand this? Don't you see this? Be assured that in your state you can no more be saved than Moors or Turks who lack and don't want the faith of Jesus Christ.[16]

Not only did Montesinos' sermon prick consciences; the intrepid missionary even refused to give his audience Holy Communion. The morning's events shocked even soldiers seasoned by years of fighting and plundering in Spain. This was not what conquistadors were used to hearing in church during advent season. The priest had even dared to degrade them as worse than infidels, the very Moors against which they had crusaded.

Probably the most stricken listener was a new priest named Bartolomé de Las Casas, who had been getting rich from his own *encomienda*. Las Casas was upset, though, by the brutal way in which his friends had conquered and divided Cuba's people into *encomiendas*, and his concern had led him to the priesthood. Montesinos' sermon was the tipping point in his life. The young priest gave up his own grant of laborers and dedicated his life to improving Native conditions. From within the very society that was helping conquer Indigenous people, then, emerged a movement to improve their situation. Using the following document, explain why the sermon angered the settlers. Would they have felt both fear and remorse if they had been getting rich? Why might the sermon have helped change the course of Caribbean events?

For Document 4.1: Montesinos' Sermon, visit www.routledge.com/9780415519120.

Growing Indigenous deaths on Hispaniola meant less income and labor for the Spanish, who moved to the surrounding islands in search of more slaves and gold. Native people on Cuba became slaves to Diego Velázquez in 1511, a Spaniard from Segovia who had arrived on Columbus' second voyage. When he conquered the island in 1511, Velázquez found enough gold to become extremely wealthy. By 1517 his "royal fifth," the 20 percent of all commodities and slaves that conquistadors by law returned to the Crown, amounted to 21,000 pesos, a huge sum. Soon after contact, Indigenous peoples on Cuba also began to die from diseases.

The Spanish Crown was disturbed at news trickling in from the colonies, such as produced by Montesinos' sermon, about the mistreatment of its new subjects. Las Casas reported that during the conquest of Cuba, soldiers killed 7,000 children in three short months. Despite the gold pouring into the royal coffers, this harsh treatment of the Natives would have to change. Montesinos traveled to Spain and so surprised King Ferdinand with his list of abuses that the monarch ordered his officials and theologians to at once write proper laws to improve the situation. The following year, 1512, the monarch signed the Laws of Burgos, which insisted on conversion and good treatment of the Indigenous people.[17] The laws regulated the *encomienda* to ensure that they worked more fairly. While laudable, the Laws of Burgos were dead even before they were announced in the Caribbean. There was simply no way to enforce their obedience so far away from the Crown. After King Ferdinand died in 1516, Cardinal Cisneros, the priest acting as regent until the next ruler was established, sent three Hieronymite monks to govern Hispaniola, but they were also incapable of enforcing better treatment.[18] Instead of allowing production to slow down because of better treatment for the Native workers, the priests imported African slaves. Europeans believed that the colonial project would only be profitable with forced labor.

Indigenous deaths continued, though, as disease spread and the Spanish divided the Native peoples among themselves as slaves. The Crown therefore issued laws meant to keep more Natives alive. The first were formal instructions to Pedro Arias Dávila to establish the *encomienda* system. Formerly named Pedro Arias de Ávila y Ortiz de Cota, but called Pedrarias Dávila for short, this administrator from Segovia led the first great Spanish expedition to the New World in 1514. The Crown also instructed Dávila to check up on his son-in-law Vasco Núñez de Balboa, given reports of his terrible administration of Darien, later known as Panama. While an inept governor, Balboa had at least kept Indigenous people alive; after all, they were his only source of gold and provisions.

Balboa first heard rumors about a rich area on the Caribbean slope of Darien from the son of Cacique Comogre. Tumaco, a leader on Panama's Pacific coast, made the conquistador a clay figure of a llama to illustrate the transportation of vast amounts of riches in that southern land. Indigenous people also lauded the skills of the Quimbayas, who lived in the swampy forests of the Chocó region, today's northwestern Colombia, and were reportedly master goldsmiths. The spirit of a gold rush was still very much in the air. On Panama's Pacific coast, an area ruled by Chief Birú came to symbolize a land of fabled riches, a reputation and name that Europeans later associated with Peru. Balboa followed tales of a land with plentiful gold to his south and eventually arrived at the Pacific Ocean. His discovery, though, was not enough to save the conquistador: Dávila finally arrested Balboa for desertion and treason and beheaded him in 1519.

Even as he authorized forced Indigenous labor, King Charles V reminded the colonists to use love and friendship to draw Native people closer to God and the Catholic faith.[19] This may have been a laudable suggestion, but the king could never enforce his mandate. Along with instructions to establish the *encomienda*, King Charles instituted the *requerimiento*, a document to invite the Indigenous people to accept Christianity. The document, an attempt to appease critics such as Las Casas, ordered officers to read it to the Natives before attacking them: "We protest that the deaths and losses which shall accrue from this are your fault, and not that of their highnesses, or ours, or of these soldiers who came with us."[20] As the writers could have predicted, even if their victims had understood Spanish, conquistadors made sure that few people actually heard the document by reading it quickly in the middle of the night and at some distance from the actual "enemy."

Given the goals of the *requerimiento*, it should not be surprising that Indigenous people protested its use. One leader from Cenu, on the northwestern coast of today's Colombia, insisted that the Pope must have been crazy when he issued the document that gave the Indigenous lands to the king of Spain, blaming the monarch even more for having come to take other peoples' lands. What is more, the chief asked why Indigenous people should believe in Christ, who the Spanish claimed as son of the true God, when they, as God's people, had never before been notified about this Church or Pope. Finally, he insisted, what gave this Pope power to take away their lands, and why did Christians claim the right to use violence to take Indigenous goods and sell their women and children as slaves?[21] These were astute questions from a leader who, like any adept politician, refused to recognize outside authority over his own territory and people.

Indigenous Peoples Defend their Communities

As the conquerors moved from the Caribbean islands to the mainland of South America, they fought over the spoils and vented their anger on the Indigenous people. After executing Balboa, Dávila set off on his own brutal search for riches. Within ten years, his soldiers killed almost all the Native people in the Urabá area of what is today northwestern Colombia, and the rest perished from diseases.[22] Such depredations spread fear: in 1517, Indigenous people on the Gulf of Panama voluntarily gave up their pearls, some the size of nuts, because the Native guides for explorer Gaspar de Morales frightened them with tales of his fierceness. Dávila had sent Morales to secure the pearls spoken of by Balboa and, once there, Morales captured 20 chieftains and let his dogs tear them to pieces.

Native people responded angrily to European abuses. On one occasion, a chief on the mainland named Chiruca hosted the Spanish overnight as the explorers made their way back to their ships. While the explorers slept in the lodgings provided, the leader set the house on fire and his warriors strangled the explorers as they staggered sleepily out of the door through the smoke. In revenge, the Spanish captured Chiruca, forced him to assemble 18 neighboring chiefs, and then chained them together until their people attempted a rescue. A young soldier named Francisco Pizarro, who had arrived with Ojeda and had turned his own leader Balboa over to Dávila, led the resulting charge against Chiruca's forces.[23] Pizarro's soldiers arrested the chiefs and then killed over 700 people in a bloody massacre. The following day, the Spanish used war dogs to kill all the detained chiefs, including Chiruca, thereby spreading even more fear.[24]

On the mainland, Indigenous people from very different sociopolitical arrangements met these new people with scary reputations. Mayans on the Yucatan met Europeans when Francisco Hernández de Córdoba sailed west from Cuba in 1517 to raid for slaves. A heavy storm drove his ships southward, to the Maya city of Ecab, on the northern point of the Yucatan Peninsula. Duly impressed, explorers called it "the Grand Cairo," and accepted an invitation to visit. "Richly dressed" people guided the sailors into an ambush, where Native soldiers attacked them. Indigenous people in the city of Campeche kindly asked the Europeans to leave. The Couohe, in the impressive city of Champoton, violently overwhelmed the disembarking Spanish and wounded Córdoba, who later died. Clearly, the Spanish reputation for violence preceded them, since many peoples in the Yucatan were not even willing to receive the European delegations.

The Aztecs in central Mexico made contact with a second Spanish expedition to the Yucatan and traded gold with them. Emperor Moctezuma, concerned about strange people and ships off his coasts, reportedly consulted priests to ask whether Quetzalcoatl's long-awaited arrival was due. Soon the isthmus and territories along the seas were rife with battles between invading explorers and Indigenous people defending their lands, gold, and families. Unleashed on the mainland, Spanish soldiers seemed to go wild, moving from community to community to rape, pillage, and steal. Still, it would be erroneous to see the Natives as defenseless; using what weapons they had against steel and gunpowder, Indigenous people fought back.

When possible, Natives on the mainland trapped the intruders in their villages, harassed them with arrows as they moved through the forests, or simply tricked them into ambushes. Chief Tataracherubi, along Panama's southern coast, brought gold to the Spanish as a peace offering and informed them of a neighboring village loaded with gold. A Spanish captain and 30 soldiers approached during the night and recited the *requerimiento*, but, as the sun rose, they found themselves surrounded by large villages full of angry, threatening people. Trying to bluff their way out, the conquerors took the chief, women, and boys as hostages and then ran. Warriors fell on them like "wild bulls" with sticks, darts, stones, and clubs, but then the Spanish apprehended their chief and threatened to run him through with a sword, bluffing their way out of the dangerous situation.[25]

Indigenous people also resisted early Spanish attempts to proselytize. At Chiribichi, on the northern coast of Tierra Firme (contemporary Venezuela), Natives grew angry when the Dominican missionaries at an early mission called Santa Fe accused them of being cannibals and tried to enslave them. Following a fight, Chief Maraguay's people routed the settlers, burned the mission, destroyed the sacramental icons, and killed the priests.[26] In other places, fear preceded the visitors and led to different encounters; Indigenous people came out of their villages loaded with gifts for the explorers, begging them to move on without stopping.

Why did the Native peoples not work together to fight off the European invasions? After all, surely a united Native military response, at least so early in the conquest, could have defeated the European forces. This seems true especially since Indigenous people knew and could use the land to their advantage. Despite the dogs and cannons, surely enough warriors fighting together could have defeated European forays into the mainland more effectively than the small groups that had defended the Caribbean islands. We tend to forget that different Indigenous peoples could not understand each other's languages, were often at odds – if not enemies – with neighboring groups, had different interests, competed for resources, and had no way of communicating over distances to coordinate resistance. For these reasons, cooperative pan-Indigenous military resistance did not occur until much later in the eighteenth century. Even then, it was only the collective colonial experience of resistance, as well as the use of Spanish as a common language and European weapons, that made it possible for Native peoples to join forces, communicate more easily, and fight the European settlers.

Despite Resistance, the Aztec Empire Falls to the Spanish

A great example of Indigenous disunity occurred during the conquest of the Aztec Empire. In February 1519, a young adventurer named Hernán Cortés set out from Cuba with a huge expedition of over 500 soldiers, 16 horses, and artillery. On the Yucatan Peninsula, Cortés found two translators who helped him immensely. The first was a shipwrecked Spaniard who had learned Mayan. The second was a Native woman, Malintzin, who both spoke her native Nahuatl and Chontal Mayan and quickly learned Spanish. Malintzin not only interpreted for the explorers but also offered them tactical advice on Aztec strategies and goals. As Cortés marched inland, warriors from states eager to overthrow the hated Aztec regime rallied behind him because the Aztecs had sacrificed their young men and squeezed tribute from them as well. The Cempoalans, impressed by the invaders' military strength, joined the Spanish. The Tlaxcalans assumed at first that the invaders were Aztec allies and fought them bitterly, but ultimately later sided with the Spanish. At Cholula, the expedition killed over 6,000 Native people to prevent a threatened attack. Aztec emperor Moctezuma tried unsuccessfully to convince Cortés to stop his invasion. The march towards Tenochtitlan shows the brutal military superiority that Europeans employed, the immense fear they instilled, huge misunderstandings on all sides, and hatred for the Aztecs among their subject peoples.

Individuals: Malintzin

Malintzin was not a traditional leader, but she played a significant enough role in the encounter that people recognized her among important Native figures in the age of conquest. A young girl of 16 years old when the Europeans arrived, Malintzin was one of 20 female slaves that a Chontal leader near the village of Cintla gave to Cortés. Malintzin was clearly a fast learner: she had grown up speaking Nahuatl, learned Chontal Maya after her family sold her into slavery, and within only a few months mastered enough Spanish to translate for Cortés. As one can imagine, her linguistic skills gave Cortés a significant advantage over the Mexica, because he could understand Nahuatl without the Mexica being able to understand Spanish. The Mexica addressed the translator with their pronunciation as Malina, adding the honorific title "-tzin" to the end, shortening it to "-tze" to indicate dignity. The Spanish heard her name Malintze as "Malinche." In helping Cortés, the translator discovered that the Totonacs were enemies of Moctezuma and helped ally them with Spanish forces. Malintzin became close to Cortés and bore him a son. Rather than recognize her as his lover, though, given current mores, the conquistador brought his own wife from Cuba, gave Malintzin some property and married her off to one of his officers. The translator died within a few years from disease before even reaching the age of 25. Some Mexicans have depicted Malintzin as a woman of ill-repute who sold out her country to the invaders.[27] Her background and past treatment, though, shows why she helped defeat the Mexica and became an important figure in the Spanish conquest of the Aztec Empire.

The Spanish invasion deeply affected the Mexica because it ended their way of life and empire. The Aztec nobility met Cortés at Tenochtitlan, welcomed him as a returning king, and housed him in a luxurious palace. The Europeans were amazed at the gardens, canals, beautiful palaces of rooms lined with cedar, and even a zoo that housed tigers, jackals, and foxes. Quickly assessing the situation, the intrepid conquistador took Emperor Moctezuma hostage to use as a bargaining chip given his precarious position: a huge Aztec population and army surrounded his small Spanish force. Despite their dangerous situation, the guests were less than gracious: Cortés belittled Mexica belief systems, drove priests from their temples, destroyed Native icons, and replaced them with crosses and images of Mary.

When Cortés returned to the coast to defeat a rival Spanish expedition sent to arrest him, the soldiers he left at Tenochtitlan attacked a defenseless crowd and killed many Mexica nobles in the central plaza. The enraged people rose up *en masse*, allowing Cortés to re-enter the city but then besieging his forces in the palace. The collapse of their world and the betrayal of their leaders obviously angered the people. When Cortés brought Moctezuma out to show the people that he was still alive, the crowd pelted Moctezuma with stones; the emperor died a few days later. Finally, the Spanish fled during what they called "the sorrowful night." Soldiers carried out so much treasure that they were easy prey to Aztec warriors, who killed over 400 Spanish and 4,000 of their Native allies during the escape.

Cortés eventually reoccupied and then destroyed Tenochtitlan out of revenge, building by building. Disease unexpectedly helped him.[28] Thousands died from smallpox, which killed from one-tenth to one-half of the Mexica. Cortés wrote in 1522 to King Charles V, "many chieftains were dying … due to the smallpox distemper which also enveloped those of these lands like those of the islands." [29] By this time, in fact, Native people on the islands were already virtually extinct. The Aztec emperor's successor, Cuitlahuac, was among the first to die of the disease, so when Cortés executed his younger brother Cuauhtemoc in 1525, the Mexica ruling line ended. The second document in this chapter is an account of the Spanish escape from the capital, and what happened to Emperor Moctezuma during the retreat, as retold years later to priest Bernardino de Sahagún. How does this document remind us that the Tlatelolcans, many of whom served as the priest's informants, disliked the emperor and his Mexica warriors?

For Document 4.2: "The Mexica account of the Noche triste," by Fray Bernardino de Sahagún, from the Florentine Codex, visit www.routledge.com/9780415519120.

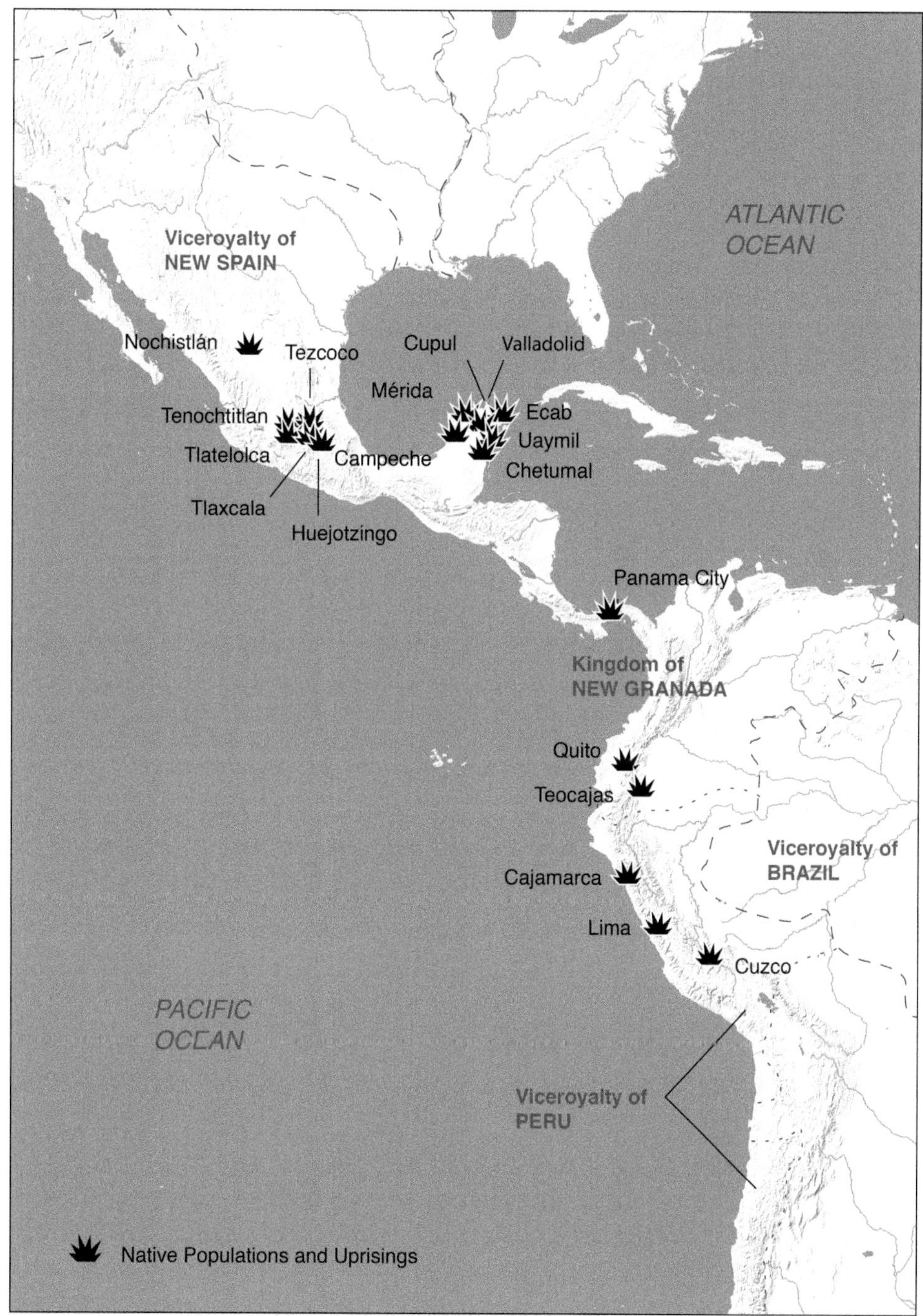

Map 4.2 Native Populations and Uprisings in the Viceroyalties of Peru and New Spain

Indigenous People on Distant Fringes Meet the Spanish

While the Mexica fought the Spanish, Native people at the southern tip of the continent met Ferdinand Magellan as they fished in a creek. The Portuguese explorer was convinced that a shorter route to the Indies existed south of Brazil, so he ventured west through southern islands. One dozen Indigenous men, women, and children in two canoes happened upon his crew quite by accident in November 1520, and promptly knelt face down, with arms extended upward as in supplication. Sailors invited the people on board, where they slept on the deck but mysteriously disappeared by morning. Superstitious sailors claimed the guests had been spirits. Once the sun set, though, the crew observed fires dotting the woods all along the southern side of the strait, and Magellan named the area "Land of Fires" (Tierra del Fuego). After a harrowing trip across the Pacific, Native Filipinos finally killed Magellan while his sailors watched, too angry to defend him because their captain had not let them search for gold.

Indigenous peoples along the northwestern Andean ridge engaged European explorers next because rumors of their wealth drew the Spanish like a magnet. On the Panamanian isthmus and in the highlands of northwestern Abya Yala, the Chibchas fed Europeans tales of vast wealth to their south. After Dávila founded the city of Panama in 1519, the Spanish set off in search of "Birú"or "Pirú" and the Quimbayas, but became embroiled in local conflicts along the way. For example, in 1522, Chief Tumaco's people convinced the explorers to help them fight their enemies in the Gulf of San Miguel. Local people thus slowed down the Spanish exploration and their meeting with the Incas.

Events: The Search for Peru

Seventeen Indigenous guides accompanied adventurers Francisco Pizarro and Diego de Almagro when they departed from Panama in 1524 to search for treasure in Peru. Pizarro was by then already among the richest and most influential citizens on the isthmus, and Dávila charged him with exploration southward along the Pacific coast. Pizarro took several years to make headway, fighting off Native people who resented the theft of their food and gold, and sending back to Panama for supplies as he went. Pizarro's first two attempts were unsuccessful. The explorers had no idea of the events happening to their south, yet it was during these same years, between 1525 and 1527, that an epidemic – possibly malaria but most likely smallpox – struck the Inca emperor, his court, and army while he was trying to subdue the Popayan and Pasto people in today's Colombia. Thousands of common people, key administrators, and the emperor himself died from European diseases even before they met the explorers rumored to be on their borders.

As they sailed south near the end of February 1527, the surprised explorers met a rigged balsa raft, a huge 30-ton ocean-going vessel manned by 20 Indigenous people. Spanish spirits surged, as the people were well dressed, wore jewels, and carried textiles and manufactured materials for trade. What is more, the three "fair-skinned" women on board were "excellent seamstresses." Note the Europeans' association of wealth and skill with lighter skin color. Five raft sailors eventually learned enough Spanish to serve Pizarro as translators, and energized the explorers with tales of Inca wealth.[30] In April 1528, Pizarro reached northern Peru, yet returned to Panama and then actually to Spain to appeal for more supplies and soldiers. Late in 1530, after years of further preparation, the soldier set out on his third trip toward Peru with 168 Spanish soldiers, 230 assistants, and several dozen horses. Finally, in September 1532, Pizarro and his 200 adventurers marched south to look for the Inca ruler in Cajamarca.

Spanish advances elsewhere wreaked havoc as they undermined the power of the caciques and divided leaders from their people. In the central Mexican valley of Cuernavaca, some leaders lost their land to the Spanish, while others took advantage of the Mexica demise to become rich. Cortés took land *and* tribute rights away from one cacique, Yaotzin, and his son Hernando (the leader's son already had a Spanish name), and in 1523 added their beautiful estate to his own. Native deaths from disease accelerated such exchanges, but the Indigenous elite also took advantage of the changes to increase their power. Native leaders adopted Spanish dress following the conquest and, with a special license from colonial authorities, even received permission to ride horses and display swords. Native intermediaries ostentatiously showed off their wealth to set themselves above the common people.[31] Europeans thus co-opted and employed Native nobles as tools to help control the masses. From the top down, the Indigenous people were changing in response to the Spanish conquest.

Another fringe area was the Yucatan Peninsula, where people resisted the conquest for over two decades, unlike the Mexica, whose empire had fallen in just two short years. Why did the people in former Maya regions resist so tenaciously? First, they had no imperial structure left to quickly collapse. Peoples lived in at least 16 former Mayan provinces and the invaders had to conquer or negotiate with these areas one by one. Cortés scouted out the Yucatan in 1525 on his way south, but it was not until two years later that his lieutenant Francisco de Montejo invaded the peninsula.

Montejo was an experienced commander, having helped conquer Panama, New Granada, and Cuba, and even shepherding the Aztec treasure back to Spain, yet Yucatan proved a different story. The dense jungle, treacherous limestone sinkholes, and especially the scarcity of gold undermined Spanish efforts. Reliance on horses and heavy armaments proved difficult and the invaders defeated but never occupied Ecab, Uaymil, and Chetumal along the eastern Caribbean coast. As we will see, between 1534 and 1535, Native peoples in the Yucatan actually evicted all Spanish forces from their territory, and for the next century and a half the Spanish retreated from territory in the peninsula that they could not effectively control.

Internal Divisions and the Lack of Steel and Horses Doom the Inca Empire

In the Andes, in a very different political and geographic context than the Caribbean, the death of Emperor Huayna Capac in 1525 or 1527 plunged the Inca Empire into civil war. Huayna Capac's son Huascar ruled in Cuzco with popular support, but a rival son, Atahualpa, was in charge of the army to the north in Quito, and they went to war against each other. Atahualpa's soldiers finally captured Huascar outside Cuzco and brutally repressed his supporters. As Pizarro's forces marched south in search of Peru, the civil war was nearing its end: towns lay in ruins and dead soldiers hung from trees along the road. Atahualpa learned of the invaders while camped at Cajamarca, high in the mountains, but the small force of outsiders could not have troubled the victor very much as he prepared for his triumphal entry into Cuzco. An envoy from Atahualpa invited Pizarro to visit as the invaders climbed along a barren savannah at 13,500 feet, probably nervous about the changing terrain.

Finally, on a Friday in mid-November, the Spanish emerged from the hills and beheld the lush, flat valley of Cajamarca. Surprised, they must have stared nervously out across the city at the encamped Inca army. As one remarked,

> The Indians' camp looked like a very beautiful city. … So many tents were visible that we were truly filled with great apprehension. We never thought that Indians could maintain such a proud estate nor have so many tents in such good order. Nothing like this had been seen in the Indies up to then. It filled all us Spaniards with fear and confusion.[32]

Putting on a brave front, the troops gathered in the main square, surrounded on three sides by buildings, and invited the Incan emperor to meet Pizarro.

The following day, Saturday, November 16, 1532, the Inca army, together with their emperor ensconced in a richly decorated litter, entered Cajamarca to meet the Europeans. Spanish soldiers – of which there were fewer than 170 – were hiding in empty buildings and streets along the main square. Pizarro's younger brother noted that many of his men were so afraid that they urinated on themselves out of sheer terror. A Dominican friar approached Atahualpa with a cross and liturgical book, reciting the *requerimiento*. The emperor demanded to see the closed book. Finally, upon opening it, Atahualpa was embarrassed at not being able to understand what he saw and threw the book at his troops. The priest ran back to Pizarro, calling on the Spanish to attack the "enemy dogs" for throwing down God's holy law. Soldiers in armor and chain-mail charged their horses into the Native crowd, who panicked and ran. Within two hours, the conquerors had captured the Inca, slaughtered 6,000 to 7,000 Native troops, and left others maimed and without limbs. Many Native soldiers fell under the horses or suffocated as they ran in panic to escape from the square.

The capture of the Inca produced rapid changes. Seeing the Spanish hoard his gold and silver, the 30-year-old emperor offered to ransom himself by filling a 22- by 17-foot-wide room half full of gold – that is, some 88 cubic meters – and a house twice over with silver, all within two months. Atahualpa also lost no time in ordering his brother Huascar murdered as the Spanish brought him from Cuzco. Once the huge ransom was assembled, Pizarro had Atahualpa strangled and set on fire, displaying his burned body in the square before its burial.

Spanish jurists, and even the monarch, were disappointed with the execution. "Nevertheless we have been displeased by the death of Atahualpa," King Charles wrote, "since he was a monarch, and particularly as it was done in the name of justice."[33] The monarch was at this time at the height of his power, having become the Spanish king in 1516 and emperor of the Holy Roman Empire in 1519. Jurists in Spain were concerned that a mere soldier like Pizarro could execute one of the most powerful emperors in the world, and that his act threatened the divine right of monarchs. Still, Charles must have been pleased with Pizarro's pillage of Cuzco and occupation of Peru, since it added a huge treasure to his war chest.

Over the following year, Native peoples of Peru changed masters as they received Spanish rulers and a different civilization replaced the Inca institutions. In June 1534, thousands of Quechua people became tributaries to the conquerors when the Spanish granted them in *encomiendas* to the conquerors. Former subjects of the Inca, who had worked for their emperor in the *mit'a* system, now began instead to send their tribute and work part of the year for the invading Spaniards. Despite receiving free new slaves, though, conquistadors were still unhappy with having to rely on Native porters to haul their food and supplies up the mountains. In 1535, Pizarro therefore founded a capital along the coast that later became Lima. Native people who left their homes to serve the European lords in their new cities, such as Lima, received the name of *yanaconas* in Peru. To the north in what became the Viceroyalty of New Spain, Indigenous people who left their communities were called *naborías*. A viceroyalty was the largest area of colonial administration, and the former Aztec and Mayan empires became the first of these in 1535. Peru became the second viceroyalty in 1542, and its territory included what later became the countries of Bolivia and Ecuador.

North of Peru, in the former Incan province of Quito, Atahualpa's general Rumiñavi named himself ruler and became a warlord, so the civil war in the Andes continued. The Spanish took advantage of the struggle and invaded Quito from both the north and the south, strengthened by Native Cañari allies eager to take revenge on their former Inca oppressors. In May 1534, opposing forces met at Teocajas and fought the largest pitched battle of the conquest. As many as 50,000 Inca troops stood against the invaders and fought them to a stalemate, using ingenious weapons such as pits filled with sharp stakes. One by one, though, rebel leaders fell and the Spanish tortured them brutally but never found Atahualpa's fabled hidden treasures. Manco Inca, son of Huayna Capac, became the next ruler in Cuzco and cooperated with the invaders to forge a new Peru.

Early Indigenous Experiences with the Imposition of Christianity

In addition to new rulers, Indigenous people also received new deities. In central areas, Native people took conversion to the gods of the conquerors for granted as a given strategy of survival under new rulers. As a traditional survival strategy, they focused on fulfilling correct rituals for the new faith in public and on continuing elements of their previous beliefs in private. Leading Indigenous communities received Spanish *doctrinas*, rural parishes right in their midst, staffed by priests who relied on Native leaders to mobilize labor to build the churches. Natives discovered that the authorities also charged such priests with enforcing *encomienda* labor, as well as making sure that the local people attended church services. Despite language barriers, the *doctrineros* – persons who dispense doctrine – began actively to try to convert the people (the word "mission" was still unknown to sixteenth-century Latin America).

The Mixtec in Tenochtitlan, Tlaxcala, Tezcoco, and Huejotzingo first received priests in 1524, when Cortés sent 12 Franciscan friars to proselytize in their cities. *Doctrineros* set up shop right in the Mixtec ceremonial center, and described it as a "transplanted hell" because of the yelling, singing, dancing, and drunken stupor they saw among Indigenous priests. "It was very pitiful to see men, created after the image of god, becoming worse than brute animals." For their part, Natives described the priests as either ill or insane, because they "do not seek joy and pleasure, but sadness and loneliness." Then, in 1528, while Indigenous people still showed little interest in the new faith, an exceptionally rainy season ruined crops and flooded houses in the area. Natives in Texcoco prayed for an end to the deluge; on that very day the rains reportedly stopped. In gratitude, the

> Indians made many crosses, banners of saints, and other ornaments to be used in processions.... Before long the Indians everywhere began to adorn churches, make altarpieces and ornaments, and to hold processions while the children learned dances to make processions more attractive.

The supposedly miraculous response to the flood helped the Catholics spread their doctrine. Priests next instituted Christian education: by 1532, over 5,000 Native children were already studying in monasteries throughout Central New Spain.[34] The transculturation of Indigenous people had begun in earnest.

More and more people received religious instruction and political organization over the following years. In 1536, only one year after New Spain became the first viceroyalty, local Natives received 60 Franciscan missionaries. Dominican missionaries traveled to the isolated south and Augustinians to the north. Native people in the Yucatan received Franciscan missionaries in 1544, and priests forced caciques to send their sons to new schools in Mérida and Campeche, on the peninsula's southwestern coast. Soon, 2,000 boys were studying Christianity, but how were they supposed to reconcile the new teachings about a loving God with the way this deity's administrators were treating their people? Peru lagged behind: a Dominican priest had arrived with Pizarro, but the delay in the area's designation as a viceroyalty set back missionary work. Native people in Brazil initially fell under a slightly different rule: Portugal divided their land into 14 strips of land from east to west into 15 lots, called captaincies, and the grantees each received a strip as a royal gift.[35] By the 1530s, Portuguese captains were fighting with Native forces and burning down villages to subdue the people into forced labor.

Most Indigenous people could not have known, but a few voices were still speaking out in their defense from within the Church. By this time, Bartolomé de Las Casas had worked in Nicaragua for two years. There he found the governor and his wife, Maria de Peñalosa, daughter of Governor Pedro Arias Dávila, running a slave business. Las Casas claimed that the couple had by this time already shipped 12,000 Native slaves to Peru and 25,000 more to Panama, even murdering their own bishop for protesting. Since Las Casas wrote to persuade the monarch to follow his suggestions, one can only assume that he stretched the truth. Despite possible exaggerations, the priest's account still paints a dire picture. Las Casas preached in Guatemala and New Spain against such abuses before returning to Europe in 1540 to request more priests for Central America. While he was in Spain, one of Las Casas' disciples in Nicaragua, Antonio de Valdivieso, took over his work in 1544. Valdivieso's assignment when he became bishop was to enforce the New Laws of 1542 (explained below), end Indigenous slavery and improve their treatment, and return to them lands stolen by *encomenderos*. The *encomenderos* responded violently to Valdivieso's work.

In Europe, meanwhile, Las Casas found Spain under the rule of Charles V, who had inherited Naples, Sicily, Spain and its colonies in the Americas and Africa, as well as the Netherlands and the German Hapsburg territories, from his paternal grandfather the Holy Roman Emperor Maximilian. Charles had grown up in Flanders, though, and could not even speak Spanish, so after his coronation he promptly moved to Germany. The persistent Las Casas railed at the emperor's advisors, denouncing abuses and demanding Native sovereignty in their own lands and an end to the *encomienda*. The most visible fruits of his persuasive lobby were the New Laws of 1542, in which the monarch recognized Natives as his own subjects, ordered an end to their slavery, terminated the *encomienda*, and forbade any more wars of conquest. Through Las Casas and supporters, Indigenous people scored an important victory. Nevertheless, how would the emperor ever enforce his new legislation?

Figure 4.1 *Lienzo de Quauhquechollan*, Mid-Sixteenth-Century Woven Nahua Document about the Conquest of Guatemala. (The Picture Art Collection/Alamy Stock Photo)

Indigenous People on the Borderlands Adjust to Colonization

Indigenous peoples largely resisted the growing extension of imperial power into their territories. As in Europe, Charles V sought to extend Spanish control over more territories in the Americas. During his rule, the Spanish pushed into the borderlands further away from the wealthy centers of New Spain and Peru. Only a few months after the founding of Lima in 1535, the Querandíes at the River Plate delta also encountered explorers. Aristocrat Pedro de Mendoza, who led the huge Spanish expedition of 16 ships that explored the delta, had hoped to defeat the Portuguese in the race to the fabled Indigenous kingdom at the center of the continent. Because his force arrived too late in the year to plant crops, Querandíes at first supplied the Spanish with food. When the explorers tried to force them to work, however, warriors besieged the Spanish and killed any who ventured out in search of food. Within a short year, the explorers were starving, eating their horses, and even each other. Native warriors gradually whittled down the expedition by two-thirds.

In search of food and the rumored Native kingdom at the continent's heart, Spaniards from the new colony at the River Plate delta sailed north along the Paraná River in 1536. Instead of gold, they found something much more valuable: a group of friendly Native people called the Guaraní. At the confluence of the Paraná and Paraguay rivers, the Guaraní were at the time warring against enemies to their west, in the Chaco, so they accepted the Spanish explorers as potential military allies. Native cooperation allowed explorers to settle where the Paraguay River turned north from the Paraná; the site became the city of Asunción. The collaboration was mutually beneficial; the Spanish helped the Guaraní fight their opponents, and they in turn supplied the Europeans with fresh corn, manioc, sweet potatoes, fish, meat, cotton, and honey. Guaraní women even served in the Spaniards' households and soon bore them children. Colonists claimed to have as many as 70 unofficial Guaraní partners apiece; by 1556, the Europeans had already fathered at least 6,000 children with Indigenous women.[36] The arrangement between the Guaraní and the Spanish suited both groups.

Continued Indigenous Resistance in Central Areas

Northwest of La Plata in Peru, Native women also served the Spanish in concubinage. Rather than household servants, the Spanish chose notable princesses who would normally have slept only with the Inca or his royal princes. Inés Huayllas Ñusta, for instance, a 15-year-old princess, bore the 56-year-old Pizarro a daughter in 1534 and a son the following year. Pizarro's younger half-brother Juan tried to take for himself Cura Ocllo, full sister and wife of Manco, the Inca ruler and Atahualpa's brother. Elders in the Indigenous army and religious institutions, however, had finally had enough of Spanish abuses. The conquerors' constant search for the fabled Incan wealth was bad enough, but the additional appropriation of their royal women finally proved too much.

In the fall of 1535, fed up with such abuses, the elders finally convinced Manco to rise up against the invaders. One night, the ruler escaped from Cuzco with his wives and servants, only to be caught as he hid in marshland along the road. While imprisoned, the Spanish urinated on the Inca and raped his wives. The Inca insurrection spread through the countryside, and Manco waited until the right time to rebel. The following holy week he escaped to the jungle northwest of Cuzco, amassed a huge rebel army of between 100,000 and 200,000 troops, and then besieged the city in an attack that reveals the ingenuity of Indigenous military tactics.

In early May, Indigenous soldiers fought their way into the center of Cuzco, using slings to shoot red-hot stones with deadly force. Juan Pizarro, the half-brother of Francisco, died when one such stone struck him in the head. Soon the city with its houses of thatched roofs was on fire, and invading forces trapped the Spaniards in their houses around the central plaza. Native troops diverted rivers into fields surrounding the city, while others tripped the horses that made it past street barricades into pits dug for that purpose. Running along the tops of the city walls, Natives threw stones and bricks at the Spanish soldiers and brought down horses with *bolas*, stones tied to llama tendons and whirled with deadly efficacy. Meanwhile, another Indigenous army besieged Lima, under orders from Manco to destroy the city, leave no house standing, and to kill all Spaniards except Pizarro. The attack went badly, however, and the Inca forces retreated. Two approaching Spanish armies rescued Cuzco from the siege and gave the Inca title to Manco's collaborator brother Paullu Inca Yupanqui, who had been off conquering the Reche in central Chile with Almagro.[37] In effect, the Europeans defeated the first great Inca uprising by co-opting its leaders. The divisions that produced this defeat, as well as the way in which *kurakas* increasingly sent their own people to work in the *obrajes*, the Spanish textile mills, reveal how rivalries and divisions within Native ranks again contributed to Indigenous losses.

During the Inca uprising, Native people in New Spain were resisting the imposition of the onerous *encomienda* system of forced labor. This was especially true in the northern

Figure 4.2 *Exploitation of Mexico by Spanish Conquistadores*, Mural by Diego Rivera. (Travelpix/Alamy Stock Photo)

mining areas of Nueva Galicia[38] and Zacatecas, where the discovery of silver created a mining rush. Mixtec and Chichimec in the area harassed the miners and attacked wagon supply lines, challenging extraction of the ore. When Governor Vázquez de Coronado left New Galicia with hundreds of Native allies in 1539 in search of the fabled cities of Cíbola, the Mixtec took advantage of his absence to overthrow Spanish rule. Encouraged by their priests, Mixtec rebels fortified their towns of Mixtón and Nochistlán and strengthened the surrounding hilltops with store-rooms of supplies in bunkers called *pañoles*. Native forces then besieged even the city of Guadalajara. Their attacks on cities and ranches led to the Mixton War in 1541, the most serious revolt in New Spain before the wars for independence. Finally, Tlaxcaltec and Aztec allies helped the Spanish recapture their frontier towns. After 40 years of forced conversion and hard labor, the Spanish had still not successfully imposed their rule upon all Indigenous peoples in New Spain.

Indigenous People in Amazonia Finally Meet the Strangers

It was Indigenous people in Amazonia who next encountered Europeans. Natives in the forest must have been surprised in 1541 when Pizarro's brother Gonzalo led an expedition down the mighty Amazon River in search of El Dorado and La Canela, the fabled land of highly prized cinnamon. Imagine trying to feed 220 soldiers and 4,000 manacled Andean

Native porters for a whole year while sailing down a river through the jungle, and it is clear why this expedition ended in disaster. Most porters simply died from exhaustion. One Spanish official, named Orellana, left Gonzalo Pizarro and for a month lived among a wealthy group of Irimarai (now called Ticuna). The Irimarai reportedly hosted this contingent because they claimed to be children of the sun. Community after community of Indigenous people seemed surprised to meet such different people. In February 1542, when the expedition entered the Amazon proper, the Machiparo attacked the Europeans, then pursued them doggedly in canoes for two days straight.[39]

The large communities located where the great river broadened impressed the explorers, but their people also resisted more effectively. Wealthy Omagua villages on the floodplain downstream amazed the Spanish with their magnificent glazed pottery and huge stocks of cotton, corn, yucca, yams, beans, fruits, game birds, and dried fish; the Paguana gave explorers pineapples and avocados. One Native village extended for six miles along the riverbank, and in one day the explorers passed more than 20 villages with landing stages built along the river. The Indigenous people learned of the invasion through their own networks, however, and villages began to refuse to receive the explorers. At the mouth of the Madeira River, Tupinambarana villages displayed posts adorned with the heads of their enemies and mounted ferocious attacks on the sailors.[40] Almost every day, flotillas of Indigenous warriors came out against the Spanish; on June 25, over 200 canoes carrying 20 or 30 warriors apiece attacked the expedition. These fierce receptions led Europeans to accuse the peoples they met of cannibalism, and scholars have debated the accounts ever since. It appears that while some Amazonian groups indeed consumed their enemies, though, the practice was not widespread.

A Silver Mountain and the Great Yucatan Revolt

A few years after the Spanish provoked Native villages in Amazonia, they discovered more precious metals in the Andes, proving a windfall for Spain and bad news for the Aymara and Quechua peoples of the region. In 1541, Pedro Díaz de Rojas located gold-mines in the coca area of Mayormarca, in southeastern Peru, and then, in 1545, a *yanacona* serving a Spaniard discovered a mountain of silver at Potosí, in Upper Peru. The area became a makeshift mining center in no time, though it took some years and a change in Spanish administration for new rulers to create a system of forced mining to extract the ore. The resulting flood of silver from Potosí boosted the economy both in the Andes and in Europe. Industries to support the miners developed around the gold-mines and the mountain of silver, including textile mills (*obrajes*), lodging sites, food, mules for transport, and prostitution. The Aymara and Quechua peoples provided the labor that kept the mines producing silver. The central Andes soon became the main powerhouse of colonial Latin American mining production.

Demands for labor and tribute increased, and many Indigenous people became understandably angrier. In places where people shared broader historical ties that were both linguistic and political, as in the Yucatan, it was easier for them to organize against the colonial impositions despite the growing demographic collapse. Chieftains in the eastern and central areas reminded their people of their successful expulsion of all the Spanish only 12 years before, without realizing that the withdrawal had resulted as much from colonial misadministration as from their own military successes. The re-imposition of the hated *encomienda* system of personal service, coupled with abuses by *encomenderos* who literally moved into Native villages to impose their will, finally became untenable. Native priests, facing their own loss of power to Spanish friars, fed the growing anger of the people. Finally, in 1546, a massive uprising took place against the invaders.

Leaders in Cupul secretly joined forces from Chikinchel, Sotuta, Tazes, Chakan, and Uaymil-Chetumal to create a united uprising. Rebels rose up on the full moon of November 8, 1546, and launched a war that Europeans called the Great Maya Revolt. The Indigenous forces attacked *encomenderos* with surprising fury and massacred as many Spanish as they could find, including the women and children. Rebels torched buildings, crucified victims under the sun, and tortured others by slowly roasting them to death over copal incense, a sweet-smelling resin from trees formerly used by the Mayans, and tearing out their hearts in traditional Mayan fashion. Insurrectionists killed Indigenous collaborators, massacring as many as 500 to 600 *naborías*, Natives who served in Spanish homes. The rebels even killed European cats, dogs, chickens, horses, and cattle, uprooting European trees and plants in their attempts to wipe out every vestige of the hated conquerors. Thousands of warriors surrounded and besieged the Spanish capital of Valladolid on the northwestern coast for two intense weeks until 40 Spanish soldiers and their 500 Native auxiliaries finally defeated the rebels in late November.[41] It took two years for colonists to subdue the rebel forces in the Yucatan: to do so the Spanish cut women to pieces, murdered children, and branded and chained men into slavery. The uprising showed that 50 years after the conquest the Spanish still did not control the colonial borderlands, and also that some Native people were still willing and able to fight.

Conclusions: Indigenous People Help Create a New World

After Indigenous people and European colonists interacted at the beginning of the sixteenth century, they began to forge a new society. Their cultures and levels of technology were so different that their resulting ways of life over the following centuries seem unprecedented. Linguistic, technological, and cultural differences obstructed easy cooperation between Native people from the beginning. Indigenous responses to European exploration at times encouraged the conquerors, as when Native peoples helped the Spanish build new settlements, traded amicably, and then spoke of great wealth beyond the next bend in the river, or when they used the Spanish as military allies. In other cases, these differences also limited and hindered exploration by violence, deliberate deception, or simple refusals by Native people to cooperate in the new colonial enterprise forced upon them. Indigenous resistance to coercive labor in the Caribbean, as well as rapid Native deaths due to diseases, forced the Europeans to seek more wealth and slaves sooner than anticipated, leading to the rapid colonization of the entire continent. The collapse of the two large Native empires, the Aztec and the Inca, revealed the relative inferiority of stone-age military technology and the relative weakness of these vast political organizations held together by force, the cult of personality, and the abuse of conquered peoples.

Native responses to European conquests and colonization amid the demographic collapse established patterns that would characterize the Colonial Period and shape the continent. Rivalries between Native leaders and the individual egos of imperial administrators limited collective resistance to the invasion; geographic isolation between groups, as well as differing languages and religions, also hampered collective Indigenous resistance. From the very start, the actions of Indigenous peoples, their cultures, and their political organizations influenced the transition from Abya Yala to Latin America.

On their part, the conquerors' Iberian heritage shaped their interaction with the Native population throughout the continent. The first legacy was the Europeans' refusal to raise crops, a result of the Spanish focus on military prowess rather than manual labor during the Reconquest. The second was the use of warfare to force religious conversion upon foreign peoples of different faiths. Both traditions led the invaders to enslave Indigenous peoples and force them to provide gold and food, rather than working for their own sustenance and enrichment.

The Reconquest also motivated the missionary enterprise that drove Spanish exploration. The conquistadors tried to convert and then incorporate Native people into the lower strata of their new society as cheap laborers, instead of excluding them as the British later did to Native Americans in North America. Advocates within the Church attracted growing attention to worsening Indigenous conditions and, surprisingly, forced Spanish monarchs to try to protect Native lives from the worst abuses. The defense of human rights through state legislation was new to both continents. While legislation failed to end many of the abuses, royal decrees did influence the future of Latin America by providing a legal and religious foundation for Indigenous resistance in later centuries, as well as by changing the course of the Catholic Church as they planted the seeds for the defense of human rights.

The huge treasure that the conquest of the Aztec and Inca empires brought to Spain bolstered the Iberian Empire, paid off creditors in the Netherlands, and in the end helped fund the Industrial Revolution in Great Britain. Massive changes in early modern Europe in turn led to still further international tensions, as nations scrambled to claim colonial territories during the age of mercantilism. The Iberian expansion to the Americas therefore marked an early stage in the monumental shift of wealth and power from the rest of the world to Western Europe. Europeans invaded and then colonized Indigenous Abya Yala, forcing them to join in the creation of a new world that would never again be the same.

Discussion Questions

1. What alternatives to military conquest could Spanish explorers have realistically employed?
2. Why did some Indigenous people help the Europeans conquer Abya Yala?
3. How can one explain divisions between the European explorers?
4. What prevented Native peoples from uniting their forces to counter European colonization?
5. What caused the downfall of the two strongest Indigenous empires?
6. How did economics influence early interaction between Native and European people?

Notes

1 King Charles was both Charles I of Spain and Charles V of the Holy Roman Empire.
2 Las Casas, *Historia de las Indias*, II, 12.
3 Bergreen, *Columbus*, 248.
4 Ibid., 268.
5 Ibid.
6 There is no way of knowing exactly who the people were that met Cabral, but by this time the Tupinamba dominated the coastal area where his fleet landed.
7 Caminha, *Carta a El Rei D. Manuel*, 67, 60, in Hemming, *Red Gold*, 4.
8 Todorov, *The Conquest of America*, 247–248.

9 Hemming, *Red Gold*, 9.
10 Jennings, *The Invasion of America*, 15.
11 McEwan, *The Incas New Perspectives*, 92.
12 Patterson, "The Inca Empire," 13.
13 Las Casas, *Historia de las Indias*, II, 507–508.
14 Ibid., 523–524.
15 Ibid., 525–526.
16 Clayton, *Bartolomé de Las Casas*, 41–42.
17 Hanke, *The Spanish Struggle*, 23–24.
18 Several religious and ascetic communities founded the Hieronymite order in fourteenth-century Spain to imitate the life of Saint Jerome and serve as a missionary order with close ties to the Spanish Crown.
19 Las Casas, *Historia de las Indias*, III, 16.
20 Ibid., 25–27; see also Burkholder and Johnson, *Colonial Latin America*, 44.
21 Las Casas, *Historia de las Indias*, III, 29–30.
22 Howe, *A People Who Would Not Kneel*, 10.
23 Francisco Pizarro later went on to conquer the Inca Empire between 1531 and 1533.
24 Las Casas, *Historia de las Indias*, III, 52, 53.
25 Ibid., 62–64.
26 Las Casas, *Obras Completas*, V, 2443–2447.
27 A thorough source on Malintzin is Townsend's *Malintzin's Choices*.
28 Díaz, *The Conquest of New Spain*, 148–149.
29 McCaa, "Spanish and Nahuatl Views," 405, 429.
30 Murphy, "The Earliest Spanish Advances," 10, 15, 18, 26, 27.
31 Haskett, "Coping in Cuernavaca," 94, 115.
32 Hemming, *The Conquest of the Incas*, 32.
33 Ibid., 81.
34 Morales, "The Native Encounter with Christianity," 139, 141, 146.
35 Twelve grantees received 14 captaincies in 15 lots as royal gifts. One of the captaincies had two sections, and two of the grantees received two captaincies apiece.
36 Horst, *The Stroessner Regime*, 6–7.
37 Hemming, *The Conquest of the Incas*, 189–220.
38 Nueva Galicia today includes the Mexican states of Jalisco, Aguascalientes, Zacatecas, Nayarit, and the northwest corner of San Luis Potosí.
39 Hemming, *Red Gold*, 188.
40 Ibid., 192.
41 Chamberlain, *The Conquest*, 243.

5 Colonial Alliances and Demographic Collapse, 1550 to 1599

Chronology

1550	King Charles V orders an end to all Spanish conquests in the Americas. Indigenous slavery formally terminated in Spanish colonies. *Congregación* system of forced settlement imposed in Central America.
1553	The Reche revolt in central Chile kills Conquistador Pedro de Valdivia.
1557	Jesuit missions founded along the Ucayali River in Amazonian Peru. Doña Beatriz Huayllas Ñusta negotiates end to standoff in Vilcabamba, Peru.
1560	Pedro de Ursua expedition along the Amazon River. Taki Onquoy movement in Peruvian highlands.
1563	The Reche besiege Fort Arauco in central Chile.
1565	Titu Cusi Yupanqui, Inca leader, leaves his fortress at Vilcabamba. The Spanish found San Miguel de Tucumán in northwestern La Plata, and enslave the Lules.
1568	*Repartimiento* system of forced labor imposed.
1569	Don Francísco de Toledo appointed fifth viceroy of Peru.
1570	The Spanish order Native settlements into villages to facilitate mission proselytism.
1570s	The Chichimecas resist increased Spanish mining in northern New Spain. Widespread Indigenous integration into colonial society in central New Spain.
1580s	Forced settlement of the Tarahumara in southeastern Sonora and northeastern Sinaloa.
1590s	Broad Indigenous cultural changes and integration, even ownership of horses.
1598	Massive Reche uprising in central Chile.
1599	Jivaro uprising in Ecuador.

Introduction: Simultaneous Indigenous Resistance and Integration into Colonial Society

Even as their societies collapsed during the sixteenth century due to virgin soil epidemics against which people in Abya Yala had no defenses, people responded creatively to the imposition of foreign hegemony. Their multiple strategies of resistance made European claims to the land tenuous and challenged the new rulers. Indigenous peoples profoundly shaped the early colonial experience, and European economic, religious, and political structures in turn altered how Natives in central areas went about their lives. Despite the growing demographic collapse, armed resistance in fringe areas increased. Europeans continued to try to decide whether Indigenous people were actually human beings; the debate and its results changed how both groups related to each other. The increasingly elaborate systems of imperial control labeled people according to their racial heritage and divided them into new categories called castes, designations that took into consideration wealth, education, and dress, as well as a fictitious classification called "race." The emerging social structure became complicated and convoluted. Europeans allowed African slaves into their own Spanish world to varying degrees, but even those who considered Indigenous people to be human beings despised them as members of a different, inferior society.

The Europeans' military advantages gave them hegemony in the central areas of the continent, but less control over the fringes of colonial society, where Native people still held the upper hand. The second 50 years of the conquest began with a mandate from the king of Spain to halt all further conquests owing to his concern for Indigenous conditions; for the time being it appeared that advocates of human rights had won the day. Soon, though, with no real way for the Crown to impose its royal will from across the ocean, conquest continued as Iberians kept trying to make Indigenous peoples fit into the European ways of life they had brought to the Americas. More and more Native people joined the societies that Europeans were creating, moving in search of work, food, and community. As they mingled in the new cities, Indigenous people and Europeans worked, ate, and slept together, had children, and interacted more and more frequently. The curious feature of this period of Indigenous history is that the more Natives resisted the foreign impositions, the more they became part of colonial society.

Indigenous People Receive New Mandates from King Charles V

The 1550s began with a momentous mandate from King Charles V of Spain. Finally, after many years, the persistent religious lobby convinced him that Natives deserved his protection. Since more Indigenous people were interacting with Europeans 50 years after Columbus' failed administration, it would seem that the invaders should have by then decided that the beings they met in the Americas were human beings. That was not the case, however, and it was not until the mid-sixteenth century that jurists finally settled the issue. Colonists had just suppressed the massive rebellion in Yucatan with huge loss of Indigenous life, and Bartolomé de Las Casas had returned to Spain from Guatemala in 1547 to argue in Spanish courts in favor of the Indigenous people. The Natives' defenders and opponents exchanged views before both the Council of the Indies and the Council of Castile in the so-called Valladolid Debate. For five long, hot, August days, Las Casas read a Latin treatise of 550 pages on Indigenous achievements that he had written for the event. He argued that all peoples of the world were legitimate human beings with similar senses and desires; Indigenous people were not "natural slaves." His opponent, Juan Ginés de Sepúlveda, a Spanish humanist philosopher and theologian, countered that the Spanish were at the refined pinnacle of human achievement and that following their example would teach the Indians manners, religion, and to abandon their cruel idolatries. The judges reached no firm decision about the debate, but history suggests that Las Casas came out ahead: the activist priest published book after book until his death, while Sepúlveda's books never came out in print. What is more, in April 1550 King Charles at last ordered an end to all military conquests in the Americas until further notice. This was an incredible declaration: historian Lewis Hanke has posited that the king's declaration was the first time a mighty emperor had halted his conquests at their height to decide whether they were just. Las Casas' 1553 treatise, written after the exchange, argued that the Spanish had no right to conquer Indigenous lands because of military superiority, and that Spain should return all wealth stolen from the Americas to the Native peoples.

As usual, it took a long time for these decrees to reach the Americas, and even then, how could the Crown enforce its legislation? In effect, administrators in the colonies commonly employed the phrase "I obey but do not comply with or execute" when they received mandates that were difficult to enforce. This acknowledgment of but not actual obedience to royal orders is worthy of analysis because, over time, such a response (ignoring the laws) came to characterize the colonists' relationships to the imperial authorities. Because of the great distance and isolation from Europe, and differences between colonial regions, the Iberian authorities had only a vague idea of actual conditions across the Atlantic at any given time. The "I obey" clause recognizes the legitimate sovereign power that, when correctly informed, would do no wrong. The second "but I will not execute" is the subordinate's postponement of obedience until the sovereign is "informed of those conditions of which he may be ignorant and without a knowledge of which an injustice may be committed." This saying, and the attitudes – such as ambiguous compliance – that it engendered, were a result of the decentralized model of authority used by the Hapsburgs in Spain to control their holdings, which allowed authorities in the colonies to ignore the new imperial laws and blame circumstances beyond their own control for their failure to defend Indigenous workers.

Given the difficulty of enforcing royal mandates imposing better relations with the Native people, it should not be surprising that the conquest continued unabated. In central Chile, Pedro de Valdivia settled Santiago in 1542 among the Muloche people, but the Huilliche, the southern Reche, put up stiff resistance after Valdivia founded the city of Concepción south along the Biobío River in 1550. Spanish settlers moved south, building forts, fighting, and distributing the Huilliche into *encomiendas*. Colonial gold prospectors struck it rich, but the Reche were not happy with the changes, especially when forced to slave in the mines. Northeast in Brazil, the coastal Tupi peoples were also fighting the Portuguese explorers during this time. The Europeans still described the Tupi as cannibals who ate their prisoners. The Portuguese used this stereotype to justify the extermination of Tupi people along Brazil's Atlantic coast.

For Document 5.1: German gunner Hans Staden describes Tupi cannibalism, visit www.routledge.com/9780415519120.

Indigenous peoples in Central America, south of the Yucatan Peninsula, also faced overseers who refused to implement royal protections. Spain had officially ended Indigenous slavery in 1550, but as Native people died from disease, more and more of them remaining in lowland communities lost their lands to colonial ranchers, poor Spanish, and people of mixed heritage who moved into the communities. Living among the Indigenous people, these people hunted wild cattle for hides, made illegal liquor, and gradually took over Native cacao plantations. This frontier society did not benefit Indigenous communities. While Native people worked all year round to produce the cacao and controlled the actual plants themselves, *encomenderos* and traders took the harvests and sold the final cocoa for their own benefit. Laws prohibited Natives from working for indigo plantations, also called *obrajes*, so African slaves and people of mixed race – *castas* – produced this dye, often on the same land used to graze cattle. Native people also lost their lands to expanding ranches and Spanish towns. Communities in the highlands, though, being further away from Spanish settlements, did not lose their lands as quickly. Instead, as the Spanish displaced them, highland peoples migrated to the lowlands. The Lacandón and Chol Manché peoples who lived there, however, fought hard to keep the highland Natives out of their territory. Colonialism gradually altered Indigenous ways of life and heightened their rivalries.

What is more, regular clergy continued to try to force Native peoples into communities managed by priests, towns called *congregaciones*, where they would be more accessible for labor and proselytism. In the *congregaciones*, however, Indigenous people perished more easily from diseases because they were concentrated in villages rather than isolated throughout the countryside. By 1600, religious orders had created some 300 such villages throughout Guatemala. To resist state pressures and escape disease, Native people fled constantly from the *congregaciones* back to their home communities.[1] Regardless of the new official Spanish legislation to protect them, it was up to Indigenous people to defend themselves from colonial impositions of labor, proselytism, and the continued loss of land.

Trends: From *Encomienda* to *Repartimiento* in Guatemala

Guatemala, a southern fringe of New Spain, offers good examples of the changing royal legislation during the long transition from the draft labor system called *encomienda* to the *repartimiento* system, in which Native communities hired out their people to Spanish businesses for wage labor. After 1568, widespread establishment of the *repartimiento* system forced Native towns to send up to one-quarter of their men to work for a token 5 *reales* per worker, per week, for up to 12 weeks every year; the system syphoned men away from communities all year except for three weeks during Holy Week and Christmas. In this system laborers farmed, herded animals, hauled loads, built houses, made bread, and even cleaned streets for Spanish settlers in Guatemala City. The *repartimiento* also forced Indigenous communities to supply labor to the silver mines and ranches. Authorities used the *repartimiento* to take over more and more *encomiendas* gradually, thus centralizing power and undermining the importance of the original conquerors. In towns that produced cocoa, as the market boomed after the mid-sixteenth century, the Crown phased out the former labor system as it cashed in on the new crop, pushing Natives into the cash economy and gradually taking control of communities and their produce. In central highland settlements, people struggled increasingly to meet *repartimiento* demands because their people were dying from disease, and the loss of workers to forced labor made it difficult for communities to raise enough food to survive.

If official impositions were not enough, Native producers also dealt with theft and forced tribute. African and casta *regatones* (middlemen) hired by Spanish *patrones*, urban businessmen or bosses, often robbed Native merchants and took advantage of them to make an easy profit when they arrived in the cities to sell their produce. To defend themselves, Native merchants traveled in groups or traded cheap products of little value. Twice a year, Indigenous communities also had to give *encomenderos* and the Crown part of their local products. Native tribute was important to the Crown: in Guatemala by the eighteenth century, these payments accounted for 80 percent of royal revenues. Only once Native people met their tribute demands were they able to grow corn for their own consumption, so one can imagine how heavily the taxes weighed on villages. Everywhere, though, the degree to which the *repartimiento* changed communities depended on the surviving population, the amount of remaining communal land, and the group's ability to retain some economic independence.[2]

As Native communities struggled with disease and the tribute payments, more people in central areas migrated to the cities to find work. Indigenous neighborhoods on the outskirts of Guatemala City, called *barrios*, varied in their success. Communities further away, such as the Cakchiquel community along Lake Quinizilapa, fared well because Spanish owners granted Native people some land. The Indigenous community of San Miguel Dueñas, on the other hand, fared poorly because freed mulattos took over low-lying lands on which the Indigenous people lived to cultivate sugar cane. There, in the lowlands, disease was also harder on Native communities, and the resulting deaths allowed the Spanish and castas to move into their midst.

In the Yucatan, as in Guatemala and throughout colonial Latin America, the Spanish authorities forced Native people into urban centers called *parcialidades*, with a formal grid structure of houses facing a central square and town hall, to make them more accessible as workers. By 1549 there were already 400 such urban resettlements of Native people in the Yucatan. The Spanish desire to concentrate Natives into cities was another result of the reconquest of Iberia, when fortified towns instead of single castles or monasteries protected the population. In the Americas, moreover, the new Renaissance emphasis on symmetry and order led Europeans to use a grid pattern for their new cities.[3] This urbanization program was an example of the imperial Spanish program to civilize Native people, and it went hand in hand with their mission efforts. Franciscans in New Spain and Central America insisted on resettlement as a precursor to mission work.[4] However, in some communities, notably Sacapulas, northwest of Guatemala City, Native people managed to hold on to their land and pay tribute as distinct Native towns.

Some resettled groups quickly joined mainstream society, but others found the arrangement furthered their Indigenous connections. Concentration in the *parcialidades* allowed Indigenous people from the neighboring countryside to form common goals and work together. Many settlements thus continued their Indigenous identities and "functioned as independently as if they had been divided by kilometers of open bush, each with their own patron saint and fiesta, its own *batab* and town council," and their own church (a *batab* had been a captain or war chief in pre-conquest Yucatan society). Some *parcialidades* even kept titles to their former lands, and a few, such as Ninkini and Halacho in the Yucatan, actually moved back to their original areas. Collective organization in the *parcialidades* shows that even as Native people joined colonial society, some tried to keep control of their lives as best they could. Most resettled communities, though, gradually joined mainstream society. As Farriss analyzed, colonial authorities "simply failed to acknowledge their existence and, by denying them any role in the colonial political system, let them wither away."[5] Spanish social engineering began to change the Native people now concentrated in the cities.

Trends: Indigenous People and the Birth of Capitalism

Conditions in late sixteenth-century Guatemala resemble those that led to the development of capitalism in early modern Europe, which also occurred during the sixteenth and seventeenth centuries. German economist Karl Marx famously analyzed the transition in Europe from feudalism, during which closed guilds monopolized production and serfs labored for lords, to the emergence of capitalism and the creation of modern world markets. To begin with, Marx argued that it was the discovery of the Americas and the resulting flow of precious metals into Western Europe that allowed the accumulation of capital necessary to build manufacturing industry.[6] Furthermore, the economist reasoned that the demise of the feudal system and the conversion of common fields into pastures for commercial agriculture, which occurred at around the same time in Western Europe, both reduced the number of workers needed for cultivation and increased the number of landless people seeking a source of income. Migrating to cities, these people became the factory laborers needed to manufacture products. Urban peasant concentration in turn created a growing demand for cloth, food, and modern manufactures, leading to industrial production, middle classes, and the emergence of a world market.[7] For Marx, then, the separation of workers from their means of production and their transition to wage labor laid down the preconditions for the evolution of capitalist production.

Arguably, the concentration of Indigenous people into *parcialidades* in early Guatemala does not equate to the birth of industrial factory work in London. The point advanced here is not that Latin America industrialized before Great Britain. Rather, that the forced relocation of peasants to towns in Central America in order to make them more available for proselytism and accessible as a labor force by severing them from their rural means of production resembles the displacement of European serfs that contributed to the emergence of modern capitalism. By resettling Indigenous people into cities, colonists severed them from independent production and made them laborers willing to exchange their work for food. Over the seventeenth century, the extension of agriculture and appropriation of communal Indigenous lands helped create landless Indigenous workers for the colonial economy. Furthermore, the profits from Indigenous labor in colonial Latin American mines, as well as the treasure stolen from the Indigenous empires, helped fund the Industrial Revolution in Europe that began in the following century.

Continuing Native Resistance in both the Andean Fringes and the Centers

Indigenous people closer to cities in colonial centers gradually joined European society due to the imposition of new forms of labor and social engineering designed to make them workers and Christians. On the less lucrative colonial fringes, though, peoples resisted the encroaching authority fiercely and creatively. The Cocama, Omagua, Conibo, Shitibo, and Setebo along the Ucayali River in the rainforests of eastern Peru received the first outsiders in 1557 with mixed results. Jesuit missionary Juan Salinas de Loyola ventured 100 leagues upstream from Iquitos, where the Ucayali drains into the Amazon, until a Native people in Benorina met him with hostility. After they finally accepted his overtures, Loyola continued on to Cocama territory. These people lived in large villages and displayed jewelry of gold and silver and "splendid pottery." The last people the dogged missionary encountered before turning back – he did not record their name – were in his view "warlike" and "very different in language and dress," living in huge villages of 4,000 to 8,000 people and with leaders who stood out clearly because of the ornaments they wore.[8] Some of these villages had actively traded products with Cuzco. Peoples along the river spoke different languages but shared similar cultures and complex social organization. The fact that Loyola mentions their pottery and adornments shows that these were large communities, because the geography – forested areas along a major river – made possible large concentrations of people, which in turn allowed settlements to display their cultural position through dress and artisanship. Communities in the Peruvian rainforest reacted differently to missionary incursions but their organization reflected their natural surroundings.

Indigenous responses in central Peru, following the conquest of the Inca Empire, also showed a complex pattern of accommodation and alliances in response to European incursions. Manco Inca, the son of Huayna Capac who Francisco Pizarro had crowned Inca in 1533, rebelled again in 1539 and had established his headquarters in Vilcabamba, in the dense Vitcos valley area of the eastern Amazonian forest. Unable to capture the rebel Inca, Pizarro brutally executed his wife, 16 of his commanders, and the leaders who had surrendered. Subsequently, opponents murdered the conquistador himself in June 1541. During this period Manco's half-brother Paullu was acting as the figurehead Inca in Cuzco, collaborating with the occupying forces. Paullu wore Spanish clothing, accepted baptism, and even owned an *encomienda*.

If Native rulers failed to unite against the Spanish, however, the invaders also fought over the Inca treasure and leadership of the new viceroyalty. Gonzalo Pizarro, brother of Francisco, raised his own army and took Cuzco. Then, during the civil war in 1544, a group of Gonzalo's rivals found refuge from Pizarro in Vilcabamba with their own plot to murder the Inca. The Inca took their arms away, allowed them to stay, and then engaged them in games of horseshoe quoits, his favorite pastime. Even in his mountain refuge, the rebel Inca still enjoyed European games. It was while playing a game, in fact, that the Spanish renegades finally murdered the rebel Inca by stabbing him from behind with a hidden dagger while he was throwing a horseshoe. The assassins fled on horseback, but Inca archers caught them on a forest path, pulled some from their mounts, and later burned the rest in a thatched hut where they had taken refuge. In the three days before he died, Manco passed on leadership of the rebel forces to his 5-year-old son Sayri-Tupac, but Manco's death dealt a significant blow to the Indigenous people because he had been the only prince left of royal lineage and was

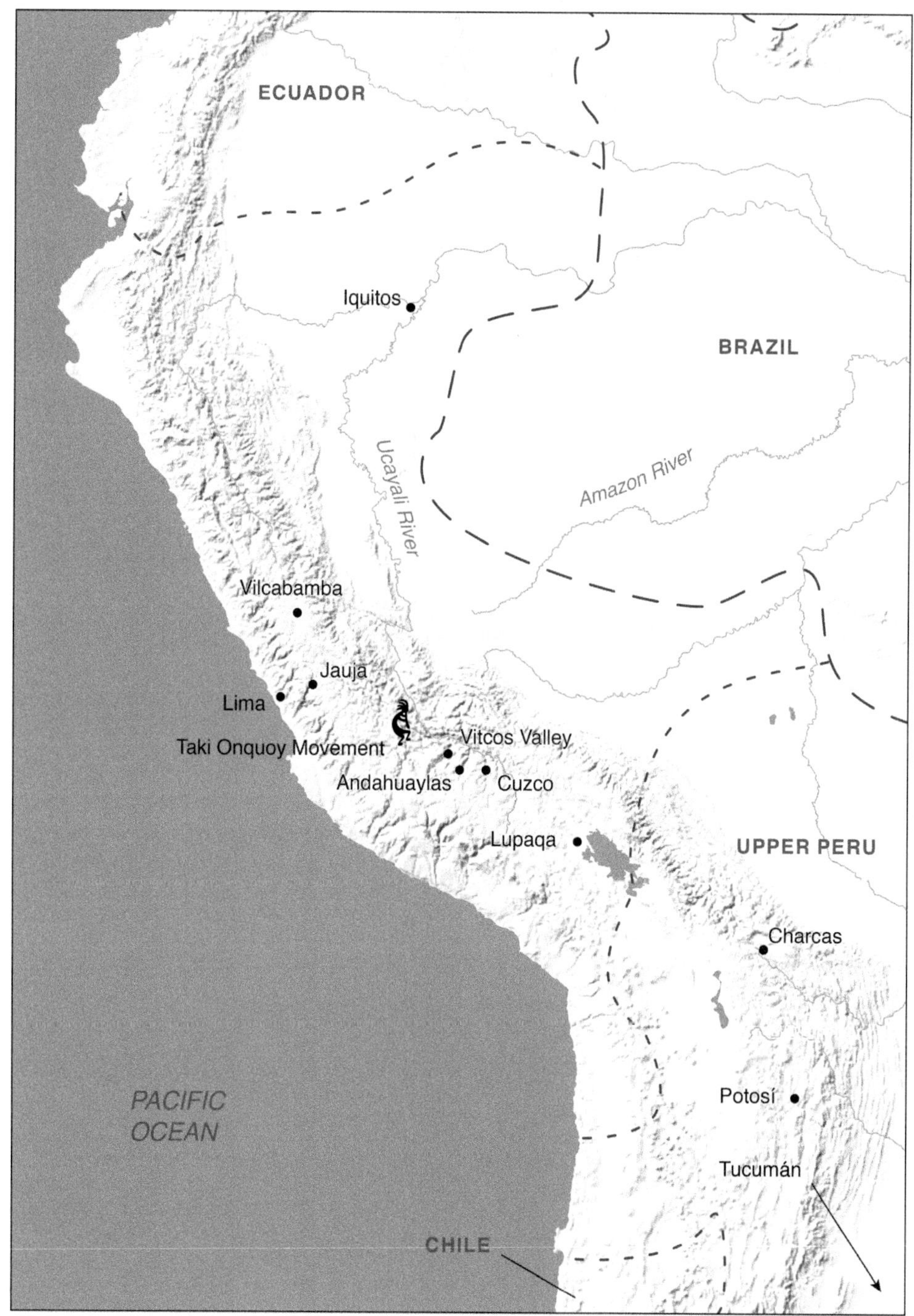

Map 5.1 The Viceroyalty of Peru in the Late Sixteenth Century

respected by both Native people and the Spanish. Manco's death led to a significant revival of Inca traditionalism.[9]

Over the next few decades, Indigenous people at the local level took advantage of new economic opportunities that came with the Spanish, and, as social divisions grew between them, the European conquest became easier. Communities everywhere exploited the Incas' former gold- and silver-mines; for instance, *kurakas*, hereditary leaders in Quechua society southeast of Lima and Ayacucho in Andahuaylas, Peru, sent people far away to mine silver veins in Potosí in response to Spanish labor demands. Native settlements also expanded coca production and used the profits to pay their Spanish tribute, purchase sheep or swine, and produce textiles to sell in Cuzco. Traditionally chosen to promote the welfare of their communities, some *kurakas* instead took full advantage of the new status they acquired after the Spanish contracted them to mobilize Native labor. These leaders used the new system to increase their wealth, renting their own people out to the Spanish as workers and pocketing the profits. Fed up with such abuses, communities denounced these leaders to the Spanish authorities, going over the heads of local *kurakas* to appeal rulings they disliked. Such litigation at times proved favorable, but it divided Native communities.[10]

Colonists capitalized and encouraged such fragmentation; in 1557, Viceroy Cañete finally begged Doña Beatriz Huayllas Ñusta, daughter of Huayna Capac and one of the most important women in Cuzco, to convince Sayri-Tupac to end the Inca rebellion at Vilcabamba. Huayllas Ñusta's negotiations were successful, as in October the Inca and his 300 warriors abandoned their fortress and traveled to Lima. As we have seen with Malintzin in New Spain and in this example from Peru, a few Native women played important but controversial roles during the conquest. The success of Huayllas Ñusta's diplomatic efforts helped end the standoff at Vilcabamba, although people who still resisted the colonizers considered her a traitor. The large estates Sayri-Tupac received for having surrendered, as well as annual tribute from their residents, made the last Inca a wealthy man. He settled outside Cuzco, married his sister Cusi Huarcai, and enjoyed the fruits of collaboration.[11] The Spanish authorities capitalized on such fragmentation within Native society by encouraging collaboration, but Indigenous people were clearly also divided by their own self-interests, and their greed assisted the imposition of colonial rule. The etching shown in Figure 5.1 of the twelfth Inca queen, Chuqui Llanto, wife of Huascar Inca, by Guaman Poma de Ayala shows how an important woman like Doña Beatriz Huayllas Ñusta might have dressed in the sixteenth century.

Individuals: Beatriz de Huayllas Ñusta Capac Coya

Beatriz Huayllas Ñusta was a resident of Cuzco who played an important role during the establishment of Spanish colonial rule. Ñusta was not a leader in the traditional sense, but she is a great example of the important roles fulfilled by some Andean women, and of how the Spanish took advantage of Native women to consolidate the hegemony they gained by deposing the Incas. The conquerors soon learned that through marriage to the *pallas*, the Inca's daughters, their sons could serve as wedges to divide Native society and gain status and recognition in Native circles for themselves. Women thus helped bridge the cultures and political transitions to colonial rule. In the 1550s, a Spanish writer observed that "in Cuzco, where Beatriz Huayllas Ñusta resided, there was no surviving lord, male or female, as important as she." Recognizing her social weight and diplomatic skills, in 1555 Viceroy Mendoza asked her to help end the ongoing Manco Inca rebellion. Beatriz was actually a sister to Manco and an aunt to Sayri-Tupac Inca, who had taken over the rebellion after Manco's death. Ms. Huayllas Ñusta and her son Mancio Sierra traveled to Vilcabamba, negotiated with Sayri-Tupac, and finally convinced him to surrender.[12] Because her son was a mestizo and had blood relations on both sides of the conflict, this important woman was able to negotiate a peaceful end to the violent standoff where others had failed. Her intervention saved many lives by avoiding an all-out Spanish assault against Vilcabamba. Still, the role that she, as an Inca princess, and others in her class played was controversial, since it helped the Spanish take control over land and Native workers by marrying the princesses who had helped rule the communities and people.

Figure 5.1 *The Twelfth Inca Queen, Chuqui Llanto*, Guaman Poma de Ayala Etching, p. 142 [142]. (Royal Danish Library, GKS 2232 4 to: Guaman Poma, Nueva corónica y buen gobierno (1615))

In the southwestern fringes of the Andes, meanwhile, the Reche had taken advantage of Spanish military technology to fortify their own resistance and they scored surprising victories. Pedro Valdivia's initial findings of gold in the area produced nuggets the size of almonds, and the conquistador was sure he had struck it rich: "From now on," he reportedly declared, "I begin to be a lord!" Then, in 1553, the Arauco, Tucapel, and Purén members of Valdivia's *encomienda* revolted. They destroyed Valdivia's Fort Tucapel east of Concepción in December and then trapped the conquistador. Lautaro, who spearheaded the attack, was an Indigenous man who Valdivia had captured as a boy and raised in his household as a groom. The boy learned Spanish ways and later escaped to instruct his people on how to defeat the invaders. The young man convinced Native leaders to torture the governor to death by filling his mouth with dirt before they reportedly ate him.[13] Even under Spanish attack, these peoples had together become so strong that the colonial authorities respectfully referred to Reche territory as "the state." Valdivia's grisly demise sparked a broad uprising that lasted for four hard years and ended only with the death of Lautaro at the young age of 23, when, on April 29, 1557, the Spanish defeated Reche troops in the Battle of Mataquito. The brutal repression of the revolt shows that the conquest of Native people proceeded despite decrees to the contrary from Spain.

On the other hand, the movement by the Reche shows tenacious Indigenous resistance to the imposition of colonial rule. By this time, the Reche had adopted defensive European-style fortifications to counter Spanish advances, transporting trees from forests in Arauco and setting them up as poles on roads running south from Santiago into their territory to stop the Spanish. Natives learned how to make gunpowder from mestizo defectors and began to use firearms. By 1563, the Reche were amassing European swords, pikes, guns, helmets, and leather jackets. European materiel and ideas fortified their resistance. Natives dug trenches and camouflaged holes to trap enemy horses, a strategy that clearly paid off when 90 Spaniards attacked a Reche fort. As they approached, horses and riders fell into the holes and warriors shot them with arrows; in their disordered retreat, the attackers lost many soldiers. Reche warriors besieged Spanish Fort Arauco in 1563 and waited, out of shooting range, for the scarce supplies in the fort to run out. Native attackers threw dead bodies and decaying trash into the only source of water for the fort. When the besieged Spanish used the water anyway, Reche soldiers dug a ditch and drained the pool. Capturing the Spanish troops who arrived to rescue the fort, the warriors displayed their heads on pikes and deceived the besieged Spanish into thinking that Concepción had fallen and that they were the only surviving Europeans left in southern Chile.[14]

Despite this effective Reche example, divisions among Indigenous peoples continued to hamper Native resistance. Collaboration with the Spanish proved too beneficial. In 1557, the Lucanas Larami people in central Peru denounced the neighboring Lucanas Andamarcas, Yauyos, and Parincochas peoples for intruding upon their hunting territory. The *encomendero* in charge of the Lucanas Larami helped them procure a viceregal ban that forbade their opponents from poaching on their land. Clearly, it was in the Spaniards' interest to keep the *encomendero*'s workers happy. The Chanca people of neighboring Andahuaylas, for instance, convinced their *encomendero* to use his soldiers to recover their coca fields in Mayomarca after Native people from Huamanga had taken them over.[15] Spanish administrators and dependent Native leaders both benefitted from such cooperation; it was to their benefit to build mutual obligations, as such liaisons lubricated colonial bureaucracy. If Native resistance continued on the borderlands, one must also acknowledge that many Indigenous leaders sided with the colonists when they benefitted economically and politically.

Ambiguous Indigenous Responses to European Exploration

The diversity of Indigenous responses to colonization highlights again how different their communities and cultures were from one another. In 1560, the Omagua people along the upper Amazon met a huge European military expedition sent to conquer them. Don Pedro de Ursúa led a force of 370 Spanish soldiers and 2,000 Native Andeans on what became a disastrous expedition, descending the river in 2 brigantines, 7 flatboats, 20 rafts, and canoes.[16] Villages of thousands of people greeted the travelers amicably along the upper Amazon. After three months, the adventurers reached the Machiparo territory on today's border between Peru and Brazil, which the Spanish described as "the richest and most populous country in the world." Yet to the Machiparo the explorers were brutal men, described as "the dregs" of Pizarro's forces, who seemingly butchered Native people for no reason.

The disastrous conclusion of the expedition reveals why it was complicated for Native people to deal with the invaders. Not only was Ursúa arbitrary and harsh as a leader, but he had brought along his beautiful mistress Doña Inés de Atienza. The leader spent more time in his tent with her than attending to his men, who claimed Ms. Atienza was in effect their real leader: the mere "whim of a whore," they held, made them liable for punishment. Ursúa intended to colonize the upper Amazon and then use his men to search for El Dorado, the fabled land of immense wealth at the heart of the continent. Fortunately, the explorers were not concerned with killing more Native people. Instead, they built a town at the mouth of the Putumayo River, where one of them murdered Ursúa in his hammock, reportedly because the leader had not allowed him to bring along his own mistress. Then the entire group rebelled against the king of Spain, appointed a Spanish noble as their figurehead "Prince of Peru," and divided huge tracts of the rainforest among themselves.[17] Divisions between European explorers sometimes curbed their attacks on the Native population.

Later, the Omagua who lived near the Tefé River intelligently directed the explorers up a tributary toward a province they described as having more silver and gold than even Peru. Aguirre, the Spaniard who mutinied and had taken over Ursúa's expedition, killed over 100 of his own followers and set ashore the remaining 170 Andean *yanaconas*, women and men who had left their communities in Peru to serve the Spanish as "dependent retainers" on the expedition. Aguirre's goal was not to seek treasure, but instead to actually take over Peru. While trekking overland across Venezuela, someone stabbed Doña Inés to death and the expedition ended in disaster. Finally, after killing anyone loyal to the king, Aguirre even murdered his 16-year-old daughter so she would not "become a concubine to villaines, nor be called the daughter of a traytor [*sic.*]."[18] The conquistador forced his crew to sail quickly down the Amazon and along the way vented his anger on the *yanaconas* he had brought from Peru; most had already died, but he abandoned the remaining 170 women and men along the shore among local peoples and beat the Spanish who protested his actions. The expedition poisoned relations with Natives in Amazonia.

Back in the central areas, where Europeans were quickly imposing their ways of life and creating a synthesis of cultures, Indigenous responses to colonial rule depended on their class and social status. *Kurakas* in Peru still cooperated with their new rulers to line their own pockets. When market forces failed to draw enough individuals and families into the mercury mines at Huancavelica, for instance, the Spanish relied on the *kurakas* to contract Native workers. Mercury was vital for the pan amalgamation, a process that combined the silver ore with salt and mercury in copper vessels and heated the mixture to extract the silver. *Kurakas* also supplied laborers to the *obrajes*, the textile mills. In 1567, the Tanquihuas people agreed to supply their *encomendero* with a rotating force of 60 workers for his *obraje* in Vilcashuamán. As Stern has shown, only traditional bonds of local kinship and reciprocity could have mobilized so many skilled people for the mass production of textiles.[19]

The image one might come away with from descriptions of leaders mobilizing villagers for textile and mine work is one of harmonious enterprise, as one might observe at a tourist site such as Colonial Williamsburg, a re-creation of a colonial village in Virginia in the United States. For people actually doing the hard and dirty work of mining or weaving, however, the picture was anything but idyllic. The 1560s was a decade of crisis for Indigenous people, especially in central Peru, where tribute payments and labor drafts had become incredibly onerous. The messengers for the *huacas*, the Andean gods, were the *taquiongos*, Native spiritual leaders. These leaders told people that the traditional *huacas* were furious that people had abandoned them, sided with the Spanish, and no long offered deities their traditional sacrifices or beer. If the Native people avoided contact with the colonizers, rejected Christianity, refused to pay tribute, evaded the labor drafts, and returned to worship their traditional deities, promised the *taquiongos*, the people would again experience good health, peace, and well-being. The spiritual leaders oversaw feasts, fasts, and confessions from people eager to regain their gods' favor; in effect, the *taquiongos* became the moral guardians of the Native communities.

Then the dancing began. The *huacas* seized Native people, possessing their bodies and making them shake, dance frenetically, and finally collapse in exhaustion. The movement that spread through central Peru after 1560, called Taki Onquoy, literally means "dancing sickness." When taken over by the spirits, people danced and sang in an uncontrollable frenzy, renounced Christianity, and channeled messages from the *huacas*.[20] Over half of the prophets were women, and the movement spread like wildfire through the Native communities. In Huamanga alone, some 8,000 of 150,000 people became active members. Perhaps the Andean women had experienced a loss of traditional power during the imposition of Hispanic culture and Christianity, and this was a way for them to recover their former influence.

The movement threatened to destroy the *kurakas*' cooperation with colonial officials, so both groups of authorities attacked the movement viciously. For two years, officials tortured, whipped, cut the hair of, humiliated, and forced followers of the Taki Onquoy to build and then serve in Christian churches. To help end the movement, Viceroy Garcia de Castro finally negotiated directly with Titu Cusi Yupanqui, the Inca who led the Incan rebels after Sayri-Tupac's surrender. Leaders signed a peace treaty in 1565, after which Yupanqui left his fortress at Vilcabamba and allowed a *corregidor*, an official who ruled a local region in Spanish America in addition to the town council, to enter the region along with a priest.[21] Garcia resettled the Natives into towns and appointed administrators called *corregidores de Indios* to supervise them. The *taquiongos* had figuratively let the *huacas* out of the bottle, though, and Native insurgencies linked to Titu Cusi spread to Jauja, Cuzco, Charcas, Tucumán, and as far south as Chile.

Figure 5.2 *Laborachera-Machasca*, A Scene that May Have Been Associated with the Taki Onquoy Uprising, Guaman Poma de Ayala Etching, p. 863 [876]. (Royal Danish Library, GKS 2232 4 to: Guaman Poma, Nueva corónica y buen gobierno (1615))

For Document 5.2: Juan de Santa Cruz Pachacuti Yamqui on the Taki Onquoy Movement, visit www.routledge.com/9780415519120.

The Taki Onquoy movement was a classic example of a millennial or prophetic movement aimed at restoring harmony to a society in disarray through promises of social transformation and liberation. These movements have often occurred in response to brutal colonial rule. The last book in the Christian Bible, Revelation, is a good example of literature that promises a harmonious future to end colonial suffering (in that case Roman) and to reward a return to traditional beliefs. Multiple examples of such religious movements in Native societies exist, even in the United States. Tenskwatawa, Handsome Lake, Smohalla, Squsachtun, and finally Jack Wovoka, who began the Ghost Dance that spread from the Paiute to the Lakota peoples across northern prairies in 1890, were all nineteenth-century Native American prophets who tried to comfort their people through religion in times of crises.[22] Much like the Taki Onquoy, examples of such movements appeared repeatedly among Indigenous societies in Latin America when conditions became too difficult.

Although colonial systems threatened some peoples, by the late 1560s, more and more Native communities had joined and were even profiting from the colonial economy. We have a unique insight into the economic structure of colonial rule in the records of the *visitas*, which were inspections of Native communities. In 1567, Peru's viceroy sent an inspector to visit the Lupaqa in a highland Aymara community of 20,000 households near Lake Titicaca to check whether they had the means to pay a larger tribute. These people traditionally had two kings who ruled together over seven provinces, as well as two authorities at every lower level, so they were politically well organized. The inspector discovered that even on the *altiplano*, a challenging plateau at one of the highest altitudes in the world, the Lupaqa made *chuñu*, freeze-dried potatoes, held huge flocks of llamas and alpacas, and wove their wool into cloth to sell to colonial traders. One Lupaqa, Juan Alanoca, was quite well to do: he owned 20,000 head of llamas![23] The people even used their animal wealth to purchase their way out of mine service and to buy commodities and food, since they sold meat and hides to the Europeans for cash. The Lupaqa example shows how quickly Native people, even those further away from the colonial centers of power, were being drawn into the colonial economic system and were managing resources to improve their situation.

Other peoples were also adopting European products, technology, and animals that they found useful. By 1568, the Reche were using horses successfully in attacks against the Spanish. Warriors advanced against Spanish forces, by this time in square formation, with infantry in the center and cavalry on both wings. The Abipon Guaicurú people in the Chaco had also adopted horses to assist in hunting, gathering, and warfare. Women especially gained mobility by using horses, and groups of women on horseback began to venture further from camp for a week at a time to gather food. Mocobí and Guaicurú settlements and camps increased dramatically in size by using horses. The Mbayá hunted wild cattle such as deer from horseback, and the Abipones stole horses from Spanish settlements to augment their own herds. In eastern South America, the Charrua also adopted horses and used them to prey on the vast herds of feral cattle that by this time had overrun the Eastern Band, the territory that later became the country of Uruguay.[24]

Events: Tightening Colonial Screws

If Indigenous people were ranging further afield and threatening colonial outposts by adopting horses and Spanish military strategies, as well as by trying to restore pre-colonial society, it should not be surprising that Spanish officials tried to recover their power in a show of strength. This backlash occurred in Peru with the appointment of a new viceroy, Don Francisco de Toledo, sent to impose greater Spanish authority. A former page of King Charles and later a steward for Philip II, Toledo was also a knight of the Order of Alcántara, a military order founded to fight the Muslims in Spain, so the new viceroy was grounded within the imperial structure and predisposed to fighting its enemies. Appointed the fifth viceroy of Peru in 1569, the new administrator spent five years inspecting his entire new realm. He then enacted an ambitious yet brutal system of reforms to increase production. The new measures that Toledo enacted forced Native people against their will into settlements under the control of Spanish *corregidores*, made the mining system more prosperous, established new systems of tribute, linked colonists' prosperity to his revised state institutions, and formally codified all these changes within the legal system. Toledo mandated a great migration that every year forced over 13,000 Natives to relocate to mine silver at Potosí. The new viceroy was also determined to destroy the neo-Inca kingdom still surviving in Vilcabamba, by this time led by Tupac Amaru, a younger brother of Titu Cusi. The independent Inca state was a lingering problem for Toledo. Historian Steve Stern has argued that the best way to explain why Toledo's reforms worked is that the collapse of the Taki Onquoy movement had so deeply demoralized Native society that they hardly opposed the politician's revisions of their world.[25]

Mixed Responses to Christian Proselytism

In New Spain, during those years of Spanish impositions the Indigenous people avoided a drastic reform such as Toledo enacted in Peru by turning to Christianity as a solution to colonial malaise. More people in New Spain remained in the colonial Catholic structure than in Peru. Indoctrination in a difficult linguistic context, though, still produced cultural misunderstandings. One example was the Christian identification of Jesus with the Sun and light and the confusion this image produced for Mixtec people, who had traditionally situated the Sun in a celestial paradise with the souls of dead warriors. In the morning, these souls took the form of "brightly colored birds" and traveled with the Sun across the sky, flying around and sucking nectar.[26] Flying souls was not the image of Christ that missionaries hoped to perpetuate. Imagine the lingering confusion that at least one generation of Native people, trying to sort out the mixed metaphors of solar deities, received during Christian indoctrination.

One way to explain why some people in New Spain more readily accepted Christianity is that the Church offered Nahua women avenues of participation within the patriarchal confines of Hispanic society. Some Indigenous women in New

Spain found a social space in the Catholic Church between the public offices held by men and their own traditional household roles. In parish churches, Indigenous women cared for convents and friaries, assisted the ill and infirm, and looked after religious brotherhoods, all of which gave them a chance to exercise public power. After 1552, Nahua women worked as officers in Indigenous religious lay-brotherhoods. They created order by cleaning religious institutions and caring for religious symbols, which had also been their tasks in their pre-contact religious institutions. Native women furthermore worked as servants in Spanish convents. Fray Mendieta, a Franciscan missionary and historian writing at the end of the sixteenth century, credited Nahua women with convincing their communities to accept and create religious societies called brotherhoods. Church authorities, who admired upper-class Native women because they bequeathed charitable donations to friaries, chapels, churches, and hospitals, highlighted these women's piety and dedication.[27]

If Catholic proselytism drew Indigenous attention in New Spain, at least for some Nahua women, many borderland peoples still rejected colonial rule and especially the forced labor. In northern New Spain, the Chichimecas mounted stiff resistance as the Spanish increased their efforts to mine silver during the 1570s. These peoples included ten separate, nomadic unrelated ethnic groups who fought together as excellent archers and skillful guerrillas. The Chichimecas joined in large confederations, used horses, and followed charismatic leaders, some of whom, like the Araucanian leader Lautaro discussed earlier, had lived among the Spanish and learned their ways.

For over a decade the Spanish tried to crush the Chichimeca threat, first by resettling the area with amicable Otomí allies from Jilotepec. By 1568, silver mining had dwindled to an end because of the deadly Chichimeca raids. Desperate, Viceroy Enríquez built presidios (forts) and defenses around the Spanish frontier towns, sent his captains out on punitive missions, and posted patrols to monitor roads and defend wagon trains. Spanish soldiers at these outposts survived by selling captured Native people into slavery, since they had to buy their own weapons, armor, and food. Chichimeca warriors nevertheless continued to defeat the Spanish frontier forces. The most effective weapons against them, New Spain's leaders finally discovered, were the missions. The viceroy sent regular orders to resettle the Indigenous people into *congregaciones*. By 1574, forced mission settlements and punitive Spanish expeditions had decreased Chichimeca raids. Additional help came from capturing and executing 80 of the notorious raiding leaders, including Paqualame, the leader who had actively helped tribute-paying Native people escape the tax collectors.[28]

In Peru, Viceroy Toledo's new laws and co-optation of Native leaders transformed Native society. In a way, Indigenous people finally officially became "Indians" during the 1570s as Toledo incorporated all individual groups of Native peoples, such as the Angaraes, Aymaras, Pariscas, Chilques, Tanquihuas, Lucanas, Huachos, Chocorvos, Yauyos, and many more into a broad, generic ethnic caste named the "Republic of Indians" to reorganize the society he intended to control. Indigenous workers in this caste, managed by both the Native elite and the colonists, provided goods, labor, and profits to the Crown and people in the superior caste called the "Republic of Spaniards." Colonial extraction syphoned silver, cloth, corn, wheat, potatoes, swine, footwear, and chickens from Native communities for Spanish use and export. To appropriate these resources, authorities imposed harsh tributes of goods and services that contradicted traditional *ayllus* (a traditional Native community in the Andes) self-reliance. Previously, Native communities had farmed small ecological areas in close cooperation with a wider community framework. People had relied on each other for labor, production, and access to communal land. Working together had allowed communities to survive in a challenging environment. Toledo's reforms drew these resources into Spanish control and ownership.

Of course, long before, under the Incas, communities had also paid tribute in labor but not in kind, that is, in goods or cash, owing to unreliable environmental conditions. Payment in kind to the Spanish proved a heavy burden, because communities actually had to come up with specific quantities of tribute, no matter what happened with the crops or the weather, and they could no longer just send workers to serve the rulers as they had for the Inca. Tribute that people in Huamanga paid during the 1550s included gold, silver, food, animals, cloth, wooden plates, vases, chairs, shoes, saddle gear, ropes, rugs, and whips, showing not only the breadth of Native production but also the extent to which Europeans depended on them. *Kurakas* sold their people's labor to the Spanish and profited from the arrangement. In 1577, a *kuraka* in Chocorvos rented 27 of his kinsmen to the Cárdenas family to transport goods and work in the fields, and received 162 pesos after their six months of work. Presumably, the *kuraka* may have redistributed such a payment to his community, but the opportunity for dishonesty is obvious.[29] Since Native leaders benefitted from such arrangements as intermediaries, they sold their own people into service, drawing people further into colonial economic systems as time passed.

If syphoning wealth and labor from communities was not enough, Toledo undermined Indigenous autonomy in other ways. Against all odds, one rebel Inca still held out in Vilcabamba. In 1572, with help from Manari informants, the Spanish finally captured that last ruler, Tupac Amaru, after a harrowing chase through the jungle. Once his entourage had accepted baptism, the Spanish tried and found Tupac Amaru guilty of the murder of Spanish priests at his jungle fortress. Tupac Amaru made a speech to the people, denouncing all that the Incas had taught as completely false. Despite his recantation, Toledo executed Tupac Amaru by decapitation in the central plaza of Cuzco.[30] Toledo destroyed holy Inca relics and the mummified bodies of earlier emperors, and then imprisoned all the descendants of the Inca rulers he could find. His attack brought the Inca Empire to a crashing end.

Even as Toledo crushed the last Incas, disease and integration into the colonial system were quickly changing other Indigenous people. The center for commerce and transport southeast of Upper Peru was Tucumán, situated between the Andes and the Chaco. The dominant people in this area were still the Diaguitas, skilled farmers and potters who also worked gold, silver, copper, tin, and bronze. The Diaguitas traded with the Chiriguanos to the north and the Comechingones to the south. Also in the area lived the Juríes, a people known for their fishing. By the time the Spanish arrived in the mid-sixteenth century, nomadic Lules from the Chaco had invaded Tucumán and were holding the Juríes in corrals made out of stakes. The Juríes were reportedly close to extinction. Clearly, the Europeans held no monopoly on violence! As they settled the area, the Spanish made quick work of the Native people as porters to transport silver from Upper Peru to Buenos Aires for shipment across the Atlantic Ocean to Spain. After founding the city of San Miguel in 1565, Spanish colonists killed off as many Native people as they could and sold the rest of them, some 8,000 people in all, as slaves to Chile and north to Charcas, the mining center of Potosí.[31] Already by 1560, not even a quarter of the population from the height of the Inca Empire survived in the area of Tucumán and its vicinities.

As their population declined and their communities collapsed, many of the remaining Indigenous people lost their ties to rural settlements and found work in Spanish cities as *yanaconas*. Some Native leaders even became wealthy. The more the leaders tightened their links to Hispanic society, the wealthier they became. Some *yanaconas* purchased and accumulated private property, making the most of opportunities to turn political influence and service to the viceroy into liquid wealth. As commerce reached further into rural networks, urban Natives purchased lands outside the cities, extended trade avenues, and became creditors to other Native people trapped in tribute, debt, and labor obligations. Doña Isabel Asto, an Indigenous widow of a Spaniard who lived in Huamanga, Peru, owned 60 *mitayo* Natives who worked her own mercury mines at Huancavelica. Out of every ten laborers contracted in Huamanga by this time, in fact, there was an Indigenous miner working for a Native entrepreneur. Some Indigenous people thus became financially successful by exploiting other Natives to enrich themselves. Indigenous miners, coca planters, and *hacienda* owners hired Native workers for wage labor, and settled dependent Native laborers on their properties. Catalina Cocachimbo, a Native woman of wealth, recruited a *yanacona* by lending them 150 pesos and contracting for repayment at 20 pesos per year. Another woman, Juana Marcaruray, lived in her own *ayllu* but secured seven private plots, including two coca fields; collection of rent from her tenants forced her own community members into debt. As they amassed wealth, these Native elites adopted European values of capital accumulation.[32]

Other pressures on Indigenous people included the viceregal decrees to use their labor or even take their children to speed up their integration into colonial society. Toledo codified the *mita de plaza* arrangement into law. This former Inca *mit'a* system, which the Spanish renamed *mita*, had brought in workers from subject communities to work on imperial jobs for limited periods. The viceroy conveniently employed the pre-Hispanic rotational labor system to recruit Native laborers to work in mines, textile *obrajes*, ranching, agriculture, construction, food production, or as domestic servants in households. The people hated Toledo's reforms because it squeezed them financially and forced them to leave their home communities; they actually tried to bribe the viceroy with a huge sum of 800,000 pesos to give up the resettlement plan, an offer he refused. One variety called the *mita de plaza*, for instance, forced 1,200 Native men from surrounding provinces to move to Lima and assemble daily in the city square. The Ward Magistrate then distributed them to Lima authorities or businesspersons, who used them as workers. Many of these men ended up staying permanently in the city after finishing their assignments, living in a neighborhood on the outskirts called Santiago del Cercado, and sending their extra income home to help their family and community.[33]

Other Indigenous people fell into the system against their will. By 1575, Natives in Canta, north of Lima, complained that their *corregidor*, and even the priests, took orphaned girls and boys, aged 6 to 8, and sent them to Spanish residents of Cañete, 75 miles south of Lima along the coast, for domestic labor.[34] These labor arrangements fragmented rural communities and changed ways of life, as these Indigenous children grew up in Spanish households and learned their customs instead of Native ways of life. Imagine the trauma of having been taken from your town and sent away to live with and work for a strange family, with all the opportunity for abuse that may have followed. These measures of forced integration resulted from Toledo's policies.

Individuals: Garcilaso de la Vega el Inca

Viceregal decrees intended to further absorb Indigenous people into colonial Spanish society slowly changed the people through transculturation. In Peru, more and more interactions between Europeans and Indigenous people continued to take place. A great example of the impact of cultural contact about this time in the Spanish colonies is the work of a Peruvian mestizo from Cuzco named Garcilaso de la Vega el Inca. This Indigenous author lived most of his life in Spain and wrote a famous book there toward the end of his life. Garcilaso's father was a conquistador and his Quechua mother claimed ascendancy as an Incan princess, so the author wrote about his experiences on both sides of the Atlantic and praised both his Indigenous and his European heritage. The author wrote his book, *Royal Commentaries of the Incas*, in smooth, erudite Spanish that reflects cultivated scholarship and serves as a good source on material culture under Inca rule and a history of the Inca Empire. The book also shows, however, the author's Spanish education and acceptance of European rule. Because Garcilaso glorified Peruvian life under the Incas and presented life in their empire as utopian, readers must approach his text carefully with that perspective in mind. On the other hand, because of its baroque perspective, many Europeans read Garcilaso's book and it has influenced popular views of ancient Peru up until today.

Widespread Indigenous Integration despite Sporadic Resistance

As Garcilaso de la Vega's example suggests, political measures to help integrate Native people were surprisingly effective in the central areas. One notable and even surprising feature of the early colonial period is the relative speed with which upper-class Indigenous people joined Hispanic society. This was especially true for the *teuctli*, the Mexica nobles, who took advantage of the European arrival to improve their own position. In the New Spanish city of Cuernavaca, just south of Mexico City, the *teuctli* boasted two-storey large houses with round arches and even wide patios for dances and fiestas. One Don Juan Jiménez, for instance, owned a *calli* (house) on a *calmilli* (an urban house lot, sometimes with an adjacent field) that consisted of a walled-in compound of several rooms facing a central court, an arrangement apparently common even before the conquest that persisted under colonial rule. Jiménez was a wealthy community member, as his will of 1579 listed 13 properties throughout the Cuernavaca region, including an irrigated field (*amiltzintli*), two lots on higher land (*tlacpactlalli*), and a private noble's property. Jiménez listed his largest lot as a *tlatocatlalli*, a designation traditionally used for public lands. The inclusion of such a property suggests that the Indigenous elite had taken over communal lands in the years following the conquest.[35]

The northern borderlands of New Spain, though, presented a completely different story. Peoples throughout frontier regions still fiercely resisted Spanish efforts to change their ways of life. When Spanish and Native allies entered Zacatecas and New Galicia for the silver boom of the mid-sixteenth century, they faced fierce Chichimeca resistance. The rugged frontier terrain northwest of the capital made these peoples' guerrilla hit-and-run tactics especially effective. In May 1570, the king ordered the authorities to settle Natives into *villas*, villages where they should "live in a civilized manner and have their organized government." When determined resistance continued, in 1580 the viceroy finally ordered a "war of fire and blood" against Chichimec rebels. Abuses followed: one Spanish miner in the Zacatecan region reportedly horrifically "cut off the feet of some and the hands of more than 300 Indians after finding a friar 'shot with arrows' and a few Indians in possession of church ornaments."[36] This total war, the complete destruction of Indigenous houses, food, crops, stock, and even the illegal trade in Native slaves was ultimately ineffective; Chichimec warriors finally attacked even the city of Zacatecas as an act of revenge.[37]

The authorities eventually realized that military strength would be unable to vanquish Native resistance, so they instead turned to religion as a tool for pacification. A new viceroy, Luis Velasco II, sent Franciscan and Jesuit missionaries to the northern provinces in 1591, along with food rations and 400 Christian families transplanted from Tlaxcala, to diminish Chichimec hostility and draw them to mission life. The resettlement of already integrated Chichimec allies nearer to the rebels is a great example of how Franciscan, Dominican, Augustinian, and Jesuit missionaries tried to reorganize Native communities and cultures. This policy was successful up until the 1590s, when additional military resistance developed in the hills of Nueva Vizcaya among the Acaxees, who revolted in 1601 and again in 1611. Their resistance fed into the Tepehuan revolt of 1616 (covered in Chapter 6). The important point for the late sixteenth century is that most peoples on the northern borderlands resisted Spanish attempts to change their ways of life.

Colonial archives allow us to examine more closely the interaction between authorities and one of the Chichimec peoples, the Guachichil. These hunter-gatherers had traditionally lived on prickly pears and mesquite seeds. Colonial travelers described them as:

> naked, very poor, and extremely barbarous ... they all live bent over and inclined towards the ground just like brutes without ever raising their eyes from it and thus their only occupation is to look for food with bow and arrow, to procreate, and to make war with each other.

By 1574, the war against the Chichimec had killed most of the Guachichil. The remainder had given up warring and settled in villages. Finally, only two elderly women in this people remained alive.

On July 19, 1599, a criminal trial took place in Tlaxcala, the former center of Guachichil life. The judicial records illuminate the relationship between Indigenous people and colonial authorities. One of the two remaining women had entered the town's churches, broken crosses, and removed religious images, reportedly "stirring up all the Indians." Neighbors clearly feared this Guachichil woman, since they accused her of being an *hechicera*, a witch who could turn herself into a coyote. Authorities claimed that the woman had insisted that people should:

> rise up and follow her in her idolatries, and that if they do not rise up that she will destroy them because she has the ability to do so, and that they should help her go to the pueblo of San Luis where the Spaniards have settled and kill them all and that if they do not go she will kill them.[38]

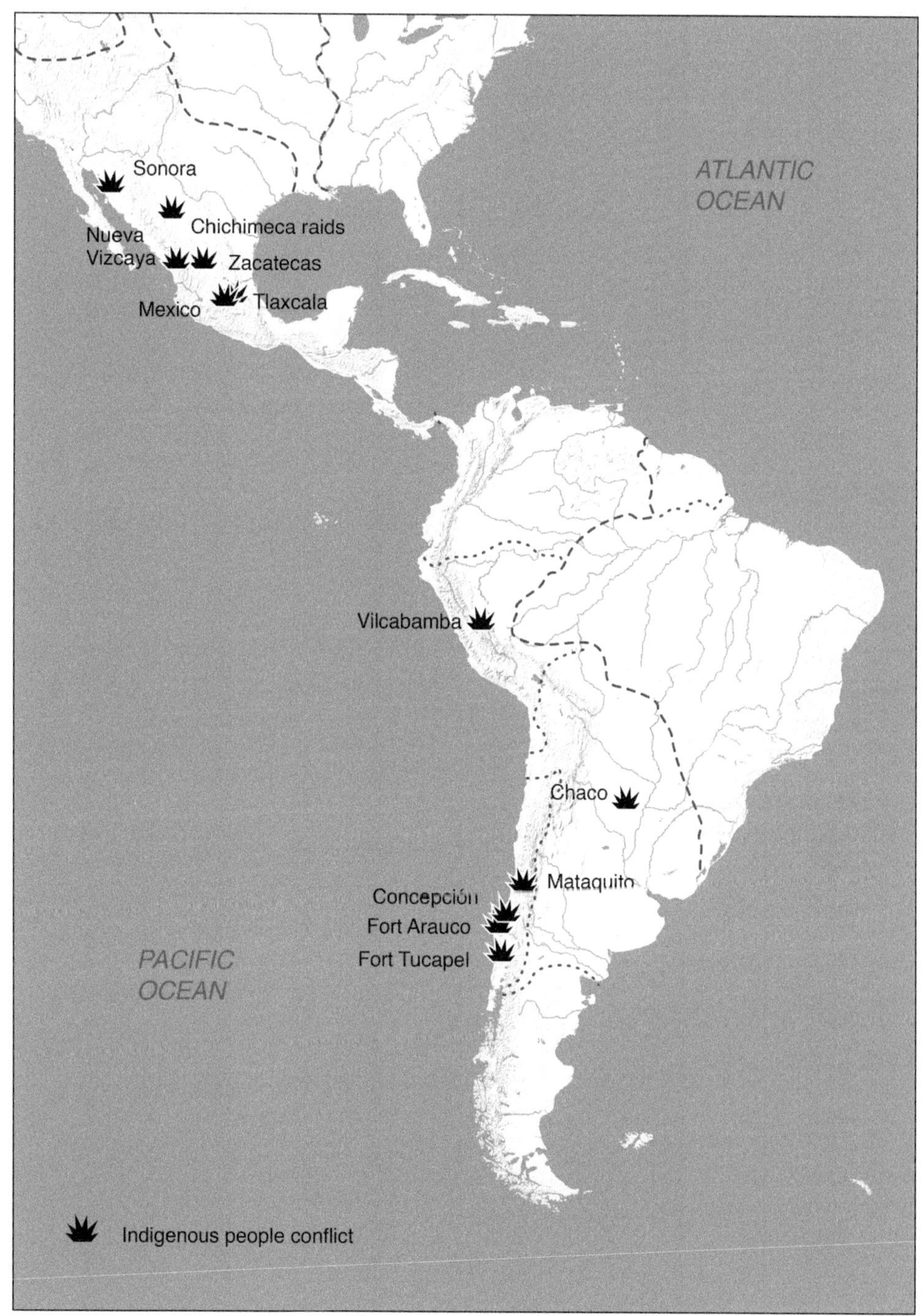

Map 5.2 Largest Indigenous Uprisings throughout the Late Sixteenth Century

At her trial, the woman denied using witchcraft and her legal defense "dismissed her visions as the drunken ravings of a crazy woman," echoing widespread attitudes toward Native alcoholism. The authorities, though, finally hung the woman out of fear that she would disturb the public peace. Courts of justice had tried such idolatry cases (sorcery, idolatry, polygamy, and seditious plots against the state and gospel) in New Spain since the 1530s.

Deeper analysis of the woman's goals in ransacking the churches reveals that she actually had plans for a broad revolt in mind: she hoped to turn Native parishioners against the authorities of both Church and state. Far from the rantings of an insane person, her plea that all her people join to kill Spaniards in order to resurrect dead Indigenous people shows her vision of a new beginning, a millenarian future without Spaniards. This was a utopian dream and the woman bravely made her request in the form of a threat, promising "to make the earth open and swallow them all with her sorcery if they did not listen."[39] Over 100 Guachichil had obeyed her initial call to assemble; this was clearly neither a crazy nor a powerless woman. Once the authorities got rid of the social threat by hanging the offender, they discovered lucrative silver-mines in the pueblo of San Luis which became so profitable that they received the name of Potosí, after the lucrative silver-mine in Upper Peru.

One notable exception to Native military resistance on the northern frontiers were the Rarámuri, who lived on the high, dry plateau of southeastern Sonora and northeastern Sinaloa, and who experienced their first contact with the Spanish in 1580. These people call themselves foot racers, using their word for foot, *rará*, and have become known for traditional foot races in which young men from different communities competed by placing their feet under a wooden or stone ball and then kicking the ball as they ran for distances as far as 100 miles. These races had spiritual dimensions: runners painted themselves, wore unique belts, employed special oils to massage their legs, and invoked magical powers by wearing the bones of their deceased ancestors. Runners used traps along the way to slow each other down and hundreds of Rarámuri lined the racetrack, illuminated with torches throughout the night, to cheer on their favorite teams. The Spanish called these people Tarahumara, and their staple food in their high-altitude and barren area was traditionally parched corn.[40] Recently, author Christopher McDougall popularized their culture and running tradition in his book *Born to Run*.

Unlike the Chichimecas, the Rarámuri initially accommodated Spanish intrusions and impositions without significantly changing their traditional ways of life. They resisted nonviolently by lying, stealing, feigning complicity, and by escaping into the surrounding hills.[41] In the final decades of the sixteenth century, though, settlers, missionaries, and stockmen moved into the area with their cattle and forced the Rarámuri into formal communities. Once gathered, the Spaniards tried to use them to mine for silver, grow crops, and watch their cattle, but, because of their semi-nomadic migration down from the high plateaus to the warmer valleys during the winter months, the Rarámuri never became a permanent labor force. Instead, they provided only part-time work for dispersed Spanish settlements.

As colonists gradually took Native lands and limited their self-sufficiency, Jesuits settled the Rarámuri on missions and distributed them for part-time labor to ranchers in a system that in effect became forced impressment. *Hacienda* owners built estates near Rarámuri communities to take advantage of their labor. The Rarámuri accepted elements of Christianity and the unavoidable Spanish cultural impositions, though, without radically changing their culture and self-identity as a people. While perhaps not as striking as an all-out war of resistance, nonviolent strategies allowed the Rarámuri to survive more successfully over the long term than surrounding Native peoples, such as the Chichimec, who fought back violently.

Indigenous People Adopt New Strategies and Weapons of Resistance

If the Rarámuri resisted colonial rule nonviolently, the Reche in the Southern Cone used a different strategy: they strengthened their fierce military opposition by adopting Spanish weapons. By the final decade of the sixteenth century, these people had amassed such a huge supply of horses that they could field several hundred mounted warriors. Reche people still fought mainly on foot, however, and used horses as auxiliaries instead of as a main weapon. Their resistance was coordinated and broad: designing their own saddles to make them very light, warriors rode nearly 50 kilometers per night to strike settlements and ranches. Their adoption of horses assisted mobility, speed, and effectiveness, but did not in the end change their main purposes of resistance. The Reche still capitalized on their own tried-and-true strategies, such as luring Europeans into traps: as the enemy drew near to their main forces, the Reche closed in behind them in "concentric rings of warriors," challenging Spanish retreats.[42] If Spanish riders turned and fled, warriors patiently ran them down on foot until they could pull them from the saddle or soldiers became entangled in the trees and underbrush. These people had traditionally run wild animals to death; now they used this strategy against the invaders.

Horses were not the only European stock which Indigenous people found useful. Throughout the Americas, Natives adopted many foreign animals and products, showing that the Columbian exchange was indeed changing Native cultures. By this time, Native people in Tlaxcala, east of Mexico City, were using chickens, goats, pigs, and sheep so extensively that they were an "inseparable part of the Indigenous household." Chickens had even become more common than native turkeys in central New Spain because they were so much cheaper. Despite official legislation forbidding the use of horses, mules, donkeys, and oxen by Native people, animals that could bear heavy loads became common in Native communities. Because of such widespread adoption, in 1597 officials relaxed legislation forbidding Natives from owning horses and allowed Indigenous traders to keep as many as six. Very wealthy individuals, such as cacica Doña Inés Cortés of Yecapixtla, could afford more livestock: by the early seventeenth century, 15 mares grazed on her large maize *hacienda*.[43]

As people improved their forces by adopting weaponry and horses and augmented food supplies with domesticated animals, it should not be surprising that resistance against colonists also increased. This was especially the case on frontier borderlands. By this time conditions in southern Chile for the Reche were desperate. One cacique described how the colonizers treated his people:

> they did not let us enjoy life in our homes, nor our sons and women. Such was their greed that each month they charged us tribute in gold, and of those who could not pay lost their clothes and coverings used against the cold in winter. Those who could not give tribute received one hundred lashes or had noses or ears cut off and were imprisoned. Women were also tributaries, spinning, weaving, [and] doing chores … in Spanish homes.[44]

The Reche in Arauco, Tucapel, Catiray, and Purén had effectively prevented the Spanish from settling their lands, but colonists pushed steadily to gain entrance. In 1598, fed up by abuses and settler pressures, the Natives finally rose in another massive rebellion against the Spanish that continued the War of Arauco begun 40 years before. Desperate to throw off European rule, warriors captured and tortured Governor Martín García de Loyola, suffocating him with dirt, although later stories exaggeratedly claimed that they poured molten gold down his throat. Warriors reportedly then used his skull as a drinking vessel at festivals.[45] The Reche rebellion raged from the Maule River to Osorno in the south, and warriors destroyed every Spanish settlement south of the Biobío River, except for Castro on the Island of Chiloé. This rebellion brought to a climax Reche resistance during the sixteenth century and for the time being effectively postponed colonial intrusions in their lands.

North in Ecuador, Indigenous people had experienced serious epidemics during the second half of the sixteenth century, especially along today's Amazonian border with Peru. A relative of Ignatious of Loyola, founder of the Jesuit order, became governor of the region in 1557. The area was the homeland of the Jívaro peoples, the Shuar, Achuar, Huambisa, and Aguaruna, who lived in thousands of kilometers of rainforest. Deep in the jungle, at 1,800 meters' altitude, Spanish prospectors discovered in the 1560s some of the largest nuggets of gold found in the Americas. A gold rush on Jívaro territory followed and Spanish administrators forced enslaved Indigenous and African people to dig shafts deep underground to mine by candlelight. Between 1561 and 1567, miners took as much as 875 kilograms of high-karat gold from vein deposits in isolated mountain camps. Over the following years, as the Spanish tried to force the Jívaro into the mines, the people understandably rebelled. In 1572, 1581, and then finally again in 1599, the Jívaro pushed back violently against the miners until they had won complete independence. Records show that rather than an outright rebellion, as some historians have argued, the Jívaro resisted in a manner more in line with their culture: they slowly attacked the Spanish through "small-scale retributive guerrilla raids followed by retreat to their isolated forest homes."[46] By the end of the sixteenth century, Indigenous people in many areas still resisted Spanish colonization and forced labor.

Conclusions: Integration amidst Ongoing Resistance

Many Indigenous people resisted colonial rule during the second half of the sixteenth century, but a significant number of them also joined European society and came under Spanish rule. Even as their societies changed and adapted, outright Native resistance seems to have pulled them further into the clutches of foreign administrators. In Central America, many Native people settled in *congregaciones* around Spanish towns as their traditional communities collapsed. Others moved to Spanish cities or even mines when pressed into forced labor; many people ended up staying in these areas after completing their work. Forced labor, the *repartimiento*, and tribute systems radically changed traditional Indigenous communities. To accommodate colonial demands, the people made alliances with each other, with colonists, and with their rulers. Native leaders collaborated with the European system and capitalized on these changes for their own benefit, selling out their own people when it helped line their pockets and becoming wealthy members of colonial society. In many borderlands, Indigenous people continued to fight colonial impositions. On the northern fringes, the Chichimeca fought New Spanish troops until the arrival of missionaries. The Reche continued a long war against the Spanish in the southern Andes, limiting European settlement in what later became

Chile. By the end of the sixteenth century, colonial forces finally crushed Reche resistance again but could not ultimately defeat them.

In the second half of the sixteenth century, Iberians finally allowed Native people to become human, so to speak, yet at the same time cast them into a social position in every way inferior to their own. Despite royal mandates for better treatment and disagreements over justice, the conquest continued unabated. These contradictions reveal the division between Spanish legislation and the reality of its implementation in the Americas. Missions increased their work during this period in cooperation with state efforts to pacify Native people. Indigenous adherents, though, tried to employ church venues to their advantage, and missions served Natives as places to meet, organize, and reconstruct their communities. The last vestiges of the Inca Empire collapsed during these years, and many Indigenous peoples on the final frontiers of northern New Spain, southern Chile, and Amazonia finally met Europeans for the first time. Europeans were in Abya Yala to stay and those Indigenous people who had survived the demographic collapse would have to either adjust to their presence or move out of their way.

Discussion Questions

1. Contrast examples of Indigenous integration into Catholic circles in New Spain with the *taquiongo* resistance to Christian proselytism in Peru. Why were Native responses to Christianity so different from place to place?
2. How did early colonial administrative impositions change Native communities, and how in turn did new forms of Indigenous labor and beliefs help shape the colonial world?
3. Why did Indigenous leaders farm out their own people to the Spanish as laborers?
4. How might experiences of Indigenous men forced into cities to work under Toledo's reforms in Peru have compared with migrants from Latin America working in the U.S. today?
5. Contrast the Indigenous leaders who took advantage of colonial rule to improve their own position with contemporary examples of opportunism by politicians.
6. Why did some peoples successfully adopt European technology and use it to their own benefit against the invaders, while others changed their ways of life and joined colonial society? What may have determined these Native choices?

Notes

1 Lutz and Lovell, "Core and Periphery in Colonial Guatemala," 40–42.
2 Ibid., 44–46.
3 Farriss, *Maya Society*, 159–161.
4 Ibid., 160.
5 Ibid., 164.
6 Marx, *Selected Writings in Sociology and Social Philosophy*, 127.
7 Ibid., 135, 168.
8 Myers, "Spanish Contacts and Social Change," 140–141.
9 Hemming, *The Conquest of the Incas*, 256, 279.
10 Patterson, "The Inca Empire," 33–34.
11 Hemming, *The Conquest of the Incas*, 291–296.
12 Lavrin, *Latin American Women*, 106.
13 Isabel Allende has written a book of historical fiction about the settlement of Chile entitled *Inés del Alma Mía*.

14 Armand, "Frontier Warfare in Colonial Chile," 127, 128.
15 Stern, "Early Spanish-Indian Accommodation in the Andes," 28.
16 A brigantine is a small two-masted ship rigged with both a fore-and-aft mainsail and a square topsail.
17 Hemming, *Red Gold*, 195–196.
18 Ibid., 197.
19 Stern, "Early Spanish-Indian Accommodation," 37.
20 Stern, *Peru's Indian Peoples*, 52, 53.
21 Hemming, *The Conquest of the Incas*, 305, 307.
22 A good source on such movements is Sylvia Thrupp's *Millennial Dreams in Action*.
23 Murra, "An Aymara Kingdom in 1567," 120.
24 Gregson, "The Influence of the Horse," 37, 38, 41.
25 Stern, *Peru's Indian Peoples*, 77.
26 Burkhart, "The Solar Christ," 239.
27 Truitt, "Courting Catholicism," 416–417.
28 Powell, "Spanish Warfare against the Chichimecas," 581, 584.
29 Stern, *Peru's Indian Peoples*, 41.
30 Hemming, *The Conquest of the Incas*, 448.
31 Nichols, "Colonial Tucuman," 471, 482.
32 Stern, *Peru's Indian Peoples*, 166.
33 Charney, "Negotiating Roots," 142.
34 Ibid., 143.
35 Haskett, "Coping in Cuernavaca," 103–104.
36 Behar, "Visions of a Guachichil Witch," 117.
37 Salmón, *Indian Revolts in Northern New Spain*, 20.
38 Behar, "Visions of a Guachichil Witch," 116, 124.
39 Ibid., 132.
40 Zingg, *Behind the Mexican Mountains*, 82–84.
41 Salmón, "Tarahumara Resistance," 379–381.
42 Padden, "Cultural Change," 112.
43 Kicza, *The Indian in Latin American History*, 97.
44 *Colección de historiadores de Chile*, 4, p. 48.
45 Ibid., p. 255.
46 Lane, *Quito 1599*, 136–149.

6 The High Colonial Period

Indigenous People Join Imperial Systems, 1600 to 1649

Chronology

1600	Huarochirí manuscript published.
	More Europeans migrate to Latin America.
1604	Franciscan missions established in the Yucatan Peninsula.
1605	The *Mita* instituted in Peru.
1609	Guaraní leader Arapizandú requests Jesuit missionaries.
	King Philip III legalizes enslavement of Indigenous people captured in war.
1610	Town council of Paraíba in Brazil declares Indigenous farming destructive.
	Office of the Holy Inquisition established in Cartagena, New Granada.
1612	French missionaries arrive in Maranhão to convert the Tupinamba and oppose the Portuguese.
1614	The Archbishop of Lima bans performances of songs and taquies (a popular dance) and orders all Native musical instruments to be burned.
1615	Guaman Poma de Ayala finishes etchings of abuses and sends them to the king of Spain.
1616	The Tepehuan revolt in northern New Spain.
1618	The Paulista *bandeirantes* begin raids west to capture Indigenous slaves.
1619	The *Colegio de Cacique* is opened in Lima for sons of *kurakas*.
1620s	Indigenous elite move to larger Spanish cities in search of jobs.
1625	*Audiencia* of Guatemala forbids Native dances; *congregación* system enforced.
1627	Campaign to capture Reche slaves in Chile.
	Harsh *Obraje* labor growing until 1630.
	Indigenous people and *cabildos* employ the Spanish legal system to address grievances.
1629	The Reche execute Spanish captives.
1630s	Four Dominican missions are sent to the Kuna.
1632	Jesuits found 12 more reductions in Mato Grosso de Sul, Brazil to escape slave raids.
1635	The Inquisition in Lima attacks the *converso* community.
	Diseases sweep the missions, killing Guaraní people.
1641	Guaraní forces from Jesuit missions defeat the Paulistas at the battle of Mbororé.
	The Spanish recognize the Biobío River as the official boundary with Reche territory.
1640s	Indigenous nobles in New Spain lease out land to Spanish colonists.
1641	A slave ship sinks at Mosquito Cays (Nicaragua); descendants called *zambos*.

1647 The Captain General in Chile forbids the game of *palin* (similar to field hockey).
1649 Jesuits resettle 4,000 Rarámuri into 12 missions north of the Conchos River.
Missionaries enter Ucayali territory in northeastern Amazonian Peru.
1651 The Kuna rebel and evict all Europeans from their territory.

Introduction: Living under European Rule

After a century of conquest, imposition of political rule, and widespread death for Indigenous people throughout the Americas, the first half of the seventeenth century showed their increasing integration into mainstream society during what became known as the High Colonial Period in Latin America. Although Spain and Portugal firmly controlled the principal colonial centers of Peru and New Spain, the collapse of the Indigenous population had decreased Native tribute and labor in mines and had opened up new territories for the Europeans. The first half of this new century saw Europeans, especially the Portuguese in Brazil, turn to African slavery to replace the Indigenous workers that had died in large numbers. Many remnants of Native communities in rural areas of Spanish colonies migrated to European urban centers to survive as best they could. During the first half of the seventeenth century, many Indigenous people accepted European rule and some form of Catholicism as their dominant faith. In Spanish America, the mining of silver dominated economic production and attracted thousands of Native people every year as miners, weavers, porters, and farmers. Royal policies directed at the Indigenous population illustrated a shift from the conquest mentality toward the creation of a profitable colonial society where Europeans benefitted from the labor of African slaves and Christian Indigenous people. Specific examples of these changes include the expansion of the *repartimiento* system and the emergence of *haciendas*, the large farms and estates that by the end of the sixteenth century produced most of the food in the colonies.

Religious proselytism came to dominate both the Spanish and Portuguese efforts to integrate Native populations during this new century. Having eliminated the Tupinamba peoples through disease and hard labor, Portuguese colonists along the coast of Brazil started importing African people to work as slaves on their sugar plantations and sent missionaries further inland. Catholic missionaries and European colonists pushed inland to convert the Indigenous peoples and take the Native land for ranching. With royal and papal support, priests tried fervently to convert Indigenous people to Christianity, to defend them from abuses by the colonizers, and to control Natives' labor by congregating them in mission compounds. In the Spanish colonies, free wage labor gradually replaced the *repartimiento* system and estate owners began to contract directly for labor with individual Native people. Throughout the first half of the seventeenth century, Indigenous peoples in central areas reconstructed their communities to fit the demands of the state and Church and to try to make the new system work for them. Adapting to the society that increasingly enveloped them, Native people nevertheless did not relinquish all the cultural markers that defined who they were as Indigenous people. In the borderlands, this period saw some examples of determined military resistance, but overall the first half of the seventeenth century was marked by the gradual and ever-increasing integration of Indigenous peoples into colonial society.

Growing Integration into Hispanic Society

Indigenous peoples in central areas overwhelmingly joined colonial society, participating in religious and legal institutions while European rule profoundly transformed their lives. As the tradition of free wage labor grew in New Spain and the Andean mining districts, the number of Indigenous people no longer reliant on their communities of origin grew steadily. More and more Native people moved to *haciendas* and cities as their reliance on cash or payments in kind increased. As they changed their ways of life, many Indigenous people left behind Native cultural markers, such as their traditional clothing, or Native rituals that European society discouraged. Some received education, and a few wrote about their changing world. Over time, many came to see themselves as peasants within the European system who no longer identified with their Indigenous heritage. Native people who lived independently from their communities of origin, who in effect became serfs like those who had served the Incas, received the name of *yanaconas* in the Andes.

In New Spain, the authorities gathered Natives into villages to change their cultures and religions to more closely resemble a "civilized" European society. The Spanish appointed colonial administrators called a *corregidor de Indios* to collect the tribute they forced Natives to pay to the Crown. Many *corregidores* were corrupt and stole from the people. To administer their own affairs, Native communities organized municipal town councils patterned after the Spanish system and also called *cabildos*, composed by members called *regidores*, 4 or 5 serving in smaller villages and up to 15 in cities. Villages in New Spain also received a governor who oversaw their *cabildo*, distributed land, and enacted justice. Growing colonial administration divided local Native leaders, the caciques, who were forced between appeasing the *corregidores'* demands for labor and honoring fellow villagers' requests for leniency. Failing to balance these competing forces correctly usually meant removal by colonial administrators or violence from their neighbors. People of mixed racial heritage occupied many of these leadership positions because they could best negotiate between the conflicting forces.

By the seventeenth century, Indigenous leaders became adept at negotiating ways for their communities to control their own production and natural resources. Often leaders balanced these forces through the *cofradías*, lay societies organized around the cult of a saint through the Catholic Church. Many *cofradías* came to own lands and cattle. By managing funds from the Church and authorities, Native leaders tried to appease both colonial authorities and their own parishioners. The number of these Native people from original communities who lived on the peripheries of colonial cities grew quickly, and by the beginning of the seventeenth century their numbers roughly equaled the number of Native people still living in rural communities of origin.

One written example that illustrates growing Indigenous integration is the Huarochirí manuscript, a collection of Andean Indigenous religious stories and traditions currently held at the National Library in Madrid. Father Francisco de Ávila, a Jesuit priest who since the late sixteenth century taught theology in Lima and ministered in the Huarochirí parish near the city, commissioned the work from his parishioners to record Indigenous religious traditions in the Andean region. The manuscript describes both the spiritual and the human worlds of Indigenous people living on the western side of the Andes, who were aware of having once lived under Inca rule but were now rooted in rural culture on the fringes of the empire. In this world, Native priests still led ceremonies to worship the *huacas*, their holy deities, but the imperial economy dominated the peoples' lives. Published in 1600, the document provides a singular window into the early colonial myths, ritual practices, and historic self-image of the Native Andean peoples. The manuscript also describes the Spanish conquerors' arrival, although the contributors' memories reflect entire lives spent under colonial rule at the turn of the century.

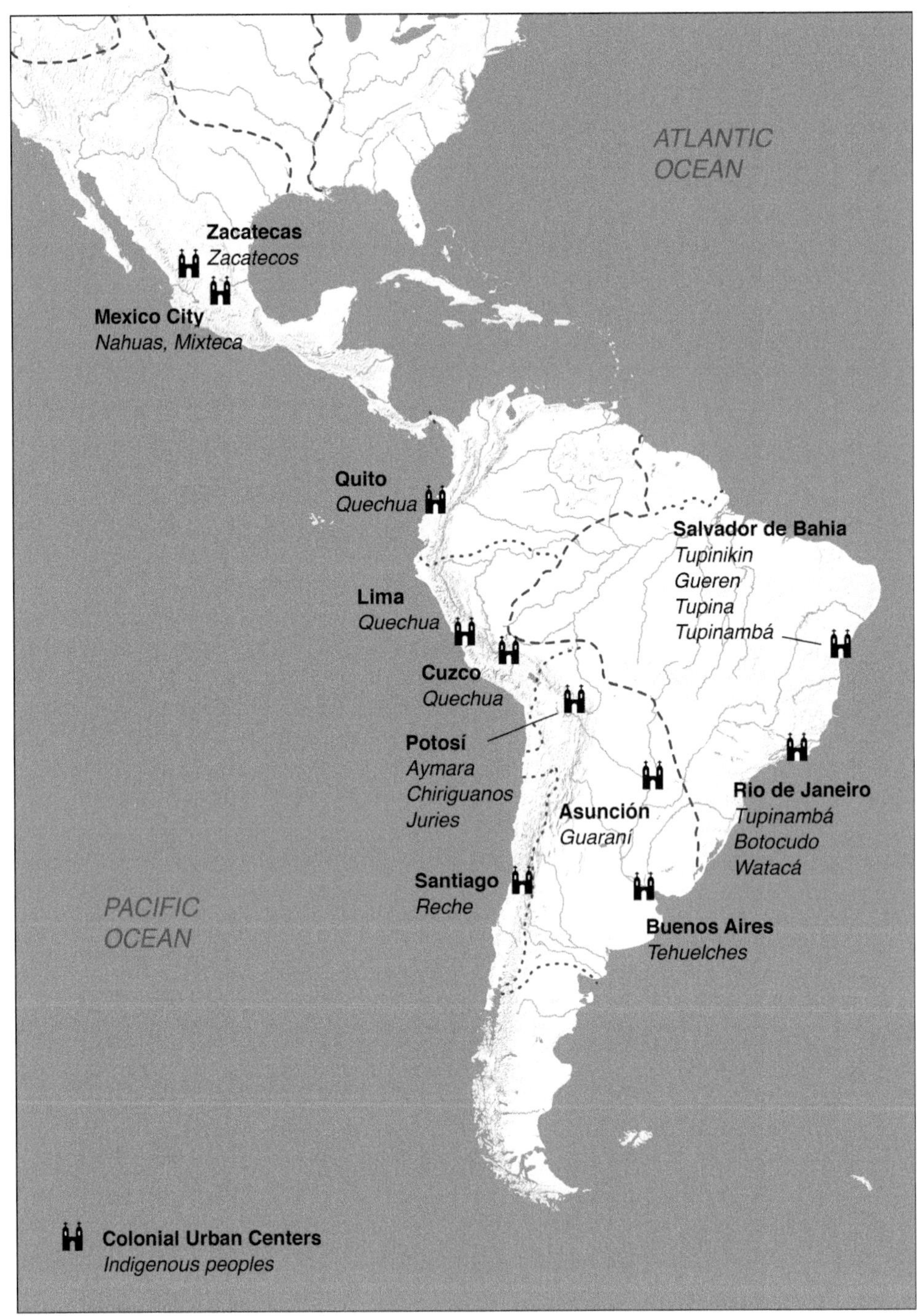

Map 6.1 Important Colonial Urban Centers and Surrounding Indigenous Peoples

Today, the manuscript is a valuable source to understanding Andean religious practices, but originally it also informed Ávila's investigations into the persistence of Indigenous religious practices under Spanish rule. This priest was specifically interested in traditional Indigenous religion, but after his Native collaborators had compiled the manuscript, Ávila employed it in 1608 to launch an official investigation to extirpate "idolatry" in the Huarochirí parish of San Damián de Checa. The results of Ávila's campaign were several broadly advertised trials, during which the priest and his allies punished Native religious leaders and demolished the Andean deities known as *huacas*. The priest's attacks, a process called *extirpation*, led to public judgments against the Indigenous practitioners by the courts of the Spanish Inquisition. To culminate Ávila's work, Lima's Archbishop oversaw the execution of the accused Native religious leaders at the stake in Lima's central square in 1609. The manuscript thus informed Ávila's successful extirpation campaign. Curiously, the priest also appears to have been getting even: Ávila apparently ordered his attacks in retaliation for the long and grim charges of "exploitation and mistreatment" that his own parishioners had leveled against him in 1607.[1] While the manuscript contains important information about Andean religious practices, it appears to have originally been Ávila's attempt to escape from an incriminating lawsuit by highlighting his own devotion.

For Document 6.1: Excerpts from *The Huarochirí Manuscript*, visit www.routledge.com/9780415519120.

This singular collection of Indigenous stories and beliefs shows that interaction between the conquerors and the ruled was growing quickly. European demands for tribute and religious fees, as well as rising Native desires for finished goods and raw materials, drew increasing numbers of Indigenous people into the colonial economy. With only limited chances to earn cash and with resources for independent subsistence dwindling, Indigenous people participated more and more in systems of credit to purchase enough subsistence rations and goods to survive. Colonial officials encouraged Native dependence on imperial markets. Within the colonial system of *reparto de bienes* or *mercancías* that developed throughout the seventeenth century, the Spanish provided raw materials and animals, including mules, to Native communities on credit, and then purchased the finished goods they made at low prices that included elevated interest on the money advanced. In this system, commonly called *repartimiento*, officials also offered goods to Natives on credit, such as textiles in the Andes, always at high prices. The elevated interest rates and substantial profits inherent to the system allowed officials to enrich themselves but kept the Natives in debt. The *repartimiento* not only provoked Indigenous anger, it also created a trade imbalance that forced Indigenous people into wage labor to repay their debts and into courts to demand reparations for the abuses they suffered. Perhaps worst of all, the system's opportunities for corruption divided neighbors from each other and leaders from their communities.

Events: The Inquisition at Work

The role that the courts of the Inquisition played in supporting Ávila's attack on Native religious leaders reveals the institution's firm establishment in the Americas. To defend and enshrine Christian orthodoxy in the colonies, the Spanish Crown had already established a Tribunal of the Holy Office of the Inquisition in

New Spain in 1569, followed by Cartagena de Indias (today's Colombia) in 1610 and then Peru. The tribunals functioned to limit "dangerous" political, religious, or philosophical ideas, although the vast majority of the cases dealt simply with immorality or blasphemy. During the sixteenth century, as officials imposed Christianity, the Inquisition took an active role in trying to change Indigenous cultures by rooting out Indigenous beliefs and "heresies," as they referred to any Native religious expression that deviated from Roman Catholic orthodoxy.

Using reports by informers as well as torture to force confessions and then expropriating the personal property of the accused, the Inquisition created an atmosphere of fear, mistrust, and strict conformity to orthodox ideas. Officials bound victims to whipping posts and then lashed them with up to 200 strokes, even for failing to report that their parents owned idols. When friars discovered evidence of Indigenous "idolatry" in the Yucatan in 1562, Bishop Diego de Landa ordered the Inquisition to torture over 4,500 Indigenous Mayan people, of which over 158 died as a direct result of their punishment.[2] For Indigenous people, who had traditionally accepted religious change and just added the gods of their conquerors to their own deities, such punishments must have been difficult to understand. The Inquisition targeted Native peoples and others of questionable faith for the next three centuries. During the course of the 1600s, the work of the office expanded to include all forms of heresies: in 1635, the Lima Inquisition attacked also the *converso* community in the city, sending some to the stake and confiscating all their goods. *Conversos* were persons who had publicly recanted their Jewish faith and had adopted Christianity under the pressure of the Spanish Inquisition. For a recent, comprehensive study of the Inquisition, please refer to Francisco Bethencourt's book *The Inquisition: A Global History 1478–1834*.

Native Resistance to Growing Colonial Impositions

Despite broad acceptance of European rule, Indigenous people also resisted such colonial abuses and increasing impositions of taxes and labor. Some Native people living within the colonial system resisted falling under complete control of the foreign authorities, mainly with daily, nonviolent resistance that subverted and complicated European rule. Native people most commonly refused to cooperate completely with imposed labor and tribute demands, trying to maintain some control of their lives as best they could. One strategy for collective resistance was flight. In Peru, many Native people ran away to escape the *mitas*, tributes, debts, and lack of food, seeking instead a life as a *forastero*, a worker who had moved away to a different community. Following their relocation, *forasteros* often married a local person and found work in their new location. Besides escaping obligations in their village of origin, one benefit of such a move was exemption from tribute and *mita* in their new community, which worked until the eighteenth century. By the late 1680s, relocations by *forasteros* cut the amount of tribute owed to the state significantly and, in Stern's analysis, constituted "a considerable Native achievement against formidable odds."[3]

Another strategy of resistance was simply to hide. To escape parish records and service in the Peruvian mines, mothers hid newborns and never baptized them. The Bishop of Huamanga noted in 1624 that so many men had either died or fled to live away in hiding "that it is impossible that one could fulfill the *mita* of Huancavelica [the mercury mine]." *Kurakas* also eased their own community's service obligations by pointing out mistakes in parish mortality records, having Spanish doctors diagnose mercury poisoning and remove sick people from tribute lists, and even by parading officials through abandoned houses to demonstrate that people had fled.[4] Indigenous claimants used lawyers in courts designed to address their cases to challenge labor quotas, the payments of statutory wages, religious abuses, and injurious relationships. While legal victories were expensive and the results often did not endure for long, Indigenous determination and persistent recurrence to Europeans' own theaters of justice shaped the colonial experience.

Occasionally, currents of Indigenous resistance burst into violent uprisings, especially around the hated mines, but Europeans crushed those challenges with overwhelming force. The authorities resorted to violence, imprisonment, and even execution to impose their rule. As the colonial economy fluctuated, Indigenous resistance on the borderlands contained European frontier expansion, which helped limit colonial profits and challenged foreign hegemony.

Indigenous people in the borderlands even drew some Europeans to their own side. Nowhere was this more evident than on the southwestern slopes of the Andes Mountains. Bolstered by their recent victory over Governor Loyola and their recovery of lands south of the Biobío River, the triumphant Reche received aid and support from defecting Spanish. In the year 1600 alone, over 60 Spanish deserters decided that Reche society was preferable to life among their own and settled among the Indigenous people, teaching them to forge iron and employ Western political skills. A mestizo showed Natives how to use volcanic sulfur, saltpeter, and charcoal to make gunpowder for captured firearms. The Natives were not emulating Spanish culture to change their own, but rather to discover European weaknesses and improve their own defenses. Even defecting priests encouraged the Reche to continue their own religious practices.[5] The Reche's refusal to submit challenged European rule in the region that later became Chile. By 1611, the Indigenous people had adopted horses so effectively as auxiliaries raided Spanish towns that their cavalry became an offensive force worthy of serious European consideration.

Yet the Reche were nevertheless fighting brutal colonizers: in 1603, the town council of Santiago began to stamp captured Native people on the face with a branding iron made of silver to indicate their impressment into legal slavery. The Spanish authorities claimed that such branding defended "pacified" peoples by distinguishing them from non-submissive peoples and identifying them as legal slaves. The military branded captured Indigenous persons and sold them into slavery. In 1627, Luis Fernández de Córdoba y Arce, Governor of Chile between 1625 and 1629, informed the king that his campaign to the province of Imperial in Araucanía had captured over 250 Reche and had killed or captured over 2,500 more in the territories of Yumbel and Arauco.[6] Soldiers on nocturnal expeditions kidnapped Reche people, branded them, and sold them as slaves to silver-miners in Peru, using one-fifth of the proceeds from the sale of each Native person to maintain the army.[7] Indigenous resistance in turn changed colonial society: besides forcing them to defend their settlements from attacks, their deaths from disease led settlers in Santiago to begin to import Indigenous slaves from Cuyo, across the Andes to the east, as sources of labor. Nevertheless, Spanish deserters continued to join Reche society.

Trends: The Colonial Economy

Indigenous peoples were key players in every aspect of the colonial economy, whether in mining, farming, or industry. Historians have long debated whether the economy of the European colonies in the Americas was feudal, mercantilist, capitalist, or some hybrid of the three. If production for markets is the paramount consideration, the colonies seem to have been partly capitalistic from the beginning. Given the wide varieties of exchanges and production in the colonies, however, a mixture of the three options prevailed. Mining was the most important of the three main economic sectors. Europeans quickly exhausted the gold, such as the great Inca treasure, that first drew *conquistadores* to the Americas. Then they turned to silver, mined largely by Indigenous people. Mining centers at Zacatecas in northern New Spain and at Potosí in Upper Peru produced most of the silver until about 1650, when smaller centers in Peru eclipsed the declining production at Potosí. From the mid-sixteenth century up until independence, Spanish colonies produced a staggering 100,000 tons of silver, 25,000 to 30,000 tons of it before 1685.[8]

Once the Indigenous population collapsed, Europeans created ranches and *haciendas*, the large family farming estates that comprised the second sector of the colonial economy. *Haciendas* spread quickly and relied almost entirely on Indigenous labor. Many estates were large enough to even have their own jails and gallows to force order and compliance. By the early seventeenth century, estates in the Spanish colonies were growing most of the crops and food for local consumption and took even more land from declining Native communities to expand their production. Indigenous workers in fields, mines, and textile mills, along with the African slaves on the sugar plantations, made the system productive for colonists.

The third economic sector included handcrafts and textile production, produced mainly in New Spain, Peru, and Central America. While Indigenous people continued to make their own clothing, pottery, and household goods, many gradually joined the cash economy to earn money needed to pay taxes and fulfill their labor quotas. Native people labored in textile workshops called *obrajes* that produced cotton and wool cloth. The *obrajes* grew until around 1630 due to the initial cost of importing cloth from Europe, and were concentrated in Puebla and Tlaxcala in New Spain, as well as in the Andes. While African slaves and sentenced criminals worked at *obrajes* in New Spain, Indigenous people also labored in such workshops in the Andes on the large sheep farms, or in their villages, to meet tribute payments. Some of the harshest labor took place in these *obrajes*: owners locked up their workers and held them against their will, as well as indebting them by using alcohol and withholding wages. One observer noted,

> In this way they have gathered in and duped many married Indians with families, who have passed into oblivion here for twenty years, or longer, or their whole lives, without their wives or children knowing anything about

them; for even if they want to get out, they cannot, thanks to the great watchfulness with which the doormen guard the exits.[9]

Europeans thus used Indigenous people to extract resources in all areas of the colonial economy.

Political Reorganization of Native Societies along Spanish Lines

As the Indigenous population collapsed from disease in central areas during the second half of the sixteenth century, the loss of traditional community support forced more and more people into Spanish communities, where they increasingly patterned their lives after the colonists. Even as their numbers declined, the Maya, Nahuas, and Mixtec in New Spain documented relations with their new rulers, adopting both the political institutions and forms of record keeping employed by colonial authorities. The principal liaisons between communities and the state in central areas were the *cabildos*, the elected municipal councils. Native *cabildos*, patterned after Spanish ones, left thousands of written administrative accounts that reflect their experiences under growing colonization. In central areas, the *cabildos* administered the political, economic, and social aspects of Native settlements, so there were plenty of details to document. *Cabildos* oversaw communal land use, woods, pastures, streets, and marketplaces, managing many aspects of Native lives. The municipal councils collected tribute and oversaw the *repartimiento*, linking their people to supervision by the colonial system, including the *audiencias*, the viceroys, and finally to the Council of the Indies in Madrid.

The *escribanos de cabildo*, the council secretaries, kept written records of these administrative bodies and their notes illustrate how the *cabildos* connected Native communities with their colonial rulers. One *escribano* in Cuzco, Pedro Quispe, who worked in the hospital for Native people, notarized documents of business conducted by Native parishioners. Quispe certified wills, death certificates, codicils, and property lists for sick patients and those close to death. Later the same *escribano* worked for a Spanish judge who addressed cases presented by Indigenous people in the city. In one lawsuit, brought by Juan Tupia, a *regidor* in a parish of Cuzco named Belén, complained that a drunken Don Gerónimo Chanca Topa had refused to work for the local church. "[H]e resisted and mistreated [Tupia], joined by some *montañeses* [a put-down for mestizos] who were his kinsmen, and they tore his shirt, and thus he displayed it before the judge and asked him to order [Don Gerónimo] punished." In the countryside outside of Cuzco, *escribanos* also notified residents in excellent Spanish of the legal changes that affected them. In 1638, the Indigenous *alcalde* of Guarocondo deposed witnesses to a fight that broke out when a "mestizo dressed like an Indian" could not pay for his gambling losses and had reportedly attacked the winner.

Throughout this entire period, *escribanos* also penned pleas for justice to church and state judges, despite efforts by the authorities to discourage such petitions. In November 1650, the *kuraka* of Oropesa, Don Diego Gualpanina, asked *escribano* Olivera to file a lawsuit before Cuzco's *corregidor* to confront a local *hacendado*, Francisco de Alarcón, who was holding an elderly Native man against his will. The authorities detained Alarcón in the Cuzco jail and interrogated him, although records do not indicate the outcome.[10] *Escribano* records show that while viceroyalties had designed *cabildos* to facilitate imperial control and check on communities' numbers, productivity, and observance of Christian rituals, Indigenous people employed these colonial agencies to protect themselves and defend their own interests. By mediating between Native communities, the Catholic Church, and the legal system, Indigenous leaders in effect "made the colonial systems work and created a hybrid colonial culture."[11]

As the examples of *escribanos de cabildo* show, the Church tried actively to reshape Indigenous cultures along imperial lines. In many areas, Catholic priests administered the *cabildos* and *cofradías* and tried to soften the impact of taxation by keeping parishioners agreeable; when the state tried to bypass religious authorities to raise taxes, Native people employed the churches to express their opposition to viceregal policies.[12]

Religious Transculturation and Indigenous Agency

Missionaries, the "shock troops" of the Church, spearheaded the push to control Native peoples. As colonial penetration grew, Indigenous people themselves employed religious organizations for protection and political advantage. In the Yucatan, where imperial control was still tenuous, the precipitous demographic decline forced many people to flee into the forests in search of independent lives or to join relatives still outside of Spanish authority. To pre-empt a military conquest of their area, the Indigenous people themselves invited the Franciscans to set up a mission in 1604. In response, Father Francisco Matías gathered over 761 Native people and their families at Tzuctok, although within only ten years a Spanish military incursion to the area prompted terrified mission residents to flee back into the forests.[13]

Along the Caribbean coast of New Spain, Carib populations and economies had been in decline long before the European arrival and contact. The Spanish referred to the area as uninhabited due to its scarce labor sources and withdrew from the coast. Then, in 1601 and 1609, the Council of the Indies issued new royal provisions that drastically lightened workloads for the Indigenous people. Regrets over the Native demographic decline played a role in this decision, but perhaps most to the point, the authorities finally came to understand that Indigenous people merited protection because they were the colonies' most important labor force. Viceroys and *audiencias* promised to obey the royal edicts, yet, in reality, they put more emphasis on keeping the economy going than on Indigenous conditions.

As did Native people in the Yucatan and Caribs, Indigenous people in northern La Plata also sought mission protection and capitalized on colonial authority. In 1609, Parané-Guaraní leader Arapizandú asked the governor of Rio de la Plata Province to send missionaries to his village. The Guaraní apparently hoped that if the Jesuits established a new mission south of the Tebicuary River, they would defend the Natives from the increasing numbers of Spanish settlers invading the area. The Guaraní also welcomed gifts of mirrors, pins, combs, scissors, glass beads, and metal fishhooks from the priests.[14] With acceptance from the Guaraní, in the early seventeenth century the Jesuits founded over 12 missions at or near Indigenous communities along the upper Paraná River, and 14 more among the Tapé Guaraní in the Eastern Band (today's Uruguay). Missionaries called their settlements "reductions," literally showing their intent – expressed in current terms – to "reduce" or "subdue" the Native people to Christianity, docile servant-hood, and life among the Europeans.

Figure 6.1 Caribs in Different Stages of Preparing Manioc to Make Cassava Cakes and Ouicou, an Alcoholic Beverage. (Public domain)

Portuguese Settlement and Indigenous People in Brazil

As the Parané and Tapé Guaraní example shows, some Indigenous people actively sought contact with missionaries. On Brazil's northeastern coast, though, Indigenous people were far less willing to move to mission settlements. By the end of the sixteenth century, the Portuguese had completed their conquest of the Atlantic seaboard and were pushing northwest toward the mouth of the Amazon. Within this area only the Waitacá people at the mouth of the Paraíba River and a few areas of Espírito Santo, Pôrto Seguro, and Ilhéus, defended by the Aimoré, remained unconquered.

The Portuguese had hoped to integrate Natives into their society as Christian subjects, but diseases killed off too many Indigenous people to make this goal viable.

Moreover, Portuguese efforts failed because the Indigenous men refused to serve as slaves in agricultural work, a job they had traditionally delegated to women. Men had routinely prepared the land for planting by burning the large trees and clearing away the underbrush, and then the women planted, harvested, and prepared the food. Traditional cultural roles based on communal, subsistent, and auto-consumptive use of farming products made Indigenous people unwilling plantation slaves.[15] Settlers tried to force Natives to weave cotton cloth and work on their sugar plantations, but differing cultural norms and the Indigenous peoples' fierce commitment to independence doomed the Portuguese efforts.[16] Life as hunter-gatherers and swidden agricultural farmers along the large rivers was completely different to slaving on sugar plantations, and Native people wanted no part in the Portuguese plans. As coastal Native societies collapsed from diseases, some peoples served the Portuguese as auxiliary troops in raids to attack their traditional enemies in the interior.

Despite their treatment, Indigenous peoples nevertheless made significant cultural contributions to Brazilian society. A few still lived in small settlements or in the dozens of missions along the coast, where they left their racial heritage, still visible today in the skin tone and high cheekbones of many Brazilians, and in the tough endurance of the wiry *caboclos*, people of Indigenous, Portuguese, and African heritage in Brazil's interior.

Additional legacies of contacts with Native people also shaped the Portuguese colony. Most geographic names in eastern Brazil today are Tupi in origin, as are many Brazilian foods, including manioc (cassava) and many dishes prepared from the manioc root, using the *tipiti*, a woven Native basket that stretches and contracts to squeeze out the poisons from the plant. Indigenous foods also facilitated Portugal's expansion to western borderlands. The Brazilian slave hunters, called *bandeirantes*, who moved west in the 1580s to explore the interior, search for gold, and raid Native communities for slaves, all relied on Indigenous guides and manioc as food to supplement game and fruit during their expeditions. From the Natives, Brazilian settlers also learned to use tobacco, pumpkins, sweet potatoes, nuts, and many fruits, including mangoes. North along the Amazon River, the raiders learned about sarsaparilla, ipecac, quinine and cinnamon, cocoa, indigo, and, much later, rubber.[17] As Indigenous peoples died from diseases, the Portuguese tried to move the remaining Native people to missions and began to replace their labor with African slaves to work the growing sugar plantations along the coast. Jesuit missionaries had been trying to resettle Native people into Christianized villages called *aldeias* since their arrival in 1549, communities that would also serve as a source of labor for sugar plantations. Tupinamba people considered agricultural labor to be women's work and refused to slave harvesting sugar cane. What is more, their rapid deaths due to disease made them an increasingly scarce labor resource.

Jesuits in Brazil had little interest in accommodating Native cultures, unlike missionaries in China and India, who perceived Asian people to be more civilized because of their architecture, technology (including gunpowder), silk, and paper, as well as their written languages. Instead, missionaries in Brazil imposed Catholicism in full as they tried to outlaw polygamy, ritual cannibalism, and even warfare between peoples. Jesuits also organized the mission *aldeias* along European lines in neat rows of houses and a church surrounding a central plaza. Through the use of Tupi, the common Indigenous language long used for trade on Brazil's coast that

Jesuits adopted for their missions even if it differed from the specific languages used by the peoples they were trying to convert, missionaries reduced Native cultures to a common base that increased detribalization.[18] The Natives resisted this forced cultural change by fleeing the missions; as early as 1556 a missionary noted that many Indigenous people preferred even to serve the colonists rather than remain at the missions.

As Portugal extended sugar plantations, pressures on Native lands increased. In 1610, the town council of Paraíba proclaimed that since sugar had become the foundation of Brazil's economy, "the harm caused by their [the Indigenous] farming was much greater than any benefits that might accrue."[19] Settlers wanted to clear Natives off the land to plant sugar. Clearly, colonial strategies had backfired for the Portuguese: the Crown had originally intended missionaries to alter Native cultures by concentrating them permanently into communities to serve the Portuguese economy. The process, though, had converted missionaries into defenders of Indigenous people against the very plantation owners who coveted Native labor. By the turn of the seventeenth century, as Native numbers collapsed (the number of mission Indians on the coast of Brazil had declined to only 4,000), and as Europe's demand for sugar grew, planters turned to African people for slave labor. By 1600, the Portuguese had imported 100,000 Africans from Guinea for work on their sugar plantations. The shift reflected not only demographics but also racial prejudice: all along the coast, where Indigenous people worked for wages, colonists valued their work less even than free blacks and paid them only in flour, cloth, and alcohol instead of cash.[20]

French Capuchin missionaries and colonists also arrived on the northeastern coast of Brazil in 1612 to establish a beachhead among the Tupinamba peoples in Maranhão. The missionaries believed that the people worshiped the devil and a host of evil spirits, even while admitting that Native legends, such as one about a great flood that had destroyed the entire world, and their belief in the immortality of the soul, closely resembled Christian traditions. For their part, the Tupinamba guided the French and helped them build chapels as a way to secure them as allies against both their Portuguese and their Native enemies. Nevertheless, the Portuguese defeated the French two years later, enslaving or killing off the Tupinamba over the following years.[21]

Besides proselytism, the early seventeenth century saw attacks on Indigenous people when they resisted colonial rule or were needed for mining. In 1609, King Philip III of the House of Hapsburg, who ruled both Spain and Portugal from 1598 to 1621, legalized the enslavement of Indigenous people captured in war. In Peru, administrators instituted the *mita* in 1605, adopting the Incas' system of forced labor for the common good to their own imperial ends. The *mita* obligated Native men to work two to four months per year in Spanish mines to mine gold and silver. The authorities whipped *kurakas* who failed to deliver their quota of laborers with braided rawhide tipped with cord, as was Omapacha chief Cristóbal de León Mullohuamani in 1612. The authorities baptized Native people to prepare them for *mita* service, so Native people understandably saw the system as slavery under the guise of education and conversion to Catholicism. Church officials also attacked Indigenous icons in their push to eliminate all vestiges of Native beliefs, as illustrated above in the case of Francísco de Ávila.

"Divide and conquer" was the key to Spanish control, and the authorities bought off leaders and separated conquered people from their communities of origin by giving kidnapped Indigenous children to surrogate Spanish parents, who raised them as servants. These young Native people grew up acculturated in the Spanish world, learning trades while apprenticed to artisans. Dislocation furthered the youth's transculturation and integration into the colonial system. Personal choice, though, clearly also played a role in cultural change as Natives moved to cities. The situation is comparable to Latin American immigrants who moved to the U.S. in recent years: parents face the tension of wanting to teach their children about their homelands of origin, yet also hope their children learn English and adapt to schools and workplaces in their new environment. Similarly, the move to the cities in the seventeenth century did not automatically mean the end of Native identity: the 1613 census in Peru shows that Indigenous migrants to the capital still paid tribute to home communities, honored loyalty to their original villages, and upheld communal ties.[22] Growing cultural change, though, was not reciprocal: in 1614 the Archbishop of Lima banned the performance of songs or *taquies* (a popular dance) either in the local dialect or in Spanish, ordering all Native musical instruments to be burned under threats of terrible punishments.[23]

Movements: European Migration during the Early Seventeenth Century[24]

Even as the Indigenous population declined, more Europeans arrived in the South American colonies. Between 1601 and 1650, an estimated 129,040 passengers and 64,776 sailors traveled to and stayed in Latin America, a total 193,816 people. Between 1601 and 1625, an average of 4,452 people arrived each year, while between 1626 and 1650, the number declined to an annual rate of 3,340 arrivals. The Crown regulated immigration and limited access to its own subjects, excluding Jews and their descendants, Protestants, Moriscos (Muslims forced to convert to Christianity rather than be expelled from Spain or Portugal), and Romani, although small numbers of each still entered the colonies. Most immigrants were at first young men interested in exploration and conquest, but after 1550, Spain instead encouraged artisans, professionals, civil officials, clerics, servants, women, and children to migrate, mostly from Andalusia in the south, Extremadura in the west, and the city of Seville. Migrants traveled to the colonies to escape growing economic problems at home and many had heard promising stories about life in the New World. By this time, ties to family had replaced adventure and conquest as the main reason for migration. Between 1570 and 1620, the Spanish population roughly trebled to around 400,000, although a decline after 1625 lowered the number and percentage of *Peninsulares* within the European population. Many immigrants moved from place to place throughout the colonies in search of better prospects, but most finally settled in or around urban centers. The European population of Potosí in Upper Peru, for instance, numbered 3,000 Spanish and 35,000 creoles by 1610. The swift rise of the foreign population led to pressure on Native lands and other changes for Indigenous people as they were drawn into greater contact with Europeans and their descendants.

Indigenous Declines Change Colonial Latin America: A Historical Debate

The Indigenous population, contrary to the European numbers, continued to decline, with varying degrees of severity. Native deaths changed the colonies at the local level. Most visibly, the lack of readily available Native people forced the Europeans to import more slaves from Africa since settlers would not do the dangerous work themselves, but other results followed. In New Spain, building projects declined along with the Indigenous population. Construction of churches and convents by the regular orders, which had depended heavily on the Native labor force, fell between 1611 and 1620 to the lowest level in 90 years. Demographer Woodrow Borah has argued that the decline resulted from the government's inability to find enough Indigenous laborers.[25] He showed similar difficulties in Guatemala, New Granada, the *Audiencia* of Quito, Upper and Lower Peru, and Tierra Firme along the coasts of northern Latin America.[26] Borah and Sherbourne Cook later argued that the Native population in central Mexico reached its lowest point of 1.1 million by the first decades of the seventeenth century.[27] Even as Native numbers bottomed out, European and African demographics grew through procreation and immigration. In the view of these economic historians, the decline of the Indigenous population helped push the empire into a depression.

Notable historians have disagreed with Cook and Borah and debated the economic results of the Indigenous collapse. Historian Henry Kamen has shown that while a cycle of economic reverses did indeed hit Spain between 1590 and 1652 due to demography, prices, trade, and production failings, the cause of this downturn was Spain's own dependent cycle of poverty rather than Indigenous deaths.[28] In Kamen's view, Spain had never actually "waxed rich and great," as some critics argued, only to later fall "away from greatness into a disaster of epic proportions that affected every sector of society." Instead, this historian suggested that the much-debated seventeenth-century decline was only a result of the persistence of the "organic weakness" long present in the Spanish economy, and was growing evidence of Spain's differences with its empire overseas. Visitors to Spain during the mid-seventeenth century described a kingdom devastated by the *Reconquista*: depopulated, demoralized by the Inquisition, environmentally degraded, experiencing widespread cultural contempt for commerce and manual labor, exporting raw materials rather than industrial goods, and facing growing indebtedness to foreign creditors. In this analysis, Spain had never been great; as its colonies in Latin America grew, they eclipsed the imperial center. The touted "decline" was, in this view, merely the extension of Spain's weak economy, conveyed by the ever-worsening differences between its strength abroad as an empire and its "organic weakness" in the imperial center.[29] Such internal decay and decline culminated in about 1640, followed by renewed population and economic growth funded by Spain's Italian, Flemish, and Jewish creditors. Trade with its colonies had, in effect, made the imperial center in turn "become a colony of European interests."[30]

Economic historian Michael Morineau has also challenged the seventeenth-century decline thesis, showing that the strong volume of trade from and value of the British and Dutch East India Companies "makes nonsense of the idea of a universal decadence" in the seventeenth century. This historian attributed the interpretation of a Spanish economic downturn to historian E.J. Hamilton, who argued erroneously in the 1930s that silver and gold production from Peru and Mexico had declined.[31] Instead, Morineau showed, growing colonial self-sufficiency in the Americas and smuggled goods from British and Dutch ports had reduced colonial demand for Spanish goods and the amount of silver being returned to Spain. By 1600, for instance, Mexico, Peru, and Chile were self-sufficient in grains and partially in wine, olive oil, ironware, and furniture. Historical evidence suggests that Spain lost American markets to growing colonial production and its own military and economic weakness, rather than to Native deaths. A decline in income for the Spanish Empire due to Native mortality might strengthen the argument for the importance of Indigenous contributions to Latin American history, but it would be historically inaccurate. European colonists experienced fiscal decline at the local level, as in the downturn of construction cited above, but they simply began to replace Natives with slaves from Africa and continued trying to make their colonies productive. The debate over seventeenth-century economics is a window into the way historians work, revising earlier theories based on emerging evidence, but it also serves as a reminder about not overstating the Native influence upon the development of the Americas without considering all the evidence. It would be up to Indigenous voices, rather than economists, to spread awareness of their colonial experiences.

Fortunately, a few Native people documented their colonial lives in writing and art. It was during this time that the life of an important source about Indigenous cultures in Peru finally ended. In 1615, at the age of 70, Guaman Poma de Ayala finally finished his long letter to the king of Spain. Since Philip II had died many years before, the Quechua author instead addressed his nearly 1,200-page missive to King Philip III and included a letter to Pope Paul V. Written in careful, flowing script, the book imitated current printing conventions such as page numbering and even placement of the first word of the next page at the bottom right-hand corner of each page, so the Native author clearly intended his work for publication. Ayala titled his book *The First New Chronicle and Good Government, On the History of the World and the Incas up to the Present.* His work documented abuses endured by Native people under colonial rule and made recommendations to the king on how to improve power relations and social interaction in his colonies. Ayala's text combined Andean Spanish with Aymara and several dialects of Quechua, so it serves as a great example of the growing transculturation of Native people and especially of the culture outside the capital, since the author was a noble from a provincial town instead of Lima or Cuzco.

Poma de Ayala's goal seems to have been to inform the monarch of ways in which his colonial administrators mistreated his Native subjects and to illustrate that previous Indigenous rulers related much less harshly to their subordinates. Shortly after finishing his life's work, Ayala himself died, leaving the world a treasure of knowledge on pre-Hispanic Andean Indigenous cultures and colonial abuses. There is no evidence that a Spanish monarch actually ever saw the finished manuscript, nor even that anyone at the time read the book, but it must have been sent first to Spain and then eventually somehow to the Royal Library of Denmark in Copenhagen, where it was discovered in 1908.[32] The book provides invaluable insights about Indigenous interaction with Europeans in the Andes, and Guaman Poma de Ayala carved the etchings that were used as illustrations in this book.

Amid Integration, Varied Native Responses to Expanding Colonial Rule

Even as colonial rule drew Indigenous people into greater interaction with Europeans, Natives still challenged their dominance on the Spanish fringes. In November 1616, the largest revolt since the Chichimeca War broke out in northern New Spain, when Tepehuan leader Francisco Goal tried to take Durango, the capital city of Nueva Vizcaya (today, this area includes the northern Mexican states of Chihuahua and Durango). The Tepehuanes had traditionally been agricultural people who lived in the hills and supplemented their crops of corn, beans, and squash by hunting. They wove cloth from cotton, yucca, and agave. Native conditions on this northern mining frontier were desperate, however, by the early seventeenth century. Devastating epidemics of *cocolitzli* (Nahuatl for smallpox), typhus, typhoid, and dysentery had decimated Indigenous communities in the 1590s, and then in 1602, 1604, and 1616. Jesuit attempts to concentrate Indigenous people into missions had only raised their mortality rate because it put people in closer contact and diseases spread more easily. In addition, as many Natives at the missions died from famines as they did from the diseases themselves.

Tepehuan rebels combined elements of their traditional faith with new Christian symbols, such as the cross and life after death, to channel their frustration; they did not intend to replace European religion with their own, but rather to repeal Spanish authority by replacing Catholic religion authorities with their own religious leaders. To undermine Goal's efforts and his allies in other communities, early on in the revolt the Spanish captured and executed 75 Tepehuan leaders and displayed their bodies along the roads surrounding Durango, which prevented a massive onslaught of Spanish settlers. Because the area was also a mission zone, Native anger at the representatives of the colonial religion figured prominently in the uprising. Nevertheless, insurrectionists killed missionaries, destroyed churches, and desecrated religious icons; at Santiago Papasquiaro, Tepehuan rebels whipped a statue of the virgin to symbolize their anger at how the priests had disciplined mission Indians, broke a cross into pieces, used the cemetery for target practice, and even burlesqued a religious procession before the assembled Jesuits.[33] Insurgents portrayed their deep hostility against the religious impositions that had forced them to move to the missions, relinquish traditional beliefs, and baptize their young, all of which had divided their communities. The uprising took a huge toll on the Tepehuan people. By the time the colonial authorities finally defeated the rebels four years later, the fighting had killed over 200 Spaniards, 10 missionaries, an unknown number of African slaves and mestizos allied with the Spanish, and as many as 4,000 Tepehuan people. Destruction to property cost as much as a million Spanish pesos.[34]

Even with the occasional uprising, the vast majority of Indigenous peoples tried to get by as best they could within the colonial system, and some of them did very well indeed. A good example of how Spanish rule was changing Native lives and cultures was the situation of the Mixteca people in the communities of Teposcolula, Coixtlahuaca, Tejupan, Yanuitlan, and other Native pueblos south of Mexico City. This highly productive land, as well as the large Mixteca population and workforce who lived there, made the area very desirable to the colonizers, who saw it as a great place from which to prosper. To augment their administrative control, Spanish authorities had, over time, converted these pueblos from *corregimientos* (provincial administrative subdivisions) into more significant *alcaldías mayores*, and placed smaller communities under the control of Spanish *escribanos*, and larger ones under a *teniente*. By the 1620s, as Native deaths grew, more and more Native caciques and wealthy *principales* in Mixtec villages, along with their families, Indigenous servants, and African slaves, moved to larger cities close to upper-class Spanish administrators and businessmen in search of jobs. In their home communities throughout this period, wealthier Natives bought up lands in the countryside to expand their farms and serve as added income, so that gradually the common lands disappeared.

One example of growing Native profit was Doña Inés Cortés, a wealthy cacica leader of her community of Ycapixtla. Cortés owned 15 mares and 35 plow oxen by 1632 on her *hacienda de labor*, a large agricultural estate that in this case produced maize. Other prosperous Native elite in the jurisdiction of Cuernavaca owned mule-trains for commerce. One noble Indigenous peddler in the town of Tepoztlán reported in 1640 that he traded "all kinds of provisions and locally produced merchandise mostly to Indigenous consumers."[35] The Native people in the common class who remained in the villages farmed, served well-to-do Spanish, mestizos, or upper-class Natives, made textiles, clothing, basketry, candles, ceramics, and durable goods, or traded plant and animal products at the markets. More and more Native people joined the hierarchical system as they accepted colonial ways of life.[36]

Increasing integration into the colonial system continued to change Native lives, but they still tried to control the extent and results of their transculturation. Another example of rising acculturation comes from Lima, where in 1619 Jesuits opened a school called the *Colegio de Cacique* to educate the heirs of Native leaders. *Kuraka* nobles began to send their sons and younger relatives to the capital to learn to read and write in Castilian under European standards. When they returned to their home villages, these youths helped change their relatives' ways of life. Growing integration, though, did not mean completely adopting colonial institutions; instead, people also turned European institutions against their rulers. As they learned to write and use Spanish, Indigenous people in large cities appealed to the Spanish legal system increasingly often to uphold their land claims, support their relatives, and strengthen religious institutions back in their rural communities. Half of the migrants to Lima also continued to pay tribute in their home communities; one tailor who had moved from Quito to Lima 20 years before continued to pay tribute in his home community.[37] Native migrants used Spanish wills to bequeath land and property to relatives and churches at home, showing that despite having moved to colonial centers, they continued ties to their rural roots of origin and their preferred religious establishments. During this time a Spanish man took one eight-year-old Native girl from Huánuco, a village nearly 140 miles northeast of Lima, to work in Lima, even though her parents had remained at home.[38] Colonial rule was changing Indigenous people as Spanish acculturation increased, but Indigenous people continued to shape their own lives as far as possible.

Growing Native integration into colonial systems also shows that rural communities continued to decline, although the rate of deaths from diseases had slowed down near Spanish cities by this time. Natives living inland were less affected by disease and the collapse of the population than those living along the coasts. By 1620, only 12 percent of the original Native population along the Pacific coast of Peru remained alive, while those in the interior survived in greater numbers. Migration to internal cities was therefore also a survival strategy for coastal Indigenous peoples. Throughout the seventeenth century the Indigenous population slowly began to stabilize. People began to regain confidence, and gradually began to claim their own identity as Native people living on the fringes of colonial structures.[39]

As the population decline gradually stabilized, colonial rule was also changing Indigenous societies culturally and politically. In some places, Hispanic culture shifted power from women to men. Women in some pre-Hispanic Indigenous societies had traditionally shared power with men on an equal basis. Societal roles had been divided along labor roles, but without the pejorative connotations attributed by European gender roles. In the Andes, women had at times even occupied political

Map 6.2 Seventeenth-Century Indigenous Migrations and Nonviolent Movements

positions of *ayllu* leadership when local leadership was passed down along the lines of matrilineal patterns of succession. Along the northern coast of Peru, women called *capullanas* had ruled Native communities by matrilineal succession, but colonial administrators imposed their patriarchal norms and altered women's roles to suit their European sensibilities and traditions. Starting in 1613, Francisca Canapaynina, a Native descendant of coastal nobility in Peru, laid claims to *kurakazgo* (chieftainship) leadership in Nariguala. By 1625, her husband Don Juan Temoche had replaced her as *kuraka* and governor, the central authority in the community. As a married woman, under Spanish rule, Francisca could no longer hold a position of independent authority, showing how quickly gender roles were changing.[40] Elsewhere in Peru, women also gradually lost positions of authority and took *kurakazgos* only if their fathers had left no male heirs. Once married, women completely lost their ability to rule.

Another way in which women lost influence occurred as priests imposed their own association of women with nature, paganism, and the devil onto Indigenous women. The establishment in 1610 of the Holy Inquisition in Cartagena, New Granada during the European Counter-Reformation led to additional attacks. To eliminate Native religions, the authorities, steeped in European beliefs of women's inherent susceptibility to diabolical influences, attacked the Natives' worship of the *huacas*, ancestors, and Indigenous deities. During the Peruvian witch-hunts of the 1620s and 1630s, the authorities tortured female herbal specialists, bone setters, and healers as enemies of the Church and the political order.[41] Indigenous gender roles changed with colonial rule and Native women often lost traditional importance as a result.

Colonial Penetration of Indigenous Territories

It was during this time that the Potiguar people of Ceará in the northeastern Portuguese captaincy of Rio Grande, who had come under Portuguese control in 1601, welcomed the French to the island of Maranhão in 1612 as allies against their Portuguese rulers. France even took six Potiguar leaders to Paris, where they were celebrated and even christened at the Notre-Dame Cathedral. But the Portuguese still had more years of experience in the area; to help expel the French they recruited Potiguar Chief Poti ("shrimp" in Tupi) and his warriors, a *mameluco* (mixed breed) and his Native Tobajara relatives, as well as warriors from Ceará. Both sides understood that Indigenous support could help determine the outcome of their colonial ownership of the area. Jesuit missionaries added 370 Native archers from their mission villages, as well as Tremembé and Ibiapaba Tobajara warriors, to the Portuguese force. This united front finally defeated the French invaders in a surprise attack on November 19, 1614 in the Bay of Maranhão; 400 Natives died in the naval battle, mostly drowning, as all their canoes were burned.[42] The Portuguese victory was disastrous for the Tupinamba, many of whom then switched their allegiance from the French to the Portuguese. The Dutch who arrived in Brazil close on French heels also actively recruited Indigenous allies. Chief Poti, who became a renowned guerrilla leader for the Portuguese, deployed warriors equipped with firearms and tracking skills against the Dutch, who for their part also employed Potiguar warriors. Most Potiguar responded eagerly to the Dutch, who promised at first to let them live and believe as they pleased. Despite initial tolerance, the Dutch eventually also forced the Potiguar to work for trivial payments in cloth as diseases decimated Native communities.[43] By 1627, there were no more than 300 bowmen left in 4 villages that had earlier housed large numbers of warriors.

In other colonial borderlands, Spanish administrators continued to try to force Native submission and acculturation through religion and settlement programs. In the Captaincy General of Guatemala, the Royal *Audiencia* decreed in 1625 a mandate forbidding "dances injurious to the Indians' consciences and the keeping of the Christian law they profess, because such dances bring to mind ancient sacrifices and rites and are an offense to Our Lord." Any Native person caught dancing the fertility *tun* or *Rabinal Achí* dance, a ceremony of words and masks that dramatized the ritual sacrifice of the son of the Quiché, would receive as punishment 100 lashes. These measures were part of the Crown's plan to impose a colonial society in Central America following so many years of war, pillage, forced migration of Native populations, and Indigenous deaths.

To help change Native ways of life, the authorities continued to resettle the people into *congregaciones*.[44] A result of such urban designing, especially near the capital Santiago de Guatemala, was that many Indigenous people lost their lands as growing numbers of poor Spanish and mestizo people moved into their communities to work on estates, hunt cattle for hides and tallow, make illegal alcoholic beverages, and take over Native cacao and indigo groves. Over time, living amidst the outsiders, many people left behind their Indigenous identity to become *ladinos*, people of mixed racial and cultural heritage.[45] What is more, friars of the Dominican, Franciscan, and Mercedarian orders continued to resettle Natives in the highlands into towns and villages to facilitate transculturation, creating some 300 *congregaciones* in Guatemala by 1600. Only in the highlands did people successfully escape forced resettlements and the diseases they fostered by fleeing back to their communities of origin.

Where royal forces were spread more thinly, as in the Panamanian borderlands, the Spanish used proselytism to undermine Indigenous authority. A young Spanish man shipwrecked along the Panamanian Caribbean coast, who had settled among the Kuna, negotiated the establishment of four Dominican missions in the 1630s. The 1,400 Kuna who fell under the jurisdiction of these priests, though, steadfastly refused conversion, especially as miners and colonists invaded in their wake. Following the mission initiatives, in 1651 Spanish authorities replaced the priests with troops, but the Kuna finally revolted in 1651 and evicted all the outsiders from their territory. Clearly, mission endeavors on the fringes faced challenges, although in central areas they contributed to widespread Indigenous integration.

Traditional rituals also empowered Native resistance, and in places they were brutal: in 1629, a Reche executioner in Araucania used a lance with three knives, representing their three strips of land, to kill a Spanish captive. After dashing out the victim's brains, the executioner reportedly cut out his heart and sucked the blood in gratitude for the victory.[46] It is important to highlight that amidst violent resistance, however, Indigenous people also used diplomacy to their advantage. The Reche could also negotiate when it was advantageous: that same year they skillfully exchanged a Spanish prisoner for three of their captive chiefs. The favorable trade demonstrates that in the southern borderlands Native people still held some power.

Indigenous Integration through Religion

As European control and Indigenous resistance increased, the Guaraní stood out because they continued to collaborate with the Europeans. Many moved to Jesuit missions in northern La Plata. Missionaries adopted Guaraní ways of life to encourage their acceptance of the foreign religious message, eating *mandi'o* (manioc) roots, bananas, sweet potatoes, and occasionally wild game, but they also introduced their own European cultural practices. The priests planted wheat for communion wafers and made the little wine brought from Asunción last for five years at a time, since deliveries from their European homeland were rare. Priests learned the Guaraní language and used a translated catechism; later on, grammars, dictionaries, and vocabularies in Guaraní written by Jesuit Antonio Ruiz de Montoya facilitated missionary efforts.

A Guaraní legend also assisted Jesuit attempts to influence Native people. The Guaraní traditionally believed that God had originally sent Sumé, a very wise man of tall stature and a white beard, to teach them how to grow manioc, harvest yerba mate, and instill good principles of religion and morality. Following his lessons, legends held, Sumé returned across the ocean and left only footprints on several hilltops. In their attempt to set their message in a local context and win Guaraní acceptance, the Jesuits replaced Sumé with St. Thomas, one of Jesus' 12 disciples, teaching that the apostle had come to the New World long before the Spanish to prepare the way for the missionaries, and had then taught the Guaraní agriculture, manufacturing, and correct beliefs. To help change Native ways of life and beliefs, missionaries and men carrying crosses then resettled the Guaraní in mission towns.[47] Jesuits used this story to expand their influence as they instructed Natives to cultivate fruit trees and wheat, practice animal husbandry, and manufacture basic goods. Understandably, missionaries faced the hostility of traditional healers because the foreign teachings undermined their own leadership, yet the Jesuit acculturation program clearly coincided with Spanish plans for colonialism.

For Document 6.2: Chief Artiguaye denounces Jesuit missionaries in Guairá, early seventeenth century, visit www.routledge.com/9780415519120.

For some Indigenous people, colonial integration led to hardship, especially when mission concentrations attracted slave raiders and forced Natives into slavery. Beginning in 1618, after Indigenous peoples along the Atlantic coast had died from diseases, Portuguese raiders from São Paulo, called Paulistas and *bandeirantes*, ventured west in search of new Indigenous slaves. Armed with muskets, shotguns, arquebuses, blunderbusses, swords, and machetes, wearing breastplates, and supported by between 1,500 and 2,000 allied Tupi warriors, these raiders trekked as far as 1,650 kilometers west into the forests to capture mission Guaraní and then marched them back in chains to Brazil as slaves. The *bandeiras*, as the marches came to be known, used Native people as well as Portuguese teenagers and African slaves as hunters, soldiers, scouts, porters, and paddlers.[48] These expeditions were rough: the raiders suffered rain, river rapids, thick vegetation, and innumerable insect bites. Snakes and other animals forced the *bandeirantes* to don leather hats, cotton shirts, coarse jackets, and heavy leather armor lined with padded cotton. Stealing food from Native villages, the expeditionaries pushed their way through hundreds of miles of dry grassy plains, swamps, and *caatingas* – dry spiny woods with thick undergrowth – relying on Native porters to carry their gear and no doubt nevertheless tumbling exhausted into their hammocks at night.[49] It is no wonder that the *bandeiras* captured the imagination of Brazilian writers over the centuries.

Approximately 70 percent of the captives in such raids were women, enslaved because of their expertise in planting and harvesting, and their children. The Portuguese forced Guaraní women to serve as concubines, wives, and servants. The long, forced marches must have been especially horrific for the prisoners. Those who survived the trip became slaves on sugar plantations and farms, or servants in the cities of Bahia, Pernambuco, São Paulo, and Rio de Janeiro. *Bandeirantes* enslaved a huge number of people; from 1628 to 1631, raiders burned down missions and forcibly deported up to 60,000 Guaraní from Guairá alone back to the coast, leaving as few as 4,000 Indigenous people behind; the raids effectively depopulated the former mission area and thus opened it up to European settlement.[50]

To escape the Paulista threat, after 1632 the Jesuits founded 12 additional reductions among the Itatín Guaraní south of the Tebicuary River, in the area that became present-day Mato Grosso de Sul, Brazil. Additional raids forced the relocation of these settlements as well, but fewer than half of the 30,000 Guaraní on settlements in Guairá moved to the new missions on the Paraná and Uruguay rivers. Those who remained behind gradually joined colonial society as peasants.

The new Itatín missions still fell under Spanish control and provided Native labor from the mission pool to local *encomenderos*. The experiment slowed down Portuguese expansion into the area, but the Indigenous people who relocated faced huge difficulties. Typhus, measles, and dysentery broke out soon after the move and as many as 5,536 mission Guaraní died from epidemics in 1634 and 1636. From 1637 to 1639, 4,600 Guaraní at the Uruguay River missions also perished from diseases. In the wake of the disaster, many Guaraní fled the missions, yet the Paulistas captured them and herded several thousand more people in chains back to São Paulo.

In a desperate measure, during the 1630s, the Jesuits armed the remaining Guaraní to repel Paulista attacks, even before permission to do so arrived from Castile in 1639. The Indigenous mission armies, armed with guns made from bamboo wrapped in hides and assisted by forest Natives who informed on the raiders' approaches, became formidable power brokers in northern La Plata. In 1641, a Guaraní force of 4,000 warriors soundly defeated an army of 400 Paulista slave raiders and their 2,700 Tupi auxiliaries at the Battle of Mbororé. A Guaraní Captain General, Nicolás Ñeengirú, and Domingo Torres, a Spanish army veteran turned missionary, led the Indigenous forces. Seventy canoes mounted with firearms on the Mbororé River supported their effort. The following year, in a second resounding victory, mission armies put a decisive end to Portuguese slave raiding and proved their military prowess to the Crown.[51] From then on, royal authorities in La Plata called upon mission troops when settlers in the northern reaches of the colony got out of hand. The irony of their own military value to the Crown, amidst Spanish prejudice and their difficult living conditions, was not lost on the Native people.

West across the Andes in southern Chile, the Reche had also organized themselves militarily and politically to fight the Spanish. The sharp contrast between the Guaraní and Reche is telling: each Native people responded to the invaders in their own way and for their own reasons. The Reche divided their region between the Biobío and Toltén rivers into three territories called *butanmapos* that ran north and south. Each of these regions had a principal chief called a *toque*, a war chief who served during times of conflict and who debated military strategy with leaders of the other two territories in a parliamentary junta. During the seventeenth century, the Reche not only added one more *butanmapo* but also extended all their territories north and south beyond their original borders. As historian Robert Padden has argued, the expansion of the Reche territory represents the growth of their strength and confidence during this second century of Spanish colonialism.[52] Evidence of Reche strength occurred in 1641, when at the Parliament of Quilín the Spanish finally recognized the Biobío

River as the official boundary between their colony and Reche territory. This was the first time in history that Spain agreed to the sovereignty of an Indigenous nation in the Americas. Clearly not all Indigenous people were peacefully joining colonial society, and differences between the Guaraní and the Reche are startling. Both had formidable military organizations, but by this time one served the empire while the other still fought the invaders.

The Transculturation of Indigenous Societies

The contrast between the Guaraní and the Reche responses to colonial rule is startling, yet it illustrates the varied and contradictory ways in which Indigenous people adapted to European rule, as well as the ways in which life among Native people had begun to influence the Europeans themselves. Clearly, Indigenous people did not respond as a single group and in a unified manner to outside impositions. Each Native people was at least as different from other groups as European peoples were from each other and certainly from African and Asian peoples and their cultures. Historian John Chasteen has defined the changing cultural process in the following insightful way:

> Imagine transculturation as a thousand tiny confrontations and tacit negotiations taking place in people's daily lives, always within the force field of hierarchy and domination. The people on top are usually able to impose the broad outlines of things, as in the case of religion, with those below contributing subtle aspects more difficult to police from above – style, rhythm, texture, mood.[53]

All that Indigenous people shared in common by this time were stories and memories of experiences from before contact and then their various relationships with the Europeans, but each group's experience was still unique, and linguistic differences made even sharing those stories a challenge. Interaction with the different Native peoples, though, also changed colonial societies in surprising ways, such as fighting the slave raids that were opening up the interior of Brazil to Portuguese expansion.

The Indigenous population's decline during these years exacerbated class divisions within Native communities, in themselves a sign of cultural changes. By the 1640s, the population of the pueblo of Tezoyuca was at its lowest ebb, and leaders in this community south of the Valley of Mexico capitalized on the situation for their own gain. Indigenous nobles had begun to lease out their urban and rural properties soon after the conquest, but as deaths made more land available, private rental agreements grew until they were as common as rentals of municipal land. In May 1642, Don Martín García, a Nahuatl cacique and attorney in Tezoyuca, leased some *pillalli* (private) land to a Spanish farmer for nine years at the price of ten pesos per year. García emphasized that he was acting by his own free will. The population of the town had reached its lowest by this time and Nahuatl demand for land was minimal. With municipal properties more available, leaders rented plots of rural and urban property to others, mostly non-Indians, for their own gain.[54] The case illustrates how market forces helped change cultural practices, in the process transferring Native land to non-Indigenous people, and shows that Indigenous people could also put personal interest above community values.

In addition, Afro-Latin Americans were joining and changing some Indigenous populations. In 1641, a ship carrying African slaves was wrecked at Mosquito Cays, on the Atlantic coast of Nicaragua. Two-thirds of the slaves escaped and settled in the mountains, where they mixed with Carib Indigenous people. Their descendants became *zambos*, a colonial caste term for people with African fathers and Indigenous mothers. Over time, foreigners identified these people with their coastal territory, first Mosquito and then Miskitu.[55]

Increasing trade continued to change Indigenous cultures, especially for Native leaders. Indigenous people near colonial cities adopted European trinkets, tools, foods, and animals that all changed their daily lives. They also borrowed European languages and apparel items, such as hats, which allowed them to better survive and distinguish themselves in a society under Spanish domination. Because the Europeans held power, their society became the accepted cultural reference point for many Indigenous people. The Native elite near urban centers imitated European practices and customs. In parts of northern Peru, *kurakas* dressed entirely in Spanish-style clothing, including hats, stockings and shoes, to show superiority. Although historians have emphasized depopulation and the serious changes it produced for Indigenous cultures, it is important to recognize that adaptation and survival were also central to Native lives in the colonies. The Nahua in central New Spain had also by this time adopted elements of Spanish culture that they could mesh with their own values, such as their self-designation. Traditionally these people had called themselves "nican titlaca," meaning "we people here." By the mid-seventeenth century, the Nahua were using Spanish names, living in Hispanic-style houses, and wearing European clothing, all while still considering themselves Indigenous.[56] Further away from the centers of power, at the same time, many Native people still lived a parallel existence or ignored Spanish society to protect their own identity from significant cultural change. Transculturation was clearly an uneven process.

Besides varying geography and cultures, Native responses also varied because the colonial authorities differed broadly in their policies, banning or endorsing Indigenous practices according to their own interests. The Reche still stubbornly resisted Hispanic impositions by continuing their own traditions. To close the noose more tightly, in 1647 the Captain General in Chile even forbid the game of *palin*, later called *chueca*, a sport resembling field hockey, in which players used curved sticks to hit a ball on a court encircled by green branches. The authorities argued that chasing a ball trained Natives for war and disturbed the peace. Even more abhorrent to them was that women and men gathered for the game clad only in feathers and skins to increase their team's hopes of winning, and even invoked their own gods for victory. Worst of all, the Reche traditionally concluded their matches in a big embrace and drank what authorities called "oceans of chichi" in a grand drunken spree.[57]

North in Peru, by contrast, with a longer and more successful history of transculturation, the Catholic Church had by this time developed a standardized form of the Quechua language to draw in the Native people through prayers, catechisms, and hymns. The Indigenous upper class in turn employed this written "mundane" Quechua to petition the authorities about abuses, turning colonial rule to their advantage. In 1643, four women from Antabamba, in the diocese of Cuzco, Peru, sought compensation from the Bishop of Cuzco for "illegal exactions by an abusive parish priest." An *escribano de cabildo* (scribe) penned the petition for compensation in Quechua and sent it up to a higher court. The outcome of the case is not included in the documents. Unlike the Nahua, rural Peruvian peasants themselves did not keep records in Quechua, though letter writing in their own language among the elite was widespread.[58]

Figure 6.2 *A Franciscan Priest Beats an Indian*, Guaman Poma de Ayala Etching, p. 499 {503}. (Royal Danish Library, GKS 2232 4 to: Guaman Poma, Nueva corónica y buen gobierno (1615))

On the colonial fringes, many Native people persisted in their opposition to growing mission influence. In the northern New Spanish province of Nueva Vizcaya, south of today's U.S. state of New Mexico, Jesuits had resettled 4,000 Rarámuri into 12 mission *reducciones* north of the Conchos River by 1649.[59] Owing to hit-and-run attacks and "continuous guerrilla warfare by Indian renegades" who refused to be settled, the priests offered food rations, clothing, tools, and trade goods to induce and try to make Native settlement permanent. Increasingly trapped by frontier colonial society, the Rarámuri turned for solace and encouragement to their shamans, who fostered hostility against the Europeans and encouraged traditional beliefs and pride in Native separateness. Strengthened by traditional religious leaders, Rarámuri forces fought the colonizers with defensive guerrilla warfare.[60] At about this time, missionaries also began to proselytize among the Ucayali peoples of northeastern Peru, who lived in villages in three main groups (Cocama, Conibo, and Piro) and spoke different languages. Sent to end "fearsome" Cocama raids, Franciscans entered the area from the south and the east, while Jesuits arrived from the north in 1644. Within a few years, thousands of Cocoama perished from what missionaries called a great pestilence: 70 percent of the people had died by the middle of the century. Disease quickly spread to the related groups and their large, complex villages.[61] Death still went hand in hand with settlement and cultural change.

Conclusions: Half a Century of Integration and Transculturation

The most notable feature of Indigenous history during the first half of the seventeenth century is that as the Indigenous population reached its lowest point, many Native remnants joined colonial society. The forces for integration and transculturation were powerful: unequal credit systems forced people into debt, difficult labor conditions, missions that physically protected Indigenous people yet changed their ways of life and beliefs, as well as the opportunity for Native leaders to improve their economic situation if they went along with the colonial systems. Caciques that adopted European ways or leased out communal land to benefit their own families, or the *kurakas* who sent their children to boarding school in the cities, all capitalized on the changing colonial system to their own advantage and fared better than the common people. Integration also challenged traditional female authority, especially through the Inquisition.

The demographic collapse itself displaced and decimated Native populations along the coasts. Beyond the deaths, however, the decline also shaped the colonial world in important ways: it began the African slave trade, diminished large construction projects, and brought Native remnants to cities for mere survival, changing urban demographics and patterns of production. The missions in particular were important forces of integration, but there also the story is mixed: the Guaraní capitalized on the Jesuit presence to defend themselves against the slave raiders, while the Tepehuan and Rarámuri lashed out at missionaries as symbols of colonial control. Despite collapsing numbers and integration, this period saw several violent responses to colonial rule, though only Reche resistance prevailed and even expanded by taking on Spanish tactics and technology. Finally, the further adoption of European culture allowed some elite Indigenous people to document their experiences artistically and in writing. Native *cabildos* kept accounts of their changing situations, and their perspectives serve as windows into colonial Latin America that help explain how Indigenous people understood and coped with their changing world during the early seventeenth century. If anything, this period reinforces the fact that Indigenous peoples were very different from each other and responded to colonialism in unique ways.

Discussion Questions

1. Did the collapse of the Indigenous population lead to an economic decline for Spain?
2. How were Indigenous resistance to colonial rule and to missionary activities related?
3. What would it have meant for European colonists in La Plata to have had Indigenous armies, armed and trained by Jesuit missionaries, operating and fighting in their midst?
4. Explain why the Guaraní and the Reche responded so differently to European colonization.
5. How did transculturation change Indigenous peoples during this period?

Notes

1 Durston, "Notes on the Authorship of the Huarochirí Manuscript," 229.
2 Clendinnen, *Ambivalent Conquests*, 76.
3 Stern, *Peru's Indian Peoples*, 114, 126, 154–155.
4 Ibid.
5 Alonso González de Nájera, "Desengaño y reparo," 10–14, 63–65, in Padden, "Cultural Adaptation," 77.
6 Korth, *Spanish Policy in Colonial Chile*, 164.
7 Jara, *Guerra y Sociedad en Chile*, 166.
8 Gerner, "Long-Term Silver Mining," 899.
9 Vásquez de Espinosa, *Compendium and Description of the West Indies*, 133–134; see also Walker, *The Tupac Amaru Rebellion*, 11.
10 Ramos and Yannakakis, *Indigenous Intellectuals*, 250–252.
11 Ibid., 3.
12 Smith, *Guatemalan Indians*, 15.
13 Chuchiak, "Fide non Armis," 130.
14 Ganson, *The Guaraní Under Spanish Rule*, 35.
15 Schwartz, "Indian Labor and New World Plantations," 46.
16 Hemming, *Red Gold*, 177–179.
17 Hemming, *Red Gold*, 179-181.
18 Schwartz, "Indian Labor and New World Plantations," 52.
19 Ibid., 54.
20 Ibid., 76.
21 Fishman, "Claude d'Abbeville and the Tupinamba," 34.
22 Charney, "Negotiating Roots," 145–147.
23 Galeano, *Memory of Fire*, 185.
24 Burkholder and Johnson, *Colonial Latin America*, 126–128.
25 Borah, *New Spain's Century of Depression*, 30.
26 Ibid., 29.
27 Cook and Borah, *Essay in Population History*, V. 2, 181.
28 Kamen, "The Decline of Spain," 49.
29 Ibid., 25.
30 Ibid., 43.
31 Morineau, "Eastern and Western Merchants," 249–250.
32 Poma de Ayala, *The First New Chronicle*, Hamilton, xviii.
33 Gradie, "The Tepehuan Revolt of 1616," 24, 154–155, 158, 167.
34 Ibid., 1.
35 Haskett, "Coping in Cuernavaca," 97–98.
36 Haskett, "Coping in Cuernavaca," 97; Spores, "Spanish Penetration," 97.
37 Charney, "Negotiating Roots," 147.

38 Ibid., 146–149.
39 Kamen, *Empire*, 360.
40 Silverblatt, *Moon, Sun, and Witches*, 151.
41 Ibid., 176.
42 Hemming, *Red Gold*, 211.
43 Galeano, *Memory of Fire*, 204.
44 Grandin, *The Blood of Guatemala*, 27.
45 Lutz and Lovell, "Core and Periphery," 39–40.
46 Padden, "Cultural Adaptation," 83.
47 Ganson, *The Guaraní Under Spanish Rule*, 30.
48 Hemming, *Red Gold*, 246–247.
49 Ibid., 248.
50 Melià, *El Guaraní Conquistado*, 88–89.
51 Ganson, *The Guaraní Under Spanish Rule*, 45–46; Hemming, *Red Gold*, 268.
52 Padden, "Cultural Adaptation," 81–82.
53 Chasteen, *Born in Blood and Fire*, 63.
54 Haskett, "Coping in Cuernavaca," 114.
55 Newson, *Indian Survival in Colonial Nicaragua*, 38–39.
56 Kamen, *Empire*, 360.
57 Pereira Salas, *Juegos y alegrías,* 127.
58 Durston, "Native-Language Literacy in Colonial Peru," 22.
59 Salmón, *Indian Revolts in Northern New Spain*, 176.
60 Salmón, "Tarahumara Resistance," 387.
61 Myers, "Spanish Contacts and Social Change," 145.

7 Transculturation, Urbanization, and Isolated Revolts, 1650 to 1699

Chronology

1650s	Four Itzá peoples at Lake Itzá, Yucatan, still excluding colonizers. Guaraní troops from Jesuit missions defend Asunción from Abipon attacks.
1651	Kuna revolt on the Atlantic coast of Panama, eviction of Capuchin missionaries.
1657–1661	Franciscans concentrate Cocama, Setebo, and Calliseca in missions, disease results.
1655	King João IV of Portugal appoints Antonio Vieira and Jesuits to proselytize and create Native mission villages administered by priests in Amazonia.
1659–1669	Zapotects in Oaxaca, New Spain, protest abuses by Magistarate Villarroel.
1661	Mbayá and Guaná-Chané attack frontier outposts and Jesuit missions in La Plata. Armed Guaraní from Jesuit missions demand protection from the king.
1664	The Carib allow the French to settle permanently in the Caribbean.
1669	Viceroy Count Lemos asks the king to decrease forced silver-mining due to abuses.
1671	British forces under Sir Henry Morgan plunder Panama City. Franciscans establish missions in northwestern New Granada and the Citaraes rebel.
1670s	Spanish Inquisition counters "idolatry" in Peru. Mixtec people in New Spain write last wills, testaments, and criminal records in Nahuatl. People throughout colonial Latin America formally appeal legal cases to the authorities.
1680	Pueblo uprising under Po'pay against the Spanish in Santa Fe de Nuevo Mexico. La Plata and Guaraní forces dislodge the Portuguese from Colonia de Sacramento. Guaraní from the Jesuit missions construct fortifications in Buenos Aires.
1684	Rebellion in Negua, Citará Province, New Granada. Peoples in the Southern Cone adopt horses. Mixtec accusation of adultery documented.

1690 Uprising in Tlapanoya, Atitalaquía (today's Hidalgo), New Spain.
Tarahumara attack Yepómera mission, Spanish defeat the revolt in 1697.
1697 Spanish finally subdue the Itzá Kingdom in Yucatan.
Guaraní forces defend the city of Buenos Aires, and again in 1701.

Introduction: Cultures Change as Most Indigenous People Join Colonial Society

By the mid-seventeenth century, most Indigenous people had come under European political control and had joined at least the fringes of colonial society. The system was weighted against them, and Native people faced challenging labor conditions and racism from the people above them in the hierarchical social structure. Economic and power differences divided some communities along class and gendered lines. European products and labor impositions continued to change the cultures of those peoples near or in urban centers, and religious missions influenced many frontier Native communities. In Latin American history, this period is called the "mature colonial period," implying a high point by which conditions created during the conquest had stabilized. Especially notable is the use of the caste system, the division of people into racial categories imposed by the Europeans to facilitate their rule. The three main groups – Indigenous, Europeans, and growing numbers of Africans – had mixed to a considerable degree, and people from diverse backgrounds received stereotypical categorizations, but racial boundaries were still visible and not as blurred as they would become a century later.

The Indigenous population stabilized and slowly began to recover during this period, entering what historians Lockhart and Schwartz have called a "trough between the quick loss at the beginning of the colonial period and the quick gain at the end of it."[1] Some peoples, notably in the Yucatan, the Pueblo in Nuevo Mexico, and a few Indigenous peoples in Brazil, tried to recover their independence and return to life as they recounted it before European control. Most Native peoples integrated instead into colonial society, adopting European animals and products, engaging in trade and labor for their rulers, and changing their traditional ways of life. The best term for this process is "transculturation," a term coined by Cuban intellectual Fernando Ortíz to describe the blend of American, European, and African cultures that created a hybrid culture in Cuba. In his book *Cuban Counterpoint*, Ortíz introduced the term to replace the concept of acculturation, which he argued reflected imperialist feelings of cultural superiority. Ortíz's term "transculturation" better illustrated the blending of cultures in Cuba.[2] The concept helps explain how people of different backgrounds created new cultures in the Americas.

Native cooperation with the Europeans strengthened the new society they were helping to create through transculturation. Communities that had grown too small as a result of forced labor or disease disappeared during this time, while peoples who adopted European technology largely survived. On the colonial fringes where royal power was still weak, this mature period also saw several massive and violent Indigenous reactions to colonial domination. Because Europeans documented these uprisings, the role of Indigenous individuals also became more visible during this period, although European perspectives shaped the way we remember these leaders, since most Native people at the time did not leave written records. Native leaders, like many politicians, organized their followers, negotiated with Europeans to promote their peoples' goals, and furthered their own interests. Native peoples in the colonial borderlands encountered Europeans during this time as the invaders sought additional resources. By the end of the seventeenth century, Indigenous people found themselves more integrated than ever. At the same time, many Natives had learned to use the colonial system to their own advantage in their ongoing and unequal struggle against imperial domination.

Widespread Cultural Changes

Although they ranked at the bottom of the caste system, Indigeous people who were able to do so took advantage of colonial structures, especially the courts and missions, to further their own interests. Their manipulation of these institutions reveals transculturation at work. Natives began to present claims in European courts as one avenue of redress against the more abusive policies of the colonial authorities. By the 1660s, the authorities in charge of Native workers still exploited their subjects and took advantage of them, but the people were now fighting back. A great example comes from Oaxaca, New Spain, where Native people used the courts to try to improve their position. Between 1659 and 1661, as many as 4,000 Zapotec people protested abuses by their *Alcalde Mayor* Villarroel (first name not listed). People recognized the position of *alcalde* as one of the most lucrative in New Spain for opportunities to exploit local people, and Villarroel took full advantage of his job to get rich through links to cotton textiles and the cochineal trade booming at the time.[i] Local Mixe communities also denounced this *alcalde*, but a *visita* found no serious infractions and allowed Villarroel to serve out his term despite the popular protests.

Document 7.1 includes a similar complaint in Nahuatl made by the town of San Martín Hidalgo (southwest of Guadalajara in central New Spain) in April 1653, against abuses by their town *alcalde* and prior. The *alcalde* forced families to work in a neighboring town, in addition to providing him each week with wood, grass for his horse, someone to watch the horse, fish, eggs, bread, fowl, water, a gardener, a guard for the church, five pesos for Easter candles, and wooden beams for construction.[3] Worst of all, the administrator never paid for these provisions or their labor. While the records do not reveal whether the authorities resolved this grievance, the documents show that the Indigenous people had begun to employ legal venues to counter abuses. With such offenses, it is no wonder that Spanish rule caused widespread resentment. The way in which Natives learned to manipulate the legal system and try to turn it to their own advantage, though, is equally notable.

For Document 7.1: Petition (in Nahuatl) from the town of San Martín Hidalgo, denouncing mistreatment by town *alcaldes* and prior, April 1653, visit www.routledge.com/9780415519120.

Meanwhile, even more abusive than the *repartimiento* was the *mita*, the system that drafted labor for the Andean mines, especially the silver mine at Potosí, still Spain's most lucrative source of wealth. Indigenous people in the Andes received no respite in their service to the empire. Officials took people from their homes to the mine by force, linked together by iron collars. The empire reaped the benefits of their labor: with its 86 churches and 200,000 residents, Potosí was by this time one of the richest cities in the world and still Spain demanded ever more silver. As the years passed, Native villages in Upper Peru grew emptier as wealth accumulated in Spanish cities. At the mine itself, in the early seventeenth century

i The cochineal is an insect native to northern Mexico and Arizona that lives on prickly pear cacti. After being dried, the carminic acid the insect produces, mixed with aluminum, forms a red dye, also called cochineal.

Map 7.1 Urban Areas and Mines with Seventeenth-Century Indigenous Integration

less than one in ten of the 58,800 Native workers were actually *mitayos*, laborers drafted through the *mita* system. The rest included 10,500 *mingas* (contractual workers) and 43,200 free wage earners. The drafted *mitayos*, though, did the deadliest work that others refused, carrying ore up the shafts to the mouth of the mine under challenging conditions.

In 1669, Viceroy Count Lemos finally asked the king to ease up on the forced mining: "There is no people in the world so exhausted. I unburden my conscience to inform Your Majesty with due clarity: It is not silver that is brought to Spain, but the blood and sweat of Indians." With great fanfare, the viceroy banned the week-long mining periods and proclaimed that Natives would work only from sunrise to sunset because "they are not slaves to spend the night in the mines."[4] Officials at Potosí ignored his decree, however, and the Council of the Indies refused to ban forced labor in the mines because silver was too lucrative. The abuses continued. The *mita* changed lives and cultures for Native people in the Andes as it forced them into the colonial economy and cities around the mines.

In Brazil, conditions were not as glamorous as in Potosí. Jesuits persisted arduously in their attempts to alter Indigenous beliefs and cultures, but like Las Casas during the Conquest, a few missionaries demanded greater justice. Jesuits had worked in the northeastern provinces of Maranhão and Pará since after the expulsion of the French in 1614, trying to convert Natives and defend them from "lawless" settlers and their sugar mills. These were the years in which the famous missionary Antonio Vieira, King João IV's close friend and advisor, began to minister in Amazonia at the age of 45. In 1655, the Crown appointed Jesuits to manage all Indigenous villages and placed Vieira at their head. To change Native cultures, Jesuits "descended" the Native groups; that is to say, they literally relocated them downstream to Portuguese settler towns and mission *aldeias* so that they would be more accessible to priests and more easily changed by European culture. Unfortunately, the process was also deadly: priests already knew that few Indigenous people survived such moves due to disease, hard labor, and despair, yet still continued the resettlements. In 1660, a "pestilential catarrh" of smallpox struck northeastern Brazil and Father Joao Betendorf described the results:

> The missionary fathers often dug graves with their own hands to bury the dead, for there were *aldeias* where there were not two Indians left on foot. Parents abandoned their children and fled into the forests in order not to be struck by that pestilential evil. Stricken Indians changed from reddish to black in colour [*sic.*]; their bodies smelt terribly; and some were struck with such force that pieces of their flesh fell off.[5]

Movements: African Slavery by the Mid-Seventeenth Century

As Indigenous slaves on Brazil's plantations died from smallpox and other diseases in the early seventeenth century, sugar barons began to replace them with slaves from agricultural and metallurgical cultures in West Africa who had experience in fieldwork and previous exposure, and therefore immunity, to the same epidemic diseases. The middle decades of the century were the peak years of Brazil's control of Europe's sugar market, and the colony's production surpassed every other place in the world. The Portuguese brought 600,000 African slaves to Brazil during the seventeenth century, while Spanish America imported nearly 300,000 people as slaves from Africa. Most slaves in Brazil worked on sugar plantations in the northeast and later inland at Minas Gerais, the General Mines, where they mined gold and diamonds, but many also cultivated indigo, tobacco, and cacao. Elsewhere, in New Granada and La Plata, African slaves were cowboys. By 1600 as many as 5,000 slaves toiled in the Potosí silver-mines. African slaves also made clothes and shoes in cities and served as carpenters, blacksmiths, and bricklayers. During the eighteenth century, as the sugar boom in the Caribbean eclipsed Brazil and established a new demand for slaves, the high mortality rate during the Middle Passage across the Atlantic became ever worse. Slaves in the Americas also lived in difficult conditions. Their quarters were mud-walled with thatched roofs and generally bare except for mattresses or hammocks. Slaves received cloth to make clothing only once in a year, and most plantation slaves went hungry. African slaves nevertheless contributed their language, music, customs, and faith to Latin American society and became an integral part of the continent's social and cultural make-up. While slaves outranked Indigenous people in the caste system, both groups mixed and began to blend cultures and races.

As they joined colonial society and came increasingly into contact with outsiders, Native people developed their use of nonviolent resistance against the vastly more powerful system stacked against them. Besides evasion and daily obstruction of labor demands, common nonviolent resistance included direct appeals to the Spanish authorities for justice. The Tarascan and Mexica people in New Spain were masters of this strategy, writing letters in Nahuatl to colonial authorities for redress of their grievances. In 1669, Indigenous people from the pueblos of Zaachila, San Martín Tilcajete, and Tlalixtac complained to their bishop about *repartimientos de mercancias* imposed by their *Alcalde Mayor*, who had been forcing them to purchase soap, wine, and 50 yokes of oxen at prices one-third to a half above the going rates. People in the town of Tlacochahuaya likewise reported their *alcalde* for obligating them to spin cotton and purchase oxen, chocolate, candles, soap, and wine; their claims show the official's profits at their expense to have been at least 200 percent. Far from "passive," as we sometimes regard nonviolent action, such Native appeals demanded bravery, knowledge of judicial institutions, determined community cooperation, and considerable expense. Indigenous people were learning how to turn the colonial system back against the very authorities who were trying to take advantage of them. Considering nonviolent strategies allows a more nuanced analysis of Indigenous history that counters the common depiction of one-sided European exploitation and reveals different facets of Indigenous agency and initiative.

The Last Free Native Communities

As Europeans extended their bureaucratic web into the corners of their empires to extract more resources, they tried to win control of even the last free Native communities. By the mid-seventeenth century, Indigenous peoples on distant frontiers had increased their attempts to keep out state emissaries and to evict colonists who had entered their lands. In northern Guatemala, in central Petén, the last unconquered Indigenous kingdom still resisted colonial domination. The Itzás had controlled the lowland tropical forests around Lake Petén Itzá since the mid-fourteenth century, and their remoteness and reputation as fierce warriors who viciously sacrificed prisoners had kept the Spanish at bay. The four Itzá peoples in the area spoke related Yucatecan languages and had arrived from Chichén Itzá during the thirteenth century, later taking surrounding lands in the early seventeenth century as buffers against the Spanish. Itzá leaders held power through royal matrilineage and enjoyed active trade with other Native towns for cacao, forest products, metal tools, and cotton cloths; they saw no reason to give in to the Spanish without a fight. Throughout the first half of the seventeenth century, the Itzá hanged, beheaded, and burned any European who ventured too close.[6] By the 1650s, interregional commerce expanded as raiding parties, refugees, and traders moved back and forth across colonial frontiers. Itzá communities also became havens for colonized Indigenous people who fled there to escape Spanish impositions and gathered around the Native monarch. In this part of New Spain, Indigenous people had long stymied the conquest; now Spanish attempts seemed even to be receding in the face of Itzá advances.[7]

Another Native People who still rejected the Spanish were the Kuna. Along the northern coast of Panama, colonial rulers posted troops in Kuna territory after Dominican missionaries left and the Capuchins replaced them. Miners and colonists followed close behind the missionaries, but the Kuna revolted in 1651, torturing two Capuchins and driving priests, soldiers, miners, and other settlers out of their land. This people kept all but a few Dominicans at bay for the remainder of the century.[8] During this time, the Kuna allied themselves with pirates based in Jamaica who frequented their coasts, and together they held off Spanish control. Alliances with outsiders would prove a successful resistance strategy against the Spanish for Native peoples along the Atlantic side of the isthmus.

In Peru, the Ucayali peoples on the eastern side of the Andes continued to resist the missionaries sent to convert them, even though diseases followed contact with outsiders. The large, complex societies along the lower Ucayali River practically disappeared during the 1650s due to disease, leading to understandable opposition among the remaining people to increased contact with Europeans. The Cocama nation met Franciscans again in 1657, when missionaries established four new mission villages. Once again, disease struck the people and spread quickly. Ignoring such deaths, missionaries congregated over 2,000 neighboring Setebo people by 1661, though many more remained in the forests. The Setebo eventually forced out the missionaries. In 1663, a mission gathered together many Calliseca people, who also evicted the missionaries after five years. Fear of death when living among the Europeans seems to have largely motivated such resistance: during the 1660s, diseases decimated the people who remained in the missions by as much as 70 percent. Natives on many colonial frontiers continued to resist mission efforts, and their opposition forced both Jesuits and Franciscans out of eastern Peru by 1668.[9]

Retreat from mission efforts was another Indigenous response to foreign intrusions, though one that ultimately failed in the long term. During the mid-seventeenth century, Portuguese colonists from Maranhão pushed west into Amazonia in search of Indigenous workers for sugar and tobacco plantations. Missionaries accompanied and competed with these incursions, ostensibly to defend Native people from the plantation owners but also to secure converts. Native people fled both advances; by the end of the century, the few remaining Omagua peoples from the Amazonian floodplains had retreated west all the way up to the river's headwaters in Peru, while the Manao and Tapajós of the middle and lower Amazon disappeared completely.[10] Evading the Portuguese colonists did not have positive results for many Amazonian peoples, but neither did integration into the expanding colonial society.

The Guaraní to the south continued to be exceptions to patterns elsewhere, even in Amazonia, especially when it came to settlement on mission compounds. These people actually gained significant political leverage by cooperating with Jesuits at the 30 missions along the Paraná and Uruguay rivers. After Guaraní troops defeated the Paulistas at Mbororé in 1641, the Jesuits kept mission troops on a war footing. The Guaraní took weapons to church in case of unexpected attacks and their possession of firearms alarmed Spanish settlers. Guaraní men, with a long tradition as warriors, volunteered to mission militias in return for greater autonomy within colonial society. Authorities in Buenos Aires and in Spain depended increasingly on the eight mission militias to keep rebellious European settlers in line. The Crown's use of Indigenous troops understandably caused great resentment among the colonists against both the Jesuits and the mission Guaraní. Not only did colonists resent the Jesuits' exemption from the *alcabala* sales tax and their free access to Indigenous labor, but the mission Natives, who they despised, now offered a formidable military advantage to the Crown when the settlers rebelled. Colonists, however, should have been more appreciative of Guaraní troops: mission armies fought practically every year during the mid-seventeenth century to defend Asunción against attacks by Abipones warriors from the Chaco region. Such military experiences empowered the Guaraní.

On the Fringes of Colonial Rule: Lingering Borderland Conflicts

On the colonial borderlands, those areas outside of direct European control, colonial expansion divided Native peoples. In Panama, pirates who attacked Spanish towns used Native warriors as auxiliaries, yet Indigenous people fought on both sides. Mission Kuna fought alongside the Spanish against Sir Henry Morgan, the infamous British admiral and privateer, who nevertheless took the city of Portobelo in 1668 and plundered Panama City in 1671. On the fields outside the city, though, other Kuna fought with Morgan against their own mission kin and the Spanish colonists. For the next two decades, the Kuna also sold their crops to pirates and guided them across the isthmus to raid Spanish gold-mines along the Pacific.[11] Figure 7.1 showing the Kuna council meeting implies that leaders met to establish consensual plans, yet Kuna actions reveal that they acted as individual communities rather than in response to a unified decision across Kuna Yala. When the Kuna fought on both sides of the European struggle for Panama City, they in effect helped the Europeans conquer new territories and undermined themselves.

During these same years, other frontiers were aflame as Indigenous peoples repelled Spanish settlers and their Native allies. Guaicurú peoples in northern La Plata attacked European settlements and missions repeatedly, threatening Spanish expansion outside of Asunción, where the Guaraní were still their allies. The Mbayá and their Guaná-Chané allies hit frontier outposts and missions in 1661, fleeing with cattle and booty. Threatened by these attacks, priests at the missions had a difficult time keeping the

Figure 7.1 "Seventeenth-Century Kuna in Council," Image, in Lionel Wafer, *A New Voyage and Description of the Isthmus of America* (London, 1699). (Public domain)

armed Guaraní in line. Five missions rose up against Jesuit control in 1661 under the leadership of a young leader, Pedro Mbaiuguá, who argued that the priests had only religious authority and that Guaraní militia captains should be responsible only to the king. Native people clearly distinguished between royal and local authorities, as well as political versus religious control. Curiously, these arguments resemble justifications that creole patriots used 150 years later when seeking to cast off Spanish control. The older Guaraní themselves, faithful to their priests, finally put down the rebellion.[12] Meanwhile, Mbayá warriors bypassed the six forts that the authorities built on the western side of the Paraguay River to stop their raids and attacked other towns. In 1673, the Mbayá raided Atyrá, capturing 120 villagers, and then joined Eyiguayegi warriors to harass additional settlements. Spanish troops finally massacred the Chaco raiders in 1678.[13]

Along South America's northwestern coasts during these years, the authorities were trying to settle and convert the five remaining Indigenous peoples in the Chocó: the Soruco, Noanama, Citará, Burgumia, and Tatamá peoples who had long kept the Spanish out of their lands. Franciscans established a mission there in 1671, about the same time that miners began prospecting in the area for gold. Local Native culture, focused on slash-and-burn agriculture and life in small communities, made settling, converting, and putting them to work difficult, but their remoteness allowed miners to make intolerable demands without repercussions. The Soruco and Burgumia remained outside of royal control for the rest of the century due to their violent resistance, though smallpox weakened them by 1670. The Tatamá built a church for missionaries in 1673, but fled as soon as they had finished. Natives refused to tolerate priests' authority and would not attend catechism nor provide the friars with food. When necessary, they escaped from mission settlements. In May 1674, and again in 1676, the Citará rebelled and tried to kill the Franciscans. Then, in 1679, leaders from the three main settlements filed legal complaints against the Franciscans and a Spanish official for having killed one of their people, for confiscating their tools, and for slaughtering their animals in an attempt to forcefully move their community. After a Spanish expeditionary force stole their food supplies the following year, Natives torched the mission settlement of Lloró, blocked roads into the area, demanded the replacement of authorities, and threatened to retreat if ignored.[14]

Finally, in January 1684, the community of Negua rose in rebellion and their insurrection spread throughout the area. Three villages launched a surprise attack on Spanish settlers, killing over 100 missionaries, miners, traders, mestizos, mulattos, slaves, and Native porters. Hundreds of Indigenous people revolted throughout the province, burning settlements and churches, and stealing church ornaments and female slaves, who they especially prized, as well as machetes, clothing, and gold used to purchase axes from settlers and traders. While some Native people seem to have focused on looting rather than killing, in Negua the rebels massacred all Spanish and mestizo residents, decapitating four victims and burning the body of the missionary, and massacring traders, slaves, servants, women, and even children. Only six Spaniards in the entire Citará province lived through the uprising, and it took three expeditionary forces of hundreds of Spanish and auxiliary Native troops to repress the rebellion. Amidst the violence, a small group of Native people remained loyal to the colonists: food suppliers, letter carriers, and informers who captured many rebels made the colonists' survival possible. The rebels actually threatened a few of these loyalists, Captains Rodrigo Pivi and Juan Mitiguirre, likely because Spanish authorities had earlier honored them with the title of Indian *gobernadores* of their settlements. These loyalists adopted Spanish names and received the title of hereditary cacique for having helped resolve the conflict. The war in Chocó lasted up until August 1687, when the authorities sent the severed head of principal rebel leader Quirubira to the Spanish king to prove they had finally defeated the uprising.[15]

On the northern reaches of the Spanish Empire, conditions had also become unbearable for the pueblo peoples, who included the Piro, Hopi, Zuñi, Tano, and Keresan groups. By 1680 there were only 17,000 people left in 40 pueblos, far fewer than the estimated 80,000 in 1598, when Oñate founded the colony of Nuevo Mexico. Since their arrival, settlers had relied on Indigenous tribute to stay alive, demanding so much in hides and food from Native stores that they destroyed trading patterns and left the people naked and starving in the winter. Periodic epidemics, such as the smallpox that had killed over 3,000 people in 1640, decimated pueblo communities. Franciscan missionaries built their churches directly on top of existing pueblos and used torture to impose Catholic doctrine and eliminate Native practices, so the people took their religion underground, both literally and figuratively, since they had worshiped their kachina deities in underground rooms and now began doing so in secret. Even the baptized Hopi rebelled regularly, killing priests to keep them silent and stop abuses. In 1640, Fray Salvador de Guerra whipped a puebloan man brutally for praying to "idols" until blood covered his victim, and then poured hot turpentine on his wounds; the man died from his torture. Priests punished rebellious youth by castration and acts of sodomy, and fathered illegitimate children with Native women. Overwhelmed by *repartimiento* demands, puebloans fled their home villages and some even allied themselves with their enemies, the Apaches, raiding Spanish settlements and supply trains.

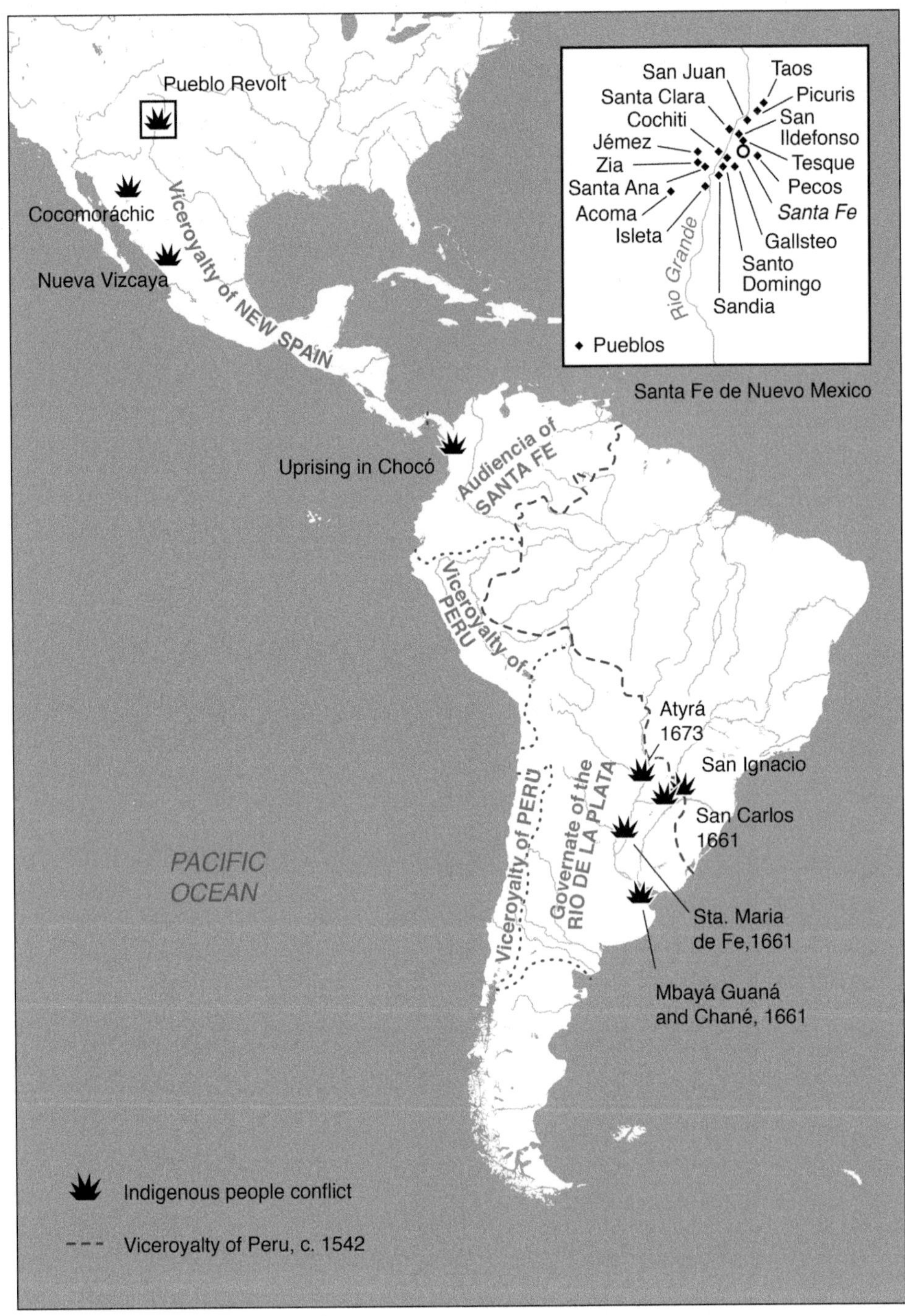

Map 7.2 Late Seventeenth-Century Indigenous Uprisings and Rebellions

Recent historians have revised early interpretations of the Pueblo Revolt focused on the Catholic displacement of Native religion. Rather than the religious causes, these newer examinations have emphasized instead catalysts such as famine and epidemics, as well as forced labor. Over the past decade especially, research on Nuevo Mexico's growing integration into the silver economy has shown that increasing exploitation of the pueblo people, including enslavement into silver mining and *obrajes*, as well as increasing numbers of Spanish raids to secure Apache slaves, pushed the pueblo peoples toward rebellion.[16]

The situation only worsened. A drought from 1666 to 1670 destroyed Native harvests, and the Europeans took the remaining staples for themselves. In desperation, Native peoples ate soaked leather boiled with herbs, yet starved nevertheless. To make this bad situation worse, in 1675, Governor Treviño, the colonial administrator, tried to detract attention by setting in motion a campaign against "idolatry." He arrested 47 pueblo "sorcerers" for practicing their kachina religion and hanged three as examples. One youth committed suicide by hanging. An army of 70 desperate pueblo warriors descended upon Santa Fe, forced their way into the governor's quarters, and threatened to kill him and revolt against the entire community unless he released their healers. The governor caved in, and one of the leaders he released, Po'pay, moved to the northernmost pueblo of Taos, and made plans to revolt. Po'pay roused the people's anger by presenting them with images of a better future that contrasted sharply with their desperate conditions.

Individuals: Po'pay and Individual Leadership within Indigenous History

Po'pay was a healer from the San Juan pueblo and an important leader of his Tema people. He was about 45 years old when the Spanish arrested and flogged him and other healers in 1675. His supporters marched to Santa Fe to demand the release of all their healers. This experience led Po'pay to consult the spirits in the Taos kiva, where he received instructions to reject everything Spanish and organize his people to drive out the colonizers. With divine sanction, in the summer of 1680, Po'pay secretly set in motion his plan to fight the Spanish. Showing exceptional skill as an organizer, the leader sent runners sworn to secrecy by pain of death to all the other pueblos. The war chiefs and even mestizo leaders joined his conspiracy. Po'pay ordered the murder of his own son-in-law, the governor of a pueblo, for fear that he might betray the uprising due to his pro-Hispanic sympathies. The healer told his followers to wash with yucca in streams to remove their Christian baptism, forbade the use of Spanish, and pressured his adherents to abandon their partners if Catholic priests had blessed their marriage. To motivate his followers, Po'pay promised what they most desired: happiness, health, and prosperity to the hungry, the same number of wives as the number of Spanish they killed, liberation, and free land for all. Once the Spanish were out of the way, he predicted, they would "break the lands and enlarge their cultivated fields … free from the labor they performed for the religious and the Spaniards." Po'pay assured his followers that if they respected the katsina, the spiritual messengers who brought rain and helped people complete their everyday activities and mediate with deities, the spirits would return to initiate a new age. The resulting uprising shows that Po'pay had an unusual ability to motivate his people.

The Pueblo rebels revolted on a dark night of the new moon in early August 1680, a few days before the resupply caravan from Mexico City was due to arrive. On August 9, Po'pay sent out runners to announce the event. The following day, pueblos throughout northern New Mexico and as far west as the Hopi mesas in today's Arizona, rose to expel the conquerors. Natives killed 19 of the 33 friars in New Mexico and massacred 380 Spanish settlers, including women and children. A few days later, 500 rebels descended upon Santa Fe, torching cornfields and villas on both sides of the Santa Fe River as they drew near. An army of 2,500 warriors besieged the city for five days until dead animals rotted and people died of thirst. Desperate, on August 20, Governor Otermín and his 100 soldiers fought their way out of the stockade, killing over 300 pueblo warriors in their escape. Only around 2,000 people of European background escaped and beat a frantic retreat south to Nueva Vizcaya. It took the Spanish 14 years to reconquer Nuevo Mexico.

Horses Change Indigenous Cultures

Even as some Indigenous people resisted Spanish expansion, they increasingly adopted European products and animals. It was in the second half of the seventeenth century that the Reche west of the Andes, the Tehuelche and Puelche east of the Andes on the Pampas, and the Abipón, Mocobí, and Q'om in the Chaco region all adopted horses, which significantly changed their ways of life. On North America's Great Plains, horses similarly improved the quality of Indigenous lives, especially for Native women, who had carried the loads when their group migrated. This cultural change also produced the decline in agriculture, a shift from female to male influence, and more raiding as the status of warriors increased. Horses became these peoples' great tool for mobility, bearing furniture and housing during seasonal moves. Warriors did not fight on horseback, but instead used the animals to escape quickly after battles. On the eastern Pampas, likewise, four groups became equestrians: northernmost were the Charrua and the Querandí, who used horses to pursue the wild cattle that overran the *Eastern Band*, as people at the time referred to the territory which became the country of Uruguay. The Tehuelche and Puelche of the northern Pampas lived in smaller groups, and horses made their hunting a group activity over a larger area rather than individual pursuits of prey. In Chile, the Reche used horses to increase their mobility, which interestingly decreased intermarriage between different groups, because communities moved more frequently and lost contact with other communities.[17]

Trends: Additional Countries and Cultures Shape Latin America

As the Spanish and Portuguese worked to change Indigenous cultures and extract wealth from their colonies, their European neighbors became interested in their imperial success. While making inroads into northeastern Brazil, the Dutch defeated the entire Spanish silver fleet near Havana in the 1620s, the same decade that the English settled in the Lesser Antilles to access tropical products. Strapped for cash, the Spanish authorities put little energy and money into defending peripheral areas such as the Caribbean or New Granada, so Northern Europeans began to trade profitably with Indigenous peoples where Spanish control was weak. By 1650, the English and French had settled the Leeward and Windward Islands and what became the English Barbados. Using indentured European servants for labor, settlers at first raised tropical crops, but soon imitated the Portuguese and brought African slaves to harvest sugar. By the late seventeenth century, private companies were producing thousands of tons of sugar for growing markets in Europe. These enterprises went hand in hand with the rise in the area of communities of transatlantic pirates. Outcasts from British and French colonies, these shipwrecked sailors and runaway servants hunted cattle to supply ships with dried beef and hides, much as the gauchos did in southern South America.

By the late seventeenth century, French pirates controlled western Hispaniola (the area that became Haiti following independence) and the island of Tortuga (Turtle). The English recognized the British pirates based in Jamaica and gave their leaders official posts to employ them as a force against Spanish rivals. During the 1680s, pirates raided Spanish ports in the Caribbean repeatedly, even crossing the isthmus to take the city of Panama. The late seventeenth century was the time of the classic pirating stories, and it was inevitable that in their marauding, these unofficial British, Dutch, and French auxiliaries would interact with Indigenous peoples and shape the history of the Caribbean.

Contact with Northern Europeans benefitted some Native Caribbean people and affected other negatively. The Carib, in the Guayana-Caribbean region between the Amazon and Orinoco rivers, traded with the Northern Europeans and served them as military allies, which benefitted their own survival. Enemies of the Spanish, the Carib allied with the English, Dutch, and French against the Iberians and manipulated these outsiders to their advantage. Northern powers in turn employed Carib warriors as "ethnic soldiers." The Dutch West India Company traders in Surinam relied on kinship ties with the Carib to facilitate trade and took Native women as concubines and even wives to cement these alliances. French treaties with the Carib people of St. Vincent and Trinidad gave them a great advantage in accessing products from the interior of South America. In 1664, the Carib allowed the French to settle permanently in the Cayenne colony, which later became the capital of French Guiana, and Jesuits followed them shortly after.[18] Over the next years, as these trade advantages declined, Europeans continued to use Indigenous people as slave hunters or as irregular militia to strengthen their missionary efforts.

Other peoples were not so successful; disease and changing political environments eliminated some groups entirely. The Querandí, northernmost of the Tehuelche peoples on the northeastern plains of La Plata, serve as one example. The Guaraní called the Querandí "people with grease" because they used guanaco (camelid animals native to South America) for wool, protein, and as pack animals. Distantly related to the Guaicurú peoples of the Chaco, the Querandí also fished from canoes and reputedly used enemies' skulls as drinking vessels, earning them a fierce reputation.[19] This nation had traditionally served as an intermediate buffer culture between the Abipones to their north in the Chaco, and the Tehuelches south on the Pampas. Although they adopted horses, the Querandí all disappeared as Western diseases spread into the Pampas during the late seventeenth century, facilitating settler expansion.

Indigenous Responses to Missions and City Life

The vast majority of Indigenous people joined colonial society rather than risk their lives trying to fight the spread of Europeans and their diseases. As they moved to the cities, many Natives lost connections to their home communities and even their ethnic identities, turning instead for support to urban guilds organized around their jobs. In Upper Peru, colonists pejoratively called these people "creole Indians," similar to today's pejorative Andean term "*cholo*," meaning urban people without clear links to rural ethnic origins but nevertheless of highland and Native descent owing to their darker skin color or physical features.

During the 1680s, Spain took a census that revealed the rapid rise of these integrated and urban Natives, so Viceroy Duque de la Palata ordered that all of them return to their home provinces. The administrator's goal here was clearly not to benefit these people by reconnecting them with their communities of origin, but instead to make more of them easier to recruit for the declining rural work levy. Adding more people to communities would have made *kurakas* pay higher tributes and send more workers to the mines. The rising number of these "non-ethnic" Native people was especially problematic to the elite because they formed the labor force of an "underground economy" in the unofficial ore mills and foundries, along with mestizos and mulattos. This informal economy diverted silver away from official mills, undermining royal returns. To degrade them, officials stereotyped these people as wild and uncontrollable barbarians outside the precepts of religion.[20] Nevertheless, these "creole Indians" played an important role in the colonial economy.

Indeed, negotiating the transition between traditional communities and new urban settings among the Spanish was challenging. Any false step might land one in prison, tortured, or even worse. Yet Indigenous people had their own tricks, and played their cards accordingly. In 1671, near Arequipa in southern Peru, visiting religious inspectors charged with rooting out idolatry in Native communities detected evidence of heresy. A woman had denounced her neighbor, Diego Vasicuio, for leading a group of Natives in a cult to an old deity. Herself charged with witchcraft, the woman instead directed the parish priest to this group, who engaged in secret worship of a deity named Sorimana. Diego Vasicuio was well over 90 years of age when he defended himself against these charges of dissidence. Having served time in the *mita*, this man had returned home and become chief priest, protector, and promoter of a *huaca*, the sacred stone representing their god Sorimana. Vasicuio regularly bathed the *huaca* in chicha, Native corn beer, offering it sacrifices of coca leaves, corn, and fodder to it while praying: "You are the one who gives, the Creator of the Earth. Look at me. I am poor. Give me strength, give me food. Have pity on me. Give me corn. I have nothing. Help me." The main request during these hard times was always simple: "give us food." When forced to surrender their idol, Vasicuio and his friends protested, but eventually turned in an impressive stone wrapped in white cloths and asked for the Christian God's assistance so they would "sin no more."[21] It is doubtful that the group actually surrendered their real deity, but by appearing to comply they were buying more time to continue their religion underground.

In the late seventeenth century, both Jesuits and Franciscans made further attempts to convert the remaining 10,000 Indigenous Piro, Conibo, Manamobobo, Campa, and Remo peoples along the upper Ucayali River in Peru. Missionaries who first entered the area in 1644 recorded that the Conibo lived in large homes of 20 to 30 persons each, in villages of 500 to 600 persons. Some of them, such as the community at San Miguel, had three chiefs and had first been gathered by the Jesuits 40 years earlier. On their return in 1686, Jesuits founded nine new mission villages during over 40 trips to the interior. The priests visited a Maspo village of 500 persons and a community of Amahuaca on the neighboring Coniguati River with 150 members. Like the Conibo, these people also lived in longhouses, similar to large bark homes used by the Iroquois in northeastern North America, with as many as 25 to 30 such dwellings in each community. While deaths from disease had diminished since the initial epidemics that had arrived with Jesuits in 1644, as explained in Chapter 6, other Native peoples who missionaries called the Semigayes and Cunivos finally attacked and burned the mission villages in 1698, killing the Jesuits. A missionary had apparently angered the neighbors in a sermon by pejoratively calling them untamable people who refused to listen to the word of God.[22] Perhaps because of their precipitous population decline, however, or because they had come to see missions as their only protection from settler invasions, Natives along the Ucayali River generally eventually accepted the missionaries during the eighteenth century.

As Indigenous people moved to missions and cities in greater numbers, many of them learned to write, a skill that helped them get along better in colonial society and appeal to the Spanish system of justice. By the 1670s, as their numbers recovered and began to grow again, Natives left more and more records which help explain how their lives were changing. From the final decades of the century until 1720, the Mixtec in larger communities such as Yanhuitlan and Teposcolula, northwest of Oaxaca in southern

Figure 7.2 "Franciscan Priest Presiding over Native Wedding Ceremony," John Carter Brown Library, Brown University, Carmack *et al.*, *Legacy of Latin America*, 209.

New Spain, left many last wills, testaments, and criminal records written in Nahuatl. These documents serve as evidence of ongoing Indigenous transculturation.

Cabildo officials, members of Indigenous town councils that administered communities near Spanish cities, wrote most of the colonial documents that survive today. Their records illustrate how the Spanish organized Indigenous communities along the lines of their own towns, appointing Spanish officials to administrate Native affairs. The *corregidor de Indios*, also called the *Alcalde Mayor*, was a Spanish magistrate who oversaw Indigenous towns and collected tribute for the Crown. *Corregidores* and their deputies, the *aguaciles*, investigated serious crimes such as homicides. If Europeans were involved in the conflict, council members called *regidores* then notified the *Alcalde Mayor*. Native people appealed local legal decisions either to the *Juzgado de Indios* (Tribunal for Indians) or to the *audiencia* in Mexico City. *Audiencias* were high courts located in major cities, and they multiplied as the number of non-Indigenous settlers increased. Later on, *audiencias* were also territorial units within viceroyalties. *Corregimientos* were districts within the *audiencias*, composed of smaller *alcaldías mayores*. European administrators still saw all Natives as mentally and morally inferior, and they especially viewed Indigenous women as the "weakest of the wretched rabble."[23] They certainly did not expect to see them as plaintiffs in court. Nevertheless, the huge amount of archival legislation shows that despite colonial prejudices, Native people employed the system in great numbers to appeal their grievances, as they would do over the next two centuries, and that legislation involved Native women as often as men.

A good example of such a grievance occurred in the town of Yanhuitlan, when in January 1684, a Mixtec man named Pedro de Caravantes saw his mestiza wife, María Montiel, talking to a local Indigenous church official. For years he had suspected that his wife was sleeping with the sacristan, Domingo de la Crúz, and believed they would be meeting that night. Pedro was already notorious for domestic violence, so two days later two neighbor women asked officials to check on his house when they did not see the couple again and feared that Pedro had abused his wife. Memories of a previous event, when Pedro had dragged his wife to a field and savagely whipped her, still haunted them. Entering the home, the officials found Maria's bloodied body wrapped in cloth, along with a letter in the Mixtec language in which Pedro explained his motives for murdering his wife. The note concluded: "In truth I swear on this paper and I make this cross + [written by the author, Pedro. This last signature file was written both in Mixtec and in Spanish]. Let the officials do all that my writing requests. Away in a shelter I wait. I do not bear [false] witness. Know that I swear as to how I seized this cloak from Justlahuaca [*sic.* this was the place where they made coats like the one he had seized from the priest on an earlier Good Friday, when he had also found him with his wife]."[24] The author did not stay to explain his motives in person: Pedro had fled the town.

At the resulting trial, neighbors testified that the husband's domestic violence and the affair had been public knowledge for at least three years. The sacristan denied the affair. His defense witnesses argued that Maria had demanded gifts from the priest and had left him alone when he refused her advances, showing her sexual freedom as a mistress who made material demands. Officials freed the sacristan but never apprehended the alleged killer Caravantes. Traditional Mixtec society had enacted harsh punishments for adultery, including hanging, whipping, exposing offenders to burning chili smoke, sale into slavery, or confiscation of goods. Sixteenth-century documents also refer to punishments given for adultery, including even the cutting off of ears or stoning. Even Poma de Ayala, the Peruvian artist who made the etchings used in chapters 2 and 5, refers to death by stoning for adultery in early sixteenth-century Peru. Both Native people and the Spanish clearly condemned adultery as a serious offense, although usually not punishable by death.

These events illustrate the complexity of changing cross-cultural customs and property practices: both Mixtec women and men held property individually in a marriage, according to both Mixtec custom and Spanish law. By placing the sacristan's cloak over his wife, Pedro also showed that clothing in his culture was an important token of identity. The letter, addressed to both Native and Spanish officials, points to the increasing literacy of the Native people. One specific insight provided by this note is that Pedro signed it in both Mixtec and Spanish, showing his written command of both languages. The region was an intersection between Mexico City and Oaxaca where Mixtec, Spanish, mestizos, and mulattos met daily. Their interaction reinforced the need to define and articulate a precise identity for a given legal purpose.[25] Colonial society was becoming increasingly multicultural, and Indigenous people were adapting to the changes as they joined a mixed-race world where people with different customs had different values yet still had to learn to get along.

Life at the Jesuit missions in La Plata had likewise drawn the Guaraní into Hispanic society as they cooperated with imperial administrators. Mission troops served authorities in La Plata on a regular basis. Guaraní soldiers marched south to defend Buenos Aires from foreign attack seven times after 1657! Mission armies also finally defeated Paulista threats in 1676, and by this time had significant numbers of weapons in their own hands. In 1680, colonial authorities called again on mission troops to dislodge the Portuguese from their base of Colonia de Sacramento on the eastern side of the Rio de la Plata. Three thousand mission troops defeated Portuguese forces and retook Colonia.[26] In all, between 1637 and 1745, mission troops fought for the king at least 50 times. Then, in 1680, the king even ordered 1,000 Guaraní families to Buenos Aires to construct new fortifications. Jesuits first protested by ignoring the command, and the Guaraní complained that the southern port city was much too cold and that even "when the more robust male adults go there for a few months, they usually get sick and die."[27] Guaraní women especially resisted, tearing out their hair and refusing to eat or make food when they heard of the king's decree. Their demands to stay in their mission towns reached royal ears: the parties compromised and Jesuits instead sent groups of 300 Guaraní volunteers to Buenos Aires for only 4 to 5 months at a time. The Guaraní had defended their own interests.

Natives on Remaining Frontiers Encounter "Civilization"

As we have seen, some Indigenous communities occasionally surprised the authorities with strong resistance to the imposition of colonial rule. Another such case occurred in July 1690, in the village of Tlapanoya, in Atitalaquía, New Spain (today the Mexican state of Hidalgo), when the Native *gobernador* arrived with an order from the *Alcalde Mayor* to apprehend two men who had fled from a neighboring town to avoid services ordered by the authorities. Villagers refused to give up the fugitives, instead renouncing the authority of the *Alcalde Mayor* as their designated judge. A mob of women and men formed and armed with clubs, rocks, plows, and other weapons threatened the officials, who fled for their lives. The *Alcalde Mayor* later tried to arrest the town official of Tlapanoya, but apprehended only the official's two sons after the villagers disappeared into the surrounding mountains.[28] This event shows that even Indigenous peoples close to centers of colonial power were capable of joining forces to defend their interests. The event also speaks to the growing ineffectiveness of the colonial authorities to administer their districts; the system had grown so corrupt by 1677 that the Crown began to sell appointments to provincial positions, such as *corregidor* and *Alcalde Mayor*, by individual cases and at differing amounts.

Rising administrative red tape, though, could only reach so far. Some fringes far from centers of power were still aflame. The pueblo revolt, for instance, proved a huge setback to Spanish frontier settlement and extension in northern New Spain. For the first time, different Indigenous peoples, including the Pima, Opata, Toboso, Concho, Tarahumara, and others had joined forces against the Spanish across the northern frontier. Unfortunately, for the missionaries to the 5,500 Tarahumara and the 150 Spanish settlers in neighboring Nueva Vizcaya, the final decade of the seventeenth century was precisely when they had chosen to expand their missions. Prospectors had also discovered a rich vein of silver ore in 1687, drawing miners, merchants, and ranchers into the area to exploit the strike. Church–state tensions were also at a high point because the military governor was accusing missionaries of encouraging Indigenous "agitation" against Spanish settlement and tribute. In November 1689, the Tarahumara governor of Cocomoráchic and seven other Indigenous mission leaders finally launched a general revolt. Native healers encouraged them and helped organize Native people throughout the province. In April 1690, warriors attacked the Yepómera mission, killing the priest, burning the church, and driving away the cattle before assaulting other missions. When a force of 50 soldiers and 250 Native auxiliaries arrived to repress the uprising, the rebels simply retreated. To purchase peace, the Spanish authorities pardoned the rebels and blamed the Jesuits for the unrest. Their attempt at pacification failed, however, and in the early 1690s the Tarahumara were still "seething with discontent."

To uncover the real problem, troops questioned and tortured some Tarahumara associated with the revolt, but the rest fled rather than face torture and arbitrary legal reviews. In March 1697, the Spanish finally shot and decapitated 30 rebels, lining the road *El Camino Real de la Tierra Adentro* with their impaled heads to threaten anyone else considering revolt.[29] In revenge for these killings, the Tarahumara joined Concho and Toboso warriors to sack and burn Tomochic, Mesachic, and five other missions. Under the leadership of a dynamic Concho leader named Puzilegi, the peoples of Upper Tarahumara finally tried to expel the Spanish from the entire province. Over 2,000 warriors attacked and burned missions, inflicting serious setbacks on the troops sent to defeat them. It was not until 1697 that the Spanish soldiers were finally able to defeat the rebels, and only after serious harm to their own forces. Tarahumara resistance in northern New Spain continued into the next century through guerrilla attacks on Spanish farms, supply caravans, and missions.

Despite occasional violent revolts, most Indigenous peoples integrated into the colonial system, learning how to use it to their advantage when possible. Events during this period in Oaxaca, southern New Spain reveal that the period from 1692 to 1702 was an especially challenging time as leaders and their factions brought cases of electoral fraud, bad leadership, sedition, and embezzlement against each other. Events show the growing use of colonial justice to solve communal political conflicts, but also the divisions that resulted for Native communities.[30] In 1695, the Native *cabildo* of the Zapotec pueblo of Yatzona, located near the town of Villa Alta, and its governor Don Pablo de Vargas, charged previous village authorities Don Francisco de Paz, Don Juan de Santiago, and Pedro Jimenez with abuse of authority. Their legal agent, the person with power of attorney to oversee their legal affairs, was Don Joseph de Celis, another cacique in Yatzona formerly charged with causing problems by encouraging village leaders to travel to Mexico City and investing 200 pesos in a lawsuit. Agents who served as legal intermediaries with Spanish authorities, such as Celis, had a tough job, because as Indigenous persons they were linked to community relationships that still remained from earlier times, such as inter-pueblo lineage and patronage links that connected him to his neighbors and friends (the Spanish authorities called these relationships "*parcialidades*"). At the same time, such caciques technically represented their people to the colonial authorities, so they needed to be on good terms with their rulers. Indigenous leaders who served as legal intermediaries had to maintain legitimacy in both contexts: in their villages and in colonial legal systems and cities.

To begin the criminal case, plaintiffs presented a detailed eight-page document signed by 113 caciques and *principales* of the town. Employing the Spanish notarial form for openings, closings, and the enumerated list that comprises the main body, the document notes 13 charges against leaders and their lawyer for crimes against the community. The accusations included not serving God and King, raising false accusations against earlier officials, and allowing the *Alcalde Mayor*'s lieutenant to steal their authority by giving him power of attorney without the pueblo's permission. The accused had reportedly imposed an illegal head tax to pay for litigation, had appointed church officials corruptly, and had abused political opponents. Finally, plaintiffs accused the officials of appointing a *repartimiento* for the son of the chief bailiff while declaring that it was for the *Alcalde Mayor* and keeping the money for themselves.[31] The records do not reveal the outcome of the case, yet one may assume that the punishments were severe if defendants were found guilty; the *Alcalde Mayor* had previously sentenced Celis and other similarly charged leaders to imprisonment, exile, and even corporal punishment.[32] As Indigenous people explored the challenge of living in both their communities and the colonial world, they were, as historian Yanna Yannakakis has argued, effectively learning how to negotiate life "in-between" places and cultures.

Another case that illustrates how Indigenous people negotiated integration into the colonial system, learning to utilize the Spanish legal system but also twist it to their advantage, occurred in Oaxaca. Between 1688 and 1696, three communities, the Nahua town of San Martín Mexicapan, the Mixtec community of San Juan Chapultepec and the Mixtec cacique of Cuilapan, Don Andrés Cortés de Velasco, all presented the Spanish authorities with "titles" in their own languages to disputed land that they all claimed. The conflict centered on whether the communities held land in common or individuals owned it and who the extant titles served: the greater community or the interests of a leader and their supporters. The documents themselves dated from the 1520s and employed events from the conquest to claim ownership of the land. Surprisingly, representatives of each party claimed to have located the documents only days before. Plaintiffs accused each other of forging the titles, pointing to "falsehoods" and "insane contradictions and defects." Over the following years, the reported authors of the documents slowly appeared in court and the parties charged each other with releasing cattle to trespass on the land, as well as denying access to forests where they all gathered wood and pastured animals.

The complexity of the legal case sheds light on the cross-cultural society in Oaxaca by the end of the seventeenth century, where people of different backgrounds were living in close proximity and interacting on a daily basis. In precolonial times, communities may have had more land available for gathering resources. The judicial documents reveal that by the late seventeenth century, different Native groups were increasingly pushed for space and conflict had grown between communities. By this time they were taking claims to the colonial authorities for resolution, appealing to their rulers for justice and the resolution of local claims. Appeals to the Spanish courts drew Indigenous people ever more closely into the very system that was changing their ways of life.

Further analysis reveals the documents to have been a forgery. First, Nahuatl and Mixtec alphabetic writing had not existed in the 1520s. The orthography and wording of the documents show purposeful attempts to imitate earlier forms of prose. The chronology is also confusing, moving back and forth from the 1500s to the end of the seventeenth century. Nahua migrants from central Mexico penned the Nahuatl title, rather than non-Nahua people who employed Nahuatl as a second language, as was most Nahuatl written in Oaxaca at the time. The Mixtec document uses words that did not become common until many years later, and drawings on the map clearly date to the seventeenth century because they include European features such as mustaches for men and unbraided hair for women. The Nahua charge against the Mixtecs as cannibals appealed to their audience's Christian sympathies by calling their enemies barbarians. Finally, the case shows how Indigenous people were trying to fit into the colonial legal system and make it work to their advantage. The authors were "reasonable people trying to meet an impossible demand – to produce a written and/or pictorial record that they either never had or had lost."[33] Unfortunately, as in most other cases from this period in the *Tierras* (Lands) files of the Mexican National Archives, it is unclear how, when, and whether the courts even resolved this case.

In the neighboring Yucatan, Spanish forces set out in 1695 to finally conquer the Itzá kingdom in the Peten, in today's northern Guatemala, which still resisted imperial control. Part of the reason was social: Indigenous people still fled to the autonomous Itzá region for refuge from colonial impositions of taxes and labor, as well as to continue their familiar ways of life. Economically, the unconquered Itzá also ran a brisk underground trade. They exchanged honey and wax for steel axes and salt from integrated Native people, who in turn sold the honey to the Spanish from central New Spain. Forcing the black market and its sources under state control must have appealed to the Spanish administrators. Officially, though, the authorities again held lofty principles. In 1686, King Charles II of Spain ordered the viceroy to "subject and pacify" the "great number of unconverted tribes" in Guatemala, Yucatan, and elsewhere "at once," but to proceed "as gently as possible," settling them in towns and "teaching them the law of God." The king was clearly out of touch with conditions across the Atlantic. With missionaries in the lead to initiate "peaceful" attempts, three expeditions at last penetrated Itzá territory in 1695. Passing through the territory of the Chols, Mopanes, and Ahiza on the way, it took the small Spanish armies several years to surround, negotiate with, and finally defeat the Itzá in late 1697, ending centuries of Native independence in the Peten. "The actual battle for the Itzá stronghold in Tayasal was brief," Nancy Farriss has explained, "culminating in a two-year campaign of encirclement and intense diplomatic pressure."[34] Divisions and intrigue among Itzá leaders facilitated their defeat. The Spanish quickly imposed labor quotas upon the newly subdued caciques to furnish workers for the construction of roads and new villages.[35] Resettlement and integration into colonial society had begun for the Itzá rebels.

For Document 7.2: Excerpt from Lisa Sousa and Kevin Terraciano, "The Original Conquest of Oaxaca: Nahua and Mixtec Accounts of the Spanish Conquest," *Ethnohistory*, 2003, V. 50, No 2, 349–400, visit www.routledge.com/9780415519120.

Economic "Success" and the "Costs" of Integration

Cooperation with the colonial authorities by some peoples, such as the Guaraní, does not fit with the popular image of noble savages fighting bravely to defend their heritage and lands from European colonizers. Neither does the idea of Native leaders becoming wealthy by joining the colonial establishment. Especially near imperial centers, though, some Indigenous leaders became part of colonial society when it served their interests. One might wishfully think that this was how they used the system to further their peoples' interests, yet evidence suggests that personal benefit was their primary motive. An interesting example shortly before the end of the century was Don Antonio de Hinojosa, who between 1671 and 1694 was the Nahua governor of the municipality of Cuernavaca, in the Valley of Mexico. Hinojosa became wealthy by renting out public land to the Native people of Acapantzinco and by amassing a huge amount of property for himself. As the most powerful figure in Cuernavaca's Indigenous society during the latter part of the seventeenth century, Don Antonio was highly literate, bilingual, and correctly called himself a cacique. The Hinojosa family and their friends claimed nobility because they were descended from early town *cabildo* members and were politically powerful. Since the conquest, they had adopted Hispanic cultural traits and intermarried with the Spanish, so Don Antonio was probably a mestizo who benefitted by claiming a Native background. Antonio had even married the daughter of another noble Native family, Doña Felipa, to solidify his ties to the colonial Indigenous elite. Claiming a mixed heritage exempted Antonio from tribute and doubly legitimized his claim to power.[36]

In the Valley of Mexico, with its large Hispanic population, there was great and intensely disruptive pressure on Native lands and culture, so Don Antonio also became "Spanish" to improve his fortune. His experience and story shows transculturation in action. Don Antonio's family lived in his great-grandparents' house, yet their furniture, including the tables, chairs, and carved chests, were all European. They also wore daggers, swords, and leather shoes; his wife owned clothing and jewelry from Europe, and the crucifixes, paintings, and weaponry that adorned their house were also Spanish. There was really nothing out of the ordinary in all this fancy display: even pre-Hispanic Aztec rulers had arrayed themselves in finery to emphasize their social rank. This wealth also allowed Hinojosa to require personal services and labor from the local Indigenous population by virtue of his status as colonial nobility and town officer. All over central New Spain, Indigenous elite took control of common land at the expense of their communities. This was roughly at the time when central Mexico underwent land title verification, called *composición* in Spanish, which was the legal transition from *encomienda*, estates based on tribute, to family farms called *haciendas*. By 1695, the Hinojosa *hacienda* included scattered parcels of 3,000 varas (2.4 kilometers), land rentals, and crops of maize and peanuts which they sold to Native consumers.[37]

Yet all this material success caught up with Don Antonio. Despite his adoption of Spanish culture, by the end of 1694, his abuse of authority and misappropriation of the town's tribute funds finally brought his small empire tumbling down. Spanish officials accused him of embezzling community rents, extortion, charging illegal fees for services, selling crops grown on community land, and owing nearly 4,000 pesos in unpaid tribute.[38] Don Antonio took refuge in the local Franciscan monastery, but the authorities still confiscated his goods and properties. His wife and daughters took part of the estate by right of dowry and inheritance and eventually reclaimed their houses, though Doña Felipa died unexpectedly. Don Antonio himself died soon after in 1697 or 1698, and his large debt, which burdened later governors, was a sum that even the sale of his huge *hacienda* could not cover. The Hinojosa family made a good life for themselves by capitalizing on their Indigenous heritage and taking advantage of their neighbors. Their success, however, seems to ultimately have helped increase European control by dividing the Indigenous community.

Conclusions: City Life, Transculturation and Varied Forms of Resistance

During this "mature" period of colonial rule, the Europeans took advantage of the steep decline in the Native population to fortify their political and economic institutions. Silver-mines were once again producing lucrative gains and, by increasing the importation of slaves from Africa, colonists still avoided fieldwork despite the Native collapse. The caste system seemed to be keeping the subject, darker peoples in their place, and the Europeans born in the Americas were not yet pushing to run their own territories by themselves. In a few places, Indigenous peoples continued to resist the seemingly inevitable extension of complete royal control in the Americas, but by the end of the century most of these groups had also collapsed. The Reche in the south and small groups in Amazonia were among the few Native peoples who still kept the Europeans at bay. Missionaries from the regular orders, however, continued to push even into these distant borderlands. The colonial and Catholic authorities seemed confident that their colonizing and religious enterprises would succeed in Latin America.

Between 1650 and 1699, the Indigenous population slowly began to rebound. Despite the occasional setbacks from disease, Native numbers stabilized. Some peoples, such as the Querandí, disappeared entirely. A few peoples, like the pueblo in Nuevo Mexico, mounted regional armed movements to evict the Spanish colonists and missionaries from their land. The vast majority of Native people in the central colonial areas of New Spain and Peru, though, joined colonial society. Some Quechua, Aymara, Zapotecs, and Mixtec peoples moved to towns, cities, or mines in search of labor and some learned to write in order to better function in the colonial world. Their documents show that Indigenous people were accessing colonial courts, sending children to schools or domestic work in cities, having love affairs, and behaving like people everywhere. Some kept alive Native religious beliefs and traditions, but, not surprisingly, many learned to speak Spanish to pass as peasants within the urban poor. Prejudice was too strong, however, to ignore for long. Cultural changes were clearly visible during this time: from the adoption of horses by plains peoples to increased literacy in Spanish to the loss of connections with Native areas of origin and participation as soldiers in the Jesuit mission armies, Native lives were clearly changing. Some Indigenous people even made it to the top of colonial society, employing connections and wealth to pass within a Hispanic world. Costs to their communities were steep, though, and "successful" Native integration ultimately helped the Europeans extend their control over colonial Latin America.

Discussion Questions

1. How did increasing contact with the Europeans lead to transculturation in Latin America?
2. Why did Indigenous recurrence to colonial courts further integrate them into the European system? What other options to address grievances would Natives have had?
3. Explain why Indigenous responses to growing colonial authority varied so much.
4. How were some Indigenous people able to integrate "successfully" into colonial society?
5. Did the Guaraní enjoy greater political advantage than other Native peoples because they had first cooperated with colonists, because they were armed and capable of mobilizing if needed by the Crown, or because the missions had partially integrated them into colonial society?
6. Explain the apparent contradiction between wealthy Indigenous leaders integrated into the Spanish colonial world and their people struggling to survive on the fringes of society.
7. If most Native people integrated into colonial society, why have accounts of the period emphasized the violent uprisings against the Spanish and Portuguese empires?

Notes

1 Lockhart and Schwartz, *Early Latin America*, 122.
2 Catoira, "Transculturacion," 185.
3 Anderson, Berdan and Lockhart, *Beyond the Codices*, 174–177.
4 Galeano, *Memory of Fire, I. Genesis*, 248–249.
5 Hemming, *Red Gold*, 338.
6 Jones, *The Conquest*, 59, 106.
7 Farriss, "Persistent Maya Resistance and Cultural Retention in Yucatán," 57.
8 Ariza, *Los Domínicos*, 63.
9 Myers, "Spanish Contacts and Social Change," 146–147.
10 Cardoso and Müller, *Amazônia*, 21; Meggers, *Amazonia: Man and Culture*, 125, 131.
11 Howe, *A People Who Would Not Kneel*, 12.
12 Susnik and Chase-Sardi, *Los Indios*, 96.
13 Susnik, *Los Aborígenes*, III, 60.
14 Williams, "Resistance and Rebellion," 404–417.
15 Ibid., 419–421.
16 Reséndez, *The Other Slavery*, 167.
17 Gregson, "The Influence of the Horse," 39, 40, 43.
18 Whitehead, "Carib Ethnic Soldiering," 366–368.
19 Sarasola, *Nuestros Paisanos*, 68.
20 Abercrombie, "To Be Indian," 113–114.
21 Whightman, "Diego Vasicuio," 39–47.
22 Chantre y Herrera, *Historia de las Misiones*, 294–295.
23 Terraciano, "Crime and Culture in Colonial Mexico," 715–717.
24 Ibid., 721.
25 Ibid., 723–733.
26 Sarasola, *Nuestros Paisanos*, 116.
27 Ganson, *The Guaraní under Spanish Rule*, 49.
28 Kicza, *The Indian in Latin American History*, 170.
29 Salmón, "Tarahumara Resistance," 387–389.

30 Yannakakis, *The Art of Being In-Between*, 58.
31 Ramos and Yannakakis, *Indigenous Intellectuals*, 94.
32 Yannakakis, *The Art of Being In-Between*, 63.
33 Sousa and Terraciano, "The Original Conquest of Oaxaca," 354, 356, 374–375, 381.
34 Farriss, "Persistent Maya Resistance and Cultural Retention in Yucatán," 67.
35 Means, *History of the Spanish Conquest*, 88, 97, 183.
36 Haskett, "Living in Two Worlds," 39–40.
37 Ibid., 45–46, 51–52.
38 Ibid., 52.

8 Demographic Recovery and Growing Insurrections, 1700 to 1749

Chronology

1700	King Charles II of Spain dies and is succeeded by King Philip V.
1701	War of Spanish Succession begins. During the war, caciques in New Spain take over Indigenous community lands. Cajonos rebellion by Zapotecs in Oaxaca.
1708–1713	Religious protest movements by Tzotzil and Tzeltal in Chiapas region of New Spain.
1712	Tzeltal revolt in Chiapas, one of the most important uprisings before independence.
1713	British defeat of Spain in the War of Spanish Succession.
1714	Spain creates four new ministries to improve government, revises colonial administration.
1719	Terrible epidemics devastate the Native population in Peru. Opposition to official survey in New Spain.
1720s	Chichimec resistance along New Spain's northern frontier, placement of *presidio* forts.
1730s	Apache raids along New Spain's northern frontier.
1732	Jesuit missions among the Guaraní reach their apex. Montevideo founded by Juan Antonio Artigas, negotiations with Charruas.
1737	Lower Pimas revolt in Sonora, Seris plunder ranches, Western Apache raids.
1739–1748	War of Jenkins' Ear between British and Spanish.
1740	Yoeme revolt in Sonora, New Spain.
1742	Juan Santos Atahualpa uprising in Peru.
1749	Seri and Pima rebellion in Sonora. Guajiro of Riohacha, New Granada, still refuse Spanish authority and Christianity.
1750	Treaty of Madrid (the sixth one) settles boundaries between Portugal and Spain.

Introduction

The Iberian Empire underwent important changes early in the eighteenth century. The death of sickly King Charles II (called "the bewitched") in November 1700 ended imperial consolidation and a disastrous reign marked by military defeats, bankruptcy, and famine. By appointing Philip of Anjou as his successor, King Charles unleashed the War of Spanish Succession. Philip belonged to the House of Bourbon, the royal family that had long ruled France; his grandfather had been King Louis XIV, and his father Louis, the Grand Dauphin, was in line to inherit the Spanish throne. Philip of Anjou received Spain's crown instead, however, because King Charles wanted Louis to become the next king of France. The appointment of Philip potentially combined the leadership of France and Spain, though, so it upset the balance of power in Europe. To prevent the union of the two nations, Great Britain and its allies – the Dutch Republic and Austria – went to war against them in 1701. With its strengthened Royal Navy, the British blockaded Spanish and French trade and finally defeated them in 1713, preventing them from joining forces. The final Treaty of Utrecht granted Britain permission to trade in the Spanish colonies. Spain had spent so much on the conflict that it relied on silver from its mines in Latin American to replenish its treasury. It was a weakened, humiliated, and cash-strapped Spanish Empire that emerged from defeat in the War of Spanish Succession, yet the Bourbons who took power ruled until Latin American independence early in the nineteenth century.

To pull the empire out of its downward tailspin and counter the Industrial Revolution in Northern Europe, the new Bourbon monarch started a program of sweeping political and economic reforms that soon changed Native lives. Imitating the French, King Philip planned to update his empire and defeat Spain's enemies in the struggle for imperial power that loomed as the eighteenth century opened. The new monarch was a child of the Enlightenment, an intellectual movement sweeping Europe that focused on reason, science, and progress rather than on tradition and faith, and his plans challenged the traditional nobility and Church. Despite the new trends, Philip was nevertheless still a monarch and bent upon retaining absolute power. The monarch's French advisors reformed the Spanish monarchy along their absolutist designs, excluding the aristocracy from state decisions to further their own dynastic ambitions. King Philip also tried to limit the Catholic Church by following the French model of regalism.[1] Already in 1709, Spanish Bishop Francisco de Solis had attacked Rome's centralism in a famous dictum: "His Majesty is permitted and even obligated to protect His kingdoms and churches from the slavery of the Roman Curia and to liberate them from it."[2] Bourbon monarchs in Spain intended to control even the Papacy.

Finance ministers also used the French example to double Spain's revenue within a few years by reviewing accounts, cutting waste, attacking smuggling, and resurrecting the royal fleet system to the colonies. By winning the war, Britain won the sole right to supply African slaves and sell 500 tons of British goods to Spain's colonies every year. Britain also took charge of the Portuguese colony of Sacramento, on the eastern side of the River Plate, an outpost that it used to smuggle goods into Buenos Aires. Britain undermined Spain's trade monopoly because even its slave ships brought contraband into the Iberian colonies. Spain tried to limit the illicit British smuggling by patrolling with private warships, but to pay for this defense King Philip had to raise taxes across the board and the Church had to draw in more tithes.

During the massive Bourbon reforms in Spain and the analogous changes in Portugal enacted by the Secretary of State Sebastião José de Carvalho e Melo, the Marquis of Pombal, the empires therefore tried to squeeze even more money from their Latin American colonies. To make his overseas holdings more profitable, Philip V reformed the imperial tax codes and raised taxes on sales of staples like cloth and wine to the Spanish colonies. As this chapter shows, Bourbon rulers also created a new viceroyalty and smaller, regional units of government called *intendencias* to increase political control. These measures raised trade and limited church power, but angered the colonists, who became frustrated with the heavy-handed royal control on the one hand and the lower castes pushing for improvements on the other. The rise of royal authority provides a venue to study how power affected the lower castes.

Even the early Bourbon reforms influenced Indigenous lives in colonial Latin America, especially through taxation. Native tribute was so important to the Crown that it was the only tax that Spain stopped farming out for collection by third parties, who had overcharged the Native people and kept the difference. Instead, royal collectors themselves began to collect Indigenous taxes. Other changes that affected Native people followed: the authorities decreased taxes on commerce, liberalized credit trade limitations, and made it easier for colonists to acquire land for agriculture. The resulting boom in export products, such as indigo in El Salvador, coffee in Guatemala, and hides in Rio de la Plata, increased pressure on Native lands and demands for their labor. Once commerce revived, the authorities monopolized and raised taxes on essentials like cloth, upon which colonists depended, to capitalize on the rise in trade. England later did much the same with cloth and salt monopolies with its own colony in India. These imperial policies cost some merchants their jobs, especially when new state businesses took control of and raised prices on products such as alcohol and tobacco. Taxation also led to additional exploration, especially the Brazilian gold rush that began later toward the end of the eighteenth century, as settlers tried to escape state controls and expanded into Native territories.

The position of Spanish and Portuguese people born in the Americas also changed during this time. Formerly at the top of the caste system, the people known as creoles lost power and influence as the new enlightened European despots undermined the authority of the viceroys in the colonies while demanding loyalty to the monarch. The number of people in the middle of the caste system, from both racially and culturally mixed heritage, also grew rapidly. Those at the lowest echelons of the caste system, the Indigenous people, felt the brunt of the increased taxation most severely, but also the demands of the onerous *repartimiento de mercancías* system and the tensions of living in between their own life choices and those that colonial society imposed upon them from above. Nevertheless, by this time Native demographics had bottomed out and begun to recover; with growing numbers the Indigenous people both joined colonial society and continued to challenge imperial rule.

Widespread Indigenous Integration and Imperial Changes

The death of Don Antonio Hinojosa and the breakup of his *hacienda* (discussed at the end of Chapter 7) occurred as the Native peoples of Latin America began to recover from their darkest hour. By the late seventeenth century, the collapse of the Indigenous population slowed down and their numbers began gradually to increase again. A few Native leaders had become wealthy members of the European colonial system. Their children and those of many other Indigenous people grew up as even more integrated participants of colonial society than their parents had been. In the cities, Indigenous arrivals gradually lost rural ties, their original languages, and even their ethnic markers, instead joining the urban poor as members of neighborhoods, specific trades, and religious associations. In the countryside, many Native people moved from home communities to missions, *haciendas*, or mines, either voluntarily or by force. After they left their traditional villages, Indigenous people forged common ties with one another. Some even began to identify more broadly in economic or caste terms as generically Indigenous or even non-ethnic peasants, rather than specifically as Mixtec, Aymara, Guaraní, or Zapotec, for instance. Common identity and causes, rising numbers of people, and access to horses and weapons gradually increased Indigenous strength; this period saw growing protests, especially where the hated mining predominated. Still, Natives were struggling against a powerful empire bent upon taking still more resources and never giving up its colonies. The beginning of the eighteenth century saw important transformations for both Indigenous peoples and the colonial rulers of Latin America.

The Process of Transculturation in the Early Eighteenth Century

Native leaders in New Spain employed this time of conflict in Europe to expand their own estates by renting additional land from Indigenous communities. One example of this practice was the case of Hilario de la Cruz, a rich cacique and leader of the community of Mazatepéc in Cuernavaca, who in 1705 requested that a Spanish noble take over the lease of his cattle ranch. De la Cruz had first rented the land from the pueblo of Ahuehuetzinco in 1700, but in order to secure a permanent lease he now argued that the ranch was too far from the pueblo for the people to use. The property was large, 21 kilometers in circumference, and de la Cruz claimed that Indigenous people had closer land available elsewhere. The noble obligingly took the land from the pueblo and then rented it back to Don Hilario for 20 pesos per year.[3] Such rentals were basically legal thefts, but they allowed wealthy individuals to amass large properties. This leader was looking out for his personal interests over the needs of his people. Another example of personal fortune-building was the estate of Don Antonio de Hinojosa, the wealthy governor of Cuernavaca (featured at the end of Chapter 7), which a court finally divided between his two daughters in 1708 after they battled over the remainders of their father's properties. The first document in this chapter is the last testament of an Otomi cacica in central New Spain, Doña Ana María de la Cruz y Alpízar, written in 1703. What does this document reveal about women holding positions of power within Native communities at this time? How did this Otomi leader influence the management of her agricultural and economic situation? Does her role fit with your image of Native women and their positions within their communities? How might colonial society have changed these Indigenous female roles?

For Document 8.1: Last Testament of Doña Ana María de la Cruz y Alpízar, Otomi Leader, 1703, visit www.routledge.com/9780415519120.

These documents from New Spain reveal that by this time some Native people, such as Doña María de la Cruz y Alpízar, had become wealthy. Native people with financial means capitalized on the conflict in Europe to take additional land from their Indigenous communities and even from each other. This is not what one might expect from the stereotypical image of Native settlements, where members freely and equally share the products of their gardens and hunting trips. Even if such idealized ways of life ever existed, many Native peoples had clearly changed by the beginning of the eighteenth century. The process of *transculturation* continued throughout Latin America. As colonial leaders imposed broad changes, such as the Catholic religion or more taxation, and people at the bottom added cultural nuances like music, holidays, dress, or foods, a new society evolved. Life in close proximity with Europeans and their descendants was changing Indigenous people: more and more they adopted the European view of themselves, and saw each other as generically "Indian" rather than by their individual group names for themselves. Colonialism was shaping their identity as Native people. Historian Ken Coates reminds us in his book *A Global History of Indigenous Peoples*, however, that colonialism was not the key determinant of *indigeneity*; that is, of Indigenous identity. Rather, it was their different values and traditions, such as a deep sense of identity to a place, or greater mobility, which were the primary determinants of Native identity. If even these core values were changing by the early eighteenth century, what was becoming of *indigeneity*?

Transculturation in Southern New Spain

Since Indigenous people were joining colonial society, one might expect that they had stopped fighting European rules and impositions. Instead, numerous examples show that as their population numbers slowly recovered, some Native people expressed their frustrations with the colonial systems ever more militantly. In the very first year of the century, Zapotec members of the Cajonos community in the district of Villa Alta, in Oaxaca, New Spain, rebelled against Spanish and Catholic abuses. Again, it was a report of "idolatry" and the resulting repression by Dominicans and their Native assistants called *fiscales* that set off the uprising. The *fiscales* were supposed to spread Catholicism among Native pueblos and report on the parishioners' (even their own relatives') misbehavior. *Fiscales* whipped villagers who missed mass or abused alcohol and collected clerical fees and parish taxes. In essence, they did the priests' and administrators' dirty work. Imagine how the *fiscales* must have aroused community anger.

In September 1700, the *fiscales* of Cajonos reported that the Saint Joseph Brotherhood was holding a wild party. With swords and guns in hand, several Spaniards and an African slave raided the gathering, and found children, women, and men, including the governor and two *alcaldes* of the pueblo, dressed in garments resembling priests' habits and repeating prayers from a suspicious-looking parchment. The people fled, but the following morning a Zapotec mob surrounded the monastery while beating drums, yelling and blowing horns. Bursting into the priests' sanctuary, the people recovered the food and tools taken from them the previous night and then demanded that the *fiscales* be turned over, threatening otherwise to set fire to the monastery and murder all those inside. The mob whipped the *fiscales* in the plaza and the Spanish never saw them again. The uprising was a long-simmering public response to the Franciscan program against idolatry begun 40 years before, along with widespread anger at the *fiscales*' betrayal of their traditional rituals. More broadly, it represents a community's response to colonial attempts to curtail their choices and autonomy.[4]

There were similar uprisings throughout the Spanish colonies, especially in southern New Spain, over the following years. East of Oaxaca in Chiapas, Church efforts to extract more money from Native communities also sparked angry uprisings. At least four protest movements organized around religious demands shook Chiapas between 1708 and 1713. The first three took place in the Tzotzil communities of Zinacantan, Santa Marta, and Chenalho, while a fourth occurred in the town of Cancuc, a Tzeltal-speaking area in the highlands.

First, a *ladino* hermit in Zinacantan, Juan Gómez, began to preach from a hollow oak tree trunk in 1708 that the Virgin had descended from heaven to help Native people and that her image was giving off rays of light. Villagers thronged to see the apparition and hear the Virgin speak through the prophet, offering her incense and food, and they eventually built her a chapel. Gómez claimed to have gone to heaven and personally met with the Holy Trinity, the Virgin Mary, Jesus Christ, and St. Peter, and had received from them authority to replace Spanish clerics with Indigenous priests in all Chiapan towns. His vision was a declaration of war against the authorities and led to a widespread uprising in 1712. An investigation revealed a small painting of St. Joseph within a hole in a tree, along with a notebook with verses encouraging penitence, but news of the disturbance spread quickly.[5]

A Native woman named Dominica López in neighboring Santa Marta, who was harvesting corn during the fall of 1711, saw the next apparition of the Virgin in the form of a living person who asked if her parents were alive. The town authorities rushed to meet this apparition, wrapped her in cloth, and placed her in a new chapel, where for three days she received offerings from Indigenous worshipers. When finally unwrapped, a wooden image had mysteriously taken her place. As Bricker has pointed out, the apparitions and cult in Santa Marta may have been a hoax, but the Virgin's appearance to an Indigenous person rather than to a European, and her offers to solve their difficulties, was the importance of the vision to Native people.[6] Natives from all over the province gathered around the Virgin for a Lenten festival in 1712, and this time she instructed them to keep her miracles secret from the Church authorities, since she had come from heaven to help only them. When local priests transported the Virgin to Ciudad Real and put Gómez and López on trial, 2,000 protesting Native people accompanied the Virgin. The authorities hid the Virgin to diffuse popular frustration, but angry villagers refused to forget her, because she had offered to solve their problems.

Religious fervor grew. In Chenalho during this time, images of two saints in the local church miraculously sweated and the image of St. Peter began to emit rays of light on Sundays, both of which greatly frightened Native parishioners.[7] Taken together, these apparitions and the resulting agitation were Indigenous attempts to create local religious cults that were acceptable to Catholic authorities yet also represented their own Native interests. Coupled with economic frustration, these movements created an explosive situation.

The charged religious situation in Chiapas finally exploded in 1712, when a new bishop increased tithe collections in Native communities, passed new church levies, and made a second expensive tour of the province. These additional impositions set off a massive Indigenous uprising in the Tzeltal area as Juan Gómez's movement become a regional revolt. Summoning Tzotzil, Tzeltal, and Chol people, Gómez proclaimed an end to the Spanish monarch, tributes, officials, bishops, and priests.[8] His ardent followers began to try to replace the entire colonial structure with Indigenous people as leaders.

The religious rebellion became political. With a new guide to channel their anger, people in 32 Native communities throughout Chiapas rose up to resurrect Emperor Montezuma and defeat the Spanish in what became the Tzeltal Revolt of 1712. Rebels employed Christian ideas to focus their movement and re-create colonial society along their own design. They cast themselves as defenders of Christ and the Virgin Mary, even while claiming that heaven was closed to the Spanish. The Tzeltales set up their own government at Cancuc and sent out "soldiers of the Virgin" to force other towns to join their new alliance. Overwhelming Spanish villages with machetes and clubs, the rebel troops executed men and children but forced Spanish women to marry their own Tzeltal men. In essence, by forcing Spanish women to grind their corn and serve as slaves, the Tzeltal rebels were turning the colonial tables upside down.[9]

As the rebels captured and executed Spanish forces in Chilon and Ocosingo, clearing Spanish and *ladino* males out of the entire region, plunder and tribute poured into their center at Cancuc. The Tzeltales appointed Native leaders who could read or write as permanent officials or priests. By donning the robes, chalices, and crosses of the expelled Catholic priests, rebels created their own version of Christianity with themselves in charge instead of the Europeans. A young Native girl named María de la Candelaria directed the masses and ceremonial feasts. By late August, the rebel army of 4,000 soldiers had moved on the capital Ciudad Real, where they met an army of 400 Spanish, mestizos, mulattos, and African slaves, 150 Chiapanec Native allies of the Spanish, and several hundred auxiliary troops from Guatemala. Armed mainly with farm equipment, the rebels could do little against such well-equipped imperial forces.[10] In November, royal troops took Cancuc after several days of fighting and executed the rebel leaders. The defeat enraged surrounding Tzeltal communities, who refused to capitulate for the rest of the year. Colonial forces finally prevailed in March 1713, replacing all the Native leaders with people under their control and bringing the famous Tzeltal uprising in Chiapas to an end.

The Tzeltal Revolt was one of the most important Indigenous uprisings in colonial Latin America. The government that the rebels created was impressively effective in its management, organization, and discipline. Leaders fielded an army of several thousand men, raised funds, and managed a two-front war that relied on extended lines of communication and supplies. Elders led villagers into war against royal forces and eventually failed due to their lack of proper arms, as well as power struggles between community political leaders and the religious overseers of the shrine, the center of the movement that housed the image of the Virgin, over the appointment of leaders for the uprising.[11] The revolts in Chiapas reflect the many ways whereby Natives had integrated Spanish customs, but also show that while many Indigenous people had adopted European commodities and even religious ideas, they still resented colonial authority and aspired to manage their own affairs as they saw best for their communities.

Because of the uprisings in Chiapas, it should not be surprising that over the next few years the Bourbon authorities tried to increase their control over their colonies, the Catholic Church, and diverse peoples even more tightly. In 1714, as part of an ongoing plan to improve colonial administration, the king created four new ministries to take over much of the work done by previous royal councils. A new Ministry of Marine and the Indies assumed many of the administrative duties of the Council of the Indies, leaving only litigation and individual issues to the former council. The new Cabinet of Ministers imposed faster, increasingly uniform, and more forceful resolutions upon the colonies, which quickly trickled down to Native people. Another measure to bring in more profit and increase royal control was the creation of new units of administration. In 1717, the Crown separated the *Audiencia* of New Granada – today's Venezuela, Colombia, and Ecuador – from the Viceroyalty of Peru, creating two large political units instead of one. This administrative change brought more protection to the Caribbean coast and to the Fort of Cartagena, attacked periodically by the French and British, as well as further oversight of the population booming in New Granada's highlands due to rising European demands for cocoa and tobacco. A few years later, Spain authorized the Caracas Company, a private enterprise, to trade with colonists in New Granada in return for keeping smugglers away from the coast. Then, in 1739, the northeastern *Audiencia* became the Viceroyalty of New Granada, with its capital at Santa Fe (currently Bogotá). The territory that is today Venezuela, with its urban center of Caracas, remained practically independent for the time being.

Trends: A Royal Power Called Regalism

Increasing anti-clericalism by Bourbon monarchs provides the opportunity to examine political power within the context of Iberian imperialism and its effects on the Native people. Regalism is the doctrine of royal supremacy over church affairs, in which a monarch attempts to control religious matters within their domain. This doctrine arrived in Iberia under the rule of King Philip V. Even though the Bourbon monarch did not follow the more strict anti-clericalism and deism growing in France during this period, his administrators sought independence from Rome by choosing their most important ministers and officials from the small middle class rather than from the notables and the Church. The new Bourbon administration intended to assert greater absolute political power over the Church within its domains and criticize its extravagance without provoking popular reactions and instability. Professional bureaucrats, appropriately called "regalists," studied current developments in imperial statecraft and "progress" as defined by Enlightenment philosophers. They then implemented strategies designed to make Spain more prosperous and politically efficient. Regalist reformers hoped to use science, reason, and progress to make Catholicism more socially useful. By the mid-eighteenth century, the movement had fragmented Spanish Catholicism into support for the Papacy, the Crown, or neither of the two.[12] As the Bourbons withdrew support for religious efforts in its colonies, regalism changed the lives of Indigenous peoples who had moved to Catholic missions and become Christians.

Even the earliest Bourbon attempts to improve fiscal administration and increase royal control of the Church changed Native lives in colonial Latin America. Because many Indigenous people had by this time moved to Spanish cities and adopted the colonizers' language and religious faith, Bourbon attempts to increase tax rates directly affected them. The tribute or head tax that the Crown required from communities by the eighteenth century was between 500 and 800 pesos per year, and most villages lacked cash. Since silver was scarce, Native governors and royal officials also accepted payments in kind – wool, maize, cochineal, for instance – and then sold the produce to merchants and passed on the proceeds to the *corregidores*. Merchants, often the *corregidores* themselves, resold the produce in the cities and mines, or exported it elsewhere. Because authorities took commodities through taxation and tithes, very little cash returned to the Indigenous people. As Arnold Bauer has shown, such syphoning created an economic imbalance that gradually, even though some farmers sold their surplus for cash, squeezed money out of the villages.[13] Despite the inflow, Bourbon leaders continued to extract still more wealth in labor and taxes from the Native people.

Seemingly trapped, some Indigenous people turned to their faith for answers and relief. Some people found sufficient motivation in their religious beliefs to risk their lives to try to cast off colonial rule. Curiously, though, they were not rallying around traditional Native faiths. Rather, it was their own understanding of Christianity, interpreted with Indigenous goals in mind, that motivated rebels in the early eighteenth century. Times had clearly changed. Native people appropriated the faith of their colonizers and tried to make it serve their own goals. Scholars of religious studies call this melding of systems of beliefs *syncretism*, and this was happening more frequently by the seventeenth century as cultures changed and blended in Latin America. What is more, the uprisings in Chiapas described above also exemplified what religious scholars call millenarian movements, the belief in a future new world of happiness and prosperity that is promised to be better than the present time of frustration and despair.

Surprisingly often, when faced with a desperate situation, people have followed a religious leader or prophet who promises them a better life in which they will recover power and their former ways of life. This happened to early Christians around the Mediterranean Sea during Roman persecution. In North America, where about this same time Native Americans were defending their lands from European settlers, Indigenous prophets rose to guide their people to a better future through religion. The Delaware prophet Neolin headed such a movement in the 1760s, an Iroquois prophet called Handsome Lake did so in 1799, and the Shawnee prophet Tenskwatawa followed suit at the turn of the nineteenth century. Similar movements in Latin America show that Indigenous people were also undergoing challenging threats and searching for religious solutions.

Indigenous Populations Forge a New Identity as Part of Colonial Society

As European rulers expanded their activities and brought even previously overlooked areas into Atlantic markets, they increasingly pressured the land base of Indigenous communities. In the colonial centers of Peru and New Spain, *haciendas* fully linked to markets grew quickly, taking over virtually all the land for crops and livestock. This expansion may not have been such a problem, except that by this time the Native population was once again recovering as people slowly built up immunity to the epidemic diseases. The Indigenous population of New Spain approximately doubled to 3.7 million throughout the eighteenth century. In Peru, the terrible epidemics of 1719 delayed the Native population recovery until toward the end of the eighteenth century. At the same time, the numbers of Europeans and people of mixed racial heritage were growing quickly as well.

As the Indigenous population slowly recovered, their communities lost traditional lands to Spanish settlement and ranching. Indigenous people moved to *haciendas* and cities in search of work, where some lost ties to their home communities as they became permanent city dwellers. Others used what they earned to help their original communities survive, much as migrants from Mexico and Central America to the U.S. might do today. In the cities, Native people met migrants from other Indigenous communities, compared stories, conveyed frustrations, and realized that despite coming from different places, they shared similar prejudices and obstacles. Slowly, Native people forged a new identity based on what they heard the colonists – the people with power – say about themselves. Natives in cities started to refer to themselves with the pejorative Spanish term *Indio*, Indian, rather than by their own word for "people" that they had previously employed in their own language to call themselves.

Here it is helpful to return to Todorov's study of the "other" introduced in Chapter 5. Recall that in his book *The Conquest of America*, the philosopher used the European conquest of Indigenous territories to explore how the different sides viewed, portrayed, and related to each other. One of Todorov's conclusions is that Europeans gained the upper hand in the Americas because they could understand the other.[14] This ability to understand the difference confirmed the conquerors' feelings of superiority and facilitated their victory over the Indigenous societies. By the early eighteenth century, after two centuries of subjugation, Native people in colonial society had internalized the Europeans' overwhelmingly negative views of themselves, in effect the other's "other." As they were drawn ever more into the Europeans' world, the colonial frame of reference colored the way Indigenous people saw themselves and their prospects.

Natives also gradually forged common ties with other Indigenous people in similar situations. The internalization of the negative stereotypes foisted upon them by the Europeans slowly forged a new identity. Indigenous people came to view themselves as "Indigenous" or even as *Indio* (Indian), along with other pejorative designations uttered by the powerful. Over a long time, the internalization of such epithets linked the various peoples of Native origins. This process varied widely from place to place, but signs of such a transformation became more evident throughout the eighteenth century. Thus the "colonial mirror" – the process of seeing reflections of oneself through the attitudes of the "other" – shaped Indigenous identity throughout the Americas.

At the same time, women of Native background continued to have children with people outside of their own Indigenous heritage. Some of these unions were consensual, but many were not. Those children grew up in a colonial world that was very different than the one of their Native grandparents. Artists at the time noted that these children did not even look as much like their parents or ancestors, but were part of a new group of people born from the great colonial mixture taking place. The first illustration in this chapter is an artist's depiction of the child of an Indigenous woman and a mestizo man, who belonged to a racial category called a "coyote." In the animal world, a coyote is the canid mammal related to the grey wolf, known for its howl and scavenging, and reputed in folklore to be a cowardly trickster. Referring to a child as a coyote would not have been flattering. Another term used was *lobo*, or wolf. What do the images, and especially the names, tell us about societal stereotypes at the time? Where would children like these have found belonging and a sense of community? What does the image suggest about the Indigenous place in colonial society?

Native Resistance Continues Despite Increasing Integration into Colonial Society

In southern Chile, the Reche still controlled their relations with the Spanish, keeping their lands between the Biobío and Toltén rivers and even extending their four territorial strips called *butanmapos* north and south. Each *butanmapo* had three superior chiefs, a commander, field commander, and diplomatic courier. In their general assembly of all the chiefs, the Reche designated a *toque-general*, a head chief over all of their territory and the only leader who could mobilize the people to war. In this highly organized government, each *butanmapo* could request military assistance from the others. Reche groups were strong enough to carry on active trade with Spanish settlers in central Chile on their own terms and with prosperous results.[15] Rather than joining colonial society, the Reche successfully resisted colonial influences.

Figure 8.1 *De mestizo y de india, coyote*, Painting by Miguel Cabrera. (Gibson Green/Alamy Stock Photo)

In Brazil, numerous Indigenous peoples resisted missionary attempts to convert and integrate them, despite ongoing deaths from diseases. In the western Amazonian savanna, Jesuit and Dominican missionaries from Peru pushed into the area of the Upper Mamoré River (where today's Bolivia and the Brazilian state of Rondonia meet) in the late seventeenth century, starting nine missions among the Arawak-speaking Moxos peoples from 1682 to 1710. In the 1690s, a people called the Moysuti, who lived in the tropical forest on the Andean slope southwest of San Ignacio in northern Peru, had burned their Dominican mission and forced the priests to flee for their lives. As the Moysuti took control of the entire western Brazilian savanna, their revolt closed trade routes from that area to the highlands and spread dissent west to Jesuit outposts. At the mission of San Borja, in what is today northern Bolivia, angry Native neophytes – those new to a belief and recent arrivals at the mission – forced missionaries to flee for their lives over the savanna during the worst part of the rainy season. Native converts were angry at the scarce supply of iron tools at the missions.

The Moysuti rebellion continued until the rains died down and the Jesuits returned with a troop of Spanish soldiers from Santa Cruz to re-impose their control. Over the following decades, missionaries pushed northwest to establish missions among the Mobima and 25 other peoples. One group was the Baure, reportedly a numerous and "civilized" people, who at first welcomed a mission on their lands. Father Cipriano Barace established an outpost but made an enemy of the powerful shaman, whose warriors ambushed and killed the missionary.[16] In retaliation, the Jesuits returned with a force of 1,000 armed and hispanicized Natives and Spanish soldiers, who hanged the leaders and marched 250 captives back to Santa Cruz to sell as slaves. Smaller Indigenous groups along the eastern slopes of the Andes also hesitated to subject themselves to Christian missionary control.

Resistance was not occurring only on the frontiers. Even in colonial centers, Native people still opposed European hegemony two centuries after the conquest. Spontaneous, popular uprisings shook New Spain throughout the eighteenth century. Most of these uprisings were short eruptions by armed villagers in response to threats from the outside that targeted imperial agents but they were not very destructive. When the church bells tolled, villagers assembled with sticks, rocks, machetes, bones, hoes, and any other tools at hand to vent their frustration against the symbols of imperial power. In 1719, a Native woman in Santa Lucia, outside the city of Oaxaca, New Spain, raised an angry mob against the priests and militiamen who had arrived to demarcate the boundaries of their town. A community's size and population determined the amount of Indian tax it owed the authorities, and the sizable Native tribute was very important to the Crown. A village of 100 tributaries, for instance, would have owed between 500 and 800 pesos a year by the eighteenth century, a heavy sum often collected in kind by the Native governors and then paid to district *corregidores*. Mariana, the tall scar-faced rebel leader in Santa Lucia, first cut the authorities' measuring rope and then took on a Spaniard in hand-to-hand combat. The unexpected leader then raised her bleeding arm to urge forward her fellow villagers armed with tools, farm implements, sticks, stones, and likely the most uniquely Indigenous weapon of all, powdered chili peppers. Armed with rocks, usually the most damaging Native weapon in such protests, they drove the surveyors back to Oaxaca.[17] As William Taylor has pointed out, Native women were often the most "aggressive, insulting, and rebellious in their behavior towards outside authorities in central New Spain, who led large and threatening crowds of Native people against the work of such inspectors."[18]

The following year, east of Oaxaca, a frightened *Alcalde Mayor* reported on his attempt to conduct another territorial survey, as shown in Document 8.2:

> When we reached the boundary of a plot of land belonging to Gabriel Martín, a Native of the pueblo of Santa Cruz ..., many Indians from Santa Cruz appeared, joining others who had assembled there. Massing together in a crowd, they sought, in disobedience of the Royal Order and Royal justice, to stop the proceedings, shouting that we would not be allowed to go beyond the said boundary. At the same time, the Indians picked up stones and threw three; they aimed one at Your representative, but it struck one of the Indian officials instead.[19]

Spontaneous uprisings show that even in centers supposedly conquered centuries before, Indigenous people kept alive their sense of community, autonomy, and entitlement. What is telling also in the example of Mariana is the growing role of the Indigenous women in leading fellow villagers to oppose colonial controls.

For Document 8.2: Description of Indigenous rock-throwing uprising in Santa Lucía, Oaxaca, New Spain, led by Mariana, 1719, against royal officials, priests, and militiamen attempting to mark town boundaries, visit www.routledge.com/9780415519120.

Throughout the eighteenth century, women played increasingly key positions in Native resistance movements. This trend should not really be surprising, given the important role that women had traditionally played in some Indigenous communities, where they shared power through complementarity rather than subordination to men. While each gender performed expected work, societies in the Andes, for instance, placed equal values on the roles filled by women and men. This was not the case for all Native societies, but the imposition of European and Christian ideals of male superiority provoked resistance among the women of some peoples. It was in the Andes, in fact, that most of the Native military uprisings took place during this time. Between 1720 and 1790, the Indigenous peoples of Peru and Upper Peru rose in violent protest against the colonial authorities well over 100 times. The example of Mariana shows that even in New Spain, some women led movements against colonial impositions.

Even more than the despised mine labor quota, it was the *reparto de mercancías*, run by the *corregidores de Indios*, that incited Indigenous hatred. In this system, local magistrates of Native communities borrowed money from merchants to purchase their own positions from royal authorities. In exchange, merchants forced the *corregidores* to sell goods at elevated prices – up to six to eight times the market cost – to the people in their district, or even to pay their workers with the goods. Products included mules, oxen, and tools, but also completely unnecessary items, such as certain cloths. The sales sometimes forced Indigenous people into mine or *hacienda* work to earn the cash they needed to repay their debts. While Spain did not legalize the system until 1754, the *reparto* had long taken the income of *kurakas* and small merchants, and even the subsistence base of many common people. Spanish administrators used the magistrates to syphon labor and assets from Indigenous people who had fallen into debt. When added to the ever-increasing taxation and religious impositions, the *reparto* created a tense situation ready to explode. In the central Andes, as historian Steve Stern has shown, by the 1740s the Spanish authorities faced an all-out actual civil war against their authority and wealth. The area was seething also because local people kept alive the legacy of the Inca king, the heritage of the stiff resistance that Aymara had offered the Spanish nearly 200 years before. Tensions were so intense that administrators who became *corregidores de Indios* during these years knowingly accepted the risk of death for the right to take advantage of Native communities in their area.

Transculturation on Frontier Borderlands

Besides Peru, royal administrators also encouraged development along New Spain's northern frontier (today Mexico's northwestern states), which had long been a fairly independent region populated by peoples the Spanish referred to as *Chichimecs*, their term for barbarians. Had it not been for rich silver strikes around Durango, Zacatecas, San Luis Potosí, and Querétaro, the area may have remained an overlooked borderland like La Plata. The push to extend the mining district north, however, brought colonists into contact with people they probably would rather not have known. Building forts called *presidios*, the Spanish slowly penetrated frontier territory by posting paid, regular troops on Indigenous lands to defend new European colonists. By the early eighteenth century, at least half of the soldiers in these forts were *castas*, integrated Native people, who received a paltry salary yet had to find their own horses, weapons, and armor. To survive in such rugged territory, frontier troops sold the local Native people they captured into slavery. By 1723 there were 17 such garrisons along northern frontiers staffed by over 1,000 soldiers, and the Indigenous peoples of the area understandably resented their presence.

Following a review of the northern *presidios* in 1729, the viceroy prohibited attacks on hostile peoples, and forbade soldiers from causing unrest and of exploiting the Natives for profit. His orders also instructed *presidio* captains not to harm local Natives if they accepted Christianity and the king's rule. The viceroy made peace overtures to the Chisos, Acoclames, and Cocoyomes peoples and tried to sign a peace treaty with the Tepehuan and Tarahumara to end their raids against frontier posts. These efforts failed, and Native attacks against the *presidios* spread. To stop harassment of mining outposts, the viceroy finally captured over 300 Native men, women, and children and shipped them as slaves to Havana, Santo Domingo, and Puerto Rico. Nearly half of the prisoners died during the forced march, but 83 escaped into the mountains around Veracruz.[20]

Despite the viceroy's "peace" overtures and misguided relocation of the prisoners, colonial expansion into northern New Spain provoked violent reactions from local Indigenous people. Pressured by settlers in Texas and to the north, the Tobosos, Conchos, and Apache peoples, including the Natagées, Mescaleros, and Lipánes, moved south during this time into the Chihuahua and Coahuila deserts of what is now Mexico, displacing other peoples and raiding Spanish missions on their way. Apache ambushes of colonial wagon trains and settlements in Nueva Vizcaya and Sonora increased frontier warfare. By the 1730s, the powerful Comanches had descended from the Rocky Mountains and, with their allies, the Utes, had displaced the Apache to trade cattle, plunder, furs, and captive slaves with Spanish pueblos in New Mexico. The colonial authorities forbade this illicit commerce with Native people in 1737, but the decree was unenforceable. The measure did divide Native allies, though, causing 50 years of war between the Utes and Comanches over access to trade goods and increasing retaliatory attacks by settlers on Native communities. It is important to note that Native people displaced and fought each other as much as they attacked the Spanish settlers. Comanche forces, for instance, killed 150 Pecos pueblo people in 1741, and access to Spanish trade goods divided other groups. Some peoples joined forces against a common enemy: Tarahumara and Mescalero Apache allies attacked and forced the closure of mines in Chihuahua, Parras, and Mapimí during this time.[21]

As frontier settlement grew, some Indigenous uprisings inflicted heavy damage to Spanish homesteads. In 1737, four years after Sonora became a province, the Lower Pimas rebelled, the Seris plundered Spanish ranches, and the Western Apaches intensified their raids. Three years later, the Yoeme people also revolted. Floods had destroyed their crops and famine ensued on northern deserts. Ranchers' demands for additional Native labor to the Jesuit missions where the Yoeme lived also increased. Yoeme leaders Muni and Bernabé finally demanded changes in the mission system for all their people.[22] The Yoeme were desperate and many individual groups joined forces to rebel in 1740, though they kept their original group independence. After achieving a specific goal important to their particular people, each group returned home. Unlike Popé's 1680 rebellion with the pueblo, the two Yoeme leaders did not intend to eradicate all the Spanish through violence, but rather sought only greater understanding with the Jesuits and other settlers. The capture and decapitation of Muni and Bernabé in 1741 ended the possibility of a negotiated compromise. The Spanish governor circulated their impaled heads to all Yoeme communities to quell their resistance. Instead, the grisly display understandably caused deep-seated resentment that only resurfaced later.

Mission Villages Prosper During this Period

Further south, in La Plata, Jesuit missions along the Paraná and Uruguay rivers were enjoying their apex. The Guaraní had adapted to life in mission villages, led by their own caciques under careful Jesuit direction. By 1732, at its peak, the mission population stood at 141,182 people. Compare this to other important mission centers: the Jesuit missions at Chiquitos in eastern Bolivia numbered 25,000 people at their apex in 1756, while Franciscan missions to the Chiriguanos (western Guaraní) in southeastern Bolivia reached only 25,000 at their highest point in 1810. Mission populations among the Guaraní fluctuated due to migrations, the numbers of people who moved from the forests to the missions, and epidemics. In 1733, for instance, 18,733 Guaraní died from disease in the 30 missions along the Paraná and Uruguay rivers. Mission populations collapsed from diseases, despite Jesuit care of the sick, owing to the high concentration of people in the dense mission village settings.[23]

The Guaraní joined the Jesuit missions because they offered some protection from European settlers and from the slave raiders, yet living under the priests' supervision also meant a loss of autonomy. Jesuit priests honored Native chiefdoms and allowed the Guaraní to choose their own leaders. The priests, though, also imposed European hierarchical structures upon Native peoples, giving Indigenous leaders and their wives the Spanish titles Don and Doña to highlight their authority over groups of 20 to 30 families in mission society. Even the chiefs and their families regularly fled the compulsory labor pressures at the missions, however, to seek independent economic opportunities in Spanish and Portuguese villages.[24] Moreover, the Jesuits ruled the missions so heavy-handedly that life must have seemed unbearable at times for the Native people.

Priests worked tenaciously to change the matrilineal and polygamous nature of Guaraní life. Jesuits enforced their regimented social hierarchy to facilitate their control of the people, appointing Native supervisors to watch over the mission's fields, gardens, and cattle. Guards patrolled the workshops, and each morning the people gathered to "give an account of their person and others." Villagers caught on the streets after curfew suffered punishments, and children informed the priests of "sins, fights and other things which happened in the pueblo." To enforce their rigid control of every detail, down to the number of crops planted, Guaraní assistants whipped offenders at a pillar in the plaza according to the severity of the infractions: homicide – 30 lashes; indecency – 30 to 60 lashes; witchcraft – 30 lashes or fewer.[25] Given such harsh cultural changes, it should not be surprising that the Guaraní regularly escaped from the missions.

Native and Colonial Interaction Increases on the Borderlands

Southeast of the missions, in the Eastern Band and in southern Brazil, it was cattle that first brought Indigenous people into contact with Europeans and only careful negotiations made European settlement possible. Natives and settlers interacted with increasing frequency as cattle introduced by the Jesuits proliferated on the fertile prairies and spread as feral stock through Native Charrua and Minuan territory. Spanish cattle hunters smuggled cowhides back and forth across the Portuguese–Spanish frontier, interacting more and more frequently with Native peoples. This marshy area was a highly contested but also porous zone claimed by both Portuguese and Spanish settlers. In 1732, Juan Antonio Artigas, a Spanish immigrant to Buenos Aires, founded the city of Montevideo along the eastern coast of the Plate River. On several occasions, when settlers feared an Indigenous attack because their community had no wall around it, Artigas negotiated with Charrua leaders and diffused tensions over settler expansion into Native lands. These repeated negotiations saved Montevideo from destruction by a Charrua attack.[26] From its earliest years, the viability of Montevideo as a Spanish colony continued only through arrangements with local Indigenous peoples.

Negotiations and interaction between Indigenous people and settlers happened more and more often throughout the European colonies as the societies and cultures slowly interacted. When possible, Natives played the foreign powers off against each other. Along Panama's northern coast during this time, the Kuna enlisted the French and British as allies against the Spanish. French settlers and Kuna forces together raided imperial outposts, but Spain soundly crushed a Native revolt in 1728. Foreign attacks posed serious threats when they involved Indigenous troops; in 1739 the British bombarded the Spanish city of Portobelo on the northern coast during the War of Jenkins' Ear and then tried to capture the city of Cartagena.[27] To create a buffer against future British attacks, Spain allowed the French to settle permanently along northern Panama, where many took Indigenous wives and began to raise cacao. From this time on, Indigenous people on Central America's Atlantic coast employed European allies, including the French but mostly the British, as allies against Spanish rule. English commanders, for their part, negotiated with the Kuna and even considered provoking a widespread Native uprising throughout Central America to weaken Spanish rule. Pressured by the Spanish to end negotiations with the British, the Kuna finally accepted Jesuit missionaries. Still, the Kuna *neles* (seers) at the new mission settlement opposed the priests so tenaciously that by 1749 those who had not perished from epidemics had deserted the mission.

As their contact with European settlers increased, Native people expressed their anger at the imposition of outside religion and foreign ways of life that infringed upon their land and customs. Indigenous people learned that when acting as a community they were stronger. In the Valley of Oaxaca, Zapotecs in the community of Macuilxóchitl fought a long-standing conflict with the Bethlehemite priests who had established a *hacienda* on their land. By the 1740s, Zapotecs regularly raided the order's estate and, when caught, received whippings from the mission overseer. The Native people finally had enough, and the next time the overseer entered the Zapotec village to whip the raiders, the townspeople instead seized and tried him. Condemned by the community, Indigenous elders sentenced the Spaniard to death and hanged him in the plaza. Royal authorities arrested some elders in retaliation, but discovered that the community as a whole had tried and executed the Bethlehemite overseer. Without specific offenders to accuse, the court only constructed a stone gallows in the plaza to threaten the community.[28] While this conflict was primarily over land, the anger vented at the religious order showed Zapotec refusal to accept the mission effort and use of their community property.

Indigenous Women Join Violent Insurrections

In 1740, a large Native uprising finally exploded in Peru's Central Sierra in a movement that eventually included Native female troops. At the root of the revolt was widespread anger at colonial impositions, especially the *reparto de mercancías*, the forced sale of European goods to indebted Indigenous communities. Added to the *reparto* was the increasingly heavy Bourbon taxation of Native communities. Much as frustration over the British Tea Act of 1773 boiled over into the American Revolution in 1776, popular anger at imperial taxation building in Latin America finally erupted against the royal authorities in Peru. Anger over the *reparto* and taxation had been building and had already broken into violence in 1736, when *kuraka* Ignacio Torote rebelled against priests at the Sonomoro Mission. Hostility grew until angry people finally gathered around a new messianic leader on the subtropical eastern slopes of the Andes.

Individuals: Juan Santos Atahualpa

The person who capitalized on growing Native hostility was Juan Santos Atahualpa, a 30-year-old man originally from Cuzco or Cajamarca, who appeared in Quisipongo in May 1742 wearing a red sleeveless cotton tunic and encouraged people to rise up against colonial administrators. Santos, called "Apu-Inca" (Inca Lord) by his followers, was a highlander who mysteriously traced his ancestry back to the Inca emperor Atahualpa himself. Like many upper-class Native people at the time, Santos had grown up in the colonial world in the highlands and had received a Jesuit education. The priests had even taken him to visit Europe and possibly even Angola in Africa, so Santos had traveled abroad.[29] Santos promised that he would divide the world into three separate kingdoms, including Spain for the Spanish, Africa for the Africans, and America for "his children the Indians and *mestizos*." In classic messianic fashion, Santos billed himself as a returned Inca leader, pledging to free all Indigenous people from their oppression under European rule and bring them prosperity. Angry Campa, Maparis, Amuesha, and Cacshibo people struggling desperately for a living in the mines, textile mills, and *haciendas* along the Ucayali River between the mountains and the jungle – mostly people no longer in original communities and desperately getting by on the fringes of colonial society – were drawn to Santos' promises of a brighter future without the Spanish. It seems logical that if increasing taxation had forced these people to leave their communities of origin, they might be angry enough to risk their lives to fight the colonizers.

This new messiah successfully united almost all the Indigenous peoples in the central jungles on Peru's eastern lowland frontier into a unique pan-Indigenous coalition never before seen in the area and even in Latin America. Natives fled missions and towns and flocked by the hundreds to join this new leader in the jungle where the uprising began. Their united movement was so successful that it kept colonizers out of the subtropical lowlands for over a century and left a legacy of resistance not matched until Tupac Amaru's rebellion in 1780, 40 years later.

Native people left missions to join the rebels and Asháninka, Amuesha, Pero, Simirinche, Cunibo, Shipibo, and Mochobo peoples from the entire central jungle, between the Ucayali and Urubamba rivers, flocked to the new leader.[30] Rebel forces marched from the jungles up into the highland territory in 1742, attacking the colonial infrastructure and especially the Franciscan missions. Santos employed guerrilla raids against the viceroy's army and expelled all non-Indigenous people, including missionaries, Spanish, Africans, and even mestizos, from the territory he took. Still, the leader himself was a controversial product of transculturation, wearing a cross, praying in Latin, and even favoring Jesuits over Franciscans. His movement became more *nativistic* and opposed to Christianity as it conquered land.[31] In 1743, Santos and his army of 2,000 followers took over the Quimirí Mission in the lower foothills east of Tarma and expelled the priests.

News of Santos' success spread to the higher sierra, and the rebel army attacked missions and *haciendas* as it climbed into the mountains. A priest reported that Natives cheered their arrival: "the Indians of Chanchamayo held grand celebrations, dances and drinking that night, celebrating like the Chunchos jungle Indians the coming of their Inca, singing that they would drink chichi beer from the skull of the priest." The following morning, a large troop of Native troops massed on the banks of the Chanchamayo River and moved toward the *haciendas*. The friar and his colleagues fled to higher altitudes.[32] Events show the significant support that highlanders gave to the jungle peoples, as well as why the viceroy desperately sent more troops and arms in what became a disastrous campaign to halt the insurrection.

In March 1746, General Don José de Llamas set out against the rebels with a force of 1,000 soldiers, intending to converge in Amuesha and Asháninka lands with a force of 400 coming from the south. Spanish forces turned back, though, due to rain, forced marches through the jungle, and the lack of provisions, leaving 14 soldiers dead of exhaustion without even seeing a single rebel.[33] Then, on October 28, 1746, an earthquake tumbled cathedrals in Lima and thrust a tidal wave against the port city of Callao and the central coast. Missionaries linked the desperate fight against Santos to the natural calamity. The viceroy rebuilt his forces and sent an army to crush the insurgents, only to be repeatedly beaten back. The Franciscans tried to retake their mission in 1747, but Native porters abandoned them in the Huanta jungle, where Asháninka warriors ambushed and killed them. A later attempt by priests to negotiate with Santos also failed.[34]

Santos and his troops finally climbed into the mountains in 1752, taking the city of Andamarca as a beachhead in the high plateau before descending to the coast and Lima. Warned by a spy about the impending arrival of royal troops, the rebels took cattle and supplies and retreated after only two days. Spies in Andamarca had facilitated Santos' invasion and the inhabitants believed the rebel would soon return to free their city, so clearly the insurrection also enjoyed growing support in the mountains.[35] The rebel incursion forced the Spanish to construct a line of forts to contain the uprising to the lowland areas of Jauja and Tarma, defenses that ultimately prevented the rebellion from spreading into the mountains. The insurrection struggled on for several more years, resisting five additional royalist expeditions, and Santos finally died of unknown reasons between 1754 and 1755. Native followers who revere the leader hold that he never died, but instead vanished in a cloud of smoke.[36] Santos' followers kept missionaries and colonial troops out of the forests for years to come.

Indigenous women played an important role as soldiers who defended the uprising against imperial troops from the highlands. Beginning in 1746, Santos' allies in the mountains organized a separate fighting unit of some 50 women who joined rebel forces

Figure 8.2 Portrait of Juan Santos Atahualpa. (The History Collection/Alamy Stock Photo)

and assisted their forays into the sierras. This female battalion challenged Spanish soldiers so effectively that during ten years of intermittent fighting the colonial authorities did not once defeat them. The leader of this female battalion was Doña Ana, a *zamba* (an ethnic designation for someone who was from both Indigenous and African heritage) from Tarma, on the eastern side of the Andes.[37] Although there is little information about this group of female soldiers, Santos' uprising frightened the colonial establishment and, as Chapter 9 shows, pushed the Bourbons to tighten royal control over the colonized people.

It was about this time that two women were born who later became important leaders in the Andean Indigenous movements of the 1770s and 1780s. The first was Micaela Bastidas Puyucahua (which means *look at the clouds* in Quechua), born in 1744 in Pampamarca, Peru to a Native woman and a man of undefined heritage. Some claim her father was a free man of African ancestry, which would therefore have made Micaela a *zamba*, a person of African and Indigenous background. Others argue that her father was a priest from neighboring Yanaoca. In either case her heritage is undecided, yet Bastidas' illegitimacy would have limited her future even in the Indigenous highlands. Micaela's family, though, belonged to the town's mainstream colonial Spanish community, since her wedding certificate listed her parents as Spanish. That people of African and Quechua heritage could pass as Spanish because of their positions reveals how fluid

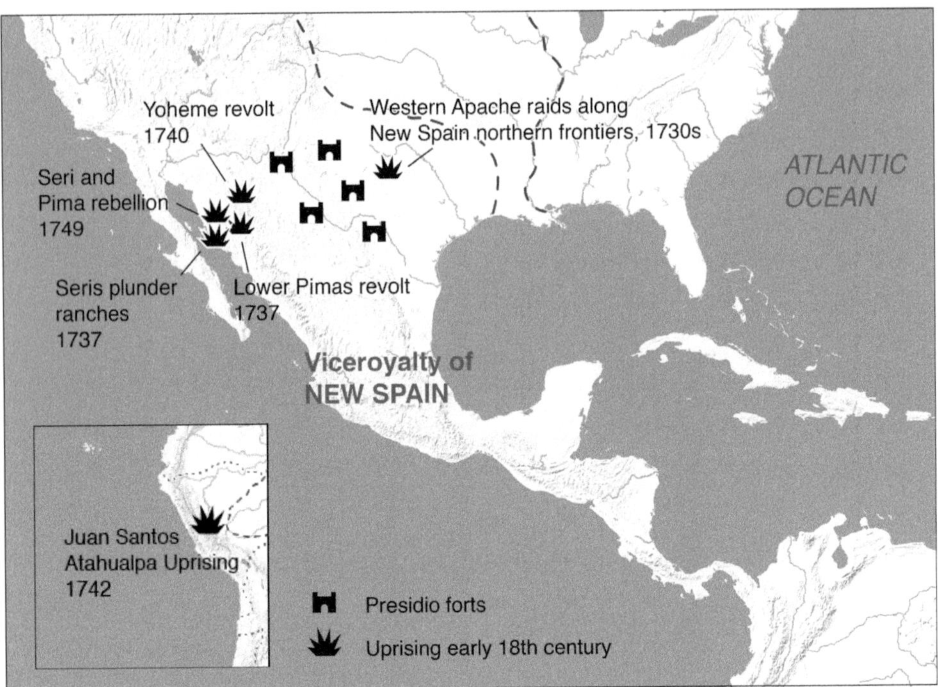

Map 8.1 Largest Early Eighteenth-Century Indigenous Uprisings

the class and racial categories had become by this time. Raised as a committed Catholic, Micaela nevertheless received little formal education and spoke Quechua much more easily than Spanish. Oral history in her community holds that as a girl she worked in an *obraje* against her will, and that at the age of 15 she married a youth of rising importance named José Condorcanqui, son of the *kuraka* who oversaw three area towns.[38] When her husband later became a revolutionary leader, Micaela played an active role at his side.

Another influential Indigenous woman born around 1750 was Tomasa Titu Condemayta Hurtado de Mendoza, who grew up to become the cacica or governor of the community of Arcos, also in Peru. Condemayta became the highest-ranking female Indigenous leader and fighter in the revolutionary Indigenous uprisings of the late 1770s, commandeering a brigade of female soldiers and even leaving her husband to join the wars.[39]

These women's lives reflect important changes in Latin America. Their multiethnic backgrounds show that by the mid-eighteenth century people in the colonies were interacting to a greater degree than ever before. That these women grew up as educated and wealthy reveals that by this time some people with Indigenous heritage could achieve positions of status and influence despite their background. The role these women later played in the insurrections suggests that, at the time of their birth, at least some children of Indigenous heritage were learning to value and honor their Native lineage. Participation in the Indigenous revolts of the later eighteenth century indicates finally that some women learned military skills and were respected, as well as that Indigenous numbers were recovering and growing sufficiently in strength to begin to challenge European rule through significant and organized military force.

Geopolitical Changes in the Hispanic Colonial World and Bourbon Consolidation of Power

Events: The 1750 Treaty of Madrid

Political arrangements in Europe continued to affect Native people in the South American colonies. In January of 1750, Portugal and Spain signed yet another Treaty of Madrid (there had been at least eight treaties of that name since 1500) to once and for all settle the shifting boundaries between their colonies. The new agreement revised the 1494 Treaty of Tordesillas, which had established the boundary between their colonies at 370 leagues west of the Azores Islands and had given Portugal the land east of this arbitrary line. Spain hoped to stop Portugal's westward expansion and force its settlers out of the Eastern Band, because the Portuguese outpost at Sacramento threatened Buenos Aires' control of trade in the area. For their part, Portugal hoped to secure the newly discovered gold- and diamond-mining areas in central Brazil, as well as the rights to use the Amazon and its affluent Tocantins, Tapajos, and Madeira rivers. Portugal in particular expected to take control of the Jesuit missions in territory that became part of Brazil. In the end, the treaty permanently changed Native lives because it gave ownership to occupants of the land, so Spain forced the Portuguese out of the Río de la Plata and in return gave up the territory of the seven prosperous Jesuit missions south of the Ybicuí River and east of the Uruguay River. The missions moved back to Spanish territory and Portugal gained control of the Amazon basin.

Diplomats in Europe seemingly gave little thought to complexities caused by the Treaty of Madrid. Imagine the logistics for moving so many missions in that time and age: there were 97,582 Indigenous people living in the 32 Spanish missions in the area, as well as 29,203 Native people in seven adjacent towns. The territory was rich with pasture, rivers, woods, orchards, cotton fields, thousands of cattle, and fields of yerba mate, which alone were valued at over 400,000 pesos. How could the priests move such wealth and resettle so many people in only the one year stipulated by the treaty? The Jesuits estimated their potential losses at 3,522,167 pesos, not including the damage to Native communities.[40] Given the prospect of being forced out of their homes and losing their property, it is no wonder that the Guaraní resisted the order to abandon their missions. As discussed in Chapter 9, their armed resistance complicated the second half of the century for European rulers.

Bourbon rulers were spending more and more money embellishing their royal trappings, extending their control, and impressing subjects with their royal power. Official plans to give away mission territory to the Portuguese directly threatened the Jesuits in Guairá, but royal problems of the Jesuits more broadly reflected the growing power struggle and tensions between the Bourbon king ruling Spain and the Catholic Church. During this time, monarchs increased their regalism and demanded greater ecclesiastical supremacy over the Catholic Church in Spanish dominions.

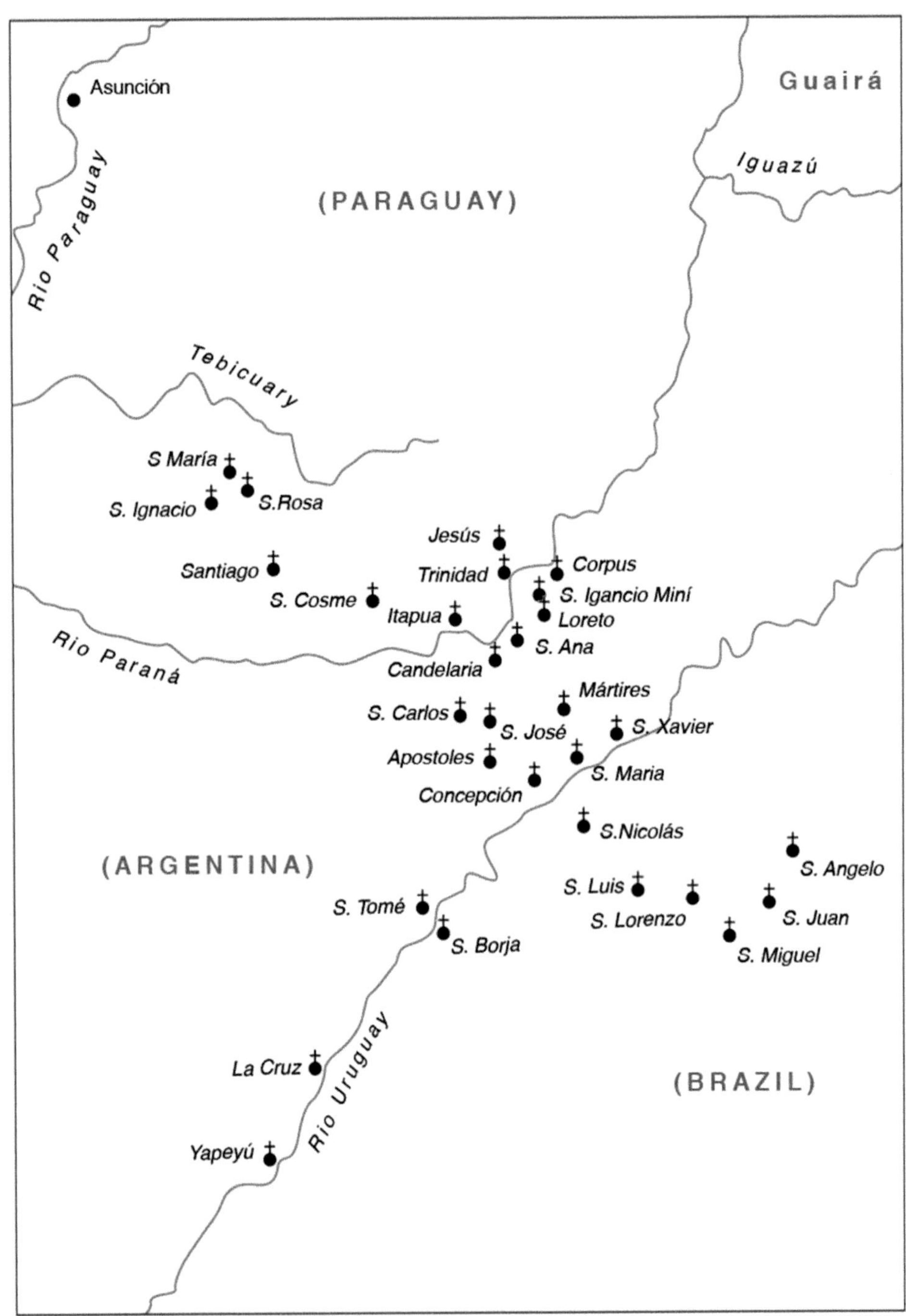

Map 8.2 Missions in the Jesuit Province of Paraguay

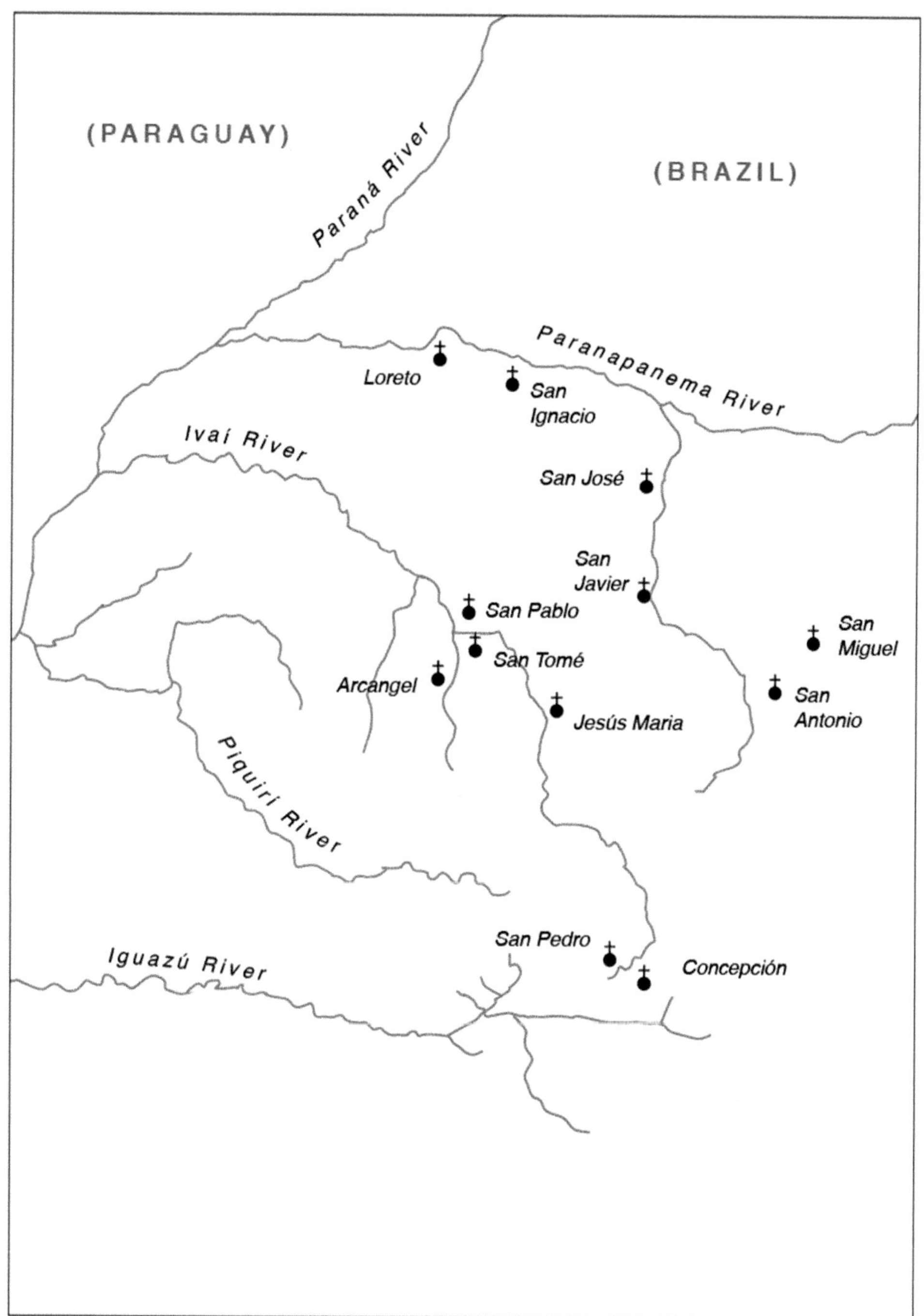

Map 8.3 Missions in the Jesuit Province of Guairá

In October 1749, the Spanish Crown issued a rescript taking control of all the parishes administered by religious orders in the diocese of New Spain and Lima, and giving them over to the secular clergy. A second order to this effect followed in 1753. Since the Crown already managed the secular clergy, Spain essentially took control of all of Rome's parishes, missions, and lucrative farms in the Americas. In less than a decade, Franciscans, Augustinians, and Dominicans all lost the parishes they had managed since the conquest.[41] The Crown implemented this mandate in 1765. Less successful was the Crown's struggle to remove all parish priests who were not fluent in Native languages, an attempt to limit the influence of regular missionaries that failed because there were not enough replacements. To extend greater administrative control, in 1749 Ferdinand VI also divided Spain into provinces and bestowed upon the royal governor of each the title of intendant and administrator of all fiscal decisions, a move he followed later for colonies in Latin America.[42] Growing pomp and circumstance reinforced the Crown's authority in its colonies. In 1747, to celebrate the coronation of Ferdinand VI, 20,000 onlookers in Mexico City watched over 95 bullfights in one wild, ten-day extravaganza. Such a show of wealth must have duly impressed villagers who lived close to European centers of power.

Further away from royal control, in the villages and countryside where most people still lived, it was more difficult to see Ferdinand's absolute power. Indigenous people still influenced many colonial frontiers. In 1749, for instance, the Seri people of Sonora, New Spain rebelled after losing their lands to frontier settlers. When the Seri and neighboring Pima elders – who faced similar losses – protested the theft of their land, the Spanish authorities exiled their families to the Yucatan and Guatemala. In retaliation, over 2,000 Seri and their Sibubapas, Piatos, Upper Pimas, and Apache allies attacked Spanish ranches and mines between Pópulo and the pueblo of Pitic. Fighting alongside 400 allied Native troops, Spanish soldiers retaliated with a war of extermination along the Cerro Prieto range against Native allies. In the end, the imperial expedition captured only a handful of Seri women and children. Over 2,000 Seri rebels continued to harass colonial troops.[43] As it turned out, though, their uprising was only a small precursor to the Upper Pima Revolt that shook the northwestern Pimeria Alta a few years later.

In fact, as the Seri revolt showed, by the mid-eighteenth century, many Indigenous people on the borderlands were relatively strong and in control of their territories. The Guajiro people in the province of Riohacha, New Granada still refused to accept Spanish authority and the Christian faith. "Among all the barbarous nations of America," a Jesuit reported in 1750, "none is more needful of reduction than the Guajiro Indians." To continue their independence, the Guajiro traded livestock, hides, and tallow to both Spanish settlers outside their communities and with foreign smugglers in exchange for weapons, manufactured goods, and liquor. By trading to their own advantage, these people and many other Indigenous societies helped sustain the settler economy without formally belonging to it. "What would the whites do without the Indians?" the Guajiros reportedly asked local Spaniards with deliberate irony.[44] Their relationship to the Spanish Empire resembled that of many other Native peoples by the mid-eighteenth century. While hindsight makes it seem like a given that regal Iberian monarchs would completely conquer the Americas, Native resistance at the time still challenged this idea.

Conclusion: What Numbers Can Do

By the early eighteenth century, the Indigenous population had begun to recover once again. Their growing numbers and especially their quickening integration into colonial urban centers and society facilitated more interaction between different Native peoples. Indigenous people in cities gradually adopted a generic, common Native identity as they joined colonial society. Their changing identification across groups, though, facilitated broader opposition along a united front that made group military opposition more feasible. Communities in many places, notably in Peru with the Santos Atahualpa rebellion and in northern New Spain with the Tarahumara, Apache, Pima, Seri, and Yoeme uprisings, challenged colonial rule with military force. Other peoples, such as the Guaraní, accepted colonial society but kept elements of their Indigenous identity, including their language, customs, and some beliefs. Everywhere, Native people and communities were changing but trying to retain some control over their lives.

The European rulers also saw important changes during this time. The Bourbon monarchs employed regalism to assert their authority more visibly over the Catholic Church. Their efforts to rebuild the home economy led to added taxation and impositions upon Indigenous peoples in the colonies, efforts that only grew over the following 50 years and ultimately contributed to widespread hostility against the empire. The remainder of the eighteenth century saw the culmination of these trends for both the European empires and the Indigenous peoples in their colonies.

Discussion Questions

1. How can one explain the mysterious apparitions of the Virgin Mary in highland Chiapas?
2. How did language use reflect transculturation in colonial Latin America?
3. In what ways did growing regalism affect Indigenous people in European colonies?
4. How did colonial rule change traditional Indigenous leadership?
5. Why might Indigenous women have taken the initiative to oppose colonial impositions?
6. How did events in Latin America during this time reveal evidence of transculturation?
7. Why did the large Indigenous military revolts of this period fail?
8. What role did religion play in the Indigenous resistance movements?

Notes

1 Regalism was an attempt by the Spanish state to exert greater control over the Catholic Church within its realm, a legacy from French Enlightenment philosophies of encyclopedic perspectives of science and economic progress.
2 Jedin and Dolin, *History of the Church*, 171.
3 Haskett, "Coping in Cuernavaca," 103–104.
4 Yannakakis, *The Art of Being In-Between*, 66–70.
5 Bricker, *The Indian Christ*, 55.
6 Ibid., 59.
7 Ibid., 57, 59.
8 Ibid., 59–61.
9 Ibid., 63.
10 Klein, "Peasant Communities in Revolt," 254–258, 260, 262.
11 Ibid., 263.
12 Smidt, "Bourbon Regalism," 26, 30.
13 Bauer, "The Colonial Economy," 26.
14 Todorov, *The Conquest of America*, 248.

15 Padden, "Cultural Adaptation," 82; Haughney, *Neoliberal Economics*, 19.
16 Block, *Mission Culture on the Upper Amazon*, 39–43.
17 Taylor, "Patterns and Variety," 160.
18 Taylor, *Drinking, Homicide and Rebellion*, 116.
19 Taylor, "Patterns and Variety," 173–174.
20 Salmón, *Indian Revolts in Northern New Spain*, 69–70.
21 Ibid., 70–71.
22 Ibid., 73.
23 Ganson, *The Guaraní under Spanish Rule*, 53.
24 Ibid., 59.
25 Sepp, *Relación*, 221.
26 Maggi, *Artigas y el lejano norte*, 29.
27 Britain and Spain fought this war with such an interesting name between 1739 and 1748. During the conflict, British Captain Robert Jenkins lost an ear to Spanish troops and later displayed it to Parliament as an incentive for his country to go to war against Spain. The actual cause of the conflict centered on forcing Spain to allow Britain to sell African slaves in the Spanish colonies. This conflict, which ended Britain's expansion into the Caribbean and Spain's invasion of Georgia, was ultimately inconclusive. The war was also the first in which Britain employed a regiment of colonial troops from New England as part of its regular army.
28 Taylor, *Drinking, Homicide and Rebellion*, 121–122.
29 Loayza, *Juan Santos, el invencible*, 9.
30 Varese, *Salt of the Mountain*, 91.
31 Galindo, *In Search of an Inca*, 74.
32 Izaguirre, 1922–1929: 2: 128–130, cited in Stern, "The Age of Andean Insurrection," 47.
33 Varese, *Salt of the Mountain*, 100.
34 Ibid., 102.
35 Stern, "The Age of Andean Insurrection," 55.
36 Varese, *Salt of the Mountain*, 109.
37 Socolow, *The Women of Colonial Latin America*, 160; see also Stern, *Resistance, Rebellion and Consciousness*, 46.
38 Walker, *The Tupac Amaru Rebellion*, 21.
39 Adams, *Notable Latin American Women*, 71; Campbell, "Women and the Great Rebellion in Peru," 186.
40 Ganson, *The Guaraní*, 89–91.
41 Prien, *Christianity in Latin America*, 248.
42 Herr, *The Eighteenth-Century Revolution in Spain*, 12.
43 Salmón, *Indian Revolts*, 74–75.
44 Kamen, *Empire. How Spain Became a World Power*, 361.

9 Religious Conflicts, Widespread Resistance, and New Countries, 1750 to 1825

Chronology

1750s	Indigenous population recovered to nearly pre-conquest numbers in central areas.
1751	Broad Kuna rebellion throughout Panama.
1753	The Pope grants Ferdinand VI the Patronato Universal as part of the Concordat of 1753.
1754–1763	Seven Years' War between Spain and Britain.
1756	Spanish and Portuguese forces kill 1,511 Guaraní at Caaíbaté; death of Chief Tiaraju.
1759	King Ferdinand VI dies and Charles III becomes king of Spain.
1761	Canek leads Maya rebellion in Yucatan.
1766	Hat and Cloak Riots in Madrid blamed on Jesuits.
	Charles III evicts Jesuits from Paraguayan missions in northern La Plata.
1767	Spain evicts Jesuits from all its territories; opposition leads to rebellions in New Spain.
1769	Portugal evicts Jesuits from its territories.
	Aymara uprising in Sicasica, Upper Peru over labor and increased taxation.
1771	Aymara in Pacajes, Upper Peru seize the provincial capital of Caquiaviri.
1772	Protests in New Spain over excessive taxation and forced labor.
1774	Reche chiefs unite against the Spanish, and by then are calling themselves Mapuche.
1778	Aymara leader Tomás Katari travels to Buenos Aires to denounce local colonial leaders.
1780	Aymara seize control of Chayanta, Upper Peru; Native riots in La Paz.
	Julián Apaza, Aymara merchant, takes charge of uprising in Upper Peru.
	José Condorcanqui (Tupac Amaru II) captures Corregidor Arriaga, begins revolt in Peru.
	November: Tupac Amaru victory at Sangarará.
	Tupac Amaru II besieges Cuzco.
1781	February: the Spanish execute Tupac Amaru II and his partner Micaela Bastidas.
	Tupac Katari besieges La Paz in Upper Peru from March to October.
	Native rebellion in Izucar de Matamoros, State of Puebla, New Spain.
1782	September: Tupac Katari executed.
	Esteban Atahualpa proclaims himself Inca in Pacajes, southern Peru.

	Felipe Velasco revolts in Huarochirí, east of Lima.
1785	The Spanish build additional forts in Panama to militarily control the Kuna.
	Increased production and exports of crops and raw materials to Europe.
	People of mixed Indigenous and European heritage (*ladinos*) become the majority in some countries.
1791	Slave revolt in Saint-Domingue initiates the process of Haitian independence from France.
1792	Indigenous protests in New Spain against increased taxation.
1793	Reign of Terror in French Revolution.
1796	Conflicts between Spanish colonists and the Charrua in the Eastern Band (today Uruguay).
1807	French troops invade Spain to reach Portugal; Spanish rebels move to Cádiz.
1808	Draught and Indigenous uprisings begin in New Spain.
1809	July: Popular Americano revolt in La Paz.
	Quechua leader Mateo Pumacahua helps defeat a revolutionary junta in La Paz.
1810	Hidalgo and Native supporters march on Guadalajara; Americanos form juntas.
1811	Spanish offensive to retake Latin American colonies.
1812	Royalists and Americanos in Upper Peru both enlist Indigenous troops.
1813	Father Morelos declares Mexican independence.
	Juana Azurday and thousands of Native soldiers fight the Spanish at Ayohuma.
1814	Antiroyalist Native force from Cuzco sacks La Paz.
	Pumacahua switches sides to fight against Spain; Royalists capture and hang him in 1815.
1821–1825	Simón Bolívar campaigns for independence against the Spanish.

Introduction

When King Ferdinand VI died in 1759, his half-brother Charles III assumed power and continued to extend royal control in the colonies. The king hoped to help Spain recover from the debts its wars had accumulated, and to compete in the Industrial Revolution underway in Northern Europe. Imperial reforms reached their height under his rule. King Charles' reign was one of "enlightened despotism," a style of absolute rule that emphasized rationality, toleration of religious differences, education and the arts, growing freedom of speech and the press, and the right to private property. On paper, more freedoms and toleration of cultural plurality seem like things that should have benefitted Native people and their cultures. The problem was that enlightened despots did not mean for their enlightenment mantras to benefit the lowest castes, but rather only those at the top. As more Indigenous people moved to growing urban centers, they pushed to claim the benefits of the economic growth of the colonies and started to influence political decisions. Moreover, increased racial mixing began to break down the caste system, furthering transculturation.

The colonial economy had recovered from its seventeenth-century decline and European-run areas saw considerable growth; by 1750, even peripheral regions had joined the market economy. In central areas, market-oriented estates and farms owned by the wealthy landed creole families spread to occupy most land appropriate for grazing and cultivation. The population growth and economic expansion into Native territories challenged Indigenous people who still depended directly on the land for sustenance. Because their traditional ways of life were not so viable anymore, many Natives left rural communities to seek employment in Spanish economic centers, cities, or estates, where they settled permanently. Some Native migrants used their earnings to help their rural communities of origin survive.

King Charles III heightened and intensified the Bourbon reforms, which reached their apex under his control. In 1753, the Pope granted Ferdinand VI the *patronato universal* as part of the Concordat of 1753, giving the monarch the right to name all bishops, clerics, and benefices in his territories, except for a few positions reserved for the Vatican. Charles III deepened his father's regalism and attacked the Jesuits, who supported the Pope instead of state churches and were confessors for the royal families; the monarch saw them as a threat to his power. The Marquis of Pombal, virtual ruler of neighboring Portugal, saw the Jesuits as a threat because of their role as confessors and barred them from his court. In September 1759, Portugal's King José I expelled the Jesuit order from Portugal and his empire.

International events worsened the conflict between state and Church. Spain's loss in the Seven Years' War (1754–1763), when it gave up Florida and almost Cuba to Britain, as well as its resulting indebtedness, forced the king to rely on his colonies for money. To boost his profits, King Charles III terminated the monopoly of the Cádiz merchant guild and allowed new companies to trade with Havana, Hispaniola, and peripheral areas. The monarch reduced duties on goods traded to his colonies, streamlined mail deliveries, and encouraged trade within Spanish America. King Charles also permitted colonial trade and agriculture to develop, which boosted the production of sugar in Cuba and other regional products, but then taxed the growing commerce. These policies worked: Spain's trade with its colonies grew by 700 percent between 1778 and 1788. Business expanded, prices decreased, and the empire reaped the benefits of the Bourbon reforms. The recovery should not be overstated though, as Spain never developed industrially. Nor was it able to control trade with its colonies during its war with Britain, when smugglers (even from the U.S.) flocked to South American ports.

Numbers Make a Difference for Indigenous People

By the mid-eighteenth century, Indigenous people in central areas of extensive contact with Europeans had built up immunity to their diseases and Native numbers recovered again to pre-conquest numbers. The Native population of New Spain doubled over the course of the eighteenth century to 3.7 million, and Peru and the *Audiencia* of Charcas (today Bolivia) still comprised clear Native majorities despite periodic epidemics. Native populations flourished, both on the fringes of royal centers of power and on the frontier borders of imperial Spanish civilization. By 1781, the area surrounding Quito was 68 percent Indigenous, while Mexico City was half Indigenous and half mestizo, along with a few Africans, mulattos, and Europeans. Native peoples predominated throughout the rest of New Spain. In frontier regions, such as the internal provinces of New Spain, Amazonia, the Chaco, and Patagonia, Native people were still in the majority. Despite growing numbers, tensions over land, leadership, labor, taxes, and changing living conditions exacerbated by the royal reforms pushed Indigenous people to the brink by the mid-eighteenth century: communities in the central areas rebelled repeatedly against the authorities. Most armed Native uprisings took place in the central Andes Mountains, site of the hated silver-mines and *obrajes*. Such rebellions responded to local tensions, and few grew into widespread movements that seriously disturbed the Crown's control. Still, *corregidores* faced a risky job in trying to manage Native communities. Women helped lead some of these local uprisings, especially in the Andes, where they had previously enjoyed gender complementarity but were by now subjugated to the patriarchal state; some fought their new situation through military force.

Native People Respond to the Bourbon Reforms

King Charles III intensified the Bourbon reforms by raising taxes on Native communities and more stringently enforcing labor demands to the Potosí silver-mine and *obrajes* that held workers as virtual prisoners. He also attacked the Church, which many Indigenous people by then revered as important. Growing *reparto de mercancías* impositions that forced Native people to purchase useless Spanish goods at elevated prices added to their burdens. Increasing commerce between the colonies, such as goods traded between Buenos Aires and Upper Peru, angered and undermined the economic positions of Native traders who had previously earned profits with their own mule trains. Royal supervision in the form of new custom houses along such regional trade routes and *corregidor* supervisors who patrolled the commerce imposed additional and more onerous restrictions upon regional Native trade. As Charles Walker has argued, such reforms "were not an abstraction for ... the Indigenous people ...; they were a daily grievance, corroding their social, political, and economic standing."[1]

By the mid-eighteenth century, Natives were increasingly frustrated with Spanish impositions. In Panama, the Kuna were angry with the Jesuit missionaries who had been proselytizing among them. At the mission of Yaviza, four *neles* (seers) called their missionary a "devil in black clothing," and staged parodies of the missionary's prayers over dead animals in the masses they acted out on their own in the chapel. In 1751, the isthmus exploded in a widespread rebellion as Kuna rose up against colonial rule and threatened Panama City. Driving out the French pirates who had settled among them, the Kuna refused to allow outsiders into their territory.[2] It took 20 years for the Spanish to re-gather the Kuna into missions.

Local impositions and protests aside, Spain and Portugal nevertheless pushed to increase royal power over their overseas dominions. The Bourbon monarchs in particular tried to limit the strength of what they perceived to be their most powerful rival, the Papacy and the Pope's so-called "shock troops," the Jesuits. The Pope had authorized King Charles to appoint almost all religious positions in the colonies by the *Patronato Universal* in 1753, which updated the *Patronato Real* of 1508, as explained in Chapter 4. The Jesuits still threatened the Crown because they answered first to the Pope, so King Charles could not control them.

Enemies of the Jesuits, most notably the Marquis of Pombal in Lisbon, accused the order of operating its own state with a private army of 6,000 Guaraní in northern La Plata. Pombal first expelled the Jesuits from his territories, but the Guaraní Mission resisted his order with force. In February 1756, Portuguese soldiers met a large force of the Guaraní Mission on the Plain of Maize, where the Portuguese governor killed their great chief Tiaraju. Some days later, Indigenous forces from the seven missions in the area fought the imperial Portuguese and Spanish armies with bamboo cannons again at Caaíbaté, but suffered 1,400 deaths. Royal forces lost only three soldiers and a few wounded in what they called the "greatest and quickest destruction of an Indian army in Brazilian history."[3]

Following Portuguese initiative, a decade later Spain also attacked the Jesuits, falsely accusing the missions of following a Jesuit ruler named Nicolás I, and for instigating the Hat and Cloak Riots that took place in March 1766 in Madrid. Although the Spanish people had risen to denounce the high prices of bread, oil, and wine, they were also angry at the reforms King Charles had imposed to modernize Spain in the style of France: short capes and three-cornered hats instead of the traditional Spanish capes and large hats that might hide the faces of criminals. Charles III used the riots to expel the Jesuits from all his territories and seize their properties. At the heart of the struggle between the Crown and the Jesuits as it spread to the colonies, though, was increased regalism and access to Indigenous converts at the missions, who European settlers still wished to use as slaves. Intensified taxation and the loss of land pressured Native communities to rise up in opposition but also changed them culturally.

Conflicts erupted throughout the colonies during the 1760s as Indigenous communities reacted to Bourbon impositions that were worsening their conditions. In the Yucatan, the Dzul (as Indigenous people called the Europeans) had pushed the Natives into towns so that the Europeans could use Native land for cattle, forcing communities to save for years to buy back their properties. Spanish cattle trampled Indigenous fields. Colonial laws forced Indigenous people to work for the Spanish and trapped them in debt peonage on the *haciendas* that took over Native lands. Settlers also raped Native women. Conditions were explosive by the time the Bourbons increased taxation. During a fiesta held in 1761 in the town of Quisteil, a drunken brawl led to the death of a Spanish merchant and scared the local priest, who fled in search of help to put down what he called a rebellion. Spanish troops tried to arrest the murderer but a Native ambush killed half of the contingent, including the commander.

Afraid because of the deaths, the local Native village leader named Jacinto fortified Quisteil and raised 1,500 troops to defend his people. Jacinto took the name of Canek, after the famed Itzá ruler from neighboring Guatemala who had fallen to the colonial authorities 64 years earlier. The Mayan Books of Chilam Balam, as explained in Chapter 3, were texts written in Spanish during the sixteenth century that had prophesied the return of an Itzá king who would drive all the foreigners back into the sea. Faced with an imminent Spanish reprisal and perhaps seeing Canek as the fulfillment of their Chilam Balam legend, villagers rallied around Jacinto and crowned him king in their church. Canek's moment of glory was short-lived: in a brief week, 2,000 Spanish soldiers retook Quisteil and slaughtered 500 of his followers. The rebel leader fled but was captured and taken to Mérida, where the authorities had him drawn and quartered in the main plaza. The Spanish garroted 8 fellow leaders, lashed 200 more rebels with 200 lashes each, and cut off one of their ears to mark them out as rebels.[4] The imperial response seems vastly out of proportion to the offenses; the punishments show that the Bourbons were nervous about restless conditions in their colonies and mounting creole fears of the darker peoples they ruled.

Then, in September 1766, Charles III heightened the conflict by forcing Paraguay's bishop to evict the Jesuits from their famous missions and replace them with secular clergy. There were so few priests in the province, however, that officials ignored the mandate. Six months later, the king finally followed France's lead of 1764, banning Jesuits from all Spanish territory and confiscating their properties. Bourbon regalism drastically changed the lives of thousands of Indigenous peoples living at the Jesuit missions.

Over the following years, local rebellions shook New Spain as authorities expelled Jesuit priests. Native people revolted not against the priests but instead attacked colonial authorities to defend their religious system and the priests they loved. This expulsion, part of the

Bourbons' regalist attempts to control the Catholic Church, shook the colonies. The eviction of the Jesuits changed Indigenous lives as missions closed and they revolted against royal authority. *Visitador General* José de Galvéz, in charge of expelling the Jesuits in New Spain, decreed harsh punishments for any rebel who rioted in defense of the priests. In the town of San Nicolás, within the *Alcaldía Major* of Michoacán, authorities executed 11 Indigenous people, cut off the town secretary's right hand, and abolished the village's political rights as a result of their protests. In the town of El Venado, royal forces executed 12 Indigenous people and exiled 72, gave 200 lashes to 7, and took away the community's rights to public lands; in San Francisco, 8 Natives were executed, 2 were whipped, and 7 imprisoned for life. Authorities in Pátzcuaro executed 2 Indigenous people and imprisoned 20 for life, lashed 24 Native people 200 times, and exiled 29 more. Following a larger uprising in San Luis Potosí against the expulsion, the authorities sent 300 Native men to prison and fined the leader of the rebellion 500 pesos, in effect condemning him to a lifetime of servitude.

The crisis caused by the evictions of the Jesuits deepened into popular movements exacerbated by coercive labor, heavy taxes, low prices paid for village products, and especially the increasing loss of land. In Tulancingo, in today's State of Hidalgo, several thousand Indigenous villagers gathered around an elderly Native man from the countryside and a woman revered as the Virgin of Guadalupe because of her Indigenous features. Proclaiming Catholic priests to be the real devils, followers of the cult appointed their own Native priests, worshiped a cross studded with images, and declared an end to the onerous clerical and state taxes. Natives dedicated their corn and chili fields to the One True God in resemblance of their traditional fertility cults. By calling for an end to taxation, demanding that colonists pay tribute to Indigenous people, and declaring a new world where Spanish bishops and priests would kiss their Native leader's hand, followers of the Virgin of Guadalupe were trying to invert the colonial world they so hated.[5] This regional cult was short-lived. José de Gálvez, the *Visitador General* of New Spain who expelled the Jesuits, brutally crushed the Tulancingo revolts.

The expulsion of the Jesuits and their replacement with secular clergy in February, 1767 led to uncertainty for the Guaraní Mission in La Plata. In Buenos Aires, Governor Bucareli proceeded cautiously to avoid another Guaraní uprising, especially because mission Natives were armed. In November, Bucareli entertained 60 Guaraní leaders from the 30 missions in his area. The following year he visited Nicolas Ñenguiru, the Guaraní leader, musician, and Native *corregidor* (magistrate) at the mission of Nuestra Señora de la Concepción, east of the Iguazú Falls in the Guairá territory which had become part of Brazil following the Treaty of Madrid (explained in Chapter 8), and showered him with gifts. Ñenguiru had already written a letter to Governor Bucareli in 1753, claiming the rights of the Guaraní to remain at the missions. Having already changed their ways of life and accepted Christianity, when the Crown expelled the Jesuits the Guaraní felt betrayed and several thousand left the missions. Many Native people did not return to the forests but instead left the area to work on ranches or as artisans in towns throughout Rio de la Plata and north of the Iguazú Falls. The Guaraní also settled in towns throughout eastern Paraguay, where, as in Brazil, measles and influenza decimated their communities.[6] The expulsion ended Guaraní resistance. Yet the fact that Governor Bucareli still personally saw the need to court the Guaraní leader shows their importance in geopolitical negotiations taking place at the time.

For Document 9.1: Nicolás Ñenguiru's Letter to the Governor of Buenos Aires (1753), visit www.routledge.com/9780415519120.

It was the Indigenous people in New Spain who expressed their discontent most loudly during the 1770s, although there were already angry rumblings in the Andes. In November 1771, the Aymara in the valley of Pacajes, Upper Peru killed their *corregidor* and his constable on All Souls' Day and seized control of the provincial capital of Caquiaviri. People were angry because over the previous religious festivities the authorities had treated celebrants brutally when their revelry had gotten out of hand. Suddenly finding themselves with new power, the Indigenous people imprisoned and even killed some of the Spanish and mestizo residents. Historian Sinclair Thomson has called the results of this uprising a "powerful notion of social transformation" that empowered anticolonial violence.[7]

Meanwhile, in the Valley of Oaxaca, New Spain, Indigenous people in the village of Zimatlán protested in 1772 because of excessive tribute, taxation, and especially the brutal punishment used to force women trapped in debt peonage to produce cochineal, the area's main export crop. European demand for the red dye had grown tremendously. Rather than admit the people's legitimate grievances, church and state authorities blamed the insurrection on the Natives' "lazy, ignorant, uncouth, vice-ridden, insolent rebellious nature or their uncivilized way of life, 'lacking god, Law and King.'" The priest attributed the uprising to the Indigenous people's "wicked style of government," because "everyone rules," including women and children.[8] The reference to practices of more egalitarian leadership shows that even in these late stages of widespread Native integration, the colonizers still saw Indigenous customs as significantly different.

Finally, as the European demand for cochineal dye grew, authorities in New Spain used coercion in Mixteca and Sierra Zapoteca villages to increase production. In 1774, townspeople throughout Teozacualco rebelled against the district lieutenant for demanding cochineal, interfering in their village affairs, and trying to tax the liquor they made.[9] Three years later, villagers in the small town of Coamelco, in the jurisdiction of Meztitlán, rose to oppose excessive taxation by their parish priest.[10] As Natives challenged abuses at the local level, they gained experience with colonial judicial systems. Their village uprisings should not have worried the colonial elite, however, since without a leader to draw broader support these rebellions rarely amounted to much. Still, the discontent from below unsettled administrators and made the creoles question the Crown's ability to defend them from the rebellious Native people.

Indigenous Transformations and Insurgencies in the Andes

While Indigenous people in New Spain protested the expulsion of the Jesuits, in South America Native peoples were also adjusting to life in the colonial Spanish world. The Reche were by this time fully engaged in trade and cattle raids, crossing the southern Andes regularly to trade their ponchos and steal livestock from ranches west of Buenos Aires along with their Huilliche allies. Both peoples also fought their common Native enemies on the plains, the Pehuenche.[11] To organize their raids and strategize, the Reche gathered periodically in large group council meetings, where they also negotiated with the Spanish authorities. At the meeting held at Tapihue in 1774, the *loncos* (leaders) defined their united policy toward Spanish threats and diminished internal dissent. Such councils eliminated those chiefs who were resisting changes and over time unified the different communities, giving authority to forward-looking caciques who prepared for life in the changing world. These broad councils also shaped Reche identity by making it more comprehensive and inclusive, but especially by forging a new identity as a people. By the 1770s, as two Franciscan sources explain, the Reche were calling themselves "Mapuche," meaning people (che) of the earth (mapu), rather than their previous designation Reche, as well as referring to their language as Mapudugu. They called peoples outside their world Espanamapu (Spanish) or Murumapu, people of other countries. As Boccara has explained, contact with outsiders had birthed a new identity for these southern people.[12]

Other Andean transformations were more violent, especially where long-conquered Indigenous people opposed the intensification of abusive labor practices and heavier taxation under the Bourbon reforms. Nowhere was anger more evident than in Peru and Upper Peru, where labor at the hated silver-mines killed Indigenous workers every year. Natives in particular hated the *repartimiento de mercancías*, the system that forced them to purchase European goods at prices well above market rates. Many of the goods were not even useful to them; for instance, razors for shaving, blue hair powder, mules, cloth from Quito, and spirits such as brandy.

Given their own frustrations with colonial rule, women also joined these uprisings. Native women in the Andes resented the male control that accompanied Catholicism. Having lived through centuries of Spanish rule, however, by this time, Native people were so thoroughly a part of colonial society and depended so much on European goods, institutions, services, and religion that a return to pre-Columbian Indigenous ways of life was no longer possible, and probably not even imagined. Indigenous people no longer hoped to eliminate all European traces and bring back Aymara and Quechua ways of life. In fact, Native rebels even took priests (or dragged them against their will) along with them to celebrate Mass, because Hispanic religious institutions, such as images of the saints, and *cofradías* (Catholic fraternities of laypeople) had become such an important part of their faith and lives.[13] Rather, Native rebels hoped only to alleviate the worst of colonial injustices.

The decades following 1760 were therefore violent as the colonial impositions worsened: simultaneous conflicts in Native communities and between their legitimate leaders and those leaders imposed by the Spanish authorities shook the Andean world at the local level and changed Indigenous people in the process. In 1769, Indigenous people in the town of Sicasica, Upper Peru, killed the *corregidor*'s agent and two years later organized a confederation of communities that besieged the town of Chulumani, with visions of establishing Native control over a new political order. Similarly, by 1771, Indigenous forces took over the provincial capital of Pacajes, Caquiaviri, and then an angry mob beat the *corregidor* to death with iron bars, smashed the skull of their ex-cacique, and killed his supporters. After cutting off all roads to the outside, the rebels contemplated massacring all the Spanish in the town and an armed march on La Paz. Neither of these options occurred, likely because the *corregidor* readied the city militias and villagers were unprepared to assume control.[14] The following year, the authorities doubled the sales tax to 4 percent. Natives then attacked other local officials. Such insurrections threatened colonial elites with the potential of spreading to the Indigenous majority; authorities in La Paz argued that only a complete revision of the *repartimiento*, or even its abolishment, might prevent disaster. Instead, administrators again raised taxes. Such an action seems suicidal, given the anger within communities, yet the internal corruption in the deteriorating colonial system explains such a move. During this time there was intense conflict over political jurisdiction and boundaries between authorities in Lima, capital of the viceroyalty, and the *audiencia* in La Plata. To make matters worse, state and church officials in La Paz increasingly threatened *corregidores* because of the way they took advantage of the political system to enrich themselves. Administrative tensions reached communities as people rejected abuses and intimidation tactics by the *reparto* agents who enforced taxation at the local level.[15]

Map 9.1 Indigenous Uprisings during the Late Eighteenth Century

Finally fed up, people reacted angrily to the Bourbon reforms and corruption. The tensions, focused in Chayanta and then in Cuzco, escalated and spread rapidly. Angry Indigenous people first threw out their traditional *kurakas*, who were getting rich at their expense, and then attacked the entire colonial system. A good example was Tomás Katari, *kuraka* of the Aymara community of Macha, north of Potosí in the province of Chayanta, who finally sparked an insurrection against the local authorities. In 1778, the leader traveled to Buenos Aires to argue before the *audiencia* (high court) that local colonial leaders were immoral and unfit to rule because they refused to recognize his title of *kuraka*; the authorities dismissed his charges. Following his arrest, villagers twice besieged the city of La Plata to demand Katari's freedom, but he was soon again behind bars.

In August 1780, villagers seized the *corregidor* and exchanged him for Katari, opening a brief period of Native self-rule in Chayanta. Energized by their success, villagers grew violent and difficult for Katari to control; in Moscari, angry Aymara killed their *kuraka* for collaboration and displayed his head outside their city. The militia head, Juán Antonio Acuña, finally arrested Katari. When the Aymara attacked his convoy, Acuña put the rebel to death. In response, angry Aymara killed Acuña and the entire troop, even piercing Acuña's eyes and leaving the bodies to rot.[16] The revolt reflected growing anger against heavy-handed colonial rule: at least 66 known revolts took place in the Andes between 1770 and 1780, some linked to leaders who claimed Inca lineage.[17]

Another leader during this time of swelling discontent was Julián Apaza, an Aymara from Sicasica in Chayanta, Upper Peru, who had grown up in poverty and suffered from childhood poliomyelitis that had left his legs and hands twisted. Apaza was a merchant who exchanged highland goods such as beef jerky for coca and baize cloth (coarse woolen fabric) from warmer valleys to the east. The merchant spoke no Spanish and was illiterate, but as a teenager he had been influenced by the community struggles in Sicasica, Yungas, and Pacajes (mentioned earlier). As he traveled, Apaza saw his people's poor conditions and experienced the "engrained, everyday modes of colonial domination, as well as the common suffering of Indians, their fears and resentment, and the yearning for release from the 'heavy yoke'."[18] As a result, Apaza began to organize Native people in the towns he visited, consulting oracles and participating in religious rituals. Like Katari, he went to Buenos Aires to speak with the viceroy about the unpopular economic reforms, but failed even to get an appointment. Trade took Apaza throughout Upper Peru, where he "made enormous efforts to persuade and mobilize the Indians, to whom he presented himself as Tomás Túpac-Katari, Inka King, and as Viceroy." Poor Native people followed Apaza because of his charisma and especially because he promised to free them from their heavy economic burdens. The leader later confessed to having "traveled to a great many towns and places and made enormous efforts to persuade and mobilize the Indians," especially his relatives.[19] The merchant likely took part in the Indigenous riots in La Paz in 1780 and then stopped paying his own tribute dues, a crime that landed his Aymara wife Bartolina Sisa in jail no fewer than five times. As Apaza gained followers, they called Bartolina "Virreina," or queen.[20]

The third Indigenous leader to organize at the time was José Gabriel Condorcanqui, an acculturated and well-educated mestizo from Cuzco, Peru, who claimed descent on his mother's Quechua side from the last Inca ruler. Condorcanqui was also a wealthy merchant who owned a train of 350 mules that traveled between Cuzco and Potosí. The

Bourbon shift of political power from Peru to La Plata, which left Lima without control of Potosí silver, directly affected him. Like Apaza, Condorcanqui traveled to Buenos Aires to talk with the viceroy, but was also unsuccessful. The leader initially promised to place an official in each town to collect a head tax for the Inca capital of Cuzco. In addition to eliminating lawyers and simplifying punishment by hanging offenders on the spot, Condorcanqui attracted followers by promising to abolish the *mita*, alcabalas, customs houses, and the *corregidores*.[21] Unlike earlier rebels, Condorcanqui professed to have received authority directly from the king to discipline his corrupt representatives. He took the name Tupac Amaru II, after the Inca leader who resisted the Spaniards in the 1500s, and tried to ally creoles, mestizos, and Indigenous people together against the *Peninsulares*, but the revolt spread out of control as his followers merged with the Katari insurrection and began to pillage in Upper Peru.

In November 1780, Tupac Amaru II ambushed and captured the despised nobleman Antonio de Arriaga, the *corregidor* in charge of collecting taxes and organizing the hated labor draft for the Potosí silver-mines, after having lunch with him in Tungasuca. Arriaga had even lent Condorcanqui money on occasion, but this time the rebel executed the official following a summary trial. Tupac Amaru II's goals became more radical: he abolished the *mita*, *repartimiento de mercancías*, African slavery and the offices of viceroy, *corregidor*, and *audiencia*, and then declared independence from Spain and the expulsion of all *Peninsulares*. Tupac Amaru II intended to rule as monarch of a restored Inca Empire, without sales taxes and large estates. The leader's views contrasted sharply with those of his angrier followers, who revived Indigenous religious practices, sacked churches, and hung priests as they attacked the cities. The cautious leader, however, failed to heed his wife's advice and did not besiege Cuzco soon enough, so Condorcanqui lost the advantage that storming the former Inca capital might have given the insurrection.

Women Join the Uprising as Leaders and Supporters

Indigenous women played important roles in the developing rebel movements. Condorcanqui's mestiza wife, Micaela Bastidas, was a strong leader in her own right; rebel troops addressed her as Señora Gobernadora. As commandant of the rebel stronghold, commissar of war, and paymaster general of the soldiers, Bastidas oversaw recruitment, supply lines, and requisitioned goods to feed the troops in the growing insurrection. She also controlled banditry and looting, posted sentinels, and watched out for spies while supervising the manufacture of arms. One tithe collector reported that Micaela had threatened to "punch him" if he did not submit.[22] In November, following Arriaga's killing, Tupac Amaru and Micaela camped in Tungasuca and solicited support from neighboring *kurakas*. Rebel troops stormed the surrounding towns and gathered people in the plaza or churches to explain their plans. Women followed the troops as camp aides, collecting rocks from the mines to use in slings, which complemented lances and pikes as effective weapons. Rebels also found a few cannons and learned to use the muskets they captured against the Spanish. A devout Catholic throughout her life, Micaela ordered troops to display palm crosses and red embroidery as insignias on their hats, "as a sign that they are good and true Christians."[23] Bastidas' directives show Gobernadora's desire that her rebel movement be legitimate to the very colonial world that she was helping overthrow. Clearly a forceful woman, Bastidas gave her husband advice on political and military strategy, and played an important role in the uprising.

Figure 9.1 Micaela Bastidas. (The Picture Art Collection/Alamy Stock Photo)

Another wealthy Quechua cacica at the time was Tomasa Tito Condemayta Hurtado de Mendoza, from Arcos, Peru, who secured silver and provided supplies to Tupac Amaru's army. She commanded a troop of women who defended the Pilpinto pass south of Cuzco from colonial forces for over a month. A member of the Arequipa militia wrote that he had never witnessed "such obstinacy and desperate defense as that of the Indian women … they can be seen with rifles raised at their breast and not only do they not ask to be pardoned, but they never cease to throw rocks and do injury to the troops." Others called the women "super-masculine" and capable of great cruelty.[24] Although women accompanied the rebel army as camp aides, few documents mention their support. A rare exception refers to one battle in Oruro, after the insurrection spread to Upper Peru, where women provided ammunition for the soldiers' slings. As one observer described, "the women dedicated themselves to continually collecting rocks, particularly big, sturdy ones they brought from the mines."[25] While often ignored in the documents, Indigenous women helped the rebellion. In the trials that followed, the authorities prosecuted and then executed both Tomasa Titu Condemayta and Micaela Bastidas.

For Document 9.2: Correspondence from Micaela Bastidas Puyucahua to José Gabriel Condorcanqui (Tupac Amaru II), 6 December, 1780, visit www.routledge.com/9780415519120.

The Uprisings Spread

Condorcanqui's massive uprising eventually spread across half the Peruvian Andes and south, out of his control, into Upper Peru. To put down the rebellion, the authorities in Cuzco sent out 1,300 soldiers, among them 722 Indigenous loyalists. The Spanish mobilized large numbers of *yanaconas*, Native people who had left their communities of origin to live among and work for the colonists, but Tupac Amaru won a decisive victory at the Battle of Sangarará in November 1780, at 12,500 feet above sea level. With 10,000 Native and 600 mestizo troops brought from neighboring towns, rebel forces surrounded royalist weapons and supplies and then attacked at four in the morning, "sounding like an earthquake."[26] The victory gave Tupac Amaru control of the entire highlands south of Puno. Rebels then marched south to the Titicaca basin in Upper Peru and joined Katari's movement, where most of the fighting in the war took place. The rebels' lack of arms and the vicious slaughter of Spanish forces and pillaging in this southern campaign, however, ended all hopes of securing creole support and dashed any idea of achieving independence from Spain.

After Tomás Katari's execution, his brothers Dámaso and Nivolas organized an army that overran mestizo towns, textile mills, and *obrajes*, putting to death all European men, women, and children. Like the French Revolution that took place ten years later, once unleashed, violence by the popular classes spun out of control in Upper Peru. Creoles rallied behind the empire against the Native insurgents, out of fear for their own lives. Rebel leaders also failed to capitalize on their victories and larger royalist forces eventually overwhelmed them.

Late in 1780, Tupac Amaru finally followed Micaela's advice and besieged Cuzco with an army reported to have numbered 40,000, but only if one includes the unofficial women and family members who cooked and gathered food and wood. The rebels mismanaged this siege: surrounding Native villagers entered the city rather than join the attacking forces as planned, where the colonial authorities terrified them "with stories of the bloodthirsty nature of the rebels and the horrific consequences for those who disobeyed and supported the rebels."[27] Nor had invading leaders considered the effect that Catholic priests would have as they convinced city dwellers to remain loyal. Despite poor conditions in their camps, including an epidemic of dysentery, rebels may have had a chance to take Cuzco had it not been for rival Indigenous troops, loyalists that finally helped the Spanish break the siege. Key among these attackers were divisions under Mateo Pumacahua, the wealthy cacique from Chinchero, north of Cuzco, who helped prevent rebels from taking the northern passes into the city.[28] The victory again shows the divisions among Indigenous peoples in Peru.

By the end of February 1781, royal reinforcements from Lima and their Indigenous allies finally overran the rebel forces, capturing Tupac Amaru and his family. When the *Visitador* (royal inspector) José Antonio de Areche demanded that Condorcanqui reveal the names of his accomplices while he was being tortured on the rack, the prisoner reportedly scornfully replied, "there are no accomplices here other than you and I. You as oppressor, I as liberator, deserve to die."[29] Royal soldiers executed Tupac Amaru's captains with unusual ferocity in Cuzco's plaza in front of over 10,000 assembled Indigenous people, and then killed his family members. Executioners cut out Micaela Bastidas' tongue, but the iron vice they used as a garrote was too large to kill her. Instead, they looped ropes around her neck and kicked at her stomach and breasts as they pulled in opposite directions until she died.[30] Finally, torturers cut out Tupac Amaru's tongue and then tied his arms and legs to four horses to quarter him, but his body would not break, so they finally beheaded him beside the gallows. The authorities finally paraded the rebel's body parts throughout Peru to illustrate the perils of rising against the empire.

The general uprising continued for another year in Upper Peru, where followers of Tupac Katari overran the Central Sierra in January 1781 and then besieged La Paz from March to October. Steep hills surrounded the city of 25,000 inhabitants that Katari's forces enclosed in March 1781, and their siege was another example of rebel mismanagement. Attackers blundered by providing food to acquaintances inside the city, and even greeting friends over the walls. As Bartolina Sisa explained, Tupac Katari inspired followers with his promise that "they would be left as the absolute owners of this place, and of its wealth." Native supporters spoke of an expected time in the near future when "they alone would rule." These Natives linked messianic expectations of greater *ayllu* power and Inca rule to visions of Indigenous emancipation, self-determination, and hegemony.[31] The importance of nativism was evident in rebel camps, where Katari ordered his troops to speak only Aymara. The insurgency spread out of control as angry troops overran ranches and towns, so the leader declared that he often could not "restrain the Indian communities due to his fear of their fury and ferocity."[32] In fact, the zeal of the rebel forces forced Katari to link with Tupac Amaru's movement in Peru.

Bartolina Sisa helped lead the Native army of around 40,000 that besieged La Paz. To frighten the city dwellers, Katari wrote letters threatening to "return the city to dust and ashes" and cut the throats and string up those who held out against him. In fact, the leader hung captives in full view of the city and his soldiers shouted throughout the night to frighten the besieged city dwellers. Despite these fear tactics, the colonial militias slowly retook advantage. Spanish forces from Buenos Aires numbering 7,000 arrived in October and quickly crushed the revolt. By then, many Indigenous followers had turned against Katari. The Spanish authorities executed the leader, his wife, and their inner circle in September 1782. The following January, the rebels signed the Peace of Sicuani, which ended major hostilities, and the authorities quickly crushed residual revolts that erupted the following year.[33]

The Andean revolt had no immediate benefits to Native peoples. In attacking Indigenous culture and the memory of the Incas in the Cuzco region, the Spanish authorities destroyed Amaru's houses, documents, clothing, pictures, and even tried to eliminate the use of the Quechua language and music. In the end, the authorities abandoned this program because it was too overwhelming to implement.[34] Repression of the insurrection in Upper Peru left thousands dead and the trials continued for years. The revolts did change the continent, however, because they heightened tensions in colonial Latin America at a critical time by challenging creole rule and threatening royal control after the Bourbon reforms had made so many enemies. The elite realized that lower castes were willing to risk even death to improve their situation, and this pressure from below ultimately helped push the creole elite to seek independence from Spain.

Additional Indigenous Challenges to Bourbon Rule

Once Indigenous people in the Andes showed that it was possible to challenge royal authority, the idea caught on and growing disaffection led to more uprisings throughout the 1780s. These movements frightened Spanish rulers because of their potential to spread dissent, and the authorities viewed local uprisings in terms of dreaded diseases like "contagion" or "cancer" that could contaminate the entire colonial system. Already in 1781, a rebellion in Izucar de Matamoros, New Spain, south of Mexico City in today's State of Puebla, made officials fear another Tupac Amaru uprising. Following more rebellions north of Mexico City, the authorities tried to prevent such insurgencies from spreading to the Chichimec and Huaxtec Indigenous people they referred to as "wild."[35] In the Viceroyalty of New Granada, lower classes calling themselves *Comuneros* rebelled in March 1781 against new taxes on tobacco and an unpopular poll tax. Thousands of peasants and artisans in the city of Socorro, northeast of Bogotá in modern Colombia, elected a central committee with a captain to represent themselves to the viceroy in the capital. While this insurrection was not carried out by Native people, Indigenous people in the isolated eastern *llanos*, the grasslands, did take advantage of the *Comunero* rebellion to rise up against white settlers and attacked missionaries in their midst, adding to the general creole elite's instability.[36] While sources do not indicate their specific name, these rebels were possibly the Hiwi – who called themselves the "people of the savannah" – because of their long history of violent resistance to outsiders that would extend well into the twentieth century.

Over the following years, a few Indigenous rebels tried to restart uprisings against the Spanish, but their efforts to mobilize supporters failed. In southern Peru, a new leader in Pacajes named Esteban Atahualpa proclaimed himself Inca in 1782, and gathered a few followers against the Spanish. Native communities, however, were battle fatigued from years of war and refused to risk their lives. There is very little information left about this leader and no trial records even exist about his capture, showing that his brief movement was insignificant compared to the earlier rebellions led by Tupac Amaru and Katari, and that Atahualpa never found much support.

The following year, shortly after the authorities executed Tupac Amaru's cousins and leading officers Diego Cristóbal and Andrés Tupac Amaru, an uprising took place in Huarochirí, east of Lima, where an Indigenous man by the name of Felipe Velasco tried to gather followers for a revolt by taking the name Túpac Inca Yupanqui. Like Esteban, though, Velasco's efforts also failed.[37] People simply had no energy left to fight. Elsewhere, on the Atlantic coast of Panama where the Kuna had long challenged both Spanish and French control, missionaries sent to remove the nose rings and anklets of the Kuna women reported some success. In 1785, the Spanish erected four additional forts along the San Blas coast and three more in southern Panama to keep out the British and control the Kuna. Regional movements had no broader significance, but they did pressure creole elites from below at an uneasy time.

Bourbon Reforms Change Colonial Society

The Bourbon monarchs pressured their colonial subjects to increase their exports to meet the growing European demand for tobacco, hides, and sugar, yet further demands undermined their control. New technology, improved roads and navigation, fewer restrictions on commerce, relaxations on the rules for borrowing credit, and easier acquisition of land all pushed the colonies away from subsistence agriculture and toward production of plantation crops such as indigo and cochineal dye for fabrics; subjects increased exports of both products during the second half of the eighteenth century. Much of the agro-export growth took place in El Salvador and especially in Guatemala, with huge changes for Native communities.

Guatemala City was a center of clerical wealth and prestige, principally for the Dominicans and Franciscans, who took advantage of local Indigenous laborers to produce crops and construct public works, often without adequate compensation. Changing from subsistence farming to export crops led to Native food shortages, since much of the land they had used for personal crops became plantations for export crops. Malnutrition spread and imports of foreign food raised prices for the common people, leading to a serious depression during the quarter-century before independence.[38]

Rising demands for land and labor for the production of export crops strained social ties and lower classes questioned the wisdom of the Crown's economic policies. In western, highland Guatemala, a rural area, Natives were wards of the state and still made tribute payments. Native rituals and distinct languages continued to set them apart enough to allow them continued identification as Indigenous people. The Church helped guard these markers of difference to protect its access to Natives' spiritual allegiance and resources. In the rest of Central America, creoles called Natives who had lost direct connection to their communities of origin and shared a mixed Indigenous and European heritage *ladinos.*

Generally not accepted by either group, many *ladinos* stopped identifying as Indigenous, worked as artisans in towns or as clients to the upper class, and became more mobile and aggressive than either Native people or Europeans.[39] As more Natives moved to cities and became *ladinos*, the disappearance of their traditional communities led to additional social *castas* and slowly broke down segregated colonial society. *Ladinos* in the cities begged, found menial work, or even turned to crime. By this time, *ladinos* made up 31 percent of the kingdom of Central America and in Nicaragua as much as 84 percent of the population.[40] Displacement of Native farmers and their loss of land to *ladino* society gradually broke down colonial productivity. The growth of the *ladino* population was one of the most important changes for Central America in the eighteenth century, and by the early 1800s Guatemala was the most integrated state in Central America. In addition to changing demographics, central Mexico faced terrible famines during those years in which thousands died of hunger and disease. An economic depression and the loss of land to export agriculture contributed to a shifting identity crisis for Native people. Uprisings in Indigenous villages reflected these tensions as they spread throughout the isthmus.

Royal programs set up to improve the Crown's political control and taxation also encountered obstacles, especially when carried out by corrupt administrators. In the jurisdiction of Metepec, southeast of Mexico City, a parish priest levied a census for tax purposes in February 1792 with the help of Indigenous assistants. The communities of San Lucas, Amanalco, and San Miguel simply refused to admit the census takers, and men and women bearing knives and throwing rocks chased them out of town. A mob made up mainly of women broke into the church, overran the jail, and freed three of their own people. Upper-class parishioners defended the priest, who fought off the mob with his blunderbuss; one Indigenous person died and three were injured in the ensuing fight, and the mob beat up the priest's Indigenous assistant for his collaboration. Following a few arrests, most of the villagers fled to the mountains.[41] The testimony from the resulting trials shows that the priest had overcharged parishioners for his services, had them whipped needlessly, and had allowed his three assistants to steal community lands for their own use.

Events: Revolutionary Changes in the Atlantic World

As if the Bourbon reforms were not enough, news of political events in the North Atlantic reached Latin America during the final decade of the eighteenth century and began to change society. Enlightenment ideas about human society circulated as forbidden books among wealthy Americanos. The Americanos were local elite of European descent who were frustrated with Iberian colonial rule and who were by this time using the term to distinguish themselves from the *Peninsulares*. While the Inquisition tried to prevent the liberalizing influence from spreading, creoles read treatises by the radical European thinkers of the day, Montesquieu, Voltaire, and Rousseau, and U.S. ships brought them the writings of Washington, Adams, and Jefferson. Imagine how thoughts of liberty, equality, and fraternity, along with John Locke's argument that governments should protect life, liberty, and property, moved creoles who were so tired of being excluded from power by the *Peninsulares*. News about the independence of the British colonies in North America aroused Americanos and their literary societies. Then, the slave revolt in 1791 that ousted the French from their Caribbean colony of Saint-Domingue and declared an independent republic of Haiti really frightened creoles. If African slaves could overpower the colonial authorities, what would prevent them and Indigenous people from doing the same throughout Latin America?

As if to add to Haiti, the Reign of Terror in 1793 that followed the French Revolution also spread fear among the Americanos. The execution and imprisonment of 40,000 nobles in France by radicals and workers, not long after Tupac Amaru's rebellion, reminded Americanos of the possibility that lower castes in Latin America could pursue similar horrors. This threatening turn of events made the Americanos decide to prevent lower castes from challenging their privileges.

Given popular discontent in the colonies and the rapid spread of radical ideas, during the final decades of the eighteenth century Bourbon rulers focused increasingly on defense. Their colonies faced attacks from the French, Dutch, and British, who repeatedly tried to steal land and riches. Spain was bankrupt because, along with France, it had lost the Seven Years' War to Great Britain in 1763. Both the Spanish and Portuguese empires foisted the cost of defending their colonies onto the colonists themselves. Low on imperial personnel, especially in the borderlands, colonial administrators increasingly employed creole and Native mercenary soldiers to fight for them, as officials in Peru had done to help repress the large Indigenous insurrections.

One unique place where Indigenous people still faced Americano expansion during these years was in the Eastern Band, the grasslands that became Uruguay. The Charrua people in the interior struggled to defend their fertile grasslands from more and more Spanish and Portuguese colonists who coveted the territory. The colony's location at the Paraná River delta also offered control to access South American resources. By the end of the eighteenth century, the Charrua people had dwindled to fewer than 1,000 people from disease and violence with the settlers, but they still harassed colonists who ventured in to herd cattle. Charrua warriors even occasionally attacked the town of Montevideo. In 1796, Americanos created a rag-tag corps of deserters, contrabandists, fugitives, cowboys called *gauchos*, and outlaws to defend the town of Montevideo and its outposts.[42] Settlers placed José Artigas, a frontiersman whose grandfather had founded Montevideo, at the head of this new troop, called the Blandengues Corps. Legends still hold that Artigas had African ancestry, had actually lived among the Charrua as a youth, and had fathered a son named Caciquillo with a Charrua woman, possibly because he was a superb horseman. More documentable is that the patriot enjoyed a unique relationship with the people, spoke their language, and that Charrua warriors helped him expel Spanish imperial forces during the wars for independence.

While Artigas received help from the Charrua to fight the empire, other colonists feared the Native people and hoped to take their fertile prairies to raise cattle. Pressure from ranchers to clear Natives off the land eventually trumped Artigas' sympathy for the Charrua. Two Blandengue expeditions attacked the Charruas in 1800/1801, and exterminated most of the people at the battles of Arapey, Sopas, and Tacuarembó. Some Charrua warriors still trusted Artigas, however, because they later helped him repel attacks by Buenos Aires and Brazil to add the Eastern Band into the new United Provinces of the River Plate, as Argentina first called itself.

Trends: Changing Politics in Spain

Although Americanos began to push back against imperial rule, it was a war in Europe that finally ended Spanish and Portuguese rule over their American colonies. King Charles IV of Spain completely mismanaged his administration, and in 1793 joined an English coalition against the new French Republic. The struggle went badly for Spain, which lost territory in the Caribbean to France. Britain eliminated Spanish shipping in the Atlantic, cutting off its communication with its colonies and attacking Buenos Aires in 1806 and again in 1807. The Americanos in La Plata fought off the British and proved the strength of their citizen militias, but the invasions destroyed the colonial Spanish administration. By the start of the nineteenth century, Spain was bankrupt. In neighboring France, Napoleon took power and in 1807 sent troops across Spain into Portugal to punish it for not having closed its ports to his British enemies. The king of Portugal and his court escaped to Brazil, but French troops occupied Spain.

Under the pretext of settling a dispute between the king and his son, Napoleon replaced them both with his brother Joseph and France took control of the Spanish Empire. Spanish resistors formed regional governing bodies in secret called juntas and launched guerrilla attacks against French occupiers. The rebels retreated to the southern port of Cádiz, where they received protection from the British and organized a secret parliament to defy the French occupiers. By 1810, French troops were closing in even on this last rebel holdout and only British naval guns kept the Spanish resistance alive. The parliament finally enacted a new constitution in 1812 that limited the monarchy and granted freedom of speech. Dependent on their colonies, though, the rebels refused to let go of their American possessions. Creole leaders in Latin America seized the opportunity offered by French occupation to take control of their own affairs in the name of captive King Charles IV.

Difficult Years for Indigenous Peoples in New Spain

Meanwhile, in the Americas, the most important way that Indigenous people contributed to independence in Latin America was by pressuring Americanos from below. Political events in Iberia as Napoleon closed the noose on Spanish rebels allowed Americanos to take charge of the colonies where they lived, but peasant and Indigenous unrest from below also pushed the creole elite to risk a rebellion against Spain. In New Spain, a severe drought in 1808 ruined crops and caused an extended agricultural crisis that raised the price of grain so severely that Native peoples faced famine conditions. The following year was even worse, and hunger and unemployment pushed peasants and Indigenous people throughout central New Spain to breaking point. Six of the most important intendencies in the colony – Oaxaca, San Luis Potosí, Guanajuato, Mexico, Mérida, and Zacatecas – lost more than two-thirds of their crops of maize, wheat, and beans in 1809. As pastures dried up, cattle died and drove up the cost of meat, transportation, and the prices of food in cities to one-third over the previous year. Native people rose up in search of work, to pillage, and to escape desperate conditions in their pueblos. By 1810, prices were the highest in a generation. Historian Eric Van Young has shown that the long drought, crop failures, and high prices devastated the working poor throughout New Spain. The agricultural crisis also affected the textile and silver-mining industries, where owners laid off workers as their own costs escalated. Bad harvests especially affected the regions of Querétaro and León, where Indigenous people joined the Hidalgo Revolt, but also influenced the centers of manufacturing in Puebla, Mexico City, and Texcoco.[43] The economic downturn pushed Indigenous people in New Spain into an explosive situation.

Native people showed little interest in the political events between Spain and its colonies. Indigenous testimonies in court cases in New Spain during those tumultuous years reveal that they were instead far more concerned about their immediate situations. The distribution of wealth and power at the grassroots level mattered far more than independence from Spain. Native people also assumed responsibility as individuals during the resulting criminal cases, insisting on having been drunk or having joined rebels out of peer pressure or under the influence of local officials, instead of as part of an angry mob pushing for political change.[44] The poor were far more concerned about putting food on their tables during those hard years.

Life under colonial rule conditioned such responses. Political scientist James C. Scott has shown that slavery, for instance, damages personal senses of self-esteem and dignity, so Native self-esteem would have been low.[45] Challenging situations during difficult years also pushed Indigenous peoples to the brink of rebellion. Native people may also have been afraid to reveal personal agendas to their judicial superiors during their trials, focusing instead on social forces such as participating in a mob. In his book *Domination and the Arts of Resistance*, Scott has argued that a subordinate person will intelligently

> conform by speech and gesture to what he knows is expected of him – even if that conformity masks a quite different offstage opinion. What is not perhaps plain enough is that, in any established system of domination, it is not just a question of masking one's feelings and producing the correct speech acts and gestures in their place. Rather, it is often a question of controlling what would be a natural impulse to rage, insult, anger, and the violence that such feelings prompt. There is no system of domination that does not produce its own routine harvest of insults and injury to

human dignity – the appropriation of labor, public humiliations, whippings, rapes, slaps, leers, contempt, ritual denigration, and so on.[46]

Colonial conditions and hidden transcripts, as well as lack of access to means of communication and interest in the affairs of colonial superiors, suggest reasons why Native people were not very interested in participating in fighting for independence from Iberia.

Rather than mobilizing for Americano political events, Native people expressed their anger against their deteriorating economic situations. First, they abandoned their unproductive lands. Desperate in draught conditions, people in the farming pueblos of Mescala, Xochipala, and Cocula, as well as in the mining camps of Palula, Sabana Grande, Coacoyula, Pedernales, Ascala, Sasamulco, all in the province of Iguala, New Spain, left behind their fields and lands in September 1809 in search of better conditions.[47] As pastures dried up and cattle died, mercury shortages also forced silver-mines to lay off their workers, leaving thousands of destitute families to seek food and work. Then Indigenous people began to attack symbols of Americano privilege and wealth.

Both in small groups and as individuals, between 1810 and 1821, Indigenous people exerted significant pressures on the Americanos from below during New Spain's war for independence. Native people sought solutions to local grievances and to defend their communities, so they mostly fought near their homes against hated symbols of unjust power relations. José Mariano, for instance, was a 28-year-old Indigenous man from Calpulalpan, northeast of Mexico City. Toward the end of April 1810, insurgents occupied his hamlet, pillaging stores and throwing goods into the streets for the poor. The rebels freed prisoners from the jail, captured José Mariano, and took him, his mule, 14 volunteers, and the *Peninsular* owner of a store along with them to kill that evening. The local priest, with an image of the Virgin of Guadalupe in hand, convinced the bandits to spare the lives of the two Spanish captives. Leaving town, the gang captured a train of mules and sacked a *hacienda*, again distributing the goods and corn to the poor. The rebels arrived in the town of Zempoala on May 3, robbing the magistrate's store and taking him captive before releasing prisoners from the jail. Four days later, the band captured the town of Tulancingo, distributed goods from stores to the poor, kept the cash, and again freed the prisoners. After they had looted other towns, a royalist force eventually caught and dispersed the bandits. José Mariano made his way home to Calpulalpan, where the authorities eventually arrested him.[48]

Such regional riots mostly lacked significant leadership and broader connections throughout New Spain. One notable exception occurred in September 1810, when Indigenous and mestizo peasants northwest of Mexico City, in the formerly rich agricultural region of Dolores, rallied behind a creole parish priest named Miguel Hidalgo. The Indigenous people of the area, who the Spanish called Chichimecas, had traditionally included Guachichiles, Pames, and Zacatecos people. Now 20,000 desperate peasants joined the priest and overran the city of Guanajuato, where over 2,000 Indigenous people in the rebel army lost their lives in the attack. The angry rebel mob grew to over 80,000 Native people and miners as it moved through Valladolid toward Mexico City. Heavy losses and low ammunition forced the rebels to disperse instead of taking Guadalajara. Even more terrorized by a lower caste uprising than by a longer struggle for independence, Americanos executed Hidalgo and disbanded his forces by the summer of 1811. To crush popular uprisings against the desperate situation, the viceroyal authorities executed thousands of peasants, posting their heads on stakes to rot beside the roads, and jailed even more, destroyed villages, and relocated poor people.[49]

Throughout Spain's Latin American colonies, Americanos assumed power in the name of the king rather than submit to French rule, most concerned with winning the right to free trade and preventing the lower castes from threatening their privileges. Demographics reveal the reason for their nervousness. By this time, estimates place the population of Spanish America at around 17 million, with 7.5 million Indigenous people, 3.2 million Europeans, 750,000 Afro-Latin Americans, and mixed *castas* comprising the remaining 5.5 million.[50] With lower castes growing rapidly, it is no wonder that Americanos were apprehensive about their hold on power. Creole elite formed their own bodies of influential men to rule in the king's name: in April 1810, a junta was formed in Caracas; Rio de la Plata created one in May, and others followed.

Indigenous People Propel the Creole Struggle for Independence

Fighting to improve their desperate conditions, Indigenous people pushed Americanos from below by attacking symbols of local injustices. In September 1811, a band of 40 armed and mounted insurgents that included 20 Indigenous men from the neighboring Otomí pueblo of Santa Mónica invaded the *hacienda* Nuestra Señora de Guadalupe near the town of Atotnilco el Grande north of Mexico City. Kicking down the door of the *hacienda* house, the attackers ran the owners through with lances, stabbed their bodies with swords, cut off their heads, and put them in bags tied to their saddles. The Otomí then sacked the *hacienda* and took most of the goods back to Santa Mónica. Testimonies at the ensuing trial highlight the collective nature of the Indigenous participation: they all went to the *hacienda* together, they all participated in the events together, they all returned to their pueblo together, and all together denied complicity in the raid.[51] In New Spain, Native people took advantage of the political chaos during these years to vent their anger collectively against symbols of wealth and authority.

Events in New Spain suggest patterns for Indigenous participation in Latin America's struggle for independence. Rather than risk their lives in the Americanos' political affairs, Indigenous people largely appear to have instead addressed injustices at the local level. Creole patriots in New Granada, who sought to unify their territories against the Europeans, started using the Inca term "Cundinamarca" to designate their region of Bogotá.[52] Creoles thought that promoting an Indigenous heritage would strengthen the new independent countries – making it seem like they did not need European oversight. Revolutionaries initially caught the Spanish by surprise, yet once they had regained control of Spain by 1815, royalist forces scrambled to retake the Americas.

Indigenous people in Upper Peru shaped the struggle for independence. Americanos in La Paz had declared themselves an independent American Republic already in July 1809. The aged leader Mateo Pumacahua, who had led royal troops against Tupac Amaru, took up arms again and helped defeat the revolutionary junta in La Paz. Royalist forces struggled for several years to crush the rebellion and Aymara troops fought on both sides. Indigenous soldiers joined the fighting to secure weapons and their participation raised the violence and struggle significantly. Over the following years, Indigenous people took advantage of the conflict to attack symbols of authority and wealth. Quechua rebels from the Cuzco region took and pillaged La Paz in a significant anti-royalist attack in mid-1814. Spanish forces overwhelmed rebels in Upper Peru and defeated three expeditions from La Plata sent to take Upper Peru. By 1816, Upper Peru was in tatters and the armed Native people had eliminated the Americanos' control of the Andean countryside.[53]

Map 9.2 Indigenous Participation in the Wars for Independence

In Peru, the aged leader Mateo Pumacahua finally switched sides and led Native troops against Spain. By this time, the Indigenous noble had become extremely wealthy as President of the Royal *Audiencia* in Cuzco. Pumacahua owned large cattle *haciendas*, houses in the city, and properties worth tens of thousands of pesos; if wealthy, why did the elderly *kuraka* switch sides? As leader of the *Audiencia*, Pumacahua had been in charge of violently repressing the growing uprisings against colonial authorities in the Peruvian countryside, a task that left him increasingly uneasy.[54] Once he heard in 1814 that King Ferdinand had died and then lost his own position on the *Audiencia*, the Aymara elder rallied between 12,000 and 14,000 Aymara troops against the royalists. His forces sacked Spanish properties and took Arequipa in November 1814. Yet like Hidalgo's forces in New Spain, they were poorly armed with slings and clubs and freely pillaged, so they did not endear themselves to either side.[55] Royal forces captured Pumacahua when they retook Arequipa and hanged him in March 1815, after which they drew and quartered his body and posted his head in Cuzco's main square, where Pizarro had displayed Atahualpa's body three centuries before. Indigenous rebellions, like those led by Pumacahua and Hidalgo, reminded Americanos that if they lost control of their revolutions the lower castes would overrun their own positions. In some places this is what happened.

Figure 9.2 Mateo Pumacahua. (The History Collection/Alamy Stock Photo)

Indigenous pressure from below also shaped Latin America's revolutions as Natives responded to Iberian policies. By early 1811, the Cortes in Cádiz launched an offensive to retake their rebellious colonies. To rally Indigenous support, Spain pledged to protect its Indigenous subjects by taxing them like everyone else. The K'iche' in Guatemala's western highlands disagreed. Beginning in 1811, K'iche' villagers revolted for 20 years against this forced tribute, making state control over their highlands tenuous. Communities refused tax payments, kept out state surveyors and census collectors, and ousted unpopular officials from their posts.[56]

Hundreds of thousands of Indigenous people lost their lives as the wars for independence raged across their continent. Native contributions were sufficiently important that Americano patriots promised to improve their situation in return for their help. When Ferdinand retook the throne following Napoleon's defeat late in 1813, he abolished the Cádiz constitution and began fighting to recover Spain's colonies. To recruit Indigenous support for his revolutionary movement, Father Morelos, the mestizo priest in New Spain who took charge following Hidalgo's demise, promised to end Native peoples' tributes when he declared Mexico's independence in 1813. As many as 500,000 communal village Indigenous people, who had worked seasonally on the *haciendas*, lost their lives and landholdings as collateral damage as the battles for independence ravaged Mexico's countryside. The resulting labor shortage forced *haciendados* to eliminate the head tax and continue communal property as an incentive to induce the rest of the Indigenous population to stay in their villages rather than move to the cities.[57]

The struggle for independence reflected the Indigenous presence and influenced their lives throughout its long process. Indigenous people participated in some of the battles, especially in the Andes. One revolutionary leader was a mestiza named Juana Azurday, born in 1780 to a Quechua mother and creole father in Chuquisaca, Upper Peru, and fluent in both Quechua and Aymara. A Spaniard had murdered her father without recrimination, so Juana hated the empire on principle. When patriots in Upper Peru began their struggle for freedom in 1809, she put on a man's uniform, found a saber, and recruited Quechuas to join the patriot army. Native troops began to call her Pachamama, Mother Earth, and she contributed 10,000 new soldiers to the rebel cause. General Belgrano, the rebel Americano who La Plata sent to fight the Spanish in Upper Peru, at first separated her Native troops from his army because they fought only with clubs and slings and he viewed them as porters.

Then, in October 1813, Azurday and thousands of her Quechua soldiers watched the Spanish defeat Belgrano's forces at Vilcapugio. Azurday and her women's battalion fought in sixteen battles. Following the battle, Azurday borrowed Belgrano's training manual and prepared her own forces. A few weeks later, when royalists again defeated Belgrano's forces at Ayohuma, the Indigenous soldiers of Azurday's faithful battalion, still fighting with slings and rocks, were among the last to leave the battlefield. Following the battle, Belgrano offered his saber to Azurday as a tribute to her soldiers' bravery. The mestiza patriot eventually lost all four of her children in the war and the Spanish displayed her husband's head on a pike until Azurday's soldiers recovered it for burial. Bolívar later visited her, awarded her a pension, promoted her to colonel, and declared to General Antonio José de Sucre, Bolivia's other patriot, that his new country should have been named "Azurday" in tribute to her bravery. Despite such recognition, years later Azurday died alone at the age of 82, forgotten and in poverty.[58]

To build broader popular support and boost morale during their wars for independence, revolutionary leaders in Latin America passed token legislation that promised Native people better conditions. Americano patriot Simón Bolívar, a wealthy landowner from New

Granada, abolished the personal service (*repartimiento*) by Indigenous peoples and their exploitation in 1820, mandating instead payment to Natives in wages agreed to in a mutual contract. His new statute regulated Indigenous labor and aimed to prevent abuses of Native workers by the religious brotherhoods. In Gran Colombia, the country Bolívar created out of New Granada, the Constituent Congress of 1821 also abolished the colonial Indian tribute and affirmed Indigenous equality with other citizens in the laws, including the payment of a personal tribute from ages 18 through 50. Rather than including Native people into the state as equals, the patriot's goal seems to have been to turn them into productive citizens working for the commonwealth rather than for their individual communities. The legislation was not something Indigenous people had asked for, and not much was done about its implementation; the law simply remained on the books as a sign of what non-Indians thought was good for the Native people.

When he arrived in Quito in 1821, Bolívar dealt first with the local groups of Indigenous people and fugitive slaves before proceeding against the Spanish. Then, as he marched south to take Peru from Spain, the poor Native conditions again disturbed the Liberator. In July 1825, Bolívar issued a decree titled "Proclamation of the Civil Rights of Indians and the Prohibition of their Exploitation by Officials, Priests, Local Authorities, and Landowners." The edict proclaimed all citizens to be equal, abolished personal service, mandated payment for any Indigenous labor in cash, and prohibited anyone from working Native people against their will.[59]

Bolívar, though, could not escape his privileged background, and he upheld a decree that divided and distributed Indigenous common lands to private owners. His goal may have been to show support for liberal notions of legal equality for Native people, which looked good on paper. Creole desires to gain control of Native lands, however, also pressured Bolívar. The process of dividing common Indigenous lands in Bolivia had similar results to the same process elsewhere. In the U.S., the Dawes Severalty Act of 1887 was a congressional provision that resembled the legislation enacted by Bolívar. The Dawes Act divided communal Native reservations and gave the allotments to individuals as private property, allegedly to encourage Natives into mainstream society and teach them habits of private property accumulation. Habits of industry and individualism were supposed to replace backward-appearing collective labor and communal landholding. Similar to what occurred later in the U.S. with this liberal legislation, though, Natives in Bolivia lost their land when the state divided and sold their common territories. Indigenous people continued to defend their territory, despite the legal attacks on their territories. After 1816, the Chiriguano retook control of the Andean foothills frontier for nearly 50 years, which made enforcement of the new official decrees difficult at best.

During the violence of the revolutionary years, moreover, there was no interest in or possibility of enforcing these new mandates: nations quickly reinstated the Indigenous tributes that Americanos abolished as a gesture of redemption toward the Native people. In both Peru and Bolivia, Americanos simply renamed tributes "Indigenous contributions," a term thought less likely to conjure up memories of Spanish taxation.[60] Liberal ideals of equality clearly influenced Bolívar's political decrees, yet he was also a first wealthy landowner, so his commitment to such legislation was a different matter. Within the decade, most countries achieved their independence: Venezuela in 1811, Argentina in 1816, Mexico and Peru in 1821, and Brazil in 1822, when Dom João returned to Portugal and left his son Pedro as emperor. Everywhere in the new states, class and caste shaped and determined the effectiveness of the creole leaders who took power to help improve Indigenous conditions in Latin America's new countries.

Conclusion: Indigenous People Face New Rulers in Latin America

The Indigenous demographic recovery of the eighteenth century coincided with royal attempts to make American colonies more productive and less expensive. Native people still predominated in many fringe areas, and as their conditions worsened and their burden of taxation increased, so did Native resistance against the Spanish. Even as Indigenous people moved to European cities and worked in the mines and on the *haciendas*, they still opposed royal efforts to streamline colonial enterprises where they worked. Native people by this time tried to employ colonial institutions to their own advantage, turning them against oppressors by challenging royal attacks against missions where they lived, by using judicial systems to counter greater government control and taxation, and by resisting coercive labor. At times, though, tensions over living conditions became intolerable, and communities in central areas rebelled violently against the authorities. Rebellions occurred especially in Andean mining areas and challenged royal control at a time when European wars also threatened Iberian rulers. These violent uprisings included the participation and leadership of Native women. By the time creoles fought for independence from imperial centers in the early nineteenth century, Indigenous people shaped continental events by pressuring the Americanos from below.

Discussion Questions

1. Explain why Indigenous people often evoked the name of an earlier Native hero when rallying support for an uprising against colonial powers.
2. Why and how did Indigenous people demonstrate against the expulsion of the Jesuits?
3. If José Artigas represented the settlers who were trying to clear Natives off their land and led the Blandengues Corps, why might Uruguayans hold that their patriot got along well with the Charrua people? Compare this anomaly with U.S. patriots who fought for independence and freedom, yet owned African slaves.
4. How can we explain similarities in attitudes and policies toward Indigenous people by leaders in both South and North America?
5. In what ways did Indigenous people influence the results of the Bourbon reforms?
6. Explain why most of the Native leaders of Andean insurrections had significant contact with the Hispanic world and colonial rulers.
7. Why did the large Indigenous rebellions in the Andes ultimately fail?
8. How did Indigenous people influence Latin America's wars for independence and why has it been difficult for creoles to recognize Native contributions?

Notes

1 Walker, *The Tupac Amaru Rebellion*, 26.
2 Howe, *A People Who Would Not Kneel*, 14.
3 Hemming, *Red Gold*, 472–473.
4 Reed, *The Caste War of Yucatan*, 44.
5 Taylor, "Patterns and Variety in Mexican Village Uprisings," 165–168. See also Beezley and Meyer, *The Oxford History of Mexico*, 206.
6 Ganson, *The Guaraní Under Spanish Rule*, 120–128.
7 Thomson, *We Alone Will Rule*, 149–152.
8 Taylor, *Drinking, Homicide and Rebellion*, 123.
9 Ibid., 126.
10 Taylor, "Patterns and Variety in Mexican Village Uprisings," 167.

11 Boccara, *Guerre et ethnogenèse*, 310.
12 Ibid., 361–362.
13 Abercrombie, "To Be Indian, to Be Bolivian," 107.
14 Thomson, *We Alone Will Rule*, 128–130.
15 Ibid., 134.
16 Walker, *The Tupac Amaru Rebellion*, 169.
17 Campbell, "Ideology and Factionalism," 119.
18 Thomson, *We Alone Will Rule*, 187.
19 Ibid.
20 Ibid., 186–187.
21 Walker, *The Tupac Amaru Rebellion*, 47–48.
22 Ibid., 22.
23 Ibid., 43.
24 Campbell, "Women and the Great Rebellion in Peru," 186.
25 Walker, *The Tupac Amaru Rebellion*, 43.
26 Ibid., 52.
27 Ibid., 122.
28 Peralta and Pinto, *Mateo Pumacahua*, 43.
29 Lewin, *La rebellion de Túpac Amaru*, cited in Galeano, *Memory of Fire*, I, 59.
30 Kirk, *The Monkey's Paw*, 73.
31 Thomson, *We Alone Will Rule*, 231.
32 Ibid., 225.
33 Campbell, "Ideology and Factionalism," 133.
34 Walker, *The Tupac Amaru Rebellion*, 258–259.
35 Taylor, *Drinking, Homicide and Rebellion*, 120.
36 Bushnell, *The Making of Modern Colombia*, 32.
37 Spalding, *Huarochirí*, 271.
38 Woodward, "The Economy of Central America," 117–120.
39 Woodward, *Central America*, 23.
40 Ibid., 78–79.
41 Taylor, *Drinking, Homicide and Rebellion*, 127–128.
42 Finozzi and Motta, *Pueblo Charrua*, 18.
43 Van Young, *The Other Rebellion*, 72, 73, 75.
44 Ibid., 128.
45 Scott, *Domination and the Arts of Resistance*, 114.
46 Ibid., 37.
47 Van Young, *The Other Rebellion*, 74.
48 Ibid., 89–90, 138.
49 Ibid., 76.
50 See, for reference, Keen and Haynes, *A History of Latin America*, 149.
51 Van Young, *The Other Rebellion*, 131.
52 Bushnell, *The Making of Modern Colombia*, 37.
53 Klein, *A Concise History of Bolivia*, 95–96.
54 Peralta and Pinto, *Mateo Pumacahua*, 47.
55 Ibid., 48.
56 Smith, "Origins of the National Questions in Guatemala," 80.
57 Bushnell and Macaulay, *The Emergence of Latin America*, 56.
58 Chasteen, *Americanos*, 177.
59 Bushnell, *Simón Bolívar, El Libertador*, 187–188.
60 Bushnell and Macaulay, *The Emergence of Latin America*, 112.

10 Indigenous Responses to New Rulers and Frontier Expansion, 1811 to 1871

Chronology

1811	Brazil wages war against the Xavante, Karajá, Apinayé, and Canoeiro Indigenous peoples.
1816	In Argentina, *Caudillo* Estanislao López distributes Native people as slaves. José Francia, "Supreme Dictator" of Paraguay, forces racial mixture, subdues Evueví.
1820–1824	Martín Rodríguez, Governor of Buenos Aires, begins to clear Natives from plains.
1823	Huge army of 5,000 Ranquels and Tehuelches attack Santa Fe and Buenos Aires.
1825	Aymara people reclaim central Andean mountain chain in Bolivia.
1826–1827	Bernardino Rivadavia, president of Argentina, fights the Ranquel people.
1830s	Comanche and Apache wars against Mexico in Nuevo Mexico, Sonora, and Chihuahua.
1831	President Rivera massacres the Charrua in Uruguay.
1831–1837	Mariano Gálvez, Governor of Guatemala, applies Livingston Codes to speed Native integration; Indigenous people secede in Los Altos.
1833	Governor Rosas in Argentina begins Campaign to the Wilderness to exterminate Ranquels.
1834	Chiriguano uprising in Bolivia.
1835	In the State of Pará, the Mura rebel against Brazil and their Mundurukú allies.
1838	Rafael Carrera "El Indio" takes power in Guatemala.
1839	Battle of Ipaguazo; Bolivia defeats Chiriguano resistance.
1840	Chiriguano Chief Ayericuay fights the Bolivians, later switches sides. The Yoheme of Sonora fight the Mexican government.
1845	Sarmiento publishes *Facundo* in opposition to Governor Rosas in Argentina, a novel that depicts Native peoples as uncivilized savages.
1846–1848	Mexico loses the Mexican–American War and almost half its territory to the U.S.
1847	Indigenous forces in the Yucatan launch the Caste War against Mexico.
1850	Liberals disassemble Native *resguardo* communities in Colombia.
1851	Liberals in Chile under Manuel Montt end Conservative protection of Mapuche lands.
1853	Cholera epidemic hits Yucatan Peninsula; *Cruzob* continue to fight Mexico.

1855	Native people in Nicaragua fight for and against the William Walker filibuster until 1857.
	The Mapuches raid towns in Buenos Aires Province, Argentina.
1856	Liberal legislation Ley Lerdo attacks communal Native lands in Mexico.
1857	Reform War begins in Mexico and lasts until 1861.
1860–1890	Foreign companies harvest products from Central America's Atlantic coast.
1864	Indigenous communities in Bolivia respond to attacks by Mariano Melgarejo.
	Native people involved on both sides of the Paraguayan war against Brazil and Argentina.
1867	Nine Tzotzil towns rise up in Chiapas, Mexico.
1869	Mapuche resistance crushed by scorched-earth campaigns in Chile.
1871	Liberals under Justo Rufino Barrios reclaim power in Guatemala, begin coffee production.
	Mexican forces invade and burn Tulum, the rebel *Cruzob* center in Yucatan.

Introduction

When over a decade of war for independence finally ended in Latin America, Indigenous people found themselves in a new and challenging situation. Although creoles had thrown off European rule and now controlled the continent, the wars had destroyed the basic infrastructure of their society: Spanish troops had looted stores, burned down cities, flooded mines, stolen crops, and executed administrators. The Americanos had employed ideas of liberty and equality to inspire and mobilize troops against the Iberians, but they also hoped that new global trade would benefit their own class as they replaced the Spanish economic monopoly. These elite were interested in Enlightenment and republican values, but had to learn how and whether to implement those ideals in their own specific Latin American contexts. Furthermore, they had never really intended to apply those lofty concepts to the lower castes of their society, including Afro-Latin American and Indigenous people. Now responsible for self-rule, the creoles drafted constitutions modeled after northern countries that had already fought revolutions, imagined what they wanted their homelands to look like, and cobbled together their own new countries.

The Americano rulers, though, had no experience running their governments, and the differences between them made political instability even worse. The main ideologies that separated the elites were political: whether they were Conservatives or Liberals, where the location of that power resided within their country, and the relationship of each creole group to the Catholic Church. Above all, the upper classes sought to keep their lands and wealth intact while continuing to use Indigenous people and African slaves as cheap laborers. The nineteenth century became a tug of war between Liberals and Conservatives struggling for power, with Native people often caught in between.

For these reasons, Americanos prevented the masses from participating in public affairs. Less than 5 percent of white male adults participated in politics during the nineteenth century, let alone everyone else. The lack of political engagement and the deep discord that ripped the new countries apart owing to the inequities perpetuated by the Americanos allowed *caudillos* to rise to power. *Caudillos* (pronounced kou ŧhē′ lyō̂, or in phonetics cow-dee-jo) were usually veterans of the struggles for independence who used personal charisma to connect with their followers, often including Indigenous people, free Afro-Latin Americans, and mestizos. The name itself comes originally from the Caribbean Arawak term *kassequa*, adopted into Spanish as cacique, or chief. By the nineteenth century, a *caudillo* was someone who ruled over a number of caciques or their people. These strongmen became the leaders of countries, or else their principal opponents, but either way they were usually large landowners with resources to staff their own army and benefit their supporters. *Caudillos* usually also decided how they would relate to the Indigenous people in their areas as they consolidated their control.

Indigenous People Compete for Land and Resources

Many European ideals remained in place in the new countries, especially the superiority of privileged people, discouragement of ethnic diversity, and the view of Indigenous and Afro-Latin American people as uncivilized and uncouth. Millions of Indigenous people remained without a legal way to express their opinions to their leaders; the disillusioned had only nonviolent resistance or outright rebellion to show their discontent. Some Native people engaged the new currents of thought. Others had given their lives in the battles for independence and then the conflicts that followed as new leaders tried to extend ranching onto their lands, so they knew that changes were taking place and focused on surviving under their new political rulers.

The economic downturn that followed Latin American independence changed outside pressures on Native land as it provoked new political tensions. Merchants loyal to Spain had returned to Europe, and the outside investment for which Americanos had hoped did not materialize because foreigners had little capital to invest abroad. Northern businessmen instead saw the new Latin American countries as markets for their own factory products, cheap cloth being most important. Economic tensions aggravated the political struggles that followed as different ideological and political factions tried to gain control of the new countries.

Trends: Conservatives and Liberals in Nineteenth-Century Latin America

In most of the new countries, political rivals battled for control even as they settled their frontiers, rebuilt their infrastructures, and tried to increase production. Two political contenders generally waged these struggles: Conservatives and Liberals. Some people can distinguish between these two camps today, using stereotypical markers that include political views, dress and attire, attitudes, place of origin, even body piercings and tattoos or lack thereof, and so forth. In the newly independent countries of Latin America, though, very few of those modern labels marked political divisions. Instead, Conservatives were generally people who had held power during the Colonial Period and wanted to keep their political and economic control following Independence. They looked back at the time when the Spanish king controlled their colonies and society had seemed ordered. Conservatives generally tried to control Indigenous people paternalistically as workers necessary to make society and production function smoothly.

The Liberals, on the other hand, were mostly creoles who had not held power before Independence and who now hoped for a turn to get rich as the new power brokers. In theory, they championed values that had become prominent during the

French and U.S. revolutions, including progress and free markets, as well as the promotion of reason and science over religious beliefs. Liberal politicians hoped to re-create their countries with an active middle class, more like the United States they idealized, as well as federal administrations, personal rights, and without special legal privileges for the military and church. To build the unified, rich and European-looking nations they imagined, Liberals tried to suppress ethnic diversity and did not apply Liberal mantras of liberty, fraternity, and equality to the people at the bottom of the former caste system. Liberals did not envision sharing power with the darker-skinned people, yet generally saw Indigenous people as obstacles to progress and modernity. As did the U.S. at around the same time, Liberals in Latin America tried to violently clear Native people off their lands. In addition, they also pushed to make Natives disappear into the lower-class peasantry through cultural change and gradual integration. Throughout the nineteenth century, Indigenous peoples faced the tensions that political struggles created throughout Latin America.

The economic downturn and political conflicts made it more difficult for Indigenous communities to work with the growing creole population, especially since the presidents of the new Latin American countries lacked the money to industrialize and focused instead on developing what they had to hand: land and natural resources. Indigenous people had controlled both of these commodities in the past. What is more, while nation states had embraced racial equality on paper, most of them determined that claiming land for agriculture and ranching meant pushing aside Native people. Ethnic cleansing and the resulting conflicts became most intense on Latin America's Great Plains or Pampas. Wherever there were broad grasslands useful for cattle and agriculture, the Liberals asked, what should we do with the Indigenous people to whom the lands belong? Countries came up with different solutions depending on their situations, but the results were often similar: Native peoples lost their lands.

One country that struggled against Indigenous people in the years following Independence was the United Provinces of the River Plate, as Argentina first called itself despite a failed attempt to assimilate Paraguay and Uruguay. In 1810, the first congress abolished forced Native labor and tribute, as well as Spanish institutions like the Inquisition. Internal political conflicts allowed British commerce to flood the new country with cheap cloth, hardware, and armaments, so the displaced Americano merchants in Buenos Aires turned instead to ranching. The failed military campaign of 1810/1811 to capture Upper Peru had alienated creole elite there by abolishing Indigenous labor services and the *mita*, still mainstays of their mining economy. Following formal independence in 1816, the leaders in La Plata expanded their internal frontiers. Estanislao López, an early *caudillo*, allied himself with Artigas, established himself in Santa Fe, defeated a force from Buenos Aires, and then fought the Indigenous people to his north. López distributed the Native people he captured as slaves among the *estancias* in Santa Fe, just as the colonial authorities had done with the *yanaconas*. To defend themselves, the Abipone people from the Chaco began to raid frontier settlements to their south.

Indigenous peoples on the Pampas grasslands in the Southern Cone soon faced genocidal campaigns.[1] Martín Rodríguez, governor of Buenos Aires from 1820 to 1824, blockaded the Paraná River to monopolize trade with Britain and then massacred

Indigenous people on the Pampas to open up his borderlands to ranching. Indigenous deaths opened up millions of acres for landed Spanish families to export salted meat and hides. To defend their lands, the Mocobí in the Santa Fe province, north of Buenos Aires, served in Governor Estanislao López's army in return for territorial demarcation. Over the following years, these warriors killed hundreds of their own people as López cleared Natives off land suitable for ranching. In Bolivia, where visions of white superiority also prevailed, rulers engaged in brutal campaigns of genocidal extermination and their push to clear land for ranching led to thousands of Native deaths over the following years.

Indigenous people responded to their new situation with a variety of creative choices. Where federal troops warred against them, as in La Plata and Bolivia, Natives harassed new settlements and fought expansion onto their lands. In some countries, Native people employed traditional strategies of resistance based on their own religious values, which by this time often included elements of Christianity. Liberal administrations in Central America used methods that were perhaps more humane in the short run, but the results were similar: states privatized communal lands to integrate Indigenous people more quickly into the rural labor force. Strong beliefs and messianic movements empowered Native people as they responded to growing national pressure for integration through nonviolent and violent resistance; religious traditions and communal organizations were worth risking death over in battles against outside forces. Some peoples in the Yucatan Peninsula used religion for much of the century to unite communities and militarily block Mexican expansion onto their lands. Religion motivated people to risk their lives against encroachment onto their lands and pressure to join national society as *ladinos* or *campesinos* (peasants), rather than as distinct Native peoples. *Ladino* is the Central American term for a person of mixed heritage, a term analogous to mestizo in Mexico. Whatever their methods, Indigenous people fought challenging odds. By 1869, the newly independent states throughout Latin America had overwhelmed Native resistance and were selling raw materials – often found on Native lands and sometimes harvested by Native labor – to markets abroad.

Indigenous Peoples Engage Latin America's New Leaders

The revolutions against European control produced political instability in the former colonies as the newly independent Americanos decided what form their own governments should take. Rising politicians applied the Enlightenment discourse of equality and fraternity to help consolidate their diverse peoples following the divisive wars of independence. Many new nations, apart from Brazil and Mexico, first adopted Liberal rule.

Indigenous people in the new country of Argentina faced Liberal attacks immediately. Bernardino Rivadavia – Liberal president from 1826 to 1827 – established the University of Buenos Aires and granted rights of long-term use of national land to settlers. The ancient Roman property system that he used, called emphyteusis, allowed people to acquire land simply by registering claims; Rivadavia's government granted 6.5 million acres to only 122 persons, 10 of whom received grants of over 130,000 acres apiece.[2] The Ranquel peoples on the plains in the Buenos Aires Province faced Prussian officer Frederick Rauch, whom President Rivadavia had sent to exterminate them. Rauch had served under Napoleon, and he bragged about his way of eliminating Native people: "to save bullets, today we have slit the throats of twenty-seven Ranquels."[3] Finally, in February 1829, Ranquel warriors defeated Rauch's troops and decapitated him in the same way he had so often killed their own warriors.

Northwest in Peru, the Quechua saw their communal lands divided by Bolívar and distributed to merchants and ranchers, who carved huge properties out of their territories. Native people in some nations faced wars between both political camps. After seceding from Colombia in 1829, factions in Venezuela fought each other for over 30 years until the Liberals finally defeated the Conservatives in 1863. Eventually Liberal politicians seized power in most nations.

Movements: President Mariano Gálvez and Liberal Rule in Guatemala

One example of the ways in which Indigenous people countered Liberal rule occurred in Guatemala, still part of a territory called the United Provinces of Central America. A civil war between 1826 and 1829 at first blocked rebuilding the infrastructure after the wars for independence. The winning Liberals pushed agro-exports, sanitation, limits on the Catholic Church, and education. They viewed Indigenous people as the main obstacle to private property and the free market, both high among their ideals, so the Liberals abolished colonial protections for Native communities and the Church. Indigenous people strongly opposed efforts by Mariano Gálvez, governor of Guatemala between 1831 and 1837, to impose Liberal "progress" upon the nation. Gálvez correctly suspected Native people of being conservative opponents to his Liberal agenda, so he tried to change them to fit the nation he imagined building through education and forced integration. The leader first confiscated church wealth and property, legalized civil marriage and divorce for everyone, and then removed Catholic teachers from Indigenous education. Native highlanders, nominal Catholics who still lived in church-administered *congregaciones*, resisted Gálvez's moves angrily.

President Gálvez's legislature next adopted a new legal system called the Livingston Codes. Named after the System of Penal Law from Napoleonic Code that U.S. jurist Edward Livingston had recently written for Louisiana in 1825, these laws granted Native people legal equality with *ladinos* and technically gave them access to more land and opportunities. On paper this move seemed positive, but in reality it strained relations between Native people and the new government because the Indigenous people were culturally different than *ladinos*, and had neither the education nor resources to avail themselves of the new laws. Instead, the legislation enabled more exploitation by limiting Native autonomy through community taxes and forced-labor projects. For example, the laws put Indigenous orphans up for adoption by *ladinos* to teach them Spanish and a trade. This step, meant to accelerate their integration, resembles the later use of Indian boarding schools in the U.S., after the Civil War, to change and integrate Native American children through education.

Predictably, Gálvez's reforms provoked a massive popular reaction. Indigenous people understood that the new law would tax their communal funds and impose labor, both dangerous attacks. Natives throughout the highlands rose up in arms against state officials to counter the 1836 decree that converted their communal *ejido* lands into private property. Gálvez's attempt to integrate Indigenous people backfired because it threatened Native autonomy and led to almost continuous Indigenous uprisings in the western highlands.[4] The unexpected spread of a cholera epidemic through Guatemala in 1837 made the situation worse. Indigenous people refused to submit to the mandatory vaccinations ordered by Gálvez, because earlier such initiatives had killed their people. *Ladinos* in the highlands blamed the spreading epidemic on "backward" Indigenous cultures and actually seceded from Guatemala in opposition to Gálvez, naming their new country Estado de los Altos, the Highlands' State.[5]

Native people in the highland towns of Quetzaltenango, Solulá, Totonicapán, and Soconusco, where most Indigenous people lived, initially joined the *ladinos* against Liberal attacks. Their independent political experiment ended only a few years later, when they backed a mestizo Conservative named Rafael Carrera, a *caudillo* nicknamed "protector of the people," who deposed Gálvez after a drawn-out revolt called the War of La Montaña (The Mountain). When Carrera's victorious rebels finally poured into the capital of Guatemala in January 1838, chanting "Long live religion and death to foreigners," between 2,000 and 3,000 Indigenous women eager to plunder and angry about vaccinations and attacks against the Church swelled their forces.[6] Indigenous resistance to the struggle between political factions in Central America aggravated racial tensions and hindered state formation.

For Document 10.1: Guatemala's 1837 Livingston Codes, visit www.routledge.com/9780415519120.

The Liberals' opponents were the Conservatives, who came from traditional families that had held power in the Colonial Period and wished to remain in control. Native people in a few nations, where colonial patterns remained strong, saw continued Conservative rule after freedom from Spain. Mexicans crowned a Conservative hero from the independence wars, General Agustín de Iturbide, as emperor in July 1822. Iturbide's pomp and circumstance lasted for only a few months and had little relevance for Native people: when he dissolved Congress, antimonarchists under *caudillo* Antonio López de Santa Ana overthrew and executed Iturbide.

Another Conservative nation was Brazil, where Prince Dom Pedro remained in Rio de Janeiro after his father John VI returned to Portugal in 1822 following Napoleon's retreat. Dom Pedro took the opportunity to declare independence from Portugal in September, thus avoiding an expensive war and arming the lower classes, which had so complicated the revolutions in the neighboring Spanish colonies. Brazil's aristocratic families pushed Dom Pedro to enact a constitution, so he approved one that gave himself complete authority to appoint ministers, convene and disband parliament at will, and even to choose provincial governors. Conservative rulers in Brazil retained power by crushing insurrections, keeping African slavery and repressing the revolts that erupted periodically. Indigenous people in Brazil's borderlands, though, violently defended their lands from missions and frontier expansion.

While most of these Conservative rulers spoke of continuing paternalistic patronage of Indigenous peoples, they were still as prejudicial as their Liberal rivals. These same politicians were also leery of solidifying the formal lip service to racial equality that had enlisted soldiers for their revolutions; real equality might force them to share power. Instead, once in charge, both Conservative and Liberal politicians embraced the vague idea of "progress" as a more unifying strategy for their rule.

Indigenous people in the Southern Cone during these years underwent heavy-handed treatment from the new states. In the Eastern Band, Americanos finally achieved independence in 1828, when Great Britain helped them defeat the Brazilians and Argentinians who had tried to integrate them. With Artigas in exile in Paraguay, Uruguayans tried to clear the Charrua off the rich grasslands colonists coveted for ranching. By this time, only about 650 Charrua remained, but their warriors harassed frontier settlements and had repeatedly defeated Blandengue attacks. Finally, President Fructuoso Rivera trapped the Charrua. Concealing 1,200 soldiers along the Queguay River, which runs west into the Uruguay River, General Rivera invited the people to sign a peace treaty to return cattle stolen by the Brazilians. On a warm day in January 1831, the remaining 400 to 500 Charrua, including women, children, five chiefs, and all their goods, presented themselves in good faith to parley with President Rivera. Many of the Charrua warriors had recently distinguished themselves fighting alongside Rivera against Brazil, so they came expecting praise and gifts. After feeding the group, soldiers instead opened fire on the people, killing most of them and marching the few survivors to be displayed as trophies in Montevideo.[7] Uruguay thus exterminated the Charrua people.

A question to consider is why the Catholic Church did not push for better treatment of the Indigenous people by these new countries. Gone were the days of Bartolomé de Las Casas and his Dominican brothers who had defended Natives during the conquest. The French Revolution and then the wars for independence had seriously weakened the Church, which had even called upon the Latin American colonies to remain under the "legitimate" authority of the Catholic king. Even if priests had spoken out for social justice, political leaders rejected Catholic authority during the 1820s and 1830s and were determined to control the Church. Priests shared the same prejudices as the upper classes and paid little if any attention to Indigenous conditions; mission work had collapsed during the wars. The only exception was Guatemala, where Gálvez's Liberal reforms made priests call for an end to discrimination against the highland Native peoples and their rightful place as "the most important element of Central American society."[8]

Events: Native People Struggle against the Brazilian Monarchy

To the north of Uruguay, the peaceful transition to Independence in Brazil made little difference to Native people. Diseases had decimated them after European contact. By the late eighteenth century, Brazil's Native population of 2.5 million had declined by three-quarters. Once relocated to Rio de Janeiro, the Portuguese authorities waged a war in 1811 against the Karajá, Xavante, Apinayé, and Canoeiro peoples. The Karajá and Xavante retaliated by destroying the Portuguese fort at Santa Maria do Araguaia. By this time there were as few as 800,000 Native people left in Brazil. In theory, Dom Pedro fancied Enlightenment ideas, but he cautiously kept the Liberals from taking popular sovereignty too far. The 1824 Brazilian Constitution assigned Pedro most of the ruling power, but when he also stacked the new cabinet with his choice of nobles the people and military rebelled.

It was a difficult situation, so Pedro abdicated in 1831 and returned to Lisbon, as his father had done only three years before. Liberal administrators called regents assumed power and ruled over a period of widespread revolts.

Many Native people contacted Brazilians during the following years as settlers moved west. To win popular support, in 1831 the regents authorized the enslavement of the Botocudo and Kaingang in Espírito Santo and Minas Gerais. Three major uprisings against the regents followed. In the most serious case, Indigenous people and peasants rose up in 1835 against authorities in Cabanagem, the State of Pará, a state with a large Native population. Two Native peoples fought in this revolt: the Mura on the side of the rebels, and the Mundurukú on behalf of the authorities. Then the economic decline during the 1830s, caused by rebellions and the falling production of sugar, gold, and cattle, complicated state relations with Native peoples.[9] Surviving Indigenous peoples along the Negro River, a northern tributary of the Amazon, many of which had been contacted earlier and were less harassed by the 1830s, received a respite from the financial downturn. In the Tocantins-Araguaia River basin and the interior of Maranhão and Piauí, frontier expansion led to peaceful contact with some Ge-speaking peoples: the Appinagé, Xerente, and Krahô on the Tocantins River, the eastern Timbira on the Maranhão, and some northern Kayapó on the Araguaio River. The Xavante retreated westward, though, becoming increasingly hostile to outsiders, and the Canoeiros in Goiás also attacked settlers. Some Bororo peoples in central Mato Grosso fought settlers during this period, but other peoples responded to intrusions peacefully, including the Terena and Guató of the upper Paraguay River, the Apiaká of the Arinos, the surviving Kayapó and Guaraní in southern Brazil, and the Karajá of Araguaia near Bananal. Finally, in 1840, Italian Capuchin priests arrived to settle Native people on compounds. Their proselytism was a failure: missionaries were unable to cope with the rigors of Amazonia, and were even worse at communicating with the Indigenous people than the Jesuits and Franciscans had been during the Colonial Period.[10]

Indigenous Peoples Face Political Instability and Conservative Rule

Indigenous people largely opposed Liberal rule during the early Independent Period. Most new Liberal administrations were unable to consolidate their new nations; internal conflicts made their task impossible. By the 1830s, Conservative *caudillos* began to replace Liberals throughout Latin America. One example was Juan Manuel de Rosas, a rancher who in 1829 took control of Rio de la Plata. Rosas came from a long-established colonial family of landowners. The Tehuelches had killed his military grandfather on his southern estate. Indigenous attacks against frontier settlement had been almost constant in Argentina: in October 1823, a huge army of 5,000 Ranquel and Tehuelche warriors attacked Santa Fe and Buenos Aires simultaneously, stealing thousands of heads of cattle from the cities. The Tehuelche also held Rosas' father, an infantry captain, as prisoner for five months until Buenos Aires ransomed him. On his mother's side, Juan Manuel belonged to one of the richest families in Argentina.

Many Indigenous peoples had enjoyed life on the Argentine Pampas. In the 1830s Native peoples on the plains, from the frontiers of Mendoza and Córdoba south to the Negro and Salado rivers, were hunters and riders who lived in tents and relied on horses for transportation, much as did the Plains Indians of North America during this period. Several nomadic peoples called the Ranquels (mixed Tehuelches and Mapuches originally from Chile) dominated the Pampas, along with the Aucazes peoples. The Pehuenches, in contrast, lived west along the Andean foothills and traded with the Europeans. The Huilliches and their allies the Puelches controlled the headwaters of the Negro and Salado rivers and north of the Colorado River, occupying the prairies from Buenos Aires to Mendoza. They exchanged ponchos and skin cloaks for goods at trading posts. Closest to the capital lived the Pampas, whom settlers regarded as savage and treacherous because they plundered ranches, stole women and cattle, lived in communal tents, and still stymied settler expansion onto their lands. Some Native people still even traded handcrafts for clothes, bread, and alcohol in the Buenos Aires marketplace. As settlers and ranchers pushed south and west into Indigenous territory after 1815 to steal their land, the people living there responded with increasing force against the pioneers and ranchers.

After becoming governor of Buenos Aires in 1829, Rosas warred against the Ranquels and Tehuelches to open up more ranch land. Rosas extended ranching because at the time a *caudillo*'s power base was landownership. Rosas purchased two *estancias* (ranches) on the Salado River along the frontier and established a farm and settlement called "Independence" as an outpost to wage war against the Native peoples. When Charles Darwin visited Rosas' ranch at Los Cerrillos, its size so impressed the scientist that he called it a fortress and town. With his cowboys (called *gauchos*) as troops, Rosas slowly pushed Indigenous people off the plains.

To secure ranchers' support, Rosas devised a massive expedition to take more land from the Ranquels. In 1831, the governor introduced his so-called Campaign to the Wilderness to his assembly: "One effort more, and our wide plains will be free forever, and we will secure the foundations of our national wealth."[11] Rosas set out toward the southwest in March 1833 with a convoy of 1,500 soldiers – mostly *gauchos*, outlaws, and vagrants – 30 wagons, 6,000 horses, and thousands of cattle to feed his troops. In a year of fighting, assisted by his allied Tehuelche chiefs Catriel and Cachul, Rosas added thousands of square kilometers of prime ranchland to his province, stretching west to the Andes and south beyond the Negro River.[12] The campaign killed 3,200 people and imprisoned 1,200 more. Supporters began to call Rosas the "Conqueror of the Wilderness." In a final peace treaty, the few remaining Ranquels offered the *caudillo* military service and peace in return for a state annuity of horses, firewater, tobacco, and salt.

The coalition of important Native chiefs who gathered regularly at Salinas Grandes, an extensive salt flat southwest of the Buenos Aires Province, signed a truce with Rosas. The governor promised them annuity payments if they stopped attacking ranches. Most prominent among these leaders was Calfucurá, a Mapuche leader who had arrived from Chile in 1835 to assist Rosas in fighting their mutual enemies, the Loncos people. The Wilderness expedition not only solidified ranching and Rosas' political career, it forced Argentinians into annuity payments for years and allowed Indigenous leaders to regroup their forces. Natives who had not capitulated to Rosas received no mercy: in 1836, the authorities caught 80 warriors after they raided Bahía Blanca, brought them in chains to the capital, and publicly shot them in groups of ten in front of the barracks.[13]

North of Argentina, Indigenous people in Paraguay faced a *caudillo* with a very different approach. Most Native people spoke Guaraní and kept some Indigenous customs while still identifying as Christians because of their earlier experience at the Jesuit missions. After Independence, an intellectual named José Francia ruled Paraguay between 1816 and 1840. Known popularly as "the doctor" and "El Supremo Dictador," Francia adopted a different approach to Native people than his neighbors in Brazil and Argentina. Paraguay's patriarch solidified his control by integrating Natives into his state. Francia recognized the remaining Guaraní communities and "strengthened their special status" by dividing land between the elites and the peasants in a Robin Hood fashion. To break the power of the wealthy landowners, Francia even forced upper-class men to marry and have children with Guaraní women. He subdued the Evueví, riverine traders with a fierce reputation, and made their canoe men escort state-owned barges of lumber down the Paraguay River. The Evueví also performed this work for later-president Solano López. Because contact with outsiders introduced them to disease, the Evueví people became extinct by the end of the nineteenth century.[14]

Relations with Indigenous people were anything but peaceful northwest of Paraguay in Bolivia, but Independence improved Native power. By 1827, there were at least 800,000 Native people in the new nation and the decline of the export sector during the wars for independence benefitted Indigenous farmers around La Paz and Cochabamba as their local agricultural markets improved. Native tribute supplied 60 percent of government income and was Bolivia's most important revenue throughout the nineteenth century.[15] Following the wars of independence, the Aymara retook control of the central Andean mountain chain up until 1860.

In the southeastern lowlands, the Chiriguano also tried to break free from the new Bolivian authorities. Because the Native economy there was agricultural, settler incursions were particularly harmful and forced the Chiriguano to leave behind their crops of corn and squash. The Chiriguano were originally Guaraní people who had migrated from eastern Paraguay in pre-Columbian times, and they were numerous enough to defend their territory fiercely from Bolivian settlers. As in Argentina, frontier violence forced the authorities in Bolivia to bribe Indigenous leaders into not raiding colonial outposts. The authorities also refused to defend colonists' expansion into Chiriguano territory. Natives used the rugged hilly terrain to their advantage, advancing through the thick underbrush of the subtropical forest and then retreating again, grouping and dispersing in typical guerrilla style.[16] Colonists stayed alive only by allying themselves with strong Chiriguano leaders. Through alliances between communities and with the Q'om to their south, Chiriguano warriors bested national forces, keeping frontier settlement at bay in southeastern Bolivia.

The Chiriguanos formerly from the Franciscan mission of Itau rose up in 1834 against local authorities after ranchers invaded more of their lands. National troops subdued the rebels, impressing 84 prisoners into the army. A few years later, the Chiriguano and the Chané, allies from Caiza and Itiyuro, almost eliminated the *haciendas* on their lands; the Chané alone stole over 400 cattle, which they traded for corn in Argentina. Over the following years, an army comprising Indigenous allies led by Chief Ayericuay, head of the important community of Ingre, attacked Bolivian settlers at will. Bolivians described Ayericuay as "an enemy who is the most powerful [leader] in this *Cordillera* [mountain range]."[17] In one campaign, Native troops stole over 5,000 cattle and 200 horses, defeating the national forces sent to avenge the thefts. Following the Battle of Ipaguazo in 1839, the first whole-scale massacre of the war occurred when Bolivian troops slaughtered Chiriguano men and captured women and children from 100 Native families to distribute as slaves in the town of Tarija. Bolivians managed such victories only when they tricked the Chiriguanos, as they did east of Tarija in Zapatera the following year, where troops ambushed Native women, men, and children on the pretext of a truce and enslaved the people in the surrounding villages.[18] Indigenous people were off to a challenging start with their new national leaders, and the fact that Natives were so numerous in Bolivia made their position all the stronger.

Highland Indigenous people in Guatemala faced a back and forth between Liberal and Conservative leaders during these years that was more typical of nineteenth-century Latin America than the frontier violence raging in Bolivia. Guatemalan political flip-flopping challenged Native people because official positions varied so much depending on who was in power. The new president Rafael Carrera was himself a mestizo, but when he took power in 1838 people referred to him as "the Indian," and his supporters lived in so-called "Indian" areas. The Maya-descended people opposed the *ladinos'* creation of Estado de Los Altos, mentioned above, and instead allied with Carrera and his conservative leaders, begging to remain part of Guatemala so that their trade with the capital could continue. Their decision shows Native preferences for life under Conservative rule, and in 1840 Indigenous people allowed state army incursions to defeat the *ladinos* of Los Altos.

Overwhelming popular support allowed Carrera to pass a constitution in 1839 that promised to "protect the Indian" as members of the weak group in society, and "improve their education, to avoid the loss of what belongs to them in common or as individuals, and so that they will not be bothered for the usages and customs learned from their ancestors."[19] Carrera thus reinstated Conservative oversight for Native communities; the late 1830s through the 1860s was practically a golden age for Indigenous autonomy in the highlands.[20] Official "protection" allowed Native people – as primary producers of market commodities – to join the cochineal dye boom that brought economic improvements to the country. This expansion offered Carrera enough support to prevent *ladino* elite from controlling Guatemala's Indigenous people for over 20 years, after which the Liberals reclaimed power.

Indigenous People on Internal Frontiers face Additional National Invasions

The 1840s saw increasing Indigenous resistance to state attempts to colonize internal frontiers. Warriors fell to government forces who defended these expansions on multiple occasions. Furthermore, changing alliances and internal conflicts weakened Native forces. In Bolivia in 1840, Ayericuay invited all the other Chiriguano leaders of the mountain *cordillera* to wage war together against Bolivian settlers. When defeated by a rival chief allied with the Bolivians, Ayericuay switched sides and assisted Bolivian forces up until 1848, when he again began to play the colonists off against each other. Bolivians were able to defeat Chiriguano resistance only when they manipulated village rivalries.[21] José Ballavián, who assumed the presidency in 1841, finally ended the war by combining his 150 national soldiers with 500 Chiriguano warriors under Chief Aracua and defeating Chief Ayericuay. Chiriguano resistance nevertheless forced Bolivian settlers, who had suffered huge losses of over 20,000 head of cattle, to capitulate. Thereafter, Bolivia's frontier remained relatively stable up until the 1850s.[22]

Similarly, numerous Indigenous peoples in Mexico rose up following Independence to oppose state attempts to incorporate and impose taxation upon frontier regions. Between

Independence and the U.S.–Mexican War of 1846, the Kiowas, Apaches, Comanches, and Navajos attacked, harassed, kidnapped, and killed thousands of northern Mexicans in a conflict called the War of a Thousand Deserts.[23] Then a serious Indigenous revolt against commercial agriculture broke out in 1842, spreading over 60,000 square miles from Michoacán to the Isthmus of Tehuantepec. Two years later, Native people revolted in the state of Mexico. The Yaquis of Sonora fought a full-scale war against Mexico between 1845 and 1846. Another insurrection broke out in Chilapa in 1849, and the last occurred in Hidalgo at the time of the Liberal Revolution of Ayutla (1854). The most famous of these Native rebellions against state control began in the Yucatan Peninsula in 1847, when Indigenous people launched the so-called Caste War that simmered throughout the remainder of the nineteenth century.

Movements: Violent Indigenous Responses to Liberal Politics in the Yucatan Peninsula

Independence created explosive social conditions in the Yucatan borderlands. The Mazehual, Indigenous people in eastern Yucatan forests, faced a challenging situation. Forced labor, as well as attacks on religious and traditional moral standards, threatened their rural communities. Mexicans at the time referred to the rural Mazehual pejoratively as Huits (loincloths). National attempts to improve Mexico's economy following Independence pressured the Mazehual because nationals needed their labor to extract the peninsula's resources. Finally desperate in the face of outside impositions, Indigenous leaders in the Yucatan masterminded a rebellion against the Mexican authorities.

The Mazehual plotters included Cecilio Chi, cacique and owner of a ranch near the village of Tepich (in today's Quintana Roo), as well as Jacinto Pat and Manual Ay. Late in February 1847, enraged Native troops struck towns throughout the peninsula, terrorizing *ladinos*. Rumors circulated that Chi and fellow rebels planned to enter the state capital of Mérida on August 15, where the Mazehual would crown Chi as king after killing all the Mexicans. Panic spread, city authorities arrested Indigenous leaders, and at sunset of the night before, the authorities lit bonfires to illuminate the town. Citizens prepared muskets, pikes, and boiling water, but in a classic turning movement the Indigenous warriors never attacked. Six months later, early in the morning of July 30, Cacique Chi instead struck his own town of Tepich, burning alive between 20 and 30 *ladino* families, children, women, and men and sparing only some girls for his soldiers to rape. As they ravaged *ladino* towns throughout the peninsula over the following years, Native people used fear to their advantage: terror of Mazehual brutality set off a general panic and *ladinos* began a witch-hunt to find and prosecute the rebels.[24]

In the face of the Mexican response, Mazehual leaders met at Tabi, southeast of Mérida, and declared a war of total extermination, without quarter, against the white race. As military reprisals failed, Mexican politicians and bishops tried to calm the rebels, attributing their anger to a decrease in their faith. Then, in February 1848, rebel leaders poignantly responded:

> And now you remember that there is a True God. While you were murdering us didn't you know that there was a True God? You were always recommending the name of God to us and you never believed in his name. And now you are not prepared nor have you the courage to accept the exchange for your blows. If we are killing now, you first showed us the way.[25]

Using rifles smuggled from British Honduras (today Belize), by 1848 Indigenous rebels controlled four-fifths of the Yucatan Peninsula, and once again besieged Mérida.

At the heart of the growing tension spreading through Latin America lay a profound contradiction: patriots had publicly spoken of popular sovereignty and the right of people to choose their own leaders through elected representatives, as a way to mobilize support for their revolutions against Spain and Portugal. Philosophers Hobbes, Locke, and Rousseau had formulated such ideas during the Enlightenment, and their ideas garnered support for the U.S., French, and then Latin America revolutions. Patriots in Latin America had employed nativism and its catchphrase "Americanos" to rally troops throughout the wars.[26] When applied to the reality of running their new nations, though, nativism was problematic. Would Enlightenment ideals of freedom and equality also apply to people of Indigenous and African heritage, who the nationals viewed as inferior and less desirable members of society? While the patriots and new leaders may have believed in the ideals, they did not intend to extend them to people in the lower castes. A similar example closer to home may help explain these contradictions. Thomas Jefferson, a U.S. patriot and author of the Declaration of Independence, Governor of Virginia, first Secretary of State, and then even the third president of the United States, firmly upheld the values of democracy and rights of individuals. At the same time, he remained a slaveholder and plantation owner throughout his life. Three hundred years of colonial racism was a heavy legacy to discard easily.

The new nations in Latin America therefore remained hierarchical and very traditional. Republican constitutions mandated equality before the law and had in theory done away with the caste system, yet these visions of new and improved societies remained utopian and fictional. Some theory helps explain this idea. In his book *Imagined Communities*, Benedict Anderson has analyzed the formation of modern nation states and the ideas that helped create them. This Professor of International and Government Studies argued that the printing press and emergence of capitalism broke down elite control of language, spreading horizontal comradeship among people. As the elite lost their power, solidarity among whites and especially the vision of a shared background based on a common heritage of race mixture finally created the idea of "nation" around the end of the eighteenth century. Most pertinent to this study, Anderson argued that nationalism among European colonists in both South and North America helped inspire the formation of modern European nation states.[27] The mostly European-descended leaders of the new Latin American countries were embarking on a new experiment in state-building, creating nations as political units to bring diverse people together in a new and virtually imagined collective. Their dreams of an ideal community help explain how upper classes in nineteenth-century Latin America united their people around visions of equality and freedom to help build the new states they envisioned, ideas in which they no doubt firmly believed, even as they still kept darker people at the bottom of their economic and political systems.

The elite endorsed European ideals of positivism and evolutionism to fortify their own positions.[28] Figuratively, though, by enacting liberal laws of freedom, they had let the darker genies out of the bottle to help fight their wars, and were now trying to return them to their former places without allowing them to take control. In their new constitutions, creoles eliminated the mixed-race divisions and classifications common in the Colonial Period, the caste system, and instead endorsed racial equality to make everyone but African slaves technically equal to one another in law. In reality, though, few elites believed in social and racial equality, as most were still socially conservative, so their problem now was how to continue to control the "liberated genies," the darker people who did their work and had helped fight the revolutions. In the U.S., conditions were no better: settlers legalized their discrimination following the Civil War in the so-called Jim Crow laws. Latin Americans formally kept racism out of their legislation yet still practiced it in their day-to-day relations. European philosophies perpetuated their prejudice and strengthened their attempts to keep undesirable people from power. Prejudice, class divisions, and the contradictions between discourse and reality are all reasons why the Liberal governments following Independence failed so quickly.

By the mid-nineteenth century, ruling groups in Latin America employed the French doctrine of positivism to suppress ethnic diversity. A good example of this manner of thinking is the way upper classes justified their attacks on Indigenous settlements and cultures using the discourse of civilization and barbarism to contrast their own ways of life (civilized) to rural folk and especially Native cultures (barbaric). The resulting contradiction between what officials said, and what they actually did, destabilized the young nations.

Indigenous–Argentine relations provide a good example of the racism that Native people faced when relating to Liberal plans to change their nations. The *caudillo* Rosas still ruled the nation with a combination of terror and patronage as Governor of Buenos Aires Province. His secret police, known as the *mazorca* or ear of corn, slit the throats of Rosas' opponents during the night to terrorize the people. State-sponsored assassinations peaked in the early 1840s, when Rosas tried to violently eliminate all his enemies.

In 1845, an Argentine teacher, statesperson, essayist, and intellectual named Domingo Sarmiento, who Rosas had exiled to Chile, published a biography of a regional *caudillo* from northwestern Argentina, Facundo Quiroga, that sheds light on relations between Indigenous people and Argentinians by this time. Sarmiento depicted Indigenous peoples as "sinister bulks of savage hordes" and "barbarian savages, avid for blood and plunder." His book *Facundo* was a thinly disguised attack on Rosas' dictatorship, yet Sarmiento employed the text to contrast rural Native cultures and "civilized" European cultures in the capital. Because Indigenous life on the plains differed from urban life in Buenos Aires, Sarmiento saw Native people as uncivilized.

> The Native town is the disgraceful other side of this coin:[29] dirty children covered in rags, living amid packs of dogs; men stretched out on the ground, in utter inactivity; filth and poverty everywhere …, miserable huts for habitation, notable for their generally barbaric and neglected appearance.[30]

This writer's view was typical of urban elite at the time, who denigrated Natives and rural folk for their different ways of life. At the root of such criticism lay the elite desire to take Indigenous lands for ranching and resentment of Native resistance. North Atlantic prejudice also allowed Latin America's upper classes to emulate European characteristics. Over the next decades, Native people in Argentina saw frontier clashes with the army that backed ranchers and settlers as a result of changing cultural mores.

By the mid-nineteenth century, Liberal administrations had failed in Guatemala, Bolivia, Mexico, and Argentina, and Conservatives replaced them. Conservatism peaked and, in places, *caudillos* fulfilled their promise to restore order and traditional ways of life. Still, they failed to make everyone wealthy. Growing prosperity in the North Atlantic world still beckoned urban Latin Americans. Most rural dwellers remained impoverished. Tensions between city and country, Conservatives and Liberals, nationals and foreigners polarized Latin American society. Conservative rule began to fall apart, and Indigenous events during the 1850s showed the transition back to Liberal governance.

Indigenous Communities Face Another Round of Liberal Attacks

Conservative *caudillos* largely failed to bring stability to Latin America despite their promises to restore order and defend private property. Most *caudillos*, like Rosas, were also landowners who favored ranching interests. These loyalties brought Conservatives into conflict with the Native communities they had traditionally overseen. In Mexico, with abundant resources and agricultural land, Conservative *caudillo* Antonio López de Santa Anna controlled the nation politically between the mid-1830s and mid-1850s. Santa Anna was the wealthy landowner from Veracruz who, as president, infamously lost almost half the national territory to the United States between 1846 and 1848. The lower classes struggled to survive as the Mexican economy faltered. Santa Anna failed to improve conditions for Indigenous people in the pueblos, whose quality of life had changed little since the Colonial Period. Natives remained impoverished and traditional, sharing their thatched huts with dogs, pigs, and chickens. Carl Sartorious, a German scientist who traveled through Mexico in 1850, described a pueblo at the time:

> Inside the hut, upon a floor of earth just as nature formed it, burns day and night the sacred fire of the domestic hearth. Near it, stands the *metate* and *metapile*, a flat and cylindrical stone for crushing the maize, and the earthen pots and dishes, a large water pitcher, a drinking cup and a dipper of gourdshell constitute the whole wealth of the Indian's cottage, a few rude carvings, representing the saints, the decoration. Neither table nor benches cumber the room within, mats of rushes or palm leaves answer for both seat and table. They serve as beds too for their rest at night, and for their final rest in the grave.[31]

As this description illustrates, conditions for Indigenous people had changed little since colonial times, even though the upper classes had embraced the North Atlantic vision of economic and social progress.[32] As European merchants flooded Latin America with cheap textiles, they undermined local urban weavers. To offset these losses, merchants turned again to the continent's traditional strengths in agricultural production, which empowered the owners of large plantations and *haciendas.*

The Conservative *caudillos* who ruled during the 1840s lived in cities but still relied on rural *haciendas* as their landed source of wealth, so they were also in contact with rural Native people. Such interaction broke down the rigid colonial caste structure and instead promoted the use of class or wealth as markers for social status. The North Atlantic concepts of progress and technological development, with all their materialistic overtones, also came to dominate the interests of Latin America's elite. To the forward-looking Liberals who took the next turn at political leadership, Indigenous people still reminded them of past colonial days.

Indigenous people throughout the continent felt the results of changing political programs. Since Independence, Liberal politicians in Gran Colombia (which included today's Colombia, Venezuela, Ecuador, Panama, northern Peru, western Guyana, and northwest Brazil) had tried without success to divide common Indigenous lands, the *resguardos*, among individual Native families, and sell the leftover lands. The Liberals who reclaimed political rule in 1850, divided and sold the *resguardo* lands. Indigenous *resguardo* communities disappeared throughout Colombia as a result of this legislation, except in the southwest, where most Native communities were located.[33] In Panama, still a Gran Colombian province, the Kuna people began moving down from the highlands to the coast during these years to have greater access to commerce as trade increased under Liberal rule. By this time the Kuna numbered between 3,000 and 10,000 people. Gradually settling on small inshore islands along the forested coastline that offered greater isolation, the Kuna profited from increased Caribbean trade and gained relief from snakes and the endemic diseases spread by Panamanian settlers.[34]

In Guatemala, Indigenous peoples enjoyed autonomous community rule and freedom from outside interference under the Conservatives, who ran the nation from the late 1830s through the 1860s. Rather than capitalizing on their isolation from the capital to build stronger communal ties and economic cooperation during Carrera's Conservative administration, though, some highland Native communities fought each other over land. The community of Santa Catarina Ixtahuacán suffered over 40 years of internal, often violent disputes with its neighbors over borders and with any state representative who intervened. Then, in the 1850s, the first synthetic organic chemical dye made from coal tar and called aniline purple replaced cochineal dye and rendered Guatemala's principal export obsolete. Native communities had generally defended their lands from agro-export investors during Conservative rule, but this changed when the Liberals retook power.[35]

Indigenous people faced difficult years as several disastrous harvests followed and Guatemala's economy shifted to coffee production. When the Liberals gained control in 1871, their leader Justo Rufino Barrios saw coffee as the solution to his country's economic struggles. While Conservatives had encouraged Native communities to produce coffee, Liberals instead promoted individual plantations, owned by their upper-class supporters, and the use of Indigenous labor to cultivate the coffee. The rise of coffee and the Liberals who promoted the crop profoundly affected the Native people, whose labor made the new crop viable.

The Mapuche people in Chile also saw the results of conflicts between ruling Liberals and Conservatives. These Indigenous people received citizenship following Independence without Chile having conquered them militarily. As a result, Chilean leaders were initially unable to force cultural changes onto Mapuche society. Conservatives extended federal protection over Native lands, but as settlers pushed south of the Biobío River, they ignored the state decrees. Liberal president Manuel Montt, elected in 1851, extended state control over education and the clergy in an attack on the Catholic institution. While Montt was in power, the price of copper plunged and sales of wheat declined, leading to revolts by miners, workers, and farmers. The president crushed the protests violently and production shifted to the north during the 1860s, where guano became the main export. Further conflicts with the Mapuche followed as Chile increased the extraction of resources from Native lands.[36]

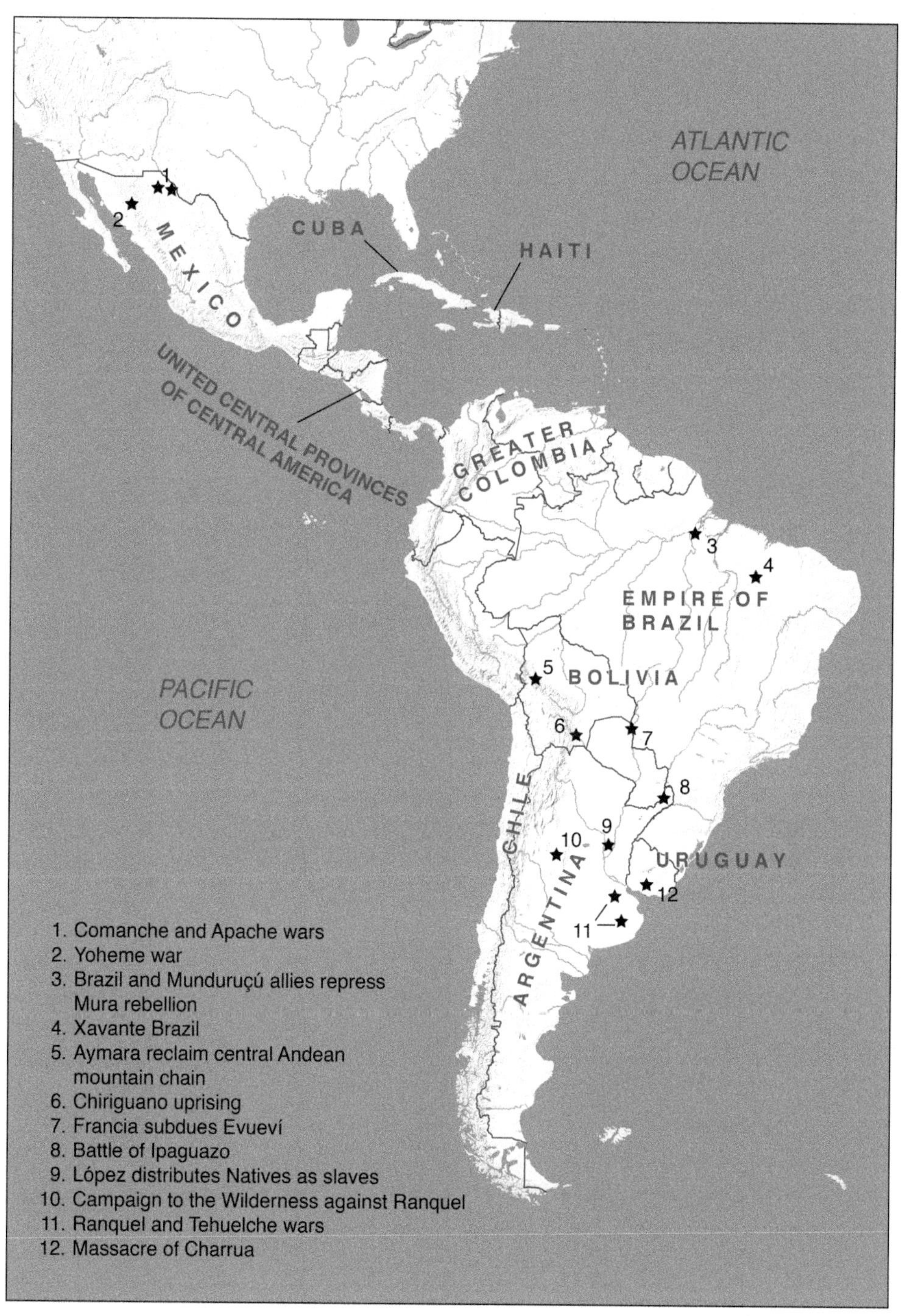

Map 10.1 Indigenous People and Liberal Rule in Nineteenth-Century Latin America

Mexico shows an even more extreme example of Liberal rule for Native people during the mid-nineteenth century. Liberal forces took control in September 1855 by deposing General Santa Anna. Their first president, backed by Indigenous people from the south, did not last long, but that mattered little because the politician who really controlled the country for the next two decades was actually an Indigenous Zapotec lawyer named Benito Juárez.

Individuals: An Indigenous Man Becomes President of Mexico

Benito Juárez was a remarkable Indigenous man and Liberal politician in Mexico. Born in 1806 in a small pueblo in the Sierra (Highlands) of Oaxaca named San Pablo Guelatao before Mexico even won its independence, an uncle raised Benito after his parents and grandparents died. As a boy, Benito worked in the fields and herded sheep. Then at the age of 12 he walked over 50 kilometers to Oaxaca City, where he found work as a domestic servant to a bookbinder. The adolescent was clearly very intelligent: he studied at the Royal School and then went on to Seminary, despite initial challenges in Spanish grammar. Benito mastered Latin and graduated four years later with "Excellent" as his grade.[37] Then, at the age of 21, Benito studied Moral Theology and finished a Seminary degree, yet decided against becoming a priest. Enrolling next in the new Institute of Science and Arts of Oaxaca, Juárez studied Living Languages, Political Economy, and Experimental Science, as well as Natural, Constitutional, and Civil Law.[38] His most influential teacher at the Institute was Miguel Méndez, a logic, ethics, and mathematics professor from the same area of the Sierra as Benito. Méndez was also a leading Liberal politician and admirer of the French Revolution, so students often met at his house to discuss politics. Benito helped Méndez organize the Oaxaca Liberal Party. At his teacher's suggestion, Benito began to study law. By the time the Conservatives took power in 1829, Juárez was teaching his own classes and finishing his law degree.

Inspired, Juárez launched a political career in Oaxaca, working as an attorney, a city councilor in 1832, and then as a state legislator. The lawyer was apparently not very impressive as a person: he was quiet, reserved and stood only a little over five feet. Juárez had a dark complexion and a long scar across his face. Still, Benito led Mexican Liberals for two decades as they battled formidable obstacles to change their country, and his legacy is huge. Making a name for himself at the local level as Secretary of the Superior Tribunal of Justice and then as a magistrate, the Zapotec lawyer then served as a congressional delegate to Mexico City. Elected governor of his State of Oaxaca in 1847, Juárez became the first Indigenous person to serve in that position in Mexico. He earned a reputation for honesty and simplicity, and helped start a national Liberal movement known as *La Reforma*, The Reform.

Juárez's Liberal legislation limited the power of the Catholic Church and Mexico's military, in imitation of the U.S., but also damaged Indigenous conditions. The law he passed in 1855, as Minister of Justice, actually bears his name, Ley Juárez. This legislation declared all citizens equal before the law and restricted the privileges of the Catholic Church, traditional defender of the Indigenous people. Then, in 1856, the Liberals also enacted the Ley Lerdo, named after Treasury Secretary Miguel Lerdo, to create a middle class in the Mexican countryside. This legislation forbade Native villages from owning communal pastures called *ejidos* and forced them to purchase land as individuals. Few Native people could afford the price, however, so, as happened earlier in Bolivia under Bolívar and as would occur later in the U.S. with the Dawes Act of 1887, Juárez's legislation opened the door for speculators to purchase communal Native lands at auction for cheap prices. Secretary Lerdo intended to eliminate Indigenous communities, which is exactly what happened during 1856. The following year, Liberals enacted a new National Constitution that enshrined Juárez's new laws and proclaimed freedom of speech, press, and assembly. Following a Conservative backlash, Juárez later returned as the national president in 1861 and served until 1872, except for the three years (1864–1867) when Mexico fell to foreign Conservative rule. The Zapotec president from Oaxaca pushed his country into the modern world at a huge cost to Indigenous people in Mexico.

Allying themselves with the Conservatives, Native people throughout Mexico protested Juárez's Liberal legislation. In 1854, government forces crushed an Indigenous rebellion in Hidalgo State. Two years later, the Huastec revolted against the sale of their communal lands in Tantoyuca. Still, the new Constitution of 1857 reflected the Liberals' principal goals: equality before the law and freedoms of speech, press, assembly, and education. The legal code also abolished slavery and compulsory service, which changed Mexico. Most devastatingly for Native people was the abolishment of the *ejido* system of communal lands. Liberals mostly intended to break up the large *haciendas* and ranching interests that had dominated the country since colonial times, but in the process they also dismantled the *ejidos*. Indigenous lands passed into the hands of private land companies and *hacienda* owners.[39] Because Natives lost their communal land to grow corn and food, Juárez's liberal laws devastated their villages; ultimately the legislation provoked a civil conflict called the Reform War. Fought between 1858 and 1861, the war cost the lives of 50,000 people, most of them Indigenous people and peasants who fought against the Liberal reformers.

Liberal Rule in Central America and the Nicaraguan Exception

Indigenous communities in Central America also experienced challenges when the Liberals took control in the 1860s and planted coffee to meet rising world demand. The political transition was ominous and quickly altered Indigenous communities. In El Salvador, to increase coffee production the government decreed in 1856 that unless two-thirds of a Native pueblo's communal lands produced coffee the state would confiscate the land. Coffee crops spread quickly during the 1860s as the Liberals assumed power.

Nicaragua was an exception. By the mid-1850s, some Indigenous people there were doing well; Natives in highland Matagalpa cultivated wheat for flour and sold sugar cane, rice, potatoes, beans, garlic, and onions to *ladino* townspeople.[40] Britain was playing an increasingly important role in the region's economy and Nicaragua was its principal source for cochineal dye. The British blockaded and then landed forces in Nicaragua during the 1840s as part of Queen Victoria's gunboat diplomacy, which undermined support for the Conservatives who had overthrown Liberal rule.

The U.S. had shown little interest in the region before 1850. Following the war with Mexico and acquisition of California and Oregon, though, the U.S. interest in Central America eclipsed Great Britain's. Then, in 1855, Nicaraguan Liberals invited U.S. adventurer William Walker to help them overthrow the ruling Conservatives. Born in Nashville, Walker was a physician and lawyer who dreamt of taking over parts of Latin America to add new slave states to the United States and make a name and fortune for himself. This was also a time of rising interest in California and Manifest Destiny, so there was growing demand for a faster route to the West. First, the adventurer tried to take Baja California and Sonora from Mexico in 1853, but failed due to a lack of supplies and Mexican opposition. Next, Walker looked toward Nicaragua, where magnate Cornelius Vanderbilt managed the most popular shipping route between the oceans at the time.

Accompanied by 300 U.S. soldiers of fortune, Walker invaded Nicaragua in 1855. With initial backing from the Liberals, the adventurer declared himself president, legalized African slavery, and proclaimed English the official language.[41] Rather than engender stability and make friends, U.S. intervention polarized Nicaraguan society and provided the chance for many groups, including Native communities, to claim further social and political rights. Some Indigenous leaders traveled far to engage Walker's assistance in their struggles against the Nicaraguan government for cultural, political, and economic autonomy, and their support strengthened his filibuster.

Native people were nevertheless divided on the filibuster. The community of Masatepe, which produced tobacco and alcoholic drinks, thought Walker would strengthen their economic position by opening up new markets. Nicaragua's government, which they referred to as "the Tyrant," had limited their business opportunities and had treated them with "contempt" because of their "caste," so they imagined U.S. rule might offer better business options.[42] That Native people would still employ the term "caste," a colonial vestige, shows the persistence of prejudicial stereotypes within Nicaraguan society. The Masatepe vision came to naught.

After Walker won the presidential elections in June 1856, neighboring Central American governments began a war to evict him. The following month, over 1,000 Guatemalan, Honduran, and Salvadoran troops invaded northwestern Nicaragua and ousted Walker's forces from León and the surrounding area. Walker's elite opponents enlisted Native people from the communities of Matagalpa and Ometepe Island, in Lake Nicaragua, to join their struggle against the U.S. forces. These Indigenous troops played a central part by assisting in the guerrilla war that elite opponents waged against Walker.[43] An alliance of Central American countries united with Nicaraguan Conservatives and finally ousted the U.S. invaders in May 1857.

Indigenous conditions on Nicaragua's Atlantic coast, meanwhile, differed markedly, because Britain had ruled the Caribbean coast of Nicaragua and Honduras informally since the early seventeenth century through its pirates. Abraham Blauvelt, a British buccaneer, had founded the town of Bluefields in the 1630s as a base for attacking Spanish ships and selling the loot to Dutch traders in New Amsterdam (today's New York City). The British traded actively with the Miskitu Indigenous people; in the 1680s, the empire had even crowned their allied Miskitu leader as king. The resulting "Miskitu Kingdom" became Britain's way of informally controlling the coast against the Spanish for the next two centuries. Empowered by their foreign alliance, the Miskitu challenged Spanish pretensions: in 1800, they destroyed the Spanish fort at Negro River and took the area until the 1840s, when they faced an independent Nicaragua and foreigners interested in a canal.

Although Nicaragua had separated from Spain in 1821, it had been part of the Federation of Central American States until 1838, when it won complete independence. The Atlantic coast of Nicaragua, populated by the Rama, Sumo, Miskitu, and other Native peoples, had remained largely isolated. In the late 1840s, the British and U.S. grew interested in a passage between the oceans through Nicaragua and almost fought when Britain took the San Juan River delta, Nicaragua's southern border. Resolving the disagreement in the Clayton–Bulwer Treaty of 1850, the foreign powers relinquished their pretensions on Nicaragua. The California Gold Rush renewed U.S. interest in a canal, though, so companies competed for the rights to cut a passage through Panama or Nicaragua. Britain took another route: it finally recognized Nicaraguan sovereignty in 1860, but reserved a self-governing enclave on the Atlantic coast for the Miskito people where the waning British Empire had long held economic control. The coastal area boomed as foreign companies began to harvest rubber during the 1860s and 1870s, mahogany and bananas in the 1880s, and finally minerals in the 1890s. The town of Bluefields became a center for export trade and its commerce brought political stability to the entire country: Conservative presidents governed Nicaragua in stable cooperation with the Liberals until 1893. The export frenzy on Nicaragua's Atlantic coast belongs in Chapter 11, which explains how Native people fared during the Neocolonial Period of Latin America.

Indigenous people on the plains of southern Latin America, meanwhile, were fighting even more desperately than the Miskitu to defend their lands. Their fertile plains were still prime real estate for ranching. Liberals from the eastern provinces finally deposed Governor Rosas in 1852. Frontier expansion took a sideline as fighting over the passage of a national constitution in 1853 divided Argentina. The conflict allowed Liberals from Buenos Aires Province to take control. During the next administrations, given the Liberal emphasis on economic development, Indigenous people on the internal frontiers intensified their attacks as ranchers spread into the borderlands.

Mapuche Chief Calfucurá, who by this time controlled the plains from Buenos Aires south to Patagonia through a broad confederation of Native leaders and peoples, presented the main obstacle to frontier expansion in Argentina. As ranchers occupied Native lands, the chief and his allies responded violently, much as Native American warriors on the Great Plains of the U.S. were fighting against pioneers during this same time. In February 1855, Calfucurá led a massive raid of 3,000 allied Ranquel warriors against the town of Azul in the Buenos Aires Province. Capturing 60,000 head of cattle, Calfucurá took 100 families captive and left 300 settlers dead. Some of these captive women and children actually voluntarily joined Native societies, even when given the chance to leave, preferring them to life among Argentinians. Next, Ranquel forces massacred a squadron of 125 Argentinian soldiers in September and then, one week later, the same 3,000 warriors attacked the town of Tandil. In desperation, Minister of War Bartolomé Mitre sent out a force of 3,000 soldiers with 12 large artillery pieces to attack Calfucurá. The chief ambushed the invading army in a large swamp named San Jacinto, west of the capital city of Buenos Aires, where his warriors killed 300 soldiers and injured many more.[44] Further Indigenous attacks and victories followed as frontier violence intensified: in 1864, Calfucurá again struck settler towns, challenging frontier expansion and settlement.

Figure 10.1 Mapuche Chief Calfucurá. (The Picture Art Collection/Alamy Stock Photo)

Indigenous peoples likewise still contested frontiers in the Yucatan Peninsula during the mid-nineteenth century by harassing the Mexican authorities from their jungle communities. Santa Anna revived the slave trade and one of his *caudillos* monopolized the sale of Native captives to Cuba. To make matters worse, a cholera epidemic struck in 1853, and Mexican troops turned back in fear. When one troop of 30 exhausted Mexican soldiers finally reached the shrine of the cross at Chan Santa Cruz, near Tulum in today's Quintana Roo and the center of the Native rebellion, they drank from a new well at the center of the town. Soon the soldiers grew dizzy, vomited, and died: Indigenous troops had infected the well with clothing from cholera victims in a case of biological warfare.[45]

By 1855, the Native rebels had fought off superior Mexican forces using pits, poisoned wells, snares, and clay bullets. Calling themselves the *Cruzob*, the Spanish term for "cross," *cruz*, joined to the Mayan plural suffix *ob*, the rebels positioned their standing army at Chan Santa Cruz. *Cruzob* warriors followed the directives of a speaking cross, housed in a large church. A ventriloquist, crouched in a pit behind the altar, issued directives, as if from God, to inspire Native followers to keep the Mexican troops at bay.[46] The wives of the priests who guarded the cross helped lead the movement. In an example of a syncretic combination of faiths, these women translated the directives of

Figure 10.2 *Cruzob* Maya with General Juan Bautista Chuc and Commander Aniceto Tzul (Dzul) Meeting with Lieutenant Governor of Yucatan Teodocio Canto in 1884 to Sign a Peace Treaty to End the Caste War.

the cross to be from the Mayan goddess Ixchel and the Christian Virgin Mary.[47] The women's role as mediators of divine instructions became important for the movement. A priestess and military strategist named María Uicab, daughter of a principal Native leader, actually led the *Cruzob* as their queen between 1863 and 1875. Queen Uicab also directed her troops into battle. In January 1871, the Mexican army burned and destroyed Tulum, kidnapping Uicab's son. Ordered by Queen Uicab, Mazehual troops retaliated by burning down the town of Chemax.[48] *Cruzob* resistance successfully kept the Mexican authorities out of their territory for the remainder of the nineteenth century.

Throughout Latin America, Conservative rulers failed to keep the order they had promised when ousting the Liberals. New Liberal *caudillos* replaced them. In Guatemala, the death of Rafael Carrera in 1865 led to six years of Liberal military and political challenges to Conservative rule. The political turmoil finally ended in 1871, when a Liberal victory ushered in a period focused on the extension of Guatemalan coffee plantations. In Colombia, where the Liberals assumed control with their victories in the civil wars of 1851, 1860 to 1863, and 1876 to 1877, participation in the military helped integrate Indigenous people into Colombian society and they employed service to their own advantage. Liberals still planned to end Native self-governance and privatize their *resguardos* as a way to turn Indigenous people into peasants and mainstream them into Colombian society without ethnic distinctions. Such programs coincided with the Liberal vision of modernity. Politicians also feared that during the civil wars, Indigenous people would side with the Conservatives who had traditionally patronized them. By 1851, Native people made up 7.9 percent of the population in the southwestern Cuaca region of Colombia. Unlike Afro-Colombians, though, who eagerly stepped forward for military service to claim citizenship and increase their political participation, Native people rarely volunteered to fight in Conservative ranks. One reason was that the

Conservatives conscripted their soldiers, which Indigenous people deeply resented. Furthermore, in 1859 the Liberals reversed plans and passed legislation that legalized the *resguardos* and thus won Native people to their side. From then on, whenever the Liberals threatened to divide their lands, Native people threatened to change sides; this strategy allowed Indigenous people the privilege of not having to fight, but only by threatening when necessary to fight for the other side.[49]

The Chiriguano during these years in Bolivia faced the brutal rule of a *caudillo* named Mariano Melgarejo Valencia, who seized power in 1864. During his six mismanaged years as president, Melgarejo attacked Indigenous communal landholdings and built fortresses to fight the Chiriguano. While not a Liberal himself, Melgarejo's gifts of Native land to ranchers resembled Liberal governments elsewhere and had similar results. Native people in the *Cordillera* highlands responded with widespread uprisings, besieging the town of Ancoraimes in 1870.

For Document 10.2: President Melgarejo of Bolivia Expropriates Communal Indigenous Landholdings, visit www.routledge.com/9780415519120.

In the Southern Cone during these years, Indigenous people participated in a massive conflict called the Paraguayan War, or the War of the Triple Alliance. Native peoples did not cause this war, but the three feuding nations fought the war largely on Indigenous lands, so they were heavily involved. Paraguay's military buildup and internal development in the 1850s destabilized the regional balance of power. When Paraguay's President Francisco Solano López marched troops into Brazil and then across Argentina in 1864 to help his friends in Uruguay, the two larger allied countries invaded Paraguay.

Native people were involved in every stage of this massive conflict that became South America's largest war. López created a regiment of Evueví spear-throwers. Indigenous people from the Chaco, notably the Q'om, also fought for Paraguay in exchange for firearms. To recruit the Kayngua from the region of Concepción, López promised to give them Paraguayan wives at the end of the war, but the Kayngua served both sides as best suited their interests. The Enlhit from the Chaco took advantage of the conflict to raid Paraguayan villages for supplies. The reward for most Indigenous cooperation, though, went to Brazil: three groups of Mbayá-Guaykurú people, focused around Fort Coimbra and Villa de Albuquerque, traded service for promises of land from Brazil. Guaykurú, Kadiwéu and Beaquéo warriors were excellent riders and attacked Paraguayan settlements for Brazil. These warriors helped defend the Brazilian Fort Coimbra, ambushed and harassed Paraguayan soldiers after they invaded the Pantanal, and served as scouts and support troops in battles. As the conflict drew to a bloody end, Brazil armed the Kadiwéu with first-rate weapons and posted them as guards along the Paraguay River. Following the war, though, smallpox devastated the Guaykurú and they never received the lands that Brazil had promised them in return for military service.[50]

The Paraguayan War allowed the Liberals to gain power in the Southern Cone and continue their efforts against Indigenous people. Bartolomé Mitre, president of Argentina from 1862 to 1868, had directed the war against Paraguay, but the booming wool economy gave him added resources (and reason) to clear Indigenous people off the plains. Sarmiento, by then Latin America's most influential Liberal, returned from exile to become president of Argentina in 1868. The new leader did wonders to extend education and promote economic development, but he also attacked Indigenous people to clear the way for ranching and "civilized" frontier settlement. As historian John Chasteen has argued, "Disappointingly, Sarmiento, the great educator, also embodies the darker side of Latin American liberalism in his thinking on race."[51]

Map 10.2 and Map 10.3 Major Nineteenth-Century Latin American Military Conflicts Involving Indigenous People

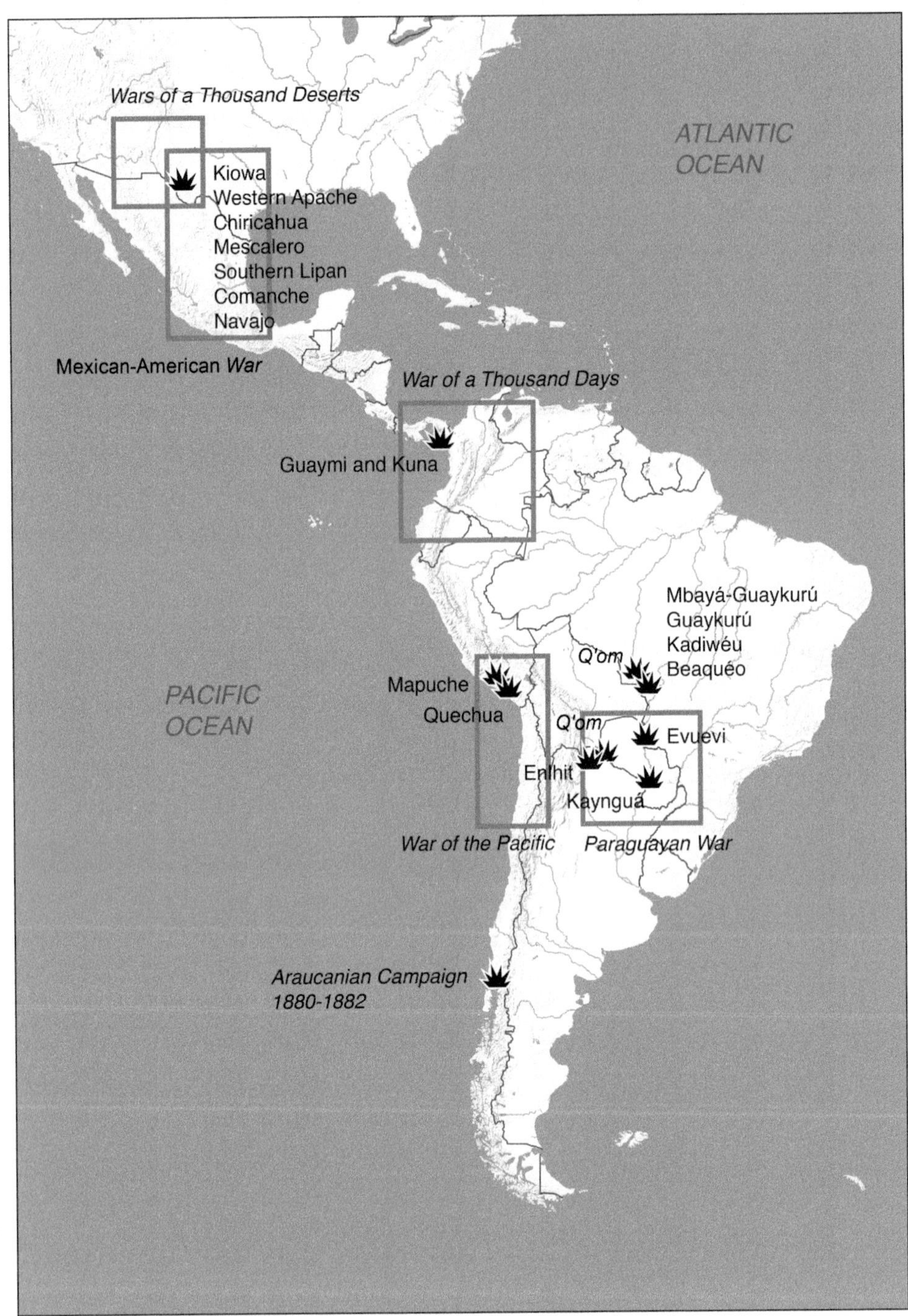

Map 10.2 and Map 10.3 Continued

Frontier conflicts proliferated during the mid-nineteenth century. The Mapuche, south of the Biobío River in their homeland of Walmapu, saw an invasion of Chilean settlers and growing conflicts resulted. Congress debated heatedly over how to proceed with the Mapuche, whom Chile had never formally conquered, though they had fought in the abortive Chilean political revolutions of 1851 and 1859. Legislators finally moved to subdue them once and for all by force. The Mapuche appealed for military support from Argentina, to no avail. In 1869, Chile crushed Mapuche resistance in a campaign of extermination noted for its scorched-earth destruction of villages and crops, as well as brutal massacres.[52] In the Southern Cone (Uruguay, Paraguay, Argentina, and Chile), Liberal leaders overwhelmingly chose to violently destroy Native peoples to quickly clear them off desirable lands.

Native people in Mexico also faced visible, if not as violent, attacks. The Liberals provoked conflicts that forced Indigenous people in Hidalgo to riot between 1869 and 1870. More significantly, the Tzotzil in highland Chiapas rebelled during 1869 and murdered three *ladino* priests, massacred Mexican colonists in several settlements, and besieged the city of San Cristobal de las Casas. The Tzotzil were angry at ongoing exploitation by *ladino* merchants and clergy who lived in their towns. Priests demanded daily domestic service like providing firewood, fodder for animals, daily supplies of maize and lard for the priest's mule, and mail services. In Chamula, officials tied the Native administrator to a post and whipped him for not having paid the priest the 28 silver coins they owed for his daily masses.[53]

Below the surface, another dynamic was also at work. The Tzotzil were struggling to legitimate their new cult of St. Rose, a movement similar to Tzotzil cults of the early eighteenth century. St. Rose was the first Americana to become a saint in 1667, and villagers celebrated her festival in August. In this instance, in December 1867, a Tzotzil girl from the village of Chamula saw miraculous stones drop from heaven. Placed in a box by her Native fiscal, the stones reportedly knocked on the box to escape. Villagers flocked to use the amazing stones' healing qualities and to listen to them speak as the movement became a regional focus of interest. On Good Friday 1868, a fiscal actually convinced his Tzotzil community to crucify someone as part of the growing movement, so the villagers nailed a 10-year-old boy named Domingo Checheb to a cross in the plaza of Tzajalhemel.[54]

When the concerned Catholic priest stole the holy stones to stop the movement, the enraged people rose up in protest. People in nine Tzotzil towns violently attacked nearby *ladinos*. Although more localized than the 1712 Tzeltal Revolt that occurred in this same area, the rebels did have contact with Yucatan's Caste War rebels and had also yearned for an Indigenous Christ. The Tzotzil never completely eliminated the *ladinos*, yet the Catholic priest never reclaimed power in Chamula and the cult of St. Rose became a regional movement against increasing Mexican authority for years to come. There are still Native priests associated with the movement of St. Rose in the area today.[55] The Tzotzil rebellion marks the beginning of a new era in Indigenous history because it achieved an Indigenous priesthood and religious freedom that lasted in the area for over a century.

Conclusions: Indigenous People Help Shape an Independent Latin America

By the mid-nineteenth century, Indigenous people responded creatively to the new leaders who took power following Latin American Independence. *Caudillos* excluded the masses from public affairs and pushed economic growth for their own benefit. Racism remained pervasive, and both Conservatives and Liberals cleared Indigenous peoples off desirable lands and took their resources as they expanded internal frontiers. Both sides sought to exterminate Native peoples, though their strategies differed: Conservatives favored manipulation and control, while Liberals more often employed brute force.

During this era, some Indigenous peoples established contact with outsiders for the first time, inevitably leading to disease and territorial tensions. Almost everywhere, Natives preferred autonomy rather than submission to the new governments. They fought state expansion into their territories by harassing the settlements, stealing cattle and people, and by rebelling forcefully when conditions became unbearable. Some Indigenous people participated in international conflicts like the Paraguayan War to further their interests, and their readiness to plunder reflects desperate conditions and Native desires for Western goods. Native people found inspiration for risking lives in various religious movements, and a Zapotec lawyer became the president of Mexico. One irony of the period is that the legislation that broke up Indigenous lands, allegedly to make landownership more egalitarian, actually concentrated land in the hands of the elite, which favored the new rulers. Another surprise is how divided Indigenous communities remained in the face of these national depredations. It was still difficult for Native peoples to join forces for common causes, and they would need all their collective strength as Neocolonialism grew over the next decades into the twentieth century.

Discussion Questions

1. Explain why President Juárez of Mexico, even if he was Zapotec, enacted legislation that dismantled Indigenous communal landholdings.
2. What is the connection or similarity between a takeover of a country by an individual (filibuster) and the use of dilatory tactics to delay or prevent actions in Congress?
3. How did religious beliefs shape Native resistance during the early nineteenth century?
4. Were Conservative and Liberal policies toward Indigenous people actually similar in their ultimate goals?
5. Indigenous responses to national policies in the new Latin American countries highlight their diverse cultures and backgrounds. Why do we assume that they would have responded to outside pressures as one collective group?

Notes

1 The term "Southern Cone" refers to the four southern countries in Latin America: Uruguay, Paraguay, Argentina, and Chile.
2 Rock, *Argentina*, 99.
3 Beyer, *Rebeldía y esperanza*, n.p., in Sarasola, "The Conquest of the Desert," 208.
4 Woodward, "Changes," 68; Smith, "Origins of the National Questions in Guatemala," 78.
5 Grandin, *The Blood of Guatemala*, 94, 98.
6 Woodward, "Social Revolution in Guatemala," 59.
7 Acosta y Lara, *La Guerra*, 190–193.
8 Prien, *Christianity in Latin America*, 275, 283, 288.
9 Burns, *A History of Brazil*, 172–173.

10 Bethell and Murilo de Carbalho, "1822–1850," in Bethell *Brazil Empire and Republic*, Note 44 on 111.
11 Rosas, *Diario de la expedición*, 55.
12 Sarasola, *Nuestros Paisanos*, 217.
13 Lynch, *Argentine Dictator*, 55.
14 Susnik, *Aborígenes del Paraguay*, 110–112. Ganson, "Evuevi of Paraguay," 486.
15 Klein, *A Concise History of Bolivia*, 104.
16 Langer, *Expecting Pears from an Elm Tree*, 42.
17 Ibid., 29.
18 Ibid., 28, 36, 37, 44, 50.
19 Smith, "Origins of the National Questions in Guatemala," 82. Grandin, *The Blood of Guatemala*, 103.
20 McCreery, citing Oliver LaFarge, "State Power, Indigenous Communities," 101.
21 Langer, *Expecting Pears from an Elm Tree*, 30, 38.
22 Ibid., 40.
23 DeLay, *War of a Thousand Deserts*, 136.
24 Reed, *The Caste War of Yucatan*, 59.
25 Ibid., 78.
26 Chasteen, *Born in Blood and Fire*, 100.
27 Anderson, *Imagined Communities*, 16, 37, 67, 140.
28 *Positivism* was a new European philosophy which argued that every rational idea can be proven scientifically or mathematically. For society, it held that government laws were rules derived logically from existing situations.

Evolutionism was a growing belief that organisms make themselves better as they inherit changes and become more complex over time.
29 The gist of "other side of the same coin" usually means a different and usually opposite idea about the same situation or subject.
30 Sarmiento, *Facundo Civilization*, 46, 50, 51.
31 Sartorius, *Mexico about 1850*, 69.
32 North Atlantic countries border the northern Atlantic Ocean, so they typically included the United Kingdom, France, Germany, the United States, and Canada.
33 Bushnell, *The Making of Modern Colombia*, 106.
34 Howe, *A People Who Would Not Kneel*, 15.
35 McCreery, "State Power, Indigenous Communities," 105.
36 Haughney, *Neoliberal Economics*, 19.
37 Roeder, *Juárez and His Mexico*, 12.
38 Ibid., 46.
39 Wolf, *Peasant Wars*, 16.
40 Gould, *To Die in this Way*, 32.
41 This type of takeover of a government by an individual, or to carry out insurrectionist activities in a foreign country, is known as a "filibuster." Note that the same word also describes the use of dilatory tactics to delay or prevent the actions of a legislative assembly, as occurs sometimes in Congress.
42 Gobat, *Confronting the American Dream*, 32.
43 Ibid., 32, 38, 39.
44 Sarasola, "The Conquest of the Desert," 210.
45 Reed, *The Caste War of Yucatan*, 152.
46 Ibid., 139.
47 Religious syncretism is the combination of different forms of beliefs and practices that at times resulted from colonial rule and the imposition of one religious faith by rulers onto colonized peoples.
48 Rosado and Rivas, "María Uicab," 136.

49 Sanders, "Subaltern Strategies of Citizenship," 30.
50 Costa, "Indigenous Peoples of Brazil," 166–172.
51 Chasteen, *Born in Blood and Fire*, 171.
52 Bengoa, *Historia del pueblo Mapuche*, 205–277.
53 Bricker, *The Indian Christ*, 119.
54 Ibid., 121.
55 Ibid., 125.

11 Struggles for Land, Labor, and Political Leverage in Neocolonial Latin America, 1870 to 1929

Chronology

1870	The *Cruzob* intensify resistance in the Yucatan.
	The Aymara besiege La Paz and overthrow President Melgarejo.
1871	Justo Rufino Barrios takes power in Guatemala, focuses on coffee exports.
1870s	Rubber War in Panama between Afro-Latin Americans, mestizos, and Kuna.
1875	Argentines begin to dig a trench to exclude Indigenous people.
1876	Porfirio Díaz becomes president of Mexico.
1877	Guatemala's new Agrarian Law divides communal Indigenous lands.
1879	The Argentine Conquest of the Wilderness exterminates the Tehuelche.
	The War of the Pacific begins between Chile against Peru and Bolivia.
1880	The Tarahumara, allied with Porfirio Díaz, defeat the Apache.
	The Yoeme begin war against the Díaz regime and Mexican army.
1881	"Pacification" and occupation of Araucania in Chile.
1883	General Victorica defeats Q'om resistance in Argentina.
1885	Atusparia Uprising, Callejón de Huaylas, Peru.
	The Quechua fight for Liberal leader Eloy Alfaro in Ecuador.
1889	Clorinda Matto de Turner publishes *Birds without a Nest* in Peru.
1892	The Chiriguano rebellion in Bolivia under Tumpa is repressed with savagery.
1894	Nicaragua invades Native territories along the Atlantic coast.
1897	General Lorenzo Winter crushes Q'om and Mocobí resistance in Argentine Chaco.
1899	Pablo Zárate Willka and the Indigenous Rebellion in Bolivia.
1899–1902	Guaymí leader and Panamanian General Victoriano Lorenzo allies with the Liberals to fight in the Thousand Days War in Colombia.
1901	Mexico defeats *Cruzob* army at Chan Santa Cruz in Yucatan.
1903	Panama declares its independence from Colombia.
1906	Sam Pitts declares himself Miskitu king in Nicaragua.
1907	Peruvian Amazon Company registered in London to harvest caucho in Peru.
1909	Opposition politician Francisco Madero demands an end to the Díaz regime in Mexico.
1910	Brazil creates the Service for Indigenous Protection.
1911	Indigenous people attack landowners throughout Mexico as the Revolution begins.

1912	President Madero recruits Yoeme, Mayos, Pimas, and Pápagos in Sonora to fight the rebels.
1913	Adventists open bible school on Nargana Island, Panama for Kuna children.
	Forced conscription of Indigenous people into the Mexican army.
	Concha Rebellion in Ecuador; Indigenous people fight on both sides.
1915	Rumi Maqui Uprising in Puno, Peru.
1916	Yoeme guerrilla sorties against Mexico.
1917	Mexico defeats Yoeme rebels at Cerro del Gallo.
	Pilagá warriors attack Fort Yunká in Formosa, Argentina.
1920	Peru's new constitution adopts an *indigenista* stance to co-opt Native insurgencies.
	The Pro-Indigenous Rights Tawantinsuyu Committee is formed in Cuzco, Peru.
1921	*Indigenistas* in Lima celebrate the First National Indigenous Congress.
1924	Massacre of 40 Mocobí at Napa'lpi in Chaco Province, Argentina.
1924–1925	*La Antorcha*, first socialist paper in Ecuador, calls for Indigenous worker protests.
1925	Kuna rebellion in Panama; Manuel Quintín Lame organizes Nasa people in Colombia.
1926	National Socialist Assembly in Quito, the first party in Ecuador to organize Native people.
1927	Aymara rebellion in Chayanta, Bolivia.
1929	Miskitu and other Indigenous people in Nicaragua support Sandino's opposition to U.S. Marine occupation.

Introduction: Neocolonialism Challenges Indigenous Communities

As the Liberals seized power throughout Latin America by the 1870s, their plans to create law and order challenged Indigenous communities. Like the Conservatives, Liberal rulers intended to exclude Native people from political rule and the benefits of development, though they did this in a more heavy-handed way. By breaking up communal Native territories, the Liberals undermined Indigenous societies and made a lot of land available for their own use. Differences between Indigenous peoples made it easier for the upper classes to divide Natives to make their own rule easier. Plans to make Latin America resemble Europe and the United States were foremost on the Liberals' agenda, but they needed money to modernize cities and infrastructure. Building factories was still unaffordable, so states instead developed resources they had to hand and could sell to businesses abroad. This chapter addresses a period of Indigenous history during which countries in Latin America turned to agrarian capitalism and sold their raw materials to companies in Europe and the United States. For some people the resulting export boom produced fabulous wealth, but for Native people the Neocolonial Period generally had a negative impact, as they lost land or entered abusive labor arrangements.

Since many Indigenous people still lived in rural areas, they often occupied lands where raw materials grew or were available. Liberal politicians either tried to force Indigenous people to harvest export products cheaply or else clear them off the land. Abolishing communal land tenure seems to have been the easiest way for national governments to take over Native lands, though where large prairies were involved, as in Argentina, outright extermination was faster and left fewer residual people. At the time, no foreigners challenged the resulting genocides. Europeans were busy watching Bismark's buildup of Germany's military strength and the U.S. was constructing its own railway, shipping, and telegraph infrastructure. More to the point, the U.S. was clearing Native people off its own Great Plains. Between 1855 and 1856, the largest groups of Native peoples on the Northern Plains ceded over 70 million acres of their homelands to the U.S., and other Native Americans also lost wars that removed them from their lands. The U.S. defeated the Modocs of Oregon and California, and Chief Joseph led the Nez Percés on their failed escape to Canada. Sitting Bull and his coalition of Lakota, Cheyenne, and Arapaho warriors wiped out Custer's forces at Little Big Horn. Warring against Native people in their own countries, foreign politicians paid little attention to Indigenous conditions in Latin America. Besides violence, other strategies for changing Native peoples during this period included missionary work and education, and Indigenous people responded creatively to both.

Theoretically, this chapter draws from literature on the role peasants have played in nation-building and the imposition of state hegemony during the transition to modern capitalist markets. In their book *Everyday Forms of State Formation*, Gilbert Joseph and Daniel Nugent outlined the creation of the modern Mexican state. Contributors to their book developed the connections between local experiences with the developing nation state, during the period between the collapse of an earlier regime and the emergence of a new government following the revolution. For Mexican leaders this was a time of insecurity, chaos, and even anarchy. People at the grassroots level, such as the Native people featured in this textbook, experienced such in-between periods as unusual times without taxes or state surveillance, and at times took the opportunity to reverse injustices. What happened to popular classes and Indigenous people during capitalist formation and as states engaged greater international trade?

Political scientist James Scott has shown that these periods of critical nation-building were "vacuums of sovereignty," a critical time that offered peasants relative autonomy and a chance to reclaim "local sovereignty."[1] This period saw popular resistance to the growing hegemony of the developing nation states. Rather than a unified front, however, Native people still resisted from individual community bases, which strengthened their defiance but challenged their collective ability to take power. Italian philosopher and politician Antonio Gramsci has shown that it is difficult for the subaltern classes, people without power, to unite until they can become a state.[2] In fact, anthropologist William Roseberry has argued that popular resistance to hegemonic state projects in Mexico during this time was stronger and more resilient precisely because of its plurality and lack of a counter-hegemonic program of its own.[3] People reached for local sovereignty in many ways, including dress, civil disobedience, religious movements, and less frequently armed resistance.

Illustrations of the multifaceted Indigenous response to state-building include the ways in which Indigenous communities also provided labor and soldiering for the Liberals' economic expansion. As foreign businesses came to control exports of natural resources, their host nations pressured the producing nations to expedite commerce. Some Latin Americans call this period "neocolonial" because they see resemblances between the export boom and their earlier colonial relationship with Portugal and Spain, and key social features of colonial interactions indeed persisted. As before, trade was at times also abusive and controlling, and the one-sided benefits did not return to most Latin Americans. Latin American nations also still traded with foreign powers, though instead of Spain and Portugal it was Britain and France, and to a lesser degree the U.S., which were the growing industrial powers.

However, there were important differences: the "gunboat diplomacy" used by the United States to control resources during this period did not last as long and was not as controlling as Iberian colonial rule. Nations were not in the business of creating long-term colonies, as in settling people from the U.S. in Latin America, and rather just focused on extracting resources. Nor were states and companies concerned with changing Latin Americans religiously, as the Catholic monarchs had done during colonial rule, though economic interactions paved the way for U.S. missionaries. Many Latin Americans now admired the U.S. as a growing power, where before they had rebelled against Iberian control. Another key change was that the products and their location were different. Instead of silver, gold, or textiles in the highlands, businesses used Native workers to harvest coffee, sugar, henequen, and rubber. Rather than force Indigenous people underground into mines, the authorities used them in fieldwork or else tried to clear them off their land to make it available for ranching. As states exported their resources, this period thus saw widespread Native labor, the defeat of some long-standing armed Indigenous resistance movements, and the incorporation of huge stretches of Native territories into ranchlands.

Indigenous people challenged the Liberals' establishment of law and order, their systems of forced labor, and the rising threats to Native lands. As nationalism grew in response to foreign influence, power, and business, nationalistic leaders took control, yet their neocolonial arrangements mainly favored their upper-class supporters. In Mexico, neocolonialism contributed to a massive revolution, and Indigenous people influenced the course of national events. In some cases, politicians employed their country's Native heritage to forge powerful nationalistic ideologies of inclusion and unity, a political strategy of forced social integration called *indigenismo*. Many Indigenous people did in fact further join national society: missions, labor, education, military service, all helped change Native cultures. Some militant Natives took advantage of national crises to fight for their own goals. More frequently, Indigenous people challenged frontier expansion, foreign intrusions, and threats to their ways of life.[i] Political leaders learned that it was increasingly more politically correct and cheaper to incorporate Native people with political strategies and cultural change than to use military force or physical barriers against them. Still, massacres occurred. By the time the Great Depression hit Latin America and politicians called populists scrambled to rebuild their economies, Indigenous people had become important participants in national events.

Positivism and Economic Changes Reach Latin America

By 1870, the Industrial Revolution was changing the world. Latin American nations were not yet industrializing, yet businesses in Europe and the U.S. required more and more raw materials such as rubber, cotton, and sugar for their factories. Liberal leaders

i This book uses the definition for the term "frontier" provided by Lamar and Thompson: "not as a boundary or line, but as a territory or zone of interpenetration between two previously distinct societies." See *The Frontier in History*, 7–8. For further exploration of frontier studies, see Colloway, *New Worlds for All*, Cayton and Teute, *Contact Points*, and Otto, *Dutch-Munsee Encounter in America*.

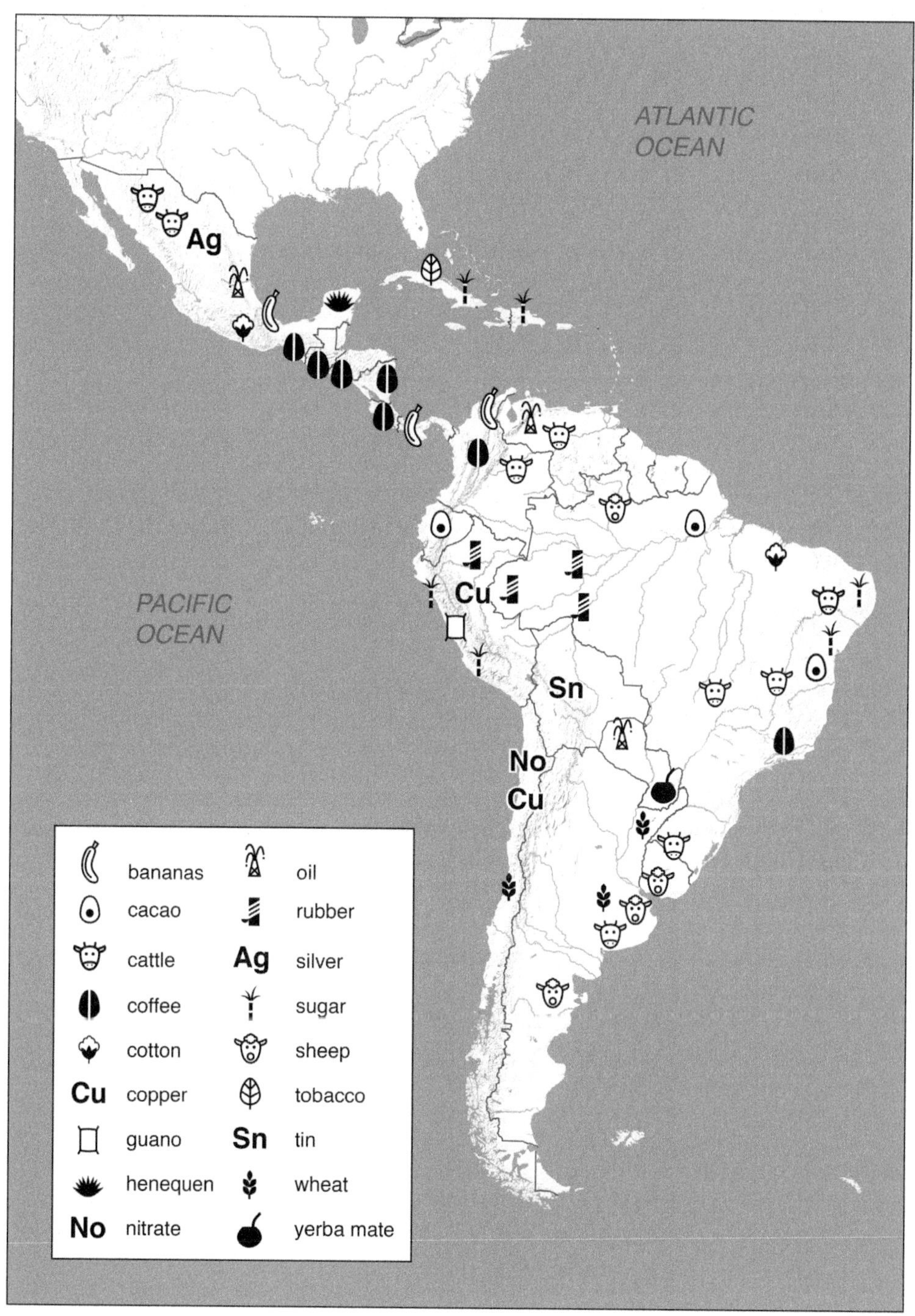

Map 11.1 Neocolonial Products in Latin America

met the demand by exporting more of those products. To legitimate their pursuit of prosperity, Latin American elites embraced a philosophy called positivism that was gaining in popularity. This social doctrine came originally from French philosopher Auguste Comte, father of sociology, who taught that political order was necessary to achieve progress and economic growth. The growing desire to establish order everywhere, especially on internal frontiers, drove the authorities to repress rebellious Indigenous peoples and impose central state authority upon Native homelands through military force.

Mexican interest in Yucatan resources grew as the market for henequen and sisal developed in the U.S., where farmers used the cactus fibers for twine to bale their hay. The *Cruzob*, the Native people still battling Mexican forces in the peninsula, serve as a good example: in August and December 1870, they revived their war by twice raiding Mexican frontier outposts without being caught. A Mexican reprisal force of 1,300 soldiers set out in January 1871 to punish the attacks, but entire *Cruzob* villages simply evacuated ahead of them. The soldiers actually turned back in fear even before reaching the movement's heartland.[4] The geography again gave Indigenous people the advantage. What does the following document, written from the highest leader of *Cruzob* authority, Bonifacio Novelo, to his *Cruzob* generals in 1866 reveal about Native resistance by this time?

For Document 11.1: Correspondence from *Cruzob* Leader Bonifacio Novelo, visit www.routledge.com/9780415519120.

Another place where the authorities tried to impose order upon a forested borderland area was Panama. Prospectors heading to California had begun crossing the isthmus by train in 1855, and mestizos and Afro-Panamanians entered Kuna territory in search of rubber. Surveyors explored sites for a possible canal across Panama. Commander Thomas Selfridge, from the U.S., traversed eastern Panama in 1870 with unwilling Kuna guides. They led his scouts through swamps and thickets to the Caledonia pass in eastern Panama, only to discover that the hilly terrain was too high for a canal. The age-old desire to bypass the long voyage around South America would have to wait.

Indigenous lands in Central America faced increasing demands for raw materials. As foreign demand for raw materials grew, market forces drew frontier regions in Mexico and Central America into capitalist relations and changed cultures in the process. In 1871, Liberal landowner and coffee planter Justo Rufino Barrios took power in Guatemala and pushed what he saw as a golden chance for his fellow elites: coffee. Demand was growing for the beverage in Europe, and Costa Rica and El Salvador were already exporting the beans. Coffee proved a great investment for Guatemalan landowners: when Barrios became president, the beverage already comprised 50 percent of exports, and under his rule production soared, doubling by 1876 and then quintupling by 1884.[5] Wealthy coffee planters built opera houses, parks, railroads, and telegraph lines in imitation of Europe. French and U.S. investors managed Guatemala's exporting infrastructure, and German immigrants taught what they believed were more efficient methods for cultivation. To harvest the beans, though, planters relied on Native smallholders, and the president remodeled his country to increase coffee production.

President Barrios had built a coffee plantation of his own on the lands of an Indigenous community in the area of San Marcos, so he knew that Native people tended to be conservative and would resist losing their communal land to coffee plantations and their self-sufficient farming to become coffee harvesters. He was also aware that peasants and Native people had led a mass uprising against Gálvez's previous Liberal reforms back in 1837 (as discussed in Chapter 10), so he favored a slower transition to a coffee economy. The new leader did not initially expropriate all communal properties (by then called *censo* lands in Central America) and replace them with private holdings, but instead enacted regulations that gradually made land available for coffee and pressured Indigenous workers into the trade.

Liberal legislation to build the coffee infrastructure in Guatemala gradually severed Indigenous people from the land, their means of subsistence. These measures culminated in 1877, when Barrios abolished communal Native properties for good. His Decree 170 declared *censo* lands to be uncultivated *terrenos baldíos*, the term for vacant public lands held without formal titles and national property, divided them into individual plots, and then sold them at prices fixed by the government.[6] If the renters themselves, usually peasants, did not "wish" to purchase the communal land, anyone could buy it as vacant property.[7] Natives in Costa Cuca lived in one community that lost its *censo* lands to coffee almost immediately, and others followed over time, especially along the coast. Then Guatemala wrote the conversion of *censo* lands to individual plots into villages' land titles, so the Liberals gradually legally whittled away at communal lands. Along with coffee, laws opened up land for cattle, rubber, chicle, and wood. The legislation forced Native people without land to grow food to earn wages as they joined the market economy.

Besides making more land available for coffee, officials helped planters secure workers for their *fincas* (coffee plantations) by forcing Indigenous villages to assign to planters the number of workers they requested for 60 to 90 days of the year. Laborers migrated from their highlands villages to the lowland coffee *fincas* to clean the groves and harvest beans. Conditions were difficult and often violent: *finca* managers called Native workers "chuchos" (dogs) and commonly beat them with fists, whips, and machete flats, attacked them with dogs, and held them in stocks or *finca* jails. Labor recruiters stole from workers, kidnapped wives and children, and burned their houses down to force compliance.[8] Planters also secured workers through indebted peonage, a system in which *finca* managers lent workers money up front to cover expenses and then held workers at the plantation until they paid their debts. By the 1920s, most of the men in the Native villages owed substantial debts to estate owners. Highland peoples lost their self-subsistence and became permanent workers on lowland coffee plantations because they had to buy food. Guatemala's entrance into the coffee market was one of the more brutal in the hemisphere.[9]

These changes seem challenging, but the transition to coffee and the loss of land varied by community. Historian David McCreery has shown that all these changes affected Indigenous communities slowly and in a variety of ways. For some coastal villages the laws were challenging: in Pochuta, Samayac, San Francisco Zapotitlán, and Coatepeque, "coffee hit the local economy and society as a tidal wave, engrossing land and converting local inhabitants into colonos (resident workers) or day laborers on the *fincas*."[10] In the western Guatlemalan department of Quetzaltenango, the new laws furthered privatization of K'iche' lands, a process already underway. The K'iche' themselves used the new laws to create individual plots out of communal lands, and landholders registered their properties for titles and purchased their own land. In fact, in this area, Native peoples themselves pushed for privatization. This change increased the annual amount of cultivated land, as well as its concentration among fewer owners.[11] Communities were changing, yet no major uprising followed privatization because President Barrios had so successfully divided Indigenous from *ladino* workers in coffee-growing regions and made the changes very slowly.[ii] Over the next 70 years, state military and political power gradually broke community self-sufficiency and made Indigenous land and labor available to the coffee growers. Guatemala's Liberal participation in the coffee market was challenging, but Indigenous people themselves shaped and furthered some of the changes.[12]

If the Liberal rulers abused Native freedoms, the Conservatives also provoked uprisings when they tried to dismantle Indigenous community structures. Thousands of angry Quechua women and men in Chimborazo, a province south of Quito in the central Ecuadorian highlands, rose up in December 1871, during the rule of Conservative president Gabriel García Moreno. Over the previous 50 years, the authorities had registered, auctioned, and sold communal lands in the parishes of Yaruquí, Punin, Cajabamba, Sicalpa, Cacha, Licto, Colta, Calpi, and Pulucate.[13] They also imposed a heavier tax of 4 to 5 *reales* to build roads, schools, bridges, and churches.

Angry peasant reactions to rising state control during the late nineteenth century, in this case the imposition of heavier taxes, illustrate popular responses to growing strategies of domination. In his study of the poor in eighteenth- and nineteenth-century England, E.P. Thompson argued that for popular cultures under domination, newer stratification by class

Figure 11.1 K'iche' Indians. (Photographed by Emil Herbruger, The Library of Nineteenth Century Photography)

ii In Guatemala, by the time of Independence the term *ladino* referred to a non-Indian, including Spaniards, mestizos and creoles. Previously, in the Colonial Period the term had referred only to Hispanicized Indians.

replaces older patterns of thought that had earlier fragmented groups of people. Roseberry has countered that the Latin American context was much more multidimensional and complex, and usually did not reveal a consensus and clear plan. As Latin American states developed their hegemony during the late nineteenth century, they developed regulative and coercive agencies to manipulate their subjects.[14] Predictably, subaltern people at times responded angrily to tightening state control.

On Monday, December 18, 1871, enraged villagers in Yaruquí finally assassinated two officials drafting workers to build a road, ripped apart the body of a tithe collector, and threatened to burn down the entire town. Over the next two days, Native people pillaged and set fire to surrounding villages. As O'Connor has shown, women played an important role in this rebellion, much as they had done in Condorcanqui's uprising a century earlier in Peru. As the uprising gained momentum, rebels crowned their principal leaders – a young man named Fernando Daquilema and his partner – as their king and queen, and organized a cavalry that attacked Ecuadorians. The authorities mobilized the National Guard and suppressed the uprising.[15] Finally, President Moreno sentenced and executed Daquilema in the plaza of Yaruquí, though he later commuted sentences to hard labor on public roads for 52 men and imprisonment for 18 women. The rebellion eased the most pressing burdens: in response, officials put off tax collections and halted forced labor. The following year, the state authorities forbade abuses in tithe and first fruit collections and forced labor.[16]

As forced labor and taxation did in Ecuador, the extraction of raw materials also pushed Indigenous people into armed struggles in Panama and Bolivia. In the early 1870s, mestizos and Afro-Panamanians invaded Panama's southern valleys of Bayano and Chucunaque searching for *castilloa* rubber. Riverine Kuna people fought off the intrusion in a local conflict called the Rubber War. In Bolivia, where 70 percent of the population were Indigenous, Natives joined forces with peasants to oppose Liberal attacks against their *ayllus*. Mariano Melgarejo, who seized power in an 1864 coup and earned the appellative "barbarous *caudillo*," tried to break up communal Native lands. The Aymara responded angrily: in the town of Macha, "an immense multitude of ferocious Indians" took over neighboring hills and recovered their *ayllus* stolen by the president's family and clients. Other protests took place in San Pedro de Tiquina, Huaicho, and Ancoraimes, northwest of La Paz, in 1870. A massive coalition of over 20,000 Aymara from highland communities finally allied themselves with Bolivians and besieged La Paz in 1871, overthrowing Melgarejo and forcing him to flee to Peru to save his life.[17] Luciano Willka, an Aymara from Huaicho, led the Native armies.

The Aymara communities largely recovered their lands from Melgarejo's cronies and clients, proving the effectiveness of alliances between Indigenous and creole communities who had joined forces in the overthrow.[18] The ability of both Natives and Bolivians to work together for a common political cause illuminates their collective response to hegemony and control. As Roseberry argues, the concept of hegemony is useful to help explain not consent but rather the struggle that subordinate people engage in against those who try to control them. People without political power use words, images, organizations, and institutions to understand, accommodate, confront, and resist their domination.[19] The Aymara and creoles did not share an ideology, yet agreed on their situation and acted together against the elite who tried to dominate them.

If the Aymara and creole alliance overthrew Melgarejo, their success was short-lived. The "Patriarchs of Silver" who led Bolivia during the mandates that followed – Presidents Pacheco (1884–1888), Arce (1888–1892), and Baptista (1892–1896) – all owned silver-mines and opened up the country to foreign capital, as if ignoring Melgarejo's example. The turmoil in Bolivia reflected Native reactions to broader changes in the national economy as local commercial and extractive businesses merged with stronger foreign sources to mine tin, silver, and other metals. The long-term result was the marginalization of Indigenous communities.[20]

Liberals in Colombia at this time also made plans in 1873 to divide Native *resguardos*, to use them instead for coffee and ranching. Over 500 Indigenous people from a coalition of villages in Southern Cauca joined forces and demanded an end to the project. They threatened to side with the Conservatives in an armed uprising if the government ignored their claim: "If the mentioned law is put into law or practice, we would find ourselves by necessity standing with the first who gave the shout of rebellion, as long as they assured us the repeal of the aforementioned law."[21] Native people in Colombia discovered that they did not need to actually volunteer to fight, but that only a threat on their part to do so was effective enough to force the Liberals to abandon their schemes.

Indigenous people in the Southern Cone also still harassed frontier settlements during these years, as pioneers and their cattle moved westward onto the Native plains. Argentine Minister of War Adolfo Alsina came up with one possible – if utopian – solution: in 1875, he ordered a gigantic trench to be dug for 1,000 kilometers across western Buenos Aires Province to stop Indigenous raiding. Frontier attacks created the urgency that pushed the project forward: the following year, an Indigenous raid just 60 leagues from Argentina's capital captured 300,000 cattle and 500 Argentine pioneers. Under pressure from Native forces, French engineer Alfred Ebelot designed the trench and workers actually dug the first 374 kilometers in 1878, before hopelessly giving up the project. Former president Sarmiento insightfully declared that trying to stop Indigenous people with a ditch was like trying to trap the wind.

Although Argentines hoped to exclude them, some Native leaders reached out to the national authorities to negotiate better relations. One such example is Document 11.2, a letter from Tehuelche Chief Vincente Pincén Calunáu to Argentine Colonel Conrado Villegas in November 1877. Chief Calunáu explains that his warriors had begun to raid frontier settlements only after having lost their own lands and families to the whites, but that he and his troops really only wished to be friends with the government and Argentinians.

For Document 11.2: Letter from Vincente Pincén Calunáu to Argentine Colonel Conrado Villegas, 1877, visit www.routledge.com/9780415519120.

Having failed to stop their raids with an unfinished ditch, and ignoring overtures for peace from Native leaders, the Argentinian authorities moved against plains Indigenous people with force. Legislators debated the wisdom of this approach, because all along their frontier Argentinian pioneers had often chosen to join Indigenous society. In the end, victorious military hawks designed a war that resembled the genocidal programs pursued by neighboring Uruguay and Chile. Minister of War General Julio A. Roca finally led five columns of troops across southern frontiers in 1879 to fight the "Conquest of the Wilderness." Military forces imprisoned, exterminated, or chased the Tehuelche and Mapuche peoples across the Andes to Chile. Natives lost over 20,000 people in the campaign, including the documented deaths of 10,513 Indigenous elders, women, and children. To prevent them from fleeing, Argentina closed its southern passes to Chile and forced the surviving Indigenous people onto reservations. Land sales financed the campaign, and following the war General Roca distributed 34 million hectares to only 381 ranchers, 24 of whom received tracts of 200,000 to 540,000 hectares each.[22] In return, the general assumed the presidency of Argentina in 1880.

Frontier development in the Western Hemisphere thus drew Indigenous people into national events. As settlers in the U.S. also moved west onto the prairies during this same period, the use of fertilizers for agriculture increased rapidly. One of the best nutrients for crops was seagull dung, called "guano," found in the 1860s along the steep Pacific coasts of Peru and Bolivia. Soon Chilean mining corporations were paying Bolivia for the right to extract guano from the dry Atacama Desert. As the prices that Bolivia demanded rose, Chilean troops occupied the Pacific port city of Antofagasta in February 1879. Bolivia and Peru in turn declared war against Chile. Chilean troops finally took Lima in 1881, but a long and messy struggle of attrition extended the War of the Pacific for two further years.

Indigenous people from all three countries participated in this war. Native peasants in Peru's central highlands provided the foundation of resistance against occupying Chilean forces, and in Cajamarca they actually fought alongside the landowning elite "in defense of a common interest they termed Peruvian."[23] Mapuche warriors, despite their long history of hostility towards outsiders, surprisingly volunteered to fight alongside Chilean forces. By 1879, over 900 Mapuche had volunteered for active duty and fought against Peru in the "Arauco" Battalion. Chile heralded them heroically as "sons of Lautaro," the Reche leader featured in Chapter 5, who had fought against the Spanish in the sixteenth century. Surprisingly, given their past interaction with Chile, some Mapuche still saw military duty as a way to further their own territorial and personal goals. These volunteers sought recognition of their traditional lands, distinctive ethnic identity, and a pluralistic, inclusive country at a time when Chileans were attacking their lands and culture. Other Mapuche contributed funds to the war effort: Don Pedro Millaleo and Don Juan Quilamán each gave 20 pesos, an important amount in 1879, to help Chile purchase a warship.[24] Indigenous participation in the conflict, even as Chile violently occupied their homeland over fierce opposition, reveals divisions within Native communities.

Events: President Porfirio Díaz of Mexico

As Chile and Argentina extended their frontiers, Mexico began its own neocolonial extractivism. The leader who made this possible was General Porfirio Díaz, who took power in 1876. The new president had been born in 1830 to a family of mixed heritage in Oaxaca, where his father had worked as a miner, blacksmith, tanner, and finally an innkeeper. His mother was part Mixtec and had raised her sons as devout Catholics. After seminary and a brief chaplaincy, Díaz studied law while Benito Juárez was governor. Díaz next joined the Oaxacan Liberal Party, became a freemason, and earned a network of political supporters. The ambitious young man entered politics in 1855, when he helped oust President Santa Anna. Díaz became an infantry captain in the Oaxaca National Guard and gained fame while fighting in the war against France.

Porfirio Díaz tried repeatedly to win the national presidency on a platform of no re-election. He lost the elections of 1871 and then rebelled unsuccessfully against Benito Juárez. When Juárez died from a heart attack in July 1872, his Chief Justice Sebastián Lerdo de Tejada succeeded him and became one of Mexico's most successful leaders to date because he was a skilled diplomat, enacted tariff reforms, and added a Senate to the national Legislature. Lerdo ran for a second term in 1876, so Díaz campaigned against him on a platform of effective suffrage and no re-election, using as a platform the ideals of the *Reforma*. Backed by Texas capitalists, Díaz finally mobilized troops and defeated federal forces in the state of Tlaxcala, occupying Mexico City and taking power in November 1876.

As president, Díaz used a heavy hand to rule Mexico over the next one-third of a century and implement a neocolonial state. Regional *caudillos* supported the new president, as did with the military, Liberals angry at Juárez failures, and Texas landowners. After stepping down between 1880 and 1884, Díaz resumed control of Mexico up until 1911. Díaz, the supposed champion of legality and no re-election, became one of the longest-lasting dictators in Latin American history.

To maintain the peace necessary to achieve economic progress, Díaz ruled by "bread and stick," rewarding supporters and clubbing opponents into submission with his *rurales*, a force of hired bandits. Using a corporate system that controlled and co-opted the army, church, landowners, and foreign business interests and prevented them from joining forces in opposition, Díaz achieved impressive growth in mining, oil, manufacturing, and transportation. Companies from abroad invested heavily in his Mexico, laying railroads, building steelworks, mining copper, gold, zinc, and lead, and exporting sugar, rubber, tobacco, henequen, and bananas. Businesses from the U.S. and Britain managed oil production, while French and Spanish businesses controlled Mexico's textile and consumer goods production.[iii] The problem was that foreign companies remitted their profits, leaving Mexico's lower classes uneducated and impoverished. Throughout the long regime, nearly one-fifth of Mexico, 389 million hectares of untitled land, became private property, an area approximately the size of California. Land became a commodity for purchase, trade, and accumulation, and values rose steeply due to agricultural demand and rising prices. The concentration of land grew worse under Díaz, and Native and peasant conditions in rural areas deteriorated.

Almost immediately, Indigenous peoples resisted Díaz's regime. During the former Liberal administrations, as Mallon has shown, Indigenous communities throughout the Sierra de Puebla had learned to expect that peasants had "original and irrevocable rights to their communal lands" they had received during the Colonial Period, and that the state should defend their rights from "predatory landowners," especially if as peasants

iii A good source on foreign interests during the Porfiriato is John Mason Hart's *Revolutionary Mexico*.

they supported the nation.[25] Díaz's threats to Native landholdings therefore prompted swift reprisals. The *Cruzob* rebels in the Yucatan, who still followed their speaking cross, challenged the new administration. By this time, cross spokesperson Aniceto Dzul was writing to the British authorities in British Honduras (today Belize), asking them to support the *Cruzob*. On the western Sierra Madre ridge that ran north through Zacatecas and Durango to Chihuahua, mountain Apache attacked and devastated the towns of Carrizal, Galeana, and Laguna.

The regime divided Indigenous people against one another, recruiting Tarahumara warriors to defeat Apache resistance at Tres Castillos and Casas Grandes in 1880.[26] Despite their support, the only payments that cooperative Native peoples received were the negative effects of economic development: by the 1880s, railroads criss-crossed sacred Tarahumara places and smoke blocked the sunlight as new tracks brought in miners and settlers. Barbed wire, installed to privatize land and protect cattle, threatened Native grazing, watering, and woodcutting. The Tarahumara faced dispossession and exploitation, even by their own caciques.[27] Some Native people joined uprisings against the new regime, however, and even on the coastal lagoons of Chiapas, so-called "bad Indians" joined outlaws and smugglers to fight Díaz's *rurales*. The fact that security forces referred to these people only as "bad Indians" rather than by their ethnic title speaks to both their prejudice and the possibility that on the borderlands, people of mixed heritage backgrounds no longer identified with a specific Native designation.

Individuals: Cajeme, the Leader Who United the Yoeme People

It was also at this time that the Yoeme (who some outsiders refer to as the Yaqui) in the northern state of Sonora organized in earnest against the Mexican authorities. Their leader was José María Leyva, a Yoeme drifter born in Sonora in 1835, who had first tried his luck among the *yori* (whites) along with his father in the 1849 California gold rush. With his earnings, Leyva learned to read and write Spanish in a private school. In 1854, the Mexican army drafted Leyva into the San Blas Battalion to fight against his own people, during their open rebellion. The soldier received his own company and served first in Mexico's War of the Reform. Then Leyva fought against the French occupation forces of Louis Napoleon Bonaparte, nephew of Napoleon I, who Mexican Conservatives had invited to rescue the Catholic Church from the Liberals. Due to his notable service, in 1872 the Governor of Sonora appointed Leyva as *Alcalde Mayor* of the Yoeme to help subdue and pacify his people. As he interacted with his own people, Leyva became aware of the Yoeme's "indomitable" desire to keep their independence; this growing awareness eventually turned Leyva around. The trooper deserted the Mexicans and returned to his people, where he became known by 1875 as Cajeme – he who does not drink – the famous leader who directed the Yoeme war against the Díaz regime.

Cajeme found the Yoeme divided. To unite them, the young leader revived communal farming, discontinued in recent decades as ranchers had taken over Native lands in Sonora. Inspired, his people declared: "God gave [us] the [whole] river, not an allotment each," and Cajeme's new guerrilla forces sought refuge in the mountains.[28] In Mexico, the 1870s were generally a period of growing peasant resistance to regime expansion: Natives in Tamazunchale also mounted an agrarian revolt against ranchers, but Yoeme resistance in Sonora became the most serious opposition to Díaz's hegemony.

Northern Sonora was by this time an increasingly disputed area: thousands of soldiers from both Mexico and the U.S. had for years been pursuing and fighting the Apache, led by Geronimo, in northern Mexico and often on Yoeme territory. The defeat of the Apache warriors occurred in 1886, even though individual Apache groups continued to harass settlers. Their demise opened the way for Mexico to declare the Yoeme homeland vacant (*terrenos baldios*), and sell the land along the Yaqui River to railroad companies and ranchers as huge properties. The Torres family purchased 400,000 hectares and the Richardson Construction Company of Los Angeles bought up 547,000 hectares of Yoeme land.[29] Díaz intended the sales to turn the landless Yoeme into submissive ranch workers, but his plans backfired and instead forced them, under Cajeme's leadership, into effective guerrilla resistance.

Joining forces with the neighboring Indigenous Mayo people, Cajeme built up Yoeme troops and pushed to reclaim regional autonomy for his people. During the 1870s, he began a guerrilla war to evict the Mexican ranchers and colonists from the United States who were buying up their so-called *terrenos baldios* (vacant lands). Cajeme stockpiled weapons and Yoeme forces raided *haciendas*, stole supplies, and burned Mexican pueblos to the ground to push the invaders out of Native lands. Yoeme opposition to the Díaz regime, as well as Cajeme's re-creation of his people into an effective resistance force, again highlights ways in which hegemony created the meaningful framework, as Roseberry emphasized, for living, talking, and reacting to social orders characterized by domination.[30]

Two Decades of War and Creative Alternatives: The 1880s and 1890s

As frontiers expanded across Latin America, the final decades of the eighteenth century saw increasing clashes and contacts between settlers and Indigenous people. The United States during this time was mopping up its own operations against Native Americans on the Great Plains, and some Latin American countries followed similar policies. In Mexico, the governor of Sonora declared a state of emergency by late 1881 in response to Yoeme raids to battle Cajeme's forces. The Yoeme example inspired the neighboring Mayos people of Cuirimpo, Navojoa, and Tesia, in western Sonora, to also reclaim leadership of their own pueblos.[31]

In the Southern Cone, it was precisely during the waning years of the War of the Pacific (1879–1883) that Chile was finally able to occupy the Mapuche homeland of Wallmapu. Rather than thank the Mapuche volunteers, Chile took advantage of the war to crush Native resistance while their warriors were away and take Mapuche land. With Chilean troops occupied in the north, colonists flooded Wallmapu, where they founded the city of Temuco in 1881 deep in Mapuche territory. Sixty enraged Mapuche chiefs finally met in March of that year and coordinated plans to resist the invasion. The result of their parliament was a general Mapuche rebellion in November, when several thousand warriors attacked Chilean towns, besieged forts, and laid waste to ranches carved out of their land. Chile, though, was militarized and had no patience for a Native uprising that distracted from its northern efforts; reinforcements from Santiago with modern weapons crushed the rebellion within a few weeks at a huge toll of Native lives. Troops relocated survivors from their homes to impoverished lives in urban centers or onto *reducciones*, forced settlements throughout the countryside. Soldiers even took children from Mapuche families and gave them to Chileans to raise as servants. The so-called "Pacification of Araucania," essentially military occupation, lasted until 1883 and terminated significant Mapuche military resistance to Chilean encapsulation.

Meanwhile, Chilean forces destroyed and left Peru in turmoil. Mobs attacked Chinese immigrant workers and their businesses in Lima and political factions struggled for power. In the highlands, peasants who had resisted Chilean forces vented their anger at their loss, taking ranches and cattle from the proprietors who they accused of collaborating with the invaders.[32] Conflicts in Lima over the presidency led to a civil war. When a prefect in the department of Ancash, north of Lima, renewed a head tax of two gold soles on peasants in the Callejon de Haylas, a long agricultural corridor between two mountain ranges, the people asked him to delay their payments because of their economic difficulties and its illegitimacy. The prefect in the city of Huaraz arrested their leader Pedro Pablo Atusparia and his 24 colleagues, cut off their braids for humiliation, and then tortured them to learn who had written their document, as the Quechua were illiterate. Soldiers fired on the people who protested the abuses in the plaza. Enraged, the following day between 4,000 and 5,000 Quechua people took Huaraz, released Atusparia, and then burned down the homes of Peruvian supporters of Provisional President Iglesias, who fell from power. Some of the more radical Quechua insurgents pushed for the elimination of all "whites" and continued to resist, but Lima sent a reprisal force that burned down Quechua villages and killed thousands of people in what became known as the Atusparia Uprising. Because Atusparia tried to restrain the radical wing of his uprising, President-elect Cáceres promised his people poll tax relief, schools, and protection of Quechua lands, a pledge he failed to keep.[33]

Even as the Quechua pushed for relief in the difficult years that followed the War of the Pacific, and Chile warred against its Indigenous population in the south, other states also attacked Native populations during this time of rising exports and expanding internal frontiers. In Argentina, officials intensified their war against the plains peoples with a campaign against Indigenous people in the northern scrub forests. General Victorica, Minister of War, led six columns into the Chaco and defeated Q'om resistance in May 1883 at Napalpí. Argentinian forces killed chiefs Juanelrai, Yaloshi, Cambá, and Meguesoxochí, taking control of an area slightly smaller than the U.S. state of Washington.[34]

Bolivia also launched an expedition against the Q'om and other Chaco peoples in 1883. To buttress their campaign, officials recruited Chiriguanos, experienced brick-makers from the Franciscan missions, to construct forts in the Chaco. One such artisan in high demand was José Yandori, and when he did not receive sufficient payment for his work, Yandori escaped to the Bolivian settlement of Caraparí, near the southeastern Bolivian border with Argentina. Skilled workers were scarce, though, so a missionary actually tracked Yandori down, arrested him for desertion, and sent him back to the fort. In the end, Yandori fell ill and escaped the heavy work regimen.[35] The experience of this skilled Chiriguano brick-maker shows how officials relied on Native laborers for frontier settlement, and that even amidst the violence, economics and labor at times drew Bolivians and Native people together.

Even while using force to clear Native people off their lands, the authorities still encouraged mission proselytism to mold Indigenous cultures into majority ways of life, a strategy as old as the Spanish Conquest. Paraguay still related differently to its Native peoples: rather than warring against them as Argentina was doing, Paraguay allowed Anglicans to open a mission for the Enxet people at Makxawaia in the lower Chaco in 1891. With government support, missionaries began to try to turn Indigenous people into agricultural peasants and workers for ranches in Paraguay's lower Chaco region.

Many governments by this time were actively encouraging religious proselytism in hopes of integrating Indigenous cultures into national society. In Bolivia by 1892 11,000 Chiriguanos were living at Franciscan missions. The last major Native uprising and massacre, in fact, were related to the missions. A young Chiriguano man named Machirope, who had grown up at a mission, began to rally Indigenous people against the Bolivians in 1892. Calling himself Tumpa, meaning "God come to earth" or "beneficial spiritual being," Machirope became their leader and virtually a deity. Chiriguanos eager to re-establish independence fled the missions and joined Tumpa's rebellion in January 1892, attacking the city of Santa Rosa with 1,300 warriors and destroying both missions and ranches. Bolivian forces put down the uprising with savagery, burning to death at least 600 Chiriguanos who were hiding in caves, and executing another 500 rebels by cutting their throats.[36] The savage repression of the Chiriguano, only two years after the Wounded Knee massacre on the Pine Ridge Lakota reservation in South Dakota, likewise effectively ended armed Indigenous resistance in Bolivia.

The violence spreading across Latin America's frontiers brought non-Indians and Native people into greater contact than ever before, often in surprising ways, and writers

Figure 11.2 First Anglican School for the Enxet at Makxawaia, Paraguay, 1890s. (Public domain)

reflected upon this experience. During the 1880s, coastal plantations in Peru used labor drafts to draw thousands of highland Indigenous people down to harvest cotton.[37] To describe how rising contacts with Native people were changing society, a writer from Cuzco named Clorinda Matto de Turner published her novel *Birds without a Nest* in 1889. This romance between a white man and an Indigenous woman explores the results of a mixed society and highlights the poor treatment of Andean Native people by the authorities. Through her novel, Matto de Turner criticized Catholic abuses (the same priest had fathered both lovers), encouraged better nutrition for Native people, and highlighted the oversight of local officials to prevent abuses in domestic service and debt peonage. The book noted Andean handicrafts, Native beliefs, music, and ceremonies, as well as creole adoption of Quechua words, dress, foods, and décor. The President of Peru praised the book for stimulating needed reforms.

The novel *Birds without a Nest* is an early expression of the political and literary movement called *indigenismo* that romanticized the Native heritage – in this Peruvian case the Incas – yet pushed to integrate contemporary Native people into national society through education and literacy in Spanish. *Indigenismo* spread quickly throughout the continent, but its popularity did not diminish the exploitation of Native peoples during the neocolonial sale of resources. Interaction between Indigenous people, intellectuals, and politicians informs the complicated relationship between coercion and consent in systems of domination, a complex dialectic that Gramsci analyzed in his study of nation states and the civil society they try to control.[38] The political strategy of *indigenismo* was an attempt by the upper classes to control the Indigenous people they needed for labor, resources, and public image, yet which at the same time they feared due to their numbers, increasing organization, and revolutionary potential.

The same year that *Birds without a Nest* was published, Peruvian entrepreneur Julio César Arana created a business to sell *caucho* (rubber latex) from Peru's eastern jungles. After his company merged with British interests, Arana's employees used brutal abuses to force Native people to harvest *caucho* in Peru's Amazonia. Both Matto de Turner and Arana used Native people to further their own goals, although rubber extraction proved much more brutal in the short term than novels.

As we have seen, during the final decades of the nineteenth century, Indigenous people in some countries faced increased violence as neocolonial extraction grew. Other Liberal governments realized that minimizing rural violence attracted more domestic and foreign investment. In Guatemala, politicians knew that violence hindered order and progress and that Native villages produced most of the country's food. Indigenous people likewise had learned that their violent responses led to further repression, so some turned to nonviolent venues to express their frustration. Communities that did rebel violently, as did the village of San Juan Ixcoy in 1898, were crushed. After neighboring *ladino* militias tried to take over this village's communal lands in 1898, the Indigenous people expelled the surveyor, set fire to the *cabildo* building, and tried to kill the rest of the *ladinos* in the village. The following day, militias from surrounding towns killed an unknown number of Native people, sending 60 more to trial in Huehuetenango.[39] Their violent response had backfired.

Indigenous people learned from such disasters. As coffee production spread slowly throughout the 1890s in Guatemala, their uprisings became less violent. Some people fled to other *fincas*, towns, or even into Belize or Mexico for refuge. Others sought legal solutions. Entire towns took conflicts over properties to court and disputed schemes to take their properties. The judicial system produced better results because pressures on lands were more gradual by this time, and because landowners offered them printed titles to lesser properties in exchange for their traditional claims to larger, untitled communal lands. Legal disputes took more time, but were a less violent compromise between Native people and the coffee growers who relied on their labor to make a profit. Over time, legal venues became effective ways for communities to defend their lands and proved less likely to bring repressive forces down upon the village. By the end of the century, violent Indigenous uprisings had gradually disappeared in Guatemala.[40]

As coffee slowly occupied Native lands in Guatemala, other commodities challenged Indigenous communities elsewhere during the export bonanza. On the Atlantic coast of Nicaragua, booms in rubber (1860s–1870s), mahogany and bananas (1880s), and minerals (1890s) turned Bluefields into an important trading center. North American businesses replaced the British interests. This change proved unfortunate for the Miskitu, who had thrown their support behind the British, long-time allies against first the Spanish and then the Nicaraguans. The growing export market on the coast attracted not only U.S. businesses but also Nicaraguan leaders, who invaded coastal Native territories in 1894.

To add foreign pressure to their territorial claims, in March the Miskitu pleaded with Queen Victoria to assist them in recovering their autonomy. "We will be in the hands of a government and people who have not the slightest interests, sympathy, or good feeling for the inhabitants of the Mosquito Reservation," they pledged, "and as our manners, customs, religion, laws and language are not in accord, there can never be a unity. We most respectfully beg … your Majesty … to take back under your protection the Mosquito nation and people, so that we may become a people of your Majesty's Empire."[41] The British Vice-Consul ignored the Miskitu missive to remain above the dispute. Growing U.S. investments during the opening years of the Gunboat Diplomacy Period, as well as U.S. interference in the Miskitu council, explain British reticence to become involved. North Americans saw the Miskitu council "dominated by Jamaican negroes so inefficient, ignorant and unequal to keep pace with the growth of the place that they were greatly dissatisfied."[42] To take control of growing business interests, Americans infiltrated the Miskitu council. Failing to secure foreign support, the Miskitu in response allied themselves with the creoles, rebelled, and prepared for a Nicaraguan attack.

In August, 500 soldiers retook Bluefield without any opposition from U.S. or British forces.[43] Nicaragua renamed the coastal region Department of Zelaya, after their president, and exiled opposing Miskitu Chief Clarence. Nicaraguans formed a compliant Miskitu government that accepted annexation of their coastal region. In November 1894, 80 Native leaders turned their land and autonomy over to the state. There is little doubt, argued anthropologist Charles Hale, that Native leaders acted against their will and in the belief that they had no other choice.[44] Forced incorporation brought taxation, state military presence, and new threats to Miskitu land from Nicaraguan entrepreneurs.

The Nicaraguan example again illustrates the late nineteenth-century attempt by Latin American leaders to link popular culture to the ruling classes and their nations. As Roseberry suggests, however, the dialectic between "the subordinate" and "the state" is not one-sided. Leaders apply their "laws, dictates, programs, and procedures" to specific regions, "each of which is characterized by distinct patterns of inequality and domination, which in turn are the uniquely configured social products of historical processes that include prior relations and tensions of center and locality." In turn, these programs create a more complex field of force when they focus on "points of rupture, areas where a common discursive framework cannot be achieved."[45] Indeed, ethnic tensions in Nicaragua continued to fester.

Economic and political tensions also drew Indigenous people into unique political alliances in Ecuador. A boom in cacao exports during the last decades of the nineteenth century, along with sales of coffee and "Panama" hats, allowed Liberal president Eloy Alfaro to take power in 1895. Native people claimed him as a "runa who desired that we all lived equally," using the Quechua term for a human being to show that Alfaro was one of their own. Regional Indigenous support for the new president shows another alliance that Native people made with Liberal politicians late in the nineteenth century to further their interests. Although coastal landowners controlled the Liberal Party, President Alfaro gained Indigenous support by expropriating church *haciendas*, rejecting territorial taxes, and canceling forced labor.

Leaders from three major Quechua communities summoned over 10,000 Indigenous troops to help Alfaro take the town of Guamote, then Chimborazo, and finally march to Quito in 1885. Natives' knowledge of local terrain and transportation of munitions and provisions were critical; in fact, communities cheered "el indio Alfaro" as his troops left for Quito, showing their acceptance of Alfaro as leader of their uprising.[46] Their support also shows that rather than always opposing Liberal rule, Native peoples were more interested in specific promises than in giving blanket support to particular parties.

While some Native people in Ecuador supported a new Liberal president, in the Southern Cone, Indigenous people still faced violent ethnic cleansing. Argentina suffered an economic crisis in 1889 after leaving the gold standard and printing too much paper currency to fund railway construction and pay off its huge foreign debt. As the economy improved, Argentinian troops returned to exterminating Indigenous people, this time in the southern Chaco. Beginning in 1897, Q'om and Mocobí south of the Bermejo River faced a four-year campaign led by General Lorenzo Winter. A series of punitive scorched-earth expeditions in 1898 slowly defeated Q'om resistance, which had persisted despite the earlier massacre at Napalpí. Soldiers burned Native settlements, killed resisters, and destroyed Q'om organization. The slaughter of hundreds of Q'om during Winter's campaign resembles the massacre of Miniconjou Sioux in South Dakota, only eight years before.

Given the massacres Indigenous people received from Liberal politicians, it is surprising that during the final years of the nineteenth century both found common causes in several nations. One example was Bolivia, where in 1899 Liberals in La Paz tried to overthrow and replace silver-mine owner and Conservative president Sergio Alonso with local federalist rule. Historians have traditionally portrayed the revolt of 1899 as a reaction to the fall of silver prices and the rise in world demand for tin, used mainly for canning. New railway networks indeed made Bolivian exports of tin to European smelters possible. The resulting boom shifted power from Potosí and Sucre to La Paz, the center for the new tin industry. Liberal elites finally aligned with angry Aymara people in the Department of La Paz to demand federalism and an end to Conservative rule, which added an Indigenous dimension to the resulting civil war.[47]

Tin may have influenced the resulting rebellion, but Indigenous history reveals a different perspective. Aymara leaders Pablo Zárate Willka and Juan Lero organized large Indigenous armies in Cochabamba, Oruro, and La Paz. Very soon, as Tristan Platt explained, the Aymara showed they had their own agenda and fought independently. The Aymara capitalized on the Liberal revolt to defend communal lands, to oppose forced labor imposed upon *ayllus*, and to claim self-rule. Native demands for a percentage of tribute funds reveal why Liberals were unable to control the uprising; the allies soon diverged.[48] On March 1, 1899, as the rebellion climaxed, Willka's soldiers sacrificed and reportedly consumed parts of 120 Bolivian soldiers, and in later battles mutilated national troops.[49] Native troops in Mohoza, between La Paz and Cochabamba, killed a contingent of Liberal soldiers to retaliate against abuses that Bolivians regularly committed in Native communities. The Aymara then established their own government in Mohoza, breaking away from Liberal rebels. After the Liberals took power in October 1899, their army chief José Manuel Pando executed Zárate Willka and 31 other Native prisoners. Liberals depicted the Aymara as "savage, bloodthirsty descendants of [Tupac] Amaru," motivated by an "insatiable thirst for revenge," who intended to end republican order.[50] The reprisal by General Pando, who became Bolivia's next president, shows that the authorities still saw Native people as unqualified for citizenship; in effect, even after Indigenous people had helped them to take power, Liberals still saw them as "enemies of the nation."[51]

Native alliances with Liberal leaders also occurred at the turn of the century in Panama, still a province of Colombia at the time. A Guaymí *corregidor* named Victoriano Lorenzo from Coclé, west of Panama City, witnessed the challenging situation of Native communities and also turned to Liberal leaders for support.[52] Liberal politicians wanted Colombia to become a federation of loosely associated states more like the United States. Conservatives in Bogotá hoped, on the contrary, to rule over regional departments in a centralist model as they saw in France, and the two sides took their differences to war. Indigenous people fought in the ensuing War of the Thousand Days, which broke out in October 1899, when Liberal rebels in Santander seized undefended villages and towns. The ferocity of the conflict marked the transition to modern warfare in the new twentieth century and resulted in as many as 100,000 deaths.[53]

In this civil war, started in 1899, the Liberals accused the Conservatives of rigging elections to stay in power. Falling world coffee prices aggravated the situation because Colombia's exports of the beans had slumped. As the violence spread west into Panama, child soldiers figured prominently in the conflict. Early on in the conflict, Victoriano Lorenzo organized Native carriers to transport supplies for Liberal leader Belisario Porras, when his army traveled toward Panama City early in 1900 and called on Lorenzo for assistance. Then, in October, Lorenzo organized a force of 300 Indigenous guerrillas that defeated Conservative forces at Aguadulce in January 1902, assuming control of the territory between Aguadulce and Panama City. Named a general, Lorenzo fought a guerrilla war from the Coclé Mountains to improve Native conditions, refusing to submit even after the Liberals signed a peace treaty arranged by the U.S. out of interests in building a canal.[54]

A New Century and Rising Indigenous Participation in National Events, 1900 to 1910

At the turn of the twentieth century, investors rushed to capitalize on the great export boom of raw materials sweeping Latin America. Brazilian coffee, Argentine wheat, Cuban sugar, Chilean guano, and Bolivian tin purchased new opportunities for elite landowners and foreign companies. Besides wealth disparity, labor and living conditions made Native situations difficult. Indigenous people continued to see venues for redress in spiritual leaders and messianic movements, political lobby, and in extreme cases, violent social revolution. The arrival of the new century, then, was for Native peoples another turn in an old cycle of continuing challenges.

Indigenous people in Mexico faced the brunt of neocolonial extraction as Porfirio Díaz reached the apex of his power. The Yoeme in Sonora had divided by the turn of the twentieth century: some worked in the central valley surrounding the capital city of Hermosillo, but the Yoeme that Mexicans called *broncos* (a pejorative term meaning wild) retreated to the eastern mountains, in the Sierra Madre Occidental Range. They vowed to die before giving up their lands and attacked the ranchers moving into their territory, even the U.S. ranchers who were growing vegetables on Native lands for the California market. Yoeme resistance became an important rural stumbling block to Porfirio Díaz's plans for development, so federal troops rounded up the Yoeme and deported them to hard labor far away in the Yucatan. Federal forces butchered women and children with Mausers (semi-automatic guns) – to force Yoeme into submission – and tortured prisoners for information up until 1908, when a downturn in the Mexican economy finally cut demand for Yoeme labor.

Expropriations were also common in the lowlands, where Mexican and foreign entrepreneurs fenced off communal Indigenous prairies and woods, limiting grazing, watering, and woodcutting.[55] As officials developed the land, some Native caciques became wealthy *rancheros*, owners of moderate *haciendas* who appropriated communal lands and added to Native inequalities. In Temosáchic, Tarahumara Cacique Encarnacion Quesada took over most of the communal lands belonging to his people, leaving them without pasture for their flocks.[56] These leaders allied themselves with the Díaz regime to dispossess and exploit their own people for personal gain. To the north, the Tarahumara experienced similar desertions by leaders and joined with mestizos in the so-called *serrano* rebellions, where Native peoples in the hills protested their turncoat leaders.

President Porfirio Díaz, now firmly in control of Mexico for over 20 years, finally moved once and for all to end the long-festering Caste War rebellion that had destroyed so many sugar plantations in southern Yucatan. Growing demand for baling twine, made from henequen fibers and used by farmers in the U.S., had by this time practically turned the peninsula into a huge plantation of henequen cactus. Díaz entrusted the campaign against the Maya rebels to his crony Ignacio Bravo, a methodical general who used 24 battalions, the Yucatecan National Guard, repeating rifles, and five cannons to crush the *Cruzob* forces. After a drawn-out campaign, General Bravo accepted the rebel surrender at Chan Santa Cruz in early May 1901. With the long war over, the *Cruzob* retreated to inaccessible swamps. Rapid development of the peninsula followed as their former lands became the new Federal Territory of Quintana Roo.

The incorporation of borderland Native territories seemed to be happening everywhere. In Nicaragua, the Indigenous Sutiaba, who lived on the Pacific coast northwest of Managua, appeared by this time to be on the brink of disappearing. Numbering only 8,500 in 1890, they owned a large communal plot west of the *ladino* town of León, and only the elders still spoke their own language fluently. The Sutiaba divided along Native lineage groups, but together opposed the ruling alliance of Liberals and Conservatives who ran the town, so the *ladinos* had a reason to see the Sutiaba disappear. More importantly, the Sutiabas' collective ownership of land irritated the town's elite, who dreamed of taking over the plot. At their demand, Liberal president José Santos Zelaya divided the Sutiabas' land in 1902 and distributed it to private cotton and sugar cane plantations. Without land, the authorities believed, the Indigenous people would gradually disappear as *ladinos*. Later that year, Congress formally abolished the community of Sutiaba. The measure should have finished off the dying Native group, but they made a surprising comeback: the group fought the privatization in court and held together as a community.[57]

On the Atlantic side of Nicaragua, other Native peoples faced similar pressures for integration. The Miskitu again received the cold shoulder from Britain when they sought support against still more Nicaraguan integration pressures. In 1906, their leader Sam Pitts rebelled and declared himself the Miskitu king. In response, Zelaya again parceled out huge grants of coastal land to his supporters. Using British leverage, the Miskitu, still inside the old reserve, fought for and received collective land titles. While they lost much of their ancestral land, the Sutiabas and Miskitu continued their fight even after Zelaya fell from power in 1909. The examples from Nicaragua show that some peoples successfully defended their lands against Liberal attacks.

Southeast along the isthmus, the Kuna were embroiled in Panama's attempt to declare independence from Colombia during the brutal War of a Thousand Days in 1903, mentioned above. The Kuna participated in Panama's push for independence because their territory lay between both countries, so both opponents courted Kuna allegiance. Indigenous leaders were divided over which country to support, Colombia or Panama, and changing leadership finally helped sway their decision toward Panama.

During those years, a Kuna man named Charly Robinson became an influential leader. While still a child, an English-speaking sea captain from an island claimed by Colombia had adopted and educated Robinson. The captain took Charly to sea and he visited ports along the Caribbean and Atlantic before returning to Nargana, the main Kuna town, where he married and opened a store. Robinson started an English school and became the head leader, but U.S. interest in a canal soon dwarfed his efforts to modernize through education. Then, in 1907, Panama attempted to change Kuna culture by sending a zealous priest named Leonardo Gassó to the coast, a Catholic missionary in Mexico and Ecuador, but Kuna opposition and Anglo affinity doomed his efforts. The Catholic mission collapsed five years later, and the Kuna instead received Protestant missionaries.[58] The U.S. demand for stability and order, central to plans for a canal, influenced the Kuna far more than Panama's efforts to change their culture.

By this time, south in the Andes, the demand for Amazonian rubber had grown to a new height, and in 1907 Julio Arana, the Peruvian rubber entrepreneur, registered his business in London. Henry Ford had founded his motor company and had discovered that automobiles ran best on tires made from rubber. Arana's Peruvian Amazon Company began supplying Ford's demand. Capitalized at £1,000,000, Arana's company employed brutal measures to force the Huitoto people in Peru's eastern forests to harvest the *caucho*, rubber latex. Even if they had been paid for their hard work, the Huitoto were self-sufficient and had no need for cash. To secure a passive labor force and force the Natives to work without pay, company managers used brutal tactics. Within a few years, rumors of abuses led the British Foreign Office to send Councilman Roger Casement to investigate. Casement was an Irishman who had investigated neocolonial extraction in 1890, when Britain sent him to the Congo during the Belgian rubber boom. While in Africa Casement met Joseph Conrad, author of *Heart of Darkness*, and witnessed the shockingly brutal treatment of the population under Belgian King Leopold's rule. Casement spent seven weeks in Peru in 1910 and, in his report, accused Arana's company of extracting 4,000 tons of *caucho* at a cost of 30,000 Native deaths.[59] He found that the company used torture and terror to force the Huitoto labor. The rubber boom in Amazonia brought wealth to some during this period – in Manaus, on the middle Amazon, where Ford was extracting *caucho* at this time, rubber barons even built a famous opera house to entertain themselves – but led to untold misery for thousands of Native people. These practices were becoming more common throughout Latin America; a similar example was taking place at this time in eastern Paraguay, where the Guaraní harvested yerba mate for the Paraguayan Industrial Company under dismal conditions of debt peonage.[60] The laborers who made such export booms possible did not benefit from the profits.

Indigenous People and the National Agrarian Revolution in Mexico, 1910 to 1911

As Latin American leaders struggled to unite their countries behind the export of raw materials, they faced a popular backlash against the labor abuses and foreign interests that dominated the trade. Most countries did not develop internally, and their industries did not grow as expected. People in the middle and lower classes suffered and lifestyles declined, causing growing anger against the elite and foreign businesses. Competition pushed countries to defend their resources and borders. Intensified hostility between states led to a rise in nationalism throughout Latin America at roughly the same time as European countries formed alliances and armed themselves before World War I. The growing urban middle classes, including millions of newly arrived Western European immigrants to Latin American countries along the Atlantic, were eager to improve their lives. To unite their growing population behind common goals of strength and prosperity, new nationalist leaders built on stereotypical images of Indigenous virility and racial uniqueness, as well as their pre-European presence in the Americas. Their strength, politicians argued, had helped forge unique, strong countries.

The collapse of the long *Cruzob* rebellion in 1901, a conflict that had dominated late nineteenth-century Mexico, actually heralded the Revolution of 1910 because the deteriorating Native conditions illustrated how Díaz's regime had made lower-class poverty progressively worse. After Díaz's army defeated the *Cruzob*, landowners in Yucatan extended commercial agriculture and political control at the expense of small and communal landholders. Elite racist attitudes only added venom: by this time many saw rural peasants as "machines that run on pulque [beer]," and contemptuously joked that "Indians only hear through their backsides." Rulers likewise hoped to kill off the Yoeme people because they stood in the way of national progress, meaning that their way of life and communal landholding potentially obstructed capitalist development.[61] As once-independent peoples lost control of both their political autonomy and ownership of production, *haciendas* and even caciques tied to the regime took charge. A depression from 1907 to 1910 raised the cost of beans and maize, and desperate Native people and peasants were infuriated. By 1910, Indigenous people throughout the country were ready to risk their lives to improve their situation.

Although Indigenous anger did not spark the Mexican Revolution, Indigenous people quickly joined the uprising; their participation was important because one-third of the people suffering under Díaz's rule were Native. By 1910, the dictator had ruled for over 30 years and his health was ailing. Wealthy elites called for a political transition. Francisco Madero, a rancher from Coahuila, demanded an end to the genocidal wars against Indigenous people and the repression of labor strikes, and suggested that moderate concessions to workers and peasants would decrease social tensions and the proliferation of radical ideas. Foreign examples of political turmoil gave the Mexican elite pause for thought: labor and political troubles in China, Russia, and the U.S. were distant rumbles, but struggles in their own nation made landowners fear that radical reforms might upset their position. Madero saw democracy as a way to control the masses by granting a few reforms and education and dissipating their growing anger. Disaffected *caudillos* not tied to Díaz eagerly joined Madero to oppose the dictator. In Chihuahua, a mule driver named Pascual Orozco and Pancho Villa, a bandit, led a rebellion in 1910 that took most of the state from federal troops. Indigenous people in the mountainous state of Morelos, who had long opposed encroaching sugar plantations, joined a mestizo named Emiliano Zapata to fight against President Díaz. Throughout the year, uprisings broke out everywhere in the country.

Change was in the air, and Natives rose throughout Mexico. The Huastecas, along the eastern coast in the State of Hidalgo, rebelled in the regions of Tancanhuitz and Tantoyuca only days after Madero issued his revolutionary manifesto in November 1910. Díaz rushed in *rurales* forces to crush the uprising, but violence spread quickly to neighboring Tantima, Tamazunchale, and Chicontepec. U.S. observers noted that these Native rebellions bore little resemblance to Madero's moderate goals. "It seems," wrote one, "that the repression of many years has resulted in a reaction, hastened by the disturbed conditions elsewhere, that no ordinary terms of peace can stop, and that there is a danger of a prolonged period of reprisal and accounting."[62] Events bore out such fears. Early on, Mexicano teenagers Domingo and Cirilio Arenas burned down the railroad station at Atlixco. In the west-central states of Jalisco and Michoacán, popular Native struggles to bring about agrarian reform – a process called agrarianism – broke out independently of official anti-Díaz movements. Social bandit Domingo Magaña took up the cause of landless Indigenous people in western Tabasco and, like the fabled Robin Hood, stole from Spanish merchants, raided plantations, and freed the peasants.[63] Madero's conservative plans for an ordered political transition soon got out of hand: by May 1911 bands of armed Indigenous people were attacking landowners in much of the country, claiming lands that had once belonged to their ancestors, and that "Madero promised we should have them, without having to pay."[64] Indigenous people were pushing Madero's revolution from below, a frightening prospect for Mexico's elite, even those who had hoped to overthrow Díaz. In 1911, the dictator finally sailed off to retire in Paris and Madero became president.

Different Approaches to "Taming" Indigenous People, 1911 to 1912

While Mexicans saw Indigenous people join their social revolution and Argentinians tried to kill the Native people, Brazilians had been preoccupied with how to move ahead without African slaves. Brazil adopted a nonviolent way to integrate Native people. Politicians had at last abolished slavery in 1888 because of British pressure and then declared a Republic. The economy shifted from sugar to coffee during the Neocolonial Period and then, in 1906, Brazil opened a direct steamship service to New York City. Brazil's transition to a modern future also altered the lives of Indigenous people. As the economy changed, German immigrants flooded the cities to work in factories and Brazilians went to the countryside to farm. In the southern state of Santa Catarina, forest Indigenous people violently opposed the invasion of their lands. In the state of São Paulo, Natives clashed with workers laying railroad tracks. The growing conflicts set off the discussion that was becoming so common throughout the continent: "What do we do with the Indians whose lands we want?" The director of São Paulo's state museum argued that Brazil should remove the savage "Indians" from the path of civilization by force.

An army engineer named Cândido Rondón proposed a different approach because Native people had earned his trust while helping him extend telegraph lines through Amazonia to Bolivia. Rondón proposed protecting Natives and attracting them to civilization by material assistance. Brazil adopted his idea in the end, because it was cheaper than military action, coincided with the nationalistic and Romantic literature of the day, and allowed Brazilians to show off their progressive goals. In 1910 the government created a new agency called the Service for Indigenous Protection to clear Indigenous people peacefully from the path of development. However, the agency was poorly funded, and all the peoples it contacted by the 1920s, including the Aimoré, Kaingang, Kagwahiva, Umutina, and Urubús, died within a few years from diseases.

In Panama, Protestant missionaries were also trying a nonviolent way to change Native cultures. Invited by Chief Robinson, Adventist missionary Anna Coope opened an English Bible school on Nargana in 1913, replacing the failed Catholic efforts to make the Kuna live like Panamanian farmers. Although Coope was good-humored and Kuna children flocked to her school, she attacked what she called their "heathen" cultural traits. The new missionary criticized the women's use of alcohol, colorful clothing, and beads, arguing that Kuna women were vain and "made of the same sinful tendencies" that she saw in women everywhere.[65] To this missionary, all "others" were essentially the same, whether in Panama or in the U.S. In a matriarchal culture such as the Kuna had, however, her misogynist approach made enemies. Then, in 1915, Panama's President Belisario Porras visited the Kuna territory of San Blas, posted police, and opened Spanish schools on the islands of Tupile, Nargana, Nusatuputo, and Playon Chico to launch a state program to change and integrate the Kuna. Inevitably, conflict with Coope's mission resulted when the authorities found that she was dissuading students from attending their state schools in favor of her own. Police ended her efforts in 1919 and placed her under house arrest, preventing her from teaching and allowing her to teach religion only at night and on Sundays.[66] Such limits kept Anna Coope from daily interaction with Kuna children. Education by missionaries and state teachers proved a difficult way to change the Kuna.

Further Indigenous Participation in National Revolutions, 1912 to 1917

In Mexico, meanwhile, more and more Indigenous people joined the revolution. After deposing Díaz, Madero proved a disastrous president and revolts against him rocked the country. Both the government and the rebels used Indigenous forces to augment their troops. During the summer of 1912, Madero recruited Yoemes, Mayos, Pimas, and Pápagos in Sonora, and 500 more acculturated *serranos* from Oaxaca to fight rebels in Chihuahua.[67] Many Native people also joined the revolution against the government out of conviction, protesting that under Díaz, life had been "all reprisals, outrages and abuses without limit."[68] Such testimonies help explain why some Natives risked their lives to fight in the civil war, but soldiering experiences also altered Indigenous views and ways of life.

All sides in Mexico's civil war relied on Indigenous people as workers and soldiers, yet also out of hope that service would change their worldviews. Rebels capitalized on Native contributions. In the State of San Luís at Palomas, the Cedillo brothers, who were *rancheros* (moderate *hacienda* owners), attracted Native fighters during March 1913 by

Map 11.2 Indigenous Participation in the Mexican Revolution

offering to return to them the lands "despoiled by the Porfirista bandits," thugs who had worked for Porfirio Díaz. Landowners just laughed at them, however, believing the threats to be worthless.[69] To some onlookers, though, the violence seemed chaotic; the U.S. consul at Veracruz wrote home in the summer of 1913 to explain that the Indians did not seem to care who was president:

> if only they can gain the liberties their ancestors enjoyed. Sometimes they cannot tell for what principle they are fighting. Nevertheless, their raids are not made in a spirit of lawlessness; abuses exist and the realization that they have suffered too long makes a reaction in such an extreme form seem lawful to this people.[70]

Indigenous people, then, fought both for and against the national government. Notably, some Yoeme served the state as troops even though they had earlier mounted such a tenacious resistance movement against Díaz. Cooperation presumably provided worthwhile benefits, such as promises of land and an end to state persecution, to some Native people.

As the regime grew desperate to repress new rebellions, it revived the Porfirian practice of Indigenous impressment – forcing Natives into the federal army. By mid-summer of 1913, President Victoriano Huerta's recruiters scoured the Puebla sierra, southeast of Mexico City, to impress Native people. Forced conscription set off a new wave of protests and a week of fighting on the sierra.[71] Indigenous bands pillaged local merchants, took advantage of villagers, extorted guns, and drank to complete intoxication to protest serving against their will. The government also impressed and then moved Native troops from one side of the country to another to divide Indigenous peoples; conscripted Mayan descendants arrived in Mérida by the trainloads to join federal forces. Impressed Yoeme from Sonora composed an entire battalion posted in Yucatan. Yet conscripted Natives did not submit easily: on Puebla's sierra and in Veracruz, opposition to forced conscription pushed even formerly peaceful communities into angry resistance, and detachments commonly mutinied, deserted, and murdered their officers.[72] Conscription worsened conditions within the dire situation already caused by the revolution.

In Ecuador, during these years after Alfaro was assassinated in 1912, Liberal factions fought each other between 1913 and 1916 in a civil war known as the Concha Rebellion. Few Native people fought in the rebellion, because Liberals still excluded them from the armed forces. Other Indigenous people joined the army to escape the debt peonage and forced labor. Even as volunteers, Native people were still targets of discrimination. Soldiers riding in trains through the northern highlands, on their way to fight revolutionaries in the province of Esmeraldas, fired drunkenly into Native houses and at Indigenous field workers and their animals in the belief that Indigenous people supported their enemies. Following the rebellion, four Liberal presidents served until 1925, during which time coastal landowners and commercial bankers controlled Ecuador and continued the neoliberal exportation of cacao until the Great Depression. Indigenous people made few visible gains for having allied with the Liberals bent on selling natural resources, although some communities gained experience that later encouraged their political participation in national events.[73]

Other Indigenous leaders turned instead to socialist politics for support. Socialists had first organized in Ecuador by 1924, calling for the defense of Indigenous rights in their paper *La Antorcha* and formally meeting in Quito two years later. The Ecuadorian Socialist Party was the first party to organize Indigenous people, and Native people employed the party as an ally in their struggle to improve their economic conditions and oppose property owner abuses. When the new socialist organization met for the first time in 1926 in Quito, Kayambi leader Jesus Gualavisí (wearing a thick red poncho) spoke to the Native situation and pushed for land reform. On Gualavisí's proposal, the Party created an office to defend the interests of peasants and workers.[74] Ecuadorian socialists used the concept of Indigenous collectivism and human rights as a foundation to organize their party and build socialism, and Native *hacienda* workers turned to urban communists for help in their own organization. Indigenous land issues thus shaped the development of socialism in Ecuador.

South of Ecuador, the rapid expansion in world trade and demand for raw materials like sugar, rubber, wool, silver, and cotton lifted Peru out of its defeat in the War of the Pacific. Despite the export boom, Peru remained divided between the elite on the coast and the Native people in the mountains. News of Russia's Bolshevik revolt and Mexico's revolution, along with a domestic leftist movement, startled Peruvian elite enough to make them form "Indian leagues" and promise to protect Native lands in hopes that "civilizing" the Native people would unite the nation and prevent violent revolution. To this end, the elite again praised the imagined legacy of Indigenous collaboration and reciprocity, and rejected racist views of Native inferiority. Peruvian leftists, notably José Carlos Mariátegui and Víctor Raúl Haya de la Torre, tried to mold socialism to their nation's reality by forming a political party in 1924 called the Popular Revolutionary Alliance of America (APRA), based on anti-imperialism and the organization of peasant and Indigenous leagues.[75]

In the countryside, meanwhile, the intellectual ferment in Lima and declining conditions were not lost on Peru's Indigenous people. Already in early December 1915, several hundred Quechua in Azángaro, Department of Puno, west and north of Lake Titicaca, attacked *haciendas* to protest authorities bent on abusively monopolizing the sale of wool at the expense of their communities. Estate employees hunted down, tortured, and executed one of the leaders of the uprising. The leader who escaped unharmed, Todomiro Gutiérrez Cuevas, was a Peruvian initially sent in 1913 to Puno to investigate local unrest. Moved by the poor conditions he saw, Gutiérrez assumed the name Rumi Maqui, Hand of Stone, and declared himself "General and Supreme Director of the indigenous pueblos and armed forces of the Federal State of Tahuantinsuyo," the new country he intended to create. While not Quechua himself, Rumi Maqui attacked abusive authorities, demanded autonomy, and called for greater "Indianness." Gutiérrez assumed Quechua identity to oppose other leaders at the time who depicted Native people as barbarians to justify using them as cheap labor in the growing wool trade. Energized by Rumi Maqui's support, in December 1915 as many as 500 Indigenous people attacked and set fire to *haciendas* in Puno. The leader named officials to positions in the new state he planned to create.[76] Peruvians finally captured Rumi Maqui, but the tenacious rebel escaped from prison and fled to Bolivia.

Revolutionaries in Mexico, in what had become a much larger civil war than in Ecuador and Peru, continued to use Indigenous people to augment their troops, and Natives served to improve their local situations. Venustiano Carranza presided over Mexico between 1914 and 1920, institutionalizing the revolution in the new 1917 National Constitution. Some Indigenous people supported Carranza, claiming he had "freed them from the slavery in which they had always lived," yet his rule was predatory. Extortions under the new president occurred far more frequently than reforms: corrupt officials speculated on food sales, supposed railway escorts stole from passengers, and even military forces seized municipal funds.[77] Crime and banditry were rampant. Mexico's national leaders understandably regarded the Indian rebellions that took place during this revolutionary time with fear and suspicion, and repressed them when possible. To build mass nationalism in a country recently torn apart, but without actually sharing their power with the masses, politicians tried to employ the upheaval that followed the toppling of Díaz to harness and pacify lower-class mobilization. Governors began promising to distribute state land to Native groups as a way to "bind" Indigenous people to Mexico, tame their activism, and indebt them to the revolution through propaganda, education, and agrarian reform.[78] Having employed Native soldiers in their armies, Mexican leaders tried to co-opt and tame Indigenous participation in the revolutionary process; to paraphrase a popular idiom, politicians now wanted to put the Indigenous genies back into the bottle before they further destabilized the new post-revolutionary system the elite were trying to forge.

The Yoeme rebels refused to submit and return to their place. They continued to fight Carranza's government and pushed authorities to take action. Six thousand warriors, women, and children in their valley, using the store of arms left over from their participation in the revolution, pressed for self-government on Native lands. Fortified in the mountains and eating mostly mescal bulbs, the Yoeme sustained themselves and were difficult to attack. By 1916, they renewed and carried out guerrilla sorties against Mexican settlements for another ten years, until the new revolutionary state, which had no place for "independent tribal enclaves," finally vanquished them at the Battle of Cerro del Gallo in 1927. Only by fighting to their last strength could the Yoeme hope to keep some land.

At the same time, the Yoeme saw small bits of their patrimony integrated into what became the Mexican revolutionary celebration of the country's Indigenous heritage through *indigenismo*, a political strategy explained in a textbox below. Economic declines made such political ceremony more urgent as a tool to unite Mexico after the revolution. One example of the downturn occurred in Veracruz, when the oil boom began its rapid decline in 1921 and thousands of Huastecs lost their jobs.[79] Military turmoil and economic decline made it necessary for Mexico's leaders to devise new political strategies to put their country back together.

State Hegemony and Lingering Indigenous Resistance between 1920 and 1930

During the Interwar Period and the worldwide Great Depression of the 1930s, Indigenous people responded to further frontier expansion through both violent resistance and nonviolent integration into majority societies. Born out of increasingly desperate conditions, both approaches were creative responses to a changing world. In some cases, Native people themselves initiated and perpetuated the violence as ranchers developed internal frontiers in countries such as Argentina. Along its swampy northern border with Paraguay, just south of the Pilcomayo River, Argentina built Fort Yunká in 1917 to monitor the frontier and discourage the local Pilagá from harassing new cattle ranches. On March 19, 1917, Pilagá warriors led by Chief Garcete attacked the fort and killed 14 Argentinian soldiers, women, and children.[80] The attack provoked a reprisal and settlement of the region, further demonstrating the social results of neocolonial expansion for Native peoples.

Trends: A Political Strategy Called *Indigenismo*

Countries with larger and recently mobilized Indigenous populations, meanwhile, devised political strategies to co-opt Native activism, especially where wars had energized Native people to express their frustrations over poor living conditions. Peruvians blamed their defeat in the War of the Pacific on their failure to integrate its Indigenous people; the large Native population made the threat of caste war loom imminently. The 1917 Bolshevik Revolution in Russia also threatened Latin America's leaders with the need to control their peasants, especially when Communist Party branches sprang up throughout Latin America. In Peru, modernizing and populist president Augusto Leguia (1919–1930) therefore sought to create a strong central state by reaching out to both the Indigenous people and the national middle class.[81] These were the interwar years when fascists were taking control with similar policies in Europe. Leguia's constitution of 1920 pledged to protect Native people, and the 1922 Patronage of the Indigenous Race decree promised legal defense of their rights. At the same time, another law obliged Indigenous Andeans to build roads without pay, revealing the program's ambiguity.

In Lima, intellectuals, landowners, and liberal *indigenistas* formed a pro-Indian rights organization in 1920, the Pro-Indigenous Rights Tawantinsuyu Committee, as an attempt to control more radical Indigenous movements in Cuzco, which politicians claimed intended to reinstate the Inca Empire and were organizing a branch of the Communist Party. The Committee started rural literacy campaigns and attempted to secure land titles for Native communities. In 1921, the Committee celebrated Peru's independence centennial with the First Indigenous Congress, which pushed for education programs in each Native community that would turn Native people into full citizens with strong-enough fists to defend their rights and become "citizens and conscientious workers, valuable for the progress of the fatherland."[82]

A group of Peruvian intellectuals who adopted Native rights to push Peru toward socialism at the time in fact collaborated with the nascent *indigenista* movement. One was journalist and philosopher José Carlos Mariátegui, who envisioned combining Inca traditions with Marxist theory. Another intellectual was Víctor Raúl Haya de la Torre, who from exile in Mexico founded a political party named the Popular American Revolutionary Alliance, to employ the Indigenous heritage against foreign imperialism in Latin America. Crowds flocked to support these radical leaders, so the army crushed the movement with executions in 1932.

In Mexico, Indigenous participation in the revolution had been even more anomalous; many Natives had fought, but apart from the Yoeme they had often done so as angry peasants instead of as members of a specific Native people. Elite politicians like Manuel Gamio therefore designed *indigenismo* as another "white/mestizo" program to resolve the "Indian problem," a way to assist the "poor and suffering race" "achieve their liberation."[83] Natives were objects of this racist strategy, not its creators, actors, or benefactors. *Indigenismo* became a method of national political control in many countries, and dominated relations between Natives and national governments for the first half of the twentieth century.

Some Indigenous people, meanwhile, showed their firm desire to control their own territory and means of production despite state overtures. In 1921, Panama finally moved to "civilize" the Kuna, who by then had moved to 50 villages on little coral islands along 150 miles of the Atlantic coast. For three years, police carefully patrolled the islands and detained Kuna who continued their own cultural practices – such as women wearing nose rings or short hair, or bathing in puberty rituals – placing them in stocks or even in jail. The Kuna used deceit, flight, and especially noncompliance with official orders to fight these mandated cultural changes. Forced integration continued until February 1925, when they finally rebelled. Armed with shotguns and rifles, the Kuna painted themselves bright red for war, took over four islands, and put the police to flight. With U.S. oversight, Kuna elders and Panamanian authorities finally met aboard the U.S. cruiser *Cleveland* and negotiated a treaty under which the Kuna gained limited regional autonomy and the removal of state police forces.

In neighboring Colombia, Native leader Manuel Quintín Lame, the "chief, representative, and general defender" of seven Páez *cabildos* (municipal regions), organized his people, known as the Páez or the Nasa, to demand land rights and even push for their separation from the country. Lame also used the Communist Party for added political weight and successfully elevated Native people to positions of authority in the party. Under his direction, the Nasa distinguished themselves from the state and defended their lands.

Indigenous people in northern Argentina during these years resisted the invasion of their lands by stealing cattle and attacking frontier forts. The authorities tried to "concentrate" them onto reservations to clear them off the land and force them to labor on sugar cane plantations. Desperate, the Native people followed messianic leaders who promised better times and the expulsion of the "whites," yet drought and hunger made their situation even worse. Throughout 1922 and 1923, police assassinations of Indigenous people created an atmosphere highly charged with fear and anger. Indigenous religious leaders encouraged attacks against settlers and mystically promised that bullets would do no harm. After ranchers and police tried to force them to pay off their debts to plantation stores, the angry people danced religiously in search of a solution; their movement resembled the Ghost Dance on the Northern Plains of the U.S.

On July 19, 1924, 130 settlers and policemen surrounded the Mocobí community of Napa'lpi, in Chaco Province, and methodically shot down over 400 Mocobí and Q'om men, women, and children with bolt-action Mauser rifles. Security forces cut up the dead with machetes, saving only severed penises and testicles as trophies.[84] In the wake of the massacre, Mocobí Cacica Dominga Mercedes, from Quitilipi, negotiated with the national authorities, encouraged her people to show loyalty by saluting the flag of Argentina, and held her communities together. Seen by some as a sell-out, the Mocobí matriarch realized that dialogue with the Argentinians was the only way to keep more of her people alive. The demand for labor to produce export commodities and the resulting disputes had again proven deadly for Indigenous workers.

Other conflicts followed as export production grew. Three years later, in southern Bolivia, one of the largest Indigenous rebellions of the twentieth century broke out in Chayanta Province, northern Potosí, when 10,000 Aymara rose in revolt against the expansion of *haciendas* onto their *ayllus.* On July 25, 1927, Natives attacked *hacienda* houses, destroyed gardens and orchards, and killed cattle to express their anger. Rebels used mock Bolivian trials, the cannibalistic consumption of a dead *hacienda* owner, and even his ritual sacrifice to their mountain deity to express their hatred. The authorities killed hundreds of people with machine guns to terminate the uprising. Although defeated, the uprising ended the extension of *haciendas* onto community lands and forced the removal of corrupt local officials.[85]

Figure 11.3 Q'om at Napalpi, Chaco Province, Argentina, 1924.

Finally, during this time in Nicaragua, Liberal patriot Augusto Sandino was still fighting against occupying U.S. Marines and National Guard forces during the last years of Gunboat Diplomacy. Given their traditional Anglo affinity, one might expect that Miskitu forces would have sided with the foreigners. Under the impact of the worldwide economic depression after 1929, though, as conditions deteriorated and export businesses left the country, a surprising number of Natives helped Sandino's forces oppose the occupiers. The rebel leader courted their support, establishing schools and agricultural support and providing health care for the Miskitu along the upper River Coco.[86] Sandino's efforts to improve Native conditions won their allegiance and some peace as Nicaragua, along with Indigenous peoples and other countries, headed into the worst years of the Great Depression.

Conclusion: Native Resistance, Exports, and Frontier Expansion in Neocolonial Latin America

During the neocolonial years of the late nineteenth century, Indigenous people faced Liberal administrations intent on moving them out of the way of economic development. The Liberals wanted land, resources, and labor to harvest lucrative export crops such as coffee, rubber, bananas, and henequen, so in areas of larger Native populations and histories of racial mixture they divided communal territories, took the land for agriculture, and created a pool of landless workers. Indigenous people experienced loss of land and strenuous labor conditions.

In societies without an historical place for Indigenous inclusion, leaders warred against Natives to clear them off ranching land. Proselytism and education were less violent ways to force Indigenous populations into national society, and Native people responded creatively to these state programs. At times they joined together to present common fronts and defeated attempts to take over their lands. In response to new strategies of integration, some Indigenous people joined the majority society. Others firmly opposed internal frontier expansion, foreign intrusions, and changes to their traditional ways of life. By the time the Great Depression hit Latin America, Native people were more involved than ever in national affairs.

While Indigenous people responded differently to Liberal attacks, they employed political alliances strategically to counter outside threats. Rather than always opposing Liberal rule, Natives were more interested in specific political policies, even if cooperation at times led to accommodation. Sometimes they signed treaties against their will to appease threats. In other cases, compliance and cooperation proved viable alternatives to costly violent resistance, and communities employed judicial courts to address local grievances. Natives also participated in wars to further their territorial claims and gain recognition as citizens. Some Native groups defended lands against Liberal attacks successfully, and thousands of Indigenous people fought in the Mexican Revolution, pushing for improvements to local grievances from below. Native resistance provoked military reprisals and even drastic measures like digging a trench for physical separation. Although they assisted in frontier development and at times supported political changes, Indigenous laborers usually saw few visible gains beyond greater collective consciousness and ethnic strength. Even peaceful contacts still resulted in decimation by disease. A few peoples negotiated treaties for limited regional autonomy, or even sent leaders to key positions in national administration and politics. In most places, Native peoples instead sought to distinguish themselves from the state and defend their lands. By the time the Great Depression struck with full force, Indigenous communities throughout Latin America had been shaped by and were helping to influence national events.

Discussion Questions

1. Did Indigenous peoples help design the policies called *indigenismo* that celebrated their Native heritage?
2. Explain the ways in which nation states employed Indigenous people and their heritage to build national hegemony during the late nineteenth century.
3. How did coffee cultivation in Guatemala compare with silver-mining in the Andes three centuries before for Indigenous workers?
4. What role did religion play in state programs to integrate Native peoples into national societies?
5. Can walls or trenches effectively separate groups of people?
6. How did Indigenous people employ religion to organize themselves?
7. What creative responses did Indigenous people find to outside threats during this period?

Notes

1 Scott, "Foreward," in Joseph and Nugent, *Everyday Forms of State Formation*, xi.
2 Gramsci, *Selections from the Prison Notebooks*, 1929, 35, and 1971, 52.
3 Roseberry, "Hegemony and the Language of Contention," 358.
4 Reed, *The Caste War of Yucatan*, 208.
5 Smith, "Origins of the National Questions," 83.
6 McCreery, "State Power," 107.
7 Williams, *States and Social Evolution: Coffee*, 61.
8 McCreery, "Hegemony and Repression in Rural Guatemala," 164.
9 Grandin, *The Blood of Guatemala*, 111.
10 McCreery, "State Power," 107.
11 Grandin, *The Blood of Guatemala*, 114.
12 Ibid., 111.
13 Ibarra, *Nos encontramos*, 22–23, 28.
14 Roseberry, "Hegemony and the Language of Contention," 357.
15 Ibarra, *Nos encontramos*, 34–35.
16 O'Connor, *Gender, Indian, Nation*, 82.
17 Mendieta, *Entre la alianza y la confrontacion*, 123–124.
18 Hylton and Thomson, *Revolutionary Horizons*, 51.
19 Roseberry, "Hegemony and the Language of Contention," 361.
20 Hylton and Thomson, *Revolutionary Horizons*, 51; Platt, "The Andean Experience of Bolivian Liberalism," 297–298.
21 Sanders, "Subaltern Strategies of Citizenship," 30.
22 Sarasola, "The Conquest of the Desert," 220.
23 Mallon, "Nationalist and Anti-State Coalitions," 233, 234, 244.
24 Crow, "Embattled Identities in Postcolonial Chile," 256.
25 Mallon, "Reflections on the Ruins," 80.
26 O'Hara, "The Slayer of Victorio Bears His Honors Quietly," 232.
27 Knight, *The Mexican Revolution*, Vol. 1, 118–120.
28 Ibid., 112.

29 Ibid., 111.
30 Roseberry, "Hegemony and the Language of Contention," 361.
31 Hu-DeHart, "Yaqui Resistance to Mexican Expansion," 222.
32 Klarén, *Peru, Society and Nationhood*, 192.
33 Ibid., 194–195.
34 Silva, *Memorias del Chaco*, 186.
35 Langer, *Expecting Pears from an Elm Tree*, 126.
36 Ibid., 188–192.
37 Favre, "The Dynamics of Indian Peasant Society," 255.
38 Roseberry, "Hegemony and the Language of Contention," 358.
39 McCreery, "State Power," 111.
40 Ibid., 110–112.
41 Petition to Queen Victoria, submitted by residents of Bluefields, March 8, 1894, cited in Hale, *Resistance and Contradiction*, 37.
42 Hale, *Resistance and Contradiction*, 42.
43 Ibid., 43.
44 Ibid., 44–45.
45 Roseberry, "Hegemony and the Language of Contention," 365–366.
46 Foote, "Monteneros and Macheteros," 84–85.
47 Klein, *A Concise History of Bolivia*, 155–156.
48 Platt, "The Andean Experience," 313–314.
49 Ibid., 315–316.
50 Hylton and Thomson, *Revolutionary Horizons*, 58.
51 Gotkowitz, *A Revolution for Our Rights*, 35–38.
52 Becker, "Victoriano Lorenzo," 234.
53 De La Pedraja, *Wars of Latin America, 1899-1941*, 5.
54 Becker, "Victoriano Lorenzo," 234.
55 Knight, *The Mexican Revolution*, Vol. 1, 112, 119–120.
56 Ibid., 120.
57 Gould, *To Die in this Way*, 117.
58 Howe, *A People Who Would Not Kneel*, 23–94.
59 Taussig, "Culture of Terror," 474.
60 Barrett, *El Dolor*, 125–129.
61 Knight, *The Mexican Revolution*, V. 1, 167.
62 Bonney, *San Luis*, March 18, May 4, 1911, cited in Knight, *The Mexican Revolution*, V. 1, 192.
63 Knight, *The Mexican Revolution*, V. 1, 224.
64 Ibid., 220, 346.
65 Howe, *A People Who Would Not Kneel*, 87.
66 Ibid., 124.
67 Knight, *The Mexican Revolution*, V. 1, 458.
68 Ibid., 153.
69 Knight, *The Mexican Revolution*, V. 2, Note 332, 51.
70 Ibid., 54.
71 Ibid., 55.
72 Ibid., 79.
73 Foote, "Monteneros and Macheteros," 100, 102.
74 Becker, "Indigenous Nationalities in Ecuadorian Marxist Thought," 12, 16, 17, 33.
75 Klarén, *Peru, Society and Nationhood*, 259; Stern, *Resistance, Rebellion, and Consciousness*, 328–329.
76 Klarén, *Peru, Society and Nationhood*, 229.
77 Knight, *The Mexican Revolution*, V. 2, 384–386.

78 Ibid., 373.
79 Santiago, "Rejecting Progress in Paradise," 181.
80 Braunstein and Sbardella, "Las dos caras," 108–119.
81 Turino, "The State and Andean Musical Production in Peru," 266.
82 De la Cadena, *Indigenous Mestizos*, 91.
83 Knight, "Racism, Revolution, and Indigenismo," 77.
84 Cordeu and Siffredi, *De la algarroba*, 89.
85 Langer, "Andean Rituals of Revolt," 230.
86 Hale, *Resistance and Contradiction*, 52–56.

12 Diverse Indigenous Paths toward Self-Determination, 1930 to 1971

Chronology

1931	Jorge Ubico becomes president of Guatemala.
1932	January: La Matanza massacre in El Salvador. July 8: U.S. stock prices collapse to their lowest level of the twentieth century. The Chaco War begins between Bolivia and Paraguay.
1933	El Zapallar gathering of Mocobí in Chaco Province, Argentina. Franklin Roosevelt declares the Good Neighbor Policy toward Latin America.
1934	Lázaro Cárdenas elected president of Mexico; *indigenismo* becomes state policy.
1936	Anastacio Somoza Garcia, Director of the National Guard, president of Nicaragua.
1937	President Getulio Vargas of Brazil declares authoritarian New State. Gold-miners invade Shuar territory in Ecuador.
1938	Panama designates Kuna Yala as the Comaraca de San Blas, a distinct territory. Ayopaya Uprising in Bolivia.
1939	Vargas appoints Rondon director of the National Service for the Protection of Indians.
1940	Mexico creates the National Indigenous Institute (INI).
1943	Roncador-Xingu Expedition to Amazonia.
1944	Patzcia attacks in Guatemala. Overthrow of Liberal president Arroyo del Rio in Ecuador. Foundation of the Ecuadorian Federation of Indians in Quito.
1945	"Tiawanaku Proclamation" at the National Indigenous Congress in Bolivia.
1946	Juan Perón becomes president of Argentina. La Violencia Civil War begins in Colombia.
1947	Pilagá gather at La Bomba, Formosa Province, Argentina, massacred by state forces.
1952	MNR Revolution in Bolivia. Jacobo Arbenz enacts land reform in Guatemala.
1953	Indigenous people in Chile organize the National Indigenous Association of Chile.
1954	Castillo Armas overthrows Arbenz and his land reform in Guatemala. Alfredo Stroessner seizes power in Paraguay.

1957	International Labour Organization supports integrating Indigenous peoples.
1959	Cuban Revolution takes power and inspires Native activism throughout the Americas.
1961	U.S. Alliance for Power enacts support for Latin American militaries.
1962–1965	Second Vatican Council in Rome.
	Rural Aymara students in La Paz found the Fifteenth of November Movement and later the MUJA Julián Apasa University Movement.
1964	Shuar Federation organized in Ecuador.
	Military forces take power in Brazil; continued development of Amazonia.
1967	Ranchers massacre 15 Cuiva Native people in Colombia.
1968	Mexico assassinates ten Aztecan Mexicano people.
	Native people in Argentina form the Indigenous Center of Buenos Aires and the Coordinating Commission of Indigenous Institutions in the Argentine Republic.
1969	President Velasco of Peru reinstitutes Quechua as the second national language.
1970	Trans-Amazonian Highway planned through lands of over 160 Indigenous peoples in Brazil.
	Natives organize the Coordinating Commission of Indigenous Institutions in the Argentine Republic (CCIIRA).
1971	Natives in Colombia form the Regional Indigenous Council of Cauca.
	Scholars gather in Barbados for the first Symposium on Interethnic Conflict.

Introduction

The worldwide economic depression that began in October 1929, with the crash of the U.S. stock market, led to serious changes for Indigenous people in Latin America. Falling prices created desperate situations for Latin American nations because their foreign trade collapsed by half, bringing down the governments that had relied on the export boom. While national leaders scrambled to find sources of income, simmering ethnic tensions exploded. Peasants who wanted access to land and labor pressured landowners. Larger nations turned to industrial development to improve fiscal matters, rallying the working classes behind these plans to sever their former reliance upon industrial goods from more developed nations. Despite these struggles for basic survival, Indigenous people took advantage of growing networks between their peoples, as well as the media, and continued to organize.

As governments developed new programs to manipulate and control peasants and Natives, these people, who lacked political power, developed their own survival strategies. When caught between opposing forces in military conflicts, Indigenous people sided with those who promised them the best long-term benefits. During wars, Native people worked as scouts, scalped enemies, guided troops through unfamiliar terrain, and then helped clean up combat zones as armies retreated. During civil struggles, as violence overwhelmed their communities, Indigenous peoples retreated or tried to survive as long as possible. When national forces seemed overpowering, some Indigenous peoples pledged their allegiance to the prevailing government to purchase time and peace during which to organize themselves. In other cases, communities accepted token gifts from the national authorities, but, rather than submit to government control, continued to act in their own interests. When desperate to defend their lands, some Native peoples used violence to evict settlers and prospectors. Politicians and state organizations tried to co-opt Indigenous leaders and divided their communities to control them. In response, Indigenous peoples forged alliances with outside advocates, including anthropologists, religious organizations, and human rights advocates. When politicians or revolutionary leaders employed their Indigenous heritage to buttress their programs, Natives contributed when it suited their interests and otherwise withdrew their support. Native people capitalized on changes in the Catholic Church to publicize their situation and link to outsiders. Expanding media, communications, and transportation options also strengthened Indigenous organization. By the 1970s, Indigenous communities had forged broad alliances with other Native peoples, with outsiders, and had forced their way into national events.

The Challenges of the Economic Downturn

Latin Americans turned to populists to lead them through the Depression years. Populist politicians, such as Juan Perón in Argentina and Getulio Vargas in Brazil, relied for political support and industrial production on the growing working class. The downturn showed that neocolonial economies, based on the export of monocultures, would not improve conditions for the majority. To break away from foreign control, Latin American leaders decided to build their own industries and replace formerly imported materials with goods made at home. To earn the workers' support and expand their industrial sectors, populists boosted social welfare programs and expanded the rights of women, workers, and minorities. Focused on industrial expansion, few populist leaders showed interest in their Indigenous populations. Still, when they needed rural workers and natural resources following the wars, states established new and more extensive contact with Native people.

For Indigenous people, the Great Depression proved extremely difficult, especially in Central America, where the sale of tropical fruits and coffee had allowed the upper class to gain control of much of the land and forced Indigenous peoples into cheap labor. The United Fruit Company, which shipped 51.6 million bunches of bananas to the U.S. every year, still dominated Guatemala. After seizing power in 1930, President Ubico kept elite support by forcing the peasants and Indigenous people to carry passes (*libretas*) to prove that they had worked at least 150 days of the year on *haciendas*, and by allowing plantation owners to commit murder to protect their properties. In Nicaragua, Sandino's war against the U.S. Marines and the Nicaraguan National Guard (1926–1933) ended with the establishment of the Somoza regime. Nicaraguans had long held their nation to be largely mestizo, yet some Native communities still resisted powerful landowners. By this time, in the Boaco municipality, the Native population had declined from 14,000 to 10,000 as *ladinos* appropriated Indigenous communal lands. Without the protection of Sandino, leaders were unable to defend their claims against the National Guard and its allies.

A Massacre in El Salvador and War in the Chaco

While Native people struggled to protect their lands in Guatemala and Nicaragua, conditions were even more difficult in El Salvador, where dwindling foreign investment and peasant evictions created a growing pool of landless workers. The international market collapse forced small farmers to sell their land as large landowners consolidated their cotton, henequen (an agave plant), and sugar production. The upper class achieved amazing levels of wealth, even as the Depression worsened.[1] Daily wages for coffee workers collapsed to only

30 cents per day by 1929. Agitation among workers grew as working and living conditions deteriorated and urban labor organizations openly opposed the regime. In December 1931, the Salvadoran military ousted Liberal president Araujo, who had tried to pass limited reforms, and installed Vice-President Martínez in his place. Labor unions and the Communist Party planned an insurrection against Martínez for January 22, 1932, and recruited peasants and Indigenous people to protest. When they discovered the plan, the government authorities seized key leaders of the movement and the rebels called off the uprising. Even without direction from Communist leaders, energized Indigenous people and peasants throughout the country still revolted. Poorly prepared, often armed only with machetes, rebels took over much of western El Salvador but soon fell to police and guard units.

The Salvadoran elite took advantage of the uprising to massacre the Native population, and Indigenous deaths following the uprising were horrific. On January 24, the National Guard killed Indigenous people in Tacuba, Juayúa, and Nahuizalco, the centers of the uprising. Troops indiscriminately slaughtered any males over 12 years of age, but in some areas, such as Tacuba, they also killed women and children. Troops massacred the unarmed Indigenous people, dumping their bodies in common graves. This vengeance was genocidal because it focused entirely on self-identified Indigenous people, and racism fueled the killing.[2] In Nahuizalco, the National Guard ambushed and slaughtered nearly 400 Indigenous men with machine guns. Military forces branded all Native males as "communists," killing over 2,500 Indigenous people in Nahuizalco and Izalco. In Juayúa and Tacuba, military forces executed over 2,000 peasants.[3] During La Matanza (The Massacre), armed forces killed over 30,000 peasants, many of them Indigenous people. The resulting trauma and terror produced for the Native population in El Salvador what social psychologists term "chains of shame and anger," argue Gould and Lauria-Santiago, because following the massacre Native people abandoned the cultural markers that had linked them to an Indigenous heritage. Indigenous women discarded the distinctive dress, such as the *refajo* skirt or wrap that branded them as Indigenous, and instead adopted the less threatening category of "peasant." Native people in western Salvador also used the Nahuatl-Pipil language less and less frequently. La Matanza devastated the Indigenous population of El Salvador.

The same year of the Salvadoran slaughter, Bolivia and Paraguay went to war over the Chaco territory between them. Bolivia sought access to the Atlantic Ocean via the Paraguay River, and Paraguay was intent on settling and claiming the dry, thorny territory fabled to harbor oil. Even before the Depression, Natives in the Chaco had helped both sides explore the sparsely populated territory, ambushing settlers and troops when they ventured into the scrub-forests. Indigenous peoples from four linguistic families lived in the Chaco: the Ayoreode and Yïshiro peoples in the north belonged to the Zamuco linguistic tree. The Enxet and the related Enlhit, and Angaité, Sanapaná, Guan'a, and Enenlhit peoples shared a Lengua-Maskoy linguistic root, while the Yofuaxa, Nivaclé, and Mak'a peoples came from Mataco-Mtaguayo ancestry and lived in central and lower areas closer to the Pilcomayo River. The Toba-Q'om people, of Guaicurúan heritage, resided in the southeastern lower Chaco. The Western Guaraní and the Guaraní Ñandeva had already migrated west from eastern Paraguay to the foothills of the Andes in pre-Columbian times. Bolivia moved military outposts into the Chaco. In 1924, Czarist immigrant General Juan Belaieff hired Mak'a and Yïshiro guides to explore the Chaco for Paraguay. Impressed by their survival skills, Belaieff requested a troop of Indigenous cavalry to patrol and defend the territory for Paraguay. However, Paraguay was far from ready to arm Indigenous people. Bolivia was the favored nation

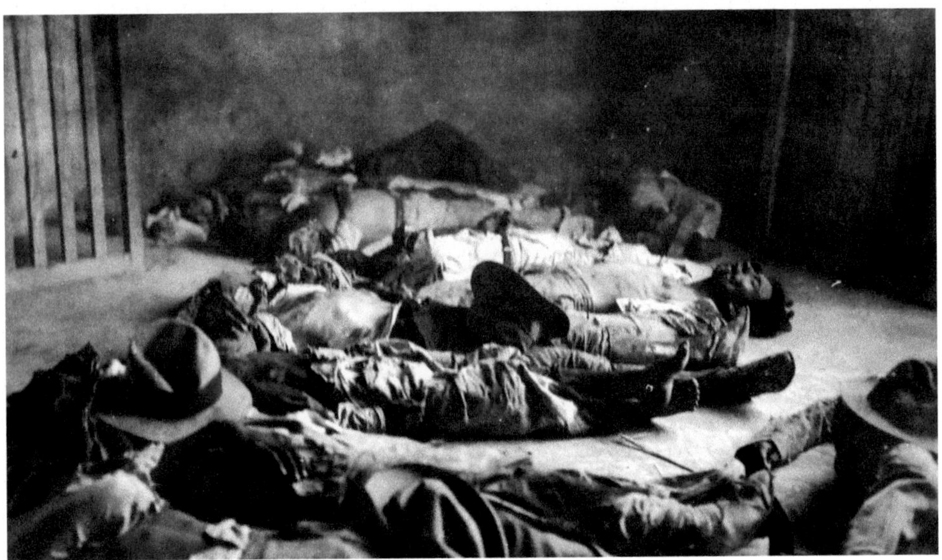

Figure 12.1 Victims of La Matanza in El Salvador Lie Dead in an Unknown Village. (Photo courtesy of the Museo de la Imagen y Palabra, Exposition 1932, San Salvador, El Salvador, www.museo.com.sv)

when war finally broke out in 1932 because it had modernized forces with obligatory military service and foreign supplies.[4]

Indigenous people served both sides of the war. Bolivia relied on Quechua and Aymara troops who ate even their pack animals to survive: "When all the mules were gone, the bones were scraped and eaten, the hides soaked and chewed."[5] Native peoples also served Paraguay as guides, scouts, and informal troops, ambushing Bolivians and trading their scalps for scraps of food and dry bread. Both armies used Indigenous languages for secret radio transmissions, much as Navajo code talkers later served the U.S. in World War II, and turncoats translated the messages of both armies. Soldiers took advantage of Native women for prostitution, and epidemics of chickenpox and mumps swept through the Native communities as a result of the increased contact, the limited mobility of each group of people to escape disease, and the dietary constraints brought on by war rations that weakened the populations. Paraguay's victory in 1935 forced entire peoples to relocate: thousands of Western Guaraní and Guaraní-Ñandeva returned from Bolivia to the Paraguayan Chaco, and the Mak'a relocated to Asunción. The Nivaclé helped clean up weapons and vehicles left in the area in return for rifles and machetes.

The Chaco War profoundly altered the lives of the Indigenous people. In the Bolivian Chaco, the high mortality of the Native people became a national emergency over labor that exacerbated Bolivia's economic depression and led to uprisings. Paraguay, on the other hand, saw the birth of *indigenismo*. A new National Indigenous Patronage office extended military control over Native people and writers glorified their Indigenous heritage. General Belaieff brought Mak'a dancers to perform in the Paraguayan capital, and a traveling Mak'a theater troupe even dramatized their role in the Chaco War at the world-famous Colon Theater in Buenos Aires, Argentina. Aside from the gaudy shows, some Native people felt ignored, as explained by Toba-Q'om leader Francisco Ramírez in the following statement about the way Paraguay ignored his people's contribution to national success in the Chaco War.[6]

For Document 12.1: Q'om Leader Francisco Ramírez Interview by René Harder Horst about the Chaco War, Asunción, May 29, 2005, visit www.routledge.com/9780415519120.

While Bolivia and Paraguay battled over the Chaco, Native people in Argentina migrated to seek work during the Depression. In 1933, at El Zapallar in the Chaco Province, 300 Mocobí gathered around a healer and prophet named Natochí after a serious drought hit the area. With wooden wands of power in hand, the people danced in expectation of a period of abundance when the Mocobí would exterminate the whites and recover their own land.[7] After the Argentinian authorities defused the messianic movement, Natochi's followers gathered nearby at Pampa del Indio around a different young prophet named Tapanaik. This charismatic leader exhorted his followers to abandon agriculture and return to hunting and gathering, promising the arrival of airplanes with material goods. The police arrested Tapanaik, but, unlike at Napa'lpi in 1924, allowed his followers to disperse peacefully. When facing desperate conditions, Native people continued to seek religious solutions and relief.

Gunboat Diplomacy Changes Native Communities in Nicaragua

The Depression years and Latin America's European heritage led the United States to extend financial credits to Latin America and solicit solidarity against European fascists. To overcome the hostility caused by the Gunboat Period, President Franklin Roosevelt promised that the U.S. would be a "good neighbor" to Central and South America. The U.S. ended its long occupations of Caribbean and Central American nations with visible effects.

The rhetorical shift in the U.S.'s relationship with Latin America, though, did not arrive soon enough for Indigenous people in Nicaragua. Since 1927, guerrilla leader Augusto Sandino had used his peasant forces to oppose the U.S. Marines and their National Guard. Highland Native people took advantage of this conflict to steal cattle from the elites and to reoccupy lands that coffee barons had stolen from them. Natives from Jinotega and San Lucas joined Sandino's army to counter the scorched-earth policies carried out by U.S. troops. To help build an anti-imperial force, Sandino had since 1927 called for the defense of the "Indo Hispanic race," employing the *indigenista* idea of a combined Indigenous and Hispanic heritage to unite his supporters. The myth of Nicaragua as a mestizo nation created an anti-imperial symbol that erased contemporary Indigenous people from public discourse even as it relegated them to history as one of many influences on the people of Nicaragua. As a result, Gould explains, by the late 1930s, full-scale marginalization and disintegration of contemporary Native communities was prevalent. Indigenous people were ultimately unable to defend their communal lands.[8] After National Guard forces assassinated Sandino in 1934, their leader General Anastasio Somoza Garcia seized power in a coup. Over the following decades, Indigenous people lost more lands and distinctive cultural markers as the dictatorship promoted *mestizaje*, race mixture. Some Natives refused to cooperate: in December 1937, after the local political boss tried to appoint non-Indians to lead their community, Indigenous people in Matagalpa refused to vote and finally had the corrupt *ladino* arrested.[9] Native opposition finally forced Nicaragua to include Indigenous people in their *indigenista* rhetoric of mestizo rule and heritage.

Natives Respond to Changing Political Strategies: Populism and *Indigenismo*

North of Central America, meanwhile, by 1934 Indigenous communities in Mexico were still recovering from the Mexican Revolution and seeking benefits from the new president, Lázaro Cárdenas. A populist leader from Michoacán with a reputation for honesty, Cárdenas distributed nearly 45 million acres of communal land to 12,000 Native communities and peasant villages. The new leader also celebrated Mexico's Native heritage. During his presidency, the state formulation of the "Indian problem" grew into a full-fledged policy called *indigenismo*, in which intellectuals proposed the "progressive, persuasive integration of the Indian into Mexican society." Mexican intellectuals formulated the policy by reviving "Indian" folklore, customs, music, and dance, coupled with images of strength, suffering, and valor to create paternalistic welfare policies geared to reap political dividends by glorifying the Native heritage. While the recent revolution changed official views about race and ethnic relations, *indigenismo* also helped create the false perception that the revolutionary violence had eliminated racism.[10] Rather, the rhetoric was another elite attempt to deal with a non-cooperative Indigenous population.

In Brazil, the new populist government of Getulio Vargas likewise began to employ images of Native strength to consolidate his rule. In 1937 Vargas crafted an authoritarian state called Estado Novo, New State. The president's focus became to settle and make Amazonia "productive," and Vargas encouraged Brazilians to "March to the West" into Native lands. The Xavante, Karajá, Bororo, and Xerente peoples were large groups in the less populated states of Mato Grosso and Goiás in central Brazil that had successfully resisted the expansion of coffee plantations and Brazilians' settlements into their lands due to their geography. Intellectuals popularized the president's pioneer initiative by glorifying the mythical Indigenous assistance given in Brazil's creation, including the Native women who had children with the conquerors. To mediate with the Natives, Vargas appointed Marshall Rondon as first director of the National Council for the Protection of Indians in 1939. Over the next decade, as the military moved into Mato Grosso, violence with Indigenous peoples resulted. When Vargas toured a Karajá village in August 1940, the first president to visit Amazonia or even a Native settlement anywhere in Brazil, he distributed axes, knives, and tools and held an Indigenous baby to pose for photographers, while the Karajá sang the national anthem in front of the Brazilian flag. The Xavante, though, were the people who could potentially challenge state plans for development, so Vargas flew to a nearby Xavante village, where he explained his plans to settle and turn them into "productive" citizens.[11]

In Central America during these years, Panama was unable to use the Kuna people for patriotic displays because the Kuna still ruled themselves following their rebellion of 1925. In 1938, Panama finally designated Kuna land as the Comarca de San Blas, a distinct territory under Indigenous administration. The 1925 uprising had given the Kuna political benefits and autonomy enjoyed by few other Native peoples. Still, as James Howe shows, the conflict had also divided the Kuna. While most communities continued their own distinctive cultural practices during the 1930s, Kuna people in Nargana and Corazón stopped wearing traditional *molas*, the colorful distinctive blouses, adopted the national education program, started working as salaried laborers, and began to use the Panamanian flag.[12] Each Kuna community chose their own path into a changing future.

Contacts between Indigenous peoples and non-Indians in Ecuador also increased during the 1930s, as prospectors entered Shuar territory in growing numbers. Miners rediscovered rich gold-mines that the Spanish had first exploited in the sixteenth century along the lower Paute, Zamora, and Upano rivers. The Shuar at first welcomed the resulting gold rush that peaked in 1937 because miners brought machetes, muzzle-loading shotguns, and paid wages for helping set up their ranches. Over half of the Shuar-Jivaro in the Upano Valley, though, died from diseases during this influx of outsiders, and the settlers took over their gardens and land. As a result, many Shuar fled the invasion, moving east and northward to the Río Chiguasa region.[13]

Artists and politicians in Mexico proceeded toward integration in a more cautious and legal manner than Ecuador, using their recent civil war to showcase the contributions that Native people, all the way back to the Mayans and Aztecs, had made to their great nation. In 1940, the government of Mexico inaugurated the National Indigenous Institute (INI) to extend health care, education, and equal legal rights to Native peoples in their nation. Later that year, the INI sponsored the first Inter-American Indigenista Congress, where Latin American nations discussed Native conditions in their countries and expressed admiration for Native cultures. The assembly created an Inter-American Indigenous Institute to integrate Indigenous peoples into mainstream Latin American society. The Institute had no legislative authority, so most Latin American nations ignored its guidelines and some created their own policies. In collecting data on Latin American Native peoples that might interest tourists, the Institute mainly ignored pressing issues such as Indigenous land rights or legal standing. Lakota historian Vine Deloria has criticized the Institute's inefficacy: "For nearly thirty years the nations met in conference, shared anecdotes, and adjourned to mourn the passing of the noble red race."[14]

Many of these reforms from above, such as the ones enacted in Mexico following the revolution, encouraged Indigenous people to take charge of their own situations. After the Chaco War crisis, Andean Native people demanded political participation and improved conditions. Bolivia's defeat angered the Indigenous peasantry in the mountainous Ayopaya region and neighboring areas of Bolivia, where, inspired by broader political changes and the new Bolivian Constitution of 1938, Native people pushed for improvements by issuing legal demands against abusive landowners. At the Yayani *hacienda*, they actually took an overseer to court for viciously assaulting a Native worker and threatening others with death. The victim and fellow workers received legal protection in Cochabamba to leave work periodically without being fired.[15] Further south in Chile, in 1939, the Mapuche founded the Frente Unico Arauco to defend their own agrarian interests. Small victories, such as the Ayopaya Rebellion and Mapuche organization, produced further activism in Andean nations throughout the 1940s.

Events: World War II and its Aftermath

World War II forced Latin American nations to become more self-sufficient. Given the massive immigration from Southwestern Europe and their historical connections, South Americans shared historical ties with Spain, Portugal, and Italy, which became fascist nations during the Great Depression. Populist presidents in South America modeled their ruling strategies on the fascist dictators – Hitler, Franco, and Mussolini – that took Europe into the war. As demand for raw materials and transportation collapsed in Europe because of the war, larger nations in South America such as Argentina, Colombia, and Brazil shifted their economies to produce industrial goods at home rather than importing them, an economic model called Import Substitution Industrialization. Leaders called "populists" gained political power throughout South America with support from factory workers and immigrants, and focused on developing the industrial sectors of their economy rather than their traditional agrarian sectors of raw materials, crops, or cattle, to substitute domestic production for imported goods and create economic independence following World War II. The strongly nationalistic focus on factory production, based on blue-collar workers, generally excluded the Indigenous people.

Populism and Indigenous Peoples

Growing Indigenous organization nevertheless also forced populist leaders to relate to Native people. At the least, populists attempted to use Indigenous issues to rally political support. The key to Brazil's development of its western territory was the Roncador–Xingu Expedition that President Vargas launched in June 1943. In preparation for the construction of new airstrips, settlements, roads, and schools along the Xingu River in Mato Grosso, military forces entered Xavante land with trepidation due to their fierce reputation. The Indian Protection Service (SPI) began to leave clothes and tools at an outpost, and the Xavante accepted the "offerings." Clearly, the Xavante were not ready to give up their independence, however, because in November they clubbed SPI officer Pimentel Barbosa and five of his assistants to death.[16] Armed confrontations continued as journalists photographed the Native people. In 1945, brothers Orlando, Claudio, and Leonardo Villas Boas, all backwoodsmen, tried to convince the Indigenous people to work for the government, especially the Kayapó. Finally, in August 1946, the SPI made peaceful exchanges with the Xavante, and *Time* magazine celebrated that "patience, suffering and love" had at last conquered them.[17] Xavante oral history shows that the SPI had "pacified" only one small splinter group, and that it took until 1966 before Brazil could occupy the main Xavante region of Norõtsu'rã further to the west. Native people shaped populist plans for "development" from below.

In areas where coffee remained an important cash crop and industrial development was only a dream, Indigenous workers were still an important labor force. In Guatemala, Native people demanded a share in the social rights that President Juán José Arevalo had implemented for others following his election in 1945. Coffee growers still relied on Indigenous workers to harvest beans, labor they secured brutally through the vagrancy law. Each year, landowners used forced labor and harsh treatment to mobilize 425,000 workers to harvest coffee on their 11,200 *fincas*. *Ladinos* in the western highlands lived in fear of Indigenous uprisings because of the pent-up Native hostility to such forced labor. On October 22, 1944, 24 Native people angrily attacked *ladino* houses in the town of Patzcia after the Liberal Party broke promises it had made to Indigenous workers about distributing land. Calling for Liberal candidate General Ponce, leader of the junta that had replaced Ubico only months before, the mob angrily demanded their land and then killed over 20 *ladinos* in the center of town. Newspapers presented the event as a revolt against the government and, with fears of El Salvador's La Matanza still present, authorities sentenced 34 Indigenous people to death or long prison terms.[18] The media widely covered the revolt, stoking fears of a widespread Indian revolution that spread quickly throughout Guatemala.

Indigenous activism proliferated throughout the continent during the last years of World War II. In Ecuador, Native people allied with women, peasants, non-commissioned officers, and students, and overthrew President Arroyo del Rio in May 1944. The Liberal leader had lost a war to Peru in 1941 and people deposed Arroyo del Rio when he tried to turn the nation into a police state. Energized Ecuadorians designed a new future. Indigenous leaders joined workers and leftists and formed the FEI, the Ecuadorian Federation of Indians, while labor leaders organized the Confederation of Ecuadorian Workers. As Marc Becker explains, this was the first time that Native people in Ecuador organized a national body under their own administration.[19] Over the next 20 years, the FEI successfully represented highland Indigenous peoples "for the defense of their class interests and oppressed nationalities," and this fueled Native mobilization. Only one month after the FEI formation, Indigenous people in Cayambe denounced abuses by *hacienda* owners. Native complaints became so numerous that newspapers could not print them all and the Minister of Government called for "constant vigilance to maintain order."[20]

As World War II ended abroad, then, Indigenous activism grew in Latin America. Native unrest in Guatemala gave rise to rumors of a widespread Indigenous uprising that was bound to engulf the entire country in conflict. When the 1946/1947 harvest was ready, Native activism forced the army to keep the peace until farmers harvested their crops. Native people obviously mobilized eagerly to ensure forward-looking president Arevalo's promises for change. The elite, for their part, repressed any sign of Indigenous uprising with excessive military force.

Rumors of violent Indigenous mobilization also spread through Bolivia, where Native people and peasants were mobilizing with increasing strength. In still trying to manage peasant discontent that grew following the Chaco War, Bolivia finally allowed Native people to organize a National Indigenous Committee in 1944. Officials knew that Mexico had hosted the Inter-American Indigenista Congress, where Latin American nations had committed to integrate Native peoples into their national collectives. Even as they permitted some Native organization, cautious Bolivian officials nevertheless arrested Luis Ramos Quevedo (called "Rumi Sonk'o" or "Heart of Stone") and Antonio Alvarez Mamani, the more radical Indigenous committee leaders, and replaced them with a state-directed steering agency.

Throughout the tumultuous 1940s, Bolivian peasants organized alongside the miners, whose lot was equally precarious. The National Agrarian Party, an Indigenous workers' political party, issued the "Tiawanaku Proclamation" in December 1945, declaring, "Bolivia was, is, and must be Indian. *Bolindia* is Indian Bolivia, for the Indian is the majority in Bolivia. Ninety percent of all Bolivians are Indian … Bolivia will be great when the Indian is free."[21] Peasant militancy grew as the state tried to co-opt their organizations, but a groundswell of nation-wide sit-down strikes finally forced President Gualberto Villarroel López, in power from 1943 to 1946, to allow a national meeting of peasants.

On May 10, 1945, President Villarroel welcomed 1,000 Native delegates to a National Indigenous Congress in La Paz. Representatives reported labor abuses and called for the abolishment of *pongueaje* (Native servitude) and *mitanaje* (the unpaid labor system inherited from pre-Columbian times). The president saluted the Native delegates with a final party that included dancing, musical bands, food, and drink.[22] On the one hand, the Congress was a clever state ploy to co-opt and undermine the growing radical Indigenous movement and control it for national ends. State goals became evident when government reports ignored the issue of land tenure. On the other hand, the Congress was the first time Native leaders formally presented demands to the nation, and Bolivia finally banned forced servitude as a result. In that regard, the congress was a path-breaking achievement for Indigenous organization in Bolivia.

For Document 12.2: The Tiwanaku Manifesto, issued in La Paz, Bolivia, in 1973, visit www.routledge.com/9780415519120.

Less pressed by specifically Native organizations, leaders in industrializing nations instead broadly courted the working classes. In Argentina, Colonel Juan Domingo Perón swept into power in 1945 with promises of a social revolution. Because Perón was the first politician to refer to Indigenous people in his campaign speeches, Native people in Argentina expected great benefits from their new president. Like populists elsewhere, Perón created a commission to "incorporate Indigenous people to civilized life" and agencies staffed with Natives to "protect" Native cultures. Peronist Party leaders also visited Indigenous communities periodically to check on their living conditions and encourage Indigenous people to vote accordingly.

Converting Native people into Peronists was the new leader's goal, and as in Guatemala, the lobbying paid dividends. Years later, after opposition Radical Party politicians hosted a particularly good barbecue to buy votes in a Q'om community, the Native leader responded with the following toast to the visiting politicians: "the wine was very good, the barbecue was very tasty, but we are all *Peronistas*." Peron invited Toba-Q'om leader Pedro Martínez to Buenos Aires in 1947 and 1948, where officials wined, dined, and showered him with gifts, land grants, and the legal permit for his people to hold religious services. One leader recalled that Perón's officials "did not call us Indians; they treated us like men."[23] Political pandering cannot be overstated; with Peronist approval, Indigenous peoples in Chaco and Formosa provinces formed large Native Pentecostal church organizations and organized religious connections between communities throughout northeastern Argentina. In return, those provinces with the highest Indigenous populations consistently voted the Peronist ticket into the 1970s. Even while pushing for industrial growth, Perón integrated the Indigenous people into his political machine.

Native Organization during the Cold War

The Cold War that followed World War II soon touched the lives of Indigenous people throughout Latin America. People have called this conflict between the U.S.S.R. and the U.S. "cold" because the two superpowers avoided using nuclear weapons and instead influenced smaller nations in Southeastern Asia and Central America. At the 1947 Inter-American Treaty of Reciprocal Assistance, also known as the Rio Treaty or the Rio Pact, Latin American leaders joined the U.S. and committed to keep their nations from moving toward socialism. Military forces throughout Latin America took power to prevent leftists from gaining control, beginning with Venezuela in 1948, Colombia in 1953, and Brazil in 1964. By the mid-1970s, military forces were running most South American nations, which challenged Native organization. Because Indigenous settlements lay outside direct state control and some used land in common, conservative governments portrayed their communities as easy targets for socialist influence.

As its influence spread through Latin America, the Cold War made nationalists nervous about peasant organization, especially in isolated Indigenous communities. Climate emergencies compounded the tense situation. A drought in 1947, combined with grasshopper swarms, ruined cotton crops in Argentina. Wildfires then destroyed cane fields and left Indigenous people without work and farmers without their crops. Three thousand Pilagá in Argentina's Western Formosa Province walked over 200 kilometers to the sugar plantations where they routinely harvested sugar cane. Landowners refused to give them work, forcing the desperate Pilagá to walk home again. In poor health, 500 Pilagá gathered in October at the community of La Bomba around a new messianic leader named Luciano. These people knew about the massacre of Q'om and Mocobí at Napa'lpi, in Chaco Province, in 1924 (discussed in Chapter 11). The Pilagá demanded to explain their worsening economic situation to President Perón, who sent them a trainload of provisions. Provincial officials delayed distribution of those goods, though, and declared that the Native assembly waiting for food was really a rebellion, ordering the people to disperse. Luciano had promised his followers that their Bibles would stop the soldiers' bullets should they attack the Pilagá, but when government troops fired on the gathering in early October, the people discovered otherwise. Over the next two months, Argentine troops in Formosa entered Pilagá communities and massacred as many as 1,500 people, taking advantage of prevailing fears of Indigenous organization to decimate the Native group.

An even more serious conflict that broke out during the time in Colombia was so devastating that people simply called it "The Violence." Between 1946 and 1953, over 200,000 people died in this Colombian civil war. Conservative and Liberal parties battled each other over political affiliations, leftist guerrillas fought state troops, landowners attacked peasants and each other over land, and the elite stifled peasant and Indigenous organization. Native people lost much of their land during the war as various groups struggled for power. The military attacked the Nasa peoples in Tierradentro as subversives because some Nasa had joined the Communist Party, even as the guerrillas attacked them for alleged ties to state security forces. Priests and missionaries struggled against what they saw as the Indigenous propensity toward liberal politics and Protestant religious affiliation. Both police and bandits looted and destroyed entire Native villages, killing cattle, ruining crops, and causing people to flee into the mountains in what became a civil war.[24] It was not until 1959 that people were able to start to rebuild their lives and traders once again entered Nasa territory. As in El Salvador, the violence created a climate of fear that affected Indigenous people in Colombia far into the future.

Violence in Bolivia also affected both Indigenous people and peasants. The 1945 Indigenous Congress failed to deliver any real results. Landowners ignored the new legislation, and waves of Native unrest swept state authority aside. Indigenous, peasant, and mining activists pushed for their rights to own land; to have safe, fair, and paid labor; and to education. Native organization around these issues came to a head in 1946 in what became the largest rural Bolivian uprising of the century.[25] During this violent event, a mob of teachers, university students, and marketplace women lynched Bolivian president Villarroel. His successor, right-wing president Enrique Herzog, finally used the army and air force to subdue the insurgents. Herzog ordered them massacred and interned their leaders in a labor camp at Chapare. The state lost control of the situation though, as more activists joined a new center-left party formed in 1941, called the National Revolutionary Movement (MNR).

Map 12.1 Indigenous Conflicts during the Mid-Twentieth Century

From 1946 on, the MNR tried a dozen coup attempts to overthrow the right-wing Herzog government. The opposition party linked miners, workers, and Indigenous peasants into a powerful organization that in August and September 1949 took over the cities of Cochabamba, Sucre, and Potosí, setting up a provisional government in Santa Crúz. After the Bolivian military annulled the MNR's 1951 electoral victory, in April 1952 the MNR armed the miners in La Paz, the movement's largest base of support. The resulting three days of battles between the miners and the police, called a National Revolution, lasted for three days and left 600 people dead. During the struggle, Native activists and miners overwhelmed state forces and installed the MNR Party to power. Peasants divided land from the *haciendas* during the upheaval and redistributed it among themselves. The new Bolivian government offered free and equal education to all citizens. The resulting 1953 Agrarian Reform Decree was the second most significant land distribution in Latin America after Cárdenas' reforms in Mexico. Native people played an important role in the Revolution, but ultimately the MNR subordinated their participation by again adopting *mestizaje* terminology to integrate Native peoples into a strong nationalist discourse and minimize their activism.

As the Cold War intensified, both the U.S. and the U.S.S.R. tried to sway Latin American countries to their side. As in Bolivia, Natives, peasants, and revolutionary forces in Guatemala pressured President Jacóbo Arbenz Guzmán, elected to follow progressive president Arévalo, to enact an Agrarian Reform Law in June 1952. Land reform was the most radical of Arbenz's programs and represented a "fundamental shift in the power relations governing Guatemala."[26] The K'iche' and other Guatemalan peasants mobilized to ensure that the reform would actually occur, and that it would be as extensive as possible.

The struggle between the K'iche' and *ladinos* that had erupted on August 24, 1947 over land in San Pedro Solomá, Hueuetenango shows how conflicts involving Indigenous people pushed President Arbenz to finally enact land reform. The new law expropriated uncultivated land from large estates of more than 672 acres; within 18 months, 100,000 peasant and Native families received land without disrupting agricultural production on the estates. By June 1954, Guatemala had expropriated over 1.4 million acres from landowners and distributed it to the peasants, benefitting 500,000 people. In Alta Verapaz, the department with the largest Mayan-descended population, the government distributed the most land: 152,633 manzanas.[27] One manzana in Central America generally measures 6,988.96 square meters, or approximately 1.7270 acres. The Mayan descendants clearly benefitted from this legislation, since they reclaimed lands they had previously owned on the Pacific coast. The land reform law drew Natives into the national process: Indigenous people eagerly sought affiliation with national agencies, such as the *Campesino* League and revolutionary political parties, to evict repressive mayors, ensure that they received lands correctly, and would be able to control them.[28]

Land reform was not happening in Nicaragua, though, where Native and peasant communities were still under attack. The Indigenous community of Camoapa became the focal point of conflict when a new mayor, Hugo Cerna Baca, a wealthy *ladino*, allowed cattle ranchers access to Native lands in the early 1950s. Accompanied by National Guard troops, Cerna himself visited the community of Salinas, where Native people shared communal land, and seized their colonial land title. The theft dealt a "crushing blow to the Indigenous leadership."[29] By the time an Indigenous man murdered Mayor Cerna in 1954 out of revenge, the Camoapa community was almost extinct.

The 1950s saw additional Indigenous political organization amid Cold War fears. In Chile, Native people organized the Asociación Nacional Indígena Chilena in 1953 and the Mapuche created the Foro de Unificación Araucana four years later in response to worsening conditions. By 1964, large landowners had taken control of 98 percent of the arable land in Chile, and per capita income in Native communities was only half the national average. Still, the situation in Chile was not yet revolutionary.

As the U.S. and the U.S.S.R. vied to influence Latin American states, Conservative military forces took advantage of the international conflict to seize power. In Guatemala, the CIA finally backed a covert operation that toppled President Arbenz in July 1954. The new leader Castillo Armas repealed Arbenz's land reform, returned expropriated property to the United Fruit Company, executed 8,000 Arbenz supporters, and turned the Guatemalan economy over to foreign businesses. Far to the south, Argentina saw a presidential change in June 1955, when the armed forces brought Perón's decade-long rule to an end. Indigenous people and workers alike lost their beloved leader to military rule.

The intensification of Cold War struggles led some governments back to policies aimed at uniting their people: *indigenismo* re-emerged as a state strategy for building patriotic unity. Intellectuals in particular saw Indigenous cultures as antiquated and barbaric ways of life that had survived into modernity but urgently needed to be changed. One example was in Peru, where anthropologist and historian Luis Valcárcel revived the image of a glorious Inca heritage to help build nationalism. Valcárcel directed national museums, taught Inca culture and history at the University of San Marcos in Lima, served as Minister of Public Education, and even taught for a period at the University of Columbia in New York. In his 1927 book *Tempest in the Andes*, Valcárcel revealed his strongly romantic vision of the noble purity of the "Indian Race" and predicted that its

> culture will radiate once again from the Andes ... For ten thousand years, the Indian has been the only worker in Peru ... [t]he Indian did it all, while the mestizo idled and the white gave himself over to his pleasures ... Inca culture is an original organism ... The Andes are an inexhaustible fountain of vitality for Peruvian culture.[30]

Similar ideas influenced popular culture. The International Labour Organization, an NGO founded in 1919 after World War I to promote peace, and which became an agency of the U.N. in 1946, approved integrationist and homogenizing policies in two documents: the Indigenous and Tribal Populations Convention (No. 107), and A Recommendation (No. 104). Latin American countries used both measures to legitimate their plans to alter Indigenous cultures and integrate Native peoples further into the mainstream national collective.

Paraguay and Brazil provide clear examples of these policies. Native people on rural frontiers were threatening settlers, and politicians during the Cold War employed their communal landholding to legitimate an attack on small communist insurrections in the Paraguayan countryside. Once he had taken power in Paraguay, Alfred Stroessner created an *indigenista* program to integrate the 17 Indigenous peoples. In 1958, the dictator named a Department of Indigenous Affairs (DAI) to settle the

Native population, to make Paraguayans more welcoming to Native integration, and to eliminate communists. That same year, frontier violence pushed a Guaraní people called the Ache to seek refuge on a ranch in eastern Paraguay, and the DAI began to supply the rancher with food and medicine to settle more of the nomadic Ache.[31] In neighboring Brazil, two Kayapó groups contacted the SPI in search of metal pots and frying pans. In return, the Kayapó ended their attacks against invading Brazilian settlers. From then on, the Kayapó discovered that they could keep the goods flowing simply by threatening to use violence against settlers, or to disappear back into the forests.[32] In both Paraguay and Brazil, leaders employed integration strategies promoted by *indigenistas* to try to integrate Indigenous peoples.

Indigenous People Mobilize in Light of Revolutionary Changes

Indigenous people responded to broader political events sweeping the continent during the Cold War. In Cuba, on January 1, 1959, Fidel Castro and his rebel forces marched into Havana after defeating Fulgencio Batista, and Native people in Cuba assisted his revolutionary forces. As many as 3,000 Taino people, known by this time as Guajiros and culturally similar to Cuban peasants, lived in Yateras in eastern Cuba and still practiced some of their Indigenous customs and beliefs. Guajiros supplied Castro's men with food during his campaign and rolled boulders and logs onto mountain paths to block federal troops. Native leaders later met with Castro, radical priest Camilo Torres, and Che Guevara in Manila, who also employed the Native heritage to help unite Cubans behind the revolution.[33] Pressured by Cuban peasants, in May, Castro passed a land reform law that expropriated farms larger than 3,333 acres, distributed the land to peasants, and, with this act, brought conflict with U.S. investors to a climax.

News of the successful Cuban Revolution spread quickly. In August 1960, two months after Velasco Ibarra assumed the presidency for the fourth time in Ecuador, 500 Indigenous workers on the Carrera *hacienda* rose up, chanting *vivas* to Cuba, Russia, and land reform. Claiming the land for their people and demanding four months of back wages, they threatened to kill the owner, who accused communist leaders of the uprising as he fled. When delegates for 200,000 Indigenous people and peasants in the highlands and coast gathered in Quito in October to demand land reform, they also asked that the government recognize Quechua along with Spanish as the official language of Ecuador, and teach it in their schools. Delegates called for universal suffrage and declared solidarity with the Cuban Revolution.

Indigenous youth were accessing formal education in larger cities. Aymara high school students from the Bolivian Province of Aroma were by this time studying in La Paz, where in the early 1960s they organized the Fifteenth of November Movement, named after the date of Tupac Katari's birth, their hero (discussed in Chapter 9), who came from their own community of Sullkawi. The group would represent rural Aymara facing life in the city, and as the students advanced, they formed the Julian Apasa University Movement. One of the principal leaders, Jenaro Flores, became secretary general of his home community and eventually represented his entire province as executive secretary of the Departmental Congress for all of La Paz. Flores focused on uniting urban Aymara through soccer championships and by supporting rural land invasions.[34] Indigenous people in cities thus used their education and connections to support rural community needs.

Events: The Alliance for Progress

If the Cuban Revolution inspired peasants and Indigenous people throughout Latin America, it should not be surprising that Conservative forces tried to discourage these radical ideals from spreading. Politicians still viewed Native people as potential supporters of communism because they sometimes held land in common and resisted control by national administrators. In certain nations, notably Ecuador, some Indigenous people joined communist organizations. To discourage the further spread of socialist revolutionary ideas and to foster democratic changes, in 1961 the U.S. president John F. Kennedy loaned Latin America $10 billion through his new Alliance for Progress to improve transportation, technology, and industry in exchange for social and political reforms. While the alliance strengthened military forces in Latin America with arms and training, over the following decade it also put many Latin American nations into debt, enriched private businesses, and fostered corruption. The most important thrust of the Alliance was the U.S. counterinsurgency training for Latin American officers, and to seal these deals Kennedy intervened in Cuba, British Guiana, and the Dominican Republic. National military forces in turn took charge in Argentina and Peru in 1962, Brazil in 1964, and in the Dominican Republic in 1965. Later applications of the Doctrines of National Security contained in the Alliance for Progress allowed nations throughout the continent to further manipulate Native peoples.

Faced with intensified national pressures to integrate into mainstream society, Indigenous peoples joined forces across traditional Native barriers. On Nicaragua's Atlantic coast, Miskitu and Mayagna (who outsiders call Sumu) people discussed their living conditions and national political events. In other countries, religious movements brought Native people closer together. Protestant denominations, especially, reported successes: between 1964 and 1970, with 890 baptisms and confirmations, most of the Enxet people joined the Paraguayan Anglican Church.[35] In Chaco Province, Argentina, the Q'om and Pilaga created the United Evangelical Church in 1959. North, in Ecuador, the Quechua organized the Asociación Indígena Evangélica de Chimborazo in 1966.[36] As communities joined religiously and politically across previous barriers, they found common ground in local grievances, religious faith, and economic goals.

In other areas, Indigenous organizations and conflicts over state development of resources on Native lands both drew some people together into the broader community and divided others. In Ecuador, the 1960s was a decade of widespread Indigenous organization. The movement culminated in a lifetime of work by Dolores Cacuango, an Indigenous woman who held a position on the Central Committee of the Ecuadorian Communist Party. By 1964, the Shuar people organized into a federation that became one of the oldest and most successful resistance organizations on the continent. Through their new union, the Shuar applied for land titles and created bilingual instructional radio programs. The programs taught the people about Shuar history, culture, and language, yet Ecuador allowed the programs because they also instilled patriotism by reminding Native people of the national context in which they lived. Through these and other initiatives, the Federación Interprovincial de Centros Shuar-Achuar (Interprovincial Federation of Shuar and Achuar Centers) successfully re-created a sense of Shuar identity and stirred up their latent hostility toward outsiders.[37]

Individuals: Dolores Cacuango and Female Indigenous Leaders

Dolores Cacuango was born in 1881 on a *hacienda* in Cayambe, Ecuador. After her parents died, she escaped to avoid a forced marriage and fled to Quito. Working as a domestic servant in the capital city, Cacuango learned Spanish. Upon returning to her area, she helped organize Indigenous uprisings pushing for better labor conditions. In 1931, soldiers burned down her house and expelled her family in an attempt to crush Native protests. The leader helped found the Ecuadorian Indian Federation in 1944 and served as its general secretary until 1950. Turning to leftist politics, Cacuango joined the Central Committee of the Communist Party. Cacuango also founded Cayambe Indigenous schools and worked in education herself for 20 years. Muriel Crespi, chief ethnographer of the U.S. National Park Service, interviewed Cacuango in the 1960s and remarked, "This remarkable woman has become one of the rural workers' most celebrated cultural heroes, and, I gather, is their only heroine."[38]

Dolores Cacuango's work highlights the role that Indigenous women have played as leaders in their communities. By perpetuating the use of Quechua to children and helping create a positive Indigenous identity as she founded schools and worked politically, Cacuango fostered pride in her Quechua identity among Native communities in Ecuador. Transmitting their language to the next generation is one important role Native women offer their people, as well as helping perpetuate cultural norms such as dress, dance, cooking practices, and other signs of indigeneity (Indigenous identity). Learning Spanish and becoming involved in Ecuadorian politics through the Communist Party may be less typical of some Indigenous women, but still fits within the Andean tradition of female leadership paralleled in other communities throughout the continent.

In Chiapas, Mexico, meanwhile, new bishop Samuel Ruíz García began to use Alliance for Progress directions to organize Native parishioners and dissuade potentially revolutionary inclinations. Chol, Tzeltal, and Tzotzil women and men began to attend two Catholic schools in 1961, where they learned to read and write. Over 10 years, 1,000 graduates of these schools taught others in the communal lowlands. During the next 20 years up until 1980, the Mexican government at the same time increased the extraction of abundant natural resources in Chiapas, especially crude oil, natural gas, lumber, and cattle ranching. Extractivism displaced tens of thousands of Indigenous villagers, who fled after evictions and began new lives in the eastern rainforests or on peripheries of cities.[39] Despite conservative inclinations, the Catholic Church remained in contact with Indigenous people. Participation in the 1968 Medellin Episcopal Conference, for instance, made Bishop Ruíz more accepting of Indigenous religious perspectives and supportive of their struggles.

During these years, Indigenous people in Brazil also saw a rise in extractivism in Amazonia, with direct results for their communities. President Juscelino Kubitschek

Figure 12.2 Dolores Cacuango, Indigenous Leader in Ecuador, 1968. (Photo by Rolf Blomberg. Courtesy of the Archivo Blomberg, Quito, Ecuador.)

began the construction of Brasilia in 1956, and later moved the federal government offices from Rio de Janeiro to the new capital city to better consolidate its interior territory and develop Amazonia. Four years later, the military seized national power. As the new leaders developed Amazonia with roads and dams and settlers flooded the area, Indigenous people made their changing situation known to outside advocates. Deforestation heightened media attention on the SPI, in charge of implementing state Indigenous policies. In 1967, Brazil's attorney general found evidence of high levels of corruption among local SPI authorities, including land theft, labor abuses, massacres, enslavement, rape, torture, and biological warfare against Native people.

In December, the Brazilian government disbanded the SPI and replaced it with the new National Indian Foundation (FUNAI). When the minister of interior Albuquerque

Lima met delegates from the Xavante, Bororo, Karajá, and Xingu in April 1969, he promised to recover and reserve their lands for them alone. Then, in July, Brazilian president Costa e Silva himself met with Xavante, Karajá, Kayapó, and Kamaiurá delegates. In the name of the Xavante people, Humberto Waomote thanked the president but announced, "We are all Brazilians. We, the Xavantes, arrived first."[40] The declaration illuminates the changing dynamics between Native peoples and outside colonizers. Waomote positioned his people both in first place over the enveloping nation by rights of earlier arrival, and yet also as members of the Brazilian state.

As Waomote's declaration to Minister Lima indicates, by the late 1960s Indigenous people voiced their concerns over extractivism and displacements to both their own leaders and the world through external media outlets. Yet in many states, Indigenous people still faced repression as settlers and ranchers cleared their lands. On the Colombian llanos, ranchers brutally killed 15 Cuiva Natives in 1967, but the judge acquitted the murderers when they declared, "[We] didn't believe it was wrong since they were Indians." The next year also saw shocking reports in Brazil, where people used arsenic, dynamite, and machine gun fire from light planes to kill Indigenous people in Rondonia and Mato Grosso.[41] Then, in August 1968, Mexican troops killed ten Indigenous speakers of Aztecan Mexicano (Nahuatl) in San Miguel Canoa, in retribution for the lynching of two stranded national students. At the time of the student movement in Mexico City and Cold War tensions, the Mexicano community had mistakenly assumed the students to be communist infiltrators.[42] One year later, in April 1969, the director of Paraguay's Department of Indigenous Affairs and his hired thugs personally visited the Q'om community at Paratodo, in the Chaco, 150 miles west of Asunción, to open up their land for ranching. Guns blazing, the director himself torched homes and forced the Q'om into the woods. After further violent threats, the Q'om refugees fled to the Franciscan mission of El Cerrito, just west of Asunción at Villa Hayes, never to return.[43]

Throughout the continent, states tried to mitigate the growing Indigenous militancy by pledging social reforms, by honoring their Indigenous heritage, and by encouraging Christian proselytism. On June 24, 1969, the National Day of the Indian, Peru's President Velasco promised to integrate the peasants further into society as new consumers for industrial goods and as recipients of his new agrarian reform. Velasco reinstituted Quechua as a second national language along with Spanish and ordered relevant legal proceedings to take place in appropriate languages. In Vaupés, Colombia, Tukanoan people employed Catholic missionaries to contact outsiders for them, as well as sources of supplies, especially food, for their schools. Indigenous people also used missionaries to block the traffic of coca paste through their territory, and to prevent paste dealers from making payments with firearms and alcohol instead of money.[44] The Second Vatican Council in 1962 counseled Catholic priests to respect Native cultures, tolerate syncretism, the merging of various religious beliefs, and to preach universal salvation. Without firm Catholic support for integration efforts, though, some states instead encouraged Protestant missions to help them alter Indigenous cultures. After Catholic bishops in Paraguay pressured Stroessner to improve his human rights record, the regime instead invited Protestant missions to increase their activities in Native communities. With national support, Protestant mission work grew quickly over the following decade.

Attacks on Indigenous people and their resources continued nevertheless. Panama's Institute of Tourism began plans in the early 1970s for the construction of a 700-room resort hotel on an artificial island in western Kuna Yala, dividing Kuna leadership over the project.[45] In 1973, an agreement signed by Kuna leaders appeared, but other leaders denounced it as a forgery. Afraid that the planned airport and workers' village would damage their plantations, Kuna mobs stymied the project until 1978, when their promise to use violence to block its completion defeated plans for the hotel complex. Similar threats occurred in Brazil, where by the late 1960s over half of the estimated total Xavante population of 2,160 lived outside their pre-contact territory due to ranching, disease, and conflicts with settlers.[46] President Médici's new Trans-Amazonian Highway cut through the lands of over 160 Indigenous peoples in 1970. Native people turned to the Indigenist Missionary Council (CIMI), which organized the earliest pan-Indigenous meetings as Brazil carved roads, hydroelectric dams, mines, and ranches through Amazonia.

Movements: The Catholic Church and Indigenous Peoples

Increased threats against Native communities coincided with important changes in the Catholic Church. The Second Vatican Council of 1962 to 1965 had encouraged respect for non-Christian religious faiths among Catholics and had promoted social justice, a position affirmed at the 1968 Bishop's Conference at Medellin, Colombia. Pressured by the Barbados Declaration of 1971, in which anthropologists demanded an end to all missionary work to Native peoples, as well as the advent of liberation theology and gains in membership by Protestant denominations, the Church acknowledged past errors and committed to support Indigenous "self-determination" and the recovery of their lands. In return, the Médici government in Brazil tried without success in 1974 to forbid Catholic missionaries from proselytizing to Native people.[47] The new Catholic approach was also an institutional attempt to counter advances that Pentecostal groups, the Church of Latter Day Saints, Jehova's Witnesses, and Seventh Day Adventists had made in Latin America since the 1960s. At the grassroots level, though, many Catholic priests were concerned with the living conditions and spiritual well-being of their Native parishioners.

Given their greater access to transportation, media outlets, and NGO advocates, the Indigenous response to development and extractivism was greater organization at the communal, national, and international levels. In 1968, Native people in Argentina formed the Indigenous Center of Buenos Aires, the first pan-Indigenous organization in the nation, to promote self-determination and the recovery of struggling Native languages. Two years later, this NGO expanded into the Coordinating Commission of Indigenous Institutions in the Argentine Republic (CCIIRA). Provincial agencies developed as well, as in Neuquén Province, where 34 Mapuche communities created their own federation. In Colombia, similarly, Native peoples in Cauca, Nariño, Putumayo, San Andrés de Sotavento, and Antioquia formed the Secretaría Indígena Nacional and later in 1971 founded the CRIC, the Regional Indigenous Council of Cauca. Formed largely by Paeces and Guambiano peoples, the CRIC protected communities from guerrillas and the military through the courts of justice and nonviolent self-defense. The organization also recovered *resguardo* lands through nonviolent occupations and organized bilingual educational initiatives, agricultural instruction, and community health care initiatives. As Native people across the continent organized, they communicated their conditions and interests to an increasing audience of outside advocates.

Learning about Indigenous conditions in Latin America directly from their organizations encouraged outside religious groups and anthropologists to focus on Native conditions. In the context of the Red Power Movement and African-American struggles in the United States, and the rise of racial consciousness more broadly, scholars began to combat racism in Latin America by drawing attention to Native conditions. As Indigenous people informed outsiders about their conditions, the World Council of Churches invited anthropologists to discuss Native situations. In January 1971, scholars gathered in Barbados for the first Symposium on Interethnic Conflict and criticized states for their harsh models of development meant to integrate or exterminate Native people. Anthropologists depicted these programs as genocidal, called for a halt to religious proselytism, and urged Indigenous people themselves to manage and determine their own futures. The media broadly publicized the symposium's encouragement for greater respect and equal rights for Native people. Indigenous people, especially, used the proceedings to demand that missionaries and governments honor the new guidelines. Over the following decades, pan-Indigenous organization grew rapidly throughout the continent.

Conclusion: Indigenous People Face the Great Depression, Populism, and the Cold War

Indigenous people faced social, economic, and political challenges during the Great Depression. As Latin American nations struggled to cope with the economic downturn, populist leaders in larger nations tried to industrialize and limit their dependencies on foreign markets. In Central America, ethnic tensions exploded into violence within highly charged political environments that challenged traditional patterns of land tenure and political power. In a few nations, authorities took advantage of the economic downturn and tried to eliminate their Indigenous peoples altogether. In other areas, the development of forest resources altered Indigenous ways of life and encouraged them to integrate into the broader population. As Native people responded to these outside threats during the Cold War, they allied with other peoples and NGOs to create stronger organizations. In some places, Indigenous peoples joined socialists, guerrilla armies, or peasant groups to counter threats. Not every option delivered the desirable results, and more often than not Indigenous people faced uphill struggles. In several surprising examples, however, Native communities and their allies pressured their governments toward greater tolerance and successfully defended their lands and resources. Early patterns of organization set in the mid-twentieth century served Indigenous people throughout the following decades, as they built on and expanded their collective influence throughout Latin America.

Discussion Questions

1. How did Indigenous lives in Latin America change during the Great Depression?
2. Why did populist governments adopt *indigenismo* policies?
3. What changes after the mid-twentieth century allowed Indigenous people to organize broadly and lobby national governments?

4. How did Native peoples respond to outside influence during this Cold War period?
5. Explain why religious organizations tried to change Indigenous peoples and whether they were successful.

Notes

1 Gould, *To Die in this Way*, 8.
2 Ibid., 219.
3 Ibid., 236.
4 Horst, "The Chaco War and Indigenous People in Paraguay," 294.
5 Zook, *The Conduct of the Chaco War*, 99.
6 Francisco Acazará, Toba-Q'om, interview with René Horst, Asunción, May 29, 2005.
7 Cordeu and Siffredi, *Del Albarrobo al Algodón*, 113.
8 Gould, *To Die in this Way*, 178.
9 Ibid., 188.
10 Knight, "Racism, Revolution, and Indigenismo," 82.
11 Garfield, "The Roots of a Plant that Today is Brazil," 749.
12 Howe, *A People Who Would Not Kneel*, 298.
13 Harner, *The Jívaro*, 32.
14 Deloria, *Behind the Trail of Broken Treaties*, 231–232.
15 Dandler and Torrico, "From the National Indigenous Congress to the Ayopaya Rebellion," 339–340.
16 Maybury-Lewis, *Akwe-Shavante Society*, 4–5.
17 *Time*, September 2, 1946.
18 Handy, "A Sea of Indians," 194–195.
19 Becker, *Indians and Leftists*, 78.
20 Ibid., 80.
21 *El País*, December 12, 1945, cited in Dandler and Torrico, "From the National Indigenous Congress to the Ayopaya Rebellion," 346.
22 Ibid., 356.
23 Miller, *Harmony and Dissonance*, 151 and 55.
24 Rappaport, *The Politics of Memory*, 146; Ortiz, *Uncertainties in Peasant Farming*, 33; González, *Las paeces*, 329–334.
25 See Dandler and Torrico, "From the National Indigenous Congress to the Ayopaya Rebellion,"356–357.
26 Grandin, *The Blood of Guatamala*, 201.
27 Gleijeses, "The Agrarian Reform of Jacobo Arbenz," 465; Handy, *Revolution in the Countryside*, 94.
28 Handy, "The Corporate Community, Campesino Organizations," 179.
29 Gould, *To Die in this Way*, 220–221.
30 Valcárcel, "Tempest in the Andes," 219–220.
31 Horst, *The Stroessner Regime*, 41.
32 Cunha, *Historia dos Indios nos Brasil*, 330; Garfield, *Indigenous Struggle*, 86.
33 Barreiro, *Panchito cacique*, 24–25, 64–67, 76.
34 Albo, "From MNRistas to Kataristas to Katari," 391–393.
35 Horst, *The Stroessner Regime*, 58.
36 Muratorio, *Etnicidad, Evangelización, y protesta*, 89.
37 Hendricks, "Symbolic Counterhegemony," 57.
38 Carrera, "Dolores Cacuango," 37.
39 Levi, "A New Dawn or a Cycle Restored?," 16.
40 *Estado de São Paulo*, April 25, 1969, reprinted in Pedro Casaldáliga, *Uma igreja de Amazônia em conflito*, 100, cited in Garfield, *Indigenous Struggle*, 143–145.

41 Bodley, *Victims of Progress*, 28.
42 Carey, *Plaza of Sacrifices*, 120–121.
43 Horst, *The Stroessner Regime*, 75.
44 Jackson, "Being and Becoming an Indian," 137.
45 Howe, "The Kuna of Panama," 87–88.
46 Garfield, *Indigenous Struggle*, 117.
47 Ibid., 178–179.

13 Indigenous Organization and Opposition to Military Rule, 1971 to 1989

Chronology

1971	Indigenous peoples in Cauca, Nariño, Putumayo, San Andrés de Sotavento, and Antioquia in Colombia form the Regional Indigenous Council of Cauca (CRIC). Settlement of the northern Ache people in eastern Paraguay. Hugo Banzer Suárez seizes power in Bolivia and attacks Native organizations.
1972	Indigenous people in Argentina organize broadly following Perón's return. Indigenist Missionary Council (CIMI) created in Brazil to help Native people organize.
1973	September 11: General Pinochet takes power in Chile, attacks Mapuche cooperatives. Colombia tries to control Native organization through the CRIVA Consejo Regional Indigena del Vaupés (Regional Indigenous Council of Vaupés). Brazil approves the Indian Statute, Law No. 6001, to "emancipate" Natives. Tiawanaku Manifesto signed in Bolivia to formalize *katarismo*.
1974	People from 327 Native communities in Chiapas, Mexico demand communal land titles. Peru recognizes the right of Amazonian Native peoples to hold communal land titles. Massacre of the Valley in Bolivia.
1975	The Kuna defend their territory from development in Panama. Second CIMI pan-Indigenous gathering in Brazil. Brazilian development of Amazonia particularly devastating during these years.
1976	Repressive "Indigenous Law" passed in Colombia. Massive earthquake in Guatemala, with disastrous results for Indigenous communities.
1977	Second Barbados Congress.
1978	Chile divides communal Mapuche land into individual private properties. Brazil launches the Xavante Project. Construction on the Itaipú Dam begins in Paraguay.

	Assassination of Chamorro in Nicaragua; Monimboseños commemorate Sandino's death.
1979	The FSLN takes power in Nicaragua in July; Native people create MISURASATA.
	CSUTCB and CIDOB created in Bolivia, massive Native blockade of La Paz.
1980	Indigenous People in Brazil organize the Union of Indigenous Nations.
	Maskoy and Q'om land disputes in Paraguay.
	Ecuador creates the Office of Indigenous Affairs.
	The Quechua and Shuar organize the Confederation of Indigenous Nationalities of the Ecuadorian Amazon (CONFENIAE).
1980s	Gold-mining and hydroelectric dams built on Native lands in Amazonia.
1981	Paraguay creates the National Indigenous Institute (INDI) after human rights charges.
1981–1983	Guatemalan forces under Rios Montt murder over 200,000 Indigenous people.
1982	Native peoples organize the National Indigenous Organization of Colombia (ONIC) and the Confederation of Indigenous Peoples of Bolivia (CIDOB).
	Xavante leader Mario Juruna is elected to Brazil's House of Representatives.
1983	Kuna in Panama organize the Project for the Study of Rural Areas (PEMASKY).
	Massacre of Ts'akiuk'um in Chiapas results in 11 K'iche' deaths.
1984	Miskitus, Sumus, and Ramas in Nicaragua demand recognition as "Sovereign Indigenous peoples."
1987	Esquipulas II Central American Peace Plan.
1988	Brazil's Constitutional Assembly; mahogany and gold rushes in Kayapó lands.
	Pope John Paul II meets with Indigenous people from four nations in Paraguay.
1989	Kayapó protest the Altamira Dam Project in Brazil.

Introduction

Between 1970 and 1990, Indigenous people in Latin America organized broadly into regional, national, and international movements. Conservative military forces and their upper- and middle-class supporters, meanwhile, struggled against the revolutionary currents that were gaining strength or had taken power in several countries, especially in Central America, Cuba, Argentina, and Colombia. Conservatives believed that radical political and societal changes threatened their positions, so they organized counter-revolutionary efforts that included military rule, religious proselytism, and financial support from abroad. Some Indigenous people allied themselves with socialist and leftist organizations when it suited their interests. Although Native traditions of using land in common seemed to coincide with Marxist ideals, some Indigenous people resented control by outside leftist leaders as much as being manipulated by the right. At the height of the Cold War, Conservative forces countered revolutionary options by taking power in countries throughout South America, aligning their efforts with the U.S., and repressing peasant and Indigenous movements struggling for social improvements along the way. Native people responded with widespread opposition to military rule throughout South America.

By the late 1960s, as technological change swept the continent, Indigenous people connected with each other and with outsiders throughout the world. Although military regimes ran many South American countries during this stage of the Cold War, Native peoples defied repression and linked causes within and beyond their own groups and areas. During the 1970s and 1980s, Indigenous people adeptly employed the media to their own advantage, capitalizing on newspaper, radio, and television reports to publicize their growing concerns over land tenure, labor situations, and access to legal representation. Native communications focused the concern of human rights organizations on the results of economic development for Indigenous peoples. Cooperation with outside advocates allowed Native peoples and Indigenous activists to challenge national policies of integration that media supporters depicted as genocidal. Such collaboration and alliances focused international attention on Native conditions and lingering abuses by the regimes, calling attention to human rights in Latin America.

As South American states scrambled to repair their international images following years of abuse toward Native people, they altered the presentation of their policies for Indigenous integration and instead promised greater Native political representation. Similar to ways in which Native Americans in the United States organized themselves through the American Indian Movement during this time, Indigenous peoples in Latin America formed alliances with NGOs and other Native peoples to demand respect, political inclusion, and the return of their lands. Some Native peoples gained access to bilingual and intercultural education, held meetings of their leaders throughout the hemisphere, and forged broad liaisons with international advocates. Working together, many Indigenous groups forced their issues for the first time into the new constitutions written following the collapse of military regimes. At the least, as they countered military rule, Native activists drew attention to their poor living conditions, abuses by the government, and punitive government policies. These successes translated into minor but tangible benefits for many Indigenous peoples.

Earlier chapters have shown ways in which Indigenous people and peasants shaped states in Latin America during the decades following national independence. This chapter examines how Native people responded to and opposed the military governments that took control in Latin America at the height of the Cold War. Indigenous leaders and communities organized political networks and alliances with human rights activists to oppose human rights abuses, counter development and extractivist programs that were taking their resources, and to defend their lands. Broad organization allowed Indigenous people to form continental political networks and movements that drew widespread attention to their causes and strengthened their demands for political participation. By the time nations moved to democracy in the 1990s, Native people had shown that their exclusion from national societies and governments perpetuated multiple conflicts and obstructed democratic rule. The Inter-American Dialogue, one of the oldest think tanks on Latin American and Western Hemisphere affairs in Washington D.C., as a result commissioned a study of Indigenous people and the transition to democracy in Latin America. In the resulting book, political scientist and editor Donna Lee Van Cott has argued that only the "satisfaction of Indian demands for greater political and economic participation, together with an embrace of the multiethnic reality of Latin America, will lead to real democracy and, ultimately, political stability" in the continent.[1] As this book shows, Indigenous opposition to military rule contributed to the return of democratic governance in Latin America.

The broad swelling for Native rights that emerged in Latin America during the late 1960s and early 1970s roughly coincided with similar social movements sweeping the United States and Europe. There were at least 40 million people in Latin America by this time who identified ethnically as Indigenous, even though they differed broadly in their cultures, languages, and integration into national societies. Technological changes and spread of communications networks by the 1970s increased networking between Native leaders and foreign advocates, and made organization more possible than ever before. Military rule inadvertently pushed Native peoples to organize more broadly and to form alliances with human rights organizations. As Alison Brysk has shown, the Native rights movement "was born transnational," encouraged by anthropologists who first met at the Barbados Conference in 1971. Cultural Survival, Oxfam, and the Inter-American Foundation all supported the creation of local Indigenous organizations and enabled networking during these years, first with international supporters and then with national organizations. Native leaders then secured support from the OAS and the International Labour Organization of the U.N., sparking a movement that by the quincentenary of 1992 included hundreds of organizations.[2] Pan-Indigenous organization in Latin America was born out of Native opposition to military rule during the late Cold War. This chapter shows that Indigenous resistance to military rule and widespread organization during the late twentieth century contributed to the continent's transition to democracy.

Indigenous Communities Counter State Plans for Rural Development

By the 1970s, Indigenous people in Latin America were increasingly concerned about protecting their resources from extractivism and national development.[i] In Colombia, Natives organized themselves around the struggle for land, following the movement started earlier by Manuel Quintin Lame, a Nasa sharecropper from the vicinity of Popayan. Lame had first served as a soldier in Colombia's War of the Thousand Days against Panama (1899–1902), and was later transferred to Tierradentro to help keep public order. Because he did not belong to a specific community (*resguardo*), Lame worked for broader Native organization and was elected by seven Indigenous *cabildos* as their "Chief, Representative, and General Defender." Lame organized the Supreme Indian Council in 1924, to unite Natives in Tierradentro, and then with José Gonzalo Sánchez, a Guambiano leader from Tolima, founded a town named San José de Indias to settle Indigenous people and consolidate surrounding communal lands. The two men organized Nasa, Guambiano, Coconuvo, and peoples from Tolima and Huila and pressed the government to honor their *resguardo* goals.[3] Lame and his followers abandoned the village, though, because they were unwilling to join Gonzalo Sánchez when he helped found the Colombian Communist Party in 1930. Lame's movement suffered from state repression during the period of *La Violencia* (1945–1953). During the 1960s, Lame worked within the legal system to recover Indigenous *resguardo* lands, to consolidate the

i Extractivism is the removal of natural resources from the earth for sale on the world market.

cabildo as the center of Native authority, to reaffirm Native cultural values and counter discrimination, and is recognized as an early Indigenous organizer in Colombia.

Building on the legacy of Lame's organizational heritage, in 1971 the Nasa and other highland Native people from Cauca, Nariño, Putumayo, San Adrés de Sotavento, and Antioquia formed the Regional Indigenous Council of Cauca (CRIC) to fight for Indigenous land rights and to oppose repression by the national armed forces and growing rebel forces in Colombia. Along with other highland Indigenous organizations, the CRIC expanded Indigenous *resguardos* and reclaimed communal land originally titled in their name by the Spanish Crown. The CRIC also fought to increase Native political authority, end sharecropping, and protect Indigenous histories, languages, and customs. The new organization was unique in that it built on existing Native institutions, notably the councils that governed the *resguardos*, rather than on Western models of organization. Within its first three years, the CRIC published *Indigenous Unity*, a paper with national reach, and reclaimed 25,000 acres of land for members by taking over *hacienda* properties.[4] In these communities, the CRIC organized cooperatives and development projects; working along with the National Association of Peasant Users (ANUC), the CRIC also advocated Indigenous rights at the national level.

Far to the south, in Argentina, Indigenous people took advantage of the return of Juan Perón from exile in 1973 and his third presidency to organize themselves. The CIIRA (successor to the CCIIRA) and the Mapuche Parliament, Futa Traun, convened a pan-Indigenous congress for Native representatives from throughout the nation and demanded land grants, state agricultural credits for farmers, free bilingual education by Indigenous teachers, health care, salaries equal to non-Indians, and participation in national decisions regarding Indigenous issues. Native people organized the Indigenous Federation of Tucumán and the Indigenous Federation of Neuquina, which united the Mapuche in southwestern Argentina. In the north, the Q'om from Chaco Province, together with Q'om and Wichi in Formosa, organized the Chaco Indigenous Federation, which promptly demanded a grant of 100 free hectares of land per family, free tools for cooperative farming, and inalienable, communal land titles. Mocobi people joined the Q'om and Wichi to call for continued study of and respect for their cultures, as well as legal representation in provincial governments. To co-opt these new organizations, Peronists formed the Indigenous Association of Argentina (AIRA) in March 1973, but after Perón died from heart failure the following year, Argentina disintegrated into chaos with inflation and guerrilla violence. To control the growing dissent, Perón's third wife, Isabela, who followed in the presidency, outlawed cooperative communities and closed the Indigenous political organizations. In the Chaco, religious organizations became a safer way for Native people to join forces, and the United Evangelical Church they had organized grew rapidly during this period.

The Kuna people along Panama's Caribbean coast, meanwhile, also resisted state intrusions, despite their divided leadership. In the late 1960s, a few caciques bypassed the Kuna General Congress and granted North Americans permission to build small resorts on the central coast. Over the next two years, the Kuna twice torched one resort after guests offended them, and finally, Panama closed the hotel for good. Other failed projects followed: in 1970, Panama proposed building a pipeline to transport oil across western Kuna Yala, so the Kuna prepared themselves to defend their lands. Early in 1975, when the National Tourism Institute proposed the construction of a 700-room hotel in western Kuna Yala, an angry Kuna mob kept officials and technicians from deplaning. When Panama redistricted Kuna Yala to ensure more compliant leadership,

Figure 13.1 Q'om United Evangelical Church Service

the Kuna simply changed their leaders again. The standoff continued until 1978, but ultimately, Panama never built the resort because the Kuna General Congress threatened to use violence to block its construction.[5] Kuna resistance forced Panama to reconsider its Indigenous policy as a whole. By 1977, the same year de facto leader Omar Torrijos and U.S. president Jimmy Carter negotiated the transfer of rights to the Panama Canal, Panama renamed the Kuna territory the *Comarca* de Kuna Yala and recognized the political structures of other Native groups in the country under Kuna-syle *comarca* political organization.[ii]

Indigenous people in Brazil also countered state development during these years, but they benefitted from the support of the radicalized Catholic Church. In 1972, the militant branch of the National Conference of Bishops of Brazil created the Indigenist Missionary Council (CIMI) to support Indigenous organization. Grounded in the Catholic Church's work with small religious groups called Christian Ecclesial Base Communities (CEBs) and landless peasants, the CIMI sponsored assemblies for Native leaders. Following the Second Vatican Council from 1962 to 1965, priests and nuns working among the poor in Latin America had organized CEBs to promote social justice, and the Catholic Church in Brazil applied this experience to foment Indigenous organization. One of the first CIMI meetings took place in Mato Grosso state, and then the Munduruku people of northern Pará state hosted a second conference in May 1975 that drew 60 Native representatives. Participants developed a new sense of pan-Native

ii A *comarca* is a traditional region or local administrative division.

solidarity that spread rapidly, based on what anthropologist Alcida Ramos termed "generalized injustice." Sampré, a Xerente, stated: "My brothers, I call you brothers because I'm an Indian. I'm a brother of the same color, the same massacre." The leader's use of the term "massacre" as an identifying marker speaks volumes about the abuses Native leaders reported. Txuãeri, a Tapirapé, declared: "I came to hear about the Indian's life ... but they are taking away our land." Claudio Nenito, a Guaraní, explained, "Down there where I live they are destroying the forest. They are selling the wood. I mean, food we used to have, we have no more.... Down there the Indian is tied up and beaten up." As Indigenous assemblies spread throughout Amazonia, the FUNAI and federal police tried unsuccessfully to block them, showing that the rise in Indigenous organization concerned Brazil's regime.[6]

As cooperation between Indigenous activists and the Catholic Church developed in Brazil, heavy-handed state settlement policies elsewhere in Latin America drew international attention. By 1970, Paraguay had settled the southern Ache people on a ranch, where half the group died from contact diseases. Although the Stroessner regime sent provisions, the corrupt overseer swindled the food and medicine and then began to settle the northern Ache. The regime tolerated the corruption to clear the Ache from the eastern forests. An anthropologist discovered the malnutrition, sexual abuse, and high Ache death rates and reported them in a series of short books after the Stroessner regime expelled him from the country.[7]

The Catholic Church took up the case of the Ache as a convenient way to tarnish the dictator. As dozens more Ache perished from simple influenza, anthropologists and priests charged Stroessner with attempted genocide.[8] The accusations spread quickly: in October 1973, the U.S. House of Representatives took up the issue, and the U.S. Senate considered terminating aid to the regime while investigating the Ache case. The ensuing scandal embarrassed Paraguay, and in 1978 the United Nations Human Rights Commission advised the regime to counteract the negative publicity by passing a new Indigenous rights law, which Stroessner finally did in 1981.[9]

Indigenous Organizations Confront Military Regimes

Native organization only increased as military regimes attacked peasants and leftists during the Cold War. After taking power in a bloody coup on September 11, 1973, Augusto Pinochet's regime tried to crush all opposition in Chile. The Mapuche had mobilized widely under the earlier government of Eduardo Frei (1964–1970), who had promised a "revolution in freedom" to address social inequalities and promoted cooperatives to alleviate Indigenous poverty. As they did not aspire to revolutionary goals in Marxist terms, in their southern Ninth Region, the Mapuche claimed only to be taking back the lands that had once been theirs as they claimed government lands. Native people then pressured Allende's Popular Unity Party, elected in 1970 to socialize Chile, to grant them financial assistance and restore their usurped lands. In response, Allende enacted an Indigenous law in September 1972 that decreed Mapuche collective property to be "indivisible," except by the agreement of community members. By August 1973, immediately before General Pinochet seized power, paramilitary troops with helicopters and machine guns attacked a Mapuche cooperative on an estate that Natives had occupied in Nehuentué, on the Pacific coast, and trials for the Mapuche activists involved took place already weeks before Pinochet's takeover.

Attacks on Indigenous rights began almost at once following the Pinochet coup. Growing Indigenous occupations of *hacienda* lands must have seemed to the military to be a result of Allende's move toward socialism. The dictator's economists, called Chicago Boys because they had studied under Milton Friedman, the economist at the University of Chicago who had advised both President Ronald Reagan and British prime minister Margaret Thatcher, opened Chilean markets as they overturned Allende's legislation. To integrate the Native people into the larger Chilean society, Decree Law 2568 of 1978 subdivided Mapuche reservations into private plots. The results in Chile resembled those of the Dawes Severalty Act of 1887 (discussed in Chapter 10), by which Native Americans lost over 90 million acres of their communal land to privatization. To make matters worse, that same year the regime actually denied the existence of Indigenous people in Chile, admitting only to the presence of "marginalized" peasants in need of social and cultural integration into the modern economy; this fiction became a convenient way to extend logging and farming activity onto Native lands. As neoliberal administrators reduced tariffs and import duties and prices for wheat fell, landowners sold out to logging companies. Military attacks that broke up Indigenous communities provoked a flurry of Mapuche protests. In 1978, 300 Mapuche activists met in Temuco under the protection of the Catholic Church and created Centros Culturales Mapuche to direct Native resistance against the regime. The new organization grew to include over 1,000 Mapuche communities (one-third of the total communities) in southern Chile.[10]

Indigenous peoples also faced heavy-handed state oversight at this time in the Vaupés region of southeastern Colombia. The Vaupés was the Amazonian home of 20,000 Tukanoan people who had traditionally lived in longhouses accommodating four to eight nuclear families of patrilineal descent. Both Catholic and Protestant missionaries proselytized among the Tukanoan people.[11] In the 1970s, Colombia codified Native land claims as either reserves, land owned by the state with rights given to inhabitants to use it as if it was their own so long as it was not destroyed, or preserves (*resguardos*), lands owned collectively and administered by Indigenous peoples through their own *cabildo*. In Vaupés, the government created a *resguardo* of 3,000,000 hectares to win the loyalty of the Native people against the 19th of April guerrilla movement, formed after the elections of 1970 had blocked former dictator Gustavo Rojas Pinilla from electoral victory. To channel the growth of Native organization, the state also created the CRIVA Consejo Regional Indigena del Vaupés (Regional Indigenous Council of Vaupés) in 1973. Because the group united over 35 different ethnic peoples, officials intended the CRIVA to mediate conflicts in inter-Native affairs and to pressure the Summer Institute of Linguistics missionaries to leave.[iii] These conservative missionaries had tried to forbid communal longhouses, dancing, mourning rites, and the consumption of manioc beer and the hallucinogen banisteriopsis, common among Amazonian Indigenous peoples. Over the next few years, the CRIVA mediated struggles between Native groups and rubber barons, settlers, and coca-paste traffickers, but also imposed outside solutions upon Indigenous members.[12] Government and mission intrusions further integrated the Tukanoans into Colombian society by pushing them to adopt non-Indian definitions of what it meant to be Indigenous, as a way to claim benefits from the state.

iii The Summer Institute of Linguistics is a Christian organization based in Texas, founded by Presbyterian minister William Cameron Towns, which promotes literacy and translates the Christian Bible into local languages.

Indigenous people in Brazil were struggling by this time under the repressive regime of Emílio Médici, the four-star general who had assumed power in October 1969. A former military attaché in Washington and head of the National Information Service, Brazil's intelligence agency, Médici continued the military hardline and the development of Amazonia. Médici built the east–west Trans-Amazonian Highway to Peru in 1970, and a north–south route between Cuiabá and Santarém, paving the way for over 5 million settlers. Rather than resolving social tensions and land distribution problems as they went along, as Médici had promised, road crews forcibly relocated entire Indigenous peoples, and the diseases they introduced ravaged the Parakanan and Kreen-Akraore. Some groups fought back against the onslaught: in 1970, the Areões Xavante community stole horses, food, and tools from ranches. When confronted by state forces, Leader Saamri threatened to "burn the ranches remaining in the area and expel residents."[13] To quieten the Xavante, the FUNAI gave them five plots of poor-quality land in the state of Tocantins; there were too many people for the land and they did not have enough food and health care. Unsatisfied, the Xavante claimed that "all these lands were theirs" and challenged the *waradzu* (non-Xavantes) to honor their promises and restore their lands.[14]

Growing protests by Indigenous peoples over the loss of their land, as well as rising criticism by international human rights organizations, forced Brazil to approve the Indian Statute, Law No. 6001, in 1973. The new legislation "emancipated" Natives in the name of equality and granted them inalienable land rights, but at the same time coerced them to join Brazilian society. At the heart of the legislation was the conflict that Indigenous people throughout the continent faced over the following decades: states forbade them from living in traditional ways but did not equip them to survive in modern society. Thirteen Indigenous peoples sent a letter to the Brazilian president in 1979, rejecting Law 6001: "We also, in the name of the Brazilian Indian Community, repudiate this emancipation.... The emancipation desired by the minister will only bring detribalization to the Indian communities, and therefore, the collective and individual destruction of their members."[15] Note their insightful use of the pan-Indigenous collective. Protests notwithstanding, the development of Amazonia continued unabated.

In Nicaragua, Native people along the Atlantic coast were by this time frustrated enough with the 45-year Somoza government that they formed their own organizations to recover their communal lands. Two Miskito students at the National University in Managua played an important role in the "ethnic awakening" of the early 1970s. The first was Brooklyn Rivera, from the Lidaukra village north of Puerto Cabezas on the Atlantic coast, and the second was Steadman Fagoth Muller, who had worked for the Somoza intelligence forces and then later, following the Sandinista Revolution of 1979, joined the CIA to oppose the FSLN.[16] The men organized the Miskitu Alliance in 1973 to replace older agricultural cooperatives along the Rio Coco, which developed into the Alliance for Progress of Miskitu and Sumu (ALPROMISU), to push for self-determination for their people. The leaders urged their people to organize against the "Spanish" (their term for Nicaraguans), whom they claimed benefitted from all the riches along the coast but left the Miskitu "dirt poor."[17] When the alliance backed the Sandinistas against Somoza, some Miskitu later fought for the FSLN. As one Miskitu recalled, "The Sandinistas said: 'You support us and when we win, you'll have your territory.' We [Miskitu] agreed and gave the Sandinistas our backing. Many Miskitu combatants lent a hand."[18]

Native people in the state of Chiapas, Mexico met in October 1974 at an Indigenous Congress on the 500th anniversary of the birth of Bartolomé de Las Casas (see Chapter 4), organized by Bishop Samuel Ruíz, the Catholic priest introduced in Chapter 12. President Echeverria inspired the conference when he pledged to revitalize Mexico's revolutionary responsibility to its workers and peasants and began a limited land distribution program. In the south, Indigenous women and men who had studied agrarian law and political economy at the INI School for Regional Development took their peoples' communal concerns to the Congress. A total of 587 Tzeltal, 330 Tzotzil, 152 Tojolabal, and 161 Chol people from 327 Indigenous communities in Mexico met and demanded the legal recognition of communal *ejido* lands and payment for processing land petitions. Beyond demanding the rights to reclaim their lands, the delegates called for state protection of Indigenous cultures, education in their own languages, and health care. The federal government may have hoped to co-opt the growing Indigenous unrest, but it failed; Bishop Ruíz insisted that the Congress belong to and represent Native concerns. The strong demands for respect and land reform drew media attention, but no real change: shortly after the conference, the army evicted Indigenous peasants from six villages in the Lacandon forest.[19]

Many Indigenous peoples faced military intrusions during the 1970s. In Peru, Commander of the Armed Forces General Juan Velasco Alvarado seized power in a 1968 coup that overthrew the Belaúnde administration. During Belaúnde's populist presidency (1963–1968), conflicts between the president's Acción Popular Party and his congressional opponents from the APRA–UNO coalition had divided the country. The resulting scandal involving the northern oilfields ended in military occupation following Velasco's coup. To stave off the social unrest growing in the countryside due to poor land distribution by the former president, Velasco enacted one of Latin America's most comprehensive land redistribution programs. The 1974 Native Communities Law for the first time recognized the right of Amazonian Native people to hold communal titles to their ancestral lands, and distributed nearly 12 million hectares of land to peasants, many of them Indigenous. President Velasco also declared Quechua a second national language on the level of Spanish and instituted obligatory Quechua instruction at all levels of education throughout the country. At the same time, though, Velasco also tried to diminish Native organization by pushing Indigenous peoples into already existing peasant federations. The leader used the term "peasants" when referring to Native peoples, renamed the Day of the Indian as the Day of the Peasant, and urged Natives to refer to themselves as peasants rather than as Indigenous people.[20]

Indigenous Organization and Military Projects for Economic Development

As the Cold War escalated, big business, ranchers, and their conservative supporters were busy developing their Latin American countries. In Brazil, President Geisel developed Amazonia as rapidly as possible. The Gaviões, Suruí, Guajajara, Amanayé, and Anambé peoples in Pará and Maranhão states saw their lands displaced by the Tucuruí dam on the Tocantins River, built in 1976 to supply energy to the huge Carajás industrial complex, a 13,000 square-kilometer area of mining, metallurgic, and agricultural development. The FUNAI moved one of the two Gaviões villages twice, and the Marabá–Belém highway cut the other village in half, leaving the FUNAI post on one side and the people on the other. The *indigenista* agency started to market Brazil nuts from Gaviões land, but by December 1976 leaders expelled the FUNAI, secured a loan from the Banco do Brasil to cover transportation, and began to market the nuts themselves.[21] With funds from the World Bank, Brazil constructed five additional hydroelectric complexes on the Xingu River and its tributary the Iriri. The resulting flooding displaced hundreds of Native people, forever changing the lives of the Juruna, Arara, Kararaô, Xikrin, Asuriní, Araweté, and Parakanã.

The development projects were most disastrous for the Parakanã, forcibly moved five times away from the road and then the flooding of the lands; their numbers dropped from 200 to a low of 82 people by 1983.[22] As many as 4,000 families from these Indigenous peoples never found land after their displacement. Construction of the Manaus–Boa Vista Highway in the 1970s was especially disastrous for the Waimiri-Atroari people; their numbers declined due to disease and mass murders from over 2,000 a century before to 332 people in 1983. After FUNAI falsely declared that there were no Indians in the northern sector, the Paranapanema Company also mined iron ore from Waimiri-Atroari lands in the early 1980s. So-called "development" proved disastrous for Native peoples in Amazonia.

Indigenous peoples and especially their organizations in Bolivia faced equally difficult challenges under the dictatorship of Hugo Banzer Suárez, who seized power in August 1971 in the city of Santa Cruz. As a colonel, Banzer had in 1970 tried to overthrow President Juan José Torres, "the most radical and left-leaning general ever to have governed Bolivia."[23] The elite in Santa Cruz supported Banzer's second coup after Torres' plans to extend agrarian reform threatened their landholdings. Banzer encouraged colonization and agricultural production in the eastern lowlands, which forced Indigenous organizations underground and their leaders into exile. Only the Tupaj Katari Cutural Center continued to operate visibly, and its broadcasts in Aymara of a program called Radio Progreso broadly educated the peasantry. Late in July 1973, the Tupaj Katari Cultural Center signed the Tiwanaku Manifesto as a way to formalize *katarismo*, an emerging Aymara political program.

President Banzer raised taxes and transportation fees by 200 percent in January 1974, increasing the costs of basic foods and approving an economic program that placed the burden for funding the government's operations on small farmers. The resulting crisis provoked a massive response. To protest, on January 22 and January 31, many thousands of Native peasants blocked the three main highways that tied Cochabamba to the rest of the country. Outside the city, at Tolata, a group of armored government trucks opened fire and killed almost 100 protesters, and more deaths happened along the blockade as far as 200 kilometers outside of Cochabamba. Aymara activists joined the blockades, especially southeast in Aroma Province. The protests and the tragic killings are together remembered as the Massacre of the Valley. Aymara leader Jenaro Flores summed up the massive mobilization and its disastrous results by using the famous promise that Tupac Katari reportedly issued at his execution.[24] Tupac Katari (Julián Apasa) had been the revolutionary Aymara leader in Upper Peru (featured in Chapter 9), whose forces had taken over the Central Sierra and had besieged La Paz in 1781. At his brutal execution, Katari's final words reportedly had been, "I die but will return tomorrow as a thousand thousands." The movement that formed after the Massacre of the Valley is known as *katarismo*, and by 1977 it became a leading political force for peasant organization in Bolivia.

Kataristas, the activists in the new movement, became the principal opponents of the Banzer dictatorship. To heighten public opposition to the regime, four wives of imprisoned tin-miners, led by Domitilla Barrios Chungara, began a hunger strike that eventually earned the support of Kataristas, one thousand followers, and the Catholic Church in Bolivia. Kataristas set up an underground government in Qullana Norte and organized provincial cells that finally joined in a National Tupaj Katari Confederation with Jenaro Flores as executive secretary. The collective strike and Katarista activism finally forced Banzer to grant amnesty to the worker unions and eventually brought down the regime itself.[25]

During the final years of the 1970s, therefore, Indigenous people organized forcefully against the national development of their lands and resources. As Native people mobilized and human rights advocates focused on specific abuses, some Latin American governments passed new laws to extend control over their Indigenous populations but disguised them as pro-Indigenous rights bills. In 1976 and 1981 Colombia tried to pass a repressive "Indigenous Law" to claim broad authority over Indigenous communities and define who was and was not an Indigenous person. Native people allied themselves with peasants and leftist organizations to prevent its passage.[26] In Panama, a commission of scientists and Indigenous activists reported on the Native situation in 1977, and as a result, President Omar Torrijos promised to demarcate Native lands by creating *comarcas.* Designation of these lands began with two large properties in Darién set aside for the Emberá-Drua in 1983, and the Kuna General Congress successfully lobbied for similar results; other Native peoples in Panama followed their example.

Very concerned about deteriorating Indigenous conditions and growing attacks on their resources and communities, 35 Indigenous people and anthropologists from throughout the continent met again in 1977 at the Second Barbados Congress. This time Native people from Guatemala and Páez representatives from Colombia risked their lives to travel secretly to Barbados. Some of the 35 Indigenous and anthropologist participants were already in hiding or in exile. Indigenous leaders quickly made clear their desire to take charge of their own ethnic affairs and political goals, which caused tensions with non-Indigenous advocates who saw Native participants as only advisors. Indigenous participants declared themselves victims of physical and cultural domination and rejected educational efforts by outsiders as attempts to divide their peoples.[27] These gatherings made Indigenous organizational goals and the limitations that Native activists faced abundantly clear: it was difficult to convince even their advocates to recognize the Native desire to achieve self-agency,[iv] self-representation, and self-determination in their own way, through their own choices and systems of knowledge.

Indigenous organization and the resulting militancy grew during the late 1970s and early 1980s. Even municipal struggles escalated: in October 1978, hundreds of Tzotzil people stormed the town hall of Chalchihuitán, in Chiapas Mexico, and demanded that the municipal president pay a fine for having mishandled his authority. That same year, Brazil's FUNAI used recent progress in agricultural technology to launch the Xavante Project, expanding mechanized monocultural rice cultivation on Native land, an effort that ignored Xavante perspectives and traditions. The initiative was part of the military's new liberalizing policy called *distensão* (the reductions of tensions), a gradual return of power to civil society aimed at raising support for the regime and implemented by limiting repression and enacting social programs. The project shows state patronage

iv Self-agency is the sense that some actions are self-generated. First studied by psychologist Benjamin Libet, the concept was developed by Daniel Wegner, who suggested three criteria of self-agency: priority, exclusivity, and consistency. The term helps explain how Indigenous people choose and then take actions on their own behalf.

of its Indigenous constituency to decrease Native militancy, especially after Indigenous people had begun to criticize the FUNAI in the media.[28]

Over the following decade, motorized farming in Mato Grosso proved disastrous for Xavante self-sufficiency and communal cohesiveness. Highly acidic soils, erratic rainfall, poorly maintained roads and bridges, as well as conflicts over the use of machinery and implements, all bedeviled the state effort. The community of Areões, where FUNAI first imposed mechanized rice, became the only community in the area to experience serious alcoholism.[29] Growing criticism of the FUNAI focused on irregularities in the agency, including patronage, corruption, and vast diversions of state funds: of the agency's budget of CR$13.5 million in 1971, only CR$1.6 was allocated for the demarcation of Native lands. The agency claimed to administer 142 Indigenous "posts" throughout the country, yet there were only 11 reservations, and these were furthermore only in the books. Widespread corruption helps explain why the FUNAI, and even its Native employees, supported efforts such as the Xavante Project that often had disastrous results.[30]

Threatened development also occurred in eastern Paraguay, where construction of the world's largest hydroelectric plant at Itaipú began in 1978. The INDI relocated four Avá Guaraní communities whose homes were in the way. Another project in the Department of Caaguazú displaced 280 families from 5 Mbyá Guaraní communities by 1980. In the Caazapá Department, in 1979 Stroessner initiated a $54.3 million U.S. program to develop small farming among the peasantry, a project that completely overran the isolated forest settlements of 400 Mbyá Guaraní.[31]

Indigenous people in Central America, meanwhile, faced the Cold War struggles that spilled into their communities. In 1978, the Somozas in Nicaragua assassinated popular journalist Pedro Joaquín Chamorro. The National Guard repressed the resulting strike by workers and then violently put down an Indigenous uprising in the town of Masaya. On February 21, 1978, thousands of Indigenous people in the barrio of Monimbo spilled into the streets to honor Sandino's death. Native animosity in this area ran deep: back in 1912, U.S. occupation troops had killed their leader Benjamin "el Indio" Zeledon. As Monimboseños marched to the cemetery for the commemoration, the Nicaraguan National Guard attacked the crowd from airplanes, and over the next few days the surviving people flew red and black Sandinista flags as they battled government-armored vehicles and helicopters with their slingshots. The violence left 200 people dead, including children, and then spread to the Sutiava Indigenous community nearby.[32]

Worsening conditions made it possible for FSLN forces to invade the presidential palace in August, capture members of the Chamber of Deputies (the Nicaraguan legislative body) along with 2,000 public employees, and force negotiations that ended President Anastacio Somoza's long rule. The cost of the revolution that brought the FSLN to power in July 1979 was enormous: 2 percent of the entire Nicaraguan population died in the war and material damage was $1.3 billion. Because the coastal Indigenous people had not fought in the revolution for either side, however, the Sandinistas portrayed them as *adormecidos*: "asleep" and "backward." These descriptions show that by 1978, coastal peoples had reversed their five-year trend toward militancy.[33] The revolution did increase state control of the Atlantic coastal regions, and because of their Anglo affinity, the coastal Natives defused any potential conflict with the FSLN by laying low until they could forcefully mobilize later against new attacks on their territory. When they joined forces in November, the Misquitu, Sumu, Rama, Asla, and Takanka created MISURASATA, an organization to oppose FSLN control over their coastal communities. Then, in the 1980s, these Indigenous people militarily opposed the Sandinistas.

During this same time, growing Indigenous resistance also led neighboring Central American countries to repress Native organization. As Native people gained education and entered professions, they formed broad organizations around Native cultural issues. In 1971, Native people in Guatemala created the Indigenous Association for Maya-K'iche' Culture to raise awareness about their Native identity and deplorable living conditions, and the following year the Seminarios Indígenas and Catholic Action's Pastoral Indígana, two religious organizations dedicated to advocating Indigenous affairs, created venues where the Ixil, Cakchiquel, and other Indigenous peoples organized themselves. By 1974, a few Indigenous people even became deputies in the national Guatemalan government.

The economic crisis of the 1970s hit Indigenous communities especially hard, though, and then on February 4, 1976, a massive earthquake shook the Guatemalan highlands and over one million people, many of them Indigenous, lost their homes. Some Native people and peasants turned for support to the Guerrilla Army of the Poor formed in northern Quiché in 1972, or the Committee for Peasant Union, an organization founded in 1978 to gain land rights, water, and food for over 200 peasant communities. Experienced organizers led the group, including Vicente Menchú, father of future activist Rigoberta Menchú, author of *I, Rigoberta Menchú, An Indian Woman in Guatemala*. As tensions rose and peasants occupied more land for their people, on Saturday, May 27, 1978, a detachment of 30 Guatemalan government troops occupied the main plaza of Panzós, where conflicts between protesters and the military had been particularly intense. Two days later a group of 600 to 700 Indigenous people, led by women, marched to the mayor's house to ask what was going to happen to their lands, but soldiers blocked their path. When the marchers drew their machetes, the soldiers opened fire and killed 34 men and women in what came to be known as the brutal Panzós massacre.[34]

The following year saw additional repression but also Indigenous mobilization in many countries. In Bolivia, where 57 percent of the population spoke one or more of 34 Indigenous languages, the Native highland peoples actively influenced politics. The Aymara formed a national union in 1979 called the Unified Syndical Confederation of Rural Workers of Bolivia (CSUTCB) as part of a struggle to end the military rule that began in 1978. Backed by the new union, in December 1979, Aymara people led a massive general blockade that paralyzed La Paz and other cities, demanding economic relief, a voice in state affairs, recognition by the government and workers' organizations, and an end to military rule. Recognition by the miners and peasant unions was important because the Indigenous workers played such a vital role in the production of tin and minerals, the base of Bolivia's economy.

Genaro Flores Santos, an Aymara leader from the town of Sicasica, organized the general blockade. Sicasica was the focal point of the Katarista Movement[v] that had dominated the Bolivian peasant movement since 1976.[35] Flores Santos had participated in trade unions and the La Paz Department Farmer-Labourers Federation up until 1968, when Aymara

v The Katarista Movement was a federation of Aymara leaders in the La Paz area, formed in 1976 to lead government peasant unions and Indigenous workers throughout Bolivia. By 1979 it became the CSUTCB (Unified Syndical Confederation of Rural Workers of Bolivia).

activists challenging state manipulation of peasant organizations appointed him as their leader. The following year Santos became leader of the La Paz Department Farmer-Labourers Federation. The rising influence of Flores Santos shows how Indigenous and peasant organizers were replacing the miners as leaders of the national confederation of workers and their allies in the urban trade unions.[36] Two years later, the eastern lowland peoples created the Confederation of Indigenous Peoples of Bolivia (CIDOB), which pressed the state for agricultural credits, water rights for both domestic and agricultural use, and access to higher education.

Development and Political Threats to Native Communities

During the 1980s, Native people organized to resist state extractivism of their resources. Latin American nations developed the lands and resources where Indigenous people lived, pushing into peripheral areas as majority populations grew and they needed resources. Growing communication nets linked people from different areas, and it became more difficult for governments to abuse Indigenous rights with impunity. Native people took advantage of the democratic transition spreading across Latin America to militate for self-determination, but rather than acknowledge the Indigenous movements as legitimate, nations portrayed their organization as treasonous or radical.[37] Still, national leaders could not simply kill off over 40 million Native people, especially as states returned to civilian rule under international scrutiny. Instead, leaders glossed over their human rights abuses, masking the actual living conditions of Native peoples with legal façades and human rights frameworks borrowed from international organizations, during a time that anthropologist Silvia Rivera Cusicanqui termed the "Era of the Permitted Indian."[38] Basically, nations allowed limited Indigenous participation in the new political scene and publicized their bestowal of token grants of rights to the Indigenous people without doing much to improve Native conditions.

Indigenous conditions in Amazonia became more precarious as Brazil built hydroelectric dams and prospectors panned for gold. The Catholic Church advocated Native land rights to pressure Brazil's military state to respect Native territories, and Indigenous people took advantage of President Geisel's move to control the repressive system and torturers, a process called liberalization, to demand more protection of their lands. Electrobrás, Brazil's energy company, made plans in the mid-1980s to build over 165 hydroelectric dams in the country by 2010, projected to affect 41 Indigenous territories. The two dams finished in the 1980s, the Tucuruí in Pará, and Balbina in Amazonas, displaced hundreds of Native people by flooding their land. In northern Mato Grosso, tensions remained high among Indigenous people, ranchers, and the authorities. Indigenous people raided cattle from the ranches, set pastures on fire, threatened ranch employees, and lobbied in Brasilia. Officials issued token concessions; some peoples, such as the Xavante at Couto Magalhães, won sizable land grants.

Another threat came from the Garimpieros, the gold-miners, who occupied Indigenous lands during the 1980s by the hundreds of thousands. By 1985, there were half a million miners in Amazonia, many on Native lands, who brought violence and widespread pollution. Miners also bribed FUNAI officials, politicians, and Indigenous leaders. Prospecting directly affected the Munduruku and Kayapó in Pará, the Waiãpi in Amapá, the Waimiri-Atroari and Tukano-Tukanoans in Amazonas, the Makushi and Yanomami in Roraima, and the Nambiquara and other peoples in Mato Grosso and Rondônia.[39] Some dynamics of the invasion resembled early colonial encounters, when Europeans entered Indigenous lands in search of gold.

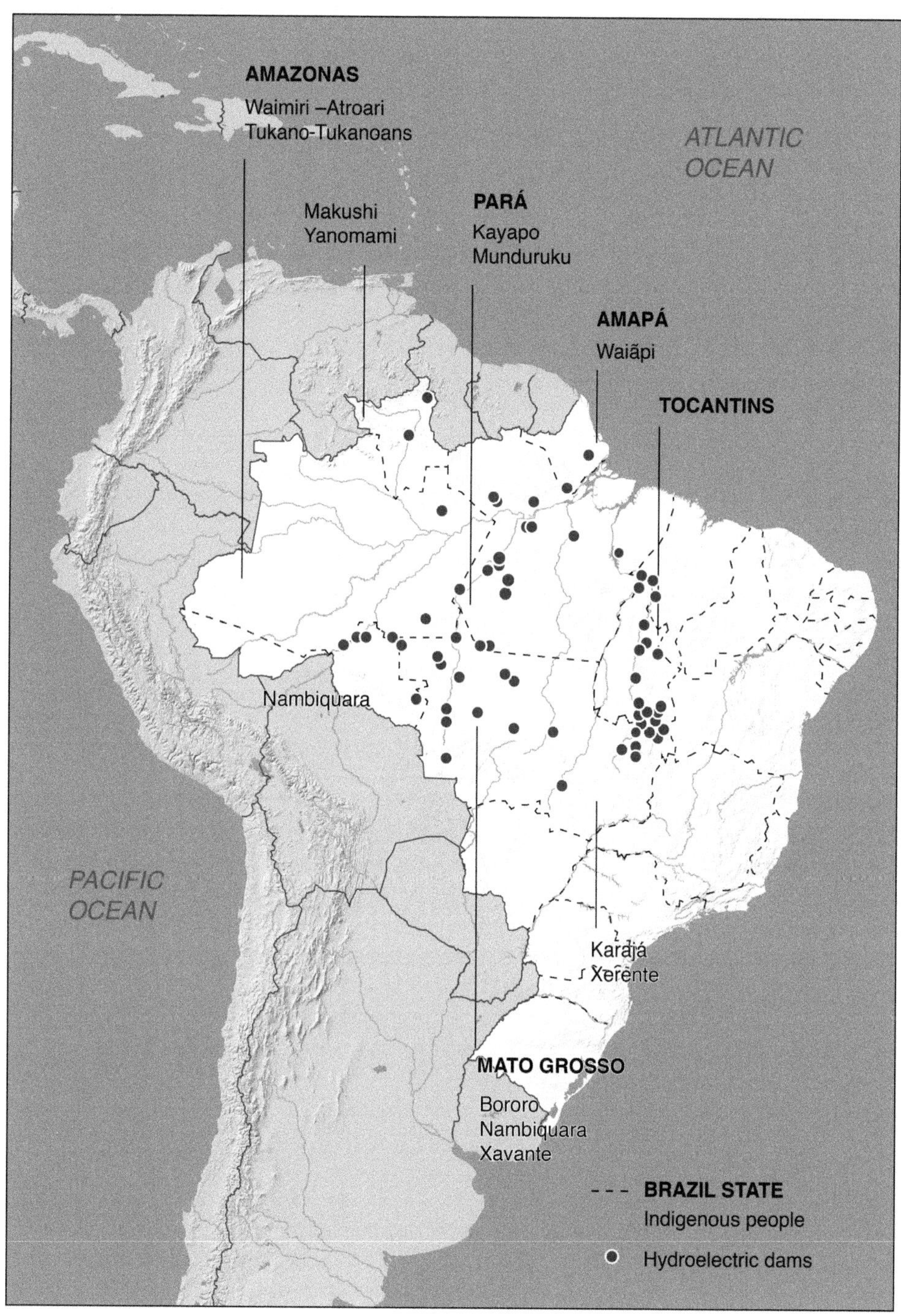

Map 13.1 Amazonia: Changes to the Environment and Indigenous Populations

For Document 13.1: David Kopenawa, Yanomami, "The Coming of the Gold Miners," 1993, Excerpts, from Alcida Rita Ramos, *Sanumá Memories*, 297–299, visit www.routledge.com/9780415519120.

Native people in Amazonian Peru also saw invasions between 1980 and 1985 by prospectors in search of petroleum, natural gas, and gold. With funds from USAID, Peru started the Amazonian Highway Project and the Pichis-Palcazu Special Project to develop roads, commercial centers, and settlements. While President Alan García's administration (1985–1990) recognized changes to Indigenous communities, severe hyper-inflation led to social unrest and severely limited how much the government could do to improve Native conditions. As in surrounding countries, Indigenous people in Peru allied with outside advocates to defend their interests. The Inter-Ethnic Association for the Development of the Peruvian Amazon and the Confederation of Amazonian Nationalities of Peru, created in 1980 and 1987 respectively, directly involved Peru's Indigenous communities in planning for their own development and protesting sales of "unproductive" lands in Peruvian Amazonia, which they claimed as their own.[40]

Indigenous people built their political influence as they defended their lands. In 1980, Native peoples in Brazil created the pan-Indigenous Union of Indigenous Nations to promote Native pride at the grassroots level and to organize effective resistance to state interference. The Catholic Church pressured Indigenous leaders to avoid confrontations, although as Native leaders in the cities lost touch with their Indigenous base the Union collapsed by the end of the 1980s. In Nicaragua, the Miskitu were not getting along with the Sandinistas, and thousands of them moved to Honduras in search of refuge. The U.S. described the scenario as an FSLN assault and many Miskitu took up arms to support U.S. Contra forces, based in Honduras, against the Sandinistas. Indigenous people in Paraguay went through two major land disputes during the 1980s. The Maskoy pressured the Stroessner regime to return their traditional lands at Riacho Mosquito in the Chaco to them by proving how dramatically close their people were to mass extinction. The judiciary branch finally allowed 200 families to occupy the property in December 1981, but Argentine president General Videla forced Stroessner to remove them because the ranchers were Argentinian. Despite widespread popular support in the national press, the Toba-Q'om likewise lost their claim to their lands at Paratodo after ranchers accused them of having communist supporters.[41] Communal landholding and contact with Catholic advocates, as well as participation in several leftist organizations, drew conservative criticism during the Cold War and contributed to the impression that Indigenous people were communists.

Indigenous Mobilization and Token Legislation

Widespread organization by Indigenous people across Latin America, as well as growing attention to human rights, finally forced countries to enact legislation favoring Native rights. In 1980, the U.N. created the Council of South American Indians, an organization to discuss Indigenous identity, as well as land and economic, social, and cultural rights. That same year, Ecuador created the Office of Indigenous Affairs to oversee and assist Natives in filing land claims. Amazonian Indigenous organizations began to self-demarcate their own territorial boundaries and their work was successful: in 1983,

Ecuador granted 67,000 hectares to 900 Huaorani people as communal territory and an additional 250,000 hectares as an exclusive "reserve" in the Amazonian provinces of Napo, Orellana, and Pastaza. President Hurtado stressed that the land was not a gift, but rather only recognition of land that had belonged to the people for centuries. Lowland Qichua and Shuar peoples promptly organized the Confederation of Indigenous Nationalities of the Ecuadorian Amazon (CONFENIAE), which recruited the Cofan, Siona-Secoya, and Huaorani peoples as well and supported their land claims.[42]

International attention to human rights also pressured Paraguay's regime, since in 1981 President Stroessner finally allowed passage of Law 904, an Indigenous Rights Bill, to dispel foreign criticism of his human rights record. Law 904 committed the regime to respect Indigenous peoples' cultures and human rights, but at the same time created a stronger state agency, the National Indigenous Institute (INDI), to oversee legislation pertaining to Native peoples. When he first saw the official law, one Native leader declared, "then we the Indigenous population will be in the service of the INDI!"[43] While the law was a regime attempt to dispel foreign criticism, Native communities rapidly employed it to focus their resistance and land claims.

Indigenous organization increased. In November 1981, the Brazilian Bar Association in Rio de Janeiro assembled Indigenous leaders and concerned professionals from throughout Brazil. Tukano leader Álvaro Tukano denounced Brazilian racism for not being in line with the Indian Statute, Law 6.001 of 1973, and claimed that Brazil had intended to control Indigenous people with the legislation. By 1982, the Brazilian Indigenous movement had become national and pan-Indigenous: leaders from throughout the country met in Brasilia for the first time.[44]

The late twentieth century therefore saw both increasing Native organization and violence. This was especially the case in Colombia, where the crisis worsened as petroleum prices quadrupled in 1974, just as the country began to depend on foreign oil. In rural areas, peasants grew desperate for land by 1973, especially since 50.7 percent of the total labor force and 67.5 percent of the rural labor force lived under the absolute poverty line. As a result, they organized guerrilla groups with the support of the Communist Party and occupied land. Peasants and some Indigenous people joined guerrilla groups such as the Armed Revolutionary Forces of Colombia (FARC), the National Liberation Army (ELN), and the 19th of April Movement that formed during the late 1960s and early 1970s to oppose the government. Indigenous people largely tried to avoid both guerrilla and government forces, instead creating their own organizations during the conflict. The most important of these groups were the Regional Indigenous Council of Cauca (CRIC) and the National Indigenous Organization of Colombia (ONIC), which negotiated peacefully with outsiders. The Comando Quintín Lame, on the other hand, was a militant Native group formed in 1974 in Cauca, Huila, and Tolima that in 1984 violently occupied several small communities in southern Cauca.

Native organization developed rapidly during this period of increasing attacks, bringing visibility and inspiring more activism. Indigenous people in Bolivia created the Confederation of Indigenous Peoples of Bolivia (CIDOB) to demand their territory back from the government and to claim the natural resources gained from that land. They also wanted equal political participation in the government. Later, the CIDOB affiliated with COICA, the Indigenous Confederation of the Amazonian Basin organized in Peru.

Also in Peru at this time, Sendero Luminoso (Shining Path) operatives went public by attacking voting sites and burning ballots in the village of Chuschi. The ensuing civil war between the insurgency and the government caught Indigenous people in between.

Map 13.2 Contemporary Resistance Movements that Included Indigenous Peoples

While sometimes labeled an Indigenous insurgency to re-establish the Inca Empire, the group was rather a leftist insurgency hoping to replace the government with what their leader called a Maoist utopia. Followers devoted their lives to armed revolution and their leader was Abimael Guzman, a philosophy professor from the San Cristóbal of Huamanga University in Peru who had studied Maoism in China and in the mid-1970s formed a resistance group.[vi] The ensuing civil war caused over 35,000 deaths during the early 1980s, many of them Indigenous people and *colonos* (mestizo colonists) in the highlands. After the civil war took the lives of the leaders of the Asháninka, Yánexha, and Nomatsiguenga people, Indigenous communities caught between the guerrillas and Peruvian troops organized patrols to defend themselves from both Sendero operatives and state counterinsurgency forces.[45]

In response to increasing Indigenous activism, some states tried to co-opt Native leaders by appointing them to administrative positions, but they continued to denounce abuses. In Brazil, the FUNAI appointed Marcos Terena, a Xane leader from the Pantanal region, as its chief of staff. This capable leader helped found numerous Native organizations, including the Union of Indigenous Nations, and later the World Conference of Indigenous Peoples on Territories, Environment and Development, where 700 Indigenous leaders from around the world appointed him as their spokesperson at the United Nations Earth Summit (UNCED) held in Rio de Janeiro in 1992. Terena also helped organize the Inter-Tribal Committee, Land is Life, the International Alliance of Indigenous-Tribal Peoples of the Tropical Forests, the Call of the Earth Circle, the Brazilian Indigenous Institute for Intellectual Property, and the World Indigenous Games Festival. Brazilians elected Mario Juruna, a Xavante leader from the village of San Marcos in the Mato Grosso State, to Brazil's House of Representatives in 1982, from where he condemned FUNAI corruption in passionate speeches. Alvaro Sampaio, a Tukano pan-Indigenous leader from the Upper Rio Negro, denounced Salesian missionaries at the 1980 Russell Tribunal on Indigenous rights in the Netherlands for causing disastrous cultural changes among his people at mission boarding schools, as well as for sending young Indigenous women to Manaus between 1965 and 1980 to work as maids-turned-prostitutes and domestic servants.[46]

Indigenous politicians in Guatemala likewise exerted political influence in the national congress, but were soon discouraged. Peasants and some Native people by this time had joined the Guerrilla Army of the Poor. The government responded to Native activism with a genocidal attack that anthropologist Richard Adams called the "1979 1984 Holocaust."[47] As in Paraguay under Stroessner, Guatemala feared that the isolation, seclusion, and diversity of the Indigenous communities, as well as Indigenous languages, were highly susceptible to communist influence. Leaders assumed that Native people were incapable of organizing on their own and portrayed their activism as evidence of outside manipulation. With financial, technical, and material support from the U.S., between 1981 and 1983, Guatemalan security forces committed over 200,000 political murders and acts of genocide against the highland Indigenous people who made up 60 percent of the population. The United Nations-administered Historical Clarification Commission (CEH) *Memory of Silence* project collected over 8,000 testimonies and condemned Guatemala for 626 massacres accounting for the disappearance or deaths of

vi A good summary of the movement is "The Shining Path," in *The Peru Reader*, 305–307.

over 200,000 people during those brief years. The CEH also accused guerrillas of 3 percent of violations and 32 collective killings.

The massacres took place during the regime of Efraín Ríos Montt (1982–1983), a minister in the California-based evangelical/Pentecostal Church of the Word and a personal friend of evangelical leaders Jerry Falwell and Pat Robertson. In their scorched-earth campaign against the assumed communists, Guatamalan security forces savagely attacked Native communities. Soldiers beat children against walls, cut off their limbs, impaled people, doused them with gasoline and burned them alive, cut out their organs, removed fetuses from pregnant women, and threw living children into graves to be crushed by adult corpses thrown on top.[48] The military also destroyed Indigenous ceremonial sites, religious places, and cultural symbols, employing the Cold War hysteria as an excuse to eliminate Indigenous people and their heritage. The counter-insurgency program killed as many as 50,000 people, forced three to five times more into exile, and displaced as many as one million more, perhaps half of the Indigenous people in Guatemala's western highlands.[49]

The genocidal attacks between 1983 and 1984 led as many as 1,300,000 Indigenous people in the Guatemalan highlands to participate in civil patrols, the army's response to guerrilla organization that followed the counterinsurgency. The state created the civil patrols to increase its presence in the highlands and reorganize communities into grid-structure "model villages" with streetlights, the most serious changes to Native society since the Spanish conquest and meant to minimize the attractiveness of guerrilla propaganda to Indigenous people.[50]

Despite occasional repression, Native people continued to organize themselves and defend their lands and heritage in many countries. Over 1,500 Mapuche communities in Chile's Temuco region formed cultural centers called Ad-Mapu to rediscover their ethnic heritage, rituals, and community values. The centers revived the practice of *gillatun*, intercommunity reciprocity, and *palin*, their sticks and ball field sport traditionally used to train warriors.[51] In 1983, the Kuna people in Panama set in motion the Project for the Study of Rural Areas (PEMASKY), funded by the Inter-American Foundation, the World Wildlife Fund, and the MacArthur Foundation, which surveyed and demarcated the threatened boundaries of their land, and evicted peasants who had settled inside Kuna Yala. The effort raised Kuna environmental awareness.[52] Panama also established the Emberá-Drua *comarca*, two large blocks of land for the Emberá and Drua peoples in the rainforest known collectively as the Chocó, which overlaps the Darien National Park and Biosphere Reserve. Indigenous people demarcated their territories in Ecuador as well, and as a result, President Osvaldo Hurtado recognized land claims by 900 Huaorani, and granted them 67,000 hectares, plus 250,000 hectares as an "exclusive" reserve.[53]

Despite such advances, further attacks continued. In Chiapas, Mexico, the people of Chalchihuitán denounced human rights violations and protested the sale of their lands by their district attorney. In March 1983, local caciques and state backers attacked the protesters in a massacre at Ts'akiuk'um, leaving 11 K'iche' dead and hundreds homeless.[54] The eleventh Native man assassinated in Brazil during 1983 was Marçal Guaraní, a community leader and nurse in Mato Grosso de Sul, who had rejected a bribe of 5 million cruzeiros to move his village off land coveted by ranchers.

The course of national events in many Latin American countries changed as the growing Indigenous presence in politics and the media affected public opinions. Argentina finally granted legal status to Indigenous people in 1983, and the following year pledged to restore traditional Native lands and provide bilingual education to Indigenous communities, plans made without Indigenous representation or adequate funding. In Nicaragua, Native peoples on the Atlantic coast pushed the FSLN to negotiate for their autonomy. Miskitus, Sumus, and Ramas peoples demanded state recognition in 1984 as "Indigenous sovereign peoples" with special rights of autonomy, and the right to free self-determination of political, economic, social, and cultural development in line with cultural traditions. With speedboats supplied by the U.S. military, MISURASATA attacked Nicaraguan coastal communities; by September 1987 they had forced the FSLN to include their Atlantic coast autonomy within the new national constitution.

Indigenous initiatives during these years varied in their results. Native conditions in Brazil were not as successful as in Nicaragua, and the return to civilian rule in 1985 complicated their relationship with the state. New politicians simply labeled the defenders of Indigenous rights as opponents of national development and threats to national sovereignty.[55] Over the following years, though, Native people in Brazil organized around specific interests: in the Vaupés region bordering Colombia, they created 18 organizations that grouped clusters of communities between 1987 and 1988. Such leadership groups countered the work of fraudulent Native leaders who, in the name of their people, allowed state or private companies to extract their minerals.[56]

Brazil's Constitutional Assembly met in 1988, preceded by serious attacks on Indigenous resources, even as Indigenous people mobilized widely to force their way into the new legislation in debate at the Assembly. Logging of Kayapó land grew rapidly, and by 1987, 69 percent of Brazilian mahogany came from their territory. By 1988, prospectors had increased mining in Yanomami lands. The resulting gold rush devastated central Yanomami communities, especially in Roraima, over the following years. Increasing extractivism prompted Indigenous people to lobby widely for more protection within Brazil's new constitution. Many Native peoples, but especially the Kayapó, arrayed themselves in ceremonial paint and feathers and posted a vigil outside the constitutional convention. Opponents of the Indigenous organizations, especially the peasant Movement of the Landless and mining companies, but also a false agency called the Christian Church World Council, used forged documents to counter Native claims about abuses and the stealing and defacing of their land. Together, these opponents defeated the article proclaiming Brazil to be a multiethnic society. Nor did Indigenous people receive protection against mining intrusions. Conservative groups argued that supporting Native rights harmed Brazil's vital interests.[57] Indigenous people, however, still won legal promises of protection for their rights to lands and ways of life.

Indigenous Peoples and Political Transitions to Democracy

The last years of the 1980s saw widespread Indigenous activism as Latin American countries moved toward democratic leadership.[58] In Nicaragua, the Miskitu, Sumu, and Rama continued to lobby for autonomy, and in September 1987 the FSLN finally designated the Atlantic coast an autonomous region but divided it into two zones by splitting the Native lobby. The Esquipulas II Central American Peace Plan of 1987 created a conciliatory venue that assisted the local Indigenous people in reaching some of their negotiation goals. In 1990 coastal peoples organized a new Indigenous political party to replace MISURASATA, called Mother Land Indigenous Communities (YATAMA), which literally means Sons of Mother Earth. The organization represented coastal peoples in the 1990 elections that ended Sandinista rule.[59]

Indigenous people demanded Catholic Church recognition in Paraguay when John Paul II visited Paraguay in 1988. The Pope met with several thousand Native people from Brazil, Bolivia, Argentina, and Paraguay in the western Paraguayan Chaco. The positive support he showed to the Indigenous people cast the flailing Stroessner regime in a negative light, and the Pope's support strengthened the resolve of the Indigenous movement in Paraguay and their commitment to opposing state abuses.[60] Native people participated in the broader popular groundswell that finally deposed the dictator in January 1989.

For Document 13.2: Enenlhit leader René Ramírez's Address to Pope John Paul II, Mariscal Estigarribia, Paraguay, May 17, 1988, visit www.routledge.com/9780415519120.

In May 2001, 12 years after the collapse of the Stroessner regime, I interviewed the Enenlhit leader who presented the Indigenous message to the pontiff. Death threats from the dictatorship had forced Ramírez into hiding in the woods for months after his speech, during which time his community clandestinely brought him food and outside news until the regime collapsed in February 1989. In our interview, during the first time that Ramírez had dared to return to Asunción, he framed his presentation to John Paul II as part of a broader Indigenous movement to oppose the dictatorship. The Enenlhit leader emphasized how he had risked his life to collect Native testimonies to the Pope and that his speech was an attempt to remedy regime abuses.

> Throughout the year before the Pope arrived, I collected how Indigenous people fared, how authorities treated them, their relations with the national police, no one knew why I was doing this, but I wrote their stories.... My just protest was that we wanted liberty in democracy and that Indigenous people be treated as humans, as people who were the original inhabitants of this country. We wanted out land, our territory, since we were no longer able to practice our culture.[61]

Ramírez clearly understood that despite possible repercussions, his presentation to the Pope was a milestone for Indigenous people throughout the Southern Cone of Latin America. The event symbolized Indigenous opposition to authoritarian rule and, as lawyer Esther Prieto has argued, helped move Paraguay toward a democratic future.[62]

While Native people in Paraguay gained media attention by demanding land and opposing the dictatorship in their meeting with the Pope, state intimidation in Chile was still heavy enough that the Ninth Region, with a significant Mapuche presence, voted to retain the Pinochet dictatorship in 1989, when the rest of the nation voted the regime out of power. One explanation is that the services on which Native communities depended, such as health care, required registry in state electoral rolls. In addition, the opposition Concertación Party featured Indigenous concerns, but only as of Chilean lower classes and not as distinct ethnic peoples, a visible slight. When Mapuche organizations presented their demands to Concertación Party candidate Patricio Aylwin, the lawyer, author, and former senator nevertheless promised to include their requests in his new constitution if he won the election. Aylwin also pledged to create a Special Commission for Indigenous Peoples (CEPI) to implement beneficial programs, presumably as an attempt to help win the Ninth Region of Chile to his side.[63]

Indigenous people throughout the continent found outside allies for added support for their political and environmental concerns. In Brazil, Kayapó leader Raoni and rock star

Sting, back from a tour in Europe, organized to defend the rainforest, gathering 3,000 Kayapó and other activists in a massive protest against the Altamira Dam Project in February 1989. The protest and the international attention it garnered successfully delayed plans for the Xingu and Iriri River dams, which would have affected 25,000 Indigenous people from 18 distinct peoples. The widespread Indigenous protests of the 1980s in Brazil and elsewhere set the stage for Native experiences in the continent's move toward neoliberal politics during the decade that followed.

Conclusion: Indigenous Organization and Authoritarian Rule in Latin America

Although many Latin American countries had moved from authoritarian rule to democracies by 1990, they overwhelmingly continued neoliberal programs of free trade and privatization begun by the regimes and supported by the Washington Consensus, the World Bank, and the IMF. The resulting austerity programs, the rapid sale of natural resources, and the privatization of state services amid very modest economic growth plunged many of Latin America's people into worse poverty. The social results of these state programs challenged Indigenous peoples. With decades of practice in resistance and organization, though, the Native peoples did not easily allow these new governments to push them aside.

This chapter has documented the widespread rise of Indigenous movements in Latin America between 1971 and 1990. Native people linked causes nationally and internationally, and employed the media to mobilize widely. Political scientist Donna Lee Van Cott and others have shown that Indigenous people contributed toward Latin America's return to democracy

Figure 13.2 Kayapó Demonstration at Altamira, Brazil. (Sue Cunningham Photographic/Alamy Stock Photo)

by drawing attention to military human rights abuses, demanding protection for their lands, and by mobilizing for inclusion in the democratic openings that spread throughout the continent. Others joined opposition forces or leftist political organizations to influence political change. At the least, Native activists drew international attention to their living conditions and lingering abuses. This repeated mobilization shook the governments of Latin America. Indigenous peoples also forged international alliances to defend their interests, and demanded to be included in new national constitutions. Most importantly, however, was the way in which Indigenous people throughout Latin America forged alliances with activists, social groups, nongovernmental organizations, and especially other Native peoples, to further their political and economic goals.

Discussion Questions

1. What organizational strategies did Indigenous people employ in the final decades of the twentieth century to oppose military rule?
2. What determined military governments' relations with Indigenous peoples?
3. In what ways did Indigenous organization draw attention to human rights abuses?
4. What technological changes made possible and encouraged Indigenous organization?
5. How have recent Indigenous movements differed from earlier ones?

Notes

1 Van Cott, *Indigenous Peoples and Democracy*, 2.
2 Brysk, "Acting Globally," 32.
3 Rappaport, *The Politics of Memory*, 114.
4 Jackson, "Caught in the Crossfire," 110.
5 Howe, "The Kuna of Panama," 88.
6 Ramos, *Indigenism*, 169–170.
7 See Münzel, *The Aché Indians*, and Arens, *Genocide in Paraguay.*
8 Horst, *The Stroessner Regime*, 82–85.
9 Ibid., 111, 117.
10 Haughney, *Neoliberal Economics*, 60.
11 The Tukanoan linguistic family includes many Indigenous peoples, among others the Uitoto, Murui, Muinane, Bora, Ocaina, Andoke, Carijona, Miraña, Cabiyarí, Inga, Siona, Letuama, Macuna, Tanimuca Yucuna, Barasano, Paez, Letuama, Matapí, Yuhup, Coreguaje, and more.
12 Jackson, "Being and Becoming an Indian," 145.
13 Garfield, *Indigenous Struggle*, 158.
14 Ibid., 160.
15 Comissão Pró-Índio, 1979c., 17–20, cited in Ramos, *Indigenism*, 247.
16 Hale, *Resistance and Contradiction*, 265, Note 50.
17 Ibid., 159.
18 Simon Gonzalez, cited in Hale, *Resistance and Contradiction*, 75.
19 Harvey, *The Chiapas Rebellion*, 78
20 Dean, *State Power*, 209; Mainwaring *et al.*, *The Crisis*, 260; Turino, "The State and Andean Musical Production," 274.
21 Ramos, *Indigenism*, 214.
22 Ibid., 205–206.
23 Klein, *A Concise History of Bolivia*, 226.
24 Albó, "From MNRistas to Kataristas to Katari," 397.
25 Ibid.

26 Jackson, "Caught in the Crossfire," 110.
27 Hernández-Ávila and Varese, "Indigenous Intellectual Sovereignties," 82.
28 Garfield, *Indigenous Struggle*, 189.
29 Ibid., 192.
30 Ramos, *Indigenism*, 230.
31 Horst, *The Stroessner Regime*, 108.
32 Black, *Triumph of the People*, 113–114.
33 Hale, *Resistance and Contradiction*, 118.
34 Grandin, *The Last Colonial Massacre*, 153–154.
35 Albó, "From MNRistas to Kataristas to Katari," 379.
36 Klein, *Bolivia*, 242.
37 Brysk, "Acting Globally," 35.
38 Hale, "Rethinking Indigenous Politics," 17.
39 Ramos, *Indigenism*, 204–209.
40 Dean, "State Power and Indigenous Peoples," 215.
41 Horst, *The Stroessner Regime*, 114–115.
42 Macdonald, "Ecuador's Indian Movement," 177–178.
43 Horst, *The Stroessner Regime*, 119.
44 Ramos, *Indigenism*, 122, 271.
45 Dean, "State Power and Indigenous Peoples," 205.
46 Ramos, *Indigenism*, 112.
47 Adams, "Strategies of Ethnic Survival in Central America," 189.
48 Grandin, "History, Motive, Law, Intent" 339–340, 350.
49 Smith, *Guatemalan Indians and the State*, 272.
50 Schirmer, "Appropriating the Indigenous, Creating Complicity," 63.
51 Stern, *Battling for Hearts and Minds*, 216; Haughney, *Neoliberal Economics*, 60.
52 Howe, "The Kuna of Panama," 92.
53 Macdonald, "Ecuador's Indian Movement," 178.
54 Levi, "A New Dawn or a Cycle Restored?," 15.
55 Maybury-Lewis, "Becoming Indian," 225.
56 Ramos, *Indigenism*, 176.
57 Maybury-Lewis, "For Reasons of State," 338.
58 For further information on Indigenous mobilization for democratic change, see Van Cott, *Indigenous Peoples and Democracy*.
59 Diskin, "Ethnic Discourse and the Challenge to Anthropology," 172.
60 Horst, *El Régimen de Stroessner*, 289.
61 René Ramírez, Enenlhit leader, personal interview, Asunción, Paraguay, May 21, 2001. See also Horst, "Consciousness and Contradiction," 124.
62 Prieto, "Indigenous People in Paraguay," 240–241.
63 Haughney, *Neoliberal Economics*, 64–65.

14 Indigenous People Enter the New Millennium, 1990 to 2010

Chronology

1990 Massive Indigenous *Levantamiento* (Uprising) in Ecuador.
First Continental Conference on Five Hundred Years of Indigenous Resistance in Quito.
Expulsion of Tukano people from Amazonas State, Brazil.
1991 Colombia enacts a new constitution that reflects "the Permitted Indian."
"March for Territory and Dignity" in Bolivia.
1992 Quincentennial of Columbus' first voyage causes widespread Indigenous organization.
Paraguay enacts a new constitution that "in theory" includes Indigenous rights.
June: U.N. Conference on Environment and Development in Rio de Janeiro.
Quiché leader Rigoberta Menchú receives the Nobel Peace Prize.
1993 Peru enacts the Law of Organic Hydrocarbons, conflict ensues with Native peoples.
CONAIE proposal for a New Multinational Nation in Ecuador.
December: Indigenous members of the Barbados Group meet in Rio de Janeiro.
1994 EZLN Zapatista movement occupies towns in Chiapas, Mexico.
1995 CIDOB and CSUTCB march to La Paz to demand radical land reform law.
1996 Brazil's Decree 1775 opens up demarcation of Native lands.
Native people in Ecuador organize the Pachacutik Movement of Plurinational Unity.
EZLN negotiations with federal authorities in Chiapas.
First National Indigenous Congress in Mexico.
Peace accords signed in Guatemala on "Identity and Rights of Indigenous Peoples."
1997 Xavante in war dress occupy Congress in Brazil.
Civil war in Colombia involves Tukanoans, Kamsá, and Quillacinga-Pasto people.
Mapuche struggle to defend their lands in Chile.
Cry of the Excluded march in Brazil.
Acteal massacre in Chiapas, Mexico.
2000 Indigenous people in Ecuador force President Mahuad from office, push pluriculturalism.
Grand Assembly of 500 Indigenous leaders in Santa Cruz.

EZLN march to Mexico City in February; Yaqui, Wixárika, and Kumiai organization.

2001 Mexican law on Indigenous rights and culture, rejected by EZLN and Native people.

Plan Puebla Panama ratified by Central American and Mexican authorities.

Guambiano leader Floro Tunabalá elected Governor of Popayán, Colombia.

2002 Garifuna in Honduras organize fraternal and development organizations.

2003 The Gas War in Bolivia and Aymara hunger strike, occupation of central plaza in La Paz.

2004 Second Continental Summit of Indigenous Peoples and Nationalities of Abya Yala.

2005 The Aymara under Evo Morales force President Carlos Mesa of Bolivia to resign.

2006 The Tzotzil in Chiapas organize the Peace and Justice Caravan to Oaxaca.

2007 Third Continental Summit of Indigenous Peoples and Nationalities of Abya Yala in Guatemala.

United Nations Declaration on the Rights of Indigenous Peoples.

2009 Fourth Continental Summit of Indigenous Peoples and Nationalities of Abya Yala in Peru.

2010 Additional attacks on Indigenous resources and people throughout the continent.

Introduction

By the final decade of the twentieth century, Latin American nations had transitioned from military rule to democratic administration, yet had largely retained the neoliberal programs of free trade and privatization begun by some regimes. Most countries also largely supported the so-called Washington Consensus, the economic reform policy guidelines for developing nations pushed by the U.S. Treasury Department, the International Monetary Fund (IMF), and the World Bank. As part of the new economic agreements with global financing institutions, governments imposed austerity programs, sold off natural resources, and privatized state services such as water delivery. Because these policies produced very modest economic growth and unequal distribution of wealth, they plunged many Latin American people into even worse poverty. Neoliberal economics forced Latin American and U.S. workers to compete against each other to manufacture the cheapest goods for North American markets. Because of their depressed economies, Latin Americans won the competition, meaning their laborers would work for lower wages. Living conditions throughout much of the continent revealed why: by 1989, according to the United Nations, 183 million Latin Americans lived under the poverty line. Following the implementation of NAFTA, poverty levels in Mexico rose from 34 percent in 1994 to 60 percent by 1999. During the final decade of the twentieth century, South American poverty levels rose from 31.5 to 38 percent of the population. The social results were especially difficult in the largest urban centers, where poverty worsened quickly, and large, underdeveloped slums appeared, but living conditions were also challenging for Indigenous peoples, both in those slums and in rural areas. Rising threats to Native land tenure made it increasingly difficult for them to enjoy independent subsistence, and the decline of state support for health and education systems contributed to the spiral of poverty. With decades of widespread political organization under their belts, though, Native peoples did not easily allow the new governments to push them aside in favor of free trade. Instead, they fought back, forming political alliances, employing the media, and linking causes with environmental NGOs to force their way into the new democratic administrations.

One inspiring development was the way in which Indigenous people continued to organize themselves during the first decade of the third millennium, as governments rushed to implement free trade and economic reforms. The neoliberal economic principle of comparative advantage gained broad support from Mexico and Guatemala to Andean nations and the Southern Cone, and leaders like Ernesto Zedillo in Mexico and Fernando Henrique Cardoso in Brazil, who had studied at Ivy League universities in the U.S., pushed free market policies in their nations. Native people mobilized themselves across national boundaries and nation states countered these efforts with further attempts to control them. Neoliberal economic changes that incentivized states to privatize natural resources, and the political sponsors of these programs tried to curtail and co-opt Indigenous organization and political influence, because it stood in their way. Joining forces with environmental activists, NGOs, and other disenfranchised minorities, Indigenous peoples worked to improve their living conditions and defend their territory and resources. Their struggles both raised national tensions and gave Native peoples the opportunity for greater political participation.

The election of Evo Morales to Bolivia's presidency in December 2005, the first Indigenous leader in Bolivia to capitalize on his indigeneity for political gain in the nation with a majority Native population, exemplified the contradictions created by Indigenous access to political power. Morales' experience illustrates the difficulty of governing nation states as neoliberalism declined and anti-imperialism championed by leaders like Fidel Castro in Cuba and Hugo Chávez in Venezuela grew in popularity during what became known as the pink tide.[1] The surprising political change in Bolivia, where Evo Morales and his MAS (Movement Toward Socialism) Party promised a cultural and democratic revolution with votes rather than bullets and connected his nationalist movement to earlier Native leaders like Tupac Katari, pointed to future challenges. Morales' rise to power shows that whatever changes now lay ahead for Latin America, Indigenous people have proven their intention of remaining important actors within the evolving social, economic, and political processes throughout the continent.

Movements by people without power and the strategies they use to improve their situation frame this chapter theoretically. Historian Howard Zinn, author of *A People's History of the United States*, wrote about the ways in which subaltern groups have shaped their lives and histories. In his book *A Power Governments Cannot Suppress*, Zinn analyzed the ways in which ordinary people in the U.S. have stood up to power and pushed for historical change. African Americans, workers, women, Native Americans, and draft dodgers all faced daunting challenges and organized in creative ways to change their situations. Many of the subaltern strategies that Zinn highlighted resemble and help explain the movements and organization by Indigenous Latin Americans during the final decades of the twentieth century.

Another useful frame of reference for this chapter is Postcolonialism, a field that emerged during the second half of the twentieth century to analyze and help understand the revolutionary history of the non-Western struggle to overthrow Western imperialism. Professor of Literature Edward Said at Columbia University and British sociologist Stuart Hall, both born in former European colonies, championed equality between cultures and peoples when they created this theoretical framework. Experience led these theorists to oppose the hierarchies that Westerners had imposed to dominate colonized regions. By the final decades of the twentieth century, states were increasingly employing politically correct terminology that nevertheless represented traditional formulations of identity to explain differences between peoples. Postcolonial writers rejected such language as a continuation of nationalist constructions of domination. They instead employed the concept of difference to analyze forces of oppression and coercive domination in the world they studied to connect intellectuals and activists. Postcolonial analysis helps explain and understand Indigenous movements that emerged during this recent period.

Widespread Indigenous Militancy Reflects 500 Years of Colonialism

The 1990s began with a massive Native uprising in Ecuador, where Indigenous people joined forces to demand land, education, economic development, and state recognition of their Indigenous nationalities. Luis Macas, leader of the Confederation of Indigenous Nationalities of Ecuador (CONAIE), the pan-Indigenous organization that directed the National Uprising, recalled, "The uprising marked a decisive change in the future of our movement. We have achieved a political space; we have entered into the political scene of the country."[2] Native people called their broad uprising *Pachakutic* (using the Quechua words *pacha* for land, and *kutik* for a return to), meaning a return to a cultural birth and reference to a revered Inca ruler. The term also described a revolution of sorts, "a turning point of cosmic dimensions and the beginning of a new era through which what was below would be on top and vice versa." This millennial concept had inspired Andean movements toward self-determination over the years.[3] The June 1990 Native demonstrations in Ecuador, called simply a *levantamiento* (uprising), paralyzed national transport systems and severed food deliveries throughout the country by peacefully blocking all roads. Then 10,000 Indigenous people marched into Quito and occupied the central plaza. The CONAIE and other Native organizations presented the government with "sixteen points," demanding bilingual education, agrarian reform, and recognition of Ecuador as a multiethnic and multicultural country. President Rodrigo Borja Cevallos, in power since 1988, had raised Native expectations by noting that Indigenous nationalities had been present "many years before we invented our states," but then once in power he failed to deliver any substantial programs to improve Indigenous conditions.

By organizing such a massive march, Native people in Ecuador were employing a time-tested strategy of nonviolent mobilization used by people without political power. Mahondas Gandhi had generated mass support to gain Indian independence from Great Britain by using similar efforts. Early in 1930, Gandhi led supporters on a march to protest Britain's salt monopoly and tax on its largest colony, India. Thousands of people joined Gandhi during the 240-mile trek to the ocean and attracted worldwide attention. Colonial forces arrested nearly 60,000 people and their leader when they made salt. Mass disobedience focused world attention on Britain's unfair monopoly on a simple product that everyone needed. Publicity of British violence set in motion the independence process, which India finally achieved in 1947.

The massive march in Ecuador also led to negotiations. Four hundred representatives from 120 Indigenous nationalities and organizations throughout the Americas met in Quito for the First Continental Conference on Five Hundred Years of Indigenous Resistance, where they prepared a response to the Columbus Quincentennary. Delegates insisted on autonomy for all Native peoples, the right to Native self-government, and national tolerance for Native customary legal and justice systems. Demanding that the conference reject the capitalist system, delegates instead proposed restructuring society into a popular power system based on pluralism and democracy. Coming so soon after the *Pachakutic* uprising, this gathering marked an important change in the tenor of the Indigenous demands, and in Ecuador opened "a decade of incredibly heightened activism with Indigenous peoples playing a key role in political developments."[4]

Native delegates then issued the "Declaration of Quito" when presenting their requests to states. They demanded recognition of "500 years of Indigenous resistance" against genocide, rather than a celebration of Columbus' voyages, a reference to the upcoming Quincentennial in 1992. To an observer, the rise of Native consciousness resembled the "awakening of a sleeping giant," as Indigenous people in Ecuador built their organizational base to its strongest force ever.

Postcolonial analysis of the Quincentennial explains that from its beginning, colonialism was an act of geographical violence directed against Indigenous people and their land rights. As Said wrote,

> Everything about human history is rooted in the earth, which has meant that people have planned to *have* more territory and therefore must do something about its indigenous residents. At some very basic level, imperialism means thinking about, settling on, controlling land that you do not possess, that is distant, that is lived on and owned by others. For all kind of reasons it attracts some people and often involves untold misery for others.[5]

Already in 1892, as interest in imperial expansion grew in the U.S., the nation capitalized on the "discovery" of America to foster public support for U.S. expansion around the world. Promoted by the Knights of Columbus after 1898 and celebrated with a national holiday in 1934, postcolonial perspectives emphasize that the celebration of Columbus in the U.S. grew to rival only George Washington, and in Europe only Queen Victoria.[6]

Energized and funded by their expulsion of Muslim and Jewish people from Granada in 1492, postcolonialists emphasize that Isabella and Ferdinand's Reconquest war culminated in a final crusade against Islam. European colonial expansion went hand in hand with the crusading mentality and the creation of the Catholic Inquisition that ended the multicultural society experienced by Iberia under Islamic rule. In addition to the traditional focus on religious crusades, postcolonial perspectives show that the voyages of exploration were also a response to the rise in European commercial expansion during the sixteenth century. Spain spent its treasure from the Americas to pay its northern creditors, and its search for precious metals fueled its expansion to the Americas.[7] Postcolonial analysis thus supported Indigenous activism.

Ecuadorian leaders in Quito finally negotiated with the Indigenous protestors and then released the detainees, so Native people removed their roadblocks, but ultimately President Rodrigo Borja Cevallos changed nothing. The 1990s thus marked the emergence of a transnational Indigenous movement as an influential political force in Latin America. No longer could states easily push Native people aside, but given the neoliberal focus spreading through the continent it would also be difficult for Indigenous peoples to make governments fulfill their social obligations.

Along with growing Native organization, threats to Indigenous resources and ways of life increased throughout Latin America. Immediately before the uprising in Ecuador, Brazil's army evicted 123 Tukano children, women, and men at gunpoint from their land in the upper Uaupés region of Amazonas State near Colombia. The Tukano had been panning for gold on the reservation where the Calha Norte Project had settled them one year earlier. To clear the area for "development," Brazilian soldiers burned down their houses and destroyed their equipment under the charge that the Tukano were smuggling gold, trafficking drugs, supporting Colombian guerrilla forces, and living outside of the designated Native area. Several years before, a few Tukano leaders had in fact allowed their land to be parceled into tracts in return for military protection and royalties from the Paranapanema mining company that was to exploit their area. This happened after years of fruitless political lobbying by the Tukano to have their lands demarcated and thus protected. Tukano attempts in Brasilia to protect their territories had often seemed to them instead like police interrogation, showing little support for the Tukano plight even from the 30 so-called nongovernmental organizations active in Brazil.[8] The mining company eventually abandoned the Tukano area after declaring it not worth the expense.

Indigenous organization in Brazil highlights the way that by the 1990s, increased attention from the press and NGOs, as well as the growing availability of media and communication outlets, made it easier for Indigenous people to contact one another and the outside world. Native people found that direct relations with each other without state or NGO intermediaries proved advantageous to broader organization and to what they called "self-determination," the ability to make their own choices.

Native self-determination was still complicated in Peru, however, where a growing civil war and authoritarian rule challenged their organization. The new president, Alberto Fujimori, in power since July 1990, tackled his nation's soaring inflation, unemployment, deficit, and widespread poverty by attracting international loans. The new leader imposed macroeconomic reforms that privatized state industries and removed barriers to trade to promote economic activity. These structural adjustments, quickly dubbed "Fujishocks" by his opponents, focused wealth upward in a system of patronage that secured elite support for his policies. The leader's populist strategies began to curb hyperinflation yet forced Peruvians into worse poverty.

Escalating internal conflict complicated the situation in Peru. To address the growing Indigenous poverty and social unrest produced by his programs, Fujimori created a new Special Project for Land Titling (PETT) and appointed National Ombudsmen for human rights abuses of Peruvian Indigenous peoples, but these legal actions did little to improve Native conditions as the nation descended into civil war. As introduced in Chapter 13, the Shining Path insurgency claimed the president's attention. Fujimori employed scorched-earth warfare to push the Shining Path operatives into the tropical forests east of the Andes. Indigenous people and *colono* peasants – mestizo farmers who lived on large rural properties in return for service – entered the conflict as both state and rebels targeted Native peoples for allegedly supporting the other side.

To deal with the growing chaos, Fujimori enacted an "autogolpe" (self-coup) in 1992, suspending the constitution and shutting down the Congress. As the resulting conflict militarized Amazonian Peru, the president instated compulsory military recruitment for poorer young Peruvian men carried out through ambushes, a practice called the *leva*. Fujimori took advantage of the war to attack Indigenous people in the path of development by labeling them dangerous to the public order.[9] Rebels and state troops alike massacred villages as the civil war escalated, killing, for example, the leaders of the Asháninka, Yánesha, and Nomatsiguenga peoples. Attacked by both sides, Native communities created self-defense patrols to protect their communities. The civil war displaced hundreds of thousands and killed over 27,000 people, including many Indigenous people, thousands of them executed without legal due process.

Native Peoples Face Different Strategies of Control

Since national governments could no longer easily sidestep Indigenous organizations, they sought new strategies to manipulate those populations. Bolivian sociologist Silvia Rivera Cusicanqui developed the idea of "Indio permitido," or "authorized Indian," to explain the shift in attitude throughout the continent during the 1990s toward the government's use of cultural rights to divide and domesticate Indigenous movements. Governments framed Native rights during this time as a reward for cooperative Native people, to allow them to organize as they wished, as long as they did not call into question the fundamental privileges of the state.[10] During the 1990s, nations for all practical purposes updated the practice of *indigenismo* by adding the current catch phrases of "Indigenous rights" and "pluricultural tolerance" into their legal frameworks, as a way to tame the growing Indigenous solidarity and placate national critics and outside observers.

Paraguay had used this strategy back in 1981 with its Indigenous Rights Bill, but Colombia was the first country to apply the "authorized Indian" strategy to a national constitution. Advocates of constitutional reform argued that the former 1886 Colombian constitution favored the Conservative upper classes and was irrelevant to a modern society marked by increased violence, widespread corruption, and the drug war. In the 1991 Constitution, Colombia included significant Native rights. Indigenous participants in the constitutional convention included lawyer Francisco Rojas Birry from the Embera people, Guambiano leader Lorenzo Muelas, and Nasa lawyer Alfonso Peña Chepe. The three representatives participated in the constitutional deliberations without legislative power. Rather, their presence symbolized the image that Colombia was attempting to project: tolerance of minorities, pluralism, a rediscovered national identity, and national political effectiveness that was inclusive of broad popular participation, even of Native rights. The constitution promised to allow "Indigenous territorial entities," collective ownership of *resguardo* lands, the right of Indigenous peoples to use lands as Natives themselves decided, and settlement of internal Native affairs according to customary law. Most potentially empowering was the writ of protection that allowed *all* Colombian citizens to appeal constitutional rights to immediate court action.[11] President César Gaviria thus sought to employ ethnic minority rights as a means to show how inclusively Colombia had incorporated even the most marginalized into the long-divided nation by offering even the Indigenous people legal protection.

Indigenous people also pushed for greater legal recognition in other nations. By the early 1990s in Bolivia, Native speakers of at least one of 34 Indigenous languages formed 57 percent of the population. Highland Aymara people numbered 1.6 million, while there were 2.4 million Quechua also in the mountains; by this time members of these peoples were working as farmers, miners, teachers, truck drivers, urban merchants, and even national congressional delegates. Native speakers in the Bolivian eastern lowlands numbered 260,000 in the Indigenous census of 1995; smaller groups there were the Araona, Paikoneka, and Yuki; the Canichana, Chácobo, and Esse Ejja numbered 2,000 to 3,000; larger peoples included the Guarayu, Ts'iman, and Movima, while the largest peoples of 40,000 to 60,000 included the Moxeño, Chiquitano [Besiro], and Guaraní. These Native peoples were largely agrarian, but also included teachers, merchants, artisans, evangelical ministers, and national bureaucrats. During 1991, the lowland and highland Indigenous people joined in the "March for Territory and Dignity," a 700-kilometer trek from the jungle to the city of La Paz to demand defense of their property from logging interests, and legal protection of their communal lands. This movement led to national recognition of four Indigenous territories and Bolivia's 1991 ratification of the ILO Indigenous and Tribal Peoples Convention on the rights of Indigenous peoples.

Additional states also included Indigenous rights in their constitutions. Having deposed ailing dictator Alfredo Stroessner in January 1989, Paraguayans enacted a new constitution. Indigenous people from the 17 Native groups in the country together forced their way into the constitutional proceedings. In May 1991, 134 representatives from 64 Indigenous settlements issued a collective request for formal participation. When the Catholic Church, two Colorado senators, labor unions, and legal agencies added their support, legislators allowed four Native delegates into the constitutional deliberations in April 1992. The fifth chapter of the new constitution marked a significant achievement for Indigenous activism: the legislation recognized Indigenous peoples as groups within Paraguay with unique cultures, granted these peoples communal landownership, and exempted them from compulsory military service. While Indigenous people saw their constitutional inclusion as a legal victory, legislators viewed the document as a way to further integrate Natives into national society.[12]

Recognition of the 500th anniversary of having discovered Columbus on their shores preoccupied Indigenous organizations throughout 1992. In June, Indigenous representatives from throughout the Americas gathered in Rio de Janeiro for the U.N. Conference on Environment and Development, also called the Earth Summit. Excluded from the proceedings, Native people met instead at an artificial village called Kari-Oca, which Rio de Janeiro built an hour from the city to keep Indigenous people away from the U.N. events. On the final day of the meetings, a busload of Indigenous people from Kari-Oca finally forced their way into the main chambers to make their demands known to the wider audience. Native defiance of Brazilian security forces and U.N. authorities resembled civil disobedience in the U.S. during the Vietnam War, when hundreds of thousands of young men burned draft cards and refused to register for the draft. Priests, nuns, and laypeople seized records from draft boards and went to prison. Even military personnel defied the authorities by refusing to embark for Vietnam, teach elite Special Forces, or even carry out bombing missions in the theater of war.[13]

At their occupation of U.N. proceedings, Kayapó leader Raoni declared,

> Now we Kayapó are thinking that when the white men finish with our land, that they will put an end to us also. Now we have to raise our heads, we have to be aware of the fight we are facing, so that we can protect ourselves from the thieves. We are not going to let you finish cutting down all the trees. White men must respect us and leave us alone. They must demarcate our lands and then leave us alone. This is what we want.[14]

The Indigenous lobby made the final U.N. Earth Summit document include recognition of Native rights in Principle 127:

> We reaffirm our commitment to continue making progress in the advancement of the human rights of the world's indigenous peoples at the local, national, regional and international levels, including through consultation and collaboration with them, and to present for adoption a final draft United Nations declaration on the rights of indigenous peoples as soon as possible.

Principle 22 recognized Native environmental stewardship:

> Indigenous people and their communities, and other local communities, have a vital role in environmental management and development because of their knowledge and traditional practices. States should recognize and duly support their identity, culture, and interests and enable their effective participation in the achievement of sustainable development.[15]

While not an enforceable directive, the clause reflected the Indigenous desire for global recognition and inclusion within international deliberations. Two months later, Brazil's government demarcated Kayapó land.

Rigoberta Menchú and the Nobel Peace Prize

Another way in which Indigenous people gained attention in 1992 occurred when a K'iche' activist from Guatemala named Rigoberta Menchú won the Nobel Peace Prize, "in recognition for her work for social justice and ethno-cultural reconciliation, based on her work for social justice and ethno-cultural reconciliation, based on respect for the rights of Indigenous peoples." Menchú accepted the distinction with the following statement:

> I consider this Prize, not as a reward to me personally, but rather as one of the greatest conquests in the struggle for peace, for Human Rights, and for the rights of the Indigenous people, who, for 500 years, have been split, fragmented, as well as the victims of genocides, repression, and discrimination.

The selection of Menchú for this prize, while celebrated by some Native activists as a victory for their cause, was already controversial due to growing questions about the historical veracity of Menchú's testimony, family history, and especially her 1984 testimonial book, edited by anthropologist Elisabeth Burgos-Debray and entitled *I, Rigoberta Menchú*.[16]

Native mobilization during the course of the Quincentennary year also took place in Ecuador, where in March 1992 2,000 Indigenous people walked 150 kilometers from the Amazonian town of Puyo to Quito, to demand that the state acknowledge pan-ethnic territories in their province of Pastaza. Thousands of Andean Indigenous supporters joined the march as it approached the capital, drawing in representatives and support from CONAIE. The marchers gathered in the central Plaza San Francisco, and their leaders met directly with the Borja government to demand respect for Indigenous rights. The Pastaza activists secured only permission for larger community landholdings of their own, rather than the broad pan-ethnic territorial claims they had requested; essentially people from Pastaza gained more communal land for themselves but not as much territory designated more broadly for all Indigenous peoples. Still, the negotiations elevated the Indigenous cause within Ecuadorian society, which respected the demonstrators for the legitimacy of their demands and their nonviolent methods.[17]

Constant Indigenous activism pressured states to enact token legislation in the Natives' favor. In Peru, President Fujimori created an investigative office called Defensoría del Pueblo to enforce the new constitutional guarantees. One Defensoría initiative was to protect the collective rights of the Peruvian Indigenous peoples and monitor land titling and electoral disputes. In preparation for the 2000 electoral campaign, the Defensoría del Pueblo offered civil rights media training and voter education in three Indigenous tongues: Asháninka, Shipibo, and Awajun. In 1993, though, Fujimori enacted the Law of Organic Hydrocarbons, encouraging petroleum extraction with unlimited access to profits. This law plunged many Indigenous communities, especially the Jivaroan and Urarina speakers of the northern Amazonian jungles, the Asháninka, Yánesha, and Nomatsiguenga of central forests, and the Harakmbut, Yine and Machiguenga peoples of southern jungles into disputes with transnational oil companies. By 1998, Chevron, Mobil, Shell, Exxon, Occidental, French Elf Aquitaine, and the Argentinian company Pluspetrol received 21 million hectares of eastern Peruvian rainforest in 34 lots for oil exploration. Indigenous people renewed efforts to title their lands. By the end of the 1990s, they had legally secured over 7 million hectares, 10 percent of Peru's rainforest. While a start, this land was less than one-third of all the rainforest land granted to the oil companies.[18]

Another example of state recognition of Native peoples occurred in Paraguay, where in 1993 President Juan Carlos Wasmosy ratified the International Labour Organization statement on the rights of Indigenous communities into Law 234/93. Paraguay thus committed to "protect the rights of the Indigenous peoples to guarantee their integrity," and defend their right "to use lands that have not been exclusively occupied by those groups, but to which they have had traditional access for their traditional and subsistence activities." While the legislation was similar to the Law 904 that Stroessner had passed in 1981 simply to quell foreign criticism of his human rights abuses, it serves as another state response to increasingly organized and assertive Native populations.

Indigenous people then raised the ante in Ecuador through the CONAIE, by issuing a proposal to the government for a "New Multinational Nation." By 1993, CONAIE was a recognized political force. The organization called for a democratic government attentive to all nationality interests and one that invites Native participation. The proposal to recognize each Native people as equal "nationalities" with separate origin, history, tradition, and territory moved Ecuador in a new direction. The lexicon later shifted from "multinational" to "plurinational," and the original claim for the recognition of nine nationalities expanded to include distinct areas of origin or pueblos, yet the basic demand remained the same: Indigenous inclusion as equal members in a plurinational state.[19]

Indigenous people continued to raise pressure for transnational legal support. In December 1993, Indigenous members of the Barbados Group, the advocates of Indigenous rights that had gathered last in 1977, met again in Rio de Janeiro. At this encounter, leaders rejected new forms of colonization in their countries that still resulted in the domination and exploitation of Native peoples.

> At the same time we confirm the Indian peoples' will to resist and to live, expressed through the multiplication of their ethno-political organizations, and of the centennial daily affirmation of cultural specificities that manifest the force of their civilizing projects.... We are witnesses in each of our countries to the repeated violations of their right to life, their dignity, and to the cultural and human universe of their local expressions.

Native delegates rejected neoliberalism, and what they called "the western-oriented integrationist market system and demanded territorial autonomy and self-determination for resource use, decision-making and cultural self-determination ... compatible with and complementary to the sovereignty of constituted national States."[20]

Movements: The Zapatista Army of National Liberation Uprising in Mexico

Indigenous opposition to neoliberalism in Mexico claimed the news in 1994. On New Year's Day, over 3,000 Indigenous people in the new Zapatista Army of National Liberation (EZLN) occupied towns in the highlands of Chiapas State – Ocosingo, San Cristóbal de las Casas, Las Margaritas, Altamirano, Oxchuc, Chanal, Oxchuc, and Huixtán – in a dramatic move that caught the world's attention. Coming from Tzoltal, Totzil, Chol, Tojolabal, and Zoque K'iche' communities, the mysterious Indigenous soldiers in black, hooded ski masks demanded land, housing, food, jobs, health care, education, freedom, independence, justice, democracy, and peace. The movement had formed in November 1983, after members of the National Peasant Confederation (CNC) attacked Indigenous Tojolabal communities in the Lacandon forest as part of a long history of repression against the Native people rooted in competition over land and resources. The peasants themselves had been victims of government and landowners' aggression following land and labor disputes but vented their frustration on Native people in the area.

Early non-Indigenous organizers of the EZLN had been members of an urban guerrilla group called the FLN, National Liberation Forces, founded by activist César Germán Yáñez Muñoz in Monterrey, State of Nuevo León, Mexico, after the Tlatelolco student massacre in 1968. Muñoz eventually linked the rebels from northern Mexican cities with Indigenous inhabitants in eastern Chiapas. Deep in the Lacandon forest, the EZLN organized quietly into armed self-defense units under the leadership of Subcomandante Marcos, an intellectual who had belonged to the FLN, and Muñoz, who trained Marcos in insurgency tactics.

The Zapatistas aimed to change the structure and nature of power and community in Mexico. Their cry of "Ya Basta" ("Enough Already") welcomed all Mexicans tired of the national political system. Since Indigenous people launched the movement and their values infused its spirit through their logo "to govern by obeying," though, the world focused on the K'iche' at the army's center.

The EZLN inspired other Native groups to push the state for increased fiscal responsibility and broader Indigenous prospects. In October 1994, the Indigenous Organization of the Highlands of Chiapas and three additional peasant organizations stormed the town hall in Chalchihuitán, forced the municipal president to resign, and then pushed for an audit. Mexico responded to the Native uprisings with a massive invasion of Chiapas. In February 1995, over 60,000 federal troops occupied the state and hunted down the Zapatistas. Instead of hurting the movement, support spread quickly and the Zapatistas created five new resistance centers called Aguascalientes deep in the Lacandon forest.

Opposition to Neoliberal Policies Spreads through Latin America

By the mid-1990s, as neoliberal reforms spread through Latin America, protests like those started by the EZLN in Mexico grew more common. In Bolivia, in the spring of 1995, the National Institute of Agrarian Reform was scheduled to pass a new land reform law. The CIDOB (the Confederation of Indigenous Peoples of Bolivia, representing 34 Indigenous groups in the eastern Bolivian lowlands) and the CSUTCB (the Unified Syndical Confederation of Rural Workers of Bolivia) together organized a massive march to La Paz to demand a more radical version of the law. The bill redistributed land to lowland Native peoples, yet it was essentially a further attempt to placate growing demands from the region, where Natives claimed 14 percent of the national territory. The march was a show of force, but it led to 11 deaths and a split between the CIDOB and the CSUTCB because as a result the lowland peoples claimed 15 million hectares, 14 percent of the national territory, while the Quechua and Aymara highland farmers received very little land, and their holdings were not increased. When the final Agrarian Reform Law passed in 1996, it reflected Indigenous pressures: the law created a more open land market that threatened small farmers, but concurrently provided a means available only to Indigenous communities to legalize their "original community lands."[21]

In a few Latin American nations, Native people were trying to make laws favor their interests by broadening the official definition of nationality, yet political conflicts undermined their progress. Indigenous people in Ecuador still pushed for plurinational recognition, meaning a nation in which different yet recognized nationalities, peoples, and cultures live together within one larger state. The well-organized Indigenous lobby advanced this goal in 1996, when the government allowed the organization and inclusion of new political parties into the political democratic process that had so often been denied. To prepare for the elections of 1996, Native people created a progressive political organization named the Pachacutik Movement of Plurinational Unity (MUUP), to broaden Ecuador's democracy to include Indigenous peoples. The MUUP won eight congressional seats in the national elections that followed. The new Native political bloc, however, distanced itself from the newly elected populist president Abdalá Bucaram, nicknamed "the madman," due to his conservativism. President Bucaram created a new Ministry of Indian Affairs and appointed two Indigenous leaders as co-ministers, though the new agency collapsed following a bribery scandal. Bucaram himself served less than six months before the National Congress declared him mentally unfit to rule and removed him from office. The fiasco delayed the MUUP's entrance onto Ecuador's political stage.

In Chiapas, meanwhile, the EZLN had garnered enough media support to force federal authorities to begin negotiations in January 1996. The National Intermediation Committee under Bishop Samuel Ruíz and the COCOPA (Commission of Concord and Pacification) negotiated an end to the standoff. In February, the Zapatistas and Mexican president Ernesto Zedillo's representatives signed the "San Andres Accords on Indigenous Rights and Culture." The four resulting agreements have been called Mexico's most important documents dealing with Indigenous rights, because they demanded a "profound transformation of the State, as well as of the political, social, cultural, and economic relationships with the Indigenous peoples, which satisfies their demands for justice." The accords stipulated an

> all-inclusive new social agreement, based on the understanding of the fundamental plurality of Mexican society and on the contribution that the Indigenous people can make to national unity, beginning with the constitutional acknowledgement of their rights, and in particular, to their right to self-determination and autonomy.[22]

If implemented, the agreements would have revolutionized the Indigenous relationship with the government.

In October, Native people from throughout Mexico sent delegates to the first National Indigenous Congress, where, along with the EZLN, they proposed new pro-Indigenous legislation. President Zedillo, however, rejected their proposal on grounds that the formations of reservations would balkanize the country. Furthermore, he opposed granting Mexico's Indians "special rights," a legacy of earlier revolutionary discourse, stating that all peasants were equal citizens in a measure that essentially annulled the EZLN demands.

A document on Indigenous identity and rights emerged in Guatemala, though, late in 1996, as Indigenous people there continued to organize themselves. This arrangement was part of peace negotiations between the government and the Guatemalan National Revolutionary Unity guerrilla group, the public front for a coalition of four leftist guerrilla groups formed in 1982 to oppose President Rios Montt's war against peasants and Indigenous people (see Chapter 13). The treaty was also a follow-up to the Esquipulas II Accord, the arrangement to end hostilities and cooperate economically signed by five Central American nations in August 1987, and led to negotiations concerning the Native peoples involved in the conflict. The resulting agreement, entitled "Identity and Rights of Indigenous Peoples," pressured Guatemala to promote Native rights, eradicate discrimination, allow Indigenous languages in education, social services, and legal systems, and finally to reform the constitution to define the nation as multiethnic, pluricultural, and multilingual. These measures appear to be significant gains for Native people, yet they again aimed to co-opt growing Native mobilization. Legislation to include Indigenous people in the national legal framework, without really improving their living and political situation, was an example of "ethnicism," a political-ideological strategy that employed "extreme culturalism to emphasize national plurality, without really changing and enforcing the laws."[23]

Additional conflicts within Indigenous territory before the end of the 1990s confirmed that token legislative changes would not by themselves improve protection for communities. By 1997, Colombia was in the midst of a multifaceted civil war between the Armed Revolutionary Forces of Colombia (FARC), still fighting since 1964 to overthrow the government, the drug cartels, the U.S. War on Drugs, and the Colombian military. Indigenous people between these forces struggled as guerrillas, paramilitaries, and Colombian forces occupied their lands and forced Natives to serve as guides, informers, and informal troops. Some Indigenous people joined either paramilitary or guerrilla forces to protect their families. The War on Drugs threatened Native communities that grew coca and poppies for opium with no viable subsistence options. The civil war grew worse by the close of 1997, when the FARC attacked Mitú, the capital city of Vaupés department, and killed 16 police and 13 Tukanoan auxiliaries, and took another 24 Tukanoan prisoners. The guerrillas bombed the homes of 3,000 people, destroyed the school and pharmacy, and damaged the hospital.

The civil war in Colombia also created tensions between Native peoples. When the Quillacinga-Pasto people established a new *cabildo* in the Valley of Sibundoy, in the highlands near the Nariño department, their legal recognition threatened the two neighboring peoples, the Inga and Kamsá, with whom the Quillacinga-Pasto shared land. In the Chocó region of Colombia, along the Pacific, some Native communities clashed with neighboring communities of Afro-Colombians over land boundaries, though both at times cooperated to fight threats to their environment.[24] As access to land and the pressures of civil war became more intense, it is no wonder that Indigenous people became more involved: by this time, Native people collectively and legally owned 28 million fully demarcated hectares, a quarter of the Colombian territory.

Indigenous organization continued to attract members and attention in the media, which added more national and international allies. Social movements on behalf of Indigenous people had gained widespread attention, and by this time there were hundreds of recognized Indigenous organizations in Brazil. One proponent of Native rights was the Catholic Church, which in September 1997 organized a march to the capital by Indigenous people, landless peasants, and workers called the "Cry of the Excluded." The demonstration responded to the senseless murder of an Indigenous Pataxó leader who had visited Brasilia to push for their land rights. While sleeping at the bus station, five young men burned Galindo to death. Because homeless people routinely suffer harm on Brazilian streets, the judge charged the attackers only with accidental death. Protestors in the Cry of the Excluded movement demonstrated in 800 towns and cities throughout the nation against such injustices, blamed on the government's neoliberal social and economic policies that were excluding so many people from economic and political recognition.

Widespread liaisons with important organizations such as the Catholic Church did not exempt Indigenous people from such violent attacks, especially in nations like Mexico, with long-standing histories of such violence. In December 1997, the Red Mask, a paramilitary group with shadowy connections to the Institutional Revolutionary Party, attacked a group of unarmed people in the community of Acteal, in the San Pedro Chenalhó municipality of Chiapas, during a Catholic prayer meeting. The resulting massacre of 45 people included children and pregnant women, all members of the pacifist group Las Abejas (the Bees), which despite nonviolent practices nevertheless supported the EZLN. Paramilitaries stabbed and deliberately shot the pregnant women to kill their unborn children. Although it lasted for hours, the nearby military post refused to stop the attack. The following morning, the soldiers themselves washed bloodstains off the church walls to clear away evidence.

By this time in Guerrero, the Insurgent People's Revolutionary Army (ERPI) operated as a guerrilla unit with many Indigenous recruits. In retaliation, on June 7, 1998, the federal army ambushed an ERPI unit in the Mixtec community of El Charco. The attack killed seven civilians and four guerrillas, and wounded five others; the army captured 24 mostly Mixteco Indigenous people.

Indigenous Experiences in the New Millennium

In January 2000, as if to usher in the new millennium, Indigenous people in Ecuador led another massive uprising in Quito that forced President Jamil Mahuad out of office. The army, frustrated with the exploding hyperinflation and collapsing economy, had joined forces with the CONAIE.[25] The coalition between the national army and the Indigenous insurgents was so strong that it shows why Indigenous people increasingly cooperated with other groups when they mobilized. Over 10,000 Indigenous people set up camp in

Map 14.1 Recent Indigenous Movements and Uprisings in Latin America

Quito. Many thousands more blocked major highways throughout the nation to paralyze the infrastructure; clearly complicit with the uprising, police and the army merely observed events without stopping the protests. On January 22, while Indigenous people besieged the National Congress and Supreme Court, the CONAIE, the military, and the former Supreme Court president then formed a Government of National Salvation. Within hours, this new governing body installed Vice-President Gustavo Noboa as the new national president.[26]

Indigenous people provided the social and numerical power necessary to force political change, yet they actually benefitted little from the uprising, because a different group of elites simply claimed power. President Noboa immediately pegged the Ecuadorian *sucre* to the U.S. dollar over fierce opposition because of the inflationary results. Inflation by this time was over 60 percent in Ecuador, the highest rate in Latin America, because the decline in oil export prices had increased public debt service during the late 1990s.[27] The Native struggle continued. Antonio Vargas, president of CONAIE, declared: "we were betrayed by a treacherous clique of generals and admirals, but our struggle is not over, and we may have to be even tougher when we mobilize again.... What occurred on January 21 was a rehearsal." Completely disillusioned, Indigenous people left the capital declaring Túpac Katari's spirited promise to return, and the next time in their millions.[28]

Indigenous people shook Latin America from end to end with protests, political mobilizations, and marches during the first year of the new millennium: the year 2000 proved momentous. In Bolivia, political and economic crises provoked by economic liberalization complicated the preparations for the 2002 presidential elections. The privatization of hydrocarbons and sales of state telecommunications, railroad, and airline industries in the late 1990s cost thousands of jobs and billions to Bolivia, making life for the peasants and Indigenous people even more difficult. Regardless, in April, Cochabamba privatized and sold the municipal water system to Aguas del Tunari, 27.5 percent of which was owned by energy company Bechtel Corporation, and which dramatically raised water distribution rates across the board. People throughout Cochabamba, including surrounding peasants, Indigenous peoples, the Strike Coordination Committee, and rural coca producers, closed down the city between January 1999 and April 2000. State employees and truck drivers across Bolivia also went on strike.

The Bolivian crisis revealed divisions between Indigenous peoples and their interests. In early July 2000, 500 Indigenous leaders gathered in Santa Cruz for a "Grand Assembly," despite cold rains and poor infrastructure. The CIDOB and the government reached agreements on health, education, and housing, yet lowland Amazonian Indigenous people disputed the deal since it did not address land demarcation. Divisions between the Aymara, led by the radical Felipe Quispe, head of the CSUTCB and known as "The Condor," and the Cocalero followers of Evo Morales, made the CSUTCB less effective; both men wanted to head up the organization. When the coca growers shut off the highways between Santa Cruz, Cochabamba, and La Paz in support of Morales, Quispe declared the creation of an independent Aymara state and military high command. Road closures and strikes in Bolivia resemble the ways in which labor organizers in the Industrial Workers of the World picketed, violated legal ordinances, and struck to unionize in the United States during the years before World War I.[29] African Americans later carried out hundreds of similar protests to defy racial segregation during the 1950s and 1960s.[30]

By September, civil disobedience had paralyzed Bolivia and critics blamed both the Aymara and the coca growers for the crisis. The CIDOB demonstrations turned violent as federal troops shot demonstrators in La Paz and Cochabamba. To help resolve the conflict, the government promised the Aymara a $26 million development project to improve their region, including 1,000 new tractors. In addition, Bolivia assigned new lands to lowland Indigenous people and appointed a Western Guaraní leader from the area to head a new Vice Ministry of Indigenous and Original Peoples' Affairs. Quispe, for his part, formed a new Indigenous political party, the MIP or "Pachakuti Indigenous Movement." By 2002, the nation had failed to keep any of these promises. Bolivian conflicts were multifaceted and complicated; they show that Indigenous people did not present a united response to neoliberal state programs, nor to broader Indigenous organizations. The atomized character of Indigenous activism challenged their effectiveness throughout the following decade.

Conditions in Chiapas, Mexico also continued to be tense as the country headed into the national elections of 2000. The victory of businessperson Vicente Fox, from the opposition National Action Party, possibly averted significant violence. During his campaign, Fox had declared that if he and Subcomandante Marcos of the Zapatistas could just talk together for 15 minutes, they would resolve all the problems in Chiapas. Indigenous people therefore pressured Fox for a resolution. Fox's first act was to push for implementation of the San Andrés Accords with the EZLN to resolve the uprising. The Zapatistas accelerated this agenda by converging in Mexico City on February 24, 2000 in the March for Dignity. Indigenous people from across Mexico joined this demonstration, and hundreds of thousands of people welcomed them to the capital. At the end of November 2000, immediately before his inauguration, the EZLN sent Fox three "good-will" provisions that they hoped he would act upon, requesting freedom for Zapatista prisoners, the demilitarization of seven Zapatista communities, and implementation of the San Andrés Accords, and waited for the new president to act.[31]

For Document 14.1: Selections from The San Andrés Peace Accords, visit www.routledge.com/9780415519120.

Other Indigenous people throughout Mexico likewise demanded greater autonomy and faced off against troops. Most notable in 2000 were the protests of the Yaqui in Sonora, and the Huichol (Wixárika) of Nayarit and Jalisco, as well as the Kumiai of northern Baja California, who all created organizations to protest ranching threats and held summits to strengthen their cultures. The Insurgent Peoples' Revolutionary Army in Guerrero, Mexico, formed in 1996 to overthrow Mexico's national government and composed mainly of Mixteco people, attacked Mexican federal troops on numerous occasions.[32] Simmering conflicts became festering challenges to Fox's new government, as well as for Native people seeking political rights.

Back in Ecuador, relations between Indigenous organizations and the state continued to be tense. President Noboa promised to repress any future strikes. Nevertheless, in January 2000, the CONAIE mobilized Indigenous people throughout the nation for yet another demonstration. As people traveled toward Quito for the strike, police pulled them off of buses and stopped their attempts to block roads. Troops surrounded the traditional campsite of the strikers and cordoned off the Salesian University to prevent food and supplies getting through to the protestors. Demonstrators won support by staying nonviolent though, in sharp contrast to the brutality of the state troops, which the media highlighted. Pressure mounted until Noboa met with CONAIE leaders and hammered out 21 points on everything from lowering gasoline prices to extending credit to small businesses. By gaining a negotiating position that achieved their key demands, the Native organization successfully pushed its agenda of "pluricultural" administration, a significant step toward political representation.[33]

Mexico under Fox, however, did not improve for Native people. Pressured by the EZLN, at the end of April 2001 Mexico's Congress passed a law on Indigenous rights and culture. Native supporters at first saw the legislation as a victory and recognition of their rights, a just reward for the Zapatista's recent March for Dignity. Yet it was soon evident that the law was another attempt to mollify Native activists. The final legislation was an altered version of the same COCOPA proposal of 1996 that completely undermined the goals of Indigenous autonomy and self-determination. Mexican legislators changed the spirit of the draft bill to make it meaningless. The new law made Indigenous people "objects of public interest" rather than "subjects of public law" to deny them rights.[34] The difference is substantive: while subjects are active, objects are only passive – instruments shaped by other forces.

The National Indigenous Congress, the EZLN, and other opposition parties immediately rejected the legislation and cut off communication with the government. Subcomandante Marcos declared that a better name for the bill would have been the "Constitutional Recognition of the Rights and Culture of the Landowners and Racists."[35] Allies filed nearly 300 constitutional complaints against this law for failing to recognize Native people as legal subjects and for denying them the right to use their own resources. If that deception were not enough, President Fox and other Central American leaders then ratified "Plan Puebla Panama," to completely develop and privatize the entire isthmus from Chiapas through Central America to Colombia.

While Indigenous people in Mexico fought privatization and state co-optation, Native cultures and ways of life continued to change. By this time, Native people worked in all types of jobs throughout the continent. In Cauca, Colombia, people elected Taita Floro Tunubalá to serve as governor of Popayán, in the *resguardo* of Guambía, between 2001 and 2004. This Guambíano leader had earned a university degree, had worked as a development consultant, and had even served as a national senator. Taita Floro highlighted his indigeneity by dressing in the traditional blue kilt, black poncho, and fedora hat, yet concurrently served the broader community; only 30 percent of his constituents considered themselves Indigenous, so his election showed broad trust in his skillful leadership.

A serious conflict developed in Cauca in June 2002, when Indigenous leaders in Caldono blocked the Pan-American Highway and demanded that Taita Floro fire their municipal mayor. *Cabildos* from across Cauca, supported by the CRIC, sent representatives to the huge tent city of hundreds of protestors protected by an Indigenous guard. Within hours, Floro negotiated the conflict and explained his quandary: as a Native politician, he represented both Indigenous and mestizo members of the broader Caucan society, each of which used sovereignty and culture to strengthen their position. Finally, the governor fell back on the Native strategy of compromise: he convinced protestors to open the highway and formed a group that finally created "Indigenous territorial entities," the geo-administrative units governed by Native people that the 1991 Constitution was supposed to have organized.[36]

On Honduras' northern Caribbean coast, meanwhile, the Garifuna people formed the Black Fraternal Organization of Honduras (OFRANEH) and the Ethnic Community Development Organization (ODECO), around their unique African-Indigenous cultural heritage, to link the Garifuna with international aid agencies. During the late 1990s, the Garifuna mobilized over 5,000 people for the "First Grand Peaceful March of the Black People of Honduras," which pressured the government to enlarge their land grant and give them the titles to their properties. As a result, by 2002 most communities had received ownership titles to significant areas of their land.[37]

Indigenous Organization in Andean Nations Reaches a High Mark

Indigenous activists in the Andes during this time were involved in the Bolivian Gas War, although internal disputes also divided their communities. Local demonstrations were part of a surge in popular opposition to the proposed Free Trade Agreement of the Americas and its local implementation, which included such neoliberal measures as privatization of water delivery and plans for the exportation of Bolivian gas to California. As part of these protests, workers and students in the neighborhood of El Alto, above La Paz, demonstrated against the sale of gas, which was supposed to raise local taxes on home construction. The CSUTCB negotiated with the government on behalf of the demonstrators, but when talks failed, Quispe led 1,000 Aymara volunteers on a hunger strike, and on top of that, threatened a civil war if the state militarized Indigenous regions. On September 15, 2003, the Aymara protestors shut down the city of Omasuyos and surrounding communities by blocking the roads; soon the entire La Paz department was inaccessible from outside and under community control.

Several organizations joined forces to lead the groundswell of opposition to neoliberal reforms in Bolivia. The first was the Coordinadora for the Defense and Recuperation of Gas, led by Oscar Olivera. Evo Morales and the political party Movement Toward Socialism (MAS) that Morales had helped found in 1998 was the second. Together, they organized over 50,000 people in La Paz and 20,000 more in Cochabamba to protest the export of gas. Olivera and Morales called for a blockade of the city, and Aymara community members traveled to La Paz by night on secret paths to avoid security forces, a strategy called Plan Añutaya after a small nocturnal fox-like animal which uses such trails. Quispe, the Aymara head of the CSUTCB, called off dialogue between his people and the state when the negotiations broke down, and prices for food doubled in the city after peasants stopped selling vegetables; in the following days, coca growers blocked roads and announced a general strike for September 30, 2003. Aymara radio stations called upon President Lozada to resign and the Aymara began a permanent mobilization. Over the next month, general strikes that included hundreds of miners who affirmed their Indigenous roots took place against the threatened export of gas. Protestors cut off the supply of gas to the city and by October had forced the military to use tanks and helicopters to bring in petroleum. In the ensuing street fights, police killed 54 civilians. The deaths strengthened liaisons within the Aymara, who presented national demands: besides the resignation of the president, the repeal of gas privatization, and rejection of the FTAA, they demanded a constitutional assembly. Over 100,000 Indigenous people and their supporters occupied Plaza San Francisco in La Paz on October 13, 2003.

Overwhelmed as the Aymara multitude took control of the city, police withdrew and the people deliberated in open assemblies as Bolivia ground to a standstill. By this time, the Aymara controlled the movement and the lack of centralized power made it difficult for the government to repress the uprising. Within three days, protestors had grown to 300,000 and hunger strikes in their favor spread to exiles in Argentina, Peru, Ecuador, and even Switzerland. Guaraní, Ayoreo, and other Native peoples in eastern Bolivia joined the hunger strike. President Sánchez de Lozada finally resigned on October 17, and when Vice-President Carlos Mesa assumed power, he promised to repeal the Hydrocarbons Law, sponsor a referendum on future hydrocarbon development, and host a new constitutional assembly.[38] Indigenous protests had rejected neoliberalism, brought down another Bolivian president, and changed their history.

Indigenous people throughout the continent continued to organize locally, in defense of their specific lands and identity, nationally in defense of their resources and rights, and internationally, to form liaisons throughout Latin America. In 2004, Indigenous people representing 64 different Native peoples throughout the Americas gathered in Quito for the Second Continental Summit of Indigenous Peoples and Nationalities of Abya Yala. After five days, the attendees issued their strongest statement yet on Native rights and demands. Nicia Maldonado, President of the National Indigenous Council of Venezuela (CONIVE), read the Declaration of Quito to conclude the meetings. The document denounced age-old abuses since the conquest and included current concerns. Indigenous people denounced the increasing use of violence to put down their mobilization. They opposed free trade pacts, as well as regional economic programs such as the South American Regional Plan for Infrastructure Integration (IIRSA), Plan Puebla Panama, Plan Patriota, Plan Colombia, Plan Dignidad, and Plan Andino.

> We also oppose the adoption of the FTAA and FTAs, which are fostered by the World Trade Organization for the benefit of the looter countries of the world. They only intend to create infrastructures to facilitate the circulation of their goods, to exploit natural resources on our lands and territories, and to protect transnational corporations. We consider them invasion plans for plundering, destruction and death.[39]

This encounter was the largest, broadest meeting of Indigenous people in Latin America to date.

Since the Indigenous people of Latin America mobilized so thoroughly and expressed themselves so vocally, it should follow that they were able to exert the political changes they desired in the nations where they constituted the large percentage of the population. Finally, conditions started to change in the political sphere. In Bolivia in May and early June 2005, between 400,000 and 500,000 Aymara from neighboring El Alto overran La Paz and forced President Carlos Mesa to resign.

Individuals: Evo Morales, Aymara President of Bolivia

The Aymara protests that ousted President Mesa called for greater control over Bolivia's natural gas reserves and showed the strength of the largest Indigenous people when they worked together. The central figure of this particular demonstration was Evo Morales, leader of 30,000 coca-farming families and head of MAS, the political party Movement Toward Socialism. An Aymara from the western department of Oruro, Morales was born into a subsistence farming family and had grown up herding llamas and selling popsicles while his father harvested sugar cane. After his formal education, Morales' family moved to Chapare Province to grow coca. Before the age of 30, Morales became the General Secretary of the Tropical Federation of Coca Growers. Activism in the coca trade led him into politics, and mobilizations for Indigenous rights led Morales to leadership of MAS. In 1997 he joined Bolivia's Congress, where he promoted Indigenous rights. In December 2005, Morales became the president of Bolivia, a nation of so many Indigenous people. Morales' story shows not only an impressive ascent to power but also the changing possibilities available to some Indigenous people.

Morales won the national election with 53.7 percent of the popular vote and confirmed his victory two and a half years later in a recall referendum, which he won by nearly two-thirds of the vote. The presidency of an Indigenous leader in a nation with such a divided population was controversial. Sociologist Silvia Rivera Cusicanqui, Morales' advisor on coca issues, argued that one problem was that MAS gradually lost its Indigenous profile and character as its power grew. Morales gradually lost the support of his Native political base. The U.S. drug eradication program also challenged Morales' rule by pressuring the coca farmers to stop growing coca, alienating the very people who had brought him to power. Seeing one of their own in the seat of power, though, encouraged Native people, despite their long road toward full equality. For example, MAS had difficulty in insisting that Bolivia offer public services in Aymara and Quechua.[40] Under Morales' rule, women's organizations, such as the Federation of Women Coca Growers, gained recognition as representatives of large women's majorities, especially Indigenous women. Postcolonial analysts have also highlighted the important role that women played throughout the world during this time as they opposed misogynist practices of concubinage, polygamy, and forms of enslavement. These movements were part of growing organization by Indigenous peoples around the world who created bonds based on ethnic, religious, and communal ties to oppose Western control and manipulation.[41] More controversial in Bolivia, though, were Morales' overtures to foreign leaders who challenged the Washington Consensus: Hugo Chávez in Venezuela and Lula da Silva in Brazil became his allies.

As their political influence grew, Indigenous people extended mutual support to other subaltern groups. In Mexico in November 2006, 200 Tzotzil women and men, members of the nonviolent Las Abejas community in Chiapas, organized a peace and justice caravan to support the Popular Assembly of the Peoples of Oaxaca, a public demonstration and a teachers' strike that had been taking place in the main square of Oaxaca City once a year for 20 years. In 2006, the teachers and public workers struck for higher wages and better working conditions and denounced the continued state and federal violence in the area. The Tzotzil delivered over three tons of food, water, and medicines to the Oaxacan Assembly, showing support for other powerless groups trying to improve their situation.

During the last week of March 2007, Indigenous people from throughout Latin America gathered in Iximché, Guatemala for the Third Continental Summit of Indigenous Peoples and Nationalities of Abya Yala, this time entitled "From Resistance to Power." Given Morales' recent rise to the presidency, conference attendees debated strategies for challenging and engaging governments. Central to their deliberations was the divisive consideration about whether to pursue ethnic "indianist" paths or rather the leftist "Popular" avenue to political influence, and which of these strategies would prove most profitable for Indigenous people. Traditional Native diversity also prevented them from declaring national sovereignty through the power of their number, but at the same time that diversity was beneficial in that it also prevented centralized powers

Figure 14.1 Cocaleros (Coca Growers) Celebrate the Popular Election of their Leader in Coroico, Bolivia. (Andres Felipe Carulla/Alamy Stock Photo)

from destroying a single Indigenous agency. The tension between strength in unity versus strength in diversity has been key to the Indigenous struggles in Latin America.[42] Delegates to the conference celebrated Morales' election in Bolivia and discussed ways to transform their own governments into states that reflected Native values of coalition, equal participation, dignity, and sustainable coexistence with the planet.[43] Even as divisions between the people emerged, the conference at Iximché reflected the highest level of unity achieved thus far by the continental Indigenous movement.

As if to more broadly recognize this Indigenous organization and its growing influence, in September 2007, the 62nd General Assembly of the United Nations adopted the Declaration on the Rights of Indigenous Peoples. The document rejected all racial and ethnic discrimination and affirmed that all peoples contribute to the diversity and richness of civilization and culture. The assembly recognized that Indigenous peoples suffered from the injustices of colonization, the dispossession of their lands and resources, and lack of control over economic, environmental, and social development that affected them. The U.N. welcomed growing Indigenous organization for political, economic, social, and cultural enhancement. The first article proclaimed:

> Indigenous peoples have the right to the full enjoyment, as a collective or as individuals, of all human rights and fundamental freedoms as recognized in the Charter of the United Nations, the Universal Declaration of Human Rights and international human rights law.

Article 11 declared:

> Indigenous peoples have the right to practice and revitalize their cultural traditions and customs. This includes the right to maintain, protect, and develop the past, present, and future manifestations of their cultures, such as archaeological and historical sites, artifacts, designs, ceremonies, technologies, and visual and performing arts and literature.

Article 12 decreed that Indigenous people have the

> right to manifest, practice, develop, and teach their spiritual and religious traditions, customs and ceremonies; the right to maintain, protect, and have access in privacy to their religious and cultural sites; the right to the use and control of their ceremonial objects; and the right to the repatriation of their human remains.[44]

The Declaration on the Rights of Indigenous Peoples carried no political weight to force compliance among nations, nor did it indicate any type of restitution for Indigenous peoples because of past injustices and loss of land. Nevertheless, the document showed that the world recognized the legitimacy of Indigenous demands for greater justice after their preceding decades of activism.

For Document 14.2: United Nations Declaration on the Rights of Indigenous Peoples, September 13, 2007, visit www.routledge.com/9780415519120.

New Strategies of Indigenous Organization

International recognition of Indigenous troubles and their demands for social justice reflected broader political and popular trends in Latin America. Pressured by the lower classes who were disillusioned by neoliberal economics and the inequalities they aggravated, as well as by the weight of the Washington Consensus, by the end of the decade some Latin American nations had turned from neoliberalism back to the time-tested strategy of nationalism. Luiz Inácio Lula da Silva began his second term as president of Brazil in 2006, and his economy weathered the global recession that began in 2008 remarkably well. In Venezuela, Hugo Chávez experimented with a pink form of populism that garnered broad popular support for his program to socialize the country; the 2009 constitutional referendum allowed him indefinite re-election. In Bolivia, Evo Morales and the MAS party enjoyed enough widespread support to enact a new constitution in 2009 and improve the situation of the Native majority. A former priest named Fernando Lugo won the presidency of Paraguay in April 2008 and positioned himself alongside Evo and Chávez as a nationalist leader. Paraguay's lower classes celebrated the ousting of Stroessner's corrupt Colorado Party in the streets of Asunción. Mexico and Colombia remained exceptions to the nationalist trend and continued as close economic and military allies of the United States.

Despite their widespread organization and opposition to neoliberal economics, Native peoples did not fare much better in the nationalist states than in the ones that remained allies of the U.S., with the exception of Bolivia and Venezuela. Indigenous people continued to organize internationally: during the last week of May 2009, 6,000 Indigenous peoples from the Americas gathered for the Fourth Continental Summit of

Indigenous Peoples and Nationalities of Abya Yala in the Peruvian highland city of Puno. Two thousand women met for the First Indigenous Women's Summit to focus on the role of Native women in forging plurinational states and in building power and democracy. The fourth Summit opened with debates about the crises in deteriorating living conditions that neoliberal policies and economics had caused for lower classes throughout the continent. Then attendees focused on improving living conditions and forging plurinational states, which became the main themes of the summit. The Quechua concept of *sumac kawsay*, of living well, symbolized the Native opposition to corporate and state programs for development usually associated with the extraction of resources such as petroleum and minerals like tin and gold.

In contrast with Western emphases for development focused on consumption and the overuse of resources, blamed for the growing environmental crisis that profoundly affects Native people, delegates at the summit proposed alternatives based on Indigenous concepts. Mario Palacios, from the Peruvian Amazon and head of the National Confederation of Communities Affected by Mining (CONACAMI), representing more than 1,200 Indigenous communities in 9 regions of Peru, declared: "Development should be in harmony with Mother Earth, with nature, not destroy it. We have to overcome the irrational use of resources and respect the rights of Indigenous peoples."[45] The pan-Indigenous gathering approved the Lake Titikaka Declaration, which called for alternatives to the capitalist crisis in Western civilization. The document requested decriminalization of the coca leaf, support for the Cuban revolution, and an end to the Israeli occupation of the Palestinian territories. More broadly, delegates recognized that Western civilization was undergoing a severe environmental and financial collapse that was destroying the planet. The alternative proposals for development included plurinationalism, following the Native model of "living well," and the formation of an international climate justice tribunal to prosecute businesses and nations that harmed the environment.[46]

For Document 14.3: The Lake Titikaka Declaration of the Fourth Continental Summit of Indigenous Peoples and Nationalities of Abya Yala, NACLA, June 2009, visit www.routledge.com/9780415519120.

Despite broad Indigenous organization, conditions at the grassroots level continued to be difficult. Multinational corporations and their local allied companies continue to extract resources throughout Central and South America, and Native peoples are faced with the results, though they are fighting back with all available tools. Recently, for instance, Mam communities in southwestern Guatemala faced attacks and even death for opposing the extraction of gold from their area in the Department of San Marcos, west of Queltzaltenango. The Canadian Goldcorp, one the world's largest gold producers, opened the Marlin mine in the highlands of San Marcos in 2006. The operation threatened the 18 Mam communities in the area and the company met their protests with violence.

Community coordinator Aniceto López and Miguel Bámaca, a farmer and public health promoter, received beatings in February 2011 for protesting the mine. Bámaca, who was shot at outside his home in July 2010, denounced the power of the company attackers, who "know what we do, where we live, when people meet ... they know everything. Who will help us? The government, the courts, the police, they are not helping." Maudilla López, a Mam woman, declared, "Our spirituality, our vision is that there is harmony between nature, people, and God, we are together and there is balance in our lives.... This mining activity puts our cultural values in danger."[47] The attempt

Figure 14.2 Fourth Continental Summit of Indigenous Peoples and Nationalities of Abya Yala. (Photo by Marc Becker)

by the Mam to counter and close the gold-mine through legal means proved a difficult, dangerous, and ultimately futile community struggle. Goldcorp's earnings continued undeterred, and by 2010 their total assets surpassed the GDP of Guatemala. As it had been during the conquest over 500 years earlier, extractivism focused on gold is still an important point of contact and conflict between Native people and outsiders. Indigenous people in Latin America have succeeded in bringing attention to their plight, and have worked together at a continental level, but these successes have still not ended abuses in many local situations where conditions continue to be difficult.

Conclusions: Opening the New Millennium

By the year 2000, Indigenous peoples had created strong alliances throughout Latin America. In a few cases, Natives and their allies toppled presidents and became leaders of states themselves. The Zapatista movement in Chiapas focused attention on their opposition to neoliberal economic programs and exposed the limits of Indigenous political participation. Joining forces with other subaltern groups, Indigenous peoples mobilized to improve their living conditions, defend their land, and protect natural resources. Even though in many cases their efforts were unsuccessful, there is no doubt that their situations would have been even worse had the Indigenous groups not protested the poor treatment of their people and the environment.

Indigenous protests during the final decades of the twentieth century largely resorted to nonviolent strategies owing to superior state firepower. Native communities refined civil disobedience strategies and engaged in marches, sit-ins, symbolic acts of sabotage, pickets, blockades, and strikes to emphasize their noncompliance with state and business policies. Still, some Native organizations employed violence when they had exhausted other options and faced seemingly unsurmountable obstacles. The EZLN forces attracted broad attention to Indigenous causes in southern Mexico and their armed resistance led to negotiations with government administrators. Their rebel demands continue to be unresolved despite repeated marches to the capital and ongoing negotiations. The militarization of Chiapas challenges the Indigenous people of the Mexican state.

Communications and transportation innovations made possible broader Indigenous unity and cooperation during this period, but also changed Indigenous ways of life as they participated more fully in national politics and events. The first decade of the second millennium saw even broader organization by Indigenous people throughout Latin America, yet also raised tensions within local communities and at the level of the nation states. Morales' rise to Bolivia's presidency highlighted the challenges prompted by Indigenous access to power, but also the benefits of broader organization amid the challenging conditions produced by the continental shift to neoliberal economic policies and their social results. Even as growing extractivism challenged their communities, Indigenous people had proven their ability to remain part of the unfolding historical tapestry of Latin America.

Discussion Questions

1. What would happen if nation states granted political autonomy to Indigenous peoples?
2. Why did the EZLN attract so much media attention?
3. Were Indigenous people in Bolivia and Ecuador better organized than in other nations?
4. How effective were the Native civil disobedience movements described in this chapter?
5. What made it difficult for Indigenous people to join forces as one united organization?

Notes

1 Postcolonial theorists included Castro among the "foreign devils" who the U.S. tried to assassinate. See Said, *Culture and Imperialism*, 315.
2 Macas, *El levantamiento indígena*, 3.
3 The name refers to the renowned Inca Pachakuti Inca Yupanqui (1438–1471), who expanded the empire by defeating the Chancas people in southeastern Peru.
4 Becker, *Indians and Leftists*, 175–176.
5 Said, *Culture and Imperialism*, 7.
6 Bush, *Imperialism and Postcolonialism*, 152.
7 Young, *Postcolonialism*, 21.
8 Ramos, *Indigenism*, 267–268.
9 Dean, "State Power and Indigenous Peoples," 203–205.
10 Hale, "Rethinking Indigenous Politics," 16–19.
11 Jackson, "Caught in the Crossfire," 112–114.
12 Horst, *The Stroessner Regime*, 156–159.
13 Zinn, *A Power Governments Cannot Suppress*, 136–137.
14 *Amazon Journal*, film by Geoffrey O'Connor.
15 United Nations, General Assembly, October 24, 2005, 60/1, *2005 World Summit Outcome.*
16 For an example of criticism of Menchu's work see Stoll, *Rigoberta Menchú and the Story of all Poor Guatemalans.*
17 Macdonald, "Ecuador's Indian Movement," 182–183.

18 Dean, "State Power and Indigenous Peoples, 212–214.
19 Macdonald, "Ecuador's Indian Movement," 184.
20 "Barbados Declaration III: Articulation of Diversity," from *Abya Yala News*.
21 Gustafson, "Paradoxes of Liberal Indigenismo," 282–283.
22 *San Andres Accords*, January 18, 1996, translated by Rosalva Bermudez-Ballin, available at http://flag.blackened.net/revolt/mexico/ezln/san_andres.html.
23 Polanco, *Indigenous Peoples in Latin America*, 73.
24 Jackson, "Caught in the Crossfire," 122, 142, 118.
25 On the deteriorating economy and escalation to the coup see O'Connor, "Indians and National Salvation," 67.
26 Macdonald, "Ecuador's Indian Movement," 170.
27 Jacome and Louis, "The Late 1990s Financial Crisis in Ecuador," 7–8.
28 Becker, *Indians and Leftists*, 186–187.
29 Zinn, *A Power Governments Cannot Suppress*, 134.
30 Zinn, *A People's History of the United States*, 450.
31 Levi, "A New Dawn or a Cycle Restored?," 36.
32 Ibid., 20–22.
33 Macdonald, "Ecuador's Indian Movement," 189.
34 Levi, "A New Dawn or a Cycle Restored?," 36.
35 Wortham, *Indigenous Media in Mexico*, 30.
36 Rappaport, "Between Sovereignty and Culture," 123–130.
37 Thorne, "Land Rights and Garífuna Identity," 24–25.
38 Hylton and Thomson, *Revolutionary Horizons*, 110–117.
39 www.cumbreindigenabyayala.org (accessed April 25, 2012).
40 Farthing, "Everything is up for Discussion," 5–7.
41 Said, *Culture and Imperialism*, 218.
42 Becker, "Third Continental Summit," 86.
43 On alternative Indigenous perspectives of political rule see Mallon, "Indian Communities," 52.
44 UN Declaration on the Rights of Indigenous Peoples.
45 Becker, "Fourth Continental Summit," 71–72.
46 Ibid., 74.
47 Hufstader, "Marlin Mine: Violence and Pollution," n.p.

Conclusion

Moving Ahead with Indigenous History in Mind

Over 500 years of history show that Native people are not going to disappear, quietly integrated into national societies as minority peoples, museum specimens of the past, or even as impoverished peasants. They are here to stay, and disease, genocidal government policies, racism, and state development projects will not destroy them. Indigenous people will increasingly become the political, economic, and public leaders helping to shape the future of the nations in which they live. It is to everyone's benefit to learn from Indigenous peoples, to invite them to share their ideas, and to honor and defend their choices, even when they diverge from nationalistic wishes. Native cultural examples also suggest that toleration of different and plural ways of political and social organization, including toleration for differing ways of being human, is in the long term beneficial to everyone.

There is much to learn from Indigenous people that can benefit humanity. Their history shows that Native people are not "tree-huggers" who are biologically driven to love and protect the natural environment. Indigenous people farmed and altered Amazonia, as Charles Mann argued, for thousands of years before the Europeans arrived. The Beni, for instance, completely altered their environment in what is today eastern Bolivia over 1,000 years ago. Archeologists Clark Erickson and William Balée have shown that these people built huge mounds upon which the forest grew, as high as 60 feet above the forest floor. Raised bridges of up to three miles in length connected the islands and served as fences to corral fish during the rainy season. Hundreds of thousands of people worked on these huge engineering projects, managing their grasslands, fish farms, and fashioning the environment to meet their needs.[1] Clearly, these people were not environmentalists in a militant sense, since they shaped, altered, and managed their surrounding forests to meet their own political, economic, and social goals. Nevertheless, they depended on their environment for a living and learned to manage it to perpetuate the longevity of their society, and their concerted work to defend their longevity is an example worthy of our consideration.

Many years of sustainable life by Indigenous people in interaction with and dependence on natural resources in ways that differ from Western models do reveal insights on how to use resources without destroying future life. Perhaps a smaller scale approach to environmental policies, rather than the imperial model, will benefit humans in the long term, despite the growth of our population. Learning from more sustainable Native approaches to the environment, even if begun on a small scale, can only improve our longer term survival prospects. Indigenous history shows that not all people need to pursue the Western path heading toward environmental challenges and the consolidation of political authority in a few imperialistic states.

Another insight gained from Indigenous history is that far too often, racism and prejudice have justified the theft of Native resources and the refusal to heed the voices and desires of the affected Native populations. Indigenous people, the majority of whom live in daily interaction with non-Indigenous society, should be treated as fully human beings capable of making their own political, economic, social, and religious choices. Non-Indigenous people and their governments must learn to respect those Native choices even if they are minority views within a larger, plural society. As our society becomes more diverse, opposition to racism and increased inclusivity should become part of every educational program. Schools could increase instruction on inclusivity, acceptance of cultural differences, and toleration of alternative ways of life. Many such efforts have already begun, with notable successes, but more can be done. To the degree that Indigenous history shows alternative models to prejudice, it points to different possible paths toward greater inclusivity. We can all benefit from embracing broader plurality and the Native model of dialogue and consensus building within communities, rather than the imposition of political choices from above in the traditional Western political framework. Listening to each other's dreams, ideas, plans, and solutions may favor our species going forward.

Indigenous histories point to concrete measures that nations should adopt in order to begin to make amends for the damages caused to Indigenous peoples. Most significantly, nations should begin to listen to Indigenous demands for respect, and safeguard their Native populations from threats by non-Indigenous people or foreign companies. Native groups should be allowed to decide for themselves the degree to which they desire interaction with national ideas and societies. They should be free to reject outside religious, cultural, and political ideas and impositions. Indigenous lands and resources should be designated for them by the government and then protected from outside invasions and exploitation. If Indigenous peoples choose to sell their resources, governments should make sure that the proceeds return completely to the Native communities. Indigenous people who refuse to sell their lands and move out of the way of "development" projects should be allowed to stay in their homes, use their own resources as they see fit, and their communal desires should be respected. Their well-being and interests should outweigh national programs. National "development" projects should be altered instead of people and their ways of life.

No one is suggesting that we turn back the clock to pre-Columbian days – rather, to recognize injustices and repair them where possible. These are some reasons why studying Indigenous histories and cultures is valuable. Each Native way of life and historical path is important because it illustrates a different way and experience of being human on our planet, a unique human adaptation to a different environmental and historical context. Just as protecting biodiversity is vital because we do not yet know which plants and animals might help us heal a disease or solve a yet-unknown future challenge, we should also learn about and protect the vast diversity of human languages, cultures, and experiences because they help us understand who we are as people and where our species has been, and how to think about ways of navigating our common future as the world continues to change.

It goes without saying that we cannot just erase more than 500 years of interaction between Indigenous, Africans, Europeans, and other peoples in the Americas. Colonial exchanges and the way they altered people and cultures around the world are historical events that cannot be changed. What we can do now is learn from past experiences, deal with the results, and hopefully try to help to make these types of exchanges more equitable for today and tomorrow. To what degree should anyone be responsible for injustices committed by their ancestors, and what measures might absolve or even correct those wrongs? If the United States could quantify all the income it earned from the African slave trade, and then pay that amount back to African and African American people, would it solve our own racial tensions and the problems in the African states? Even if European governments would deconstruct all their cities, empty their bank accounts, turn over all the silver taken from Abya Yala back to the Native people, and then all return to Europe, it would not resolve Indigenous problems and would in fact only create more. No, we must live and learn from our past, using it to plan creatively for the future.

What is needed instead is greater respect for cultural differences and alternative priorities, as well as lots of dialogue. Both Indigenous peoples and national governments have the opportunity to make the future better by talking and then working together. Native people should recognize that past injustices were committed by other people in vastly different contexts that cannot and will not be relived, and instead agree to move forward to negotiate and resolve current challenges. Many Indigenous people are working hard to improve their current situations through education, lobbying political structures to protect their lands and resources, and reaching across group barriers to organize themselves as Indigenous blocs that can exert political influence and change. Such changes take time, however, and can often seem futile or hopeless given the obstacles. Part of the struggle is to keep alive and pass on to one's children those Indigenous languages, traditions, worldviews, and stories that make each people unique, even while learning to survive and live in an environment controlled by others, some of whom are prejudiced and bigoted. Persistence and time have sometimes worked successfully for some peoples in such struggles.

A more difficult option toward achieving greater social parity is to take or gain political control of nations. This experience presents both answers and further challenges, as Morales' recent path in Bolivia shows; still, where they have a numerical advantage, Indigenous people might consider political power to be their best option. History nevertheless shows that taking power by force, as did the Spanish and Portuguese colonists, as well as the Mexica and Quechua people, is a temporary measure that often creates more problems than it solves. Working within the established legal and political system to protect and defend their indigeneity and resources seems to be the best viable option for Native peoples.

National governments, for their part, should listen to and honor Indigenous wishes for greater self-governance, respect, and ownership of their lands and resources. Where Native groups desire autonomy, their areas should be demarcated and tribal lands returned, their territorial choices respected, and the resources on their lands protected by the authorities. Indigenous people should receive fair compensation for the sale of their labor, resources, and products. They should equally be respected should they choose not to participate in the broader market economy. Those groups that wish for greater involvement in national political decisions and economies should have the opportunity to compete for representation in governments and in the choices that shape the course of the countries in which they live. Educational systems throughout the Americas can play a vital role in positive change. Further instruction in acceptance, inclusion, in the toleration of diversity and ethnic differences, and the encouragement of respect for differing cultural and religious traditions may increase respect and enhance tolerance. We outsiders could learn to better understand but not commodify ethnic and cultural differences, to tolerate and respect different ways of life, and to ensure that state services are shared fairly among people within our national borders.

There are different models that a future together might adopt. One option for relating to Indigenous people is the expansion of the reservation system used already in several Latin American countries, including Colombia and Argentina, where Indigenous peoples have very limited self-control over specified portions of land within the broader nation state. Allowing Native peoples to choose their own patterns and degrees of interaction with outsiders within an enveloping state seems to be another viable option, as is occurring already in some nations, although national political choices always have Indigenous possibilities. The designation of parts of cities, counties, or even nations as Indigenous territories or homelands, and then encouraging those areas to grow economically through interaction with outside market forces, may also be a viable option, although South Africa has shown the challenges this model presents for economic distribution.[2]

Another possibility would be to grant Native people self-rule and political independence, allowing the creation of small Indigenous nation states or small independent states encapsulated within the larger established nations. While at first the idea of reshaping countries may seem impossible because national borders are defended and seemingly already permanent, remember that the concept of national sovereignty is a recent development in human history and that it will likely change again in the future. If this idea also seems impractical, recall that currently some very small nations in Europe, such as Monaco, Andorra, and the Vatican City, function very effectively as independent states. Some of them, like Israel, rely heavily on foreign support for survival. Why could not small, independent, Indigenous states encapsulated within larger nations in Latin America work with similar success? Native people could capitalize on ecotourism, gambling, or industry to turn a profit. Given the patriotic fervor with which countries defend their national patrimony, however, it seems unlikely that they might willingly give up sections of their territory to Native peoples for the creation of smaller independent states within their national borders.

The challenges at the heart of all these options seem to focus on differing economic conceptions of resource use, basically the differences between surplus or subsistence approaches to the use of natural resources.[3] The Western economic system and model of development is based on using natural resources to create staples and surplus commodities to then be sold to people who trade their labor for cash to buy those products. This structure ensures that the producers have an advantage over the consumers. Many smaller scale Native economies, on the other hand, have for a variety of reasons traditionally harvested resources without rapidly depleting the environment on which they depended, allowing them to live in the same area for a longer time without great wealth disparities. Even though Native societies also changed their ecosystems and environments over time, often radically so, their alterations were not drastic or fast enough in relation to their population size to completely destroy their life-support systems. Or, if they did, as in small-scale slash-and-burn societies, they would migrate periodically to allow the environment to recover. Different economic models and approaches to resource use such as green architecture that resemble or are even based on traditional Indigenous models and are more sustainable in the long term may be critical for our survival as a species. Without glorifying a utopian Native past that likely never existed, it is in our interest as a species on a global scale to seriously rethink our current capitalist economic model of interaction with the Earth, our life-support system, with a Native perspective of greater respect for our environment in mind. Given our limited resources, ballooning global population, and our current technical challenges for the colonization of space, it is also in our human interest to explore and reconsider ideas from Indigenous models of subsistence while we still depend for survival on planet Earth.

There are many ways to stay involved and to continue exploring the lives and experiences of Indigenous Latin Americans. Reading Indigenous history and learning more about Native experiences around the world is a great place to begin. Interacting with and learning from Indigenous people is another rewarding step. Visiting Latin America is also a way to learn more about its peoples. Becoming politically active and helping improve state policies for Indigenous people in one's own area or in Latin America from afar is also a path that some people find possible. Indigenous histories in Latin America show that Native people are not going to disappear. They are here to stay as important members of our societies, who will help to shape our future. The sooner governments and institutions begin to respect them and listen to their wishes, protect their lands, and defend their resources, and the sooner their rights are honored, the better off the communities, nations, and our entire continents will be. People throughout the Americas should take concrete steps to incorporate Indigenous peoples' political, social, religious, and economic choices into their national considerations. Educational programs along these lines are important, and we should work at learning from Native choices, ideas, and plans and then honoring those options as viable patterns to help guide our civilization. Listening to each other is critical, not only for Indigenous people but also for everyone. Peoples and their cultures are different in many ways, but all have a collective interest in living sustainably on Earth until other options become possible.

Notes

1 Mann, *1491*, 3–5. For more on archeologists Erickson and Balée see the Bibliography.
2 Anthropologist Héctor Díaz Polanco explores different political options for Native people in Part Two of his book *Indigenous Peoples in Latin America, the Quest for Self-Determination.*
3 Coates has an interesting discussion on similar ideas in *A Global History of Indigenous Peoples*, 268.

Glossary

Abya Yala Kuna name for "land of maturity" or "land of vital blood." Employed by Indigenous peoples to refer to the lands in the Americas before and outside of European heritage.

alcalde magistrate of a township; higher ranking alcaldes were referred to as *Alcalde Mayor*.

Americanos people of European descent who were born in the Americas, in order to distinguish themselves from those born in Europe, the Peninsulares.

audiencia Spanish judicial court used to administer royal authority.

ayllu an Indigenous community and local government in Andean regions.

Book of Chilam Balam Mayan prophetic text from the sixteenth to eighteenth centuries that foretold a return of the old ways and of the expulsion of white invaders.

butanmapo Reche strips of territories that were independently governed but also jointly ruled by a general assembly of chieftains from each territory. A toque-general ruled over all of the territories and was in charge of mobilizing warriors.

cabildo Native town councils in Mesoamerica.

cacica *see* cacique.

cacique governor of Indigenous communities in Mesoamerica, often of Indigenous descent, but frequently manipulated by Europeans governors of the territory. Also called a kuraka in the Andean region. A cacica is a female cacique.

caucho rubber latex, harvested from the Peruvian and Brazilian rainforest.

caudillo a political leader who ruled over multiple caciques through personal loyalty.

Chichimec bands of nomadic or semi-nomadic Indigenous people in present-day northern Mexico who were characterized by the Spanish as barbarians and raiders.

congregaciones Indigenous communities built around Spanish settlements as the traditional Indigenous communities changed. These Spanish settlements were often originally missions.

conquistador Spanish for "conqueror." Spanish soldiers who invaded the Americas during the fifteenth and sixteenth centuries.

corregidor royal official who governed districts, also an appointed Indigenous town leader.

creole a person of pure Spanish descent but born in the Americas. Also called a criollo.

criollo *see* creole.

Cruzob a nineteenth-century Indigenous rebellion in the Yucatan Peninsula.

ejido Indigenous communal lands in Mesoamerica; called resguardo in South America.

encomenderos recipients of encomiendas.

encomienda grant of Indigenous workers given to Spanish conquerors in return for converting the Natives to Christianity. Replaced by the repartimiento system of rotational labor after 1550.

fiscales Native assistants of Spanish Catholic leaders who collected taxes for the Church.

hacienda a large family farm or estate owned by one family to produce crops for local consumption.

hegemony social control exerted by one people over another, sometimes through negotiation.

huaca local spiritual objects or places often associated with origin stories.

indigeneity the self-identification of being an Indigenous person.

indigenismo political strategy to incorporate Indigenous peoples into the national society.

kuraka *see* cacique.

ladinos people of mixed Indigenous and Spanish heritage who were viewed as having lost their connection with their native community.

mercancías literally meaning merchandise, a system employed in the colonial system in which officials forced Indigenous people to purchase raw goods on credit for a high price and purchased the finished goods at a lower cost. Also called repartimiento.

mestizo a person of mixed race, usually of European and Indigenous heritage.

mit'a mandatory labor by Indigenous people to the ruling government. Originally started by the Inca Empire and then intensified by the Spanish colonial system and called mita.

mulatto a person of mixed European and African ancestry.

neocolonialism practice of one country controlling another country through economic pressure.

Peninsulares European people who lived in the New World but were born on the Iberian Peninsula.

pluricultural a person or people with multiple cultural identity, which allows them to belong to multiple cultural groups.

proselytism the act of attempting to convert a people to a different religion.

repartimiento *see* mercancías and encomienda.

requerimiento the document read out by Spanish soldiers before attacking an Indigenous village that gave people a chance to convert before being enslaved.

resguardo Indigenous communal lands in northwestern Latin America; *see* ejido.

royal fifth the 20 percent tax on mining collected by the Spanish Crown.

Serrano highland peoples in New Spain.

syncretism blending or fusion of different systems of beliefs.

transculturation the process of merging different cultures to create a new culture.

Triple Alliance a Mesoamerican alliance between Texcoco, Tlacopan, and Tenochtitlan city states that would form the Aztec Empire.

yanacona servants that ayllus sent to work on the Inca's private estates. Under Spanish rule, these were Native people who left communities to work in cities or on haciendas for cash to pay tribute and the repartimiento de mercancías.

Bibliography

Abercrombie, Thomas, "To Be Indian, to Be Bolivian: 'Ethnic' and 'National' Discourses of Identity," in Urban and Sherzer, *Nation-States and Indians in Latin America*, 95–130.

Acosta y Lara, Eduardo, *La Guerra de los Charruas en la Banda Oriental*, Montevideo, A. Monteverde y Cía, S.A., 1969.

Adams, Jerome R., *Notable Latin American Women: Twenty-Nine Leaders, Rebels, Poets, Battlers, and Spies, 1500–1900*, Jefferson, McFarland & Co, 1995.

Adams, Richard, "Strategies of Ethnic Survival in Central America," in Urban and Sherzer, *Nation-States and Indians in Latin America*, 181–206.

Adams, Richard, "Ethnic Images and Strategies in 1944," in Smith, *Guatemala Indians and the State*, 142–162.

Adrien, Kenneth and Adorno, Rolena, *Transatlantic Encounters, Europeans and Andeans in the Sixteenth Century*, Berkeley, University of California Press, 1991.

Albó, Xavier, "From MNRistas to Kataristas to Katari," in Stern, *Resistance, Rebellion, and Consciousness*, 379–419.

Álvaro, Jara, *Guerra y sociedad en Chile*, Santiago, Editorial Universitaria, 1961.

Anderson, Arthur J.O., Berdan, Frances, and Lockhart, James, *Beyond the Codices, The Nahua View of Colonial Mexico*, Berkeley, University of California Press, 1976.

Anderson, Benedict, *Imagined Communities, Reflections on the Origin and Spread of Nationalism*, London and New York, Verso, 1983, 1991–2003.

Arens, Richard, ed., *Genocide in Paraguay*, Philadelphia, PA, Temple University Press, 1976.

Ariza, S. and Alberto, E.O.P., Fr., *Los Domínicos en Panama*, Bogota, Cooperativa Nacional de Artes Gráficas, 1964.

Armand, Louis De, "Frontier Warfare in Colonial Chile," *Pacific Historical Review*, 23, 2, 1954, 125–132.

Arreola, Pablo Raúl, "Reorganization of Chile's Frontier Administration," *Canadian Journal of Latin American and Caribbean Studies*, 25, 50, 2000, 131–167.

Barreiro, José, *Panchito cacique de montaña: testimonio guajiro-taino de Francisco Ramírez Rojas*, Santiago de Cuba, Ediciones Catedral, 2001.

Barreiro, José and Johnson, Tim, *America is Indian Country, Opinions and Perspectives from Indian Country Today*, Golden, Fulcrum Publishing, 2005.

Barrett, Rafael, *El Dolor Paraguayo*, Caracas, Biblioteca Ayacucho, 1978.

Bauer, Arnold, "The Colonial Economy," in Hoberman and Socolow, *The Countryside in Colonial Latin America*, Albuquerque, University of New Mexico Press, 1996.

Bawden, Garth, *The Moche*, Cambridge, Blackwell, 1996.

Becker, Marc, *Indians and Leftists in the Making of Ecuador's Modern Indigenous Movements*, Durham and London, Duke University Press, 2008.

Becker, Marc, "Indigenous Nationalities in Ecuadorian Marxist Thought," *A Contra Corriente*, 5, 2, 2008, 1–46.

Becker, Marc, "Third Continental Summit of Indigenous Peoples and Nationalities of Abya Yala: From Resistance to Power," *Latin American and Caribbean Ethnic Studies*, 3, 1, 2008, 85–107.

Becker, Marc, "Fourth Continental Summit of Indigenous Peoples and Nationalities of Abya Yala," *Dialogo*, No. 13, summer 2010.

Becker, Marc, "Victoriano Lorenzo, the cholo guerrillero," *Canadian Journal of Latin American and Caribbean Studies*, 39, 2, 2014, 229–243.

Beezley, William H. and Meyer, Michael C., *The Oxford History of Mexico*, New York, Oxford University Press, 2000.

Behar, Ruth, "The Visions of a Guachichil Witch in 1599: A Window on the Subjugation of Mexico's Hunter-Gatherers," *Ethnohistory*, 34, 2, 1987, 115–138.

Belaieff, Juán, "Final Belaieff Report," in file "Reserved Notes on Troop Movements," Archives of Ministry of Defense, Asunción, September 10, 1928, 461–462.

Bengoa, José, *Historia del pueblo Mapuche (siglo XIX e XX)*, Santiago, Ediciones Sur, 1985.

Benson, Elizabeth P., *The Mochica, A Culture of Peru*, New York and Washington, Praeger Publishers, 1972.

Berger, Julian, *Report from the Frontier, The State of the World's Indigenous Peoples*, London, Zed Books, and Cambridge, Cultural Survival, 1987.

Bergreen, Laurence, *Columbus: The Four Voyages*, New York, Viking, 2011.

Bethell, Leslie, ed., *Brazil Empire and Republic, 1822–1930*, Cambridge, Cambridge University Press, 1989.

Bethencourt, Francisco, *The Inquisition: A Global History 1478–1834*, Cambridge, Cambridge University Press, 2009.

Beyer, Osvaldo, *Rebeldía y esperanza*, Buenos Aires, Group Editorial Zeta, 1993.

Binford, Leigh, *The El Mozote Massacre*, Tucson, The University of Arizona Press, 1996.

Black, George, *Triumph of the People: The Sandinista Revolution in Nicaragua*, London, Zed Press, 1981.

Block, David, *Mission Culture on the Upper Amazon, Native Tradition, Jesuit Enterprise, & Secular Policy in Moxos, 1660–1880*, Lincoln and London, University of Nebraska Press, 1994.

Boccara, Guillaume, *Guerre et ethnogenèse mapuche dans le chili colonial: l'invention du soi*, Paris and Montréal, L'Harmattan, 1998.

Bodley, John H., *Victims of Progress*, Menlo Park, Cummings Publishing, 1975.

Borah, Woodrow, *New Spain's Century of Depression*, Berkeley and Los Angeles, University of California Press, 1951.

Braunstein, José and Sbardella, Cirilo, "Las dos caras de la tragedia de Fortín Yunká," in *Hacia una nueva carta étnica del Gran Chaco*, II, 107–131.

Bricker, Victoria Reifler, *The Indian Christ, the Indian King: The Historical Substrate of Maya Myth and Ritual*, Austin, University of Texas Press, 1981.

Brysk, Alison, "Acting Globally: Indian Rights and International Politics in Latin America," in Van Cott, *Indigenous Peoples and Democracy*, 29–54.

Burkhart, Louise M., "The Solar Christ in Nahuatl Doctrinal Texts of Early Colonial Mexico," *Ethnohistory*, 35, 3, 1988, 234–256.

Burkholder, Mark and Johnson, Lyman, *Colonial Latin America* (8th edn), New York and Oxford, Oxford University Press, 2012.

Burns, E. Bradford, *A History of Brazil* (2nd edn), New York, Columbia University Press, 1980.

Bush, Barbara, *Imperialism and Postcolonialism*, London and New York, Pearson Longman, 2006.

Bushnell, David, *The Making of Modern Colombia, A Nation in Spite of Itself*, Berkeley, University of California Press, 1993.

Bushnell, David, ed., *Simón Bolivar, El Libertador, Writings of Simón Bolivar*, New York, Oxford University Press, 2003.

Bushnell, David and Macaulay, Neill, *The Emergence of Latin America in the Nineteenth Century*, New York, Oxford University Press, 1988.

Caminha, Pero Vaz de, *Carta a El Rei D. Manuel*, São Paulo, Dominus Editora S.A., 1963.

Campbell, Leon, "Ideology and Factionalism during the Great Rebellion, 1780–1782," in Stern, *Resistance, Rebellion, and Consciousness*, 110–139.

Campbell, Leon, "Women and the Great Rebellion in Peru, 1780–1783," *The Americas*, 42, 2, 1985, 163–196.

Caplan, Karen D., *Indigenous Citizens, Local Liberalism in Early National Oaxaca and Yucatán*, Stanford, CA, Stanford University Press, 2010.

Caraman, Philip, *The Lost Paradise, the Jesuit Republic in South America*, New York, Seabury Press, 1976.

Carcamo, Taren, *Grupos étnicos de Honduras*, available at www.monografias.com/trabajos93/grupos-etnicos-honduras/grupos-etnicos-honduras.shtml.

Cardoso, Fernando Henrique and Müller, Geraldo, *Amazônia: Expansão do capitalismo*, São Paulo, Brasiliense/ Centro Brasileiro de Análise e Planejamento, 1978.

Carey, Elaine, *Plaza of Sacrifices, Gender, Power, and Terror in 1968 Mexico*, Albuquerque, University of New Mexico Press, 2005.

Carrazzoni, José Andrés, *La epopeya del indio Andresito*, Buenos Aires, Editorial Dunken, 1999.

Carrera, Gabriela Bernal, "Dolores Cacuango and the Origin of the Mother Country: Seed for the Kichwizacion of the World," in Natividad Gutiérrez Chong, ed., *Women, Ethnicity and Nationalisms in Latin America*, Burlington, Ashgate Publishing Company, 2007, 29–52.

Carter, Miguel, *El Papel de la Iglesia en la Caida de Stroessner*, Asunción, RP Ediciones, 1989.

Casaldáliga, Pedro, *Uma igreja da Amazônia em conflito com o latifúndio e a marginalizaçao Social*, Mato Grosso, n.p., 1971. Cited in Garfield, *Indigenous Struggle at the Heart of Brazil*, 283.

Catoira, Patricia, "Transculturación à la Ajiaco: A Recipe for Modernity," in Mauricio Augusto Font and Alfonso W. Quiroz, *Cuban Counterpoints: The Legacy of Fernando Ortíz*, Lanham, MD, Lexington Books, 2005, 181–192.

Cayton, Andrew R.L. and Teute, Fredrika J., *Contact Points: American Frontiers from the Mohawk Valley to the Mississippi, 1750–1830*, Chapel Hill, University of North Carolina Press, 1998.

Chamberlain, Robert S., *The Conquest and Colonization of Yucatan, 1517–1550*, New York, Octagon Books, 1966.

Chance, John K., *Race and Class in Colonial Oaxaca*, Stanford, CA, Stanford University Press, 1978.

Chance, John K., *Conquest of the Sierra, Spaniards and Indians in Colonial Oaxaca*, Norman, University of Oklahma Press, 1989.

Chantre y Herrera, José, *Historia de las Misiones de la Campañia de Jesus en el Marañon Español, 1637–1767*, Madrid, Imprenta de A. Avrial, 1901.

Charney, Paul, "Negotiating Roots: Indian Migrants in the Lima Valley during the Colonial Period," in Kicza, *The Indian in Latin American History* (revised edn), 2000, ch. 6. First published 1993.

Chasteen, John Charles, *Born in Blood and Fire* (4th edn), New York and London, W.W. Norton, 2016.

Chaudhury, Sushil and Morineau, Michel, *Merchants, Companies and Trade, Europe and Asia in the Early Modern Era*, Cambridge, Cambridge University Press, 1999.

Chong, Natividad Gutierrez, ed., *Women, Ethnicity and Nationalisms in Latin America*, Hampshire and Burlington, Ashgate Publishing, 2007.

Christian, David, *Maps of Time, An Introduction to Big History*, Berkeley, Los Angeles, and London, University of California Press, 2005.

Chuchiak, John E., "'Fide non Armis': Franciscan reducciones, the Frontier Mission Experience and the Subjugation of the Mayan Hinterland, 1602–1640," in Schwaller, *Francis in the Americas*, 119–142.

"CLACS Welcomes Indigenous Rights Activist to Duke," Duke University Center for Latin America and Caribbean Studies, 2017.

Clayton, Lawrence A., *Bartolomé de las Casas and the Conquest of the Americas*, West Sussex, Blackwell, 2011.

Cleary, Edward L. and Steigenga, Timothy J., eds, *Resurgent Voices in Latin America. Indigenous Peoples, Political Mobilization and Religious Change*, New Brunswick and London, Rutgers University Press, 2001.

Clegern, Wayne M., *Origins of Liberal Dictatorship in Central America: Guatemala, 1864–1973*, Niwot, University of Colorado, 1994.

Clendinnen, Inga, *Ambivalent Conquests, Maya and Spaniard in Yucatan, 1517–1570*, Cambridge, Cambridge University Press, 1987.

Coates, Ken S., *A Global History of Indigenous Peoples, Struggle and Survival*, Basingstoke and New York, Palgrave Macmillan, 2004.

Cobo, Bernabe, *Inca Religion and Customs*, trans. Roland Hamilton, Austin, University of Texas Press, 1990.

Codice Chimalpopoca: Leyenda de los Soles, fol. 76–77, from the Annals of Cuauhtitlan, sixteenth-century manuscript in Nahuatl at the National Museum of Anthropology, Mexico City, cited in Leon-Portilla, *Native Mesoamerican Spirituality*, 281.

Colección de historiadores de Chile y documentos relativos a la historia nacional, Vols 3 and 4, Santiago, 1861.

Columbus, Christopher, *The Journal: Account of the First Voyage and Discovery of the Indies* (English edn), Rome, Instituto Poligrafico e Zecca Dello Stato, 1992, Part 1.

Comissão Pró-Índio, Antropólogos manifestam-se contra projecto de emancipaçao de grupos indígenas. In *A questão da emancipaçao*, Cadernos da Comissão Pró-Índio/SP No. 1, pp. 17–20, São Paulo, Global Editora, 1979, cited in Ramos, *Indigenism*, 247.

Conejo, Daniel Rojas, *Dilema e identidad del pueblo Bribri*, San José, Editorial Universidad de Costa Rica, 2009.

Consejo Asesor Hondureño para el Desarrollo de las Etnias Autoctonas, *Pueblos Étnicos de Honduras*, Tegucigalpa, Litografía López, 1988.

Cook, Noble David, *Demographic Collapse, Indian Perú, 1520–1620*, Cambridge, Cambridge University Press, 1981.

Cook, Noble David, "Sickness, Starvation, and Death in Early Hispaniola," *Journal of Interdisciplinary History*, 32, 3, 2002, 349–386.

Cook, Sherburne F. and Borah, Woodrow, *Essays in Population History: Mexico and the Caribbean*, Vol. 1, Berkeley, University of California Press, 1971.

Cook, Sherburne F. and Borah, Woodrow, *Essays in Population History: Mexico and the Caribbean*, Vol. 2, Berkeley, University of California Press, 1974.

Cordeu, Edgardo and Siffredi, Alejandra, *De la algarroba al algodón; movimiento mesiánico de los guaycurú*, Buenos Aires, Juarez Editor, 1971.

Costa, Maria de Fátima, "Indigenous Peoples of Brazil and the War of the Triple Alliance, 1864–1870," in Foote and Horst, *Military Struggle and Identity Formation in Latin America*, 159–174.

Crosby, Alfred W., *The Columbian Exchange; Biological and Cultural Consequences of 1492*, Westport, CT, Greenwood Publishing, 1972.

Crosby, Alfred W., "Infectious Disease and the Demography of the Atlantic Peoples," *Journal of World History*, 2, 2, 1991, 119–133.

Crow, Joanna, "Embattled Identities in Postcolonial Chile: Race, Region, and Nation during the War of the Pacific, 1879–1884," in Foote and Horst, *Military Struggle and Identity Formation in Latin America*, 243–262.

Crow, Joanna, *The Mapuche in Modern Chile, A Cultural History*, Gainesville, University Press of Florida, 2013.

Cunha, Manuela Carneiro, ed., *História dos Indios no Brasil*, São Paulo, Editora Schwarcz, 1998.

Cunningham, Richard L., "The Biological Impacts of 1492," in Samuel Wilson, ed., *The Indigenous People of the Caribbean*, Gainesville, University Press of Florida, 1997, 29–35.

Dandler, Jorge and Torrico, A. Juan, "From the National Indigenous Congress to the Ayopaya Rebellion: Bolivia, 1945–1947," in Stern, *Resistance, Rebellion, and Consciousness*, 339–340.

De Civrieux, Marc, *Watunna, Mitología Makiritare*, Caracas, Monte Avila Editores, 1970.

De Civrieux, Marc, *Watunna, An Orinoco Creation Cycle*, Austin, University of Texas Press, 1997.

De La Cadena, Marisol, *Indigenous Mestizos, The Politics of Race and Culture in Cuzco, Peru, 1919–1991*, Durham, NC, Duke University Press, 2000.

De La Pedraja, René, *Wars of Latin America, 1899–1941*, Jefferson, MO: McFarland & Company, 2006.

De Ste. Croix, G.E.M., "Suffragium: From Vote to Patronage," *British Journal of Sociology*, 5, 1954, 33–48.

Dean, Bartholomew, "State Power and Indigenous Peoples in Peruvian Amazonia: A Lost Decade, 1990–2000," in Maybury-Lewis, *The Politics of Ethnicity*, 199–238.

DeBoer, Warren R., "The Machete and the Cross: Conibo Trade in the Late Seventeenth Century," in Francis *et al.*, *Networks of the Past*, 31–48.

DeLay, Brian, *War of a Thousand Deserts, Indian Raids and the U.S.-Mexican War*, New Haven, CT, and London, Yale University Press, 2008.

Deloria Jr., Vine, *Behind the Trail of Broken Treaties: An Indian Declaration of Independence*, Austin, University of Texas Press, 1985.

Denevan, William M., "Estimating the Aboriginal Population of Latin America in 1492: Methodological Synthesis," *Conference of Latin Americanist Geographers*, Vol. 5, Austin, University of Texas Press, 1976.

Denevan, William M., ed., *The Native Population of the Americas in 1492*, Madison, University of Wisconsin Press, 1976.

Diamond, Jared, *Guns, Germs, and Steel, The Fates of Human Societies*, New York and London, W.W. Norton & Company, 1999.

Díaz, Bernal, *The Conquest of New Spain*, New York, Penguin Books, 1963, 148–149.

"Discurso Indígena de Bienvenida dirigida a Su Santidad Juan Pablo Segundo," Mariscal Estigarríbia, Equipo Nacional de Misiones, May 17, 1988.

Diskin, Martin, "Ethnic Discourse and the Challenge to Anthropology," in Urban and Sherzer, *Nation-States and Indians in Latin America*, 156–180.

Dobyns, Henry F., "Estimating Aboriginal American Population: An Appraisal of Techniques with a New Hemispheric Estimate," *Current Anthropology*, 7, 1966, 395–416.

Dobyns, Henry F., *Peru. A Cultural History*, New York, Oxford University Press, 1976.

Dunbar-Ortiz, Roxanne, *An Indigenous People's History of the United States*, Boston, MA, Beacon Press, 2014.

Dunbar-Ortiz, Roxanne and Dina Gilio-Whitaker, *"All the Real Indians Died Off", and 20 Other Myths about Native Americans*, Boston, MA, Beacon Press, 2016.

Durston, Alan, "Notes on the Authorship of the Huarochirí Manuscript," *Colonial Latin American Review*, 16, 2, 2007, 227–241.

Durston, Alan, "Native-Language Literacy in Colonial Peru: The Question of Mundane Quechua Writing Revisited," *Hispanic American Historical Review*, 88, 1, 2008, 41–70.

Erickson, C.L., "Prehistoric Landscape Management in the Andean Highlands: Raised Field Agriculture and its Environmental Impact," *Population and Environment*, 13, 4, 1992, 285–300.

Espinosa, Vásquez de, *Compendium and Description of the West Indies*, Washington D.C., Smithsonian, 1942, 133–134.

Estévez, Juan José, *Pincén Vida y Leyenda*, Buenos Aires, Editorial Biblos, 2011.

Ewers, John Canfield, *The Horse in Blackfoot Indian Culture: With Comparative Material from other Western Tribes*, Washington D.C., Smithsonian Institution Press, 1980.

Faron, Louis C., "Effects of Conquest on the Araucanian Picunche during the Spanish Colonization of Chile: 1536–1635," *Ethnohistory*, 7, 3, 1960, 239–307.

Farriss, Nancy M., *Maya Society under Colonial Rule, the Collective Enterprise of Survival*, Princeton, NJ, Princeton University Press, 1984.

Farriss, Nancy M., "Persistent Maya Resistance and Cultural Retention in Yucatán," in Kicza, *The Indian in Latin American History* (revised edn), 53–70.

Farthing, Linda, "Everything Is Up for Discussion," *NACLA*, 40, 4, 5–7.

Favre, Henri, "The Dynamics of Indian Peasant Society and Migration to Coastal Plantations in Central Peru," in Kenneth Duncan and Ian Rutledge, eds, *Land and Labour in Latin America, Essays on the Development of Agrarian Capitalism in the Nineteenth and Twentieth Centuries*, Cambridge Latin American Studies, No. 26, Cambridge, Cambridge University Press, 1978.

Fernández-Armesto, Felipe, *The Americas, A Hemispheric History*, New York, The Modern Library, 2003.

Finozzi, Gabrial and Motta, Carlos, *Pueblo Charrúa*, Montevideo, Fundación de Cultura Universitaria, 2000.

Fisher, William H., *Rain Forest Exchanges, Industry and Community on an Amazonian Frontier*, Washington D.C., and London, Smithsonian Institutional Press, 2000.

Fishman, Laura, "Claude d'Abbeville and the Tupinamba: Problems and Goals of French Missionary Work in Early Seventeenth-Century Brazil," *Church History*, 58, 1, 1989, 20–35.

Flores, Francisco A., *Realidad Indígena Hondureña*, Tegucigalpa, Instituto Hondureño de Antropología e Historia, 1977.

Florney, Bertrand, *Jivaro, Among the Headshrinkers of the Amazon*, London and New York, Elek, 1953.

Foote, Nicola, "Monteneros and Macheteros, Afro-Ecuadorian and Indigenous Experiences of Military Struggle in Liberal Ecuador, 1895–1930," in Foote and Horst, *Military Struggle and Identity Formation in Latin America*, 83–106.

Foote, Nicola and Horst, René, *Military Struggle and Identity Formation in Latin America*, Gainesville, University of Florida Press, 2010.

Fowler Jr., William R., *The Cultural Evolution of Ancient Nahua Civilizations: The Pipil-Nicarao of Central America*, Norman and London, University of Oklahoma Press, 1989.

Francis, Peter D., Kense, F.J., and Duke, P.G., *Networks of the Past: Regional Interaction in Archaeology, Proceedings of the Twelfth Annual Conference*, Calgary, The Archaeological Association of the University of Calgary, 1981 and 1984.

Gabbert, Wolfgang, *Becoming Maya, Ethnicity and Social Inequality in Yucatán since 1500*, Tucson, University of Arizona Press, 2004.

Galeano, Eduardo, *Memory of Fire, I. Genesis*, New York, Pantheon Books, 1985.

Galeano, Eduardo, *Memory of Fire, II. Faces and Masks*, New York, Pantheon Books, 1987.

Galiano, Eva Herrero and Serna, David Berná, "Los Maká," *Suplemento Antropológico*, 39, 2, 2004, 13–122.

Galindo, Alberto Flores, *In Search of an Inca, Identity and Utopia in the Andes*, Cambridge, Cambridge University Press, 2010.

Ganson, Barbara, *The Guaraní Under Spanish Rule in the Río de la Plata*, Stanford, CA, Stanford University Press, 2003.

Ganson, Barbara, "The Evuevi of Paraguay: Adaptive Strategies and Responses to Colonialism, 1528–1811," *The Americas*, 74, S2, 2017, 461–488.

Garfield, Seth, "'The Roots of a Plant that Today is Brazil': Indians and the Nation-State under the Brazilian Estado Novo," *Journal of Latin American Studies*, 29, 1997, 747–768.

Garfield, Seth, *Indigenous Struggle at the Heart of Brazil, State Policy, Frontier Expansion, and the Xavante Indians, 1937–1988*, Durham, NC, and London, Duke University Press, 2001.

Gellately, Robert and Kiernan, Ben, *The Specter of Genocide, Mass Murder in Historical Perspective*, Cambridge, Cambridge University Press, 2003.

Gerner, Richard, L., "Long-Term Silver Mining Trends in Spanish America: A Comparative Analysis of Peru and Mexico," *The American Historical Review*, 93, 4, 1988, 898–935.

Gliejesis, Piero, "The Agrarian Reform of Jacobo Arbenz," *Journal of Latin American Studies*, 21, 3, 1989, 453–480.

Gobat, Michel, *Confronting the American Dream, Nicaragua under U.S. Imperial Rule*, Durham, NC, Duke University Press, 2005.

Goetz, Delia and Morley, Sylvanus G., *Popol Vuh, The Sacred Book of the Ancient Quiché Maya*, Norman, University of Oklahoma Press, 1950.

González, David, *Las paeces; o, genocidio y luchas indígenas en Colombia*, Editorial La Rueda Suelta, 1977.

Gotkowitz, Laura, *A Revolution for Our Rights: Indigenous Struggles for Land and Justice in Bolivia, 1880–1952*, Durham, NC, and London, Duke University Press, 2007.

Gotkowitz, Laura, "'Under the Dominion of the Indian': Rural Mobilization, the Law, and Revolutionary Nationalism in Bolivia in the 1940s," in Jacobsen and Losada, *Political Cultures in the Andes*, 137–159.

Gould, Jeffrey, *To Die in this Way, Nicaraguan Indians and the Myth of Mestizaje, 1880–1965*, Durham, NC, and London, Duke University Press, 1998.

Gould, Jeffrey and Lauria-Santiago, Aldo A., *To Rise in Darkness, Revolution, Repression, and Memory in El Salvador, 1920–1932*, Durham, NC, and London, Duke University Press, 2008.

Gradie, Charlotte M., *The Tepehuan Revolt of 1616: Militarism, Evangelism and Colonialism in Seventeenth Century Nueva Vizcaya*, Salt Lake City, University of Utah Press, 2000.

Graham, Richard, *The Idea of Race in Latin America, 1870–1940*, Austin, University of Texas Press, 1990.

Gramsci, Antonio, *Selections from the Prison Notebooks* [1921–1935], New York, International Publishers, 1971.

Grandin, Greg, "History, Motive, Law, Intent: Combining History and Legal Methods in Understanding Guatemala's 1981–1983 Genocide," in Gellately and Kiernan, *The Specter of Genocide*, 339–352.

Grandin, Greg, *The Blood of Guatemala, A History of Race and Nation*, Durham, NC, Duke University Press, 2000.

Grandin, Greg, *The Last Colonial Massacre, Latin America in the Cold War*, Chicago, IL, and London, University of Chicago Press, 2011.

Gregson, Ronald E., "The Influence of the Horse on Indian Cultures of Lowland South America," *Ethnohistory*, 16, 1, 1969, 33–50.

Guardino, Peter, *Peasants, Politics, and the Formation of Mexico's National State, Guerrero, 1800–1857*, Stanford, CA, Stanford University Press, 1996.

Gustafson, Bret, "Paradoxes of Liberal Indigenismo: Indigenous Movements, State Processes, and Intercultural Reform in Bolivia," in Maybury-Lewis, *The Politics of Ethnicity*, 267–308.

Gutierrez, Ramón A., *When Jesus Came, the Corn Mothers Went Away, Marriage, Sexuality, and Power in New Mexico, 1500–1846*, Stanford, CA, Stanford University Press, 1991.

Gutierrez Chong, Natividad, *Women, Ethnicity and Nationalisms in Latin America*, Hampshire and Burlington, VA, Ashgate Publishing, 2007.

Hahner, June, *Women in Latin American History. Their Lives and Views*, Los Angeles, CA, UCLA Latin American Center Publications, 1976.

Hale, Charles R., *Resistance and Contradiction, Miskitu Indians and the Nicaraguan State, 1894–1987*, Stanford, CA, Stanford University Press, 1994.

Hale, Charles R., "Rethinking Indigenous Politics in the Era of the 'Indio Permitido'," *NACLA Report on the Americas*, 38, 2, 2004, 16–20.

Handy, Jim, "'The Most Precious Fruit of the Revolution': The Guatemalan Agrarian Reform, 1952–54," *The Hispanic American Historical Review*, 68, 4, 1988, 675–705.

Handy, Jim, "'A Sea of Indians': Ethnic Conflict and the Guatemalan Revolution, 1944–1952," *The Americas*, 46, 2, 1989, 189–204.

Handy, Jim, "The Corporate Community, Campesino Organizations, and Agrarian Reform: 1950–1954," in Smith, *Guatemala Indians and the State*, 163–182.

Handy, Jim, *Revolution in the Countryside, Rural Conflict and Agrarian Reform in Guatemala, 1944–1954*, Chapel Hill and London, The University of North Carolina Press, 1994.

Hanke, Lewis, *The Spanish Struggle for Justice in the Conquest of America*, Philadelphia, University of Pennsylvania Press, 1949.

Hardenburg, Walter, *The Putumayo: The Devil's Paradise*, 1912, cited in Taussig, "Culture of Terror – Space of Death," 475.

Harner, Michael, *The Jívaro, People of the Sacred Waterfalls*, Berkeley and Los Angeles, University of California Press, 1972.

Hart, John Mason, *Revolutionary Mexico, The Coming and Process of the Mexican Revolution*, Berkeley, University of California Press, 1987.

Harvey, Neil, *The Chiapas Rebellion, The Struggle for Land and Democracy*, Durham, NC, and London, Duke University Press, 1998.

Haskett, Robert, "Coping in Cuernavaca with the Cultural Conquest," in Kicza, *The Indian in Latin American History* (revised edn), 2000, ch. 5.

Haskett, Robert, "Living in Two Worlds: Cultural Continuity and Change among Cuernavaca's Colonial Indigenous Ruling Elite," *Ethnohistory*, 35, 1, 1988, 34–59.

Haughney, Diane, *Neoliberal Economics, Democratic Transition, and Mapuche Demands for Rights in Chile*, Gainesville, University Press of Florida, 2006.

Hemming, John, *The Conquest of the Incas*, New York, Harcourt, 1970.

Hemming, John, *Red Gold, The Conquest of the Brazilian Indians*, Cambridge, MA, Harvard University Press, 1978.

Hemming, John, *Amazon Frontier, The Defeat of the Brazilian Indians*, Cambridge, MA, Harvard University Press, 1987.

Hemming, John, "Indians and the Frontier," in Leslie Bethell, ed., *Colonial Brazil*, Cambridge, Cambridge University Press, 1991, 145–189.

Hendricks, Janet, "Symbolic Counterhegemony among the Ecuadorian Shuar," in Urban and Sherzer, *Nation-States and Indians in Latin America*, 53–71.

Hernandez-Ávila, Inés and Varese, Stefano, "Indigenous Intellectual Sovereignties: A Hemispheric Convocation. An Overview and Reflections on a United States/Mexico Binational Two-Part Conference," *Micazo Sa Review*, 14, 2, 1999, 77–91.

Herr, Richard, *The Eighteenth-Century Revolution in Spain*, Princeton, NJ, Princeton University Press, 1958.

Hoberman, Luisa Schell and Socolow, Susan Migden, *The Countryside in Colonial Latin America*, Albuquerque, University of New Mexico Press, 1996.

Hoffmann, Curtiss, *The Seven Story Tower, A Mythic Journey through Space and Time*, Cambridge, Perseus Publishing, 1999.

Holder, Preston, *The Hoe and the Horse on the Plains: A Study of Cultural Development among North American Indians*, Lincoln, University of Nebraska Press, 1970.

Horst, René Harder, "Consciousness and Contradiction: Indigenous Peoples and Paraguay's Transition to Democracy," in Langer and Muñoz, *Contemporary Indigenous Movements in Latin America*, 103–132.

Horst, René Harder, *The Stroessner Regime and Indigenous Resistance in Paraguay*, Gainesville, University of Florida Press, 2007.

Horst, René Harder, "The Chaco War and Indigenous People in Paraguay," in Foote and Horst, *Military Struggle and Identity Formation in Latin America*, 286–306.

Horst, René Harder, "Indigenous Integration and Legal Changes in Paraguay," in O'Connor and Garofalo, *Documenting Latin America Gender, Race and Nation*, Vol. 2, 213–220.

Horst, René Harder, *El Régimen de Stroessner y la Resistencia Indígena*, Asunción, Centro de Estudios Antropológicos de la Universidad Católica, 2011.

Horst, Willis, *Misión Sin Conquista, Acompañamiento de comunidades indígenas autóctonas como práctica misionera alternativa*, Buenos Aires, Kairos, 2009.

Howe, James, *A People Who Would Not Kneel. Panama, the United States, and the San Blas Kuna*, Washington D. C. and London, Smithsonian Institution Press, 1998.

Howe, James, "The Kuna of Panama: Continuing Threats to Land and Autonomy," in Maybury-Lewis, *The Politics of Ethnicity*, 81–106.

Hu-DeHart, Evelyn, "Yaqui Resistance to Mexican Expansion," in Kicza, *The Indian in Latin American History, Resistance, Resilience, and Acculturation* (revised edn), 2000, 213–241.

Hufstader, Chris, "Marlin Mine: Violence and Pollution Lead to Call for Suspension," Oxfam America, October 17, 2011, available at https://www.oxfamamerica.org/explore/stories/marlin-mine-violence-and-pollution-lead-to-call-for–suspension.

Hylton, Forrest and Thomson, Sinclair, *Revolutionary Horizons, Past and Present in Bolivian Politics*, London and New York, Verso, 2007.

Ibarra, Hernán, *"Nos encontramos amenazados por todita la indiada," el levantamiento de Daquilema (Chimborazo 1871)*, Quito, SEDIS, 1993.

Jackson, Jean, "Being and Becoming an Indian in the Vaupés," in Urban and Sherzer, *Nation-States and Indians in Latin America*, 131–155.

Jackson, Jean, "Caught in the Crossfire: Colombia's Indigenous Peoples during the 1990s," in Maybury-Lewis, *The Politics of Ethnicity*, 107–134.

Jacobsen, Nils, *Mirages of Transition, The Peruvian Altiplano, 1780–1930*, Berkeley, University of California Press, 1993.

Jacobsen, Nils and Losada, Cristóbal Aljovín de, *Political Cultures in the Andes, 1750–1950*, Durham, NC, and London, Duke University Press, 2005.

Jacome, H. and Louis, I., "The Late 1990s Financial Crisis in Ecuador: Institutional Weaknesses, Fiscal Rigidities, and Financial Dollarization at Work," International Monetary Fund Working Paper, January 2004.

Jamison, James Carson, *With Walker in Nicaragua, or Reminiscences of an Officer of the American Phalanx*, Columbia, MO, E.W. Stephens Publishing, 1909.

Jane, Cecil, *The Journal of Christopher Columbus*, New York, Clarkson N. Potter, 1960.

Jara, Álvaro, *Guerra y Sociedad en Chile; la transformación de la Guerra de Arauco y la esclavitud de los indios*, Santiago, Editorial Universitaria, S.A., 1971.

Jara, Carla Victoria, *I Ttè Historias Bribris*, San José, Editorial de la Universidad de Costa Rica, 1993.

Jedin, Hubert and Dolan, John, *History of the Church*, New York, Seabury Press, 1980.

Jennings, Francis, *The Invasion of America. Indians, Colonialism and the Cant of Conquest*, Chapel Hill, University of North Carolina Press, 1975.

Jones, Grant D., *The Conquest of the Last Maya Kingdom*, Stanford, CA, Stanford University Press, 1998.

Joseph, Gilbert and Nugent, Daniel, *Everyday Forms of State Formation, Revolution and the Negotiation of Rule in Modern Mexico*, Durham, NC, Duke University Press, 1994.

"Juán Pablo II y Los Indígenas, Mariscal Estigarríbia-17 de mayo de 1988," Asunción, Equipo Nacional de Misiones, 1988.

Kamen, Henry, "The Decline of Spain: A Historical Myth?," *Past and Present*, *81*, Oxford, Past and Present Society, 1978, in Kamen, *Crisis and Change in Early Modern Spain*, 24–50.

Kamen, Henry, *Crisis and Change in Early Modern Spain*, Aldershot, Ashgate Publishing, 1993.

Kamen, Henry, *Empire. How Spain Became a World Power, 1492–1763*, New York, Harper Collins, 2003.

Katzew, Ilona, *Casta Painting, Images of Race in Eighteenth-Century Mexico*, New Haven, CT, and London, Yale University Press, 2004.

Keen, Benjamin and Haynes, Keith, *A History of Latin America* (7th edn), Boston and New York, Houghton Mifflin, 2004.

Kellog, Susan, *Weaving the Past, A History of Latin America's Indigenous Women from the Prehispanic Period to the Present*, Oxford, Oxford University Press, 2005.

Kicza, John E., ed., *The Indian in Latin American History, Resistance, Resilience, and Acculturation* (revised edn), Lanham, MD, Boulder, CO, and New York, SR Books, 2004.

Kicza, John E., *Resilient Cultures, America's Native Peoples Confront European Colonization, 1500–1800*, Upper Saddle River, CO, Pearson Education, 2013.

Kirk, Robin, *The Monkey's Paw, New Chronicles from Peru*, Amherst, University of Massachusetts Press, 1997.

Klaren, Peter, *Peru, Society and Nationhood in the Andes*, New York, Oxford University Press, 2000.

Klein, Herbert S., "Peasant Communities in Revolt, the Tzeltal Republic of 1712," *Pacific Historical Review*, 35, 3, 1966, 247–263.

Klein, Herbert S., *African Slavery in Latin America and the Caribbean*, New York and Oxford, Oxford University Press, 1986.

Klein, Herbert S., *A Concise History of Bolivia* (2nd edn), New York, Cambridge University Press, 2011.

Knaut, Andrew L., *The Pueblo Revolt of 1680. Conquest and Resistance in Seventeenth-Century New Mexico*, Norman and London, University of Oklahoma Press, 1995.

Knight, Alan, *The Mexican Revolution*, Vol. 1, Lincoln and London, University of Nebraska Press, 1990.

Knight, Alan, "Racism, Revolution, and Indigenismo, Mexico, 1910–1940," in Graham, *The Idea of Race in Latin America*, 71–113.

Knowlton, Timothy and Aveni, Anthony, *Maya Creation Myths: Words and Worlds of the Chilam Balam*, Boulder, University Press of Colorado, 2010.

Korth, Eugene H., *Spanish Policy in Colonial Chile, The Struggle for Social Justice, 1535–1700*, Stanford, CA, Stanford University Press, 1968.

LaFeber, Walter, *Inevitable Revolutions. The United States in Central America* (2nd edn), New York and London, W.W. Norton, 1993.

Lamar, Howard and Leonard Thompson, *The Frontier in History: North America and South Africa Compared*, New Haven, CT, Yale University Press, 1981.

Lane, Kris, *Quito 1599 City and Colony in Transition*, Albuquerque, University of New Mexico Press, 2002.

Langer, Erick, "Andean Rituals of Revolt: The Chayanta Rebellion of 1927," *Ethnohistory*, 37, 3, 1990, 227–253.

Langer, Erick, *Expecting Pears from an Elm Tree, Franciscan Missions on the Chiriguano Frontier in the Heart of South America, 1830–1949*, Durham, NC, Duke University Press, 2009.

Langer, Erick and Muñoz, Elena, *Contemporary Indigenous Movements in Latin America*, Wilmington, DE, Scholarly Resources, 2003.

Las Casas, Bartolomé de, *Historia de las Indias*, Vols I, II, III, México and Buenos Aires, Fondo de Cultura Económica, 1965.

Las Casas, Bartolomé de, *Obras Completas, Historia de las Indias*, 5, Vol. III, Madrid, Alianza Editorial, 1988.

Lauria-Santiago, Aldo A., *An Agrarian Republic, Commercial Agriculture and the Politics of Peasant Communities in El Salvador*, 1823–1914, Pittsburgh, University of Pittsburgh Press, 1999.

Lavrin, Asunción, *Latin American Women, Historical Perspectives*, Westport, CT, Greenwood Press, 1978.

Leakey, Richard E., *The Making of Mankind*, Sphere Books, 1982.

León-Portilla, Miguel, ed., *Native Mesoamerican Spirituality, Ancient Myths, Discourses, Stories, Doctrines, Hymns, Poems from the Aztec, Yucatec, Quiche-Maya and other Sacred Traditions*, New York, Paulist Press, 1980.

León-Portilla, Miguel, *Pre-Columbian Literatures of Mexico*, Norman, University of Oklahoma Press, 1986.

Levi, Jerome M., "A New Dawn or a Cycle Restored? Regional Dynamics and Cultural Politics in Indigenous Mexico, 1978–2001," in Maybury-Lewis, *The Politics of Ethnicity*, 3–50.

Lewin, Boleslao, *La Rebelión de Tupac Amaru*, Buenos Aires, Sociedad Editorial Latino Americana, 1967.

Loayza, Francisco A., *Juan Santos, el invencible*, Lima, Editorial Domingo Miranda, 1942.

Lockhart, James, ed., *We People Here: Nahuatl Accounts of the Conquest of Mexico*, Berkeley, University of California Press, 1993.

Lockhart, James and Schwartz, Stuart B., *Early Latin America, A History of Colonial Spanish America and Brazil*, Cambridge and New York, Cambridge University Press, 1983.

López-Hernández, Miguelángel, *Encuentros de los Senderos de Abya Yala*, La Habana, Casa de las Américas, 2001.

Lutz, Christopher H. and Lovell, W. George, "Core and Periphery in Colonial Guatemala," in Smith, *Guatemalan Indians and the State*, 35–51.

Lynch, John, *Argentine Dictator Juan Manuel de Rosas, 1829–1852*, Oxford, Clarendon Press, 1981.

Lynch, John, *San Martín, Argentine Soldier, American Hero*, New Haven, CT, Yale University Press, 2009.

Macas, Luis, *El levantamiento indígena visto por sus protagonistas*, Quito, Instituto Científico de Culturals Indígenas (ICCI), 1991, cited in Becker, *Indians and Leftists*, 166.

Macaulay, Neill, *Dom Pedro: The Struggle for Liberty in Brazil and Portugal, 1798–1834*, Durham, NC, Duke University Press, 1986.

Macdonald, Theodore Jr., "Ecuador's Indian Movement," in Maybury-Lewis, *The Politics of Ethnicity*, 169–198.

Maggi, Carlos, *Artigas y el lejano norte: refutación de la historia patria*, Montevideo, Editorial Fin de Siglo, 1999.

Mainwaring, Scott, Bejarano, Ana María, and Leongómez, Eduarco Pizarro, eds, *The Crisis of Democratic Representation in the Andes*, Stanford, CA, Stanford University Press, 2006.

Mallon, Florencia, "Nationalist and Anti-State Coalitions in the War of the Pacific: Junín and Cajamarca, 1879–1902," in Stern, *Resistance, Rebellion, and Consciousness*, 232–279.

Mallon, Florencia, "Indian Communities, Political Cultures, and the State in Latin America, 1780–1990," *Journal of Latin American Studies*, 24, 1992, 35–53.

Mallon, Florencia, "Reflections on the Ruins: Everyday Forms of State Formation in Nineteenth Century Mexico," in Joseph and Nugent, *Everyday Forms of State Formation*, 69–106.

Mallon, Florencia, *Peasant and Nation: The Making of Postcolonial Mexico and Peru*, Berkeley, University of California Press, 1995.

Mann, Charles C., *1491, New Revelations of the Americas before Columbus*, New York, Alfred A. Knopf, 2005.

Mann, Charles C., *1493, Uncovering the New World Columbus Created*, New York, Alfred A. Knopf, 2011.

Mario, Rodríguez, *The Livingston Codes in the Guatemalan Crisis of 1837–1838*, Middle American Research Institute, Publication No. 23, 1955.

Marx, Karl, *Selected Writings in Sociology and Social Philosophy*, London, C.A. Watts, 1956.

Maybury-Lewis, David, *Akwe-Shavante Society*, Oxford, Clarendon Press, 1971.

Maybury-Lewis, David, "Becoming Indian in Lowland South America," in Urban and Sherzer, *Nation-States and Indians in Latin America*, 205–235.

Maybury-Lewis, David, *Indigenous Peoples, Ethnic Groups, and the State*, Boston, MA, Allyn and Bacon, 1997.

Maybury-Lewis, David, ed., *The Politics of Ethnicity: Indigenous Peoples in Latin American States*, Cambridge, MA, Harvard University Press, 2002.

Maybury-Lewis, David, "For Reasons of State: Paradoxes of Indigenist Policy in Brazil," in Maybury-Lewis, *The Politics of Ethnicity*, 329–346.

McCaa, Robert, "Spanish and Nahuatl Views on Smallpox and Demographic Collapse in Mexico," *Journal of Interdisciplinary History*, 25, 3, 1995, 397–431.

McCreery, David, "Hegemony and Repression in Rural Guatemala, 1871–1940," *Journal of Peasant Studies*, 17, 3, 1990, 157–177.

McCreery, David, "State Power, Indigenous Communities, and Land in Nineteenth-Century Guatemala, 1820–1920," in Smith, *Guatemalan Indians and the State*, 96–115.

McEwan, Gordon F., *The Incas New Perspectives*, New York and London, W.W. Norton, 2006.

Means, Philip Ainsworth, *History of the Spanish Conquest of Yucatan and of the Itzas*, Cambridge, MA, Peabody Museum of American Archaeology and Ethnology, Harvard University, 1917.

Meggers, Betty Jane, *Amazonia: Man and Culture in a Counterfeit Paradise*, Washington D.C., Smithsonian Institution Press, 1996.

Melià, Bartomeu, *El Guaraní Conquistado y Reducido*, Biblioteca Paraguaya de antropología, Vol. 5, Centro de Estudios Antropológicos, Universidad Católica, Asunción, 1988.

Mendieta, Pilar, *Entre la alianza y la confrontación: Pablo Zárate Willka y la rebelión indígena de 1899 en Bolivia*, Instituto Francés de Estudios Andinos, 2010.

Métraux, Alfred, *Myths of the Toba and Pilagá Indians of the Gran Chaco*, Philadelphia, PA, American Folklore Society and Baltimore, The Waverly Press, 1946.

Metzner, Ralph, ed., *Sacred Vine of Spirits: Ayahuasca*, Rochester, Park Street Press, 2006.

Miller, Elmer S., "Toba Kin Terms," *Ethnology*, 5, 2, 1966, 194–201.

Miller, Elmer S., *Los Tobas Argentinos: Armonía y disonancia en una sociedad*, Buenos Aires, Siglo Veintiuno Argentina Editores, 1979.

Moncayo, José Flores, *Legislación boliviana del indio*, La Paz, Ministerio de Asuntos Campesinos, Departamento de Publicaciones del Instituto Indigenista Boliviano, 1953.

Morales, Francisco, "The Native Encounter with Christianity: Franciscans and Nahuas in Sixteenth-Century Mexico," *The Americas*, 65, 2, 2008, 137–159.

Morineau, Michel, "Eastern and Western Merchants from the Sixteenth to the Eighteenth Centuries," in Sushil Chaudhury and Michel Moreneau, *Merchants, Companies and Trade, Europe and Asia in the Early Modern Era*, Cambridge, Cambridge University Press, 1999, 116–114.

Müller, Wolfgang, Jedin, Hubert, Dolan, John, *et al.*, *History of the Church VI, The Church in the Age of Absolutism and Enlightenment*, New York, The Crossroad Publishing Company, 1981.

Münzel, Mark, *The Aché Indians: Genocide in Paraguay*, Doc. 11, Copenhagen, International World Group for Indigenous Affairs, 1973.

Muratorio, Blanca, *Etnicidad, evangelización, y protesta en el Ecuador, Una perspectiva antropológica*, Quito, Ediciones CIESE, 1982.

Muratorio, Blanca, *The Life and Times of Grandfather Alonso, Culture and History in the Upper Amazon*, New Brunswick, NJ, Rutgers University Press, 1991.

Murphy, Robert Cushman, "The Earliest Spanish Advances Southward from Panama along the West Coast of South America," *Hispanic American Historical Review*, 21, 1, 1941, 3–28.

Murra, John V., "An Aymara Kingdom in 1567," *Ethnohistory*, 15, 2, 1968, 115–151.

Myers, Thomas P., "Spanish Contacts and Social Change on the Ucayali River, Peru," *Ethnohistory*, 21, 2, 1974, 135–157.

Nabokov, Peter, *Native American Testimony. A Chronicle of Indian–White Relations from Prophecy to the Present, 1492–2000*, New York, Penguin Books, 1999.

Nájera, Alonso González de, "Desengaño y reparo de la Guerra de Chile" (CHC, XVI, 10–14, 63–65, *passim*), in Padden, "Cultural Adaptation and Militant Autonomy," 87.

Nelson, Diane, available at https://latinamericancaribbean.duke.edu/clacs-welcomes-indigenous-rights-activist-duke.

Newson, Linda A., *Indian Survival in Colonial Nicaragua*, Norman and London, University of Oklahoma Press, 1987.

Nichols, Madaline W., "Colonial Tucuman," *Hispanic American Historical Review*, 18, 4, 1938, 461–485.

O'Connor, Erin, "Indians and National Salvation: Placing Ecuador's Indigenous Coup of January 2000 in Historical Perspective," in Langer, *Contemporary Indigenous Movements in Latin America*, 65–80.

O'Connor, Erin, *Gender, Indian, Nation, the Contradictions of making Ecuador, 1830–1925*, Tucson, The University of Arizona Press, 2007.

O'Connor, Erin and Garofalo, Leo, *Documenting Latin America Gender, Race and Nation*, Vol. 2, Boston, MA, Prentice Hall, 2011.

O'Hara, Julia, "'The Slayer of Victorio Bears His Honors Quietly,' Tarahumaras and the Apache Wars in Nineteenth-Century Mexico," in Foote and Horst, *Military Struggle and Identity Formation in Latin America*, 224–242.

Ortíz, Sutti Reissig, *Uncertainties in Peasant Farming. A Colombian Case*, London, University of London the Athlone Press, 1973.

Otto, Paul Andrew, *The Dutch–Munsee Encounter in America: The Struggle for Sovereignty in the Hudson Valley*, New York, Berghahn Books, 2006.

Padden, Robert Charles, "Cultural Change and Military Resistance in Araucanian Chile," *Southwestern Journal of Anthropology*, 13, 1, 1957, 103–121.

Padden, Robert Charles, "Cultural Adaptation and Militant Autonomy among the Araucanians of Chile," in Kicza, *The Indian in Latin American History* (revised edn), 71–91.

Pané, Fray Ramón, *Relación acerca de las antigüedades de los indios* (accessed at http://webs.advance.com.ar/pfernando/DocsIglLA/Pane_Relacion.html).

Patterson, Thomas C., "The Inca Empire and Its Subject Peoples," in Kicza, *The Indian in Latin American History*, 1–21.

Peloso, Vincent C., *Work, Protest, and Identity in Latin America*, Jaguar Books on Latin America, No. 26, Wilmington, DE, Scholarly Resources, 2003.

Peralta, Luz and Pinto, Miguel, *Mateo Pumacahua, En torno a la personalidad del Cacique de Chinchero*, Universidad Nacional Mayor de San Marcos, Lima, 2003.

Pereira Salas, Eugenio, *Juegos y alegrías coloniales en Chile*, Santiago, Epresa Editora Zig-Zag, S.A., 1947.

Perry, Richard J., *From Time Immemorial, Indigenous Peoples and State Systems*, Austin, University of Texas Press, 1996.

Phelan, John L., "Authority and Flexibility in the Spanish Imperial Bureaucracy," *Administrative Science Quarterly*, 5, 1, 1960, 47–65.

Pietrobruno, Sheenagh, *Salsa and Its Transnational Moves*, Lanham, MD, Lexington Books, 2006.

Platt, Tristan, "The Andean Experience of Bolivian Liberalism, 1825–1900: Roots of Rebellion in 19th-Century Chayanta (Potosí)," in Stern, *Resistance, Rebellion, and Consciousness*, 280–326.

Pohl, Frederick J., *The Viking Settlements of North America*, New York, Clarkson N. Potter, 1972.

Polanco, Héctor Díaz, *Indigenous Peoples in Latin America, the Quest for Self-Determination*, Boulder, CO, Westview Press, 86.

Poma de Ayala, Felipe Guaman, *The First New Chronicle and Good Government. On the History of the World and the Incas up to 1615*, translated and edited by Roland Hamilton, Austin, University of Texas Press, 2009.

Powell, Philip Wayne, "Spanish Warfare against the Chichimecas in the 1570's," *The Hispanic American Historical Review*, 24, 4, 1944, 580–604.

Prien, Hans-Jürgen, *Christianity in Latin America*, Leiden, and Boston, MA, Brill, 2013.

Prieto, Esther, "Indigenous Peoples in Paraguay," in Van Cott, *Indigenous Peoples and Democracy in Latin America*, 235–258.

Rabben, Linda, *Unnatural Selection, The Yanomami, the Kayapó and the Onslaught of Civilisation*, Seattle, University of Washington Press, 1998.

Rabben, Linda, *Brazil's Indians and the Onslaught of Civilization: The Yanomami and the Kayapó*, Seattle, University of Washington Press, 2004.

Ramírez, Francísco, Q'om leader, interview with author, Asunción, Paraguay, May 29, 2005.

Ramírez, René, "Discurso de bienvenida dirigida a su santidad Juan Pablo Segundo," Unpublished manuscript, Mariscal Estigarribia, Archive Equipo Nacional de Misiones, Asunción, 1988.

Ramírez, René, Enenlhit leader, interview with author, Asunción, May 21, 2001.

Ramos, Alcida Rita, *Sanumá Memories, Yanomami Ethnography in Times of Crisis*, Madison, University of Wisconsin Press, 1995.

Ramos, Alcida Rita, *Indigenism, Ethnic Politics in Brazil*, Madison, University of Wisconsin Press, 1998.

Ramos, Gabriela and Yanna Yannakakis, eds, *Indigenous Intellectuals, Knowledge, Power, and Colonial Culture in Mexico and the Andes*, Durham, NC, Duke University Press, 2014.

Rappaport, Joanne, *The Politics of Memory. Native Historical Interpretation in the Colombian Andes*, Durham, NC, and London, Duke University Press, 1998.

Rappaport, Joanne, "Between Sovereignty and Culture: Who is an Indigenous Intellectual in Colombia?," *International Review of Social History*, 49, 2004, supplement, 111–132.

Reed, Nelson, *The Caste War of Yucatan*, Stanford, CA, Stanford University Press, 1964.

Reichel-Dolmatoff, Gerardo, "The Cultural Context of an Aboriginal Hallucinogen: Banisteriopsis Caapi," in Peter Furst, *Flesh of the Gods the Ritual Use of Hallucinogens*, Long Grove, Waveland Press, 1972, ch. 3.

Reséndez, Andrés, *The Other Slavery, the Uncovered Story of Indian Enslavement in America*, Boston, MA, and New York, Houghton Mifflin Harcourt, 2016.

Rivas, Ramón, *Pueblos indígenas y garífuna de Honduras*, Tegucigalpa, Editorial Guaymuras, 1993.

Roberts, David, *The Pueblo Revolt, The Secret Rebellion that Drove the Spaniards Out of the Southwest*, New York, Simon and Schuster, 2004.

Robins, Nicholas A., *Native Insurgencies and the Genocidal Impulse in the Americas*, Bloomington, Indiana University Press, 2005.

Rock, David, *Argentina, 1516–1987, From Spanish Colonization to Alfonsín*, Berkeley and Los Angeles, University of California Press, 1987.

Rodas, Raquel, *Dolores Cacuango: gran lider del pueblo indio*, Quito, Ediciones Banco Central del Ecuador, 2005.

Roe, Frank Gilbert, *The Indian and the Horse*, Norman, University of Oklahoma Press, 1955.

Roeder, Ralph, *Juárez and his Mexico; A Biographical History*, New York, Viking Press, 1947.

Rojas Conejo, Daniel, *Dilema e indentidad del pueblo Bribri*, San José, Editorial Universidad de Costa Rica, 2009.

Roldan, Mary, *Blood and Fire, La Violencia in Antioquia, Colombia, 1946–1953*, Durham, NC, Duke University Press, 2000.

Romero, Simon, "Discoveries Challenge Beliefs on Humans' Arrival in the Americas," *The New York Times*, March 28, 2014, A5.

Rosado Rosado, Georgina and Rivas, Landy, "María Uicab: Reina, Sacerdotiza y Jefa Militar de los Mayas Rebeldes de Yucatan, 1863–1875," *Plumsock Mesoamerican Studies*, 29, 50, 2008, 112–139.

Rosas, Manuel de, *Diario de la expedición al desierto, (1833–1834)*, Buenos Aires, Ediciones Plus Ultra, 1965.

Roseberry, William, "Hegemony and the Language of Contention," in Joseph and Nugent, *Everyday Forms of State Formation*, 355–366.

Roys, Ralph, *The Book of Chilam Balaam of Chumayel*, Washington D.C., Carnegie Institution, 1933. Available at www.mayaweb.nl/mayaweb/chilam.pdf.

Said, Edward, *Culture and Imperialism*, New York, Alfred Knopf, 1993.

Salmón, Roberto Mario, "Tarahumara Resistance to Mission Congregation in Northern New Spain, 1580–1710," *Ethnohistory*, 24, 4, 1977, 379–393.

Salmón, Roberto Mario, *Indian Revolts in Northern New Spain, a Synthesis of Resistance (1680–1786)*, Lanham, MD, New York, and London, University Press of America, 1991.

Salomon, Frank and Urioste, George L., *The Huarochirí Manuscript, A Testament of Ancient and Colonial Andean Religion*, Austin, University of Texas Press, 1991.

San Andrés Accords, January 18, 1996, translated by Bermudez-Ballin, Rosalva, available at http://flag.blackened.net/revolt/mexico/ezln/san_andres.html.

Sanderlin, George, ed., *Witness Writings of Bartolomé de Las Casas* (2nd edn), Maryknoll, Orbis Books, 1993.

Sanders, James E., "Subaltern Strategies of Citizenship and Soldiering in Colombia's Civil Wars: Afro- and Indigenous Colombians' Experiences in the Cauca, 1851–1877," in Foote and Harder Horst, *Military Struggle and Identity Formation in Latin America*, 25–42.

Santiago, Myrna, "Rejecting Progress in Paradise: Huastecs, the Environment, and the Oil Industry in Veracruz, Mexico, 1900–1935," *Environmental History*, 3, 2, 1998, 169–188.

Sarasola, Carlos Martínez, *Nuestros Paisanos Los Indios*, Buenos Aires, Emecé Editores, S.A., 1992.

Sarasola, Carlos Martínez, "The Conquest of the Desert and the Free Indigenous Communities of the Argentine Plains," in Foote and Horst, *Military Struggle and Identity Formation in Latin America*, 204–223.

Sarasola, Carlos Martínez, *La Argentina de los caciques O el país que no fue {The Argentina of the Chiefs or the Country that did not Happen}*, Buenos Aires, Del Nuevo Extremo, 2012.

Sarmiento, Domingo Faustino, *Facundo Civilization and Barbarism*, Berkeley, Los Angeles and London, University of California Press, 2003.

Sartorius, Carl, *Mexico about 1850*, Stuttgart, F.A. Brockhaus, 1961.

Sauer, Carl Ortwin, *The Early Spanish Main*, Berkeley and Los Angeles, University of California Press, 1966.

Schirmer, Jennifer, "Appropriating the Indigenous, Creating Complicity: The Guatemalan Military and the Sanctioned Maya," in Maybury-Lewis, *The Politics of Ethnicity*, 51–80.

Schwaller, John F., *The Church in Colonial Latin America*, Wilmington, DE, Scholarly Resources, 2000.

Schwaller, John F., ed., *Francis in the Americas: Essays on the Franciscan Family in North and South America*, Berkeley, CA, Academy of American Franciscan History, 2005.

Schwartz, Stuart B., "Indian Labor and New World Plantations: European Demands and Indian Responses in Northeastern Brazil," *The American Historical Review*, 83, 1, 1978, 43–79.

Schwartz, Stuart B., *Victors and Vanquished, Spanish and Nahua Views of the Conquest of Mexico*, New York, Bedford/St. Martin's Press, 2000.

Scott, James, *Domination and the Arts of Resistance, Hidden Transcripts*, Newhaven, CT, Yale University Press, 1990.

Scott, James, "Foreward," in Joseph and Nugent, *Everyday Forms of State Formation*, vii–xii.

Sepp, Antonio, S.J., *Relación de Viaje a las Misiones Jesuíticas*, Buenos Aires, Editorial Universitaria de Buenos Aires, 1971.

Sieder, Rachel, *Multiculturalism in Latin America, Indigenous Rights, Diversity and Democracy*, New York, Palgrave Macmillan, 2002.

Silva, Mercedes, *Memorias del Chaco, Primera Parte*, Resistencia, Edipen, 1997.

Silverblatt, Irene, *Moon, Sun, and Witches, Gender Ideologies and Class in Inca and Colonial Peru*, Princeton, NJ, Princeton University Press, 1987.

Smidt, Andrea J., "Bourbon Regalism and the Importation of Gallicanism: The Political Path for a State Religion in Eighteenth-Century Spain," *Anuario de Historia de la Iglesia*, 19, 2010, 25–35.

Smith, Carol A., ed., *Guatemalan Indians and the State: 1540 to 1988*, Austin, University of Texas Press, 1990.

Smith, Carol, "Origins of the National Questions in Guatemala, a Hypothesis," in *Guatemalan Indians and the State*, 72–95.

Smith, Gavin, *Livelihood and Resistance, Peasants and the Politics of Land in Peru*, Berkeley, University of California Press, 1989.

Socolow, Susan, *The Women of Colonial Latin America*, Cambridge and New York, Cambridge University Press, 2000.

Sousa, Lisa and Terraciano, Kevin, "The Original Conquest of Oaxaca: Nahua and Mixtec Accounts of the Spanish Conquest," *Ethnohistory*, 50, 2, 2003, 349–400.

Spalding, Karen, *Huarochirí: An Andean Society Under Inca and Spanish Rule*, Stanford, CA, Stanford University Press, 1984.

Spores, Ronald, "Spanish Penetration and Cultural Change in Early Colonial Mexico," in Kicza, *The Indian in Latin American History*, 1993, 89–108.

Staden, Hans, *Hans Staden's True History, An Account of Cannibal Captivity in Brazil*, translated by Neil L. Whitehead and Michael Harbsmeier, Durham, NC, Duke University Press, 2008.

Starn, Orin, Degregori, Carlos Iván, and Kirk, Robin, *The Peru Reader, History, Culture, Politics* (2nd edn), Durham, NC, and London, Duke University Press, 2005.

Stavenhagen, Rodolfo, "Indigenous Peoples and the State in Latin America: An Ongoing Debate," in Rachel Sieder, ed., *Multiculturalism in Latin America, Indigenous Rights, Diversity and Democracy*, New York, Palgrave Macmillan, 2002, 24–44.

Stepan, Alfred, ed., *Americas: New Interpretive Essays*, New York and Oxford, Oxford University Press, 1992.

Stern, Steve J., ed., *Resistance, Rebellion, and Consciousness in the Andean Peasant World, 18th to 20th Centuries*, Madison, University of Wisconsin Press, 1987.

Stern, Steve J., *Peru's Indian Peoples and the Challenge of Spanish Conquest. Huamanga to 1640*, Madison, University of Wisconsin Press, 1982, 1993.

Stern, Steve J., "Early Spanish–Indian Accommodation in the Andes," in Kicza, *The Indian in Latin American History*, 23–52.

Stern, Steve J., *Battling for Hearts and Minds, Memory Struggles in Pinochet's Chile, 1973–1988*, Durham, NC, Duke University Press, 2006.

Stern, Steve J., "The Age of Andean Insurrection, 1742–1782: A Reappraisal," in Stern, ed., *Resistance, Rebellion, and Consciousness*, 34–93.

Steward, Julian H. and Faron, Louis C., *Native Peoples of South America*, New York, McGraw-Hill, 1959.

Stoll, David, *Rigoberta Menchú and the Story of all Poor Guatemalans*, Philadelphia, PA, Westview Press, 2008.

Stringer, Christopher and McKie, Robin, *African Exodus, the Origins of Modern Humanity*, New York, Henry Holt, 1997.

Susnik, Branislava, *Los Aborígenes del Paraguay, III, 1, Ethnohistoria de los Chaqueños, 1650–1910*, Asunción, Museo Etnográfico Andrés Barbero, 1981.

Susnik, Branislava and Chase-Sardi, Miguel, *Los Indios del Paraguay*, Madrid, Ediciones Mapfre, 1995.

Sweet, David and Nash, Gary B., *Struggle & Survival in Colonial America*, Berkeley and Los Angeles, University of California Press, 1981.

Taussig, Michael, "Culture of Terror – Space of Death. Roger Casement's Putumayo Report and the Explanation of Torture," *Comparative Studies in Society and History*, 26, 3, 1984, 467–497.

Taylor, William B., *Drinking, Homicide and Rebellion in Colonial Mexican Villages*, Stanford, CA, Stanford University Press, 1979.

Taylor, William B., "Patterns and Variety in Mexican Village Uprisings," in Kicza, *The Indian in Latin American History* (revised edn), 157–189.

Terán, Buenaventura, *Lo que cuentan los tobas*, Buenos Aires, Ediciones del Sol, 1994.

Terraciano, Kevin, "Crime and Culture in Colonial Mexico: The Case of the Mixtec Murder Note," *Ethnohistory*, 45, 4, 1998, 709–745.

Thomson, Sinclair, *We Alone Will Rule, Native Andean Politics in the Age of Insurgency*, Madison, University of Wisconsin Press, 2002.

Thorne, Eva T., "Land Rights and Garífuna Identity," *NACLA*, 38, 2, 2004, 21–25.

Thrupp, Sylvia, *Millennial Dreams in Action: Studies in Revolutionary Religious Movements*, New York, Schocken, 1970.

Todorov, Tzvetan, *The Conquest of America, The Question of the Other*, New York, Harper & Row, 1984.

Torquemada, Juan de, *Monarquía Indiana*, 3 Vols, Mexico City, Editorial Porrúa, 1969.

Townsend, Camilla, *Malintzin's Choices, An Indian Woman in the Conquest of Mexico*, Albuquerque, University of New Mexico Press, 2006.

Truitt, Jonathan, "Courting Catholicism: Nahua Women and the Catholic Church in Colonial Mexico City," *Ethnohistory*, 57, 3, 415–444.

Turino, Thomas, "The State and Andean Musical Production in Peru," in Urban and Sherzer, *Nation-States and Indians in Latin America*, 259–285.

United Nations Declaration on the Rights of Indigenous Peoples (UNDRIP), UNESCO, March 2008.

United Nations General Assembly, October 24, 2005, 60/1, 2005 World Summit Outcome.

Urban, Greg and Sherzer, Joel, *Nation-States and Indians in Latin America*, Austin, University of Texas Press, 1991.

Valcárcel, Luís, "Tempest in the Andes," in Starn *et al.*, *The Peru Reader, History, Culture, Politics*, Durham, NC, and London, Duke University Press, 2005, 231–234.

Van Cott, Donna Lee, ed., *Indigenous Peoples and Democracy in Latin America*, New York, St. Martin's Press, 1994.

Van Cott, Donna Lee, *The Friendly Liquidation of the Past: The Politics of Diversity in Latin America*, Pittsburgh, PA, University of Pittsburgh, Digital Research Library, 2009.

Van Young, Eric, *The Other Rebellion, Popular Violence, Ideology, and the Mexican Struggle for Independence, 1810–1821*, Stanford, CA, Stanford University Press, 2001.

Varese, Stefano, *Salt of the Mountain, Campa Asháninka, History and Resistance in the Peruvian Jungle*, Norman, University of Oklahoma Press, 2002.

Varese, Stefano, *La sal de los Cerros, Resistencia y Utopía en la Amazonía Peruana*, Lima, Fondo Editorial del congreso del Perú, 2006.

Vásquez, Alfredo Barrera and Rendón, Silvia, *El Libro de los Libros de Chilam Balam*, México, Fondo de Cultura Económica, 1972.

Vásquez de Espinosa, Antonio, *Description of the West Indies*, translated by C.U. Clark, Washington D.C., The Smithsonian Institution, 1942.

Walker, Charles F., *The Tupac Amaru Rebellion*, Cambridge and London, The Belknap Press of Harvard University Press, 2014.

Warren, Kay B., "Transforming Memories and Histories: The Meanings of Ethnic Resurgence for Mayan Indians," in Stepan, *Americas: New Interpretive Essays*, 189–219.

Warren, Kay B., *Indigenous Movements and their Critics. Pan-Maya Activism in Guatemala*, Princeton, NJ, Princeton University Press, 1998.

Warren, Kay B. and Jackson, Jean E., *Indigenous Movements, Self-Representation and the State in Latin America*, Austin, University of Texas Press, 2002.

Whightman, Ann M., "Diego Vasicuio: Native Priest," in Sweet and Nash, *Struggle and Survival in Colonial America*, 38–48.

Whitehead, Neil Lancelot, "Carib Ethnic Soldiering in Venezuela, the Guianas, and the Antilles, 1492–1820," *Ethnohistory*, 37, 4, 1990, 357–385.

Williams, Caroline A., "Resistance and Rebellion on the Spanish Frontier: Native Responses to Colonization in the Colombian Chocó, 1670–1690," *The Hispanic American Historical Review*, 79, 3, 1999, 397–424.

Williams, Robert Gregory, *States and Social Evolution: Coffee and the Rise of National Governments in Central America*, Chapel Hill, University of North Carolina Press, 1994.

Wilson, David, *Indigenous South Americans of the Past and Present, an Ecological Perspective*, Boulder, CO, Westview Press, 1999.

Wilson, Samuel M., *Hispaniola: Caribbean Chiefdoms in the Age of Columbus*, Tuscaloosa, University of Alabama Press, 1990.

Winn, Peter, *Americas, the Changing Face of Latin America and the Caribbean*, Berkeley, University of California Press, 1992.

Wolf, Eric, *Peasant Wars of the Twentieth Century*, New York, Doubleday, 1969.

Woodward, Ralph Lee Jr., "Social Revolution in Guatemala, the Carrera Revolt," Publication No. 23, *Applied Enlightenment: 19th Century Liberalism*, No. 3, Middle American Research Institute, New Orleans, Tulane University, 1971, 48–70.

Woodward, Ralph Lee Jr., "The Economy of Central America at the Close of the Colonial Period," in Duncan Kinkead, ed., *Estudios del Reino de Guatemala: homenaje al professor S. D. Markman, 117–134*, Sevilla, Escuela de Estudios Hispano-Americanos, 1985.

Woodward, Ralph Lee Jr., "Changes in the Nineteenth-Century Guatemalan State and Its Indian Policies," in Smith, *Guatemalan Indians and the State*, 61.

Woodward, Ralph Lee Jr., *Central America a Nation Divided*, New York and Oxford, Oxford University Press, 1999.

Wortham, Erica Cusi, *Indigenous Media in Mexico, Culture, Community, and the State*, Durham, NC, and London, Duke University Press, 2013.

Yannakakis, Yanna, *The Art of Being In-Between, Native Intermediaries, Indian Identity, and Local Rule in Colonial Oaxaca*, Durham, NC, and London, Duke University Press, 2008.

Yannakakis, Yanna and Ramos, Gabriela, eds, *Indigenous Intellectuals, Knowledge, Power, and Colonial Culture in Mexico and the Andes*, Durham, NC, Duke University Press, 2014.

Yashar, Deborah J., "Indigenous Politics in the Andes: Changing Patterns of Recognition, Reform, and Representation,"in Mainwaring *et al.*, *The Crisis of Democratic Representation in the Andes*, 257–291.

Yetman, David, *Conflict in Colonial Sonora, Indians, Priests, and Settlers*, Albuquerque, University of New Mexico Press, 2012.

Young, Robert J.C., *Postcolonialism: An Historical Introduction*, West Sussex, Wiley Blackwell, 2016.

Zambrano, Ramos, "Rumi Maqui, Movimientos Campesinos de Azangaro (Punol)," Puno, Centro de Investigaciones Para El Desarrollo Social Del Altiplano, 1986.

Zingg, Robert, *Behind the Mexican Mountains*, Austin, University of Texas Press, 2001.

Zinn, Howard, *A People's History of the United States, 1492–Present*, New York, Harper Perennial, 2003.

Zinn, Howard, *A Power Governments Cannot Suppress*, San Francisco, CA, City Lights Books, 2007.

Zook, David, *The Conduct of the Chaco War*, New Haven, CT, Bookman Associates, 1960.

Appendix 1

Organization Abbreviations

CCIIRA	Coordinating Commission of Indigenous Institutions in the Argentine Republic
CIDOB	Confederation of Indigenous Peoples of Bolivia
CIMI	Indigenist Missionary Council
COCOPA	Commission of Concord and Pacification
CONAIE	Confederation of Indigenous Nationalities of Ecuador
CRIC	Regional Indigenous Council of Cauca
CRIVA	Consejo Regional Indigena del Vaupés (Regional Indigenous Council of Vaupés)
CSUTCB	Unified Syndical Confederation of Rural Workers of Bolivia
DAI	Department of Indigenous Affairs
ERPI	Insurgent People's Revolutionary Army
EZLN	Zapatista Army of National Liberation
FSLN	Sandinista National Liberation Front
FTAA	Free Trade Area of the Americas
FUNAI	National Indian Foundation
IAII	Inter-American Indigenist Congress
ILO	International Labour Organization
INDI	National Indigenous Institute (Paraguay)
INI	National Indigenous Institute (Mexico)
MAS	Movement Toward Socialism
MISURASATA	MIskito, SUmo, RAma and SAndinista, Asla, TAkanka (working together). An organization of the Miskitu, Contra, and other Atlantic coastal indigenous people
MNR	National Revolutionary Movement
MUUP	Pachacutik Movement of Plurinational Unity
NGO	Non-Governmental Organization
ONIC	National Indigenous (Indian) Organization of Colombia
SPI	Indian Protection Service
U.N.	United Nations

Appendix 2
Indigenous People

Mesoamerica

Ache
Ahiza
Apache
Asla
Bokota
Bri Bri
Cakchiqueles
Care
Carib
Cempoalan
Cerquín
Chichimeca
Chols
Chorotega
Chortis
Concho
Corobici
Couohe
Cuirimpo
Embera-Wounan
Garifuna
Guaymí
Hopi
Huaxtec
Huit
Ixil
Kaqchikel
Keresan
K'iche'
Kumiai
Kuna
Lencas
Maleku
Mam

Maribio
Mario
Matagalpa
Matambú
Mayangna
Mexica
Misquitu
Mixtec
Monimboseño
Mopanes
Movere
Murire
Nahua
Nahua Pipil
Napo Runa
Navojoa
Ngo'ba
Ngo'be-Buglé
Nicarao
Ocos
Olmec
Opata
Otomi
Pech
Pima
Piro
Pokoman
Potón
Q'eqchi
Rama
Seri
Sumu
Takanka
Talamanca
Tano
Tarahumara
Tarascan
Tawahka
Tepehuan
Teribe
Tesia
Tewa
Tiwa
Tlaxcalan
Toboso
Toltec

Tompiro
Towa
Tzeltal
Tzotzil
Tzutujil
Xinca
Yaqui
Yekuana
Zapatista
Zapotec
Zuñi

Caribbean

Arawak
Caribs (Kalinago)
Ciboney

Northern South America

Burgumia
Carangues
Cayambia
Chibcha
Chocó
Citará
Huancavelica
Noanama
Pastos
Popayan
Quillacinga-Pasto
Quiriquire
Quitos
Shuar
Soruco
Tatamá
Tukano
Ucayali
Warrau

Amazonia

Aimoré
Apiaká
Apinayé
Appinagé

Arara
Araweté
Asuriní
Awá
Bororo
Canoeiro
Carijó
Cocama
Cofan
Conibo
Guató
Huaorani
Irimarai
Juruna
Kagwahiva
Kaingang
Karajá
Kararaô
Kayapó
Krahô
Machiparo
Makushi
Manao
Munduruku
Mura
Nambiquara
Omagua
Parakanã
Runa
Setebo
Shitibo
Siona-Secoya
Tapajós
Tapirapé
Terena
Ticuna
Tukano-Tukanoans
Tupinambá
Tupinambarana
Tupinikin
Umutina
Urubús
Waiãpi
Waimiri-Atroari
Xavante
Xerente
Xikrin
Yanomami

Andean

Angara
Arauco
Ayaviri
Aymara
Canares
Cañari
Candires
Caracara
Cashinawa
Chavin
Chilqu
Chocorvo
Chumbivilca
Colla
Diaguita
Huacho
Itzá
Jurí
Lucanas
Lupaqa
Mapuche
Moche
Nazca
Parisca
Purén
Quechua
Quimbaya
Soras
Tanquihua
Tiwanaku
Tucapel
Wari
Yauyo

Southern Cone

Abipón
Alakaluf
Aucazes
Ayoreode
Beaquéo
Caingang
Chane
Charrúa
Chiriguano
Chonecas

Enenlhit
Enlhit
Enxet
Evueví
Guaikurú
Guan'a
Guaraní
Guaycuru
Guaykurú
Huarpes
Huilliches
Kadiwéu
Mak'a
Maskoy
Mbayá
Mbayá-Guaykurú
Minuane
Mocobí
Nivaclé
Ona
Patagones
Pehuenches
Pilagá
Puelche
Querandí
Q'om
Ranquel
Reche
Sanapaná
Tehuelche
Tequenica *see* Yaghan
Toba-Q'om
Tupi
Wichi
Yagán *see* Yaghan
Yaghan (also called Yagán, Yahgan, Yámana, Yamana, or Tequenica)
Yámana *see* Yaghan
Yishïro
Yofuaxa
Zamuco

Index